Latinos and Criminal Justice

Latinos and Criminal Justice

AN ENCYCLOPEDIA

José Luis Morín, Editor

GREENWOOD™

An Imprint of ABC-CLIO, LLC
Santa Barbara, California • Denver, Colorado

Library of Congress Cataloging-in-Publication Data

Names: Morín, José Luis, editor.
Title: Latinos and criminal justice : an encyclopedia / José Luis Morín, editor.
Description: Santa Barbara : Greenwood, 2016.
Identifiers: LCCN 2015036612| ISBN 9780313356605 (hardback) | ISBN 9780313356612 (ebook)
Subjects: LCSH: Alien criminals—United States. | Latin Americans—United States. | Crime—United States—Sociological aspects. | Criminal justice, Administration of—United States. | BISAC: SOCIAL SCIENCE / Ethnic Studies / Hispanic American Studies. | SOCIAL SCIENCE / Criminology. | SOCIAL SCIENCE / Ethnic Studies / General.
Classification: LCC HV6791 .L38 2016 | DDC 364.3/46807303—dc23
LC record available at http://lccn.loc.gov/2015036612

ISBN: 978-0-313-35660-5
EISBN: 978-0-313-35661-2

20 19 18 17 16 1 2 3 4 5

This book is also available on the World Wide Web as an eBook.
Visit www.abc-clio.com for details.

Greenwood
An Imprint of ABC-CLIO, LLC

ABC-CLIO, LLC
130 Cremona Drive, P.O. Box 1911
Santa Barbara, California 93116-1911

This book is printed on acid-free paper ♾

Manufactured in the United States of America

To Elisa and Velia

Contents

A to Z Entries on Latinas/os and Criminal Justice and Cross References

Guide to Related Topics

Sleepy Lagoon
Transnational Crime
Uniform Crime Report
Violence

Criminology

Cultural Criminology

Culture

Cultural Competency
Family Issues
Gangs in the United States and Latina/o Communities
Hispanics/Latinas/os
Machismo
Marianismo
Salinas, Raúl R. (raúlrsalinas) (1934–2008)

Discrimination, Bias, and Stereotypes

De Facto Segregation
De Jure Segregation
Driving While Brown
Felon Disenfranchisement
Halo Effect
Implicit Bias
Incarceration and Latinas/os in the United States
Institutional Racism
Media Depictions
Racial and Ethnic Discrimination
Racial Profiling
Residential Segregation
Segregation
Selective Prosecutions
Sentencing Project, The

Gangs/Street Organizations

Gangs in the United States and Latina/o Communities
Gangs/Street Organizations
Greaser Act
Homies Unidos
Mara Salvatrucha
Sánchez, Alex (1971–)
Sleepy Lagoon
Terrorism
Transnational Crime
Young Lords
Zoot Suit Riots

Gender and Sexuality

Femicide
Gender Issues
Intimate Partner Violence/Domestic Violence
Latinas and the U.S. Criminal Justice System
Lesbian, Gay, Bisexual, and Transgender (LGBT)
Machismo
Marianismo
Sex Crimes

Immigration and Deportation

Border Crime
Border Patrol
Crime and the U.S.-Mexican Border
Crimmigration
Deportation
Deportation Laws
Dominicans
Immigrant Detention Centers
Immigration and Customs Enforcement (ICE)
Immigration and Law Enforcement
Immigration and Naturalization Service (INS) v. Lopez-Mendoza et al., 468 U.S. 1032 (1984)
Nativism
Plyler v. Doe, 457 U.S. 202 (1982)
Removal
Vigilantism

Incarceration

Incarceration and Latinas/os in the United States
Latina/o Youth and Criminal Justice
Mass Imprisonment/Mass Incarceration

Language

Latin America/Latin Americans

Law

Law Enforcement

Legal Profession

People

Race and Ethnicity

Victimization

Vigilantism
Violence

Youth

Brown Berets
Gangs
Juvenile Delinquency
Latina/o Youth and Criminal Justice
School-to-Prison Pipeline
"Talk, The"
Violence Prevention
Young Lords
Youth
Youth Crime

Introduction

José Luis Morín

In modern times, it seems that no other country in the world is more preoccupied with criminal justice than the United States. It is a country that incarcerates far more persons than any other nation in the world; it has the highest recidivism rate of any country on the planet; and it is known for its glaring racial and ethnic disparities in criminal justice outcomes and its persistent controversies centered on police practices. Matters relating to race and criminal justice continue to grip the nation. Most often the question of "race" is what divides communities of color and police. African Americans, undoubtedly, comprise a significant percentage of people who are most disproportionately incarcerated and who criminologists identify as being most affected by bias in the criminal justice. Latinas/os—persons in the United States who typically trace their ancestry back to a country in Latin America—also are among the groups most disproportionately incarcerated and most vulnerable to unequal treatment by the criminal justice system. Although information, research, and analyses have been more readily available about African Americans in relation to the U.S. criminal justice system, the same has not been the case for Latinas/os. This book attempts to bridge that gap by bringing together in a unique way the available information on Latinas/os and their experience of criminal justice in the United States.

Latinas/os accounted for more than half of the population growth in the United States occurring from 2000 to 2010 (Ennis, Ríos-Vargas, & Albert 2011, 2). As one of the fastest growing demographic groups in the United States, Latinas/os have the potential to dramatically affect the political, economic, and social trajectory of the country, attracting increasing interest of the news media, government officials, and others in the public and private sectors. In spite of their rising presence and importance, "Latinos"—or "Hispanics," as they are commonly referred to in U.S. government reports—remain relatively unfamiliar to other people in the United States. Although they often are perceived or depicted in the media and in public discourse as a recent immigrant group, most Latinas/os are born in the United States. Only 37 percent of Latinas/os in the United States are foreign born, and nearly three out of every four Latinas/os are U.S. citizens (Motel & Patten 2012).

The presence of persons of Latin American descent in the United States is not new and has its origins in the long history of U.S.–Latin American relations. In fact, the presence of the two largest Latina/o populations in the United States—Mexicans followed by Puerto Ricans—can be traced back to the U.S. wars of the 1800s. In a war with Mexico, the United States in 1848 wrested half of the country of Mexico, and with those new territories it acquired some 75,000 to 100,000 Mexicans. As a result of armed conflict with Spain in 1898, the United States acquired Puerto Rico as a prize of war, and by 1917 Puerto Ricans were made U.S. citizens. (For a more extensive discussion of U.S.–Latin America relations and the history of the presence of Latinas/os in the United States, see "Latinas/os and the U.S. Criminal Justice System: An Overview of Socio-Historic and Contemporary Issues" in this volume.)

Yet, despite their presence throughout U.S. history, Latinas/os generally remain poorly understood and often are overlooked in many areas of academic inquiry. A collective lack of understanding in the United States of the historical inequities, challenges, and circumstances that have given rise to the U.S. Latina/o population endures. One area that has received insufficient attention over time has been the Latina/o experience with the criminal justice system. Scholars note that until recently Latinas/os have been "virtually invisible" in major criminal justice studies and policy debates. Indeed, **Latina/o "invisibility"** frequently is cited by academics as an enduring characteristic of the Latina/o experience, as there is a scarcity of reliable information about Latinas/os, Latinas/os often are not accurately portrayed in the media, and Latinas/os lack sufficient representation in many important sectors of the society. The absence of Latinas/os has been especially noticeable in the criminal justice field; there have been few Latina/o lawyers, judges, prosecutors, and police officers.

The dearth of adequate data, social scientific research, and analysis has left an information gap that too often is filled by misperceptions, misconceptions, and stereotypes. It is a commonly held belief, for example, that Latina/o immigration results in an increase in crime rates. To the contrary, social scientific studies show that Latina/o immigrants tend to be less inclined to engage in criminal behavior than are U.S.-born persons. Studies show that immigrants to the United States in reality have lesser rates of incarceration than those of other groups in the population. It also has been demonstrated that immigration by and large does not increase homicide rates, but rather it stabilizes communities, thereby curbing criminal violence. Immigrants tend to stimulate economic activity and revitalize neighborhoods, and as a result recent studies point to immigration playing a key role in reducing crime in cities such as New York, home to a significant Latina/o immigrant population. As one study has shown, each one percent increase in a New York City police precinct's immigrant population has resulted in an average of 966 fewer crimes committed every year (Vigdor 2014). Los Angeles—another city with a sizable Latina/o immigrant population—has similarly experienced a reduction in violent crime. Latino/a immigrants, specifically, not only have been found to be no more susceptible to commit crime than are other groups, and after accounting for factors including age and vulnerability to pretrial detention, Latino/a immigrants typically are *less* likely to be involved in crime than U.S.–born citizens.

Overrepresented in detention facilities in the United States, it has been easy to characterize Latina/o incarceration rates as simply a function of being more criminally predisposed than other racial or ethnic groups. But research results increasingly have differed from this conclusion. Contrary to popular belief, studies indicate that Latinas/os are no more likely to use illicit drugs that other groups; they are less likely to be involved in violent crimes than other groups; and, when convicted of a crime, they most often are incarcerated for relatively minor, nonviolent offenses. This data notwithstanding, it also is the case that Latinas/os are more likely to be arrested and charged with drug offenses than are whites; Latinas/os are less likely to be given pretrial release than are whites; and Latinas/os are more likely to have been detained before trial when convicted of crimes than are whites.

An Encyclopedia to Broaden Understanding

Accurate and readily available information about Latinas/os and the criminal justice system—such as the data just cited—has been wanting. The need to fill the void of information on the subject is what gave impetus to creating this volume, *Latinos and Criminal Justice: An Encyclopedia*. Composed of long essays on major topics followed by a series of short entries and additional materials, this book provides readers information that is accessible and that imparts insights into many dimensions of the Latina/o experience with the U.S. criminal justice system.

The present volume seeks to bring together current research on areas of major concern and debate in the field of criminal justice in relation to the most prominent groups of people of Latin American descent in the United States. Although this book attempts to cover as broad a range of criminal justice topics and experiences of Latinas/os as is possible, it does not purport to cover every conceivable issue in the field of criminal justice, only those that seem to most directly affect Latinas/os. This book also does not attempt to cover the experience of every individual Latina/o group member residing in the United States, but instead it focuses on the experiences of the largest groups of Latinas/os in the country for which data is available and those whose history and interactions with the U.S. criminal justice system has been the longest and most representative. Mexican Americans, for instance, make up almost two-thirds of all Latinas/os in the United States (Lopez, Gonzalez-Barrera, & Cuddington 2013). Mexicans have been present in the United States in significant numbers for the longest period by far, and also have interacted with the criminal justice system for the longest time. Hence, this book delves deeply into their trajectory and that of other U.S. Latina/o populations in relation to how the U.S. criminal justice system has perceived and treated persons of Latin American descent, both historically and into the present.

This book concentrates on an emergent area of inquiry, deserving of further research and analysis. For this reason, this volume decidedly is *an* encyclopedia, not *the* encyclopedia on the subject. In view of nationwide concerns about crime and criminal justice policies, accurate information and critical analyses are necessities. This book endeavors to improve knowledge and understanding as well as dispel popular misconceptions about Latinas/os, crime, and the criminal justice system in the United States. The experts, scholars, practitioners, and others who have contributed to this book were attracted to this project as a means of disseminating information on this very important—but much neglected and poorly understood—topic. In their efforts to do so, they amassed information and data that in many instances contributes to the literature in the fields of criminal justice and Latina/o studies. Although the editor is conscious of the need for ongoing research in this area, this book is designed to serve as a reference and resource on the Latina/o experience with the U.S. criminal justice system. *Latinos and Criminal Justice: An Encyclopedia* is intended to expose a broader audience of readers to a variety of critical analyses and information in a relatively concise manner, and also to serve as a quick reference for those readers seeking to identify areas for further research.

How This Book Is Organized

Unlike a traditional encyclopedia with entries simply covering topics alphabetically (A through Z), this book contains longer essays that ensure the contextualization of a topic and contains shorter entries that are cross-referenced with related topic areas. This volume is divided into two basic parts. Part I consists of lengthier topical essays that provide depth of analysis and context. Essays in Part I typically are subdivided into specific subtopics or areas of significance that are cross-referenced. Part II provides a series of short entries on specific topics and is organized in a traditional encyclopedia style (A to Z), and it also provides cross references for topics that are discussed in essays or entries found else elsewhere in the book. At the end of each essay or entry is a list of related topics that can be found elsewhere in the book.

The study of criminal justice draws from many disciplines and areas of study—including history, sociology, law, anthropology, and political science. This book is organized with the goal of providing the reader with the opportunity to read essays that examine the many social, economic, historical, and other dimensions that must be explored in forging a better understanding of the conditions and circumstances affecting Latinas/os in relation to criminal justice matters. The various components of the book—long and short essays and cross-referenced entries—help provide the reader a range of information about the subject matter not usually found in a traditional encyclopedia. These components also provide an overview of and information on the topic that are not readily available in one publication.

Examining the contemporary situation of Latinas/os in relation to the U.S. criminal justice system necessitates an understanding of significant historical events that shaped the current state of affairs. Hence, the longer essays in Part I of this book are designed to explore the historical and social contexts of the Latina/o experience in the United States and the ways Latinas/os continue to be affected by enduring historical and structural inequities and tendencies. For instance, the challenges posed by racism, segregation, xenophobia, and discrimination have been ubiquitous throughout U.S. history, from the country's earliest years to the present. The existence of racism, segregation, xenophobia, and discrimination—both institutionalized and in less overt forms—has not only influenced criminal justice policy, practices, and laws, but it has had a long-lasting impact on how Latinas/os are viewed and treated by the criminal justice system. This volume explores the connections between history and social conditions and their impact on criminal justice. Although not often taught or understood as such, Latinas/os are part of both the history and the future of the United States. How well Latinas/os will do in the United States going forward will increasingly and inexorably depend on how they will fare in relation to issues of justice.

How to Use This Book

Readers can access information according to topic in several ways. The **Table of Contents** in the beginning of the book gives an overview of the two parts of the book: **Part I**, the longer subject matter essays and **Part II**, A through Z entries and cross-referencing of entry topics. The Table of Contents is especially useful in identifying the longer essays on major topics that provide context and depth. Each long essay integrates other topics that are germane to the central theme of that essay. At the end of a long essay, related topics are listed which the reader can find elsewhere in the volume.

Following the Table of Contents and the A to Z Entries is a **Guide to Related Topics**. This guide separates all topics found in the book and lists them under their appropriate general category. A particular topic or essay can be found in the Table of Contents, List of Entries, and the Guide to Related Topics. Finally, an essay or entry could include words or phrases in **bold**. A word or phrase in bold signifies that it is a topic in the book for which additional information is available elsewhere in the volume.

Terminology ("Latina/o" or "Hispanic")

The question of which term—"Latina/o" or "Hispanic"—is more appropriate has been a subject of considerable discussion. Formally adopted by the U.S. government in the 1970s, "Hispanic" has been the category used in government agency studies and reports. It is a term that identifies a person by tracing their ethnic identity to Spain and those from countries that were part of the former Spanish colonial empire. The term "Hispanic" has been deemed unsatisfactory and imprecise as it homogenizes the identities and experiences of diverse groups of people from numerous countries of Latin America, not those from Spain. Persons from Latin America, whose presence in the United States is central to the subject matter of this book, are diverse peoples. They come from countries with varying cultural and historical experiences, and they do not necessarily share Spanish as a common language (many indigenous languages are spoken throughout Latin American countries). Objections to the term "Hispanic" also have been registered because "Hispanic" appears to value only that derived from European and Spanish colonialism, invalidating the diverse indigenous and African heritages that also are part of the identity of persons from Latin America and the Caribbean. This issue is not a simple matter when considering that racial difference, frequently discussed in this book, is at the core of how Latinas/os are viewed and treated or mistreated by the U.S. criminal justice system.

Surveys indicate that when given the option, Latinas/os prefer to identify themselves by the country of origin—Colombian, Dominican, Panamanian, and so forth—but many also share a sense of belonging as part of a community of persons of Latin American ancestry in the United States (Pew Hispanic Center/Kaiser Family Foundation 2002). The term "Latino" has come into greater use over time as a term describing a shared identity and experience in the United States. In acknowledging the increased use of the term, government agencies, including the Census Bureau, have begun to use the term "Latino" interchangeably with "Hispanic."

The term most often used by contributors to this book throughout this book is "Latina" or "Latino." The use of "Latina/o" is used to recognize both genders. The term "Hispanic" is also used in this book, primarily in reference to sources, such as a U.S. government report where the term was used originally. Another identifier applied frequently to Latinas/os is "minority." Typically used to identify a disadvantaged racial or ethnic group in the United States, the term can carry negative connotations as being "less than" and therefore "people of color" and "communities of color" are used most often in this text instead.

Race, Ethnicity, and Data on Latinas/os

The federal government defines "Hispanic" as an ethnic classification, as it considers that Hispanics could be of any of the racial categories it uses. The four basic racial categories U.S. government agencies originally used were black, white, Asian, and American Indian. These classifications have undergone some modifications. The National Crime Victimization Survey (NCVS), for example, collects information on victimization and the racial categories NCVS lists in its most recent surveys are: "white, black/African American, American Indian/Alaska Native, Asian/Native Hawaiian/other Pacific Islander, and other race" (Bureau of Justice Statistics 2015). As an "ethnic" group, Hispanics/Latinas/os fall outside of these racial categories. As a result, criminal justice agencies across the United States have not necessarily kept consistent and accurate data about Latinas/os, or have kept none at all. Some agencies place Latinas/os in the category of "white," for example, and thereby overstate the numbers of whites and ignore Latinas/os.

More government agencies—such as NCVS—are gathering statistics on race and include the category "Hispanic/Latino." But deficiencies in the information available on Latinas/os persist. Data available by state about arrests, racial profiling, pretrial detainment, sentencing, and community reintegration can differ greatly, as there is no national standard or mandate to maintain such data or uniformity in including Latinas/os. In fact, the usefulness of the **Uniform Crime Reports** (UCR) issued by the Federal Bureau of Investigation (FBI) is limited when it comes to matters related to race, ethnicity, and crime because data collected on "crimes known to police" excludes race, and there is no separate category for "Hispanics" when data is gathered on arrests (Walker, Spohn & DeLone 2012, 19). Advocates and analysts alike are among those calling for improvements in data collection to include not only the category of "Latina/o," but also data that provides a breakdown of Latina/o national origin groups (*see, e.g.,* Californians for Safety and Justice, 2014). Disaggregating the data into the specific national origin group could provide useful information about how to better serve the needs of particular groups. Cognizant of the statistical shortcomings, the contributors to this book have sought to use the best available data that includes Latinas/os.

Advisory Board for This Volume

This book was supported by the efforts of an advisory board that provided valuable insights and comments on various entries and portions of this volume. The following individuals served as advisory board members: Kevin R. Johnson, dean, Mabie-Apallas professor of Public Interest Law, and professor of Chicana/o Studies at the University of California at Davis School of Law; Francisco A. Villarruel, associate chair for Education and Outreach, Department of Human Development and Family Studies, and University Outreach and Engagement Senior Fellow at Michigan State University; Sandra Del Valle, civil rights attorney and educator; and Louis Kontos, assistant professor at John Jay College of Criminal Justice. I extend my appreciation to them for their assistance and inspiring work. Responsibility for the contents of this book solely resides with the editor and not with the advisory board members.

Acknowledgments

A book of this magnitude requires the dedication and efforts of many people. I wish to thank the contributors of the entries for their work and for their engagement and commitment to this project: Luis Barrios, Leonard Baynes,

Juan Cartagena, Ric Curtis, Sandra Del Valle, Nitza Milagros Escalera, Hernando A. Estévez, Rosa Maria Gonzalez-Guarda, Nancy Guarneros, Melissa Guzman, David Manuel Hernández, Manuel A. Huerta, Joshua G. Kellison, Louis Kontos, Yolanda C. Martín, Isabel Martínez, Ramiro Martínez, Jr., Louis Mendoza, Brian Montes, Marco Fernando Navarro, Judith Perez Caro, Lisandro Pérez, François Restrepo-Serrano, Robert Riggs, Victor M. Rios, Jenny Rivera, Evin R. Rodkey, Hector W. Soto, Maria Swimm, Manuel D. Vargas, and Charles R. Venator-Santiago. Biographical information on each of the contributors can be found at the end of this book.

I want to recognize and thank the many others who provided logistical, editing, and other forms of support in organizing and compiling this volume, including Maria Swimm, Brian Montes, Isabel Martínez, Yolanda C. Martín, Sandra Del Valle, and Jodie Roure. Maria (Mady) Swimm is deserving of a special word of praise for her extraordinary work in assisting with editing and helping with this project in a myriad of other ways. I am also grateful for the support provided by John Jay College students, Anthony Albertorio and Harrison Garcia, and my colleagues at the Latin American and Latina/o Studies Department at John Jay College of Criminal Justice. This project would not have been possible without the team at Greenwood Press. I thank them, and most especially Kim Kennedy-White, Senior Acquisitions Editor, American Mosaic, for her support and patience. Finally, I thank my wife, Jeanette Guillén-Morín, for all she does to assist and sustain me in all my endeavors.

Further Reading

Bureau of Justice Statistics. 2015. "Race /ethnicity." Washington, DC: Bureau of Justice Statistics, U.S. Department of Justice. http://www.bjs.gov/index.cfm?ty=tp&tid=922.

Butcher, Kristen F., and Anne Morrison Piehl. 2005. "Why are immigrants' incarceration rates so low? Evidence on selective immigration deterrence, and deportation." *Working Papers 2005–19*. Chicago: Federal Reserve Bank of Chicago, http://www.chicagofed.org/publications/workingpapers/wp2005_19.pdf.

Californians for Safety and Justice. (2014). *Latino voices: The Impacts of crime and criminal justice on Latinos.* Oakland, CA: Californians for Safety and Justice. http://libcloud.s3.amazonaws.com/211/04/1/430/LatinoReport_7.8.14v1.pdf.

Delgado, Richard, Juan F. Perea, and Jean Stefancic. 2008. *Latinos and the law: Cases and materials.* St. Paul, MN: Thomson/West.

Ennis, Sharon R., Merarys Ríos-Vargas, and Nora G. Albert. 2011. The Hispanic Population: 2010. U.S. Census Bureau. http://www.census.gov/prod/cen2010/briefs/c2010br-04.pdf. Accessed November 12, 2015.

Hagan, John, and Alberto Palloni. 1999. "Sociological criminology and the mythology of Hispanic immigration and crime." *Social Problems* 46 (4): 617–32.

Karman, Andrew. 2000. *New York murder mystery: The true story behind the crime crash of the 1990s.* New York: New York University Press.

Lee, Matthew. 2003. *Crime on the border: Immigration and homicide in urban communities.* New York: LFB Scholarly Publishing.

Lopez, Mark Hugo, Ana Gonzalez-Barrera, and Danielle Cuddington. 2013. Diverse origins: The nation's 14 largest Hispanic-origin groups. Washington, DC: Pew Research Center/Hispanic Trends. http://www.pewhispanic.org/2013/06/19/diverse-origins-the-nations-14-largest-hispanic-origin-groups/. Accessed November 12, 2015.

MacDonald, John M., John R. Hipp, and Charlotte Gill. 2013. "The effects of immigrant concentration on changes in neighborhood crime rates." *Journal of Quantitative Criminology,* 29 (2):191–215. doi 10.1007/s10940-012-9176-8.

Martínez, Jr., Ramiro. 2002. *Latino homicide: Immigration, violence and community*. New York: Routledge.

Morín, José Luis. 2009. *Latino/a rights and justice in the United States: Perspectives and approaches*, 2nd ed. Durham, NC: Carolina Academic Press.

Motel, Seth, and Eileen Patten. 2012. "The 10 Largest Hispanic Origin Groups: Characteristics, Rankings, Top Counties." Washington, DC: Pew Hispanic Center. http://www.pewhispanic.org/2012/06/27/the-10-largest-hispanic-origin-groups-characteristics-rankings-top-counties/. Accessed November 12, 2015.

Oboler, Suzanne. 1995. *Ethnic labels, Latino lives: Identity and the politics of representation in the United States*. Minneapolis, Minnesota: University of Minnesota Press.

Pew Hispanic Center/Kaiser Family Foundation. 2002. *2002 National Survey of Latinos*. Washington, DC: Pew Hispanic Center/Kaiser Family Foundation.

Rumbaut, Rubén G., and Walter A. Ewing. 2007. "The myth of immigrant criminality and the paradox of assimilation." Immigration Policy Center. http://www.immigrationpolicy.org/special-reports/myth-immigrant-criminality-and-paradox-assimilation. Accessed November 12, 2015.

Vigdor, Jacob L. 2014. *Immigration and New York City: The contributions of foreign-born Americans to New York's renaissance,* 1975–2013. New York: Americas Society/Council of the Americas.

Villarruel, Francisco A., and Nancy E. Walker, with Pamela Minifree, Omara Rivera-Vázquez, Susan Peterson, and Kristen Perry. 2002. *¿Dónde está la justicia? A call to action on behalf of Latino and Latina youth in the U.S. justice system.* Washington, DC: Michigan State University/Building Blocks for Youth.

Walker, Nancy E., J. Michael Senger, Francisco A. Villarruel, and Angela M. Arboleda. 2004. *Lost opportunities: The reality of Latinos in the U.S. criminal justice system*. Washington, DC: National Council of La Raza.

Walker, Samuel, Cassia Spohn, and Miriam DeLone. 2012. *The color of justice: Race, ethnicity, and crime in America.* 5th ed. Belmont, CA: Thomson/Wadsworth.

Part I

Essays on Latinas/os and Criminal Justice

Latinas/os and the U.S. Criminal Justice System: An Overview of Socio-Historic and Contemporary Issues

José Luis Morín

Latinas/os are one of the fastest growing demographic groups in the United States, and it is expected that—along with their numbers—their social, economic, and political significance to the country also will rise. Yet, Latinas/os generally are not well understood, and in relation to crime and the U.S. criminal system, they have been more often than not absent or ignored in the scholarly research. Their invisibility in academic studies and publications and in the collection of vital criminal justice data has resulted in their exclusion from key policy criminal justice deliberations. The void of adequate and accurate information about the reality and experience of Latinas/os in relation to crime and the U.S. criminal justice system has too frequently been filled with stereotypes, myths, and mistaken assumptions. Although there still is much to be studied and understood, social scientific studies and research in recent years have been providing a certain amount of clarity on the subject, dispelling many popular misperceptions and portrayals of U.S. Latinas/os in relation to crime.

This essay presents an overview of major facets of the U.S. Latina/o experience of criminal justice, grounded in contemporary research and empirical studies. The departure point of this synopsis is the overarching demographic, historical, social, political, and economic context of U.S. relations and policies towards Latin America and its peoples as well as the trajectory of Latinas/os within the United States in relation to questions of justice and injustice. This overview does not attempt to summarize all of the entries in this book, as it is not possible to cover every criminal justice issue affecting Latinas/os. It does, however, seek to provide a background, contextual data, and information for topics discussed more extensively throughout this volume.

Data reveal that Latinas/os have been incarcerated at rates that are disproportionate to their representation in the overall population in the United States. Based solely on this fact, one would assume that Latinas/os simply are committing more crimes. But a closer and more thorough examination of the research suggests a different conclusion. Studies consistently show that disparities between Latinas/os and whites point to persistent problems of unequal treatment and racial and ethnic bias in the criminal justice system. Prominent criminologists assert that—based on the evidence—one would be mistaken or remiss to believe that race and ethnicity do not play crucial roles in the treatment of persons of color—Latinas/os and African Americans, in particular—in the criminal justice system. In addition to race and ethnicity, Latinas/os also experience a range of social, economic, and other forms of disadvantage that often are deeply rooted in U.S. history and society that influence in the criminal justice arena.

How the United States viewed and treated Latin America and its peoples from the earliest years of its founding influenced how U.S. society would treat persons of Latin American descent within its borders in later years in every aspect of society, including matters of law and justice. Inequities and injustices that befell past generations have had a lasting impact on present-day Latina/o communities. Thus, the persistence of unequal treatment and of myths and misperceptions about Latinas/os becomes relevant shaping current criminal justice policies and practices. In addition to addressing these dimensions of the U.S. Latina/o experience, this essay outlines the many enduring racial and ethnic disparities within the criminal justice system that affect Latina/o communities. At a time when concerns are mounting with regard to a system that seemingly does not mete out justice fairly across racial and ethnic lines, this essay examines contemporary issues confronting U.S. society, and the trends and needs to be addressed to reduce disparities and promote a more equitable system for all, including Latinas/os.

Demographics: Latinas/os in the United States

An examination of criminal justice issues and Latinas/os in the United States invariably must include a look at the **demographic** trends and data that shed light on the importance of this particular segment of the population and aid in understanding questions related to criminal justice. In recent years, census data has shown that the Latino/a population in the United States is growing rapidly. By 2012, the Latinas/os population had grown to 53 million people in the United States—a 50 percent rise from 2000 and a six-fold increase since 1970. Latinas/os accounted for half of the country's growth from 2000 to 2012—the overall population rose just 12 percent during that same period (Brown 2014). As of July 2013, Latinas/os represented 17 percent of the U.S. population, with the Census Bureau projecting that the group would reach 28 percent by 2050 (U.S. Bureau of the Census 2014).

This increasing segment of the country's population, however, is not homogeneous. Latinas/os originate from different countries in Latin America and Spain. (Although Latinas/os most often are associated with persons of Latin American origin, the U.S. Bureau of the Census includes Spaniards in the count of "Hispanics/Latinos.") Similarities notwithstanding, each group has its own distinct culture, history, traditions, linguistic variations, and economic and social conditions. The geographic area where each group is found in greatest numbers within the United States also varies. In the West and Southwest regions of the United States, it is most common to find Latinas/os of Mexican ancestry, and on the East coast of the United States, Latinas/os from the Spanish-speaking Caribbean are more predominant. These regional differences often are linked to historical events, such as the U.S. war against Mexico that resulted in the United States taking possession of the northern half of Mexico in 1848 that now comprises U.S. states where some of the largest Mexican populations reside.

Of all Latinas/os residing in the 50 states and the District of Columbia today, 64.6 percent (more than 33 million) are persons of Mexican origin, with Puerto Ricans being the second largest Latina/o group at 9.5 percent (Lopez, Gonzalez-Barrera, & Cuddington 2013.). Mexicans—the largest of all Latina/o groups—comprise a majority of Latinas/os in all but 11 states. Puerto Ricans represent the

Latina/o Population in the United States: Highlights

- U.S. Latina/o Population in 2014: 53,027,708, a 50% increase since 2000
- Only 37 percent of Latinas/os were foreign-born in 2012
- 74% of Latinas/os are U.S. citizens
- Approximately two-thirds of all U.S. Latinas/os are of Mexican origin

Population	Numbers	Percentage of Latinas/os
Mexicans	33,539,000	64.6
Puerto Ricans	4,916,000	9.5*
Salvadorans	1,952,000	3.8
Cubans	1,889,000	3.6
Dominicans	1,528,000	2.9
Guatemalans	1,216,000	2.3
Colombians	989,000	1.9
Spaniards	707,000	1.4
Hondurans	702,000	1.4
Ecuadorians	645,000	1.2
Peruvians	556,000	1.1
Nicaraguans	395,000	0.5
Argentineans	242,000	0.5

* Population and percentage numbers do not include Puerto Ricans living on the island of Puerto Rico.

Sources: Brown, Anna. 2014. The U.S. Hispanic population has increased six-fold since 1970. Washington, DC: Pew Research Center/Pew Hispanic Center. http://www.pewresearch.org/fact-tank/2014/02/26/the-u-s-hispanic-population-has-increased-sixfold-since-1970/.

Lopez, Mark Hugo, Ana Gonzalez-Barrera, and Danielle Cuddington. 2013. Diverse origins: The nation's 14 largest Hispanic-origin groups. Washington, DC: Pew Research Center/Hispanic Trends. http://www.pewhispanic.org/2013/06/19/diverse-origins-the-nations-14-largest-hispanic-origin-groups/.

Motel, Seth, and Eileen Patten. 2012. The 10 largest Hispanic origin groups: Characteristics, rankings, top counties. Washington, DC: Pew Hispanic Center. http://www.pewhispanic.org/2012/06/27/the-10-largest-hispanic-origin-groups-characteristics-rankings-top-counties/.

U.S. Bureau of the Census. 2014. Facts for features: Hispanic heritage month 2014, Sept. 15 –Oct. 15. http://www.census.gov/content/dam/Census/newsroom/facts-for-features/2014/cb14ff-22_hispanic.pdf.

largest Latina/o group in New York and New Jersey, and Cubans are most concentrated in Florida. A close look at Latina/o groups reveals discernible differences among them. The population of Mexican descent tend to be the youngest of all Latinas/os—median age 25 years—in contrast to Cubans' median age of 40 years. Although Venezuelans have the highest rate of college degree attainment at 51 percent, Salvadorans and Guatemalans are at 7 percent each (Brown 2014).

Nativity and U.S. Citizenship

Recent data also show that one would be mistaken to believe that most Latinas/os are foreign born, noncitizens. Thirty-seven percent of Latinas/os are foreign born, and close to three-out-of-four (74%) Latinas/os are U.S. citizens (Motel & Patten 2012). Moreover, as the flow of foreign-born immigrants from Mexico and Latin America has slowed in recently years, U.S.-born Latinas/os are driving the fast growth of the Latina/o population in the United States.

English Language Proficiency and Educational Attainment

Other recent data point to the progress that Latinas/os have made as well as the challenges ahead. Contrary to the popular notion that most Latinas/os are not learning English, a substantial number of Latinas/os speak English proficiently—68 percent in 2013 (Krogstad, Stepler & Lopez 2015). As for educational achievement, 26 percent of Latinas/os aged 25 years or older only have a high school diploma, as compared to 28 percent of the total U.S. population, with Puerto Ricans at the higher end (30 percent) and Guatemalans on the lower end of high school diploma attainment (22 percent). Approximately 13 percent of Latinas/os aged 25 years or older have obtained a bachelor's degree, as compared to 28 percent of the total U.S. population, with Colombians at some of the highest levels of attainment among Latinas/os (32 percent) and Salvadorans having the lowest rate (7 percent) (Motel & Patten 2012).

Income, Poverty, and Health Insurance

Economically, Latina/o median household income in 2010 was $40,000, which is lower than the $49,800 median income for the total U.S. population. Of all Latina/o groups, Ecuadorians had the highest median household income at $50,000, followed by Colombians ($49,500) and Peruvians ($48,000). Among the groups with the lowest median household income were Dominicans ($34,000), Puerto Ricans ($36,000), and Hondurans ($38,900). In 2010, Latinas/os endured an overall poverty rate of 25 percent, as compared to only 15 percent for the total U.S. population. Compared to all other racial/ethnic groups, the largest group living in poverty in the United States is Latina/o children. At 27 percent, Mexicans, Puerto Ricans, and Hondurans have the greatest poverty rates, with Dominicans and Guatemalans at 26 percent. Colombians (13 percent) and Peruvians (14 percent) had a lower poverty rate than the total U.S. rate of 15 percent in 2010 (Motel & Patten 2012). The income disparities between Latinas/os and whites are especially concerning when gender is considered. Census data show that, on average, women in the United States generally are paid only 77 cents for every dollar paid to men. Women of color fare much worse, however, earning 70 cents for every dollar paid to men, and **Latinas** earn just 55 cents for every dollar paid to white men (*Huffington Post* 2013).

With respect to healthcare, Latinas/os do not fare well as compared to the rest of the population. An estimated 31 percent of

Latinas/os lack health insurance, in contrast to 16 percent of the total U.S. population. Hondurans, in particular, experience the worst situation, with half being uninsured. Guatemalans at 48 percent and Salvadorans at 41 percent are among the most uninsured Latinas/os. Puerto Ricans at 15 percent, Dominicans at 22 percent, and Cubans at 25 percent are more likely to have health insurance (Motel & Patten 2012).

The Impact of Low Socioeconomic Conditions and Segregation

Socioeconomic conditions and challenges that Latinas/os face have an impact on their vulnerability to interactions with crime, the criminal justice system, and their ability to navigate the system. Latinas/os are disproportionately poor compared to whites (one-in-four Latinas/os are poor in contrast to one-in-nine whites) and Latinas/os are three times more likely than whites to not have health insurance (Walker et al. 2004, 7). Poverty strongly correlates with high rates of incarceration, and Latinas/os—who are disproportionately affected by poverty—tend to experience many challenges in their dealings with the criminal justice system. For example, criminologists and other analysts have identified low socioeconomic circumstances as impacting one's ability to

- Seek help for substance abuse and thereby prevent encounters with law enforcement,
- Obtain adequate legal representation to ensure a fair outcome in the criminal justice system, and
- Make bail and thereby avoid receiving harsher treatment by the criminal justice system (as a consequence for not making bail).

Racial and ethnic **segregation** in schools and housing has been implicated in exacerbating and contributing directly to problems related to crime. From 1968 to 2011, schools around the country became increasingly segregated, and dramatic changes in school enrollment have taken place—enrollment by white students dropped by 28 percent, African American student enrollment rose 19 percent, and Latina/o student enrollment grew a startling 495 percent (Orfield & Frankenberg 2014, 6). The end result is that Latina/o children experience extremely high levels of school segregation around the United States today.

Segregation, a problem that historically was most associated with the Southern states of the country, is a national problem. New York State, for example, a state with an overall Latina/o population of 18.4 percent in 2013, has been deemed to have the most segregated school system in the country (U.S. Census Bureau 2015a). It surpasses all other states in African American and Latina/o students attending highly segregated schools—that is, schools where whites are less than 10 percent of student enrollment (Kucsera with Orfield, 2014, 3). New York City, with a 28.6 percent overall Latina/o population, also is recognized as having one of the most segregated public school systems in the nation (U.S. Census Bureau 2015b; Kucsera with Orfield 2014, 3).

Socioeconomic Conditions and Victimization

Latinas/os experience high levels of **victimization** in the United States, particularly as compared to the experience of whites. Data from 1994 to 2011 show that Latinas/os were more likely to be victims of shootings than whites, but were less likely than African Americans (Planty & Truman 2013). Studies also suggest Latinas/os to be more vulnerable to being victims of crime than whites. Along with African Americans, Latinas/os tend to

Latinas/os and Segregation in the United States: Findings of the Civil Rights Project/*Proyecto Derechos Civiles* at the University of California Los Angeles, 2014.

Excerpt from the Report

The growth of segregation has been most dramatic for Latino students, particularly in the West, where there was substantial integration in the 1960s, and segregation has soared. A clear pattern is developing of black and Latino students sharing the same schools; it deserves serious attention from educators and policy makers.

Segregation is typically segregation by both race and poverty. Black and Latino students tend to be in schools with a substantial majority of poor children, but white and Asian students are typically in middle-class schools.

Segregation is by far the most serious in the central cities of the largest metropolitan areas, but it is also severe in central cities of all sizes and suburbs of the largest metro areas, which are now half nonwhite. Latinos are significantly more segregated than blacks in suburban America.

The Supreme Court has fundamentally changed desegregation law, and many major court orders have been dropped. Our statistical analysis shows that segregation increased substantially after the plans were terminated in many large districts (Orfield et al. 2014, 2).

be robbed and assaulted by strangers more than whites, especially during times of economic downturn. Overall, Latinas/os endured higher rates of home break-ins than whites, lesser rates than for African Americans.

Researchers have linked low socioeconomic status and conditions to increased susceptibility to **victimization** and exposure to crime (Walker, Spohn, & DeLone 2012; California Endowment 2010). A number of studies have shown that social and economic disadvantage is a factor in homicide rates in various cities in the United States. In the state of California, where many Latinas/os face difficult economic and social conditions, the Latina/o homicide rate is double that of whites, and Latinas/os are more likely to be victims of multiple crimes—three or more in the last five years (Californians for Safety and Justice 2014, 6). Research suggests that a more equitable economic and social structure would have a stabilizing effect because poverty, education, and other socioeconomic differences appear to account for differences between Latina/o and white victimization (Phillips 2002).

Socioeconomic disparities have had a devastating impact on children of color, with African American and Latina/o children being 3.5 times more likely to grow up in poverty than white children and with approximately half of all African American and Latina/o fourth graders attending schools under conditions of extreme poverty. Health risks run high for Latinas/os, who are 2.5 times less likely to have access to healthcare services than whites, and are 4.8 times more likely to not have health insurance. Latino boys and young men experience post-traumatic stress disorder at a rate 4.1 times greater than white boys and young men (California Endowment 2010, 5–6).

Racial and ethnic segregation tends to concentrate crime, low educational and job opportunities, poverty, and mental and physical health problems in neighborhoods of color. As studies have shown, Latina/o and African American children are disproportionately exposed to high levels of violence; often are deprived of healthy foods; suffer unduly from illnesses, such as asthma; are the most susceptible to school suspensions and expulsions associated with the "**school-to-prison pipeline**"; and have increased chances of contact with the criminal justice system or problems related to criminal justice (California Endowment 2010).

Race and Racialization: Historical Perspective

The impact and role of race and ethnicity in the U.S. criminal justice system cannot be fully understood without an examination of the historical context to aid in explaining the roots of present-day perceptions and misperceptions that influence criminal justice decisions, policies, and practices. The idea of "race" and the significance that was placed on distinguishing people based on differences in skin color profoundly affected the lives of those living in the United States—some reaping tremendous advantages and privileges, and others enduring oppression, discrimination, and hardship. In the United States, those with any African ancestry were commonly viewed as an inferior race, undeserving of respect or equality, and subjected to the scourge of slavery. Even after slavery was abolished, racial segregation and injustice remained legally sanctioned for many years. Racial and ethnic prejudice and inequality continues today, despite the many efforts of the civil rights movement and legislation—such as the Civil Rights Act of 1964 and other laws—designed to eradicate racial and other forms of discrimination.

Similar to the African American experience, Latinas/os have had to face "racial" discrimination, and they have often been "racialized" in the United States—that is, thought to be "other" or "less than" in association with racial and ethnic characteristics. Race and the **racialization** of Latinas/os in many ways is part of what helps explain the Latina/o presence in the United States, as many of the first Latinas/os in the United States were not immigrants who crossed the border; instead, the border crossed over them. In fact, the presence of the two largest Latino/a groups in the United States today—Mexicans and Puerto Ricans—can be traced to U.S. expansionist endeavors of the 19th century, and sizable numbers of these respective populations were in the territories taken under United States control in the 1800s. In large measure, the justification for these territorial conquests was the supposed inherent racial inferiority of the peoples of Latin America.

Scholars note that Latin America experienced a "double conquest"—first by European powers, most notably Spain, and later the United States. As many Latin American countries sought freedom from Spain and other European countries in the 1800s, the United States surged ahead with designs of becoming a regional and global power of its own that could rival Europe's most powerful countries, extending its territory, economic markets, and political sphere of influence.

Very early on, founders of the United States embraced expansionist ambitions. As early as 1767, Benjamin Franklin spoke of acquiring Mexico and Cuba for a country that had not yet gained independence from Britain. Thomas Jefferson envisioned the United States having the "hemisphere to itself . . . a separate system of interest which must not be subordinated to those of Europe," and by the

1780s Jefferson called for the undoing and taking of the Spanish empire "peice by peice [*sic*]" (quoted in Smith 2013, 19). The historical record shows that the United States did not come upon an empire by accident, but rather by design. United States policy makers intentionally set out to "take" lands, as Secretary of State James Blaine had done in 1891 by identifying "three places that are of value enough to be taken that are not continental. . . . One is Hawaii and the others are Cuba and Porto Rico [*sic*]" (quoted in LaFeber [1963] 1998, 110). Because the United States initially was a slave-owning country, with many of its founders being slave-owners themselves, race profoundly shaped the lens through which U.S. decision makers viewed the world and the prerogatives they considered were rightfully theirs as white people.

Manifest Destiny

Coined by journalist John O'Sullivan in 1845, "manifest destiny" is a term that was both a catchphrase and a rationale for U.S. territorial expansionism in the 19th century. Ideologically, it resonated with policy makers and the Anglo-American public alike, effectively justifying U.S. expansionism based on what was believed to be self-evident: that white Anglo-Americans possessed a God-given right to territorial expansion based on their superiority in race, religion, culture, and intellect, as compared to all other "races" found in North America, Latin America, Asia, or Africa. The acquisition of territories after the wars with the newly independent state of Mexico in the 1840s and the war against Spain in 1898 were justified, in good part, on the assumption that Mexicans, Puerto Ricans, Filipinos, and other populations living in the lands the United States conquered were racially inferior to Anglo-Americans—so inferior that they could only benefit from Anglo-American domination.

Among policy makers, the racial inferiority of Latin Americans often was part of the public discourse. In the 1800s, many prominent political figures—including James Buchanan—regularly made reference to the "Mexican race" as a "mongrel" race incapable of participation in a democracy (Horsman 1981, 251). Senator John C. Calhoun opposed U.S. expansionists' ventures into Mexico for fear of what it would mean to "incorporate" Mexicans into the United States. In his words, "Ours, sir, is the Government of a white race . . . it would be a fatal error of placing these colored races on an equality with the white race" (Cong. Globe, 30th Cong., 1st Sess. 96–98 (Jan. 4, 1848); quoted in Perea et al. 2007, 295).

President James K. Polk, a staunch advocate for manifest destiny, succeeded in instigating a war with Mexico in 1846 by placing U.S. troops on the border of the United States and Mexico. By 1848, Polk fulfilled the dream of wresting approximately half of the entire country of Mexico—roughly one-third of the continental United States today that are now the states of California, Texas, New Mexico, Arizona, Nevada, and portions of Colorado, Utah, and Kansas. Along with Mexican lands seized by the U.S. government at the end of the war, approximately 75,000 to 100,000 Mexican residents remained. The fear of giving this "mongrel" race equality with whites resulted in severe restrictions in their ability to assert rights under U.S. law.

The Treaty of Guadalupe Hidalgo of 1848, which ended the war between the United States and Mexico, not only forced Mexico to surrender vast regions of its country (that were rich in resources) to the United States—notwithstanding the mere $15 million payment to provide a veil of legitimacy for the seizure of this land—but the treaty also failed to adequately protect the rights of those Mexicans who remained in the conquered territories. To placate fears that white political, social, and economic domination and authority might be threatened, article IX of the Treaty of Guadalupe Hidalgo was amended to assure that Mexicans in the conquered territories would not be extended full citizenship rights immediately, but rather at a "proper time" to be decided by the U.S. Congress. Additionally, article X of the treaty, which sought to ensure that "[a]ll grants of land made by the Mexican government or by the competent authorities, in the territories previously appertaining to Mexico" could remain in the possession of the original Mexican owners was deleted from the final document, virtually guaranteeing the loss of the Mexican owners' lands to Anglo-Americans settlers (Delgado, Perea, & Stefancic 2008, 16). The changes to the treaty in contravention of international law standards; land claims courts that failed to protect land rights of Mexican Americans; and racially hostile white settlers who used legal and illegal means—including violence—to secure their control over land all worked in combination to marginalize Mexicans and essentially reduce them to persons without rights.

In keeping with the racial assumptions intrinsic to manifest destiny, all Latin Americans—not just Mexicans—were viewed as and treated by U.S. policy makers as being racially inferior. Latin Americans—including Puerto Ricans, Cubans, Nicaraguans, and other Central and South Americans—were presumed to be so racially deficient that they, as with Mexicans, endured incursions into their lands and violations of their rights to political, economic, social, and cultural self-determination throughout the 19th century and beyond. Such was and continues to be the case for Puerto Ricans, who today make up the second largest Latina/o group in the United States. As in the case of Mexico, the United States engaged in war—in this instance with Spain in 1898—to expand its territory and take control of island nations in

Restricting Latina/o Rights: 1848

Restrictions on the ability of Mexicans to exercise full rights as U.S. citizens in the territories wrested by the United States after the U.S. war with Mexico included the amendment to article IX of the Treaty of Guadalupe-Hidalgo of 1848 (shown in italics below), to provide the U.S. Congress the power to determine when complete rights can be accorded, allaying racial fears that white political and economic domination and authority might be threatened.

> Article IX:
>
> The Mexicans who, in the territories aforesaid, shall not preserve the character of citizens of the Mexican Republic, conformably with what is stipulated in the preceding article, shall be incorporated into the Union of the United States and be admitted, *at the proper time (to be judged of by the Congress of the United States)* to the enjoyment of all the rights of citizens of the United States, according to the principles of the Constitution; and in the meantime, shall be maintained and protected in the free enjoyment of their liberty and property, and secured in the free exercise of their religion without restriction [emphasis added] (quoted in Delgado, Perea, & Stefancic 2008, 18–19).

the Pacific and the Caribbean, including the Philippines, Guam, Cuba, and Puerto Rico. Puerto Rico became a territorial possession, but the rights of Puerto Ricans residing in their homeland have been strictly constrained under U.S. law.

Among the U.S. Supreme Court cases that still define Puerto Rico's relationship to the United States today (the *Insular Cases*) is the 1901 case of *Downes v. Bidwell*. The *Downes* case—a case decided by many of the same justices who decided the infamous 1896 *Plessy v. Ferguson* case—held that Puerto Rico was as an "unincorporated" territory "belonging to but not a part of" the United States (Torruella 1988; Trías Monge 1997). Similar to the fear raised about "incorporating" Mexicans into the Union because they were an inferior "mongrel" race, the *Downes* case posits the view that Puerto Ricans and other peoples within the newly acquired U.S. territories were "alien races" incapable of understanding the virtues of a democratic government and, as such, they were not intended to be incorporated into the United States and were not worthy of equal rights under the U.S. Constitution or U.S. laws.

Even after the U.S. Congress imposed U.S. "citizenship" on Puerto Ricans without their consent in 1917, as residents of an "unincorporated territory" Puerto Ricans still were not accorded—and continue not to possess—full rights as U.S. citizens. In 1917, the U.S. Congress passed the Jones Act making Puerto Ricans U.S. citizens, ignoring a vote by the Puerto Rican legislature to retain Puerto Rican citizenship. In a lawsuit challenging the idea that Puerto Ricans could be denied equal rights under the U.S. Constitution even though they are U.S. citizens, the U.S. Supreme Court in *Balzac v. People of Porto Rico* [sic] (1922) ruled that Puerto Rico remains an "unincorporated territory," and, in accordance with the Territorial Clause of the U.S. Constitution, article IV, section 3, paragraph 2, Congress continues to exercise absolute or "plenary" power to grant or deny rights to Puerto Ricans, even though they are called U.S. "citizens." Plenary powers also were granted to Congress under article IX of the Treaty of Paris, which ended the U.S. war with Spain. Congress was granted the authority to decide the civil rights of Puerto Ricans and the political status of Puerto Rico. Based on this reasoning, the Court in the *Balzac* case found that the basic right to a jury trial under the U.S. Constitution was inapplicable to Puerto Ricans, unless Congress expressly grants that right.

The congressional record also is clear. Congress never intended to give Puerto Ricans rights as full U.S. citizens, and instead applied the term "citizen" to Puerto Ricans so that the United States would not appear to possess colonial subjects. As a result, Puerto Ricans born on their homeland today are considered U.S. "citizens," but their rights are severely restricted. To this day, the United States reserves the right to limit the basic rights of Puerto Ricans under a legal framework devised by U.S. Supreme Court decisions grounded in racially biased reasoning.

The *Downes* and *Balzac* cases—having never been overturned by the U.S. Supreme Court—still apply today. Puerto Ricans born on their island nation are U.S. "citizens" at birth, but are not afforded equal rights under U.S. law. Puerto Ricans cannot vote in presidential elections, although the President of the United States can order them to fight in U.S. wars, which they have done since World War I. Puerto Ricans have no voting representation or meaningful voice in the U.S. Congress, even though Congress passes laws that affect them. Puerto Ricans have no control over treaties or foreign matters that

> In accordance with the Jones Act which was passed into law by the U.S. Congress in 1917, persons born in Puerto Rico are U.S. citizens. In the debate about what "citizenship" was to actually mean, however, the Congressional Record makes clear that "those people" (Puerto Ricans) were not going to have any rights that the American people did not see fit to give them, as expressed by Senator Joseph B. Foraker of Ohio on the "granting" of U.S. "citizenship" to Puerto Ricans:
>
> > We considered very carefully what status in a political sense we would give to the people of [Puerto Rico], and we reported that provision not thoughtlessly. . . . We concluded . . . that the inhabitants of that island must be either citizens or subjects or aliens. We did not want to treat our own as aliens, and we do not propose to have any subjects. Therefore, we adopted the term "citizens." *In adopting the term "citizen" we did not understand, however, that we were giving to those people any right that the American people do not want them to have.* "Citizens" is a word that indicates, according to Story's work on the Constitution of the United States, allegiance on the one hand and protection on the other (Cabranes 1979, 37, quoting Sen. Foraker, 33 Cong. Rec. 2473–74 [1900]) [emphasis added].

affect Puerto Rico; the United States controls all trade, maritime, immigration, and monetary policies. Social Security and other federal benefits to Puerto Ricans are not equal to citizens living in the continental United States. Puerto Ricans are subject to the jurisdiction of the U.S. federal court system—which conducts its business entirely in English, not Spanish. The United States has had free reign to use Puerto Rico's land for military bases, bombing exercises, and other purposes without compensation. Although Puerto Rican residents do not pay federal taxes, they pay taxes on income earned within the 50 states, as well as local and municipal taxes. Based on current circumstances and the U.S. law governing the island nation, many scholars and analysts—as well as all major political parties on the island—conclude that Puerto Rico's political status, despite the use of the term "commonwealth," remains that of a colony.

By the early 1950s, the U.S. Congress passed legislation to allow Puerto Rico to be considered a "commonwealth." But the legislative record makes plain that "The bill [S.3336] under consideration would not change Puerto Rico's fundamental political, social and economic relationship to the United States" (House of Representatives, 82nd Congress, 2nd session, Report 1832, April 30, 1952, p. 3, quoted in Fernandez 1994, 85). As such, the U.S. Congress has preserved complete authority over Puerto Rico, including the power to supersede Puerto Rico's Constitution—which it did, removing Article 2, Section 20, on economic and social rights from the original 1952 Commonwealth Constitution.

Presently, the case of Puerto Rico's colonial situation is heard annually before the United Nations Special Committee in charge of decolonization and the implementation of General Assembly Resolution 1514 (XV) of 1960, the Declaration on the Granting of Independence to Colonial Countries and Peoples, considered the authoritative international law document on decolonization.

Since the 1970s, the U.N. Special Committee has received testimony regarding the colonial relationship with the United States; it has approved numerous resolutions recognizing the inalienable right of Puerto Ricans to the exercise of self-determination under international law; and it has called on the United States to uphold internationally recognized standards for decolonization. That Puerto Ricans are still considered an "alien" race under U.S. Supreme Court decisions and that the political status of Puerto Rico is beholden to a legal framework imbued with outmoded, illegitimate racial paradigms continues to be a cause for deep concern and consternation.

Beyond Mexico and Puerto Rico, "race" has had a lasting impact on the U.S. policies toward other Latin American countries and their peoples. The notion that Latin American countries were "banana republics" run by inept leaders of an inferior race became a narrative equivalent to the British "White Man's Burden" that the U.S. government successfully utilized to justify military interventions throughout the 19th and the 20th centuries. From 1898 to 1934, the United States used its military might—or what President Teddy Roosevelt called the "big stick"—to repeatedly intervene in Latin American countries to consolidate U.S. economic power in the region. Done in the name of "spreading democracy," consecutive U.S. presidents and Congresses oversaw the propping up of brutal dictators—Trujillo in the Dominican Republic, Batista in Cuba, the Somoza dynasty in Nicaragua, the Duvaliers in Haiti, the infamous Fourteen Families in El Salvador, and countless military juntas and strong men in Honduras, Panama, Argentina, Brazil, Paraguay, and Chile. Well into the 20th century, U.S. corporations and agencies within the U.S. government—most notably, the Central Intelligence Agency—devised coup d'états in countries such as Guatemala, Chile, and many others, in support of right-wing regimes that committed horrific crimes and human rights violations against their own people.

Years of economic strife, war, and human rights atrocities throughout Latin America led many people to flee their homelands to come to the United States to seek sanctuary. Over the years, U.S. policies and influence have played an enormous role in "pushing" Latin Americans to leave their homelands to come to the United States. In other instances, U.S. business interests "pulled" Latin Americans to come to the United States. For example, sweeping changes in Puerto Rico's economy (beginning in the late 1940s) triggered thousands of Puerto Ricans to come to the United States in search of employment. As repressive U.S.-backed regimes fought rebel groups throughout Central America in the 1980s, thousands of Latin Americans came to the United States to escape the conflict. Additionally, U.S. agricultural and corporate interests have for many years lured Mexicans and other Latin Americans to work as cheap labor on farms and in factories in the United States. The idea that Central America, the Caribbean, and the rest of Latin America was the United States' "backyard"—and that the peoples of those regions were racially "other" and "less than"—contributed in justifying U.S. actions in the region, including actions that led to violations of human rights.

Race, Racialization, and the Criminalization of Latinas/os Post-1848

In a manner similar to how Latin Americans were perceived historically as racially inferior to white Americans, so, too, were the Latin Americans who came to live in the United States—who today we call

Latinas/os. After 1848, Mexicans were systematically denied rights that white persons enjoyed. It was assumed that racial inferiority rendered Latinas/os incapable of participating in civic life, and therefore testifying in court or serving on juries was prohibited. Stereotypes that Latinas/os are criminally prone are rooted in those times, and continue to have an enduring impact on Latinas/os, likely for many years to come.

In *People v. Hall*, 4 Cal. 399 (1854), the California Supreme Court decided that a Chinese person could not testify against a white defendant, and the same was deemed true for Mexicans. In 1857, Manuel Dominguez was a prominent wealthy landowner, supervisor of Los Angeles County, and an original delegate to the California Constitution who signed the document in 1849. When Dominguez was found to be of Mexican mestizo ancestry, however, he was denied the right to testify as a witness in court.

By 1855, California law also legally had sanctioned **racial profiling** of persons who were of Mexican or Latin American descent. Pursuant to an anti-vagrancy law commonly known as the "**Greaser Act**" of 1855, the Act of April 30, 1855, ch. 175, § 2, 1855, Cal. Stat. 217, states, "all persons who are commonly known as 'Greasers' or the issue [children] of Spanish and Indian blood . . . and who go armed and are not peaceable and quiet persons" singled out persons who were Mexican or Mexican American using the racially derogatory term "Greaser." The term typically was applied to Mexicans and carried the connotation that they were dirty and criminally predisposed. Similar to the narrative made popular in the 1915 D. W. Griffith film *Birth of a Nation*, which depicted African American men as sexual threats to white women, Greasers were pegged as sexual predators who desire white women. Scholars consider the Greaser Act a forerunner to modern-day racial profiling and laws and practices that are seemingly race-neutral but have a disproportionate impact on communities of color, such as anti-loitering laws, anti-gang laws, and police "**stops and frisks**."

After 1848, **hate crimes** against Latinas/os became a regular occurrence. Of the most extreme forms of hate were Latina/o **lynchings**. Akin to the terror and violence levied on African Americans, Latinas/os experienced this horrific form of hate into the 20th century. Anglo-American settlers' diaries and other documentation reveal a history of prejudice and anti-Mexican/Latina/o mob violence that included lynching in the Western and Southwestern United States. Although research on the subject is continuing, some estimate that, although not as extensive in number as African American lynchings, more than 597 Latinas/os were lynched in the United States, and most occurred during the same period when African American lynchings were most prevalent (Delgado 2009). The justifications for lynching Latinas/os tended to be very similar to the motives behind lynching African Americans, such as posing a threat to white women. Latina/o lynchings, however, also were occasioned by a person speaking Spanish or exhibiting another public display of distinct Latina/o cultural identity.

Segregation and Discrimination Against Latinas/os

After 1848, generations of persons of Mexican and Latin American descent were perceived and treated as racial "others" and, as a result, Latinas/os—along with African Americans—endured the degradation and indignity of segregation in many facets of their lives. It was not unusual for restaurants, schools, and many public and private facilities to exclude Latinas/os. Viewed as a threat to health and morality, Mexicans were restricted to certain

Lynching of Latinas/os: Common Motives or "Justifications"

[S]imilar [to African Americans]—acting "uppity," taking away jobs, making advances toward a white woman, cheating at cards, practicing "witchcraft," and refusing to leave land that Anglos coveted—with one exception . . . acting "too Mexican"—speaking Spanish too loudly or reminding Anglos too defiantly of their Mexicanness. As with African Americans, Latino lynching went on with the knowledge and, in some cases, active participation of Anglo law enforcement authorities, especially the Texas Rangers (Delgado 2009, 299).

areas of town and could only purchase "miserable little houses" in isolated Mexican "barrios." They also were subject to the indignity of segregated movie theaters (balcony seating only), and to using the public swimming pools only on "Mexican day"—the day of the week when the pool was its dirtiest, prior to being cleaned (Arriola 1995).

In the 1940s, a case brought by a group of Mexican American World War II veterans in California that included Gonzalo Mendez, a tenant farmer, and his wife Felicitas, a native of Puerto Rico, successfully challenged the segregation of Latina/o children in public schools in federal court. The case, *Mendez v. Westminster School District of Orange County* (1947), affirmed that "the methods of segregation prevalent in the defendant school districts foster antagonisms in the children and suggest inferiority among them where none exists." A precursor to the landmark 1954 Supreme Court decision in *Brown v. Board of Education*, the *Mendez* decision is recognized today as laying the groundwork for further legal challenges to **de jure segregation** and the finding of the principle of "separate but equal" to be unconstitutional.

The courts also were a venue in which Latinas/os encountered segregation and exclusion. Handed down two weeks before the *Brown v. Board of Education* decision, the U.S. Supreme Court in the 1954 case of ***Hernandez v. Texas*** found that persons of Mexican descent had been systematically excluded as jurors in criminal trials in violation of the U.S. Constitution, and also noted the larger problem of unjust segregation against Mexicans in many other aspects of life in the United States. The Court made reference to ubiquitous signs outside restaurants reading "No Mexicans Served" and observed that certain courthouse restrooms specifically indicated "Colored Men" and "Hombres Aquí" ("Men Here") (Olivas 2006). In declaring illegal the practice of excluding persons of Mexican descent from service as jury commissioners, grand jurors, and petit jurors, the Court for the first time acknowledged that Latinas/os are a "cognizable minority group for equal protection purposes" under the Constitution's Fourteenth Amendment. Going forward, civil rights matters involving discrimination issues within U.S. jurisprudence were not to be limited as only between African Americans and whites. Referred to as the "**Black/White binary paradigm**" in which race issues in the United States traditionally have been perceived and debated as a matter solely between African Americans and whites, the 1954 *Hernandez v. Texas* decision was seminal in broadening discussions about discrimination to include Latinas/os in relation to race, ethnicity, and national origin.

Despite the victories and advances made as a result of the *Mendez* and *Hernandez* cases, Latinas/os continued to face discriminatory treatment. The end of World War II and the beginning of the Cold War era brought an increase in anti-immigrant and anti-Mexican animus, with Mexicans and Latinas/os being viewed with suspicion as potentially dangerous "foreigners." By the 1950s, the federal government initiated "**Operation Wetback**," a military operation to deport undocumented Mexicans from the United States. From 1954 through 1959, more than 3.7 million Latinas/os were deported under Operation Wetback (Carrasco 1997, 197). Not unexpectedly given the use of the disrespectful and pejorative term "Wetback," Latinas/os were abused and mistreated during Operation Wetback. Illegal and discriminatory searches and seizures were rampant in this campaign to deport masses of Mexicans, including those who were U.S. citizens. Only 63,500 persons actually went through formal deportation proceedings before being forced out, and many had their human and civil rights violated (Carrasco 1997, 197–98).

Latinas/os have encountered discrimination in other areas, including voting rights, education, and housing. Puerto Ricans—who have been U.S. citizens since 1917—in New York City were subjected to literacy tests similar to those used to exclude African Americans from participation in elections in the South. Puerto Ricans living in the continental United States were not free from discriminatory literacy tests until the 1966 U.S. Supreme Court decision in *Katzenbach v. Morgan*, which ruled that New York City was in violation of the 1965 Voting Rights Act for excluding Puerto Ricans educated in Spanish from voting in city elections.

Numerous cases of unconstitutional treatment in schools and housing filed in federal and state courts over the years suggest that discrimination against Latinas/os has not been occasional or incidental, but rather is part of a larger pattern of institutionalized forms of unequal treatment. Among the many cases is the groundbreaking case of *United States, et al. v. Yonkers Board of Education, et al.* (1988). In this case, the court ruled that the City of Yonkers and the Yonkers Board of Education had intentionally discriminated against African Americans and Latinas/os for decades by creating housing and schools separate and apart from whites in the city in violation of Title VIII of the Civil Rights Act of 1968 and the Fourteenth Amendment of the U.S. Constitution.

The lengthy history of discrimination against Latinas/os is well documented (Delgado, Perea, & Stefancic 2008; Delgado & Stefancic 2011). It is in this context that Latinas/os have endured and—as many analysts and scholars point out—continue to endure unequal treatment in the area of criminal justice (*see, e.g.*, Urbina 2012; Californians for Safety and Justice 2014; Walker et al. 2004; Arya et al. 2009). Even the success in the 1954 case of *Hernandez v. Texas* in the view of many analysts has suffered a major setback.

In 1991, in ***Hernandez v. New York***—a criminal case in which a Spanish-speaking defendant required a translator—the U.S. Supreme Court determined that it was constitutional for a prosecutor to use peremptory challenges to reject potential Latino/a jurors who understood Spanish under the presumption that they would not adhere to the official translation. The Court reasoned that the prosecutor's actions did not constitute racial, ethnic, or national origin discrimination because anyone—not just Latinas/os—can be proficient in Spanish. The decision still provokes controversy today, however, as many scholars and analysts contend that the Court underestimated the disparate impact that the decision would have on the right to a jury of one's peers in New York City, where Latinas/os most often would be Spanish speakers in the pool of potential jurors.

Overrepresentation and Unequal Treatment of Latinas/os

Over the years, Latinas/os consistently have been overrepresented in the criminal justice system—that is, their numbers in the population in different stages in the criminal justice system are disproportionate to their numbers in the general population. With more than 60 percent of persons in prison being persons of color, Latinas/os represented 21.6 percent of persons in state and federal prisons in 2013, even though they made up only 17 percent of the overall U.S. population (Sentencing Project 2015; Carson 2014; U.S. Bureau of the Census 2014). Although African American incarceration rates exceed that of Latinas/os, Latino men are still 2.4 times more likely to be incarcerated than white men (Sentencing Project 2015; Carson 2014). One-in-six Latino men are likely to be imprisoned in their lifetime as compared to 1-in-17 white men and 1-in-3 African American men (Sentencing Project 2015; Bonczar 2003). Latinas are incarcerated at 1.4 times the rate of white women—71 per 100,000 as opposed to 51 per 100,000 for white women (Carson & Sabol 2012).

Research has shown that, much like African Americans, Latinas/os have been incarcerated at higher rates, particularly after the 1970s when stricter policies were adopted that led to unprecedented increases in the number of persons imprisoned in the United States. The term "**mass imprisonment**" has come to signify the historically unique and high rates of incarceration that distinguish the United States as the nation with the most incarcerated persons in the world and as a nation that disproportionately incarcerates certain racial and ethnic groups—in this case, African Americans and Latinas/os. With 2.2 million persons in some form of detention or imprisonment, the United States by far exceeds the rate of imprisonment of any other country—717 persons per 100,000 people in the United States, as compared to Rwanda at 492 per 100,000, which in 2012–2013 ranked second in the world after the United States (Travis & Western 2014; Sentencing Project 2015, 1).

Extraordinarily high rates of incarceration in the United States attributable, in large part, to tough law-and-order policies that began with President Richard Nixon's administration, generally have continued to the present. As "get-tough" stances became more popular and politically expedient, harsh "war on drugs" and "war on crime" legislation was passed in Washington and throughout the states, including the **Rockefeller drug laws**, mandatory minimum sentences, and three-strikes laws. Controversy mounted over time, however, as it became clear that this legislation was producing severe racial and ethnic disparities in the criminal justice system that could hardly be justified. Studies indicate that African Americans and Latinas/os have borne the brunt of harsher criminal penalties enacted over the last 40 years (Travis & Western 2014). Although greater rates of imprisonment might have had some impact on reducing crime in the United States, most studies raise doubt that the impact was substantial, and even the effectiveness and efficiency of lengthy sentences have come into question because recidivism rates drop precipitously with age.

Bias in Criminal Justice and Policing and Latina/o Communities

Although disparities in criminal justice are not automatically dispositive of bias in the criminal justice system, studies over the years point to a long trajectory of implicit and explicit forms of bias in the criminal justice system. The **Texas Rangers** in the mid-1800s were known for their abuse and harassment of Mexicans. They readily deemed persons of Mexican descent "*bandidos*" (bandits) and freely killed Mexicans and Native Americans in a manner that resembled **vigilantism** rather than conduct becoming of proper law enforcement agents.

In later years, racial profiling of Latinas/os became a fixture of policing in cities such as Los Angeles. In the 1940s, police targeted Mexican youth who wore **zoot suits**, flashy attire that was popular among young Latinos at the time. Racialized **media** images of young Mexican Americans as hoodlums and **gang** members in zoot suits instilled fear among white communities and encouraged police crackdowns on crime. Mexican youths became synonymous with crime. The 1942 **Sleepy Lagoon** case, in which youths not involved in the murder were imprisoned, and the 1943 **Zoot Suit Riots**, in which many Mexican Americans were attacked indiscriminately in the "*barrio*" during several days of unrest, were emblematic of the ways in which criminality had been projected onto an entire community. In response to the dominant perception of Mexicans as criminals, the criminal justice system turned to aggressive policing and sentencing. Many observers of how Latinas/os are policed and prosecuted today draw analogies with police and Mexican American community relations of the 1940s. It has been noted that in California today, Latina/o youths wind up in gang databases without any verification performed and without their knowledge. This can result in harsher sentences even for offenses that are not gang-related. Not too dissimilar from the targeting of Latina/o youths in 1940s Los Angeles, a federal judge in New York in 2013, in the case of *Floyd et al. v. City of New York*, found that the manner in which city police implemented **stops and frisks** of Latinas/os and African Americans amounted to "indirect racial profiling," based on evidence that officers were instructed to go after "the right people."

As has been documented, negative stereotypes of Latinas/os have persisted over time, influencing the operations of the criminal justice system and police practices throughout the country. Throughout the 1960s and 1970s, Mexican Americans continued to be frequently excluded from juries by judges who summarily viewed them as incapable of carrying out that responsibility based on their ancestry and social status. Mexican American youths engaged in the Chicano movement were viewed not as persons with the constitutional rights to protest and assemble, but as lawbreakers undeserving of equal treatment in encounters with law enforcement agents and the criminal justice process.

The excessive use of force by law enforcement officers—typically referred to as police brutality—is not limited to past decades. Complaints made by Latinas/os of brutality and biased treatment and abuse at the hands of police and throughout the criminal justice system have been longstanding. Throughout the 1990s and into the present, Latina/o fatalities caused by police in Los Angeles, New York City, and other parts of the country have been documented by noted human rights organizations (Amnesty International 1998; Human Rights Watch 1998; Johnson 2003). Reminiscent of Los Angeles in the 1940s, Latina/o and African American youths in Chicago and other cities, when found in "particular areas, wearing certain clothes, or simply out on the street" have been deemed gang members and targeted by police for harassment, according to Amnesty International. Instances in which the police never were disciplined or prosecuted, or were acquitted, have over the years been a source of consternation and have bred distrust for police in Latina/o communities. In New York, 20 years after **Anthony Báez** was killed by a police officer who used a chokehold that had been banned by the NYPD, Báez's death still resonates in the city and police use of the banned chokehold persists, as was brought to light by the recent death of Eric Garner in Staten Island.

Police and law enforcement relations with persons of Latin American descent around the country more often than not have been characterized as strained, and virtually no sector of the Latina/o population has been immune to incidents of police misconduct. Cases of racially motivated violence and homophobia intersecting and of police use of excessive force against **lesbian, gay, bisexual, and transgender (LGBT)** Latinas/os and African Americans have been documented (*see* McArdle 2001; Amnesty International 1998). Recent studies have sought to divulge the extent to which excessive police force, unjust arrests, and other forms of police misconduct against LGBT persons of color are substantial throughout the United States (National Coalition of Anti-Violence Programs 2014).

High incarceration rates and mass imprisonment have been linked to aggressive policing strategies that have gone under the rubric of the "broken windows" theory, "zero tolerance" policies, and "quality-of-life" policing. These forms of policing have focused police attention and efforts on minor offenses under the theory that enforcing laws that prohibit loitering, panhandling, and other lesser offenses deter more serious crimes. Aggressive police practices have been popular, particularly in the 1990s, but the efficacy of such tactics in a rising number of studies has brought these practices into question. Vast racial and ethnic disparities in outcomes between how communities of color and whites have been a byproduct of the manner in which "get-tough" police practices have been implemented. Considerable scrutiny and criticism have spurred lawsuits challenging the constitutionality of police tactics, such as **stops and frisks**. As referenced above, a legal case of this type in New York City (*Floyd et al. v. City of New York*) exposed evidence of such disproportionate and biased policing that the court in 2013 declared the police department's practices unconstitutional. The city has since made significant reductions in the use of this practice with no appreciable rise in crime. (For more on policing policies and practices see "Policing and Latina/o Communities" in this volume.)

Disparities in Criminal Justice Outcomes for Latinas/os

Criminal justice data on racial and ethnic disparities consistently point to Latinas/os as experiencing significant and discernable gaps in treatment when compared to that of whites. Studies make plain that Latinas/os are less likely to be released on their own recognizance before trial; when offered bail it often is set at higher levels for Latinas/os than similarly situated whites or African Americans; only 33 percent of Latina/o defendants are able to post bail in contrast to 58 percent of whites and 47 percent of African Americans; and 51 percent of Latinas/os are incarcerated before trial as compared to 32 percent of whites (Schlesinger 2005). Studies also find that courts in the United States tend to incarcerate Latinos at a rate 44 percent greater than that of whites for property crimes and a 53 percent greater rate than that of whites for drug offenses. Additionally, Latinas/os are more likely than other groups to be convicted of crimes carrying "mandatory minimum" sentences where judicial discretion is restricted (Demuth &

Steffensmeier 2004; United States Sentencing Commission 2011; McGovern, Demuth & Jacoby 2009).

Latina/o Youth and Gangs

Criminal justice statistics show that Latina/o youth—among all Latinas/os—are especially vulnerable to unequal treatment. Compared to similarly situated white youths, Latina/o youths are "4% more likely than white youth to be petitioned; 16% more likely than white youth to be adjudicated delinquent; 28% more likely than white youth to be detained; 41% more likely than white youth to receive an out-of-home placement; 43% more likely than white youth to be waived to the adult system; and 40% more likely to be admitted to adult prison" (Arya et al. 2009, 6). Additionally, most Latina/o youths are incarcerated for nonviolent offenses, and almost 18,000 Latina/o youths are incarcerated in any given day (Arya et al. 2009, 6).

Studies on anti-gang laws have been indicating that Latina/o youths are being swept into the criminal justice system by laws and practices that seek to identify persons with any association with a gang. California Penal Code 186.22, for instance, although intended to deter gang involvement, has been criticized for helping to amass a database identifying anyone with a supposed gang affiliation. Actual gang membership does not need to be proven, and Latina/o youths listed in the database who might not be gang members nonetheless receive harsher sentences under the law. In California, Latinas/os make up two-thirds of those included in the database of people believed to have gang affiliations and, if convicted of a crime, a harsher sentence is handed down even if the offense for which the person was convicted is not related to gang activity.

Emerging research on gangs in Latina/o communities is exploring the motivations and conditions that give rise to gang affiliation. Social and economic conditions—including underfunded schools, high unemployment rates, and the lack of adequate healthcare and housing—provide the circumstances in which youth marginalization and dislocation intensify. Thus the search for interconnectedness, community, self-esteem, identity, and dignity drive Latina/o youth to associate with street organizations known as gangs.

The marginalization of Latina/o youth is a phenomenon that has been observed for many years. As was the case in 1940s Los Angeles, Mexican American youths wore the zoot suits as on expression of social cohesion and identity in response to racial and ethnic segregation and anti-Mexican bias of the time. So too, it has been observed that Latina/o youths of today respond to social conditions.

Despite the many millions of dollars spent on get-tough police strategies and harsher sentences around the country, gang activity has not disappeared. Some analysts have called for a reassessment of traditional strategies, calling for less-punitive measures and more evidence-based efforts that focus on improvements in job and educational opportunities geared toward youths and the realities they face. Many academics and advocacy groups engaged in studying and working in Latina/o communities point to successful examples of community-based organizations that provide vital services to youths and effectively work to address gang affiliation and youth marginalization. Homeboys Industries, **Homies Unidos**, Southwest Key Programs, Barrios Unidos, and other programs designed and run at a grassroots level have been cited in reports for their efficacy and outreach to Latina/o youths.

Latinas/os, Illicit Drugs, and Implicit Bias

Stereotypes linking Latinas/os to illicit drug activity have been persistent and long lasting. (For a further discussion of this issue, see in this volume **The U.S. War on Drugs and Latina/o Communities**.) Studies on racial and ethnic group drug use, however, contradict conventional beliefs that people in communities of color necessarily use drugs more frequently than people in white communities do. Government data reveal that Latinas/os generally use illegal drugs at lesser rates than those of most other groups in the United States (Substance Abuse and Mental Health Data Archive 2014). This is especially true when comparing Latinas/os with whites. Data from 2013 for persons 12 years old and older show that the rate of previous-month illicit drug use by whites was 9.5 percent, and for Latinas/os the previous-month illegal drug use was only 8.8 percent (U.S. Department of Health and Human Services 2014, 26). In fact, previous-month illicit drug use data by race/ethnicity from 2002 through 2013 indicates that Latinas/os as a group consistently use illegal drugs of all types at lesser rates than that of whites (U.S. Department of Health and Human Services 2014, 27). In 2013, for every category of substances—cigarettes, alcohol, cocaine, crack, hallucinogens, heroin, inhalants, marijuana, pain relievers, sedatives, stimulants, and tranquilizers—Latina/o use was lower than that of whites.

In spite of data to the contrary, government and law enforcement drug policies and practices have tended to have a severely disproportionate impact on communities of color, particularly as the "war on drugs" in the United States gained momentum and popularity in the United States. Academics have discerned **implicit bias**—unconscious prejudice that influences policies and practices—operating in the criminal justice system in ways that have a disparate impact on certain racial and ethnic groups. For instance, scholars point to federal law imposing harsher sentences for crack cocaine—a substance used more often in communities of color than powder cocaine, which is more prevalent among whites—as an example of a decision that appears neutral but actually harbors an underlying bias favoring whites. As a result, people of color are more severely punished, even though scientifically there is no significant difference between crack and powder cocaine that justifies differential sentencing.

Drug-courier profiles also tend to be implicitly biased against communities of color, and Latinas/os in particular. Law enforcement training programs in which drug enforcement agents identify "Latino males traveling together" or specific Latino groups—Dominicans, Colombians, and Puerto Ricans, for example—are among the ways bias has been reinforced. Federal drug-courier profiles that single out "Hispanics" carry the insinuation that racial profiling of Latinas/os is appropriate. Studies repeatedly find that drug enforcement has been a driving force in racial profiling by police and other law enforcement agencies and that the "war on drugs" principally has been waged in communities of color.

Latina/o Immigrants

It is a popular belief that immigrants to the United States are criminally prone and bring crime into the country. Research, however, posits the contrary, making evident that immigrants to the United States have lower incarceration rates than do other groups. As a whole, immigrants come to the country highly motivated to use their skills to better their lives, and encounters with the criminal justice system undermine their ambitions for employment and a better life. Studies also reveal that recent immigration generally has not led to increases in homicides. Instead, research suggests that immigration helps stabilize communities and reduces crime because immigrants promote economic activity in neighborhoods—for example, they open new businesses not previously in the area which, in turn, act to suppress criminal behavior (Lee 2003; Karmen 2000).

Latina/o immigrants, as scholars report, are no more prone to commit crime than are other groups. After taking into consideration factors such as age and vulnerability to pretrial detention, research suggests that Latino/a immigrants actually are *less* inclined to engage in criminal behavior. Among the reasons for this finding is that Latino/a immigrants have cultural and family values and traditions that discourage criminal conduct. Some scholars have concluded that the assumed link between crime and Latino/a immigrants is mirrored and promoted in part by the criminal justice system itself, along with immigration laws, policies, and practices that tend to underpin an inaccurate narrative about immigrants.

As to whether immigrants "bring" crime into the country, the data indicates that unauthorized immigration does not correlate with greater crime rates. States with greater immigration rates tend to have some of the lowest crime rates in the country. In Arizona, for example, prior to the enactment of its strict immigration laws crime rates had been dropping for years at the same time that unauthorized immigration into the state was rising. Violent crime rates declined in Arizona from 545.4 incidents per 100,000 people in 2006 to 481.1 per 100,000 people in 2008, and the property crime rate dropped from 5,849.8 incidents per 100,000 people in 2002 to 4,087.3 per 100,000 people in 2008 (Immigration Policy Center, 2010).

Hate Crimes

Hate crimes—criminal offenses involving an element of racial, ethnic, or other form of prejudice (e.g., bias based on national origin, religion, sexual orientation, disability, and gender)—have been part of the Latinas/os experience in the United States for as long as there have been persons of Latin American origin in the country. Often rooted in negative stereotypes and racialized notions of Latinas/os as undersirable "others," hate crimes further marginalize and dehumanize Latinas/os. The lynching of Latinas/os, as described earlier, represents one example of how these communities were marginalized and dehumanized historically through terror and violence.

Today, hate crimes are still a reality for Latinas/os. There is some evidence that the proliferation of anti-immigrant sentiment in recent years has resulted in a rise in anti-Latina/o crimes. FBI data show a 40 percent increase in hate crimes targeting Latinos in the United States from 2003 to 2007 (Southern Poverty Law Center 2008). The upsurge in hate crimes coincides with increases in anti-immigrant propaganda by hate groups. In 2012, Latinas/os endured higher rates of violent hate crime than did whites and African Americans—2.0 victimizations per 1,000 residents, as compared to 0.8 per 1,000 for whites and 1.1 per 1,000 for African Americans. From 2011 to 2012, hate crimes against Latinas/os more than tripled—"0.6 per 1,000 persons age 12 or older in 2011 to 2.0 per 1,000 in 2012" (Wilson 2014, 6).

The traditional narrative about race in the United States postulates that whites should fear becoming victims of crimes committed by Latinas/os and African Americans. The available data belie this narrative. Whites actually are three times more likely to be victimized by other whites than by a person of color (Dorfman & Schiraldi 2001, 3). Nevertheless, over the last decade increases in the number of hate groups have been detected. Among radical right-wing groups that espouse prejudice against Latinas/os, hate groups, nativist extremist groups, and "patriot" organizations grew from 1,753 groups in 2009 to 2,145 in 2010—an increase of 22 percent—which was preceded by a 40 percent increase from 2008 to 2009 (Southern Poverty Law Center 2011). Nativist extremist groups—organizations known for targeting assumed undocumented immigrants where they work or at the border—also have experienced increases. From 2008 to 2009, the number of such groups increased nearly 80 percent (from 173 to 309), and after the passage of Arizona's tough immigration law (S.B. 1070) the number climbed to roughly 319 (Beirich 2011).

Media and Crime

An area of concern and study is the absence of positive Latina/o characters on television and the negative portrayals on the evening news. Studies find that Latinas/os have not only been underrepresented in the mass media, but when they are presented on newscasts or entertainment media, they more often than not are depicted inaccurately or in a negative light. The filmmaking industry in the United States has a long history of producing an overabundance of negative images of Latinas/os—from Westerns in which Latinos played the stereotypical Mexican bandit to more recent films where Latinas/os regularly play the role of irredeemable urban criminals or **drug users**. The most popular and memorable images of Latinos have been the violent, pathological bandit ("bandito"), switchblade-carrying juvenile delinquents, the ruthless drug-dealer, and the gang member.

As the National Council of Crime and Delinquency points out, public perceptions about violent crime to a great extent have been shaped by the media's coverage of crime, and most importantly, crimes committed by youths. Studies show that media leave powerful and exaggerated impressions about crime that tend to spread fear and alarm, especially about crime committed by youths of color. Latina/o and African American youths have been found to be overrepresented as violent offenders on evening newscasts at levels greater than their actual rates of crime, and crimes committed by whites are underrepresented in evening television news stories, even when the actual crime rates are greater than those depicted on the news.

Reports issued by the National Association of Hispanic Journalists (NAHJ) found that network news items about Latinas/os tend to focus on negative stories involving crime, terrorism, and illegal immigration. Other studies reveal not only that crime is a top news story featuring Latinas/os, but that in most of those news stories Latinas/os are the perpetrators of crime, not the victims. In view of this pattern, concerns continue to be raised that media reinforce preexisting biases and negative stereotypes and influence the thinking and decision-making behavior of those who set criminal justice policy.

Cultural Competency, Reentry, and Reforms

Cultural Competency

Despite their long history in the United States and their rapidly increasing presence, a substantial gap in what is generally known about Latinas/os exists. Studies reveal that the U.S. society still falls short in overcoming longstanding racial and ethnic

Media Images of Latinas/os

The most popular and enduring images of Latinos have been the violent, pathological bandit ("*bandido*"), switchblade-carrying juvenile delinquents, the ruthless drug dealer, and the gang member. Below are but a few examples of movies, plays, and television shows that are consistent with a negative narrative about Latinas/os in the United States.

Examples

Movies

- *The Cowboy Baby* (1910)
- *Tony the Greaser* (1911)
- *Broncho Billy and the Greaser* (1914)
- *The Young Savages* (1961)
- *West Side Story* (1961)
- *Dirty Harry* (1971)
- *The French Connection* (1971)
- *Badge 373* (1973)
- *The Seven-Ups* (1973)
- *Fort Apache: The Bronx* (1974)
- *The Exterminator* (1980)
- *Scarface* (1983)
- *Colors* (1988)
- *American Me* (1992)
- *Falling Down* (1993)
- *Carlito's Way* (1993)
- *Traffic* (2000)

Theater

- *West Side Story*
- *Capeman*

Television

- *Cops*
- *American Undercover*

Sources: Berg, Charles Ramírez. 2002. *Latino images in film: Stereotypes, subversion, resistance*. Austin, TX: University of Texas Press.

Gonzalez, Juan. 2011. *Harvest of Empire: A history of Latinos in America*. Revised ed. New York: Penguin Books.

Martínez, Ramiro, Jr. 2002. *Latino homicide: Immigration, violence and community*. New York: Routledge.

myths, misconceptions, and stereotypes—particularly as it concerns Latinas/os and the criminal justice system. Many analysts and advocacy groups have called for expanding our knowledge and understanding of Latinas/os as an important first step in being able to provide culturally competent services—services that effectively serve populations of diverse cultural and linguistic backgrounds. In their view, an increasingly diverse country requires a deeper awareness and appreciation of racial and ethnic differences. It also necessitates institutional changes to ensure that adequate services are provided to all who interact with the criminal justice system so that fairness and justice can be advanced.

Many evidence-based programs—programs that use data to assess and determine the efficacy of their service model—have been shown to be effective for many youths. Most of these programs have been designed and validated for non-Latina/o youths, however, and have not necessarily been shown to produce successful results for them. Consequently, research and Latina/o advocacy organizations including the **National Council of La Raza** have advocated for evidence-based programs that incorporate culturally competent approaches—that is, evidence-based programs that also embrace the cultural and linguistic values and concepts typically found among Latinas/os. In addition to offering services in Spanish, understanding Latina/o proclivities for family, respect, and spirituality, for example, can make agencies more effective at reaching and serving Latinas/os.

Cultural competency does not simply entail the provision of translation services. It represents a broader approach to service delivery in which the agency—and in this instance, the criminal justice system—adopts system-wide measures that enhance and institutionalize awareness, attitudes, policies, and practices that enable an agency and its personnel to work effectively across different cultural and linguistic experiences. It is an approach that works to address the cross-cultural dimensions and context of those people needing services. Culturally competent agencies engage in an ongoing process of valuing diversity, of becoming adept at managing cross-cultural dynamics, of institutionalizing cultural understanding among all of its staff, and of constantly assessing and adopting strategies that improve services (Ayra et al. 2009).

The inability of the criminal justice system to operate effectively in a diverse society can lead to unequal outcomes for those outside the mainstream. Harsher sentences for youths can result when a judge misinterprets a Latina/o youth's efforts to be polite as a form of disrespect or when a court fails to consider the support that an extended family can lend as part of an alternative to institutionalizing a youth far away from family and the community. Building culturally competent agencies requires recruiting, training, and promoting personnel at all levels, in addition to adopting and implementing policies and practices consistent with servicing the needs of diverse populations.

Reinforcing positive Latina/o community cultural and linguistic attributes is consonant with research that indicates that traditional Latina/o cultural values and norms inhibit delinquency and socially counterproductive behavior. A study focusing on Latino/a homicide rates in five major U.S. cities—Chicago, El Paso, Houston, Miami, and San Diego—reveals that strong social networks within Latino/a communities help deter criminal activity (Martínez, Jr. 2002). Culture-based approaches appear to be especially relevant in working with Latina/o youths. Culture-based youth initiatives, such

Cultural Competence: Five Basic Elements

"*Valuing Diversity*

[S]elf-assessment (the ability as an individual or agency to examine yourself and/or your organization);

[T]he ability to manage the dynamics of difference (being prepared with the awareness, knowledge, and skills to assist in smoothing out, negotiating, or navigating those differences);

[I]nstitutionalizing cultural knowledge (making sure that not just one person in your organization or on your staff has the knowledge or the skill to work with a particular cultural group or community, but ensuring that the organization is aware of this knowledge or skill and is making it a part of the organization's knowledge and skill set); and

[M]aking adaptations to policies, service delivery, structures, attitudes, and behaviors" (Arya et al. 2009, 55–56) [emphasis added].

as John Jay College of Criminal Justice's *Palenque* and similar projects that work with youths at a community level, serve as models for assisting Latinas/os nationwide (Morín 2009).

Recidivism, Reentry, and Reforms

Data on recidivism for state prisoners released in 30 states in 2005 reveal that approximately two-thirds or 67.8 percent of released prisoners were arrested for a new crime within three years, and three-quarters, or 76.6 percent, were arrested for a new crime within five years (Durose, Cooper, & Snyder 2014, 1). The data also show that Latina/o recidivism rates are similar to the recidivism rates of whites—70.7 percent for Latinas/os compared to 68.8 percent for whites and 74 percent for African Americans in 2005. Although re-arrest and reconviction rates between Latinas/os and whites are generally comparable, Latinas/os experience a re-incarceration rate for those convictions that is greater than for whites. One study posits that the more punitive outcomes for Latinas/os might be the result of bias—namely, that Latinas/os are viewed as more culpable or as posing a greater risk to the public than whites or African Americans. In reaching this finding, the study controlled for factors such as the seriousness of the offense and prior record (McGovern, Demuth, & Jacoby 2009).

Despite having the highest incarceration rate of any country in the world, the United States appears not to be succeeding in deterring offenders from recommitting crime. The United States holds the added distinction of having the greatest recidivism rate of any nation on the planet. Comparing incarceration policies and practices of the United States with other developed countries raises the question about how to justify a system that holds 25 percent of the world's prisoners when the total U.S. population is only roughly 5 percent of the world's population (Deady 2014). Norway's criminal justice system, for example, is much less punitive; it houses significantly fewer prisoners and it provides prisoners with a range of social

U.S. Recidivism Rates

Population-adjusted percent of prisoners arrested for a new crime within 3 years following release in 12 states in 1994 and 2005 by demographic characteristics

Characteristic	1994	2005
Race/Hispanic origin		
White	61.7%	68.8%
Black/African American	71.9	74.0
Hispanic/Latino	64.6	70.7
Other	53.6	72.6

Source: Compiled from Durose, Matthew R., Alexia D. Cooper, and Howard N. Snyder. 2014. *Recidivism of prisoners released in 30 states in 2005: Patterns from 2005 to 2010* (NCJ 244205). Washington, DC: Bureau of Justice Statistics.

services, including education and employment opportunities, that are unimaginable in the United States. Yet, at 20 percent, Norway maintains one of the lowest recidivism rates in the world (Ploeg 2012; Jilani 2011; Deady 2014). Norway's model deemphasizes punishment in favor of practices that ensure that persons released from prison can reintegrate successful into society (**prisoner reentry**). If the goal is to reduce recidivism, then it is a model that some criminologists and analysts suggest works. It also is an approach that resonates with the research and trends in advocacy around crime reduction in Latina/o communities and Latina/o reentry.

Many recommendations to improve the situation of Latinas/os in the context of criminal justice emphasize creating access to more and better healthcare, including mental health services, and reducing the stigmas attached to mental health services; prioritizing the development of new initiatives and the support of successful existing initiatives that link Latinas/os—particularly youths and persons reentering society—to jobs, housing, education, and treatment programs; and addressing systemic and institutional policies and practices that drive children out of schools and into the criminal justice system. Proposals for reforming the current criminal justice system pay particular attention to public health problems—such as drug addiction and mental health issues—and the need to solve public health problems with public health solutions.

Many analysts and advocacy organizations call for making the criminal justice system culturally competent at every level—the courts, police departments, prosecutor offices, and all other agencies and personnel engaged in the system—to enhance the opportunities for a fair and just process. In addition to developing culturally competent services for Latina/o youths, research shows that working through community-based organizations, enhancing family engagement in treatment, and actively engaging youth in developing a strength-based plan improve outcomes much more so than do traditional institutions that are focused on punishment.

Criminal justice system reforms can encompass a wide range of proposals. Some reforms which analysts believe to be most germane to Latinas/os include diversifying the criminal justice system—from police officers to lawyers and judges; ending aggressive police practices frequently associated with racial and ethnic disparities; and redirecting youth to programs that emphasize treatment, education, or other services that help rebuild a young person's life as an alternative to incarceration in adult facilities. Instead of a system that emphasizes punishment, studies suggest that restorative justice approaches—initiatives that seek to repair the harm done to victims and reestablish the relationship between the offender and the community—can successfully reintegrate people back into society and thereby reduce recidivism. With respect to rebuilding the broken trust between police departments and communities of color, **community policing** and neighborhood policing—models that promote communication and cooperation between law enforcement and individuals and groups in communities—currently are viewed as promising alternatives to "get-tough" policing associated with disparate criminal justice outcomes for communities of color.

Looking ahead, **community-based Latina/o advocacy organizations**, **legal advocacy groups,** and **political activist groups**—both old and new—can, as they have in the past, play a key role in advancing changes in laws and other reforms to address the needs of Latina/o communities. They, along with public interest organizations, can be at the forefront of pressing for a more culturally competent criminal justice system and can be working to protect the rights of Latina/o immigrants, Latinas, Latina/o youths, LGBT Latinas/os, and all other Latinas/os seeking just and equitable outcomes.

A growing number of Latina/o academic scholars have added their analyses and recommendations. Quantitative and qualitative studies that include Latinas/os are providing invaluable insights and are helping to dispel persistent and counterproductive myths and stereotypes. International perspectives on policing, recidivism, drugs, the death penalty, social and economic inequality, and many other issues provide other ways to approach problems that communities of color face in the United States. **International human rights** laws, norms, principles, and mechanisms, in particular, add to the ways of viewing and handling questions of justice as they affect Latinas/os. Scholars in the areas of **LatCrit: Latina Latino Critical Legal Theory** and **cultural criminology** are among those providing a deeper understanding of the challenges that Latinas/os encounter in the criminal justice system. Such scholars have broadened the ways of thinking of, looking at, and addressing longstanding, complex issues.

Further Reading

Acuña, Rodolfo. 2007. *Occupied America: A history of Chicanos*, 6th ed. New York: Pearson Longman.

Amnesty International. 1998. *United States of America: Rights for all.* New York: Amnesty International Publications.

Arriola, Christopher. 1995. Knocking on the schoolhouse door: *Mendez v. Westminster*, equal protection, public education, and Mexican Americans in the 1940s. *La Raza Law Journal* 8: 166–207.

Arya, Neelum, Francisco Villarruel, Cassandra Villanueva, and Ian Augarten. 2009. America's invisible children: Latino youth and the failure of justice. Washington, DC: Campaign for Youth Justice and National Council of La Raza. http://www.campaignforyouthjustice.org/documents/CFYJPB_InvisibleChildren.pdf.

Baker, Al, and J. David Goodman. 2015 (January 12). Despite scrutiny, police chokeholds persist in New York City. *New York Times*. http://www.nytimes.com/2015/01/13/nyregion/police-keep-using-chokeholds-despite-bans-and-scrutiny.html.

Balko, Radley. 2013. *Rise of the warrior cop: The militarization of America's police forces*. New York: Public Affairs.

Beirich, Heidi. 2011. The year in nativism, 2010. *Intelligence Report* (Spring): 141.

Bender, Steven W. 2003. *Greasers and gringos: Latinos, law, and the American imagination*. New York: New York University Press.

Berg, Charles Ramírez. 2002. *Latino images in film: Stereotypes, subversion, resistance*. Austin, TX: University of Texas Press.

Bonczar, Thomas P. 2003. *Prevalence of Imprisonment in the U.S. Population, 1974–2001* (NCJ 197976). Washington, DC: Bureau of Justice Statistics. http://www.bjs.gov/content/pub/pdf/piusp01.pdf.

Brotherton, David (ed.). 2015. *Youth street gangs: A critical appraisal*. New York: Routledge.

Brotherton, David, and Luis Barrios. 2004. *The Almighty Latin King and Queen Nation: Street politics and the transformation of a New York City gang*. New York: Columbia University Press.

Brown, Anna. 2014. The U.S. Hispanic population has increased six-fold since 1970. Washington, DC: Pew Research Center/Pew Hispanic Center. http://www.pewresearch.org/fact-tank/2014/02/26/the-u-s-hispanic-population-has-increased-sixfold-since-1970/.

Butcher, Kristen F., and Anne Morrison Piehl. 2005. Why are immigrants' incarceration rates so low? Evidence on selective immigration deterrence and deportation. Working Papers 2005–19. Chicago: Federal Reserve Bank of Chicago. http://www.chicagofed.org/publications/workingpapers/wp2005_19.pdf.

Cabranes, José, A. 1979. *Citizenship and the American empire*. New Haven: Yale University Press.

California Endowment. 2010. Healthy communities matter: The importance of place to the health of boys of color. Los Angeles, CA: Author.

Californians for Safety and Justice. 2014. Latino voices: The Impacts of crime and criminal justice on Latinos. Oakland, CA: Californians for Safety and Justice. http://libcloud.s3.amazonaws.com/211/04/1/430/LatinoReport_7.8.14v1.pdf.

Carrasco, Gilbert Paul. 1997. Latinos in the United States: Invitation and exile. In *Immigrants out! The new nativism and the anti-immigrant impulse in the United States*, edited by Juan F. Perea, 190–204. New York: New York University Press.

Carrigan, William D., and Clive Webb. 2013. *Forgotten dead: Mob violence against Mexicans in the United States, 1848–1928*. Oxford: Oxford University Press.

Carson, E. Ann. 2014. *Prisoners in 2013* (NCJ 247282). Washington, DC: Bureau of Justice Statistics. http://www.bjs.gov/content/pub/pdf/p13.pdf.

Carson, E. Ann, and William J. Sabol. 2012. *Prisoners in 2011* (NCJ 239808). Washington, DC: Bureau of Justice Statistics. http://www.bjs.gov/content/pub/pdf/p11.pdf.

Cobas, José A., Jorge Duany, and Joe R. Feagin. 2009. *How the United States racializes Latinos: White hegemony and its consequences*. Boulder, CO: Paradigm Publishers.

Cole, David. 1999. *No equal justice: Race and class in the American criminal justice system*. New York: New Press.

Cole, David. 2001. Formalism, realism, and the war on drugs. *Suffolk University Law Review* 35: 241–55.

Deady, Carolyn W. 2014. Incarceration and recidivism: Lessons from abroad. *Report of the Pell Center for International Relations and Public Policy, Salve Regina University*. http://www.salve.edu/sites/default/files

/filesfield/documents/Incarceration_and_Recidivism.pdf.

Delgado, Richard. 2009. The law of the noose: A history of Latino lynching. *Harvard Civil Rights and Civil Liberties Review* 44: 297–312.

Delgado, Richard, Juan F. Perea, and Jean Stefancic. 2008. *Latinos and the law: Cases and materials.* St. Paul, Minnesota: Thomson/West.

Delgado, Richard, and Jean Stefancic (eds.). 2011. *The Latino/a condition: A critical reader*, 2nd ed. New York: New York University Press.

Demuth, Stephen, and Darrell Steffensmeier. 2004. Ethnicity effects on sentence outcomes in large urban courts: Comparisons among white, black, and Hispanic defendants. *Social Science Quarterly,* 85(4): 994–1011.

Denis, Nelson A. 2015. *War against all Puerto Ricans: Revolution and terror in America's colony.* New York: Nation Books.

Dorfman, L., and V. Schiraldi (2001). *Off balance: Youth, race and crime in the news.* Washington, DC: Building Blocks for Youth.

Dunn, Christopher. 2014. Stop-and-frisk during the Bloomberg administration (2002–2013), NYCLU briefing. New York: New York Civil Liberties Union.

Durose, Matthew R., Alexia D. Cooper, and Howard N. Snyder. 2014. *Recidivism of prisoners released in 30 states in 2005: Patterns from 2005 to 2010* (NCJ 244205). Washington, DC: Bureau of Justice Statistics.

Escobar, Edward J. 1999. *Race, police, and the making of a political identity: Mexican Americans and the Los Angeles Police Department 1900–1945.* Berkeley: University of California Press.

Fernandez, Ronald. 1994. *Prisoners of colonialism: The struggle for justice in Puerto Rico.* Monroe, ME: Common Courage Press.

Garland, David (ed.). 2001. *Mass imprisonment: Social causes and consequences.* London: Sage.

Gautier Mayoral, Carmen, and María Del Pilar Argüelles. 1978. *Puerto Rico y la ONU.* Río Piedras, Puerto Rico: Editorial Edil.

Gonzales-Day, Ken. 2006. *Lynching in the West: 1850–1935.* Durham, NC: Duke University Press.

Gonzalez, Juan. 2011. *Harvest of empire: A history of Latinos in America,* revised ed. New York: Penguin Books.

Grandin, Greg. 2006. *Empire's workshop: Latin America, the United States and the rise of the new imperialism.* New York: Metropolitan Books.

Griswold del Castillo, Richard. 1990. *The Treaty of Guadalupe Hidalgo: A legacy of conflict.* Norman: University of Oklahoma Press.

Hagan, John, and Alberto Palloni. 1999. Sociological Criminology and the mythology of Hispanic immigration and crime. *Social Problems* 46(4): 617–32.

Haney López, Ian F. 1996. *White by law: The legal construction of race.* New York: New York University Press.

Haney López, Ian F. 2003. *Racism on trial: The Chicano fight for justice.* Cambridge, MA: Belknap/Harvard University Press.

Harcourt, Bernard E. 2001. *Illusion of order: The false promise of broken windows policing.* Cambridge, MA: Harvard University Press.

Harcourt, Bernard E. 2002. Policing disorder: Can we reduce serious crime by punishing petty offenses? *Boston Review* (April 01). http://www.bostonreview.net/us/bernard-e-harcourt-policing-disorder.

Harcourt, Bernard E. 2013. "Punitive preventive justice." In *Prevention and the limits of the criminal law*, edited by Andrew Asworth, Lucia Zedner, and Patrick Tomlin, 252–72. Oxford: Oxford University Press.

Harcourt, Bernard E., and Jens Ludwig. 2006. "Broken windows: New evidence from New York City and a five-city social experiment." *University of Chicago Law Review* 73: 271–320.

Harcourt, Bernard E., and Jens Ludwig. 2007. Reefer madness: Broken windows policing and misdemeanor marijuana arrests in New York City, 1989–2000. *Criminology & Public Policy* 6(1): 165–82.

Harris, David A. 2002. *Profiles in injustice: Why racial profiling cannot work.* New York: The New Press.

Horsman, Reginald. 1981. *Race and Manifest Destiny: The origins of American racial Anglo-Saxonism.* Cambridge, MA: Harvard University Press.

Huffington Post. 2013 (January 29). Wage gap hits African-American, Latina women hardest, report shows. http://www.huffingtonpost.com/2013/01/29/wage-gap-african-american-women-infographic_n_2568838.html.

Human Rights Watch. 1998. *Shielded from justice: Police brutality and accountability in the United States.* New York: Human Rights Watch.

Immigration Policy Center. 2010. Arizona's punishment doesn't fit the crime: Studies show decrease in Arizona crime rates over time. http://www.immigrationpolicy.org/just-facts/arizona%E2%80%99s-punishment-doesn%E2%80%99t-fit-crime-studies-show-decrease-arizona-crime-rates.

Jilani, Zaid. 2011, July 25. As the right bemoans Norway's criminal justice system, it is one of the safest countries on earth. *Think Progress.* http://thinkprogress.org/justice/2011/07/25/277771/norway-is-safe/.

Johnson, Marilynn. 2003. *Street justice: A history of police violence in New York City.* Boston: Beacon Press.

Jones-Brown, Delores. 2015. Neighborhood policing: A safe, respectful and effective community policing strategy. Testimony before the Task Force on 21st Century Policing. Phoenix, AZ. February 13, 2015. http://www.cops.usdoj.gov/pdf/taskforce/submissions/Jones_Brown_Delores_Testimony.pdf.

Karman, Andrew. 2000. *New York murder mystery: The true story behind the crime crash of the 1990s.* New York: New York University Press.

Kinzer, Stephen. 2006. *Overthrow: America's century of regime change from Hawaii to Iraq.* New York: Times Books.

Kontos, Louis, David Brotherton, and Luis Barrios (eds.). 2003. *Gangs and society: Alternative perspectives.* New York: Colombia University Press.

Kornbluh, Peter. 2003. *The Pinochet file: A declassified dossier on atrocity and accountability.* New York: New Press.

Koss-Chioino, Joan D., and Luis A. Vargas. 1999. *Working with Latino youth: Culture, development, and context.* San Francisco, CA: Jossey-Bass Publishers.

Krisberg, Barry, Christopher Hartney, Angela Wolf, and Fabiana Silva. 2009. *Youth violence myths and realities: A tale of three cities—the different story of delinquent youth as told by the media and by juvenile justice system professionals and the youth national council on crime and delinquency.* Oakland, CA: National Council on Crime and Delinquency.

Krogstad, Jens Manuel, and Mark Hugo Lopez. 2014. Hispanic nativity shift: U.S. births drive population growth as immigration stalls. Washington, DC: Pew Research Center/Hispanic Trends. http://www.pewhispanic.org/2014/04/29/hispanic-nativity-shift/.

Krogstad, Jens Manuel, Renee Stepler, and Mark Hugo Lopez. 2015. English proficiency on the rise among Latinos: U.S. born driving language changes. Washington, DC: Pew Research Center. http://www.pewhispanic.org/2015/05/12/english-proficiency-on-the-rise-among-latinos/.

Kucsera, John, with Gary Orfield. 2014. New York State's extreme school segregation inequality, inaction and a damaged future. Los Angeles, CA: The Civil Rights Project/*Proyecto Derechos Civiles*, UCLA.

LaFeber, Walter. [1963] 1998. *The new empire: An interpretation of American expansionism, 1860–1898.* Reprint, with a new preface by W. LaFeber. Ithaca, NY: Cornell University Press.

LaFeber, Walter. 1993. *Inevitable revolutions: The United States in Central America,* 2d ed. New York: W. W. Norton.

Lauritsen, Janet L., and Karen Heimer. 2010. Violent victimization among males and economic conditions. *Criminology and Public Policy* 9(4): 665–92.

Lee, Matthew. 2003. *Crime on the border: Immigration and homicide in urban communities.* New York: LFB Scholarly Publishing.

Lee, Matthew T., Ramiro Martínez, Jr., and Richard Rosenfeld. 2001. Does immigration increase homicide? Negative evidence from three border cities. *Sociological Quarterly* 42(4): 559–80.

Lopez, Mark Hugo, Ana Gonzalez-Barrera, and Danielle Cuddington. 2013. Diverse origins: The nation's 14 largest Hispanic-origin groups. Washington, DC: Pew Research Center/Hispanic Trends. http://www.pewhispanic.org/2013/06/19/diverse-origins-the-nations-14-largest-hispanic-origin-groups/.

Maldonado-Denis, Manuel. 1972. *Puerto Rico: A socio-historic interpretation.* New York: Vintage.

Martínez, Jr., Ramiro. 1996. Latinos and lethal violence: The impact of poverty and inequality. *Social Problems* 43(2): 131–46.

Martínez, Jr., Ramiro. 2002. *Latino homicide: Immigration, violence and community.* New York: Routledge.

Martínez, Jr., Ramiro, Jacob I. Stowell, and Jeffrey M. Cancino. 2008. A tale of two border cities: Community context, ethnicity, and homicide. *Social Science Quarterly* 89(1): 1–16.

Martínez, Jr., Ramiro, Jacob I. Stowell, and Matthew T. Lee. 2010. Immigration and crime in an era of transformation: A longitudinal analysis of homicides in San Diego neighborhoods, 1980–2000. *Criminology* 48(3): 797–829.

McArdle, Andrea. 2001. Introduction. In *Zero tolerance: Quality of life and the new police brutality in New York City,* edited by Andrea McArdle and Tanya Erzen, 1–16. New York: New York University Press.

McGovern, Virginia, Stephen Demuth, and Joseph E. Jacoby. 2009. Racial and ethnic recidivism risks: A comparison of postincarceration rearrest, reconviction, and reincarceration among white, black, and Hispanic releases. *The Prison Journal* 89(3): 309–27. doi: 10.1177/0032885509339507.

Méndez-Méndez, Serafín, and Diana Alverio. 2003. *Network brownout 2003: The portrayal of Latinos in network television news, 2002.* Washington, DC: National Association of Hispanic Journalists.

Mirandé, Alfredo. 1987. *Gringo justice.* Notre Dame, IN: University of Notre Dame Press.

Montalvo, Daniela. 2006. *Network brownout 2006: The portrayal of Latinos and Latino issues on network television news, 2005.* Washington, DC: National Association of Hispanic Journalists. http://www.nahj.org/resources/2006Brownout.pdf.

Morín, José Luis. 2009. *Latino/a rights and justice in the United States: Perspectives and approaches,* 2nd ed. Durham, NC: Carolina Academic Press.

Motel, Seth, and Eileen Patten. 2012. The 10 largest Hispanic origin groups: Characteristics, rankings, top counties. Washington, DC: Pew Hispanic Center. http://www.pewhispanic.org/2012/06/27/the-10-largest-hispanic-origin-groups-characteristics-rankings-top-counties/.

National Coalition of Anti-Violence Programs. 2014. Hate violence in 2013. New York: Author. http://avp.org/storage/documents/2013_ncavp_hvreport_final.pdf.

National Council of La Raza. 2008. *Overcoming language and culture barriers using evidence based-practice.* Washington, DC: Author.

Nieto, Clara. 2003. *Masters of war: Latin America and U.S. aggression from the Cuban Revolution through the Clinton years.* New York: Seven Stories Press.

Ogletree, Charles, Robert J. Smith, and Johanna Wald. 2012. "Coloring punishment: Implicit social cognition and criminal justice." In *Implicit racial bias across the law*, edited by Justin D. Levinson and Robert J. Smith, 45–60. New York: Cambridge University Press.

Olivas, Michael A. (ed.). 2006. *"Colored men" and "Hombres aquí": Hernandez v. Texas and the emergence of Mexican-American lawyering.* Houston, Texas: Arte Público Press.

Orfield, Gary, and Erica Frankenberg, with Jongyeon Ee, and John Kuscera. 2014. Brown at 60: Great progress, a long retreat and an uncertain future. Los Angeles, CA: UCLA, The Civil Rights Project/*Proyecto Derechos Civiles*, UCLA.

Pagán, Eduardo Obregón. 2003. *Murder at the Sleepy Lagoon: Zoot suits, race, and riot in Wartime L.A.* Chapel Hill, North Carolina: University of North Carolina Press.

Perea, Juan F. 1997. The black/white binary paradigm of race: The "normal science" of American racial thought. *California Law Review* 85: 1213–58.

Perea, Juan F., Richard Delgado, Angela P. Harris, Jean Stefancic, and Stephanie M. Wildman. 2007. *Race and races: Cases and resources for a diverse America*, 2d ed. St. Paul, MN: West Group.

Peters, Jeremy W. 2009, March 4. Albany takes step to repeal '70s-era drug laws. *New York Times*. http://www.nytimes.com/2009/03/05/nyregion/05rockefeller.html?fta=y.

Phillips, Julie A. 2002. White, black, and Latino homicide rates: Why the difference? *Social Problems* 49(3): 349–73.

Planty, Michael, and Jennifer L. Truman. 2013. Firearm violence, 1993–2011 (NCJ 241730). U.S. Department of Justice/Bureau of Justice Statistics.

Ploeg, Gerhard. 2012, December 18. Norway's prisons are doing something right. *New York Times*. http://www.nytimes.com/roomfordebate/2012/12/18/prison-could-be-productive/norways-prisons-are-doing-something-right.

Reiman, Jeffrey, and Paul Leighton. 2010. *The rich get richer and the poor get prison: Ideology, class, and criminal justice*, 9th ed. Boston: Allyn and Bacon.

Rivera Ramos, Efrén. 2001. *The legal construction of identity: The judicial and social legacy of American colonialism in Puerto Rico.* Washington, DC: American Psychological Association.

Rodríguez, Clara E. 1998. *Latin looks: Images of Latinas and Latinos in the U.S. media.* Boulder, CO: Westview.

Rodriguez, Nancy. 2007. Restorative justice at work: Examining the impact of restorative justice resolutions on juvenile recidivism. *Crime & Delinquency* 53(3): 355–79.

Rodriguez, Orlando. 1996. *The new immigrant Hispanic population: An integrated approach to preventing delinquency and crime.* National Institute of Justice, Research Review: U.S. Department of Justice.

Rumbaut, R. G., and Ewing, W. A. (2007, Spring). The myth of immigrant criminality and the paradox of assimilation. Immigration Policy Center. http://www.immigrationpolicy.org/special-reports/myth-immigrant-criminality-and-paradox-assimilation.

Salinas, Lupe S. 2015. *U.S. Latinos and criminal injustice.* East Lansing, MI: Michigan State University Press.

Schlesinger, Traci. 2005. Racial and ethnic disparity in pretrial criminal processing. *Justice Quarterly* 22(2): 170–92.

Schmitz, David F. 1999. *Thank God they're on our side: The United States and right-wing dictatorships, 1921–1965.* Chapel Hill, North Carolina: University of North Carolina Press.

Sentencing Project 2015. Fact sheet: Trends in U.S. corrections. Washington, DC: Author. http://www.sentencingproject.org/doc/publications/cc_HiT_CriminalRecords_profile_1.pdf.

Smith, Peter H. 2013. *Talons of the eagle: Latin America, the United States, and the world*, 4th ed. New York: Oxford University Press.

Southern Poverty Law Center. 2008. Anti-Latino hate crimes rise for fourth year in a row. *SPLC Intelligence Report*, Winter: 7–8.

Southern Poverty Law Center. 2011. U.S. hate groups top 1,000. *Intelligence Report*. http://www.splcenter.org/get-informed/news/us-hate-groups-top-100.

Stacey, Michele, Kristin Carbone-López, and Richard Rosenfeld. 2011. Demographic change and ethnically motivated crime: The impact of immigration on anti-Hispanic hate crime in the United States. *Journal of Contemporary Criminal Justice,* 27(3): 278–98.

Substance Abuse and Mental Health Data Archive. 2014. List of available quick tables for the National Survey on Drug Use and Health, 2013. Rockville, MD: U.S. Department of Health and Human Services (HHS). http://www.icpsr.umich.edu/quicktables/quickconfig.do?35509-0001_all.

Torruella, Juan R. 1988. *The Supreme Court and Puerto Rico: The doctrine of separate and unequal.* Río Piedras, Puerto Rico: Universidad de Puerto Rico.

Travis, Jeremy, and Bruce Western (eds.). 2014. *The growth of incarceration in the United States: Exploring causes and consequences.* Washington, DC: National Academies Press.

Treaty of Guadalupe Hidalgo. 1848. *Treaty of peace, friendship, limits, and settlement.* Done at Guadalupe Hidalgo, February 2, 1848. Entered into force May 30, 1848. 9 Stat. 922; T.S. No. 207; 9 Bevans 791.

Trías Monge, José. 1997. *Puerto Rico: The trials of the oldest colony in the world.* New Haven: Yale University Press.

Urbina, Martin G. (ed.). 2012. *Hispanics in the U.S. criminal justice system: The new American demography.* Springfield, IL: Charles C. Thomas.

U.S. Bureau of the Census. 2014. Facts for features: Hispanic Heritage Month 2014, Sept. 15 to Oct. 15. http://www.census.gov/content/dam/Census/newsroom/facts-for-features/2014/cb14ff-22_hispanic.pdf.

U.S. Census Bureau. 2015a. State and County QuickFacts: New York. http://quickfacts.census.gov/qfd/states/36000.html.

U.S. Census Bureau. 2015b. State and County QuickFacts: New York (city), New York. http://quickfacts.census.gov/qfd/states/36/3651000.html.

U.S. Department of Health and Human Services. 2014. National Survey on Drug Use and Health, 2013. ICPSR35509-v1. Ann Arbor, MI: Substance Abuse and Mental Health Services Administration. Center for Behavioral Health Statistics and Quality. Inter-university Consortium for Political and Social Research [distributor], 2014-11-18. http://doi.org/10.3886/ICPSR35509.v1.

United States Sentencing Commission. 2011. *Report to the Congress: Mandatory minimum penalties in the federal criminal justice system.* http://www.ussc.gov/news/congressional-testimony-and-reports/mandatory-minimum-penalties/report-congress-mandatory-minimum-penalties-federal-criminal-justice-system.

Villarruel, Francisco A., and Nancy E. Walker, with Pamela Minifree, Omara Rivera-Vázquez, Susan Peterson, and Kristen Perry. 2002. *¿Dónde está la justicia? A call to action on behalf of Latino and Latina youth in the U.S. justice system.* Washington, DC: Michigan State University/Building Blocks for Youth.

Waldrep, Christopher (ed.). 2006. *Lynching in America: A history in documents,* New York: New York University Press.

Walker, Nancy, E., J. Michael Senger, Francisco A. Villarruel, and Angela M. Arboleda. 2004. *Lost opportunities: The reality of Latinos in the U.S. criminal justice system.* Washington, DC: National Council of La Raza.

Walker, Samuel, Cassia Spohn, and Miriam DeLone. 2012. *The color of justice: Race, ethnicity, and crime in America,* 5th ed. Belmont, California: Thomson/Wadsworth.

Walters, Jennifer Hardison, Andrew Moore, Marcus Berzofsky, and Lynn Langton. 2013. Household burglary, 1994–2011

(NCJ 241754). U.S. Department of Justice/ Bureau of Justice Statistics.

Wilson, Meagan Meuchel. 2014. *Hate crime victimization, 2004–2012—Statistical tables* (NCJ 244409). Washington, DC: Bureau of Justice Statistics.

Youth Justice Coalition's REALSEARCH Action Research Center. 2012. *Tracked and trapped: Youth of color, gang databases and gang injunctions. December 2012.* http://www.youth4justice.org/wp-content/uploads/2012/12/TrackedandTrapped.pdf.

Zeff, Blake. 2015, January 10. America's over-policing bombshell: How new data proves "stop & frisk" critics were right all along. *Salon.* http://www.salon.com/2015/01/10/americas_over_policing_bombshell_how_new_data_proves_stop_frisk_critics_were_right_all_along/.

Zinn, Howard. 2003. *People's history of the United States: 1492 to present.* New York: Perennial Classics.

Cases Cited

Balzac v. People of Porto Rico [sic], 258 U.S. 298 (1922).

Brown v. Board of Education, 347 U.S. 483 (1954).

Downes v. Bidwell, 182 U.S. 244 (1901).

Floyd et al. v. City of New York, 959 F. Supp. 2d 540 (S.D.N.Y. 2013).

Hernandez v. Texas, 347 U.S. 475, 479–80 (1954).

Katzenbach v. Morgan, 384 U.S. 641 (1966).

Mendez v. Westminster School District of Orange County, 64 F. Supp. 544, 549 (S.D. Cal. 1946), *aff'd*, 161 F.2d 774 (9th Cir. 1947).

People v. Hall, 4 Cal. 399 (1854).

Plessy v. Ferguson, 163 U.S. 537 (1896).

United States et al. v. Yonkers Board of Education, et al., 624 F. Supp. 1276 (S.D.N.Y. 1985); *aff'd*, 837 F. 2d 1181 (2d Cir. 1987); *cert. denied* 486 U.S. 1055 (1988).

Latina/o Immigrants, Crime, and Justice

Ramiro Martínez, Jr.

The lack of Latina/o crime and justice research is one of the most enduring shortcomings in the evolvement of race/ethnicity/criminal justice system scholarship. This oversight is curious considering that scholars in the seminal 1931 Wickersham Commission report focused on Mexican immigrants—a topic central to early work on immigrants, crime, and justice, and one pivotal to early studies on the consequences of Mexican immigration into the United States. Pioneering research on Latinas/os and police also includes studies on **Border Patrol** mistreatment of Mexican border-crossers, Texas police abuse of people of Mexican-origin, and the contentious relationship between Latinas/os and urban police departments during World War II. The latter was highlighted by the "**zoot suit** hysteria" and police misconduct in the 1940s, when the singling out of Latinas/os by various facets of the criminal justice system laid the foundation for protracted animosity between the Los Angeles Police Department (LAPD) and the city's Mexican-origin community. In fact, scholars contend that even in the absence of solid data on this topic, the LAPD and general community has stereotyped **youth** of Mexican origin as inherently delinquent for the last half of the 20th century.

Even though early research existed on immigrants and the police, contemporary research on Latina/o perception of local police, encounters with federal police agents (i.e., **Immigration and Customs Enforcement**), encounters with city police by residents of heavily immigrant communities across the United States, and efforts enabling local police to act as federal immigration agents is scarce (*see* Engel & Calnon 2004; Kane 2002; Hagan, Shedd, & Payne 2005; Menjívar & Bejarano 2004; Reitzel, Rice, & Piquero 2004; Weitzer & Tuch 2005). This includes the failure to examine the consequences of increased enforcement of federal immigration policies by local police or police raids on businesses in search of "illegal" immigrants (see Capps et al. 2007, for recent exception). The present lack of research is obvious. A recent search of articles published between 1990 and 2006 with keywords "Hispanic" or "Latino" and "police" in *Criminal Justice Abstracts,* for example, netted 68 items but a similar search using "black" or "African American" and "police" provided 485 articles on this topic. Scholars understandably have directed attention to black and white attitudinal differences towards the police and documented the perception and prevalence of police misconduct in some African American areas, particularly in extremely poor communities where aggressive police strategies are concentrated. Still, researchers interested in examining racial and ethnic variations in experiences with the police and other criminal justice agencies are just now extending attention to Latinas/os and foreign-born newcomers.

This is important to consider because the Latina/o crime and justice experience varies from that of non-Latina/o whites and blacks, and distinctions vary among Latina/o subgroups (e.g., Mexican, Puerto Rican, Cuban). Beyond immigration and legality status, distinctions also include variations in terms of historical, cultural, political, demographic, economic, and religious patterns (*see* Rodríguez, Sáenz, & Menjívar 2008). These differences also have important consequences.

In an era of concern over the growth of immigration, the most recent Federal Bureau of Investigation hate crime statistics report shows a significant increase in **hate crimes** committed against Latinas/os in the United States between 2004 and 2006. According to the report, *Hate Crime Statistics, 2006*, Latinas/os (Hispanics) comprise 63 percent of **victims** of crimes motivated by a bias toward the victims' ethnicity or national origin. In 2004, the comparable figure was 52 percent; thus, there has been a steady growth of anti-Latina/o hate crimes during a period of increased Latina/o immigration.

Latinas/os also disproportionately reside in high-poverty communities, and research on the impact of community characteristics on Latina/o crime and justice should be expanded. This work could probe the impact of neighborhood disadvantage on violent crime—which also is linked to research on satisfaction with **police** and other criminal justice professionals in extremely poor communities. Moreover, ecological characteristics of policing also include the use of physical and deadly force, officer misconduct, response times in communities, and determinants of police killings highlighting research indicating that attitudes toward the police could be a function of neighborhood context. Police actions disproportionately impact young black males, but the impact on Latina/o youths is an open issue. The same holds true for the role of recent immigration in shaping police encounters, including what happens when local police assume federal immigration-monitoring functions. These issues potentially appear to construct a different story with respect to immigrant Latinas/os, crime, and justice.

The recent Latina/o population growth has implications for the United States. Stereotypes regarding the Latina/o population proliferate in public discourse in the United States. Fueled by media reports and perpetuated by some politicians, most often stereotyping goes unchallenged even though it contributes to the notion that Latina/o immigrants are a dangerous threat. These include stereotypes that Latinas/os are uneducated peasants, drug dealers, welfare recipients, crime prone, and are "illegal." Moreover, new policy mandates for tightening the **border** and singling-out undocumented immigrants who are primarily of Mexican origin is encouraged by politicians and commentators for the sake of enhancing "national security." Actions considered include the deployment of the National Guard, building a fence on the U.S.-Mexico border and labeling undocumented immigrants as "criminal aliens" (*see* Martínez 2008).

Historical Background

Although the founders of American criminology directed attention to European immigrants, some important pioneering research in the 1920s and 1930s also was conducted on the Mexican-origin population. The 1931 Wickersham Commission Report of *Crime and the Foreign Born* focused on "The

Mexican Immigrant and the Problem of Crime and Criminal Justice," a section containing several chapters that were the first to systematically examine crime committed in several urban cities and rural towns by people of Mexican origin. Most of these research sites were in the Southwestern United States, an area where Mexican Latinas/os were long-time identifiable residents. Unfortunately, with the exception of this report, the Mexican-origin population in particular and Latinas/os in general largely were ignored by American criminologists for several decades.

Building on early research, including the 1931 report, historians have contributed to the nascent body of research on Latina/o crime and justice and have made important contributions towards an understanding of immigration trends in the early 1900s. This data includes Mexican immigrants' response to the U.S. criminal justice system, to crime and **violence** within that system, and to non-Latina/o white hostility which emerged during the era of massive Mexican immigration (the 1890s to 1930s). Moreover, historians remind us that the border problems of that time—such as the smuggling of liquor during Prohibition, illegal **drugs** and "illegal" immigrants—persist in contemporary society, as did concerns about an emerging "Mexican problem"—a foible attributing an innate propensity to crime to newcomers from south of the Rio Grande (Rosales 1999, 3–4). This stereotype still is reflected in contemporary society by politicians and the media, but now targets "illegal immigrants"—a demographic group most likely to include persons of Mexican origin (*see* Martínez 2008 for examples of stereotypes). For a review of research on Latina/o crime and justice issues and early 1900s immigration trends, see Rosales (1999, 75–98); Warnshuis (1931); and Gamio (1931 [1971], 140–182). Gamio—the revered Mexican social scientist—produced pioneering research on Mexican immigration to the United States (Gamio 1930 [1969]). His study of Mexican labor and migration during 1926–27 (funded through the Social Science Research Council) generated an enormous amount of data and two books. The life histories of the Mexican immigrants include rich information on their encounters with border patrols and local police.

Regarding crime and justice, the 1931 Report contends that immigrant Mexicans experienced the "negative presence of the police system" as soon as they landed on U.S. soil. Many Mexican immigrants were disproportionately arrested for disorderly conduct, a "colorless charge" used to "keep them in check" and indicated that "indiscriminate dragnets and brutal arrest tactics" were routine in "Latina/o" communities (Rosales 1999, 75). These activities were undoubtedly linked to the widespread stereotype that Mexicans were inclined toward criminality. Warnshuis (1931) also quotes a Chicago police sergeant as stating, "You know, Indian and Negro blood does not mix very well. That is the trouble with the Mexican; he has too much Negro blood" (Warnshuis 1931, 267; *see also* Martínez 2006).

In fact, not only did the notion that Mexican Americans were "born criminals" endure, it eventually contributed to national concern about this group, culminating in harsh measures singling out Mexican youths and young adults. By 1943, many residents of the Los Angeles (LA) *barrios* believed that the LAPD regularly violated the rights of Mexican Americans and that police misconduct in the Latina/o community was routine. In one nationally publicized incident, from June 3 to June 10, 1943, white military servicemen, civilians, and policemen attacked Mexican American youths who were dressed in distinct "zoot suits." Many were assaulted, shaved, and left naked in the LA streets. During the riot, LAPD officers allowed servicemen to beat and strip the "zoot suiters," usually arresting the Mexican American youths for disturbing the peace. In fact, police officers only arrested a handful of servicemen but jailed more than 600 Mexican Americans. As the police watched, servicemen entered bars, theaters, dance halls, restaurants, and even private homes in search of victims. By the end of the rioting, servicemen were targeting *all* Mexican Americans and even some African Americans. Clearly, for some people, hostility and animosity probably defined the relationship between the Latina/o community and the LAPD even long after the end of World War II.

Yet, the extent of this enmity largely was ignored by criminology researchers as the nation directed its attention to race and crime for several decades. This is unfortunate because a research foundation existed that could be built upon to improve current research, including learning more from the well-documented police mistreatment of Mexican immigrants in the early half of the century. As early as 1919, the **Texas Rangers**, a state police force, were involved in "murder; intimidation of citizens; threats against the lives of others; torture and brutality; flogging, horsewhipping, pistol whipping, and mistreatment of suspected persons; incompetency; and disregard for the law" (Samora, Bernal & Peña 1979, 12). The U.S. Border Patrol also regularly restricted or relaxed the movement of "illegal Mexican aliens" according to business cycles in the agriculture industry through at least the 1970s. The relaxation of immigrant policy, border-crossing enforcement, and the employment of "illegals" were linked to ebbs and flows in the U.S. economy. When crops needed to be harvested, the Border Patrol participated in getting workers to the fields. In contrast, when harvest season ended and the workers were no longer needed the number of apprehensions and **deportations** spiked. Thus, the periodic deportation of "illegals" was linked to agriculture industry policy and law enforcement practices (*see* Samora 1971). (In 1953 Professor Samora was the first Mexican American to earn a doctorate in sociology. For more on his pioneering research in immigration, civil rights, public health, and rural poverty, see http://www.samoralegacy.com. The premier Latina/o research center in the Midwest bears his name (http://www.jsri.msu.edu.))

Latina/o Immigrant Neighborhood Research

Much of the recent research on race and ethnicity and crime has been conducted for the community level using official data reported to the police (*see* Peterson & Krivo 2005; Sampson & Bean 2006). This literature largely considers variations in violent crime victimization or offending across places such as metropolitan areas or cities. Ecological research on crime and violence also draws attention to the relationship between race/ethnicity and place (city, metropolitan area, or community) and proposes that racial disparities are linked to the varying social contexts in which population groups exist. A consistent finding in this literature is that violent crime rates—both offending and victimization—are higher in places with greater proportions of African Americans, and this finding persists over time. Most of these studies use **homicide** or violent crime rates or counts of race- and ethnicity-specific violence as the dependent variable because homicides routinely are detected and reported to the police, but even these studies typically focus on black or white crime differences (*see* Martínez 2014 for exceptions).

These studies are valuable because they demonstrate the need to consider racial disparities in crime and, in some cases, they encourage scholars to push conceptions of race and crime to include Latina/o composition in crime studies. Indeed, researchers recently evaluated whether the neighborhood conditions relevant for black and white violence also apply to Latinas/os. Latina/o-specific homicides were analyzed either alone or in comparison with models for native-born blacks and whites, and sometimes including immigrant Haitians, Jamaicans, and Latina/o groups such as the Mariel Cubans (*see* Martínez 2008; Martínez & Lee 2000). All of these are racial, ethnic, and immigrant groups that reside in high-crime and disadvantaged communities in need of police services and which regularly encounter police officers, but the extent of positive or negative police-citizen interactions is not clear. Moreover, Latinas/os usually follow the familiar pattern as found for black and white communities in terms of the all-encompassing effect of concentrated disadvantage or heightened economic problems even though some predictors of Latina/o homicide to some extent are distinct. Thus, the basic linkages among disadvantage and homicide hold for African Americans, Haitians, and Latinas/os even in areas that are dominated by immigrants. This suggests that further examination of the interactions between police and residents and levels of police treatment is warranted because—by extension—the study of Latinas/os and police encounters at the community level could vary from results of studies of blacks or whites.

This body of work is important because there is a strong relationship between economic disadvantage, affluence, and violent crime and this connection has received a great deal of attention given the racial and ethnic differences in the strength of the association between crime and socioeconomic context at the community level. Thus, the premise is that community-level patterns of racial inequality give rise to the social isolation and ecological concentration of the truly disadvantaged, which in turn leads to structural barriers and cultural adaptations that undermine social organization and shape crime. Therefore "race" is not a cause of violence, but rather is a marker deriving from a set of social contexts reflecting racial disparity in U.S. society. This thesis has become known as the "racial invariance" in the fundamental causes of violent crime. The racial invariance thesis rarely has been applied to Latina/o immigrants and justice, however. Although other conceptual or theoretical overviews of Latina/o crime and delinquency exist, attention is directed to macro-level approaches because it is where the bulk of Latina/o violence research is found.

The study of neighborhood disadvantage and violence generated similar findings for blacks and Latinas/os in San Diego, California, and El Paso, Texas (*see* Lee, Martínez, & Rosenfeld 2001), and the characteristics of black, white, and Latina/o homicides in Miami, Chicago, Houston, and Los Angeles (*see* Peterson & Krivo 2005). The research controlled for social and economic determinants of crime that are thought to shape racial/ethnic disparities across neighborhoods. No evidence that more immigration means more homicides in a given area has been found. For the most part, these studies also led to the conclusion that the disadvantage link to homicide is similar for African Americans and Latinas/os.

Therefore, the impact of disadvantage holds in the case of Latinas/os and might be extended to ethnic variations in terms of community-level causes of violence. By extension, it also appears that residents of communities that are heavily of Mexican origin might have enhanced contact with federal and local police who are increasingly engaged in aggressive crime-control strategies designed to stop the movement of undocumented workers into the United States. Intentionally or unintentionally, local efforts enabling the police to act as federal immigration agents could have important consequences. Perceptions of unfair and disrespectful treatment, together with increased targeting by police in search of immigration violations and undocumented workers to deport, could impact Latino males' perception of police. As immigration crackdowns increase, young Latina/o adults are singled out regardless of nativity status—which shapes views of police and increases distrust and negative interactions with criminal justice officials. The aggressive targeting by local police engaging in federal immigration efforts typically occurs in poor Latina/o communities and potentially strains relationships with community members and law enforcement officials. Moreover, negative perceptions of local police likely will increase if the police assume a more active role in immigration enforcement and turn back the clock on criminal justice initiatives designed to enhance trust and cooperation between the police and the communities they serve.

Future Research on Immigrants, Crime, and Justice

There are a number of other important questions that should be addressed in the future. For example, what happens when law enforcement targets specific areas populated by working-poor Latinas/os with aggressive policing tactics designed to subdue immigration policy violations but not necessarily crime? What is the effect of current deportation methods (workplace raids) on immigration trends? Will native-born Latinas/os be content with these tactics when pulled off the streets in these sweeps along with documented and undocumented immigrants? What happens when local police act as federal immigration agents?

It is not surprising that Latinas/os disapprove of recent stepped-up immigration enforcement. In a 2007 survey by the Pew Hispanic Center, Latinas/os wholeheartedly disapprove of a variety of enforcement measures. More than 80 percent say that immigration enforcement should be left mainly to the federal authorities rather than the local police; about 76 percent disapprove of workplace raids; 73 percent disapprove of the criminal prosecution of undocumented immigrants; and 70 percent disapprove of the criminal prosecution of employers who hire undocumented immigrants. Most Latinas/os agree that there has been an increase in immigration enforcement actions targeted at undocumented immigrants; more than one-third of surveyed Latinas/os say there has been an increase in anti-immigrant sentiment, and a majority of Latinas/os worry about deportation (Pew Hispanic Center 2007).

Legality aside, Latina/o concern about aggressive enforcement actions and recent anti-immigrant legislation are obvious. A new Arizona law called the "Support Our Law Enforcement and Safe Neighborhoods Act" (SB 1070) was passed—and proponents argue that it is needed—to prevent "illegal alien crime." A prominent claim by politicians and anti-immigrant supporters is that SB 1070 is needed to fight immigrant crime given rising levels of violence. There is little if any systematic evidence to support this claim because violent crime is not increasing in the area, nor is there any evidence that immigrants are disproportionately involved in perpetrating violence (Martínez 2010).

The legislation creates new crimes and enhances police powers by forcing police officers to investigate, detain, and arrest people for perceived immigration violations based on a reasonable suspicion that they are in the country without documentation. Moreover, SB 1070 also makes it a state crime to lack immigration papers, requires local police to determine whether people they encounter are in the country illegally, and makes attribution through enforcement the policy of all state and local agencies. This legislation moves beyond federal law by creating new and more severe penalties than seen in current enforcement of immigration policy and civil violations of immigration law. The future will prove whether SB 1070 will have a long-term significance in Arizona and in other states.

The potential increase of profiling among Latinas/os is an important topic to consider. The tactic has the potential to create fear and distrust of the police in many Latina/o communities where some families are "blended" with immigrant parents and children born and raised in the United States.

What is the impact of public or police corruption in the home country for Latina/o immigrants? It is possible that, as disadvantaged as conditions might be, immigrants can use their native countries—which could have even worse economic and political conditions—as reference points when assessing their economic position relative to others, but the impact on police encounters requires more research. For example, research on human smuggling suggests that law enforcement officials actively aid in facilitating "illegal" immigrants exiting their country of origin to enter the United States. Some public officials openly request money and gifts to facilitate the immigration process to the extent that smugglers consider public corruption a cost of doing business. Public and police corruption and the extraction of bribes—which cuts into the smugglers' profit margins in the end—are part of the price built into the smuggling business. These activities probably shape immigrants' perceptions, expectations, and tolerance of American policing. It very well might be that prior experience in the country of origin has set such a low standard of expectation that it affects what immigrants expect and what they will tolerate in the United States. The past experiences of immigrants could shape how they perceive police and the criminal justice system. Given the widespread popularity of immigration crackdowns, researchers should reconsider what works and what doesn't work when trying to improve police-citizen relations in Latina/o communities.

Undocumented Latinas/os are now being targeted by local and federal police agencies and singled out from others in disadvantaged communities, which sets the stage for potential conflict between police and residents. Much like the neighborhoods studied by pioneering researchers in 1931, these activities are concentrated in economically disadvantaged communities—a reminder that economic conditions shape crime, violence, and perhaps police reactions to residents examining SB 1070–type legislation. In the Pew survey, nearly one in ten Latinas/os—native-born and foreign-born—report that in the past year the police or other authorities have stopped them and asked about their immigration status. Whether Latina/o profiling will increase hand in hand with police strategies reacting to the growth of immigration across some poor neighborhoods is an area for further research. The outcomes of criminal justice tactics are under-examined for Latinas/os, and many questions remain unanswered about Latinas/os and reactions to the police.

Although much of the Latina/o population growth is in traditional settlement areas in the Southwestern United States, there is substantial movement to new places or places where few Latinas/os have resided in previous decades. The emergence of anti-immigrant laws or ordinances such as SB 1070 has proliferated in these new destinations. Such laws aim to prevent "illegals" from securing housing, punish business owners, and enable local police to search for "illegals" or ask about legality status—an issue typically in the federal domain (*see* Esbenshade 2007). The village of Hazleton, Pennsylvania, is a prime example. According to the 2000 census, Hazleton had approximately 23,000 residents and about 5 percent were Hispanic or Latina/o. In 2006, local officials passed the Illegal Immigration Relief Act—a measure that would have resulted in **racial profiling**, discrimination, and denial of benefits even to legal immigrants. This ordinance also imposed fines of up to $1,000 to landlords who rented to "illegal" immigrants, denied business permits to corporations that employed undocumented immigrants, and made English the official language of the village. Latinas/os bore the brunt of the latest anti-immigrant hysteria in Hazelton and other places that implemented similar restrictions. The consequences of anti-immigrant and Latina/o initiatives are that *all* Latinas/os, legality aside, are singled out by politicians and the media and presumed to be "illegals" (Rodríguez, Sáenz & Menjívar 2008).

Clearly, scholars should broaden their focus beyond blacks and whites to include immigrant Latinas/os and Latina/o groups whenever possible in future research on the criminal justice system. The incorporation of Latinas/os will help scholars of violent crime, serious delinquency, justice, and policing to produce a broader understanding of race, ethnicity, and violent crime linkages and expand the focus to include the diverse ecological contexts in which blacks, whites, and Latinas/os reside. Until Latinas/os and immigrants are brought into the study of crime and justice, any understanding of **race and ethnicity** remains underdeveloped.

See also: Part I essays: Latinas/os and the U.S. Criminal Justice System: An Overview of Socio-Historic and Contemporary Issues; The U.S. War on Drugs and Latina/o Communities; Incarceration and Latinas/os in the United States; Crime and the U.S.-Mexican Border. Part II entries: Deportation; Deportation Laws; Hate Crimes; Homicide; Texas Rangers; Victims.

Further Reading

Alpert, Geoffrey P., Roger G. Dunham, and Michael R. Smith. 2007. Investigating the racial profiling by the Miami-Dade Police Department: A multimethod approach. *Criminology & Public Policy* 6: 25–56.

Capps, Randy, Rosa Maria Castañeda, Ajay Chaudry, and Robert Santos. 2007. *Paying the price: The impact of immigration raids on America's children.* A report by The Urban Institute for the National Council of La Raza. http://www.nclr.org/content/publications/download/49166.

Chavez, Leo R. 2008. *The Latino threat: Constructing immigrants, citizens, and the nation.* Stanford, CA: Stanford University Press.

Culver, Leigh. 2004. The impact of new immigration patterns on the provision of police service in Midwestern communities. *Journal of Criminal Justice* 32: 329–44.

Engel, Robin, and Jennifer M. Calnon. 2004. Examining the influence of drivers' characteristics during traffic stops by police. *Justice Quarterly* 21: 49–90.

Esbenshade, Jill. 2007. *Division and dislocation: Regulating immigration through local housing ordinances.* Washington DC: Immigration Policy Center Special Report. http://www.immigrationpolicy.org/special-reports/division-and-dislocation-regulating-immigration-through-local-housing-ordinances. Accessed November 12, 2015.

Escobar, Edward J. 1999. *Race, police, and the making of a political identity: Mexican Americans and the Los Angeles Police Department, 1900–1945*. Berkeley, CA: University of California Press.

Gamio, Manuel. 1969 (1930). *Mexican immigration to the United States*. New York, NY: Arno Press and the New York Times.

Gamio, Manuel. 1971 (1931). *The life story of the Mexican immigrant*. New York, NY: Dover Publications.

Hagan, John, Carla Shedd, and M. R. Payne. 2005. Race, ethnicity and youth perceptions of criminal justice. *American Sociological Review* 70: 381–407.

Kane, Robert J. 2002. The social ecology of police misconduct. *Criminology* 40: 867–96.

Lee, Matthew T., Ramiro Martínez, Jr., and Richard Rosenfeld. 2001. Does immigration increase homicide? Negative evidence from three border cities. *The Sociological Quarterly* 42: 559–80.

Lopez, Mark Hugo, and Susan Minushkin. 2008. *2008 national survey of Latinos: Hispanics see their situation in the U.S. deteriorating; oppose key immigration enforcement measures.* Washington, DC: Pew Hispanic Center.

Martínez, Ramiro, Jr. 2006. Coming to America: The impact of the new immigration on crime. In *Immigration and Crime,* edited by R. Martínez, Jr. and A. Valenzuela, 1–19. New York, NY: New York University Press.

Martínez, Ramiro, Jr. 2007. Incorporating Latinos and immigrants into policing research. *Criminology & Public Policy* 6: 57–64.

Martínez, Ramiro, Jr. 2008. Editorial introduction: The impact of immigration policy on criminological research. *Criminology & Public Policy* 7: 53–58.

Martínez, Ramiro, Jr. 2010. Policy essay: Economic conditions and racial/ethnic variations in violence: Immigration, the Latino paradox and future research. *Criminology & Public Policy* 9(4): 707–13.

Martínez, Ramiro, Jr. and Matthew T. Lee. 2000. On immigration and crime. In *Criminal justice 2000: The nature of crime: continuity and change,* edited by R. J. Bursik, Jr., J. F. Short, Jr., and R. B. Taylor, 485–524. Washington DC: National Institute of Justice.

Martínez, Ramiro, Jr. 2014. *Latino homicide: Immigration, violence and community*. 2nd edition. New York, NY: Routledge.

Mazon, Mauricio. 1984. *The Zoot-Suit Riots*. Austin, TX: Center for Mexican American Studies and the University of Texas Press.

Menjívar, Cecilia, and Cynthia L. Bejarano. 2004. Latino immigrants' perceptions of crime and police authorities in the United States: A case study. *Ethnic and Racial Studies* 27: 120–48.

Moore, Joan, and Raquel Pinderhughes. 1993. *In the barrios: Latinos and the underclass debate*. New York, NY: Russell Sage Foundation.

Nielsen, Amie L., Matthew T. Lee, and Ramiro Martínez, Jr. 2005. Integrating race, place, and motive in social disorganization theory: Lessons from a comparison of black and Latino homicide types in two immigrant destination cities. *Criminology* 43: 837–72.

Nielsen, Amie, and Ramiro Martínez, Jr. 2006. Multiple disadvantages and crime among black immigrants: Exploring Haitian violence in Miami's communities. In *Immigration and crime: Race, ethnicity and violence,* edited by R. Martínez, Jr., and A. Valenzuela, 212–34. New York, NY: New York University Press.

Ong, M., and D. A. Jenks. 2004. Hispanic perceptions of community policing: Is community policing working in the city? *Journal of Ethnicity in Criminal Justice* 2: 53–66.

Peterson, Ruth D., and Lauren J. Krivo. 2005. Macrostructural analyses of race, ethnicity, and violent crime: Recent lessons and new directions for research. *Annual Review of Sociology* 31: 331–56.

Pew Hispanic Center. 2007 (December). *2007 National survey of Latinos: As illegal immigration issue heats up, Hispanics feel a chill.* Washington, DC. http://pewhispanic.org/files/reports/84.pdf.

Pew Hispanic Center. 2008. *Statistical portrait of Hispanics in the United States, 2006.* http://pewhispanic.org/factsheets/factsheet.php?FactsheetID=35.

Reitzel, John D., Stephen K. Rice, and Alex Piquero. 2004. Lines and shadows: Perceptions of racial profiling and the Hispanic experience. *Journal of Criminal Justice* 32: 607–16.

Rodríguez, Havidán, Rogelio Sáenz, and Cecilia Menjívar. 2008. Preface. In *Latinas/os in the United States: Changing the face of América.* New York, NY: Springer.

Rosales, F. Arturo. 1999. *¡Pobre raza¡ Violence, justice, and mobilization among Mexico Lindo immigrants, 1900–1936.* Austin, TX: University of Texas Press.

Rosenbaum, Dennis P., Amie M. Schuck, Sandra K. Costello, Darnell F. Hawkins, and Marianne K. Ring. 2005. Attitudes toward the police: The effects of direct and vicarious experience. *Police Quarterly* 8: 343–65.

Sáenz, Rogelio. 2004. *Latinos and the changing face of America.* The American People Series, Census 2000. New York, NY: Russell Sage and Population Reference Bureau.

Samora, Julian. 1971. *Los mojados: The wetback story.* Notre Dame, IN: University of Notre Dame Press.

Samora, Julian, Joe Bernal, and Albert Peña. 1979. *Gunpowder justice.* Notre Dame, IN: University of Notre Dame Press.

Sampson, Robert J. 2008. Rethinking crime and immigration. *Contexts* 7: 28–33.

Sampson, Robert J., and Dawn Jeglum Bartusch. 1998. Legal cynicism and (subcultural?) tolerance of deviance: The neighborhood context of racial differences. *Law and Society Review* 32: 777–804.

Sampson, Robert J., and Lydia Bean. 2006. Cultural mechanisms and killing fields: A revised theory of community-level racial inequality. In *The many colors of crime: inequalities of race, ethnicity and crime in America*, edited by R. Peterson, L. Krivo, and J. Hagan, 8–36. New York: New York University Press.

Sampson, Robert J., and William J. Wilson. 1995. Toward a theory of race, crime, and urban inequality. In *Crime and inequality,* edited by J. Hagan and R. Peterson, 37–56. Stanford, CA: Stanford University Press.

Skogan, Wesley G., and Lynn Steiner. 2004. Crime, disorder and decay in Chicago's Latino Community. *Journal of Ethnicity in Criminal Justice* 2: 7–26.

Vásquez, Manuel A., Chad E. Seales, and Marie Friedmann Marquardt. 2008. New Latino destinations. In *Latinas/os in the United States: Changing the face of América,* edited by H. Rodríguez, R. Sáenz, and C. Menjívar, 19–35. New York, NY: Springer.

Warnshuis, Paul L. 1931. Crime and criminal justice among the Mexicans of Illinois. In *Report on crime and the foreign born*, no. 10, National Commission on Law observance and enforcement report. Washington, DC: U.S. Government Printing Office: 265–329.

Weitzer, Ronald, and Steven A. Tuch. 2002. Perceptions of racial profiling: Race, class and personal experience. *Criminology* 40: 435–57.

Weitzer, Ronald, and Steven A. Tuch. 2005. Racially biased policing: Determinants of citizen perceptions. *Social Forces* 83: 1009–30.

Zhang, Sheldon, and Ko-lin Chin. 2002. Enter the dragon: Inside Chinese human smuggling organizations. *Criminology* 40: 737–68.

Policing and Latina/o Communities

José Luis Morín

In the United States, few criminal justice topics evoke as much disquiet and debate as policing in communities of color, both when discussing the Latinas/os experience of the U.S. criminal justice system, and when examining the experience of African Americans. Tensions between law enforcement agencies and Latina/o communities in more recent years are inextricably linked to a longer history of strained relations—a history that can be traced back to the earliest days of U.S. relations with Mexico and other Latin American countries.

Persons of Mexican descent are among the earliest of Latinas/os present in significant numbers in the United States. They did not immigrate to the United States, but rather were residents and owners of the lands that were once part of Mexico, prior to the 1846–1848 U.S. war with Mexico. From their earliest experiences with law enforcement officials and practices, Mexican Americans were likely to encounter law enforcement agents and a U.S. justice system more predisposed to serving and protecting Anglo-American interests in the territories of the west and southwest than with protecting Mexican American rights to person and property. Since then, police and law enforcement relations with Mexican Americans and others peoples from Latin America who have come to comprise today's U.S. Latina/o population, more often than not, have been characterized as strained. Over time, complaints of biased and discriminatory treatment at the hands of police and throughout the criminal justice system have been common.

This essay provides a synopsis of the historical antecedents to today's relations between law enforcement and U.S. Latinas/os. Perceptions and assumptions of Latinas/os in the United States as racial and cultural "others" within the established U.S. racial framework and dynamic of each historical period laid the foundation for the unequal treatment of Latinas/os by law enforcement personnel and the criminal justice system. The history of U.S. Latinas/os is replete with examples of **vigilantism**, **hate crimes, racial profiling**, and **police brutality** and other forms of abuse at the hands of law enforcement officers. Indeed, **police brutality**—defined as excessive force or the use of physical force greater than that which is needed to complete a lawful police end—has become an all-too-common occurrence in the Latina/o experience of policing in their communities.

Contemporary issues between police and Latina/o communities often are viewed by scholars as stemming from longstanding problems linked to racial and ethnic bias in law enforcement, policing policies and tactics, police corruption and brutality, and questions about police culture. Demands for reforms and for increasing diversity in the ranks of law enforcement officers and agents have led to an increase in Latina/o representation among rank-and-file officers in some jurisdictions around the country. This essay also examines the experience of Latina/o officers and whether greater diversity has necessarily improved relations between law enforcement and Latina/o communities. As for other reforms to promote better police-community relations, enhanced police accountability, expansion of **community policing**, and greater community empowerment are among the salient recommendations that have been posited and that are covered in this essay.

Law Enforcement and Latina/o Community Relations: A Brief Historical Overview

1800s–1950s

Tensions between Latina/o communities and law enforcement agencies in the United States can be traced at least as far back as the 1800s. After having defeated Mexico in a war that ended in 1848, the United States secured possession of approximately half of the northern territory of Mexico that currently constitutes roughly one-third of the continental United States. Mexicans, living on what previously was Mexico's sovereign land were forced to decide whether to remain in the United States or leave and lose their land and property. Those who remained from that moment forward faced many challenges to being accepted and treated as equals by the dominant Anglo-American society. In the United States, a country where race-based slavery was legal in 1848, racial attitudes strongly influenced laws, policies, and practices that related to Mexicans and other persons of Latin American origin. Thus, the racial, ethnic, socioeconomic, and political divide that runs through the history of the United States provided a foundation for past and present frictions between law enforcement and Latina/o communities.

In 1848, slavery and racial discrimination were the norm in the United States. As detailed in the overview of Latinas/os and the criminal justice system provided in this volume, the U.S. conquest of the territories that were previously part of Mexico was premised on the idea of **Manifest Destiny**. Manifest Destiny was an ideology that not only argued that the United States was fated to expand its territory, but that it was justified in doing so based on Anglo-American racial, religious, and cultural superiority. Mexicans and other groups from Latin America generally were regarded as belonging to an inferior race, given their mixed Spanish, indigenous, and African ancestry. The racial and cultural superiority of persons of Anglo-Saxon heritage in the United States went largely unquestioned well into the 20th century, as the institution of slavery was replaced by a system of de jure racial segregation and discrimination during a period now commonly referred to as the "Jim Crow era."

Although the Mexicans who remained in the territories acquired by the United States after 1848 had not crossed the border as unauthorized persons (instead, the border had "crossed over" them), the dominant Anglo-American population viewed Mexican Americans as foreigners and racial "others" not worthy of being accorded the rights and privileges of "true Americans"—that is, persons of white Anglo Saxon origin. Tensions rose as Anglo-Americans increasingly sought to settle in the territories of west and southwest, which today comprise in part or in whole the states of California, Texas, New

Mexico, Arizona, and Nevada, and include parts of Colorado, Utah, and Kansas.

In the years following the U.S.-Mexico War, countless numbers of Mexican Americans lost possession of their lands and other property to white settlers, who were able to use U.S. laws and the courts to their advantage to wrest land and property previously governed under Mexican or Spanish law or were able to take possession of land belonging to Mexican Americans through force with the tacit approval or active participation of law enforcement authorities. Widely held and promoted notions of Mexicans as violent bandits ("*bandidos*" or "*banditos*") helped justify actions taken by law enforcement officials in the territories that were once part of Mexico to protect Anglo-American power and privileges at the expense of Mexican Americans' rights and claims to land. Mexican Americans were treated unequally and unfairly and even subject to brutality and physical violence. **Lynchings** and other forms of mistreatment at the hands of Anglo-American vigilantes and law enforcement agents, such as the **Texas Rangers**, became commonplace.

In the 1800s, U.S. laws and policies mirrored prevailing anti-Latino and anti-Mexican biases and sentiments, having a direct impact on how police and the criminal justice system treated Latinas/os. California's 1855 anti-vagrancy law, most often referred to as the "the **Greaser Act**," enshrined into law the use of a racially pejorative term ("**Greaser**") for Mexican or Latina/o and empowered law enforcement officers to racially profile and arrest for vagrancy or loitering "all persons who are commonly known as 'Greasers' or the issue [children] of Spanish and Indian blood . . . and who go armed and are not peaceable and quiet persons" (Act of April 30, 1855, ch. 175, § 2, 1855, Cal. Stat. 217; quoted in Haney López, 1996, 145). De jure discrimination and the racial profiling of Mexicans and Latinas/os had become the order of the day.

Stereotyping and profiling Latinas/os as criminals was also the accepted norm in the day-to-day operations of the judicial system as well as in law enforcement. Mexicans—and hence Latinas/os—were prohibited by law from testifying in court against white defendants. Such was the case of Manuel Domínguez, a Mexican-American mestizo. In 1857, Domínguez—a prominent citizen, a delegate to California's Constitutional Convention, and a signatory to the state's constitution—was denied the opportunity to testify in a trial against a white defendant when a judge acceded to the argument that his mixed racial ancestry was grounds to exclude his testimony, in keeping with legal precedent—*People v. Hall* (1854)—that excluded persons of Chinese descent from testifying against a white defendant. In a court of law, only a "white" person could be deemed competent, and persons of mixed or non-white ancestry automatically were incompetent based on race.

Mexicans and other Latinas/os in the United States have experienced discriminatory segregation in many facets of their lives. Into the 20th century, it was not uncommon for Latina/o children to be required to attend segregated schools or for Latinas/os to be excluded from restaurants and other public accommodations including public pools, as it was generally taken at face value that Mexicans were inferior. Widely accepted forms of unequal treatment and segregation were replicated in the judicial system. Texas courthouses, for example, explicitly denied Mexican Americans attorneys and Latinos generally the use of whites-only men's restrooms. Other facilities on the courthouse grounds were marked "Colored Men" and "*Hombres Aquí*" ("Men Here") for Latinos and other persons of color. It was not until ***Hernandez v. Texas*** (1954) that Mexican American lawyers were successful in having the U.S. Supreme Court end the overt and systematic exclusion of Latinas/os as jurors, as had been the case until then.

Scholars point out, however, that the *Hernandez* case did not end the exclusion and underrepresentation of Latinas/os on juries. Bias in the selection of jurors and other impediments, such as the use of peremptory challenges, have played a role limiting the ability of Latinas/os to serve on juries for many years after the 1954 Texas case. Indeed, the 1991 U.S. Supreme Court decision in ***Hernandez v. New York***, allowing prosecutors to use peremptory challenges to exclude Spanish speakers from juries for fear that the official court translation might be disregarded continues to raise concerns that *Hernandez v. New York* serves as a modern-day means of curtailing Latina/o representation on juries. The exclusion of and bias toward Latinas/os prevalent in U.S. history extended to other parts of the criminal justice system, including the daily operations of law enforcement agents and police officers. The general ethos that Latinas/os are sufficiently unfit and undesirable has been reinforced throughout history with adverse consequences for Latina/o relations with law enforcement.

As the presence of persons of Latin American ancestry grew in the United States, negative perceptions of them as foreigners prone to criminal behavior have persisted, resulting in adverse treatment by law enforcement officials and the justice system. Police and other law enforcement personnel functioned in a social and legal milieu that had long accepted the exclusion and unequal treatment of Mexicans and other Latinas/os. By the late1920s, fear over crime committed by "foreigners" prompted a study by the U.S. National Commission on Law Observance and Enforcement, commonly referred to as the "Wickersham Commission." Issued in 1931, the commission's report made note of the widely held view of Mexicans as foreigners, even those who were born in the United States. It linked negative perceptions of Mexicans to numerous instances where police treated Mexicans unfairly and often with brutality and deadly force. After its publication, the commission report essentially was overlooked in favor of an initiative to combat marijuana, as it was presumed that marijuana use by Mexican Americans resulted in increased violence.

Residential segregation typified the existence of Mexican Americans in the United States by the 1940s and 1950s. The *barrio*—segregated enclaves in which Mexicans lived—did not just isolate Mexicans from white/Anglo society, it stood as an obstacle to understanding the Mexican community and perpetuated media stereotypes about Mexicans as being inferior, lazy, and prone to criminality. As some analysts point out, police played an indispensable role in maintaining and enforcing Mexican isolation to keep Anglo society "safe." Hence police encounters with Mexicans often turned brutal.

In response to their unequal standing and circumstances, many young Mexican American men in Los Angeles in the early 1940s began wearing ostentatious clothing known as the "**zoot suit**," in affirmation of their sense of identity and independence. For Anglo society, the mass media, and—most importantly—law enforcement, the zoot suit became synonymous with criminality. Only someone predisposed to criminal conduct would wear a zoot suit. Because the zoot suit was so closely associated with Mexicans, as scholars note, the zoot suit served as a proxy for race. In 1943, several days of physical confrontations erupted in Los Angeles between white military servicemen and Mexican Americans. In the **Zoot Suit Riots**, as they became known, the servicemen entered the Mexican barrio, targeting Mexicans regardless of whether they were wearing zoot suits, and the police were implicated in the brutality and violence that ensued. Despite denials on the part of the mayor, an independent investigation revealed that race was indeed a central factor in the riots.

Fear of foreign "subversives" and "communists" during the 1950s only reinforced widely held stereotypes and suspicions about Mexican American immigrants and provided further justification for the use of extraordinary law enforcement measures to rid the country of "illegals." From 1954 to 1959, the federal government instituted what is popularly known as "**Operation Wetback**," a military-style campaign to round up and deport undocumented Mexican immigrants. As its name suggests, this campaign to deport went a long way to be disrespectful of Mexicans and to violate their rights and civil liberties. The operation included house-to-house raids that intimidated Mexican communities. More than 3.7 million Mexicans were deported, among them countless U.S. citizens (Mirandé 1987, 21–22; Carrasco 1997, 197–98).

1960s–1970s

Police Corruption and Police Brutality

Ongoing racial and ethnic inequality and discrimination in U.S. society provoked discontent in many urban neighborhoods where people of color lived—from California to New York. The Kerner Commission was convened to study the causes of the riots and disturbances that arose in the 1960s. In 1968, the commission issued a groundbreaking report that spoke of the frustrations and despair of the African American community caused by social and economic discrimination. It pointed to the need to address police brutality, corruption and a "double standard" within the justice system. The recurring themes of police corruption and police brutality—defined as the excessive use of force and its impact on communities of color, toward African Americans and Latinas/os, in particular—also resonated in future studies that examined policing.

As with African Americans, Latinas/os in the 1960s and '70s commonly resided in poor communities and were separated from whites. Pegged as criminally prone, living in segregated neighborhoods, and too often economically unable to mount a legal defense or challenge in court, Latinas/os, like African Americans, were vulnerable to police excesses. The political activism of the time did give rise to new ways of organizing against police use of excessive force. A younger generation of Latinas/os engaged in activism that made combating police brutality in their communities a high priority.

On the West Coast of the United States, young Mexican Americans increasingly became conscious of the social and economic injustices that their community faced in the United States and their growing awareness led them to organize what became known as the "**Chicano** movement," with the word "Chicana/o" embodying a sense of racial and ethnic identity and pride, as well as a resolve to stand up for their rights. Chicana/o activists went on to found the **Brown Berets**, whose militancy challenged the discrimination that they saw permeating society, including institutions such the police department and the criminal justice system in general.

On the East Coast, Puerto Rican youth emboldened with a greater sense of national identity also organized efforts to counter unequal treatment that disadvantaged and oppressed their communities. Among the groups they formed were the **Young Lords**, whose goal was to address many political, social, and economic inequities they experienced, including abuse and brutality at the hands of law enforcement officers.

In the face of ongoing and blatant disparities in education, housing, healthcare, and other public services, Latina/o youth in communities around the country mobilized protests. In Los Angeles, students organized school walkouts to protest inferior education in Mexican communities. Protests often led to beatings by police, arrests, and criminal trials of activists that brought to light inequities in the justice system. Chicano activists not only experienced police brutality and arrests but regularly faced judges and all-white juries predisposed to rule against them. As one prominent academic who has studied this period notes, racism in the criminal justice system functioned as a matter of "common sense" (Haney López 2003). That is, judges and others who worked in the justice system did not need to intentionally seek to discriminate; it was understood (common sense) that whites were qualified to be jurors and persons of Mexican ancestry were not, and that Mexican Americans were plainly degenerates, criminally prone, and therefore deserving of harsher treatment and punishment (Haney López 2003). In the late 1960s, police brutality in Mexican American communities, such as East Los Angeles, was rampant and routine. Hundreds of cases of police misconduct and excessive use of force against residents of East Los Angeles were documented by the American Civil Liberties Union of Southern California.

Similarly, Puerto Rican activists in eastern cities such as New York mobilized to protest the denial of adequate basic services to their community, including health care, education, and seemingly mundane needs such as regular garbage collection. The Young Lords, in particular, occupied hospitals and buildings—including Lincoln Hospital in the Bronx and a church in East Harlem (El Barrio) in New York City—as part of their efforts to seek redress for the daily injustice they saw their communities as having to endure.

As with Chicana/os on the West Coast, violence and harsh treatment by police was common in East Coast Latina/o communities, and organizations such as the Young Lords viewed police brutality as a major concern. In 1970, Julio Roldán, a Vietnam veteran active in the Young Lords, was arrested by police and was unable to make bail. He was sent to jail pending adjudication of his case. By the next day, he was declared dead by hanging in his jail cell—a death that authorities subsequently claimed was a "suicide." But many in the Puerto Rican community disputed that conclusion, especially after an autopsy revealed Roldán had broken bones and signs of having been beaten. In the Puerto Rican and Latina/o community, the Roldán case became emblematic of the ongoing problem of police violence against Latinas/os, along with many other cases that followed.

The connection between police corruption and police brutality has a long history in major urban centers such as Los Angeles and New York City. Latinas/os have been particularly vulnerable to the excesses of corruption and brutality, which frequently go hand in hand. The targeting, stereotyping, and mistreatment of the Mexican Americans by law enforcement officers under the guise of fighting criminally inclined zoot suit wearers in the 1940s continued with the targeting, stereotyping, and mistreatment of Chicana/o activists in the 1960s and 1970s. In the early 1970s, the Knapp Commission, a special committee impaneled to investigate allegations of graft and misconduct in the New York City Police Department (NYPD), uncovered rampant corruption and brutality on the heels of disclosures by police officer and whistleblower Frank Serpico. In spite of the public outcries and attempts at reform in the 1960s and 1970s, abuses at the hands of police personnel were to continue, not just in New York City, but in Los Angeles and wherever Latinas/os were to be found throughout the United States.

Policing and the War on Drugs

By the late 1960s, President Richard Nixon had gravitated toward a law-and-order political platform in which drugs became a focal point. Despite evidence pointing to the efficacy of **drug treatment** programs and a 1971 report by the Bureau of Narcotics and Dangerous Drugs that the link between illicit **drug use** and violent crime was overblown and misguided, declaring a "**war on drugs**" and tough law-and-order stance was determined to be more politically expedient in winning over "middle America" (Balko 2013, 67–96). Thus, the Nixon administration pressed ahead with legislation permitting police officers to conduct "no-knock raids" on homes of suspected **drug users**. Although there were serious concerns about the constitutionality of such a law and its potential for abuse, legislators were more concerned with not appearing weak on crime. Regardless of political party, politicians have since been loath to run campaigns that could be perceived as soft on crime.

By the early 1970s, Governor Nelson Rockefeller secured passage of a series of strict laws, known as the "**Rockefeller Drug Laws**." These laws included a "no-knock" provision that set aside the requirement that police knock and announce themselves when in pursuit of illegal drugs, measures empowering police to "stop and frisk" individuals, and strict penalties for drug offenses. The get-tough Rockefeller Drug Laws were replicated in many states throughout the country. Stricter drug laws became mired in controversy over the decades, however, as it became increasingly clear that these tougher police tactics and harsh mandatory sentences disproportionately affected the poor and African American and Latina/o communities. The mass incarceration of the poor and people of color resulting from the war on drugs and its pursuit of low-level offenders and minor violators eventually led to calls for repeal of the Rockefeller Drug Laws, which only became a reality in 2009.

1980s to the Present

Ronald Reagan's presidency in the 1980s couched the "war on drugs" as a matter of national security. Drug use was further demonized, the notion of decriminalization of any substance—including the least harmful, marijuana—was summarily dismissed, and efforts to curtail Fourth Amendment rights under the U.S. Constitution were advanced as part of the "war on drugs." Aggressive policing and the war on drugs, although politically popular, were to have severe consequences for Latinas/os and African Americans.

Militarized Policing

By the 1990s, the police approach to fighting this "war" was not only more aggressive, it was markedly more militarized. The deployment of military-style equipment, training, and tactics—including SWAT teams—that originated with the Los Angeles Police Department (LAPD) after the Watts riots of the 1960s, became accepted and ubiquitous throughout the United States. Police departments continued acquiring surplus military armaments, vehicles, and other equipment to be used in increasing numbers of drug raids and arrests. But too often the "war" on drugs has been found to be waged in communities of color. Among the cases documented by the American Civil Liberties Union pointing to the excessive use of military force by police is that of José Guerena. While at home with his wife and child, Guerena, a 26-year-old Iraq War veteran from Tucson, Arizona, was shot 71 times and killed by a SWAT team that broke into his home at about 9:30 in the morning. No drugs were found in his home, and he was left to die without medical attention. Similar raids conducted throughout his neighborhood retrieved only a small quantity of marijuana in one house.

As in previous decades, police corruption and police brutality were shown to be inextricably linked, with communities of color frequently bearing the brunt of excessive uses of force. Twenty years after the Knapp Commission, another investigation of police corruption in New York City was launched. The Mollen Commission, which operated from 1993 to 1994, heard gripping testimony by NYPD officers Bernard Cawley and Michael Dowd, who exposed the routine nature of excessive police force and the generally accepted practice among police personnel not to report such acts committed by their colleagues. In describing why he was nicknamed "The Mechanic," Officer Cawley explained that his role was to "tune people up"—that is, beat up people—"to show who is in charge" (quoted in Human Rights Watch 1998, 268). As Officer Dowd made clear in his testimony, police brutality was an essential part of the job; it was also how police officers obtained acceptance from fellow officers.

Among cities with large Latinas/os populations with long histories of police–Latinas/os community tensions and police misconduct is Los Angeles. In 1991, the videotaped police beating of Rodney King and the police officers' subsequent acquittal of state charges not only struck a chord with the African American community, it was similarly felt in the Los Angeles Latina/o community. Latinas/os in Los Angeles appeared to have released pent-up frustrations and dissatisfaction with their treatment by LADP so much so that in the days of upheaval following the acquittal of the police in the King case, a majority of those arrested were Latina/o and as much as 49 percent of the damage was in Latinas/os sections of Los Angeles (Martínez 1993, 469; Pastor 1993). The King case brought to the fore, once again, the issue of police brutality and its impact on racial and ethnic groups. Indeed, the Christopher Commission, constituted to investigate the LAPD after the Rodney King beating and headed by attorney Warren Christopher, concluded that "an officer's prejudice towards the suspect's race may lead to the use of excessive force" (Independent Commission on the Los Angeles Police Department 1991, 69).

In the late 1990s, Los Angeles police became the focus of attention again when it was disclosed that its elite anti-drug unit, known as the CRASH (Community Resources Against Street Hoodlums) unit, was involved in an array of illegal conduct, including drug trafficking and profiteering. To cover up their criminal behavior, the LAPD systematically used excessive force and framed individuals. The CRASH unit focused attention on the area of Los Angeles called "**Rampart**," a neighborhood with a sizable Latina/o population and where the impact of the police corruption and brutality for Latinas/os was significant. As one analysis states, the infamous Rampart CRASH unit engaged in "[p]olice work targeting predominantly Latinos/as and Latino/a 'suspected gang members' in Los Angeles . . .

[it] framed thousands of innocent people by planting evidence on them, committed perjury in court to gain convictions, and physically brutalized innocent youth and adults" (Villarruel et al. 2002, 64). One of the many victims of the Rampart CRASH unit was a Latino who the police planted false evidence on to conceal their own criminality. He also was wrongfully charged and was paralyzed by the brutal beating he received at the hands of the police. His testimony in court was key in breaking open the case against the police.

Although Latinas/os were frequent victims of the CRASH unit, it is equally telling that one of the LAPD officers who played a central role in the police corruption scheme was himself Latino. The police officer, Rafael Pérez, a Puerto Rican, explained at his sentencing that he had become "consumed by the 'us-against-them ethos of the overzealous cop' after he transferred to Rampart Crash" (Cannon 2000, 32). He disclosed that corrupt behavior was explicitly sanctioned by supervisors who "specifically instructed him to lie on police reports in order to have a more successful prosecution" (Chemerinsky 2001, 637 n. 183). Even judges who had long suspected that police were perjuring themselves in court to secure convictions often turned a blind eye to police wrongdoings, and some Los Angeles county judges even admitted that they were also "hostile to the defense" and biased in favor of prosecutors (Cannon 2000, 32).

In the 1980s and 1990s, get-tough policing was brought to new levels, and despite some recent efforts to rein in the excessive racial and ethnic disparities and tensions that have been associated with aggressive policing, get-tough police policies and practices remain a source of controversy and consternation, particularly in Latina/o and African American communities. Glaring disparities in the incarceration rates of African American and Latinas/os as compared with whites, and innumerable cases of police misconduct and brutality in communities of color from the 1980s to the present have brought into question many of the policing strategies and practices utilized to wage "war" on drugs and crime. Introduced and implemented in the 1980s and 1990s, "broken-windows," "zero tolerance," and "quality of life" became catch phrases for forms of aggressive policing that were promoted to reduce crime. For some political figures and heads of police departments, such policing is and continues to be indispensable to reducing crime rates. Others dispute the efficacy of these strategies as unproven and laden with deleterious consequences. Many in Latina/o and African American communities, in desiring greater safety and security in their communities, feel that they have fallen prey to police policies and practices that paint their communities with a broad brush and render their communities susceptible to the excessive use of force and other forms of abuse at the hands of police officers.

Broken-Windows Policing, and Zero Tolerance and Quality of Life Policing

The 1982 article in the *Atlantic Monthly* by George Kelling and James Q. Wilson posited the "broken-windows" theory of policing—a theory that was to become both influential and controversial. Under this theory, authorizing police to target low-level offenders would, in turn, deter more serious crimes. In the 1990s, the most visibly ardent proponents of broken-windows policing became New York City Mayor Rudolph Giuliani and his police commissioner, William Bratton. Both embraced this theory as part of a "zero tolerance" approach intended to improve the "quality of life" of the city by mandating that police more stringently enforce laws against minor offenders—that is, persons engaged in such offenses as truancy, graffiti writing, street peddling, panhandling, public drinking, subway turnstile jumping, public urination, and squeegee window washing. As a result, policing became decidedly aggressive and focused on areas identified as "high-crime-rate" neighborhoods.

The notion that minor infractions, if ignored, result in more serious crime has had its adherents who have maintained over time that "broken windows" as a causal theory of crime has proven to be valid. Former police commissioner William Bratton, who most recently resumed charge of the NYPD under Mayor Bill de Blasio, has remained steadfast that zero tolerance and broken-windows policing are effective, that the drop in crime in New York City would not have been possible without broken-windows policing, and that critics are mistaken.

The theory that there is a causal connection between minor infractions and disorders and serious crimes, and the notion that broken-windows policing (also referred to as "order maintenance") reduces serious crime have been studied. Some studies have suggested that a causal connection does exist between minor disorder and serious crimes (e.g., Skogan 1990). Others have posited that aggressive policing strategies, such as increasing stops and arrests, deter crime (e.g., Wilson & Boland 1981; Kelling & Sousa 2001).

A range of other studies cast doubt on the broken-windows theory (*see, e.g.,* Harcourt 2001; Eck & Maguire 2000). One study found only a modest correlation between disorder and major crimes. Among its conclusions is that aggressive broken-windows policing might be popular but is not necessarily strong in reducing crime (Sampson & Raudenbush 1999). Another study of several large cities that have implemented forms of broken-windows policing—including New York, Chicago, and Los Angeles—showed overall that that neighborhood disorders do not lead to serious crimes (Harcourt & Ludwig 2006).

Crime rates dropped in parts of the country where such aggressive police tactics were not being implemented, and a myriad of social science research has pointed to many factors other than aggressive broken-windows policing that account for the significant decline in crime since the 1990s, including the rise in incarceration, additional police, the waning of the crack epidemic, and the legalization of abortion. Other social and economic factors have been identified by scholars—including the effect of immigration on the revitalization of neighborhoods in cities such as New York—that appear to have played a role in reducing crime. New York City, known for broken-windows policing, is where massive real estate development and the redistribution of wealth have been taking place since the 1990s, and the impact of neighborhood gentrification, commercial development, and sky-rocketing property values has been understood to have contributed to the crime-rate drop to a much greater extent than have policing tactics.

Focusing police enforcement where "broken windows" could be found meant that police would target identified "high crime rate neighborhoods." In New York City, high-crime neighborhoods almost invariably have been low-income, African American, and Latina/o communities. Researchers, however, have shown that in deploying police where crime is said to be prevelant, unequal criminal justice outcomes often have resulted.

"Broken windows," not just in theory but in practice, has embraced the aggressive pursuit of minor arrests (Eck & Maguire 2000, 225). Among the types of low-level arrests that have been most common has been the public use or display of marijuana. In New York City from 1994 to 2000, misdemeanor arrests involving marijuana grew from 1,851 in 1994 to 51,267 in 2000—a 2,670 percent increase—and even though African Americans and Latinas/os were each roughly 25 percent of New York City's population, from 2001 to 2003, 52 percent of those arrested on marijuana charges were African American and 32 percent were Latinas/os (Harcourt & Ludwig 2007, 165). Moreover, African Americans and Latinas/os arrested for these marijuana offenses were found to have been treated more severely in the criminal justice system than similarly situated whites. African Americans were 2.66 times and Latinas/os 1.85 times more likely than whites to be detained before arraignment, they were both two times more likely than whites to be convicted, and African Americans were four times and Latinas/os three times more likely than whites to receive harsher sentences (Golub, Johnson, & Dunlap 2007).

With regard to illicit drug use, previous-month illicit drug use data by race/ethnicity from 2002 through 2013 show that Latinas/os, as a group, consistently use illegal drugs at lesser rates than whites do (United States Department of Health and Human Services 2014, 27), and national government statistics also reveal that both Latinas/os and African Americans tend to use marijuana at lesser rates than whites do (Substance Abuse and Mental Health Data Archive 2014). The disparate impact that broken-windows policing has had on Latinas/os and African Americans coupled with the enormous expense and the absence of sufficient evidence of its effectiveness in reducing serious crime have raised doubts about New York City's reliance on this form of policing. Many in the Latina/o and African American communities have continued to raise concerns about the effects of broken windows, as have international human rights groups and major news media (*see, e.g.,* McArdle & Erzen 2001; Human Rights Watch 1998; Amnesty International 1998; *New York Times* 2014).

Police Brutality

National data compiled by the U.S. Justice Department's Bureau of Justice Statistics (BJS) for 2002 and 2005 show that white, African American, and Latina/o drivers were stopped by police at similar rates, but African American and Latina/o drivers were searched more often than whites (Durose, Smith, & Langan 2007, 1). Although approximately 9 out of 10 residents who had face-to-face contact with police in 2005 felt they were treated properly, African Americans and Latinas/os were more likely than whites to experience the use of police force. Among all persons experiencing force, about 83 percent felt that the police force used was excessive, with Latinas/os at 85.6%, whites at 84.3 percent, and African Americans at 81.5 percent (Durose, Smith, & Langan 2007, 3, 8). Criminologists maintain that incidents of police use of excessive force for those in communities of color have particular significance in the larger context of social inequality and discrimination. Additionally, studies show that Latinas/os are reluctant to report crimes and file complaints for a variety of reasons, including language barriers, immigration status, and low levels of confidence in the police and the justice system. This suggests that incidents of police use of force and excessive force as well as crimes committed against Latinas/os could be greater than official statistics indicate (*see* Walker, Spohn, & DeLone 2012, 171; Californians for Safety and Justice 2014, 9–10, 19–20).

Aggressive broken-windows policing—with which zero tolerance and quality of life approaches are associated—have been

Nationally, the rate of police stops of whites, African Americans, and Latinas/os were similar in 2002 and 2005, but African Americans and Latinas/os were searched more often than whites.

	Percent of Drivers Stopped by Police		Percent of Drivers Stopped Drivers Searched by Police	
Race/Ethnicity	**2002**	**2005**	**2002**	**2005**
Total	8.8%	8.8%	5.0%	4.8%
Latina/o	8.6	8.9	11.4	8.8
White	8.8	8.9	3.5	3.6
African American	9.2	8.1	10.2	9.5

Percent of contacts with police in which force was used in 2002 and 2005, by race/ethnicity

	Percent of contacts with police in which force was used		Percent of persons who felt police use of force was excessive
Race/Ethnicity	**2002**	**2005**	**2005**
Latina/o	2.5%	2.3%	85.6%
White	1.1	1.2	82.9
African American	3.5	4.4	81.5

Source: Compiled from Durose, Matthew R., Erica L. Smith, and Patrick A. Langan. 2007. Contacts between police and the public, 2005. NCJ 215243. Washington, DC: Bureau of Justice Statistics, U.S. Department of Justice, pp. 1, 8.

criticized as having detrimental consequences for relations between the police and communities of color, and are linked to many cases of excessive force on the part of police officers charged with implementing aggressive tactics. During Rudolph Giuliani's term as mayor of New York City, charges of excessive police force against African Americans and Latinas/os sharply increased. The brutal beating and sodomizing of Abner Louima in a Brooklyn police precinct in 1997 and the death of the unarmed African immigrant, Amadou Dialo, who was shot 41 times by plainclothes officers of the NYPD's Street Crimes Unit in the Bronx in 1999, are just a couple of the many cases that caused alarm and spurred a wave of mass protests during Giuliani's time as mayor (McArdle & Erzen 2001).

Latina/o communities of New York City experienced their share of excessive police force cases during that period as well. In

1994, a young Puerto Rican, **Anthony Báez**, died at the hands of police officer Frances Livoti. Livoti, infuriated that Báez's football accidently fell onto his police car, killed Báez using a chokehold prohibited under police guidelines. An officer with at least 11 civilian complaints of police brutality in 11 years of service, Livoti was acquitted in state court, but was dismissed from the police force for violating department rules and later was sentenced to seven and one-half years for violating federal civil rights laws. More recently, in 2014, Eric Garner was confronted by police for allegedly selling loose, untaxed cigarettes on the street and was killed by the same banned chokehold technique used on Anthony Báez. This incident sparked outrage throughout New York City and prompted *The New York Times* editorial page to voice concern at the high cost of adhering to a theory that is merely hypothetical, when many other localities around the country have seen major reductions in crime without broken-windows policing. In the Garner case, no indictments were issued by the local district attorney.

Although procedures for filing **civilian complaints against police officers** for excessive use of force or other misconduct have been in place in a number of cities like New York for some time, the efficacy of such complaint processes at times have been questioned. A year after the Anthony Báez death in the Bronx at the hands of an NYPD officer, Antonio Rosario (age 18) and Hilton Vega (age 22) were shot dead by two police officers—one of whom served as a bodyguard for Mayor Giuliani. Although Rosario and Vega and a third individual, 18-year-old Freddie Bonilla, were reported to have been armed, forensic reports appeared to show that the men were shot in the back while lying prone on the ground. After conducting an investigation, the Civilian Complaint Review Board concluded, based on the evidence, that excessive force had been used. Its findings, however, were ignored by the police commissioner and no departmental charges were brought against the officers. The case has been cited as one that undercut the reputation of the civilian complaint process and its credibility as an agency capable of effectively investigating, substantiating, and moving substantiated cases forward for further disciplinary or other appropriate action.

In New York City, tensions between the police and Latina/o and African American communities were reaching a high point during the Giuliani years. The Báez and other cases—including the Rosario and Vega cases—became exemplars for all that could go wrong for victims of excessive police force seeking redress and justice. By the end of the 1990s, polls showed that concerns over police brutality had intensified. A 1997 poll revealed that 73 percent of Latinas/os believed that police brutality was a grave problem in New York (Human Rights Watch 1998, 275).

Around the country, numerous other instances of police brutality in Latina/o communities have been documented over the years, with many linked to the wave of aggressive policing. Latina/o immigrants have been especially vulnerable to excessive police force and other forms of police abuse. In 1996, Latina/o immigrants **Leticia Gonzalez** and **Enrique Funes Flores** in Riverside County, California, were videotaped being beaten by police. In 1997, Los Angeles police shot Efrain Lopez nine times, and although the case was settled out of court none of the police officers were prosecuted or disciplined.

Incidents of police brutality and misconduct occurring in Latina/o communities have continued into the 2000s. In New York City, protests and charges of police brutality arose in 2007 with the death of **Fermin Arzu**, a Honduran immigrant who was shot by a police officer. By 2008, Latina/o community complaints grew, as it became increasingly apparent that Suffolk County police on Long Island were failing to investigate and attend to hate crimes committed against Latinas/os. In spite of a Justice Department investigation and an agreement by the county to address discriminatory police practices, six years later Suffolk County police were once again mired in a police abuse scandal. In 2014, a Suffolk County police officer was discovered to have been systematically robbing Latinas/os who he suspected to be undocumented, reigniting concerns that the measures taken to correct police misconduct and discrimination were ineffective.

On the heels of the police killing of Michael Brown in Ferguson, Missouri, the killing of **Antonio Zambrano-Montes**, a 35-year-old Latino shot by police in Pasco, Washington, gave rise to protests and comparisons to the events and the situation faced by the Ferguson community, where a majority of the town's population is not adequately represented in the police force or positions of political power. Although Zambrano-Montes was reported to have been throwing rocks earlier, a video of the incident appears to show him running away from the police unarmed then raising his hands at the moment he was shot. The Latina/o community response was vehement in its opposition to how police handled the situation. In a city where Latinas/os comprise 56 percent of the population of 68,000 persons, only 14 of the 68 police officers are Latina/o, only 12 officers speak Spanish, and—in a school system that is 70 percent Latina/o—Latinas/os have no representation in 2015 on the five-member school board. All this is very similar to the conditions African Americans endure in Ferguson, Missouri (Turkewitz & Oppel, Jr. 2015).

The rate of civilian deaths caused by police using firearms in the United States far exceeds the rate of other developed countries in the world. Based on the best available data, in 2013, 409 people in the United States were shot dead by police—more than one person per day over the course of a year. By comparison, Britain and Japan had no deaths, and Germany had eight deaths resulting from police shootings (*The Economist* 2014).

Despite the many high-profile police killings and shootings that have garnered national and international attention and sparked numerous protests, the more than 17,000 law enforcement agencies throughout the United States are not required to maintain comprehensive data on police shootings. Instead, the Federal Bureau of Investigation's annual report on "justifiable homicides" relies on voluntary self-reporting by agencies around the country, of which only approximately 750 agencies participate. In any given year, the FBI reports that nationally police officers are involved in about 400 "justifiable homicides" (Lowery 2014). The lack of comprehensive data has led to criticism that the

Deaths by Police Shootings in 2013

Japan	0
Britain	0
Germany	8
United States	409

Source: *The Economist*. 2014 (August 23). Overkill: Police in a Missouri suburb demonstrate how not to quell a riot. http://www.economist.com/news/united-states/21613272-police-missouri-suburb-demonstrate-how-not-quell-riot-overkill.

government does not want the public to know how many die at the hands of police, spurring demands for national legislation mandating the collection of such data.

Based on available data, data compiled by the Centers for Disease Control and Prevention indicates that Africana Americans—particularly those between the ages of 20 and 24 years—were the most likely group to be killed by police officers in the United States at 7.1 per million in the population per year from 1999 to 2011. The average for all races was 1.3 per million. The data also show that Latinas/os were killed by police at a rate 30 percent greater than the national average and almost twice (1.9 times) the rate of whites (Males 2014).

Code of Silence and the Impact of Police Corruption

As had been the case for many years, studies show that police tend to hold fast to an unwritten oath among fraternal colleagues known as the "**code of silence**"—or alternatively, the "blue wall of silence"—to keep secret any information that can incriminate a fellow officer. Police corruption investigations in Los Angeles and in New York—the Christopher Commission and Mollen Commission, respectively—uncovered patterns of police secrecy and deceit that were prevalent and that work to undermine investigations and prosecutions of officers engaged in wrongdoing. It is an aspect of police behavior that is among the most difficult to eradicate, as self-preservation, self-interests, and fraternity among officers can take precedence over the truth.

Under the code of silence, it is typical for police officers to present false testimony in court. Such was the case in the Anthony Báez police brutality case involving police officer Frances Livoti who killed Báez using a chokehold banned by NYPD regulations. Even though Officer Livoti was acquitted at trial in a state court, it was apparent to the judge that there was insufficient evidence against Livoti presented because police officers who testified at trial, in the words of the judge, had engaged in "a nest of perjury" (Human Rights Watch 1998, 290). At the federal civil rights case in which Livoti was found guilty, the judge in sentencing him to prison acknowledged the lies that were used to cover up Livoti's crime.

One of the officers who witnessed Anthony Báez die of the banned chokehold, however, was a Latina, Daisy Boria. Because she had not adhered to the code of silence at a hearing on police perjury and obstruction of justice testimony related to the Báez case, her fellow officers engaged in a series of retaliatory actions to harass her and render her without protection in dangerous situations. Under the pressure, she was compelled to resign from the police force.

The code of silence was a palpable facet of the scandal involving Los Angeles Police Department's CRASH unit. Police officers in this specialized unit systematically and regularly committed perjury to ensure the prosecution of innocent persons and to conceal their own drug-related profiteering enterprise. When confronted in court, Officer Rafael Pérez, a key member of the corruption and brutality plot, testified that it was generally accepted behavior. He disclosed that his own supervisors "specifically instructed him to lie on police reports in order to have a more successful prosecution" (Chemerinsky 2001, 637 n. 183).

Police corruption has been found to be especially deleterious to the poor and communities of color. As communities that lack the economic and political power to defend themselves, low-income, Latina/o, and African American communities are vulnerable to the authority and power that a police officer can exert. Police corruption thus tends to concentrate on these communities in ways that are discriminatory. Corrupt police allow illegal activity, such as drug sales and use, to thrive in communities of color, as the police might be intimately involved in or profiting from the illicit activity. These activities, in turn, diminish the standard of living in the communities of color and can spur on other illegal conduct. Ultimately, confidence in the police and relations between communities of color and police will be strained.

Stop-and-Frisk Police Tactics

In recent years, a source of enormous tension between communities of color and police has been the implementation of police stop-and-frisk tactics. Present-day **stops and frisks** have their origins in the 1968 U.S. Supreme Court decision in ***Terry v. Ohio***. In the *Terry* case, the Court relaxed the probable cause requirement to the U.S. Constitution's Fourth Amendment to allow law enforcement agents to use a less rigorous "reasonable suspicion" standard to stop, question, and frisk someone that the police encounter. As aggressive police tactics became increasingly popular with politicians as well as with the public over the last several decades, stop-and-frisk tactics were being utilized with greater frequency. Proponents of stop-and-frisk tactics argue that it is a strategy that concentrates in neighborhoods with high crime rates based on police data-gathering systems (in New York it is called CompStat), and therefore police stops and frisks are not discriminatory against communities of color.

Although the Supreme Court in the *Terry* case did not intend stops to be based on mere hunches, critics of the tactic charge that the lesser standard set by the Court in *Terry* has provided police and law enforcement considerable leeway to use stops in a manner that is arbitrary and discriminatory. Consistent with the broken-windows theory of policing, police stops and frisks frequently have targeted neighborhood disorder and not necessarily serious crime, leaving African American and Latina/o communities especially vulnerable to excessive stops and frisks in a manner more akin to **racial profiling** than maintaining public safety and order.

Perhaps no jurisdiction in the country has been more aggressive at using stop-and-frisk tactics and has received more attention for doing so than New York City. By the late 1990s, stop-and-frisk tactics had become a major concern in the city, as cases of the excessive use of force by the police and other forms of police abuse garnered growing attention of the public and the media. In 1999, a report by the New York State Attorney General revealed that there were noticeable racial and ethnic disparities resulting from police stops and frisks in New York City (Spitzer 1999). The disparities between Latinas/os and whites as well as between African Americans and whites and the use of these tactics were so great that the data appeared to point to the illegal practice of racial profiling—that is, the use of race and ethnicity as the sole criterion for law enforcement action.

The State Attorney General's report was compelling and it challenged the assumption that Latinos/as and African Americans are stopped and frisked at greater rates than other racial groups because they live in high crime rate neighborhoods. With respect to Latinas/os, the report found that even when taking into consideration differences in crime rates of the various communities in the city, Latinos/as were still stopped 39 percent more often than whites across all crime categories. Even though Latinas/os in 1999 were 23.7 percent of the population of New York City, they comprised 33.0 percent of all persons stopped by police. The report also raised doubts about the effectiveness and arbitrariness of the strategy, as the number of frisks far exceeded the number of arrests resulting from the frisks. In 1998, of 27,061 persons frisked only 4,647 were arrested (Spitzer 1999, vii–x).

Michael Bloomberg succeeded Rudolph Giuliani as mayor of New York City with a promise to ease community-police tensions. The Street Crimes Unit, known for its aggressive undercover operations and for the shooting death of unarmed Amadou Dialo in the Bronx, had been disbanded. Under Mayor Bloomberg, a staunch defender of the stop-and-frisk police approach, however, the number of stops and frisks swelled to unprecedented proportions. In 2002, at the beginning of Bloomberg's administration, police stopped 97,296 persons in all of New York City. By 2011, that number was approaching 700,000 (685,724) (Dunn 2014, 2).

As African Americans and Latinas/os increasingly complained of being harassed, embarrassed, and mistreated by police stops and frisks in their communities, civil rights organizations sued the NYPD to force the department to make public the data it compiled on the number of stops and frisks police had been conducting. The data showed striking racial and ethnic disparities and became central in a subsequent lawsuit challenging the NYPD's stop-and-frisk practices. Data amassed during years in which Bloomberg was in office show that African Americans and Latinas/os were overwhelmingly targets of police stops and frisks. African Americans and Latinas/os together made up 86.2 percent of the persons stopped from 2003 to 2013 (Dunn 2014, 4). For the same years, Latinas/os, who comprised 28.6 percent of the population in 2010, made up 32 percent of those stopped by police in New York City. Whites, who made up 33.3 of the city's population, were stopped at a rate of only 10.3 percent over that period (U.S. Census Bureau 2015; Dunn 2014, 4).

Annual Police Stops in New York City, 2002–2013

Year	Number of Stops
2013	191,851
2012	532,911
2011	685,724
2010	601,285
2009	581,168
2008	540,302
2007	475,096
2006	506,491
2005	398,191
2004	313,523
2003	160,851
2002	97,296

Source: Compiled from Dunn, Christopher. 2014. Stop-and-frisk during the Bloomberg administration (2002–2013), NYCLU briefing. New York: New York Civil Liberties Union, p. 2.

Disparities in the data are more glaring when examining the police stops of young men ages 14 years to 24 years. Although the percentage of New York City's Latina/o population of 14- to 24-year olds was 2.8 percent, they comprised 15.1 percent of the persons stopped by police. By comparison, white youths aged 14 to 24 years, were 2.0 percent of the city's population and 4.4 percent of those stopped. From 2003 to 2013, 825,403 Latinas/os were frisked, and 194,909 whites were frisked. The percentage of stops involving police use of force also

Stops By Race/Ethnicity 2002–2013

	Stops	Percentage of New York City's Population (2010)
Latinas/os	32%	28.6%
African American	54.2%	25.5%
White	10.3%	33.3%
Asian/American Indian	3.6%	13.4%

Sources: Compiled from:

Dunn, Christopher. 2014. Stop-and-frisk during the Bloomberg administration (2002–2013), NYCLU briefing. New York: New York Civil Liberties Union, p. 2.

U.S. Census Bureau. 2015. State & County QuickFacts: New York (City), New York. http://quickfacts.census.gov/qfd/states/36/3651000.html.

was greater among African Americans and Latinas/os (23.4 percent) as compared to whites (17.1 percent) (Dunn 2014, 6, 9, 12).

As the number of stops increased over the years, community protests and concerns that communities of color were paying a heavy price for maintaining this police practice continued to mount. That stops and frisks were resulting in innocent people being harassed, subjected to humiliation in public, or otherwise ruining people's lives mobilized efforts to call into question the policy and to advocate for change. Scholars have questioned whether adherence to the stop-and-frisk practice was worth the damage to police-community relations. Studies in other cities where stop-and-frisk practices were adopted also show that many of those people subjected to stops reported being treated in a harsh and discourteous manner by police. In a study of African American and Latino/a high school students in Chicago stopped by police, 63 percent of the Latina/o students and 62 percent of the African American students reported being treated disrespectfully by the police (Freidman & Hott 1995, 111).

Stop-and frisk tactics have been defended as indispensable in reducing serious crime in the city, but NYPD data has not aligned with that position. Most of the people stopped (more than 4 million) from 2003 to 2013 were innocent persons—individuals not arrested or given a summons. The position that persons of color are disproportionately engaged in violent crime which accounted for why persons of color were stopped disproportionately also was undercut by the data, because more than 90 percent of all stops from 2003 to 2013 had no relation to violent crimes. Supporters of stop-and frisk tactics also have argued that the tactic has been essential in getting guns off the streets. Of all the frisks conducted from 2003 to 2013, however, only 2 percent resulted in the seizure of a weapon. Retrieving one gun required nearly 600 stops (593) to be made (Dunn 2014, 2, 4, 7).

In 2013, a federal district court judge ruled in *Floyd et al. v. City of New York*—a case challenging NYPD stop-and-frisk tactics—that the practice as implemented by the police was unconstitutional. The court

Stops of Young Men (ages 14 to 24) In New York City—2002–2013

Race/Ethnicity	Stops	Percentage of New York City's Population
Latinas/os	15.1%	2.8%
African American	25.4%	1.9%
White	4.4%	2.0%

Frisks by Race/Ethnicity 2002–2013

	Frisks
Latinas/os	825,403
African American	1,393,741
White	194,909
Asian/American Indian	72,163

Source: Compiled from Dunn, Christopher. 2014. Stop-and-frisk during the Bloomberg administration (2002–2013), NYCLU briefing. New York: New York Civil Liberties Union, pp. 6, 9.

Stops and Frisks During New York City Mayor Bloomberg's Term

In 2014, the New York Civil Liberties Union released an analysis of the NYPD stop and frisk data for all years during which Michael Bloomberg was mayor except for 2002, a year for which only the total number of stops is available. Below is the NYCLU's summary of its analysis of 2003 to 2013 data.

- During the 12 years of the Bloomberg administration, NYPD officers recorded 5,081,689 stops. Annual stops were at a low of 97,296 in 2002, rose to a high of 685,724 in 2011, and then dropped dramatically to 191,851 in 2013.
- As stops skyrocketed from 2002 until 2011, the number of guns recovered, shooting victims, and murders changed modestly, moving up and down. When stops plummeted in 2012 and 2013, shootings and murders declined substantially, with murders falling in 2013 to the lowest level ever recorded.
- Between 2003 and 2013 there were nearly 4.4 million stops of innocent people (as evidenced by the fact they were neither arrested nor given a summons). The 75th Precinct in Brooklyn led the city with 236,324 stops of innocent people. Excluding the Central Park Precinct, the 17th Precinct on the Upper East Side of Manhattan had the fewest with 12,553.

- In 70 out of 76 precincts, black and Latino New Yorkers accounted for more than 50 percent of stops, and in 32 precincts they accounted for more than 90 percent of stops. In 6 of the 10 precincts with the lowest black and Latino populations (such as the 6th Precinct in Greenwich Village), blacks and Latinos accounted for about 70 percent or more of stops.
- Young black and Latino men were the targets of a hugely disproportionate number of stops. Though they accounted for only 4.7 percent of the city's population, black and Latino males between the ages of 14 and 24 accounted for 41 percent of stops between 2003 and 2013. Nearly 90 percent of young black and Latino men stopped were innocent.
- Though frisks can legally be conducted only in the unusual situation when an officer reasonably suspects the person has a weapon that might endanger officer safety, 52 percent of those stopped were frisked. Of those frisked, a weapon was found only 2 percent of the time. And police officers conducted frisks in one-half of the 4.4 million stops of innocent people.
- Black and Latino New Yorkers were more likely to be frisked than white New Yorkers and, among those frisked, were less likely to be found with a weapon.
- Throughout the Bloomberg era, stops yielded a tiny number of guns. Between 2003 and 2013 (figures are not available for 2002), it took 593 stops to recover a single gun (Dunn 2014, 1).

Source: Dunn, Christopher. 2014. Stop-and-frisk during the Bloomberg administration (2002–2013), NYCLU briefing. New York: New York Civil Liberties Union, p. 1.

reviewed NYPD data that showed vast racial and ethnic disparities in the stop-and-frisk practice, and it heard testimony and examined evidence that superiors pressed officers into maintaining a certain number or quota of summons and arrests. Evidence also was entered into the record that officers were told to target "the right people," that police training in this tactic was inadequate, and that the NYPD routinely refused to discipline officers who conducted unconstitutional stops. Based on the evidence, the court found that the police were carrying out stops and frisks in an unconstitutional manner and that encouraging officers to target "the right people" was an "indirect form of racial profiling." The court held the city liable for violation of Fourth and Fourteenth Amendment rights under the U.S. Constitution and ordered remedial action that included the appointment of an independent monitor to oversee the changes mandated by the court.

New York City's new mayor, Bill de Blasio, who ran on an anti-stop-and-frisk platform during his mayoral campaign, readily embraced reforming stop-and-frisk practices. The rate of stops and frisks dropped dramatically in subsequent years, from a high of 685,724 in 2011 to 191,851 in 2013 (Dunn 2014). As of mid-2015, the concern raised by proponents of the tactic—that without stops and frisks the crime rate would soar once again—had not been realized. Crime continued its decline even with sharp decreases in the number of stops and frisks.

Other major cities in the United States have employed stop-and-frisk police tactics. The American Civil Liberties Union of Illinois reported that for 2014 in comparing "stops to population, Chicagoans were stopped more than four times as often as New Yorkers at the height of New York City's stop and frisk practice" (ACLU 2015b, 3). The data show people of color in 2014 were stopped disproportionately more often than were whites.

Although African Americans were stopped at proportionately greater rates than Latinas/os overall, Latinas/os in 2014 were stopped at greater rates in proportion to their population in predominantly white neighborhoods, which include District 18 (Near North), District 19 (Town Hall), and District 16 (Jefferson Park). In District 18 (Near North), Latinas/os comprised 5.0 percent of the population, but were 10.5 percent of all persons stopped; in District 19 (Town Hall), Latinas/os made up 10.0 percent of the population, but were 16.3 percent of all persons stopped; and in District 16 (Jefferson Park), Latinas/os comprised 22.8 percent of the population, but were 31.2 percent of all persons stopped (ACLU 2015b, 10). Concern over unjustified and unconstitutional stops and racial and ethnic disparities have prompted calls for improvements in data collection and transparency to assess the frequency of arrests after stops and to gain a clearer picture of who is being frisked, the reasons for frisking, and the rate at which contraband is secured through frisks.

Los Angeles, a U.S. city with a sizable Latina/o population, has a long history of poor police and community relations. As a result of a complaint filed by the U.S. Justice Department alleging that police officers in the city engaged in "a pattern or practice of unconstitutional or otherwise unlawful conduct that has been made possible by the failure of the City defendants to adopt and implement proper management practices and procedures," the City of Los Angeles entered into a consent decree requiring that it collect and maintain stop-and-frisk data (Consent Decree in *United States v. City of Los Angeles* 2000, 1). Analyses of data from 2003 to 2004 showed significant disparities between communities of color and whites in relation to vehicle and pedestrian stops, frisks, and arrests following police stops. This raised serious concerns about biased policing. Similar

In 2014, Stops per 1,000 People in Chicago Surpassed the Rate of Stops in New York City

Chicago	2014	93.6 per 1000 people
New York City	2014	1.6
New York City	2013	5.7
New York City	2012	15.4
New York City	2011	22.9

Source: Compiled from American Civil Liberties Union. 2015b. *Stop and frisk in Chicago.* Chicago, IL: ACLU. http://www.aclu-il.org/stop-and-frisk-in-chicago1/.

to studies of stops and frisks in New York City, African American and Latinas/os were found to be much more likely to be stopped, frisked, and arrested than whites were, and the African Americans and Latinas/os who were searched were less likely to possess contraband (Ayers & Borowsky 2008, 27).

In 2011, the City of Philadelphia entered into a consent decree as a result of a lawsuit challenging that city's police stop-and-frisk tactics. Progress in improving racial and ethnic disparities in policing has been elusive, however, as periodic reports required under the consent decree apparently reveal. In 2015, the fifth monitoring report showed that although African Americans comprise 43.22 percent of the population—with Latinas/os at 8.5 percent and whites at 42.26 percent—people of color comprise 80.23 percent of the persons stopped by police and 89.15 percent of those frisked in Philadelphia (ACLU 2015a). The report points out that tens of thousands of persons continue to be subject to stops and frisks that are not legally justifiable and that factors other than race and ethnicity do not account for the vast racially disparities that persists.

Halo Effect

The question that relates to the issue of racial profiling and bias in policing is whether Latinas/os and other people of color are treated differently from whites. A concept called the "racial **halo effect**" has been defined by criminologists as the "dynamic whereby being White American, in and of

Findings of a 2008 Study on Racially Disparate Outcomes in Policing in Los Angeles

The following is an excerpt of the findings of a 2008 study that closely examined pedestrian and vehicle stop data over a one-year period (July 2003 to June 2004) prepared for the ACLU of Southern California by Yale Law School professor Ian Ayers and Jonathan Borowsky.

> The results of this study raise grave concerns that African Americans and Hispanics are over-stopped, over-frisked, over-searched, and over-arrested. After controlling for the violent and property crime rates in the specific reporting district and a host of other variables, we find that:

- Per 10,000 residents, the black stop rate is 3,400 stops higher than the white stop rate and the Hispanic stop rate is almost 360 stops higher.
- Relative to stopped whites, stopped blacks are 127% more likely to be frisked and stopped Hispanics are 43% more likely to be frisked.
- Relative to stopped whites, stopped blacks are 76% more likely to be searched and stopped Hispanics are 16% more likely to be searched.
- Relative to stopped whites, stopped blacks are 29% more likely to be arrested and stopped Hispanics are 32% more likely to be arrested.

(Ayers and Borowsky 2008, 27)

itself, reduces the odds of being viewed with suspicion or being questioned by an officer" (Weitzer & Tuch 2006, 19; see also Weitzer 1999). This concept attempts to explain different outcomes of a police encounter when a police officer makes contact with a white person as compared to making contact with a Latina/o or African American person.

Latinas/os have a long history of struggling to gain acceptance, respect, and full rights in the United States. With respect to crime, Latina/o immigrants, in particular, have been typically stereotyped as persons who bring criminality into the country or are inclined to criminal behavior. Misperceptions and stereotypes of Latinas/os have persisted, regardless of the facts and studies to the contrary. Social scientific studies actually show that immigrants—and Latina/o immigrants specifically—have lower rates of criminality and they are *less* prone to criminal conduct than are U.S.-born citizens. Contemporary and popular movies and television programs—*The Untouchables*, *Scarface*, *Miami Vice*, among many others—perpetuate the image of Latinas/os as predisposed to criminal behavior and reinforce negative stereotypes. Not surprisingly, in national surveys, such as the National Opinion Research Center's 2000 General Social Survey, almost three-quarters of those polled believe that there is a causal relationship between immigration and crime and a clear majority believe that U.S. citizens are likely to lose their jobs because of immigrants. The belief and fear that immigration results in greater crime rate also have prompted legislation, such as the "Illegal Immigration Relief Act Ordinance" of 2006 passed by the city council of Hazleton, Pennsylvania, in 2006. The ordinance sought to take measures to protect against this impending immigrant threat to peace and security.

Analyses of law enforcement personnel interactions with Latinas/os invariably include the deeply entrenched ideas and perceptions that Latinas/os represent a criminal element in U.S. society. Scholars have examined the history of the social construction of Mexican identity by those who command power and privilege in U.S. society. From the earliest images of Mexicans as bandits and as "dirty Mexican[s]," Mexicans and Latinas/os generally have become susceptible today to police stops and are targeted for racial profiling while driving—a situation also known as "**driving while brown**" (Aguirre 2012; Crawford 2012; Romero & Sánchez 2012; Mucchetti 2005). The practice of racial profiling would represent that inverse of a racial halo and to the extent that whites are exempt from being targeted in such a fashion they are perceived to have a racial halo. (See "Racial Profiling" section below.)

Some criminologists make the point that race and ethnicity are significant and both play a role in determining criminal justice outcomes and in explaining disparities in the operations of the U.S. criminal justice system. In examining the experience of Latinas/os in the U.S. justice system, scholars have discovered that negative stereotypes and media images linking Latinas/os to criminality reinforce longstanding biases that surface in the operations of the criminal justice system—including how police perceive and treat those who comprise Latina/o communities throughout the United States.

Racial Profiling

The singling out of persons for unequal treatment by law enforcement personnel based on their race or ethnicity—known as racial profiling—is unlawful. Yet, the racial profiling of Latinas/os by police and other law enforcement agents has a long history. A clear and blatant example of the history of racial profiling of Latinas/os is California's 1855 "**Greaser Act**," a vagrancy law that allowed law enforcement officers to target so-called "**Greasers**." Incidents of racial profiling of Latinas/os in present-day U.S. society have been numerous, and many civil rights advocates and analysts find that there are sufficient cases that are well-documented enough to show a regular pattern of such cases around the country.

The Latina/o civil rights group, the **National Council of La Raza**, has singled out many other examples of racial profiling of Latinas/os. Among the incidents noted were

- Raids conducted by immigration agents in 2001 in New York City who based the searches on people's skin color and Spanish accents;
- A 1990s investigation of the Florida Sheriff's Department in Volusia County that showed that Latinas/os and African Americans comprised only 5 percent of the drivers on a section of Interstate 95 that ran through the county, but were nearly 70 percent of drivers who were stopped on that section of the freeway;
- The 2001 ejection of four Latina/o businessmen from a Delta Airlines flight because they appeared to be Middle Eastern; and
- The case brought by the Mexican-American Legal Defense and Education Fund (MALDEF) against the City of Rogers, Arkansas, for racial profiling performed by its police force (the case was settled in 2003) (Walker et al. 2004, 60).

Many studies—including a study of high school students who were stopped by police in Chicago in the 1990s—suggest a pattern of racial profiling. In Chicago, 80 percent of African American high school students and 62 percent of Latino/a high school students in the study reported having been stopped by police (Freidman & Hott 1995).

Latinas/os typically are profiled as being among the persons who most "look like" a drug trafficker or other criminal. Louisiana State Police viewed training films that encouraged them to stop and search persons for illicit drugs, especially people who were "males of foreign nationalities, mainly Cubans, Colombians, Puerto Ricans, or other swarthy outlanders" (Walker et al. 2004, 60). Similar profiles used by the Drug Enforcement Agency (DEA) listed "Hispanics" and Colombians, Dominicans, and Puerto Ricans as being among the most likely narcotics traffickers (Harris 2002, 49; *see also* Cole 1999, 49).

Surveys of Latinas/os also point to racial profiling by the police as being prevalent. A 2001 survey conducted by the Public Policy Institute of California indicated that 65 percent of Latinas/os held that racial profiling by the police was pervasive, and 82 percent of African Americans and 43 percent of whites believed the same (Hajnal & Baldassare 2001, 15). Analysts point to these types of results as contributing to a broken relationship between Latina/o communities and law enforcement.

Latina/o populations have begun to increase in parts of the United States outside of the areas of the country where they traditionally have been found in significant numbers, such as the Western or Southwestern regions or the major East-coast cities. Towns and cities in the Midwest and Southeast are places where waves of Latinas/os have settled in recent years. Tulsa, Oklahoma, for instance, experienced a 303 percent increase in its Latina/o population between 1980 and 2000; Latina/o population grew 630 percent in

Nashville, Tennessee; and Raleigh, North Carolina's Latina/o population increased 1,180 percent (Mucchetti 2005, 4). Along with population increases has come a noticeable increase in discriminatory treatment directed at newly arrived Latinas/os. In some states with sharp increases in Latinas/os in rural areas, such as Missouri, police stops of Latinas/os have been as much as 12 percent to 1,250 percent greater than the proportion of Latinas/os in the local population (Mucchetti 2005, 4–5).

Driving While Brown

In the African American community, the expression "driving while black" has become a common refrain. Analysts, however, also have observed the phenomenon of "driving while brown" (Mucchetti 2005). Similar to "driving while black," "driving while brown" refers to the unlawful targeting of Latinas/os by police and other law enforcement agents based on their racial or ethnic features, particularly Latinas/os who are behind the steering wheel of a car. New Jersey state troopers were found to have systematically targeted African Americans and Latina/o drivers on the New Jersey Turnpike for stops and searches under the premise of intercepting the trafficking of illicit drugs. Throughout the 1990s, 8 of every 10 cars searched by state troopers for illegal drugs were driven by a Latina/o or African American, even though whites were more likely to be transporting contraband than either Latinas/os or African Americans (Kocieniewski & Hanley 2000, A1; Harris 2002, 80). In a state court case brought to end this practice—*State v. Pedro Soto* (1996)—it was proven that New Jersey troopers had engaged in racially profiling Latinas/os and African Americans.

Undocumented Latina/o immigrants and anyone who "appears Mexican" are especially vulnerable to police stops and ostensibly racial profiling, as some U.S. Supreme Court decisions have made it legally permissible for law enforcement agents to use "Mexican appearance" as a factor in justifying a vehicle stop, as long as it is not the sole reason. In 1968, the U.S. Supreme Court in the ***Terry v. Ohio*** case made it permissible for police to use a lesser standard to justify stops, namely "reasonable suspicion" over the "probable cause" standard found in the U.S. Constitution's Fourth Amendment. The Court determined that "reasonable suspicion" was acceptable given the experience and training of police officers.

In 1975, however, the Supreme Court in ***United States v. Brignoni-Ponce*** took the further step of ruling that "Mexican appearance" could be a factor used in justifying vehicle stops by the U.S. Border Patrol, but it could not be the only factor. In 1976, the Court in ***United States v. Martinez-Fuerte*** made it permissible for law enforcement officers to briefly stop vehicles at permanent checkpoints even if there is no reason to suspect that undocumented persons are in the vehicle. In a dissenting opinion in the *Martinez-Fuerte* case, Justice William Brennan warned that the U.S. Supreme Court had gone too far in eroding the Fourth Amendment's protections from unreasonable searches and seizures. Justice Brennan concluded that, from that point on, anyone who appeared Mexican would be susceptible to intrusive law enforcement stops and searches that could be discriminatory and humiliating to persons of Mexican ancestry, causing "deep resentment." Among Latina/o scholars, these court decisions have come to be known as "Mexican exception" to the Constitution's Fourth Amendment (Mirandé 2003).

In recent years, cases involving racial profiling by police officers have attracted national attention and have resulted in U.S.

Justice William Brennan's dissent in the 1976 *United States v. Martinez-Fuerte* decision

Excerpts

Every American citizen of Mexican ancestry and every Mexican alien lawfully in this country must know after today's decision that he travels the fixed checkpoint highways at the risk of being subjected not only to a stop, but also to detention and interrogation, both prolonged and to an extent far more than for non-Mexican appearing motorists.... [F]or the arbitrarily selected motorists who must suffer the delay and humiliation of detention and interrogation, the experience can obviously be upsetting. In addition, that experience is particularly vexing for the motorist of Mexican ancestry who is selectively referred, knowing that the officers' target is the Mexican alien. That deep resentment will be stirred by a sense of unfair discrimination is not difficult to foresee (428 U.S. 543, 572–573 [1976]).

Footnote 4 of Justice Brennan's dissent

Though today's decision would clearly permit detentions to be based solely on Mexican ancestry, the Court takes comfort in what appears to be the Border Patrol practice of not relying on Mexican ancestry standing alone in referring motorists for secondary detentions.... Good faith on the part of law enforcement officials, however, has never sufficed in this tribunal to substitute as a safeguard for personal freedoms or to remit our duty to effectuate constitutional guarantees. Indeed, with particular regard to the Fourth Amendment, *Terry v. Ohio,* 392 U.S. 1, 22 (1968), held that " 'simple' good faith on the part of the arresting officer is not enough." ... If subjective good faith alone were the test, the protections of the Fourth Amendment would evaporate, and the people would be "secure in their persons, houses, papers, and effects," only in the discretion of the police. (428 U.S. 543, 573 (1976), n.4)

Department of Justice investigations and monitoring. In Suffolk County, Long Island, after a series of **hate crimes** in which Latino immigrants were assaulted by whites—including the 2008 beating and death of Ecuadorean immigrant, **Marcelo Lucero** at the hands of a group of white youths—police were implicated in failing to properly investigate hate crimes committed against Latinas/os. After the Justice Department intervened, the Suffolk County police department entered into an agreement to implement new nondiscriminatory police policies. Despite this effort to correct discriminatory police practices directed at Latinas/os, however, by 2014 new allegations surfaced that police were racially profiling Latina/o drivers thought to be undocumented so that officers could steal money from the drivers' wallets when examining a driver's license. A police sergeant, Scott A. Greene, was arrested after complaints were filed, but Latinas/os remained reluctant to come forward publicly due to fear of police retaliation (Semple 2014).

East Haven, Connecticut, a town that has seen a marked increase in its Latina/o population in recent years, also has become known for anti-Latino police practices. After years of sustaining police harassment and violence, members of the Latina/o community in East Haven organized and came forward to expose a pattern of racial profiling. Among Latina/o store owners and other Latinas/os, East Haven earned a reputation as a venue where police were free to intimidate, abuse, and conduct false arrests against the Latina/o population. The systematic racial profiling and mistreatment of Latinas/os prompted the intervention of the U.S. Justice Department. Even after four police officers were arrested in 2012 for related misconduct, however, the town's mayor, Joseph Maturo, Jr., drew national attention for responding to the need to reach out to the Latina/o community by blithely stating that he "might have tacos" (Yee 2013). After reaching a settlement, the East Haven police department was placed under Justice Department monitoring and was required to implement reforms.

"The Talk"

Imparting parental advice to children about the dangers of police stops and racial profiling has become known as "the Talk" (Harris 2002, 110). As in the African American community, "**the Talk**" has become common among Latina/o families. "The Talk" consists of what youth of color need to know about how to behave when approached by a police officer. It is a conversation that is not limited to those who live in poor and underserved neighborhoods that are commonly designated by police as being high crime areas. It includes any person of color regardless of income, education, or other status or position in society. As scholars have noted, this is because race and ethnicity are at the heart of racial profiling—an immutable aspect of one's being that police are targeting.

"The Talk," has become emblematic of the anxiety and distrust found in African American and Latina/o communities, and of the ways that police policies and practices—which should be race-neutral—are perceived and understood to be driven by race and ethnicity. Analysts observe that each generation of Latinas/os and African Americans has had to confront the reality that one cannot expect that policing will be colorblind and fair and therefore it becomes intrinsic to fear the very people who are supposed to serve and protect you.

Latinas/os in Law Enforcement

With an ever-growing Latina/o population in the United States, it would appear self-evident that Latina/o representation in the ranks of police officers and other law enforcement agencies would result. Studies show that the ability to have Latina/o officers who can effectively communicate and work with communities can be a great asset. But access to the profession has not necessarily been easy. In California and New York,

"The Talk"

Northeastern University School of Law Professor Deborah Ramirez contemplating what she will tell her son about police encounters: "Sit up straight. If you slouch to the right or the left, the police are gonna think you're carrying a gun. Put both hands on the wheel so the police can see you don't have a weapon in your hands" (Harris 2002, 111).

discrimination cases were necessary to break down barriers to people of color being admitted into the police force. In New York, the police organization known as the **Hispanic Society of the New York City Police Department** served as a plaintiff in groundbreaking litigation to end police admissions tests that contained questions that were not job related and that had a disparate effect on the success rates of Latina/o applicants. For those Latinas/os already in the police force, Latinas/os police associations—such as the National Latino Peace Officers Association (NLPOA)—have sued to ensure that Latina/o officers would not be treated discriminatorily. Latina/o officers have been found to suffer from high levels of posttraumatic stress disorder (PTSD), and ensuring the well-being of Latina/o officers is an important function of **Latina/o fraternal law enforcement organizations.**

In recent years, the number of Latinas/os in law enforcement has improved, primarily in larger cities and locations where there are active Latina/o officer organizations. In smaller communities, Latinas/os have experienced greater marginalization and lack the resources and political power to increase representation in their police departments and other important government positions. Such appears to be the case in Pasco, Washington, where a Latino male being shot dead by local police in 2015 has opened up questions about the lack of Latina/o representation in the ranks of the police.

Research suggests that increasing the number of Latina/o police officers alone will not necessarily reduce incidents of excessive force. In one study conducted in Miami, Latina/o officers used force most often on Latinas/os rather than white or African American officers (Alpert & Dunham 2004). Police departments also are hierarchical and quasi-military in how they function and how decisions are made. Officers are expected to take orders and follow directives and policies that might have a disparate impact on Latinas/os. Persons active in Latina/o police organizations have noted that there is pressure to fit in and belong and representation of Latinas/os at the highest levels of decision making might be negligible. Examples in which Latinas/os have fallen into corruption also exist, such as in the case of LAPD Officer Rafael Pérez, a key figure in the Rampart CRASH corruption scandal. Pérez has admitted being "consumed by the 'us-against-them ethos of the overzealous cop' after he transferred to Rampart Crash" (Cannon 2000, 32). He also has conceded that superiors "specifically instructed him to lie on police reports in order to have a more successful prosecution" (Chemerinsky 2001, 637 n. 183).

Low Confidence in Policing

In the midst of a series of police excessive force cases in the 1990s, polls registered that Latinas/os demonstrated a high level of discontent with policing. A 1997 survey in New York City showed that 73 percent of Latinas/os and 81 percent of African Americans believed that police brutality was a severe problem (Human Rights Watch 1998, 275). Human rights organizations also reported that dissatisfaction with policing nationally was endemic among communities of color.

More recent polls continue to show that there is low confidence in the criminal justice system. In a 2009 survey conducted by the nonpartisan Pew Hispanic Center, only 45 percent of Latinas/os stated that they believed that police treat Latina/o communities fairly. In comparison, 74 percent of whites and 37 percent of African Americans state they have confidence that the police will treat African Americans and whites equally (Lopez & Livingston 2009, 4).

A 2014 survey confirms that Latina/o confidence in local police remains low as compared to that of whites. Only 46 percent of Latinos affirm that they have "a great deal or fair amount of confidence in local police to treat Hispanics and whites equally," but 72 percent of whites say that they do. Just 45 percent of Latinas/os express a great or a fair amount of confidence in local police not using excessive force on suspects, as opposed to 74 percent of whites saying they have a great or fair amount of confidence in tactics of local police (Krogstad 2014).

Community Policing, Problem-Oriented Policing, Neighborhood Policing, and Cultural Competency

Controversies centered on police practices and the vast racial and ethnic disparities in criminal justice outcomes have prompted demands for less aggressive policing and more "**community policing**." Community policing is a form of police work that seeks to engage law enforcement personnel in ways that promote improved police-community relations. Such initiatives often focus on holding regular meetings between the community members and patrol officers, such as Chicago Alternative Police Services (CAPS). Researchers have found that persons in the community who perceive that community policing is being implemented tend to view policing more positively, and believe that the regularity of police use of excessive force is reduced (Weitzer & Tuch 2004).

Other scholars have also found community policing to have a similar positive effect, except in situations where portions of the community are not aware of or are not engaged in the community policing initiative. This phenomenon was observed in Chicago, where Spanish-speaking Latinas/os were often unacquainted with and detached from the program (Skogan & Hartnett 1997).

Problems identified with policing strategies that fall short of enhancing community-police relations include instances in which there is little or no community input or dialogue. A popular form of policing that has been adopted across the country is a strategy known as "problem-oriented policing" (POP), an evidence-based approach to policing communities that focuses on how to effectively achieve the goals of preventing and controlling crime in communities. As some academics point out, however, this approach has failed in many cases, particularly when—among other things—community collaboration is absent. Some scholars emphasize the need for a "neighborhood policing" approach, a form of community policing that combines serving the community with enforcement techniques, such as POP, and encourages police to adjust to the circumstances in the neighborhood, as needed (Jones-Brown 2015).

There is evidence that some cities that implemented community-policing or neighborhood-policing approaches instead of get-tough or order-maintenance measures (such as "broken-windows," "quality-of-life," or "zero-tolerance" policing), experienced reductions in crime rates as much as or greater than had occurred in New York City. San Diego geared its policing practices toward greater community involvement along with POP approaches and experienced a drop in homicides and robberies between 1991 and 1998 that surpassed New York City's decline in crime—a 76.4 percent decline in homicides as compared to New York City's 70.6 percent drop, and a 62.6 percent reduction in robberies as compared to New York City's 60.1 percent decrease (Harcourt 2002). Other cities that adopted community-policing approaches, such as San Francisco, were similarly successful. Unlike the case of New York City, in which order-maintenance policies and practices disproportionately affected communities of color and exacerbated racial and ethnic tensions between communities and the police, community-oriented approaches appear to be viable and effective at reducing crime.

After years of being besieged by crime, poverty, and despair, the City of Camden, New Jersey, took the radical measure of dismantling its police force and rebuilding it to be more community oriented. Rather than a militarized presence in a city with a significant Latina/o and African American population (95 percent of the population is composed of people of color), police now interact daily with the community, attend community baseball games, and have established a more cooperative and congenial relationship with the Camden residents. Officers are trained to be more community focused, and more racially, ethnically, and linguistically diverse police personnel (including Spanish, Haitian, Creole, and speakers of nine other languages) have been recruited. In turn, preliminary results show a sharp decrease in crime—a 43 percent decline in shootings in two years and a 22 percent drop in violent crime—and a much-improved relationship between community members and the police (Zernike 2014).

It should be noted that some analysts are skeptical about community policing. Community policing requires a level of community cohesion and empowerment that is uncommon, and police officers—who tend to see themselves as authorities on crime fighting—can be resistant to meaningful community oversight and input. Whether the current push and promising efforts toward community policing will bring substantive change could be a question of time.

Advocates for effective reforms have called for greater "**cultural competency**" in policing (Arya, Villarruel, Villanueva & Augarten 2009). Cultural and linguistic barriers can result in detrimental and unjust consequences. For a Latina/o youth whose parents do not understand English well, the inability to have translations or documents available in the parent's native language could affect important decisions about a youth's detention, probation, incarceration, and out-of-court agreements, or can present obstacles in effective interactions with police or other authorities and have negative outcomes for the child.

The concept of cultural competency, however, is not limited to assuring the availability of translators or documents translated into another language. It involves an institutional commitment that police departments and all other agencies and offices in the criminal justice system will become knowledgeable about the cultural, language, and ethnic differences found within Latina/o communities and in other racial and ethnic groups. Such institutional commitment includes the adoption of measures that facilitate a change in an organization's outlook, behavior, personnel, practices, and policies, enabling and empowering the organization to effectively work across cultures to serve diverse constituencies in many ways other than just providing for adequate translation services.

Although Latinas/os often share many similar attributes, they also originate from different countries in Latin America—each with its own traditions and cultural and linguistic variations. Culturally competent criminal justice agencies and personnel—police officers, judges, prosecutors, public defenders, and others—would be familiar with cultural nuances, community characteristics, and other differences, and not simply have a basic knowledge of the language. A Latino youth remaining silent, for instance, can be misinterpreted as a sign of disrespect to criminal justice authorities, when it actually indicates that the youth is attempting to be polite or does not understand English well.

Concomitant with the goal of making institutions culturally competent is the need to diversify the criminal justice system. Specifically with respect to diversity in law enforcement, New York City is among the large urban centers that by court order has been required to recruit greater numbers of Latina/o and African American police officers. Nationally, however, the lack of racial and ethnic diversity in hundreds of police departments remains a glaring problem. Around the country, the number of whites in police departments is more than 30 percentage points greater than the number of residents in the communities in which officers work, with research indicating that greater diversity enhances the credibility of police forces (Ashkenas & Park 2014). Given the growing Latina/o population across the United States, it stands to reason that the country should aim to increase Latinas/os representation among the ranks in police departments nationally, with the goal of not only making police forces more diverse, but also making them more culturally competent.

See also: Part I essays: Latinas/os and the U.S. Criminal Justice System; Latinas and the U.S. Criminal Justice System; Crime and the U.S.-Mexican Border. Part II entries: Latina/o Fraternal Law Enforcement Organizations.

Further Reading

Acuña, Rodolfo. 2011. *Occupied America: A history of Chicanos*. 7th ed. New York: Longman.

Aguirre, Jr., Adalberto. 2012. Criminalizing Mexican identity: Privilege, power, and identity formation. In *Hispanics in the U.S. criminal justice system: The new American demography*, edited by Martin G. Urbina, 131–44. Springfield, IL: Charles C. Thomas.

Alpert, Geoffrey P., and Roger G. Dunham. 2004. *Understanding police use of force: Officers, suspects, and reciprocity*. Cambridge: Cambridge University Press.

American Civil Liberties Union (ACLU). 2014. *War comes home: The excessive militarization of American policing*. New York, NY: ACLU. https://www.aclu.org/sites/default/files/assets/jus14-warcomeshome-report-web-rel1.pdf.

American Civil Liberties Union (ACLU). 2015a (February 24). Philadelphia police continue to stop tens of thousands illegally. https://www.aclu.org/news/philadelphia-police-continue-stop-tens-thousands-illegally?redirect=criminal-law-reform/philadelphia-police-continue-stop-tens-thousands-illegally.

American Civil Liberties Union (ACLU). 2015b. *Stop and frisk in Chicago*. Chicago, IL: ACLU. http://www.aclu-il.org/stop-and-frisk-in-chicago1/.

Amnesty International. 1998. *United States of America: Rights for all*. New York: Amnesty International Publications.

Arya, Neelum, Francisco Villarruel, Cassandra Villanueva, and Ian Augarten. 2009. America's invisible children: Latino youth and the failure of justice. Washington, DC: Campaign for Youth Justice and National Council of La Raza. http://www.campaignforyouthjustice.org/documents/CFYJPB_InvisibleChildren.pdf.

Ashkenas, Jeremy, and Haeyoun Park. 2014 (September 4). "The race gap in America's police departments." *New York Times*. http://www.nytimes.com/interactive/2014/09/03/us/the-race-gap-in-americas-police-departments.html?emc=edit_th_20140904&nl=todaysheadlines&nlid=18654451&_r=1.

Ayers, Ian, and Jonathan Borowsky. 2008. A study of racially disparate outcomes in the Los Angeles Police Department. Los Angeles, CA: ACLU of Southern California.

http://islandia.law.yale.edu/ayers/Ayres%20LAPD%20Report.pdf.

Balko, Radley. 2013. *Rise of the warrior cop: The militarization of America's police forces*. New York: Public Affairs.

Blumstein, Alfred, and Joel Wallman (eds.). 2000. *The crime drop in America*. New York: Cambridge University Press.

Burns, Sarah. 2011. *The Central Park five*. New York: Vintage Books.

Cabán, Pedro A. 1999. *Constructing a colonial people: Puerto Rico and the United States, 1898–1932*. Boulder, Colorado: Westview Press.

Californians for Safety and Justice. 2014. *Latino voices: The impacts of crime and criminal justice on Latinos*. Oakland, CA: Californians for Safety and Justice. http://libcloud.s3.amazonaws.com/211/04/1/430/LatinoReport_7.8.14v1.pdf.

Cannon, Lou. 2000 (October 1). One bad cop. *New York Times Magazine*.

Carrasco, Gilbert Paul. 1997. Latinos in the United States: Invitation and exile. In *Immigrants out! The new nativism and the anti-immigrant impulse in the United States,* edited by Juan F. Perea, 190–204. New York: New York University Press.

Center for Constitutional Rights. 2012. *Stop and frisk: The human impact*. New York: Center for Constitutional Rights. http://stopandfrisk.org/the-human-impact-report.pdf.

Chemerinsky, Erwin. 2001. "Symposium: The Rampart scandal: Policing the criminal justice system: An independent analysis of the Los Angeles Police Department's Board of Inquiry report on the Rampart scandal." *Loyola of Los Angeles Law Review* 34: 545–655.

Cole, David. 1999. *No equal justice: Race and class in the American criminal justice system*. New York: New Press.

Cole, David. 2001. Formalism, realism, and the war on drugs. *Suffolk University Law Review* 35: 241–55.

Consent Decree in *United States v. City of Los Angeles*. 2000. LAPDOnline.org. http://assets.lapdonline.org/assets/pdf/final_consent_decree.pdf. Accessed November 22, 2015.

Crawford, Charles. 2012. The historical dynamics of ethnicity in law enforcement. In *Hispanics in the U.S. criminal justice system: The new American demography*, edited by Martin G. Urbina, 23–41. Springfield, IL: Charles C. Thomas.

Delgado, Richard, Juan F. Perea, and Jean Stefancic (eds.). 2008. *Latinos and the law: Case and materials*. St. Paul: Thomson West.

Delgado, Richard, and Jean Stefancic (eds.). 2011. *The Latino/a condition: A critical reader*. 2nd ed. New York: New York University Press.

Dockterman, Daniel. 2011. Country of origin profiles. Washington, DC: Pew Hispanic Research Center. http://www.pewhispanic.org/2011/05/26/country-of-origin-profiles/.

Dunn, Christopher. 2014. Stop-and-frisk during the Bloomberg administration (2002–2013), NYCLU briefing. New York: New York Civil Liberties Union.

Durán, Robert J. 2012. Policing the barrios: Exposing the shadows to the brightness of a new day. In *Hispanics in the U.S. criminal justice system: The new American demography*, edited by Martin G. Urbina, 42–62. Springfield, IL: Charles C. Thomas.

Durose, Matthew R., Erica L. Smith, and Patrick A. Langan. 2007. Contacts between police and the public, 2005. NCJ 215243. Washington, DC: Bureau of Justice Statistics, U.S. Department of Justice.

Eck, John E., and Edward R. Maguire. 2000. "Have changes in policing reduced violent crime? An assessment of the evidence." In *The crime drop in America,* edited by Alfred Blumstein and Joel Wallman, 207–65. New York: Cambridge University Press.

Enck-Wanzer, Darrel (ed.). 2010. *The Young Lords: A reader*. New York: New York University Press.

Fernandez, Manny. 2007 (May 27). Remembrance, and protest, for a man slain by an officer. *New York Times*.

Freidman, Warren, and Martha Hott. 1995. *Young people and the police: Respect, fear and the future of community policing in Chicago*. Chicago: Chicago Alliance for Neighborhood Safety.

Golub, Andrew, Bruce D. Johnson, and Eloise Dunlap. 2007. The race/ethnicity disparity in misdemeanor marijuana arrests in New York City. *Criminology & Public Policy* 6(1): 131–64.

Gonzalez, Juan. 1996 (September 27). Her bravery shatters blue wall. *New York Daily News*.

Gonzalez, Juan. 2011. *Harvest of Empire: A history of Latinos in America*, revised edition. New York: Penguin Books.

Hagan, John, and Alberto Palloni. 1999. "Sociological criminology and the mythology of Hispanic immigration and crime." *Social Problems* 46(4): 617–32.

Hajnal, Zoltan, and Mark Baldassare. 2001. *Finding common ground: Racial and ethnic attitudes in California*. San Francisco, CA: Public Policy Institute of California.

Haney López, Ian F. 1996. *White by law: The legal construction of race*. New York: New York University Press.

Haney López, Ian F. 2003. *Racism on trial: The Chicano fight for justice*. Cambridge, MA: Belknap/Harvard University Press.

Harcourt, Bernard E. 2001. *Illusion of order: The false promise of broken windows policing*. Cambridge, MA: Harvard University Press.

Harcourt, Bernard E. 2002 (April 1). Policing disorder: Can we reduce serious crime by punishing petty offenses? *Boston Review*. http://www.bostonreview.net/us/bernard-e-harcourt-policing-disorder.

Harcourt, Bernard E. 2013. "Punitive preventive justice." In *Prevention and the limits of the criminal law*, edited by Andrew Asworth, Lucia Zedner, and Patrick Tomlin, 252–72. Oxford: Oxford University Press.

Harcourt, Bernard E., and Jens Ludwig. 2006. "Broken windows: New evidence from New York City and a five-city social experiment." *University of Chicago Law Review* 73: 271–320.

Harcourt, Bernard E., and Jens Ludwig. 2007. Reefer madness: Broken windows policing and misdemeanor marijuana arrests in New York City, 1989–2000. *Criminology & Public Policy* 6(1): 165–82.

Harris, David A. 2002. *Profiles in injustice: Why racial profiling cannot work*. New York: The New Press.

Herbert, Steve. 2006. *Citizens, cops, and power: Recognizing the limits of community*. Chicago: University of Chicago Press.

Horsman, Reginald. 1981. *Race and Manifest Destiny: The origins of American racial Anglo-Saxonism*. Cambridge, MA: Harvard University Press.

Human Rights Watch. 1998. *Shielded from justice: Police brutality and accountability in the United States*. New York: Human Rights Watch.

Independent Commission on the Los Angeles Police Department. 1991. *Report of the Independent Commission on the Los Angeles Police Department*. Los Angeles, CA: The Commission.

Isquith, Elias. 2014 (September 11). "NYPD Commissioner Bill Bratton: 'Broken windows' critics 'just don't get it.'" *Salon*. http://www.salon.com/2014/09/11/nypd_commissioner_bill_bratton_broken_windows_critics_just_dont_get_it/.

Johnson, Kevin R. 2006. *Hernandez v. Texas*: Legacies of justice and injustice. In *"Colored men" and "Hombres aquí": Hernandez v. Texas and the emergence of Mexican-American lawyering*, edited by Michael A. Olivas, 53–90. Houston, TX: Arte Público Press.

Johnson, Marilynn. 2003. *Street justice: A history of police violence in New York City*. Boston: Beacon Press.

Jones-Brown, Delores. 2015. Neighborhood policing: A safe, respectful and effective community policing strategy. Testimony before the Task Force on 21st Century Policing. Phoenix, AZ, February 13, 2015. http://www.cops.usdoj.gov/pdf/taskforce/submissions/Jones_Brown_Delores_Testimony.pdf.

Kelling, George, and Catherine Coles. 1996. *Fixing broken windows: Restoring order and reducing crime in our communities*. New York, NY: Touchstone.

Kelling, George L., and William H. Sousa. 2001. Do police matter? An analysis of the impact of New York City's police reforms. *Center for Civic Innovation at the Manhattan Institute, Civic Report No. 22.* http://www.manhattan-institute.org/pdf/cr_22.pdf.

Kelling, George L., and James Q. Wilson. 1982 (March 1). Broken windows: The police and neighborhood safety. *The Atlantic*. http://www.theatlantic.com/magazine/archive/1982/03/broken-windows/304465/?single_page=true.

Kenny, Dennis. 2011. Presentation on the failures of problem oriented policing. Problem Oriented Policing Conference, September 12, 2011, Seattle, Washington. https://www.youtube.com/watch?v=9hBBXFplaaU.

Kocieniewski, David, and Robert Hanley. 2000 (November 28). "Racial profiling was routine." *New York Times*.

Krogstad, Jens Manuel. 2014. Latino confidence in local police lower than among whites. Pew Research Center. http://www.pewresearch.org/fact-tank/2014/08/28/latino-confidence-in-local-police-lower-than-among-whites/.

Laughland, Oliver. 2015 (February 19). "Pasco shooting: police will not say how many bullets fired at unarmed man." *The Guardian*. http://www.theguardian.com/us-news/2015/feb/19/police-pasco-shooting-bullets-antonio-zambrano-montes?CMP=ema_565.

Levitt, Steven D. 2004. "Understanding why crime fell in the 1990s: Four factors that explain the decline and six that do not." *Journal of Economic Perspectives* 18(1): 163–90.

Lopez, Mark Hugo, and Gretchen Livingston. 2009. "Hispanics and the criminal justice system: Low confidence, high exposure." Pew Hispanic Center, Washington, DC.

Lowery, Wesley. 2014 (September 8). "How many police shootings a year? No one knows." *Washington Post*. http://www.washingtonpost.com/news/post-nation/wp/2014/09/08/how-many-police-shootings-a-year-no-one-knows/.

Mac Donald, Heather. 2010 (June 25). Fighting crime where the criminals are. *New York Times*. http://www.nytimes.com/2010/06/26/opinion/26macdonald.html.

Males, Mike. 2014 (August 26). "Who are police killing?" *Center on Juvenile and Criminal Justice*. http://www.cjcj.org/news/8113.

Martínez, Elizabeth. 1993. "Beyond black/white: The racisms of our time." *Social Justice* 20(1–2): 22–34.

McArdle, Andrea. 2001. Introduction. In *Zero tolerance: Quality of life and the new police brutality in New York City*, edited by A. McArdle and T. Erzen, 1–16. New York: New York University Press.

McArdle, Andrea, and Tanya Erzen (eds.). 2001. *Zero tolerance: Quality of life and the new police brutality in New York City*. New York: New York University Press.

Meeks, Kenneth. 2000. *Driving while black*. New York: Broadway Books.

Meléndez, Miguel. 2003. *We took the streets: Fighting for Latino rights with the Young Lords*. New York: St. Martin's Press.

Mirandé, Alfredo. 1987. *Gringo justice*. Notre Dame, IN: University of Notre Dame Press.

Mirandé, Alfredo. 2003. "Is there a 'Mexican exception' to the Fourth Amendment?" *Florida Law Review* 55: 365–89.

Morín, José Luis. 2009. *Latino/a rights and justice in the United States: Perspectives and approaches*, 2nd ed. Durham, NC: Carolina Academic Press.

Moskos, Peter. 2008. *Cop in the hood: My year policing Baltimore's Eastern District*. Princeton, NJ: Princeton University Press.

Mucchetti, Anthony E. 2005. "Driving while brown: A proposal for ending racial profiling in emerging Latino communities." 8 *Harvard Latino Law Review* 8: 1–32.

New York Times. 2009 (March 9). "End the Rockefeller Drug Laws". http://www.nytimes.com/2009/03/10/opinion/10tue3.html?_r=0.

New York Times. 2014 (July 26). "Broken windows, broken lives" [Editorial]. A20.

Olivas, Michael A. 2006. *"Colored men" and "Hombres aquí":* Hernandez v. Texas *and the emergence of Mexican-American lawyering*. Houston, TX: Arte Público Press.

Pastor, Manuel, Jr. 1993. *Latinos and the L.A. uprising*. Tomás Rivera Study Center, Occidental College, California.

Perea, Juan F., Richard Delgado, Angela P. Harris, Jean Stefancic, and Stephanie M. Wildman. 2007. *Race and races: Cases and resources for a diverse America*, 2nd ed. St. Paul, MN: West Group.

Peters, Jeremy W. 2009 (March 4). "Albany takes step to repeal '70s-Era drug laws." http://www.nytimes.com/2009/03/05/nyregion/05rockefeller.html?fta=y.

Press, Eyal. 2006 (December 3). Do immigrants make us safer? *New York Times*. nytimes.com.

Rios, Victor. *Punished: Policing the lives of black and Latino boys*. New York: New York University Press.

Romero, Mary, and Gabriella Sánchez. 2012. Critical issues facing Hispanic defendants: From detection to arrest. In *Hispanics in the U.S. criminal justice system: The new American demography*, edited by Martin G. Urbina, 63–79. Springfield, IL: Charles C. Thomas.

Rosenbaum, Robert J. 1998. *Mexicano resistance in the Southwest*. Dallas TX: Southern Methodist University.

Rumbaut, Rubén G., and Walter A. Ewing. 2007. The myth of immigrant criminality. New York: Social Science Research Council. http://borderbattles.ssrc.org/Rumbault_Ewing/.

Sampson, Robert J., and Stephen W. Raudenbush. 1999. Systematic social observation of public spaces: A new look at disorder in urban neighborhoods. *American Journal of Sociology* 105(3): 603–51.

Semple, Kirk. 2014 (March 2). "Latino drivers report thefts by officers." *New York Times*. http://www.nytimes.com/2014/03/03/nyregion/latino-drivers-report-thefts-by-officers.html?_r=0.

Sheridan, Clare. 2006. Peremptory challenges: Lessons from *Hernandez v. Texas*. In *"Colored Men" and "Hombres Aquí":* Hernandez v. Texas *and the emergence of Mexican-American lawyering,* edited by Michael A. Olivas, 143–60. Houston, TX: Arte Público Press.

Skogan, Wesley G. 1990. *Disorder and decline: Crime and the spiral of decay in American neighborhoods*. Berkeley, CA: University of California Press.

Skogan, Wesley G., and Susan M. Hartnett. 1997. *Community policing: Chicago style*. Oxford: Oxford University Press.

Soltero, Carlos R. 2006. *Latinos and American law: Landmark Supreme Court cases*. Austin, TX: University of Texas Press.

Spitzer, Eliot. 1999. *The New York City Police Department's "stop and frisk" practices: A report to the people of the State of New York from the attorney general*. New York: Civil Rights Bureau.

Substance Abuse and Mental Health Data Archive. 2014. List of available Quick Tables for the National Survey on Drug Use and Health, 2013. Rockville, MD: U.S. Department of Health and Human Services (HHS). http://www.icpsr.umich.edu/quicktables/quickconfig.do?35509-0001_all.

The Economist. 2014 (August 23). Overkill: Police in a Missouri suburb demonstrate how not to quell a riot. http://www.economist.com/news/united-states/21613272-police-missouri-suburb-demonstrate-how-not-quell-riot-overkill.

Turkewitz, Julie, and Richard A. Oppel, Jr. 2015 (February 16). "Killing in Washington

State offers 'Ferguson' moment for Hispanics: Pasco Police's shooting of rock thrower draws comparisons to Michael Brown case." *New York Times*. http://www.nytimes.com/2015/02/17/us/killing-in-washington-state-offers-ferguson-moment-for-hispanics.html?hp&action=click&pgtype=Homepage&module=second-column-region&region=top-news&WT.nav=top-news&_r=0#.

Urbina, Martin G. (ed.). 2012. *Hispanics in the U.S. criminal justice system: The new American demography*. Springfield, IL: Charles C. Thomas.

United States Department of Health and Human Services. 2014. National survey on drug use and health, 2013. ICPSR35509-v1. Ann Arbor, MI: Substance Abuse and Mental Health Services Administration. Center for Behavioral Health Statistics and Quality. Inter-university Consortium for Political and Social Research [distributor], 2014-11-18. http://doi.org/10.3886/ICPSR35509.v1.

U.S. Census Bureau. 2015. State & County QuickFacts: New York (City), New York. http://quickfacts.census.gov/qfd/states/36/3651000.html.

U.S. Commission on Civil Rights. 2000. *Police practices and civil rights in New York City: A report of the United States Commission on Civil Rights*. Washington, DC.

U.S. National Commission on Law Observance and Enforcement. 1931. Report on crime and the foreign born. Washington, DC: U.S. Government Printing Office.

Vera Institute of Justice. 2007. *If parents don't speak English well, will their kids get locked up? Language barriers and disproportionate minority contact in the juvenile justice system*. New York, NY: Author.

Villarruel, Francisco A., and Nancy E. Walker, with Pamela Minifree, Omara Rivera-Vázquez, Susan Peterson, and Kristen Perry. 2002. *¿Dónde está la justicia? A call to action on behalf of Latino and Latina youth in the U.S. justice system*. Washington, DC: Michigan State University/Building Blocks for Youth.

Walker, Nancy, E., J. Michael Senger, Francisco A. Villarruel, and Angela M. Arboleda. 2004. *Lost Opportunities: The reality of Latinos in the U.S. criminal justice system*. Washington, DC: National Council of La Raza.

Walker, Samuel, Cassia Spohn, and Miriam DeLone. 2012. *The color of justice: Race, ethnicity, and crime in America*. 5th ed. Belmont, CA: Thomson/Wadsworth.

Way, Lori Beth, and Ryan Patten. 2013. *Hunting for dirtbags: Why cops over-police the poor and racial minorities*. Boston, MA: Northeastern University Press.

Weisburd, David, Cody W. Telep, Joshua C. Hinkle, and John E. Eck. 2008. The effects of problem-oriented policing on crime and disorder. *Campbell Systematic Reviews* 14. doi: 10.4073/csr.2008.14.

Weiser, Benjamin. 1998 (June 25). U.S. asserts police officer planned to lie. *New York Times*.

Weiser, Benjamin. 1998 (October 9). "Former officer gets 7 1/2 years in man's death." *New York Times*. http://www.nytimes.com/1998/10/09/nyregion/former-officer-gets-7-1-2-years-in-man-s-death.html.

Weitzer, Ronald. 1999. "Citizens' perceptions of police misconduct: Race and neighborhood context." *Justice Quarterly* 16: 819–46.

Weitzer, Ronald, and Steven A. Tuch. 2004. Race and perceptions of police misconduct. *Social Problems* 51(3): 305–25.

Weitzer, Ronald, and Steven A. Tuch. 2006. *Race and policing in America: Conflict and reform*. New York: Cambridge University Press.

Wilson, James Q., and Barbara Boland. 1981. "The effects of the police on crime: A response to Jacob and Rich." *Law and Society Review* 16(1): 163–70.

Yee, Vivian. 2013 (January 23). Hispanics in East Haven are wary of kinder tone. *New York Times*. http://www.nytimes.com/2013/01/24/nyregion/in-east-haven-hispanics-are-wary-of-towns-kinder-tone.html.

Zeff, Blake. 2015 (January 10). America's over-policing bombshell: How new data proves "stop & frisk" critics were right all along. *Salon.* http://www.salon.com/2015/01/10/americas_over_policing_bombshell_how_new_data_proves_stop_frisk_critics_were_right_all_along/.

Zernike, Kate. 2014 (August 31). "Camden turns around with new police force." *New York Times.* http://www.nytimes.com/2014/09/01/nyregion/camden-turns-around-with-new-police-force.html.

Cases Cited

Floyd et al. v. City of New York, 959 F. Supp. 2d 540 (S.D.N.Y. 2013).

Hernandez v. New York, 500 U.S. 352 (1991).

Hernandez v. Texas, 347 U.S. 475 (1954).

Mendez v. Westminster School District of Orange County, 64 F. Supp. 544, 549 (S.D. Cal. 1946), *aff'd* 161 F.2d 774 (9th Cir. 1947).

People v. Hall, 4 Cal. 399 (1854).

State v. Pedro Soto, 324 N.J. Super. 66, 85; 734 A.2d 350, 361 (1996).

Terry v. Ohio, 392 U.S. 1 (1968).

United States v. Brignoni-Ponce, 422 U.S. 873 (1975).

United States v. Martinez-Fuerte, 428 U.S. 543 (1976).

The U.S. War on Drugs and Latina/o Communities

Ric Curtis and Robert Riggs

Despite popular views and iconic American imagery, Latina/o involvement with illegal **drugs** in the United States historically has been less than or comparable to that of other ethnic groups. Greatly contributing to the perception that Latinas/os are intimately and routinely involved in the production, distribution, and use of illegal drugs in the United States has been mainstream knowledge that some illegal drugs are produced in and imported from a few Latin American countries. The perceived but misinformed connection between Latinas/os and illegal drugs has generated an inordinate amount of attention to Latina/o neighborhoods from the criminal justice system and law enforcement. This focus on Latinas/os as a major part of the drug problem in the United States in turn had a detrimental impact on Latinas/os and their communities. From no source have these negative effects emerged more steadily and forcefully than from the "**War on Drugs**."

The War on Drugs: Its Origin and History

First articulated in the United States by President Nixon in 1969, the term "War on Drugs" referred to attempts by the U.S. government to reduce and ultimately eliminate the production, distribution, and use of substances it deemed "illegal." The phrase was meant to evoke President Lyndon Johnson's "War on Poverty" of 1964. The war on poverty, however, was intended as a metaphor to convey the government's serious commitment to addressing the problem of poverty; the war on drugs turned out to be an actual war with real victims. Considering this observation, it is very ironic that the war on drugs ended up focusing on the very same people who had been identified in the war on poverty as needing help and being worthy of assistance—namely impoverished African Americans and Latinas/os.

Even before Nixon popularized the rhetoric of a drug "war," however, ethnicity and illicit drugs were linked in the American social imagination. Indeed, the demonization of illegal **drug use**, its association with particular racial or ethnic groups, and racialized targeting by law enforcement has a history that spans the whole 20th century. Latinas/os, in particular, were first systematically targeted as a group during the Great Depression when a large number of Mexican migrants flooded into the United States in search of employment. Although marijuana use had been present and largely unproblematic in some Southern black communities and some Southwest Mexican communities from the turn of the 20th century, the substance suddenly leapt into prominence as a major threat to the social order in the 1930s during a wave of anti-immigrant sentiment.

Suddenly demonized, marijuana served as a convenient foil for states and the federal government to deport and otherwise remove large numbers of Latina/o immigrants from the U.S. labor market. Tellingly, an infamous 1937 article by the head of the powerful Federal Bureau of Narcotics described marijuana as a drug that drives users to commit heinous acts, including murder and suicide, and referred to the purveyors of this "evil drug" as "tamale vendors" (Anslinger & Cooper 1937). Thus, long before the war on drugs was officially declared, Latinas/os were being systematically targeted by law enforcement, especially in connection with illicit substances.

More recently, policy makers and law enforcement professionals have been criticized for the disproportionate effects of the war on drugs on communities of color. Those in law enforcement typically assert that the methods and techniques they use to identify targets in the war on drugs are not based upon racial or ethnic criteria, yet almost all of the available data on arrests and prosecutions for drug-related offenses strongly suggest that **racial profiling** has been a central pillar in the war on drugs. Some scholars have complicated the calculus of detecting racial bias by suggesting that secondary factors, such as differential access to private space, have been critical in determining whether communities of color have a problem with drugs. This, in turn, has fed the perception that drug distribution and use have become integral parts of life in neighborhoods with high concentrations of African Americans or Latinas/os. In essence, this argument maintains that poor people do not have access to private spaces to buy or use drugs and, hence, their involvements with illegal drugs take place in public spaces where they are visible and more easily targeted by law enforcement. There is merit to the argument that overcrowding in poor neighborhoods causes drug activities to take place in the street and that the atmosphere of an open-air drug bazaar leads to the formation of large drug markets that draw users and distributors, thus provoking the attention of the police. Public drug use, however, was widespread from the 1960s through the early 1990s, and it often was just as obvious in white and middle-class neighborhoods as it was in African-American and Latina/o lower-class neighborhoods. Nevertheless, poor communities of color more often were the recipients of drug **policing** initiatives than white communities were. The impact of this war on drugs on Latina/o communities has had profound and lasting consequences.

Latinas/os, Drug Stereotypes, and Gangs

The war on drugs is fundamentally different from typical wars fought by the United States in that the definition of the enemy is not as explicit as it was in wars against other sovereign nations. The war on drugs, in short, was a war in need of an enemy. Defining this enemy merely in terms of individuals or groups who broke the law would not have been enough to justify an all-out war. The enemy in the war on drugs had to be constructed as organized and dangerous "others" whose violent and amoral subcultural values posed an imminent threat to mainstream U.S. society. Often cast in this role, Latinas/os have proven useful targets for those leading the charge in the war on drugs.

Whatever theories researchers advance to explain why communities of color became ground zero in the war on drugs, many people—including policy makers and law enforcement professionals—believed that minorities were especially susceptible to problems with drugs. Minorities, it was said, became involved with drugs because they were poor and needed money, because they were uneducated about the dangers of drugs, because they became ensnared in gang activities, because they had multi-problem families, and because of a wide variety of additional reasons advanced over the years. Coincidental to this perception that African Americans and Latinas/os, in particular, were overly susceptible to drug problems was a belief that minority families and communities were incapable of dealing effectively with the problem on their own. Thus, only an aggressive approach spearheaded by law enforcement could root out the growing drug menace in poor communities of color. In this highly racialized conception of the drug problem, young minority males were singled out as especially worthy of blame and particularly deserving of harsh punishment. Absent in this narrative are any possibilities for treatment and rehabilitation. These "superpredators" were universally constructed as dangerous to society and in need of neutralization via incarceration or **deportation**. Undoubtedly, the stereotyped figure of the "superpredator" inevitably wore brown or black skin.

Additionally, stereotyped images of drug "pushers" as being alien "others" who represent real threats to mainstream society have taken on many forms in reference to Latinas/os. It is important to note, however, that drug stereotyping has not been confined to Latinas/os. The Chinese, for example, were subjected to similar processes when a moral crusade against opium smoking in the late 19th and early 20th centuries served as an effective mechanism by which to control cheap labor from Asia.

The archvillains of the drug world always have been portrayed as amoral sociopaths, and Latina/o stereotypes generally are no exception. Due to **media** images, news reports, and law enforcement press conferences, the figures of the Latina/o drug courier, drug trafficker, and drug "pusher" have become seemingly inextricable components of the social imaginary. It certainly is true that the dim-witted, bumbling Latina/o **drug user** is a frequent theme in comedy—from the routines made famous by Cheech and Chong since the 1970s, to the comedy of John Leguizamo in the 1990s and 2000s caricaturing Latinas/os as having problematic relationships with substances such as marijuana, cocaine, and heroin. The dominant Latina/o image relative to drugs is that of the violent drug dealer—and no single media portrayal has been more emblematic of that image than Cuban drug dealer Tony Montana, as played by Al Pacino in the movie *Scarface*. Moderately successful when first released, the movie has since grown into a cult classic. The images in *Scarface* have spread across the globe as the emblem of cutthroat Latina/o gangsterism financed by international **drug trafficking**, much as the iconic image of Che Guevara became detached from its historical context and evolved into an international symbol of youthful protest. After *Scarface*, a nefarious connection between Latinas/os and drugs was indelibly etched in the global psyche.

The association between Latina/o **gangs** in the United States and drug dealing also is well-established in academic literature, but the degree to which highly organized gangs actually dominate drug markets is disputed among experts in the field. In some cities, especially on the West coast and in the Midwest, some Latina/o gangs have lengthy histories of involvement with drug distribution, but the degree to which they dominate local drug markets to the exclusion of other distributors has been challenged by scholars and by law enforcement data suggesting that the markets are not so tightly controlled by gangs (Hagedorn 1994; Klein, Maxson, & Cunningham 1991). Indeed, on the East coast—especially in New York City—drug dealing throughout the 1970s and 1980s was dominated by large corporate organizations (run by men such as Nicky Barnes and Frank Lucas, who became the subjects of Hollywood movies). Street gangs were largely inconsequential in the drug market. In the mid-1990s in New York City, after the corporate-style drug organizations were dismantled, gangs resurged but never became a large, systematized presence in drug markets. In fact, the decision of whether to deal drugs often was left to individual gang members.

At the start of the new millennium, new forms of highly organized Latina/o gangs began gaining prominence in drug distribution—drug trafficking organizations (DTOs) that were based in Mexico. These gangs were not the local variants that had been the subject of much scholarly work and police attention over the years; rather, they were groups that sought to extend their drug distribution networks across the United States. Dealing primarily in methamphetamine imported from Mexico (although they also sold other drugs), these DTOs were formed specifically for the purpose of making money in the drug business, and they have been remarkably successful in capturing significant portions of the American market in the many cities in which they operate—especially after federal regulations on precursor chemicals curtailed the ability of local methamphetamine dealers to manufacture the drug.

In the United States, the widespread perception that Latinas/os are deeply involved in drugs and drug trafficking has been fed by a variety of sources including the media. The effect has been to homogenize the image of the Latina/o population as a monolithic, undifferentiated group. No matter that there are vast differences between the cultures of various Latina/o groups in the United States, or that geographic differences within the United States have led to the further elaborations of those cultures, the Latina/o community often is painted with a broad brush. Yet the experience that Latina/o communities in the United States have had with drugs varies tremendously. In some communities drugs seem virtually absent, in others—particularly **border** communities—drug trafficking and smuggling contraband across the border has a long and colorful history that has generated a culture all its own, including its own form of music called *narcocorridos*. *Narcocorridos* celebrates the lives and exploits of high-level drug traffickers and primarily is of Mexican origin, but has become enormously popular in some Southwest Latina/o communities. Social scientists have noted that in some of these communities the drug trade is a "normal part of life," and that social gatherings nearly always feature the telling of "drug stories" that act to memorialize significant events in the lives of community members (Campbell 2005). Clearly, the Latina/o experience with drugs in the United States is complex and multifaceted, but the dominant Latina/o stereotypes do not capture this complexity.

Drug Use and Latina/o Communities: What We Know

Latina/o communities in the United States are remarkably varied and differ in a variety of ways, including residents' nationality, class, political orientation, and geographic location. These differences have affected the trajectories of community members' substance use. In general, Latinas/os use illegal drugs at a lesser rate than those of most other groups in the United States (Substance Abuse and Mental Health Data Archive

(SAMHDA) 2014). This is especially true when comparing Latinas/os with whites. Data for 2013 for persons 12 years old or older show that the rate of previous-month illicit drug use by whites was 9.5 percent, and Latinas/os' previous-month illegal drug use was 8.8 percent (United States Department of Health and Human Services (USDHHS) 2014, 26). In fact, previous-month illicit drug use data by race/ethnicity from 2002 through 2013 indicate that Latinas/os, as a group, consistently use illegal drugs at lower rates than whites (USDHHS 2014, 27). In 2013, for every category of substances—cigarettes, alcohol, cocaine, crack, hallucinogens, heroin, inhalants, marijuana, pain relievers, sedatives, stimulants, and tranquilizers—Latina/o use is lower than for whites (SAMHDA 2014).

National data, however, indicate that substance use by Latinas/os is not always uniformly lower as compared with other racial and ethnic groups, particularly with respect to subcategories of use. For instance, the results of the 2010 National Household Survey on Drug Use and Health show that Latinas/os surpass other racial and ethnic groups in the rate of binge (not heavy) alcohol use at 25.1 percent, compared to whites at 24.0 percent, blacks/African Americans at 19.8 percent, American Indians/Alaskan Natives at 24.7 percent, Asians at 12.4 percent, and persons reporting two or more races at 21.5 percent (Substance Abuse and Mental Health Services Administration 2011, 30).

Regional differences in substance use also appear in national data. For example, among Latinas/os 12 years of age or older for 2004 and 2005, the previous-month use of any illicit drug was 7.4 percent, which was less than the percentage of any illicit drug use in the overall population in large metropolitan counties (8.2 percent) and small metropolitan counties (8.4 percent), but greater than the overall population in non-metropolitan counties (6.6 percent) (Office of Applied Studies 2007, 2). For 2004 and 2005, the previous-month use of marijuana among Latinas/os was 5 percent, which was less than the percentage of marijuana use in the overall population in large metropolitan counties (6.3 percent) and small metropolitan counties (6.4 percent), and only slightly greater than the overall population in non-metropolitan counties (4.8 percent) (Office of Applied Studies 2007, 2). Nonmedical prescription drug use by Latinas/os at 2.4 percent was similar or lower when compared to all racial and ethnic groups 12 years or older for 2004 and 2005 in large metropolitan counties (2.4 percent), small metropolitan counties (2.9 percent), and non-metropolitan counties (Office of Applied Studies 2007, 2).

Because Latinas/os are so varied in ethnic composition, data in national surveys of drug use suggest some variations in the rates at which Latina/o subgroups use illegal drugs. Greater rates of past and present drug use among Mexican Americans and Puerto Ricans have been reported as compared to Cuban Americans. Variations in high or low rates of drug involvement by Latina/o subgroups were believed to include a range of factors, such as proximity to trafficking routes or to street-level retail markets.

One factor that researchers routinely point out, however, is that Latinas/os born in the United States are more likely to use illegal drugs than are those who were born elsewhere. One study from the late 1980s, for example, found that Latinas/os "who preferred to be interviewed in English were two to three times as likely ever to have used drugs" as Latinas/os who "preferred to be interviewed in Spanish" (Office of Applied Studies 2008). The point is that Latinas/os who were more assimilated into U.S. culture and society were more likely to be involved with illegal drugs. More recent data continues to support this view, but the globalization of illegal drug markets over the last several decades no longer assures that Latinas/os arrive in the United States without any experience with illegal drugs. Central Americans in the United States continue to exhibit lower rates of involvement with illegal drugs than that of Puerto Ricans, for example. The growth of internal drug markets in certain Latinas/os' home countries (for instance, in El Salvador, where crack markets boomed near the turn of the new millennium), however, assures that new arrivals to the United States are more experienced with or less hostile to illegal drugs.

Although it is true that assimilated second-, third-, and fourth-generation Latinas/os use illegal drugs at greater rates than those of new Latina/o arrivals, it is *not* necessarily true that they consume large quantities of illicit substances, especially in comparison to whites and other ethnic groups (USDHHS 2014; SAMHDA 2014). Even in Latina/o neighborhoods that once featured street-level drug "supermarkets" offering a wide range of illegal drugs, the rates that local people used these drugs appeared to drop precipitously in the mid-1990s. For example, a 1994–95 study of one Latina/o neighborhood in Brooklyn, NY, having large crack, cocaine, and heroin markets, found that only 3 percent of 18- to 21-year-olds in the neighborhood used heroin and that there was widespread local stigma against the use of crack and other hard drugs (Friedman et al. 1997). Clearly, the pendulum of drug use among young, assimilated Latinas/os in this neighborhood was swinging toward more moderate levels of consumption.

The point is that drugs and drug use have increased and decreased in popularity over time in Latina/o communities in the same way that they have in other communities. The stereotyped image of the Latina/o drug user not only is inaccurate but also is detrimental to understanding the trends of drug use in Latina/o communities in the United States. Understanding these trends requires far less stereotyping and law enforcement targeting, and performance of far more research specifically focused on Latina/o communities.

The War on Drugs and Its Impact on Latina/o Communities

The war on drugs has claimed many victims over the last several decades. Indeed, in the last three decades the number of drug arrests in the United States has more than tripled—going from about 581,000 arrests annually in 1980 to more than 1.8 million per year in 2005 (Mauer 2009). These figures represent a "body count" in the war on drugs, but they do not measure the full impact arrests have on the families and communities of arrestees. Much has been written about the detrimental impact of the war on drugs on poor communities of people of color in general, but there is little scholarly work that provides a detailed account of the war's effects specifically on Latina/o communities in the United States. Notable exceptions include works from a growing body of literature written by ethnographers and other qualitative researchers that highlight the complexity and dimensions of the problem in ways that statistics or overviews cannot convey. In many ways, the paucity of extensive or reliable data on Latina/o communities is surprising, because the drugs that have been the primary targets of the war on drugs in the United States over the decades—cocaine/crack, heroin, marijuana, and methamphetamine—often originate in or are trafficked through Latin American and Central American countries. This fact certainly has appeared to justify law enforcement's intense focus on Latina/o communities. Ironically, however, it has not provoked the same focus from researchers. Indeed, there are shockingly few statistics that accurately portray the impact that the war on drugs has had on these targeted Latina/o communities.

One area where the drug war's detrimental impact upon Latinas/os is amply demonstrated with empirical evidence is in the disproportionate number of Latinas/os in federal and state prisons, the majority of them convicted of drug-related offenses. Beginning in the crack era of the mid-1980s—a period in which crack-cocaine use was exploding out of control—and extending well into the 21st century, the annual growth of the imprisoned Latina/o population outpaced that of all other groups in the United States. By 2004, the proportion of Latinas/os in federal prison was more than double the proportion of Latinas/os in the population as a whole. The crack era sparked new vigor in the war on drugs, but crack use leveled off in the United States during the mid-1990s. Despite a steep decline in crack use in communities of color, great numbers of blacks and Latinas/os continued to be arrested and incarcerated throughout the decade.

At the turn of the century, however, a new trend emerged: widespread methamphetamine use. Methamphetamine spread across the country during this time and was concentrated in rural areas where whites were the principal users and sellers. As one would expect, whites began to be arrested at greater rates for drug-related offenses during this period, and rates of drug arrests among blacks dropped, although it remained disproportionately high. Throughout this entire period, however, Latina/o incarceration rates remained largely stable at about 20 percent of the population of state prisons across the United States and 32 percent of the federal prison population. In other words, Latinas/os continued to be arrested and incarcerated at consistently and disproportionately high rates relative to their representation in the population as a whole (Mauer 2009). Clearly, Latina/o communities, groups, and individuals remain in the crosshairs of those tasked with prosecuting the war on drugs in the United States.

Despite the lack of many details about the impact of the war on drugs on Latinas/os, it is clear that they always have been overrepresented in the statistics on arrests and prosecutions for drug-related offenses in the United States. It also is clear that during the last two decades of the 20th century, the number of Latinas/os imprisoned for drug offenses grew exponentially, as reflected in statistics revealing that by 2005 one of every eight arrests nationwide was for drugs. Despite consistent data collected through national surveys and indicating that whites used drugs at considerably greater rates than that for blacks and Latinas/os (USDHHS 2014; SAMHDA 2014), blacks and Latinas/os were arrested and incarcerated at far greater rates than whites were (Mauer 2009).

The vast majority of those arrested for drugs in the United States since the war on drugs was declared by the Nixon administration have come from black and Latina/o communities, and their sentences often have been considerably harsher than those meted out to whites. In 1995, for example, an individual could possess "100 times more powder cocaine," which often is viewed as a white middle-class drug, "than crack," which often is described as a minority drug, "before facing the same mandatory minimum jail term" (Wytsma 1995). In other words, there was a 100:1 ratio between two substances that differed significantly only in terms of the racial groups most associated with the substances. It did not matter that cocaine easily could be converted to crack in less than 5 minutes with a few ounces of water and a pinch of baking soda or that whites consistently used crack at greater rates than those of blacks or Latinas/os. The fact is that the demonization of crack and its association with particular racial and ethnic groups had become firmly entrenched in the public's imagination, and policy makers were eager to capitalize on this misperception.

Although it undoubtedly is true that the African American community was greatly affected by the war on drugs and the harsh sentences that accompanied it, Latinas/os also bore a substantial weight, often in ways that were unique to them. At the height of the crack era, for example, the "aggravated felon" category of offender was created by the federal criminal justice system, and it allowed prosecutors to deport thousands of Latinas/os in a new twist in the war on drugs. In 1990, barely 8,000 immigrants were deported because of criminal charges, but by the late 1990s that number had increased to more than 50,000 deportations per year (Yates, Collins & Chin 2005). During the decade of the 1990s, drug offenses became the foremost reason for deportation—more than all other categories combined. This outcome makes Latinas/os victims of the war on drugs in ways that other groups have not had to endure. Often, the Latinas/os deported for drug-related offenses were fully assimilated into American culture, and sending them back to the countries in which they were born meant returning them to places where they were stigmatized as pariahs, unfamiliar with local cultures and sometimes unable even to speak Spanish.

Alternatives to the War: Treatment, Harm Reduction, and Reform

As the number of Latinas/os sent to prison and jail for drug-related offenses began to increase in the 1980s and to grow further through the start of the new millennium, court-mandated **drug treatment** became an important tool in the war on drugs. Diversion to drug treatment was touted as a cost-saving measure: it allowed the criminal justice system to supervise a much greater number of people than could possibly be accommodated in prisons and jails. Mandatory drug treatment programs—including outpatient day programs and "therapeutic communities"—typically have very modest rates of success. Bad outcomes in treatment, however, generally are depicted not as a failure of the programs but rather as a failure of the individual clients. There are a variety of stereotypes about the type of people that typically fail these programs, and Latinas/os are included. Many treatment providers think that Latino culture is an impediment to general well-being and that it leads Latinas/os to view Anglo providers with suspicion, causing them to avoid drug treatment and health care in general. Yet very few culturally appropriate drug treatment programs exist in the United States, and the relatively low success rate for Latinas/os in drug treatment programs needs to be understood in light of that deficit.

Two of the major types of drug-treatment modalities serving as alternatives to sending drug arrestees to prison or jail are outpatient day programs and therapeutic communities. Outpatient day programs require individuals to attend various types of activities in a community setting over several months, often at a local non-governmental social service agency. Included among the activities in which patients are required to engage are individual, family, and group counseling sessions as well as job readiness and life-skills training sessions. One problem with outpatient programs is that they often do not differentiate between clients, a problem that fails to recognize that different patients have different problems and different needs. For example, marijuana users whose primary language is Spanish could be placed in a therapeutic group setting with users of heroin and crack whose only language is English.

Unlike outpatient programs, therapeutic communities require patients to live in the facility—sometimes for as long as 18 months—to be "re-socialized" before they can reenter society. This approach generally attempts to help individuals whose lives have become dysfunctional to confront and shed the problematic attitudes, orientations, and behaviors that caused their troubles and then to reassemble them into productive citizens. Many therapeutic community programs utilize a confrontational approach to achieve these goals. Although this approach might be effective for some people, it often proves far less successful for others.

The poor success rates of court-mandated drug-treatment programs ensure that the facilities that operate them serve as a constant source of bodies for prisons and jails, and often, these are Latina/o bodies. Failure in a treatment program results in a "technical violation" of the court agreement or the terms of probation or parole, an outcome that often results in a trip back into the criminal justice system. Indeed, the number of technical violations served on parolees and probationers in the last two decades escalated to such extraordinary heights that prisons became dangerously overcrowded, draining state coffers and posing a threat to public health. In 2009, overcrowding in California's prison system—where Latinas/os are extremely disproportionately represented in the prison population—became so untenable that a panel of federal judges ruled that the state had to reduce its nearly 150,000-person prison population by 40,000 people because the state was simply unable to provide adequate health care for inmates. The failure of treatment programs and the resulting explosion of "technical violations" deserve close attention for contributing to the problem of prison overcrowding.

In the midst of the failure of treatment programs, some Latina/o communities—alarmed by the twin threat of AIDS and an amped-up war on drugs during the 1990s—embarked on a new path toward managing drug-use problems: "harm reduction" strategies. Harm reduction programs seek to minimize the harms associated with drug use, and they partner with clients to improve health and total quality of life (*see, e.g.,* Harm Reduction Coalition [n.d.]). One controversial aspect of some harm-reduction programs includes syringe exchange services through which drug users can trade their used syringes for sterile ones as a way to reduce the spread of the HIV virus. These grassroots community programs, which ultimately have been proved efficacious in reducing the spread of HIV, were pioneered in Latina/o communities in the United States. These efforts have been at the forefront of the fight against the AIDS epidemic and a variety of other drug-related problems that afflict Latina/o communities, including drug overdose, Hepatitis B and C, and tuberculosis. In addition to these innovative approaches, harm reduction programs have introduced new methods and techniques to address the negative consequences of opiate addiction, including the distribution of Naloxone to prevent overdose and the prescription of Suboxone in place of methadone. Methadone is a synthetic "opiate" used throughout the United States to treat heroin addiction, but it has an onerous reputation in Latina/o communities because it locks patients into taking daily doses at a local clinic, thereby preventing many from leading normal lives.

As the first decade of the new century came to a close, many politicians and policy makers have claimed that the war on drugs is being scaled back. In New York State, for example, the "reform" of the infamous 1970s-era **Rockefeller drug laws** that took effect on October 1, 2009, was hailed as a milestone in rolling back some of the most pernicious features of the war on drugs, especially the extraordinarily long sentences that routinely had been given to relatively minor drug offenders. It should be noted that Latinas/os were instrumental in the push toward reform of these draconian laws in an effort to reduce the legislations' severely detrimental effect on Latina/o communities in New York. Essentially, the reforms eliminated mandatory minimum sentences, restored judicial discretion in some cases, expanded funding for alternatives to incarceration and treatment programs, and made it possible for roughly 1,500 people in prison for minor drug offenses to apply for resentencing (Drug Policy Alliance 2009). The so-called reforms, however, represented a legislative victory but did not go nearly far enough to mitigate the negative effects of years of systematic targeting of Latinas/os in the war on drugs. Indeed, the reforms are a component of what seems a larger organized effort to change the tone and rhetoric of the fight against illicit substances. In the very same month that New York State passed the reform of the Rockefeller Drug Laws, the Obama administration announced that the Justice Department would no longer seek to prosecute users and distributors of medical marijuana who were compliant with the laws in states that allow medical marijuana.

These attempts to ameliorate the effects of the war on drugs do not mean that the war is over, however, even if policy makers realize that the "war" metaphor has outlived its usefulness and begin to employ new language to describe their approach to drugs. Indeed, evidence suggests that the war on drugs has become an ingrained feature of the landscape in the United States and that it has a dynamic trajectory all its own—enriching law enforcement agencies and calling forth vast bureaucracies to manage it. In New York City, for example, the NYPD recently has come under intense public scrutiny for an aggressive "stop and frisk" policy that it insisted was not racially biased, even though the vast majority of those stopped were blacks and Latinas/os, and the largest group of drug users, percentage-wise and overwhelmingly in absolute numbers, continued to be white people. The department's aggressive campaign to root out criminals was conceived and carried out despite consistent declines in the crime rate every year between 1993 and 2009. In 2008, for example, the city made more than 40,000 arrests for marijuana, and the overwhelming majority of those arrested were blacks and Latinas/os (Levine 2013). Thus, despite new rhetoric suggesting that the "war" on drugs is over and notwithstanding dramatic reductions in crime in some places, the campaign against illegal drugs has become institutionalized in the United States. Additionally, the businesses that experienced growth as a result of the war—such as drug-treatment programs and **prisoner reentry** services—are increasing rather than decreasing in number and size. Latinas/os continue to be among the primary users of these "services," and they continue to be disproportionally targeted and affected by society's response to illegal drugs given the modest levels of drug involvement they exhibit as a group.

See also: Part I essays: Incarceration and Latinas/os in the United States; Gangs in the United States and Latina/o Communities; Latina/o Youth and Criminal Justice. Part II entries: Central Americans; Colombians; Cubans.

Further Reading

Anslinger, Harry J., and Courtney Ryley Cooper. 1937, 2011. Marijuana: Assassin of youth. In *The American drug scene: An anthology,* edited by J. Inciardi, James and K. McElrath, 64–69. New York, NY: Oxford University Press.

Bennett, William J., John J. Dilulio, and John P. Walters. 1996. *Body count: Moral poverty . . . and how to win America's war against crime and drugs*. New York, NY: Simon and Schuster.

Bourgois, Philippe. 2002. *In search of respect: Selling crack in el barrio.* 2nd ed. Cambridge, UK: Cambridge University Press.

Brotherton, David C., and Luis Barrios. 2009. Displacement and stigma: The social-psychological crisis of the deportee. *Crime, Media, Culture: An International Journal* 5(1): 29–55.

Campbell, Howard. 2005. Drug trafficking stories: Everyday forms of narco-folklore on the U.S-Mexico border. *International Journal of Drug Policy* 16 (5): 326–33.

Drug Policy Alliance. 2006. Ferrer, Rivera, Aubry and NYC Latino Coalition urge Governor Pataki to keep his promise to "dramatically reform" Rockefeller drug laws. http://www.drugpolicy.org/news/pressroom/pressrelease/pr_december06_01.cfm. Accessed October 22, 2015.

Drug Policy Alliance. 2009. NYS legislation passes historic Rockefeller Drug Law reform, bill now awaits governor's signature. http://www.drugpolicy.org/news/pressroom/pressrelease/pr004039.cfm. Accessed October 22, 2015.

Friedman, Samuel R., Richard Curtis, Benny Jose, Alan Neaigus, Jonathan Zenilman, Joan Culpepper-Morgan, Lisa Borg, Mary Jeanne Kreek, Denise Paone, and Don C. Des Jarlais. 1997. Sex, drugs, and infections among youth: Parenterally and sexually transmitted diseases in a high-risk neighborhood. *Sexually Transmitted Diseases* 24(6): 322–26.

Gelman, Andrew, Jeffrey Fagan, and Alex Kiss. 2007. "An analysis of the New York City police department's 'stop-and-frisk' policy in the context of claims of racial bias." *Journal of the American Statistical Association* 102(479): 813–23. doi: 10.1198/016214506000001040.

Hagedorn, John M. 1994. Homeboys, dope fiends, legits, and new Jacks. *Criminology* 32(2): 197–219.

Harm Reduction Coalition. n.d. http://www.harmreduction.org/. Accessed October 22, 2015.

Klein, Malcolm W., Cheryl L. Maxson, and Lea C. Cunningham. 1991. Crack, street gangs, and violence. *Criminology* 29: 623–50.

Levine, Harry. 2013, November 18. "The Scandal of Racist Marijuana Arrests." *The Nation.* http://www.thenation.com/article/176915/scandal-racist-marijuana-arrests-and-what-do-about-it. Accessed October 22, 2015.

Maher, Lisa. 1997. *Sexed work: Gender, race and resistance in a Brooklyn drug market.* New York, NY: Oxford University Press.

Mauer, Marc. 2009. The changing racial dynamics of the war on drugs. Washington, DC: The Sentencing Project. http://www.sentencingproject.org/doc/dp_raceanddrugs.pdf.

Monitoring the future. 2014. Ann Arbor, MI: University of Michigan. http://monitoringthefuture.org/.

Musto, David F. 1999. *The American disease: Origins of narcotic control.* New York: Oxford University Press.

National Drug Intelligence Center. 2004. National Drug Threat Assessment, April 2004: Methamphetamine. Washington, DC: U.S. Department of Justice. http://www.justice.gov/archive/ndic/pubs8/8731/meth.htm.

Office of Applied Studies. 2007. Illicit drug use, by race/ethnicity, in metropolitan and non-metropolitan counties: 2004 and 2005. *The NSDUH* [National Survey on Drug Use and Health] *Report.* Rockville, MD: Substance Abuse and Mental Health Services

Administration. http://www.oas.samhsa.gov/2k7/popDensity/popDensity.pdf.

Office of Applied Studies. 2008. Prevalence of substance use among racial & ethnic subgroups in the U.S. Rockville, MD: Substance Abuse and Mental Health Services Administration. http://www.oas.samhsa.gov/NHSDA/Ethnic/toc.htm.

Padilla, Felix M. 1992. *The gang and an American enterprise*. New Brunswick, NJ: Rutgers University Press.

Sanchez-Jankowski, Martin. 1991. *Islands in the street: Gangs and American urban society*. Berkeley, CA: University of California Press.

Substance Abuse and Mental Health Data Archive. 2014. List of available quick tables for the National Survey on Drug Use and Health, 2013. Rockville, MD: U.S. Department of Health and Human Services (HHS). http://www.icpsr.umich.edu/quicktables/quickconfig.do?35509-0001_all.

Substance Abuse and Mental Health Services Administration. 2011. *Results from the 2010 National Survey on Drug Use and Health: Summary of national findings*, NSDUH Series H-41, HHS Publication No. (SMA) 11-4658. Rockville, MD: Substance Abuse and Mental Health Services Administration.

Substance Abuse and Mental Health Services Administration. 2014. *Results from the 2013 National Survey on Drug Use and Health: Summary of National Findings*, NSDUH Series H-48, HHS Publication No. (SMA) 14-4863. Rockville, MD: Substance Abuse and Mental Health Services Administration. http://www.samhsa.gov/data/sites/default/files/NSDUHresultsPDFWHTML2013/Web/NSDUHresults2013.pdf.

Taylor, Carl S. 1990. *Dangerous society*. East Lansing, MI: Michigan State University Press.

United States Department of Health and Human Services. 2014. National Survey on Drug Use and Health, 2013. ICPSR35509-v1. Ann Arbor, MI: Substance Abuse and Mental Health Services Administration. Center for Behavioral Health Statistics and Quality. Inter-university Consortium for Political and Social Research [distributor], 2014-11-18. http://doi.org/10.3886/ICPSR35509.v1.

Williams, Terry. 1989. *The cocaine kids: The inside story of a teenage drug ring*. Reading, MA: Addison-Wesley.

Wytsma, Laura A. 1995. Punishment just for us: A constitutional analysis of the crack cocaine sentencing statutes. *George Mason Law Review* 3(2): 473–513.

Yates, Jeff, Todd A. Collins, and Gabriel J. Chin. 2005. War on drugs or a war on immigrants? Expanding the definition of "drug trafficking" in determining aggravated felon status for noncitizens. *Maryland Law Review* 64(3): 875–909.

Latinas and the U.S. Criminal Justice System

Sandra Del Valle, José Luis Morín, Maria Swimm, and Nitza Milagros Escalera

Many Latinas in the United States face challenges that increase the chances that they will be exposed to **violence**, crime, or harsh treatment within the criminal justice system. Socioeconomic conditions, language barriers, and immigration status are factors that often contribute to the vulnerability of these women to violence and unequal treatment in the context of U.S. society and its system of justice. Initiatives and reforms to address the issue of violence and disparities in treatment that Latinas experience have been proposed and, in some instances, have been enacted. The limitations of what has been done within localities and under domestic laws in the United States, however, has led advocates, scholars, as well as municipal legislative bodies in the United States to look to developing principles, norms, and laws in **international human rights** as a model for the creation of new standards and remedies for the promotion and protection of women in the United States. Economic, social, and cultural rights recognized under international human rights laws and standards are especially relevant to the socioeconomic, cultural, and linguistic needs of Latinas in relation to violence, crime, and the U.S. criminal justice system.

A Social, Economic, and Demographic Portrait of Latinas in the United States

Latinas in the United States are a dynamic and diverse population. They are young, are more likely to have children than are white women, and are engaged in the workforce. They are challenged by a number of social stressors which have kept their wages low and their educational attainment limited, however, and which leave many Latinas across the country continually living in poverty.

According to a Pew Hispanic Center report revised in 2008, of the more than 30 million adult Latinas/os in the United States, more than 48 percent are women (Gonzales 2008). The report provides important insights into the situation of Latinas in the United States: Almost half the Latina population was born either in the United States or born abroad to U.S. citizen parents; the other half was born abroad. Sixty percent of immigrant Latinas are from Mexico and the rest are from Central America, South America, or the Caribbean. Latinas tend to be younger than the white female population and are more likely to be within the traditional child-bearing age range. The median age for Latinas in the United States is 41 years old and for white women is 47 years old. The Latina population born in the United States is even younger—the median age is 39 years old. Whether native-born or immigrant, Latinas have a greater fertility rate than their white counterparts. Although 55 percent of Latinas reported that they speak either only English at home or speak English very well, more than 70 percent of immigrant Latinas reported not speaking English well. Latinas also tend to have less formal education than white women have. More than 35 percent of immigrant Latinas do not have a high school diploma as compared to just 10 percent of white women. Further, only 12 percent of immigrant Latinas have a college degree versus 28 percent of white women.

Although Latinas participate in the workforce at about the same rate as white women (approximately 60 percent), they earn significantly less regardless of their place of birth. One significant factor complicating the lives of many Latinas is that they are much less likely than non-Latina immigrants to be naturalized citizens. Only 31 percent of Latinas are naturalized versus 55 percent of non-Latina immigrant women. Together with family responsibilities, lack of formal education, and—for immigrant women—limited English skills, combined with entrenched **institutional racism**, Latinas often are relegated to the lowest rungs of the U.S. socioeconomic ladder. Latinas are twice as likely to live in poverty as are white women, 20 percent versus 11 percent (Gonzales 2008).

One cause of Latina poverty stems from their low educational attainment. For instance, 41 percent of Latinas fail to graduate high school on time with a standard diploma as compared to 22 percent of white girls. This has huge implications for the course of their lives; half of the Latinas without a high school diploma between the ages of 25 and 64 are not employed, and the annual average income of those that are employed is approximately $15,000. Teen pregnancy is a significant issue for Latinas; they are more likely to become pregnant before the age of 20 than are women of any other racial or ethnic group. Consequently, their high school careers are jeopardized and aspirations of higher education are never realized. For those Latinas who do go on to college, many likely will not obtain a bachelor's degree (National Women's Law Center 2009).

Most Latinas, however, begin high school with high aspirations. Ninety-eight percent expect to get their high school diploma and 80 percent want to obtain a college degree (National Women's Law Center and Mexican American Legal Defense and Educational Fund 2009, 6). That so many never obtain their high school diploma is demonstrative of the difficulty that Latinas experience achieving educational advancement. The reasons for this disconnect between aspiration and reality are complex, but they present in microcosm some of the most significant issues facing Latinas generally—childhood poverty that puts them at a disadvantage from the beginning of their educational careers and compounded over the years, the low expectations of educators, and pressure to conform to gender-role expectations that emphasize undertaking family responsibilities (National Women's Law Center 2009).

Although there is no research focusing exclusively on the experiences of Latinas in college, research on Latino college participation and completion indicates that the disparities between Latino and white degree attainment is even starker than the disparities in high school completion. Although 300,000 Latinos will enroll in a four-year college, only 60,000 will obtain a bachelor's degree (Fry 2004).

Some Latina girls turn to **gangs** to help them confront and negotiate the harsh realities which comprise their lives. Approximately 15 percent of gang members are Latinas; the majority are teenagers. In Southern California, **Chicana/o** (or **Mexican American**) gangs have existed since the 1920s. Chicanas have formed part of mixed Chicana/o gangs from the beginning. Some Chicanas formed their own gangs and others formed cliques within Chicano gangs (Díaz-Cotto 2006, 76).

Although Latinas join gangs for multiple reasons, gang culture provides a means for them to renegotiate the power structures of their lives. Many Latina girls must confront problems associated with poverty, inadequate school systems, discrimination, restricted gender roles, and fractured families, and some also have been the victims of physical or sexual abuse. As Molidor (1996) asserts, these disempowering phenomena can lead young Latinas to seek out gangs as alternative family structures. Poverty alone has been found to correlate with gang involvement, and increases in poverty levels in the 20th century and the 21st century have been followed by increased numbers of female gangs. Although it is legitimate to view female gang members as victims, some of them also engage in asocial conduct.

Studies indicate that girls need strong relationships with caring adults to help them maneuver through their teenage years successfully. They need positive role models, opportunities to explore sexuality at their own pace, and a chance to develop a sense of competency and worth. Many Latina teens, however, live in environments where exactly this type of support is missing, thus increasing the likelihood that they will end up involved in the criminal justice system.

Further, community-based resources often focus on the needs of boys. Consequently, without practical alternatives, once caught in the juvenile justice system girls are more likely to be detained for less-serious offenses than boys are, and they are detained for much longer. Racial and ethnic disparities follow Latina girls into the incarceration system as well. African American and Latina girls often are found to be overrepresented in secure detention. In 1994, 13 percent of the girls in secure detention were Latinas (Office of Juvenile Justice and Delinquency Prevention 1998, 2).

Latinas and Incarceration

Latinas' status in the United States as women, socio-economically poor, and challenged by discriminatory policies, accounts for their growing presence in the nation's incarceration system. The Bureau of Justice Statistics (2008b) indicates that Latinas represented more than 16 percent of women incarcerated in federal or state prisons and jails. **The Sentencing Project**, a national sentencing reform organization, however, has found that Latinas comprise approximately only 10 percent of the U.S. female population. In recent years, Latina presence in the nation's prisons and jails has grown. Between 1990 and 1996, the number of Latina prisoners increased by 71 percent (Human Rights Watch 2002). From 2000 to 2006, Latinas' portion of the incarcerated population grew by 4.9 percent compared to the overall 3.4 percent increase in the female population. Although the imprisonment rate for Latinos decreased between 2000 and 2007, the rate for Latinas grew from 2000 to 2006 and then stagnated. Latinas were more than 1.5 times more likely than white women to be incarcerated (Bureau of Justice Statistics 2008b). One out of every 45 Latinas can expect to go to prison during her lifetime (Bonczar 2003, 8).

One significant reason for the increased incarceration of Latinas is the United States' declared war against **drugs.** Human Rights Watch notes (2003) that the focus of the drug war has been almost exclusively on the zealous enforcement of anti-drug laws and the adoption of punitive sentencing policies that disproportionately affect—if not outright target—people of color. Supporting that argument, the Bureau of Justice Statistics indicates that in 1999, 46 percent of defendants charged with a drug offense were Latinas/os (Scalia 2001, 5). Further, The Sentencing Project (2003) notes that despite equal **drug use** proportionate to their population, Latinas/os were twice as likely as whites to be sent to a state prison for a drug offense.

In 1968, Richard Nixon declared a war on drugs, and in 1973 he created the Drug Enforcement Administration. Since then, the rhetoric against drug crimes has intensified, the budget for drug enforcement has increased exponentially, the expansion of anti-drug activity has broken through international borders, and mandatory sentencing laws have increased the prison population (Garland 2001; Scalia 2001), fueling an explosion in prison construction and making the United States the world's leader in incarceration rates (Garland 2001). As with men of color, Latinas were increasingly subsumed by the mass incarceration phenomenon, often unable to navigate a criminal justice system that required resources that were beyond their means. By 1990, 78.9 percent of felony sentences for women in New York were for drug violations, and Latinas—who comprised 28.8 percent of women arrested, made up 41.2 percent of women sentenced for drug offenses (Mann 1995, 128).

Over the last several decades, the United States also targeted crack cocaine users. Crack is the type of cocaine most often used by low-income **drug users**, as opposed to powder cocaine which is more often used by middle- and upper-class whites. The Anti-Drug Abuse Act of 1986 mandated stiffer sentences for possession of crack than of powder cocaine. In 1999, the average prison term in federal prisons was 77 months for powder cocaine and 114 months for crack (Scalia 2001, 9). Other laws requiring tough mandatory minimum sentences—including the harsh **Rockefeller drug laws** of New York—were enacted throughout the country with the intent to imprison major drug traffickers or so-called drug "kingpins." It has been noted, however, that these laws actually have done more to incarcerate low level drug offenders than kingpins. Only 16 percent of the incarcerated drug offenders reported being an importer, grower, or manufacturer of illicit drugs. Twenty-five percent reported that they distributed drugs to street-level dealers (Scalia 2001, 1).

National data specifically focused on the drug-related incarceration of Latinas is not available. In New York, however, Latinas comprise 14 percent of the state's prison population but constitute 44 percent of women sentenced to prison for drug offenses (Mauer, Potler, & Wolf 1999). Although Latinas use drugs less frequently than do white women, they are more likely to be incarcerated for drug violations. In 1990, Latinas comprised 18.7 percent of women arrested for drug violations but more than 26 percent of those imprisoned for drug offenses, and white women accounted for more than 48 percent of the women arrested for drug offenses but only 38 percent of those sentenced to prison (Mann 1995).

Latinas who are involved in the drug trade often are on the lowest rungs of the drug-enterprise ladder. Although they are underpaid for their dangerous work, they face stiff prison sentences. Further, because they have little access to the most powerful drug lords, they are less likely to have

The Experience of Latinas and the Criminal Justice System in the 1990s

Studies point to Latinas being sentenced to prison for felonies—most often for drug-related offenses—at a greater rate than that for African American or white women in California, New York, and Florida in the 1990s (Mann 1995; Díaz-Cotto 2006, 23–24). The following passage describes a common occurrence for Latinas entering New York's criminal justice system for drug violations.

> Latinas, particularly those with no previous arrest records, tended to reject plea-bargain offers, believing that they would be found innocent. However, most did not have the financial resources to post bails or hire private attorneys as did middle- and upper-class women charged with similar crimes. Other Latinas, even when innocent, frequently pled guilty to a lesser offense in order to get a reduced sentence. Likewise, poor women could not afford to pay the cost of private recovery programs accessible to women with higher incomes. Thus, addicted Latinas often ended up in the criminal justice system, where treatment was usually not an option due to lack of available programs and to mandatory sentencing laws (Díaz-Cotto 2006, 24).

Sources: Díaz-Cotto, Juanita. 2006. *Chicana lives and criminal justice.* Austin, TX: University of Texas Press.

Mann, Coramae Richey. 1995. Women of color and the criminal justice system. In *The criminal justice system and women.* 2nd ed. Edited by Barbara Raffel Price and Natalie J. Sokoloff, 118–35. New York: McGraw-Hill.

valuable information to trade with prosecutors for reduced charges. Immigrant Latinas sometimes are used as "mules" transporting drugs for powerful Latinos engaged in transnational **drug trafficking**. Latinas who lack proper immigration documentation also are reported to **Immigration and Customs Enforcement** (ICE) agencies for **deportation**.

Overall, once arrested, Latinas/os are less likely to be channeled into alternative-to-incarceration programs than are African Americans and whites, leading to their overrepresentation in pretrial detention centers. Those Latinas/os already in detention are more likely to ultimately be sentenced to prison than are those participating in treatment or alternative-to-incarceration programs at the time of sentencing. Additionally, in 1997, Latinas/os composed the smallest percentage of the federal prison population receiving any form of substance abuse treatment at 36.4 percent, as compared with whites at 53.7 percent and African Americans at 48.4 percent (Arboleda 2002, 8). Thus, as with their male counterparts, Latinas face severe obstacles to receiving alternative sentences or access to **drug treatment** once imprisoned.

The disparities in sentencing that inequities resulting from tougher sentences for crack cocaine (which is found in greater use in Latina/o and African American communities) as compared to powder cocaine (used more frequently by whites), only recently have been addressed in new legislation. The Fair Sentencing Act passed by the U.S.

Congress in 2010 provides for new federal sentencing guidelines that increase the five-year mandatory minimum sentence level from 5 grams of crack to 28 grams and the 10-year mandatory minimum sentence level from 50 grams to 280 grams. Although some defendants might receive a fairer sentence, some people think that much will not change. For instance, the new law increases penalties for an aggravated felony for drug kingpins who coerce a girlfriend or family member into drug dealing, but federal prosecutors and judges had already been taking that into consideration. Federal public defenders believe that the law does not go far enough to create fairness, and critics of the law point out that people imprisoned since the 1980s and 1990s are not able to benefit from the changes, and continue to serve their sentences rendered under the old laws.

States nationwide also recently have begun scaling back strict drug laws that have been in the books for decades in an effort to address unfair outcomes and the disproportionate impact on African American and Latina/o communities. In 2009, three states—Minnesota, New York and Rhode Island—reduced mandatory minimum drug sentences, with New York reforming its much criticized **Rockefeller Drug Laws** by eradicating mandatory minimums for the first and second offense for certain drug charges and allowing the resentencing of approximately 1,500 people who were sentenced under the previous laws (Porter 2010). The impact of these recent changes on the growing incarceration rates of Latinas and Latinos is still unclear.

Racial and immigrant profiling, selective enforcement of drug laws, and sentencing disparities all make it more likely that Latinas will be caught within the criminal justice system and face long jail sentences. Immigrant profiling is a phenomenon in which law enforcement personnel rely on Latino physical and linguistic characteristics to stop, question, and even search individuals who they believe might not have proper immigration documentation. Studies show that Latinas/os are vulnerable to harsher penalties because of racial biases that unfairly associate Latinas/os with illegal drug activity, low intelligence, and a rise in neighborhood crime. Further, difficulties in obtaining adequate legal assistance, insufficient resources for posting bail, lack of family to provide a network of support, and the failure to provide translated court documents for recently immigrated Latinas make it more likely that Latinas will be incarcerated or receive long sentences.

The Impact of Incarceration on Latinas

Incarceration affects almost every aspect of a Latina's life, and reentry into the social and civic lives of their communities is enormously challenging. Imprisonment results in many—sometimes unforeseen—consequences for Latinas. One common outcome is that incarcerated Latinas face the possibility of losing custody of their children while incarcerated. The Adoption and Safe Families Act passed by Congress in 1997 requires states to terminate the parental rights of children who have been in foster care for 15 of the prior 22 months, subject to limited exceptions. In 2006, the median sentence imposed by state courts for nonviolent drug offenses was 36 months, and for property offenses was 24 months (Cohen & Kyckelhahn 2010, 13). Thus, Latinas are likely to receive sentences long enough to jeopardize custody of their children. As of 2006, Latina/o children comprised 15 percent of those in foster care—a 4 percent increase since 2000—and make up the only racial or ethnic population that experienced a rise in foster care placement (Child Welfare

Information Gateway 2009). At least one state had argued that parental rights ought to be terminated when parents had been in prison since the date the child was placed in foster care, because incarceration made it impossible for parents to have addressed the issues that caused the child's removal.

Private housing is more difficult to find when there is no recent record of employment or credit history, and felony or drug convictions disqualify Latinas from obtaining public housing. Employment also is vastly more difficult to attain. Many employers conduct background checks and some employment opportunities are completely foreclosed to individuals with criminal convictions. Some of those employment possibilities, such as working in a child-care setting, attract women in particular and could be a route out of poverty for previously incarcerated Latinas. Escaping poverty has been made even more difficult by the Personal Responsibility and Work Opportunity Reconciliation Act, passed in 1996, which allows states to restrict access to public benefits for anyone with a drug-related conviction—which includes more than half of the women reentering communities.

As the rate of Latina incarceration has continued increasing without indication that it will subside, it is important to examine the conditions that make it difficult for incarcerated Latinas to succeed. The **war on drugs** and national incarceration policies that targeted people of color and the poor; the lasting impact of the country's economic downturn and the ever-growing gap between rich and poor; and discrimination and abuses against immigrants are among the multiple factors that contribute to rendering U.S. Latinas vulnerable to the excesses and consequences of the criminal justice system.

Latina Victimization

The various aspects surrounding the victimization of Latin American women are wide-ranging and complex. Each day Latinas are the **victims** of physical and sexual violence in their homes and in their communities, at the hands of partners, spouses, and others who use various methods to intimidate, oppress, and further disenfranchise them. Latinas endure additional burdens stemming from societal norms that further complicate and inhibit their ability to overcome ill-treatment. Sexual and **intimate partner violence** continue to plague the Latina female population at alarming rates, and **human trafficking** and **femicide** have exhibited international dimensions. Latina victimization in combination with inexorable governmental disregard, has laid the foundation for a shameful history of gender injustice within the Latina community.

According to the National Crime Victimization Survey, there were 255,630 rapes and sexual assaults in 2006. Among these incidences, approximately 60 percent were committed by someone known to the victim, such as an intimate partner, friend, relative, or acquaintance (Bureau of Justice Statistics 2008a). Although comprehensive data on Latina victims of sexual violence is not available, it is widely understood by practitioners and community advocates that women of color are at serious risk for rape and sexual assault, although reported incidences are less than those for white women. Results from the 2000 National Violence Against Women Survey—an effort based on projections from a national sample survey—indicate that approximately 7.9 percent of Latinas will be raped over the course of their lifetime (Young Women's Christian Association 2009).

The stigma associated with women's sexuality and legal issues surrounding immigration status appear to keep many victims from reporting or talking about their experiences to law enforcement agencies and others who might be able to provide medical assistance or psychological support. Those Latinas in the United States who attempt to seek redress for intimate partner violence face innumerable obstacles, including linguistic barriers in the criminal justice system and the lack of adequate culturally competent services.

Intimate partner violence—commonly referred to as **domestic violence**—can involve physical, psychological, and emotional abuse. The domestic episodes experienced by women range from isolated incidences of physical battery to daily occurrences of emotional torment over an extended period. The violent domination of women by men has been so common as to make it socially accepted to use emotional and physical punishment as a means for Latino men to maintain the control of their partners, creating a cycle of violence within homes and communities. Intimate partner violence is not a crime unique to the Latina/o communities, however. In fact, in a study of intimate partner violence cases in large urban countries throughout the United States, the Bureau of Justice Statistics found that both victims and defendants in intimate partner violence cases were about equal percentages of white, African American, and Latina/o.

Gender and Race/Hispanic (Latino) origin of intimate partner violence victims and defendants in 16 large urban counties, May 2002

Demographic characteristic	Percent of intimate partner violence	
	Victims	Defendants
Total	100%	100%
Gender		
Male	14.0%	86.3%
Female	86.0	13.7
Race/Hispanic (Latino) origin		
White non-Hispanic	37.1%	33.6%
Black non-Hispanic	26.4	33.5
Hispanic	33.6	30.8
Other non-Hispanic	2.8	2.0

Source: Smith, Erica L., and Donald J. Farole, Jr. 2009. *Profile of intimate partner violence cases in large urban counties.* NCJ 228193. Washington, DC: Bureau of Justice Statistics. http://bjs.ojp.usdoj.gov/content/pub/pdf/pipvcluc.pdf (p. 3).

Whereas "***machismo***" refers to male characteristics that are valued within a social and cultural context, such as physical strength and sexual prowess, "***marianismo***" centers on the ideas of feminized passivity and sexual purity, and the ideal Latina is submissive, compliant, and loyal. Rigid gender-role identification and the expectation that a woman should submit to the control of her male mate aid in the creation of oppressive conditions in which violence and degradation thrive. Any deviance from these prescribed behaviors is believed to be the fault of the woman which, in turn promotes a culture of self-blaming by victims of sexual and intimate partner violence. These widely accepted behavioral norms for men and women have directly affected the way Latinas view themselves and how they deal with their victimization. Many women are silenced for fear of being ridiculed by their communities and rejected by their families. To further exacerbate the seriousness of this problem, victimization in both childhood and adulthood is viewed by professionals and practitioners to be closely related to the ever-increasing number of Latinas abusing substances to cope with their emotional, psychological, and physical distress.

Contemporary Forms of Slavery and Femicide Among Indigenous and Non-Indigenous Latinas

Human trafficking involves the "recruitment, transportation, transfer, harboring, or receipt of a person by threat or use of force, abduction, deception, or abuse of power or vulnerability for the purpose of exploitation, including sexual exploitation, forced labor, **slavery**, or similar practice" (United Nations Office on Drugs and Crime 2010). Although the most recent statistics indicate that more than 12.3 million adults and children were known to have been forced into labor and prostitution around the world, human trafficking has long been viewed as a women's issue. At the end of fiscal year 2009, the U.S. Department of State (2010) reported that women comprised 56 percent of the world's known trafficking victims. Human trafficking specifically affects Latinas who come from impoverished communities where financial and civic opportunities are scarce and gender inequity is commonplace. Although firm numbers of individuals who have been trafficked to the United States from Latin America are unknown, the primary foreign countries or origins of victims certified by the United States in 2009 included Mexico, Guatemala, and the Dominican Republic.

The majority of human trafficking in the world takes the form of forced labor, but trafficked women also are threatened and coerced into working in all facets of the sex trade, risking their lives and health. The contemporary sex-trafficking industry involves the systematic rape, exploitation, and even murder of Latinas, many of whom are exposed to HIV and sexually transmitted infections and often suffer acute drug and alcohol addictions. Indigenous women from Brazil, El Salvador, and Mexico, have been specifically targeted for **sex crimes** consistently over time and with impunity. Forced sterilization, the targeting of women for rape by national armies and other organizations, and the commercial sexual exploitation of young girls long have remained ever-present obstacles for native Latinas. Blatant disregard for the indigenous community—rooted in ethnic intolerance and socio-economic discrimination—remains an impediment that governments must acknowledge if women are to be given the rightful protection they deserve.

Femicide, commonly defined as the gender-motivated murder of women, remains the most extreme and disconcerting crime suffered by Latina victims. At the forefront of the international human rights agenda of Latina/o activists, researchers, and supporters, femicide has devastated the women of Mexico and Guatemala. In the border town of Ciudad Juárez, more than 400 murders have been reported since 1993, with many of the Mexican victims having been "abducted, raped, sexually assaulted, tortured, and, in some cases, mutilated" (Beltrán & Freeman 2007, 2). An estimated 2,500 women have been violently killed in Guatemala since 2001, with recorded cases increasing consistently each year thereafter. The eruption of murders has been directly attributed to the growing perception of women as rejecting the culturally prescribed gender identities which demand that they remain docile, subservient, and modest.

A significant number of femicide victims have worked in *maquiladoras*—sweatshop-type factories linked to free trade zones that employ women at low and often insufficient wages—supporting the notion that class discrimination is a contributing factor in femicide. Corrupt, ill-equipped authorities have historically done little to investigate or prosecute those responsible for the murders and have been known to extract confessions from scapegoats through unlawful methods. Many cases have been inadequately investigated as law enforcement and judicial institutions remain shrouded by gender biases, resulting in a failure to prosecute and punish those responsible and further contributing to a climate of impunity.

Social and economic barriers are persistent across nations for many women who have been victimized. Such unrelenting conditions force women and girls to remain unaware about their legal protections and unable to adequately exercise their rights. Latinas also must deal with culturally generated gender biases that prevent law enforcement from appropriately responding to the urgency of their victimization and further impose on their ability to seek the support they require. Scholars and advocates alike find that Latina victimization cannot be addressed without a comprehensive, multinational reevaluation of the value placed on Latina lives.

Latinas and the Legal Profession

On August 6, 2009, Justice Sonia Sotomayor was sworn in as the first Latina and the third woman to be a member of the United States Supreme Court. Although the Latina/o community celebrated this milestone, it was also evident that Latinas—along with other women of color—still are too few in number and that those in the profession often are not viewed or treated as equals. For Latina/o communities, the dearth of Latina and Latino lawyers also means that there are few attorneys familiar with Latina/o communities and their needs and too few are available to meet the many needs for legal services within the growing Latina/o population.

A study by the American Bar Association's Commission on Women in the Profession (2006) found that women of color are typically invisible in the legal profession. Although their numbers have increased, they still are underrepresented in proportion to their numbers in the general population and are marginalized in traditional law firm settings. Many women of color abandon the profession to seek other types of work.

In 2009, the Hispanic National Bar Association (NHBA) issued a specific report on the situation of Latinas in the legal profession, *Few and Far Between: The Reality of Latina Lawyers*. According to the study, "Latinas—who make up 7% of the total U.S. population and are part of the largest and fastest-growing ethnic and racial group in the United States—represent only 1.3% of the nation's lawyers, the lowest representation of any ethnic or racial group as compared to their overall presence in the nation" (Cruz & Molina 2009).

The number of Latinas who are judges is even smaller. "There are 49 women of color serving as federal judges across the country. Of this total, 18 are [Latinas]" (National Women's Law Center & Mexican American Legal Defense and Educational Fund 2009). Precise data on the number of Latinas who serve as state judges is unavailable. In 2002, however, **LatinoJustice/PRLDEF** issued a report that found that Latinas/os "held only 3.8 percent of the judgeships at the state level" (Falcón 2002, 3). Increasing the number of Latina judges at the federal, state, and municipal levels is considered important not simply because the racial-ethnic composition of the bench should reflect the diversity of the larger society, but

Women of Color in the Legal Profession

The American Bar Association's Commission on Women in the Profession issued a report on the status of women of color in the profession, *Visible Invisibility: Women of color in law.* Below are some of the Commission's key findings.

- Almost half of the associates in private law firms are now women and 15% are attorneys of color, but in 2004 only 17% of law partners were women and only 4% were attorneys of color. In the late 1990s, the National Association of Law Placement (NALP) found that more than 75% of minority female associates had left their jobs in private law firms within five years of being hired, and after eight years the percentage of those leaving rose to 86%. By 2005, 81% of minority female associates had left their law firms within five years of being hired.
- Nearly half of women of color but only 3% of white men experienced demeaning comments or harassment.
- Nearly two-thirds of the women of color but only 4% of white men were excluded from informal and formal networking opportunities, marginalized, and peripheral to professional networks within the firm. They felt lonely and deprived of colleagues with whom they could share important career-related information.
- Forty-four percent of women of color but only 2% of white men reported having been denied desirable assignments.
- Nearly one-third of women of color but less than 1% of white men felt they received unfair performance evaluations.
- The stress of second-class citizenship in law firms led many women of color to reconsider their career goals. The retention rates of women of color and white men reflected their lopsided experiences: 53% of women of color and 72% of white men chose to remain in law firms (Commission on Women in the Profession 2006, 9–10).

because Latina judges could bring a greater understanding of the culture of the parties that utilize the courts.

Research indicates that Latinas face many hurdles to entering and being accepted into the legal profession. Gaining access to legal careers is not easy for Latinas because they often lack exposure to the profession and lack role models who can serve as mentors or guides. Latinas typically experience isolation and alienation in law school because they can be the only Latina in the class or be one of a few Latinas. These women often believe that they must work harder to fit into the law school environment. Because of their gender, race, and ethnicity, Latinas frequently experience bias—their abilities and qualifications often are questioned, and professional advancement is hindered. As a result, there is a clear need to improve and expand mentoring programs, to recruit more role models, increase outreach efforts to Latinas enrolled in law schools, and to educate the greater society about the gross **underrepresentation** of Latinas in the legal profession.

Latinas and the Law

The 2009 National Hispanic Bar Association study on Latina lawyers provides insights into what many Latinas face in becoming a lawyer and in attempting to advance in the profession. The following are some of the major findings from the report.

The Importance of Strong Attorney and Latina Role Models

The vast majority of Latinas in the study were not exposed to attorneys growing up. As a result, they did not consider a career in the legal profession until college or later.

Parental Support for Education

The parents of the Latinas in the study placed a high value on being well-educated as a means to a better life; this was an important factor in the Latinas' ability to overcome significant educational barriers, including institutionalized discouragement. The path to law school was indirect and serendipitous for most of the Latinas in this study. However, the high value their parents placed on education served as a catalyst for them to eventually pursue this route.

The Law School Cultural Divide

The Latinas in the study were often one of the very few Latinas—or the only Latina—in their law schools. This minority status led to feelings of isolation and alienation, exacerbated by a significant cultural divide that distanced them socially and academically from their non-Latina peers. This contributed to feelings of self-doubt and the belief that they needed to work harder than others to fit in and succeed.

The Intersection of Gender, Ethnicity, and Race

As ethnically and racially diverse females, the Latinas appear to have encountered a multilayered glass ceiling that acts as a three-way threat to their careers. Although gender, ethnicity, and race are intertwined, gender bias and stereotyping appear to be the greatest obstacles to their retention and career advancement. At their workplaces, the Latinas have confronted gender and cultural expectations and assumptions about their roles as attorneys. They have been subjected to overt sexism, have lacked influential mentors, and have struggled with the conflicting demands of career and motherhood.

Devaluation of Qualifications and Abilities

The Latinas believe their legitimacy, qualifications, and abilities as attorneys are often questioned or devalued by their employers, coworkers, clients, and the general population. For example, they are often mistaken for someone other than the attorney (e.g., court reporter, interpreter, paralegal) both in the workplace and in court. Moreover, from admission into law school and throughout their careers, their place within the legal profession is questioned and devalued.

Isolation in the Workplace

The lack of Latina attorneys in the legal profession contributes to their feelings of isolation and alienation as one of the few or only Latinas in their workplaces. They are often placed in token positions and burdened by additional diversity-related roles and responsibilities. Their sense of "otherness" compels many to mask or disavow their Latina identity to assimilate within the dominant culture of their workplaces.

Race Matters

Latinas' experiences in the legal profession have varied according to others' perceptions of their racial identity. The Latinas who believe they can "pass as white" acknowledge that they are treated better and afforded more opportunities in the legal profession than darker-skinned Latinas (Cruz & Molina 2009).

Latinas in the Legal Profession

A number of Latina attorneys who attained national prominence are profiled in *Notable Hispanic American Women, Book I*. Among the attorneys whose careers are featured are those listed below.

- *Lourdes G. Baird*, born in 1935, graduated from law school in 1977, became a superior court judge in 1988 and later was nominated to be United States Attorney General for California's Central District.
- *Vilma S. Martinez*, born in 1943, graduated from Columbia University School of Law in 1967. That same year she joined the legal staff at the NAACP Legal Defense Fund and in 1973 was appointed president and general counsel of the Mexican American Legal Defense and Educational Fund (MALDEF). Ms. Martinez later rose to serve as the U. S. Ambassador to Argentina.
- *Irma Vidal,* born in 1924, graduated from Brooklyn Law School in 1961. That same year she became the first Puerto Rican woman admitted to the New York State Bar, and in 1983 she became the first Puerto Rican to win a seat on the New York State Supreme Court. Throughout her career she belonged to community groups that advanced the rights of Puerto Ricans in New York City.
- *Grace Olivarez,* born in 1922, in 1970 became the first woman and Latina graduate of Notre Dame Law School. She was a professor of law at the University of New Mexico Law School, was appointed by President Johnson to the National Advisory Council on the War on Poverty and by President Carter as the Director of the Community Services Administration (Telgen & Kamp 1993).

Latinas in Law Enforcement, Corrections, and Probation

As of 2003, women filled about 12.7 percent of the sworn positions in large law-enforcement agencies nationwide. Women of color, however, comprise just 4.8 percent of this workforce (National Center for Women & Policing 2003, 2). The absence of any precise data about Latinas in law enforcement exemplifies the persistent **invisibility of Latinas** in law enforcement agencies, including in police, corrections, and probation agencies. Historians, for instance, have documented the hiring of the first female police officer in the nation, Alice Stebbins Wells, a white woman, in 1910 and the hiring of the first African-American female officer, Georgina Robinson, in 1920. To date, however, there is no research documenting when the first Latina police officer was hired at the local, state, or federal level. Similar to the lack of Latina lawyers and judges, low numbers of Latinas in law enforcement translates not only into an absence of representation of a significant segment of the U.S. population, it also signals an absence of participation, decision making, and the ability to effect change in the field of law enforcement.

Latina/o police societies in New York City and Texas can be credited for providing some of the history that exists about Latina police officers. During the 1950s, the New York City Police Department (NYPD) had at least one Latina on its force. The archives of the **Hispanic Society of the New York City Police Department** indicate that Police Officer Isabel Barber and a handful of her male colleagues were the founders of the NYPD's Hispanic Society in 1957 (New York Police Department Hispanic Society [n.d.]).

In 1966, Sheriff Barbara Ponza joined the Santa Clara Sheriff's Department and then became a member of the National Latino Peace Officers Association (NLPOA) when it was founded in 1974. The NLPOA made history when it elected Officer Barbara Ponza to the board of its national office. She became the first Latina law enforcement officer to hold national office in a Hispanic police society. Officer Cindy Villarreal also made the list of the firsts in 1975 when she "became the first Latina officer at the Dallas Police Department" (Malaspina [n.d.]). Despite these advances, even in the 21st century Latinas still can earn the bittersweet achievement of being the *first* Latinas in many police departments.

The passage of **civil rights** legislation in the 1960s and the Equal Employment Opportunity Act of 1972 greatly enhanced opportunities for women to enter the field of **policing**. Noting that the presence of women in large police agencies increased about one-half of a percentage point each year from 1972 to 1999, the National Center for Women & Policing has expressed concern that that trend might be on the decline or reversing. Data shows that in 2000 and 2001 the numbers of women in large law-enforcement police agencies declined from the previous years—14.3 percent in 1999, to 13.0 percent in 2000, and down to 12.7 percent in 2001. At that rate, "women will not achieve equality in large police agencies for several generations if at all" given the existing barriers within the profession and "few agencies have specific strategies for increasing the number of women within their ranks" (National Center for Women & Policing 2003).

Although many law enforcement departments have adopted affirmative action programs, gender-equality policies, and cultural-sensitivity programs, the field of law enforcement continues to be a domain that is not always hospitable, respectful, or accepting of women.

Harassment and discrimination based on gender and race or ethnicity has been a recurring problem for Latinas and African American women in law enforcement. In 2007, the Guardians Association, an NYPD fraternal organization championing the rights of African American NYPD officers, filed a federal lawsuit against the NYPD alleging that three "African American women and Latina Police Officers . . . were targeted and demeaned at a precinct roll call and called 'hos' and 'nappy headed hos' by their sergeant and then by a male cop who followed suit" (Guardians Association 2007). In July 2008, eight Latina employees of the San Luis Obispo Probation Department filed suit against the county, claiming harassment and discrimination because of their race and gender. The employees alleged that they were subject to unequal treatment in promotions, training, workload, and supervisory requirements. The Probations Department Human Resource Manager, Antonia Herrera, claimed that racial slurs and discriminatory and harassing conduct was tolerated. The lawsuit also stated that complaints were ignored and that a 2007 county investigation found allegations of harassment and intimidation by a male officer to be accurate.

Increasing the presence of Latina police, corrections, and probation officers might produce positive results for Latino communities and the entire criminal justice system. As the National Center for Women and Policing (2003) had noted, women, generally, benefit police departments because women are less likely to use excessive force, are more likely to implement "community oriented policing," and are more responsive to crimes of violence. Gender-based discrimination and harassment against women also are less likely to occur in departments having a substantial female presence. Consistent with a growing concern about the absence of culturally competent services, Latina criminal justice professionals, in particular, would also add the important cultural and linguistic capacity that the criminal justice system sorely needs. Latinas afraid of reporting intimate partner violence to the police might feel more comfortable if there were Spanish-speaking or culturally sensitive Latina officers and employees with whom to speak. Increasing the number of Latinas in positions in the criminal justice system would increase the likelihood that they will participate in policy making decisions. Bringing their culturally relevant experiences and depth of knowledge to the table, they could promote policies that could have a positive impact on the lives of Latinas/os in the criminal justice system and in their communities.

Some efforts that can help increase the number of Latinas in law enforcement include establishing mentoring programs within law enforcement departments, establishing "family-friendly" work polices that allow women to achieve a greater balance between their home and work lives, and reaching into the civilian workforce for promotion opportunities.

Latinas and Criminal Justice: Moving Forward

In the United States, the challenges Latinas face are significant and complex. They involve issues concerning language, culture, immigration status, and gender. The United States, for its part, has not adequately responded. The result is that many Latinas live in poverty, join gangs, drop out of school, or never enter post-secondary institutions. Additionally, numerous cases of domestic abuse go unreported. In other instances, many Latina immigrants bring with them the scars of negative experiences in their native countries—such as women who have been the victims of **human trafficking**. At the same time, Latina presence in jails and prisons continues to increase.

To address inequities and to make the criminal justice system more responsive to the needs of Latinas, some criminal justice scholars and nonprofit monitoring and advocacy agencies—including the American Civil Liberties Union and the Brennan Center for Justice at New York University School of Law—have called for multidimensional and comprehensive changes in national policies and priorities (*see, e.g.,* American Civil Liberties Union 2005). Among the reforms commonly called for by such groups are the elimination of mandatory minimum sentences and the use of alternatives to incarceration (*see also*, Human Rights Watch 2003). Attention to specific issues affecting Latinas has been called for, including the need to repeal laws that penalize women for their association with people involved in drug activities rather than for their own conduct; the ending of racial and immigrant profiling performed by law enforcement personnel; requiring collection and publication of ethnic/racial/immigration status data by all federal enforcement agencies; and increasing the linguistic and cultural competence of the courts and all other parts of the criminal justice system.

Women in prison, including Latinas, are severely affected by the lack of adequate drug treatment, physical and mental health services, educational, and employment programs, and the absence of sufficient safe and affordable housing and employment opportunities to successfully reenter society upon release. To increase Latina achievement and diminish their vulnerability in encounters with the criminal justice system, changes in society's priorities and efforts that have garnered support by many academics and advocacy groups. Such changes include reforming the educational system to make it more responsive to Latinas' needs, including providing quality bilingual education programs; recruiting more Latina teachers at all educational levels so as to provide more role models; providing more mentoring opportunities; improving efforts to prevent teen pregnancy and improving programs to keep teen mothers in schools; increasing parental participation through extensive outreach and innovative programming; teaching to high academic standards and ensuring college readiness; and expanding early diagnostic services and early childhood education.

Latina victims of intimate partner violence commonly experience many complications as a result of a criminal justice system that too often is not responsive to their needs. Although Congress passed the Violence Against Women Act (VAWA) in 2000, which included the Battered Immigrant Women Protection Act, services and protections for immigrant women generally are considered lacking. Greater access to legal services and public benefits, and improvements in the way courts and judges adjudicate cases of gender violence are among the areas requiring additional attention. The reauthorization of the Violence Against Women Act in 2013 helped secure existing protections and services and in some instances expanded safeguards and services. The VAWA now assures **lesbian, gay, bisexual,** and **transgender** survivors access to the services; domestic violence victims in publicly subsidized housing can more easily relocate to different and safer locations; and college students are afforded increased protections.

Scholars and Latina/o advocates also have prioritized issues on their agendas for social change: The creation of culturally sensitive outreach programs and emergency services for Latina victims of violence, as well as the establishing of formal and informal linguistically appropriate, community-based support systems; and improving access to affordable legal assistance, specifically for those Latinas who are undocumented or whose immigration status otherwise might be in question.

Recruitment of multilingual and multicultural criminal justice professionals and ensuring that the criminal justice systems are consistently, strictly, and efficiently responding to intimate partner violence assaults and enforcing anti-trafficking laws are among the other public-policy priorities that frequently are cited. With respect to improving the perception and treatment of Latinas overall, the creation of comprehensive educational programs that concentrate on promoting the intrinsic value of Latinas, and efforts to combat negative stereotyping and *machismo* within and outside the Latinas' communities also are cited as important initiatives.

International Standards for Supporting Reform

Inadequacies or limitations in domestic laws and remedies have led women in the United States and around the world to look to developing laws, principles, norms, and remedies at the international level. As other groups have done, Latinas and Latinos have begun to look at the application and relevance of international human rights norms, principles, and treaties to their situations in the United States (*see, e.g.,* Morín 2009; Hernández-Truyol 1997). Among the major international human rights instruments adopted to promote and protect the rights of women is the Convention on the Elimination of all Forms of Discrimination Against Women (CEDAW).

The Convention on the Elimination of all Forms of Discrimination Against Women defines discrimination against women within the social, economic, political, and cultural context in which progress should be measured. It calls upon nations to take affirmative steps to not only overturn discrimination laws and practices, but to also enact new legislation and establish new institutions that ensure greater equality and justice for women. Article 1 of the Convention defines discrimination against women as "any distinction, exclusion or restriction made on the basis of sex which has the effect or purpose of impairing or nullifying the recognition, enjoyment or exercise by women, irrespective of their marital status, on a basis of equality of men and women, of human rights and fundamental freedoms in the political, economic, social, cultural, civil or any other field." Pursuant to article 3, CEDAW obligates all States to take "all appropriate measures, including legislation, to ensure the full development and advancement of women, for the purpose of guaranteeing them the exercise and enjoyment of human rights and fundamental freedoms on a basis of equality with men" (United Nations 1979).

For Latinas, the significance of the economic, social, and cultural dimensions of CEDAW cannot be overstated. Economic inequity—along with racial, ethnic, and linguistic discrimination—long has been a hallmark of the Latina experience in the United States. The lack of bilingual and bicultural legal and social service programs and Latinas' low socio-economic status present enormous obstacles for Latinas caught in violent circumstances or other forms of abuse. Many women and numerous countries around the world have used CEDAW as a model for affecting change in laws and practices that once were detrimental to women. The United Nations has documented numerous successes in securing the rights of women on issues of family law reform, land rights, inheritance, sexual harassment, and violence through the implementation of CEDAW in countries such as Morocco, Kyrgyzstan, Tajikistan, Bangladesh, Hungary, Kenya, and Mexico.

As of October 23, 2015, 189 out of 193 United Nations member states ratified CEDAW. The United States, however, together with a select few countries such as Iran, Sudan, and Somalia, have not ratified this treaty. Nonetheless, many human rights groups—such as Amnesty International and Human Rights Watch—view CEDAW as a vital tool for improving the status of women in the United States and advocate for its ratification and enforcement in the United States. In calling for U.S. ratification of CEDAW, Human Rights Watch (2009) points out that CEDAW would protect women's right to life, enhance women's equality in the workplace, and would take necessary action on the issue of trafficking of women and girls for exploitation as labor or prostitution. These issues are of particular relevance to Latinas in the United States.

Amnesty International (AI) (1999) has documented numerous human rights violations and abuses of women who are incarcerated in prisons and jails throughout the United States, including instances in which women have been subjected to sexual abuse by male guards, or instances of women in labor or women who were very ill or dying being kept handcuffed or chained to their beds. It has also noted that African American women, Latinas, and other women of color are disproportionately represented among incarcerated women. In accordance with the 1995 Beijing Declaration and Platform for Action, adopted at the Fourth World Conference on Women, AI has called for the United States to adhere to international treaties that it has ratified—such as the International Covenant on Civil and Political Rights of 1966—which prohibits torture or cruel, inhuman, or degrading treatment or punishment (Article 7); and which defines the right of any detained person to be treated with humanity and with respect for the inherent dignity of the human person (Article 10).

Amnesty International also has urged the United States to withdraw its reservations to the International Covenant on Civil and Political Rights, the Convention Against Torture and Other Cruel, Inhuman or Degrading Treatment or Punishment, and the International Convention on the Elimination of All Forms of Racial Discrimination, so that full protections under these treaties—which the United States has ratified—can be realized. The organization continues to urge the United States to ratify without reservations the Convention on the Elimination of All Forms of Discrimination Against Women as well as regional human rights instruments, such as the Inter-American Convention on the Prevention, Punishment and Eradication of Violence Against Women and the American Convention on Human Rights.

International human rights treaties that promote economic, social, and cultural rights, such as CEDAW and the 1966 Covenant on Economic, Social and Cultural Rights, have special significance for Latinas in the United States. International human rights law envisions meeting a range of economic, social, and cultural needs of Latinas who lack the financial resources to seek proper legal and other assistance and who are adversely affected by the dearth of linguistically and culturally competent services in the criminal justice and prison systems.

Limitations in obtaining justice in cases of violence against women in the United States have generated interest in international human rights organizations as venues for seeking redress. After exhausting all remedies in U.S. courts, Jessica Gonzales, a woman of Latina and Native American descent, filed a case with the Inter-American Commission on Human Rights (Inter-American Commission), a quasi-judicial organ of the

Organization of American States of which the United States is a member nation. Pursuant to the Commission's rules a case can be brought against a member state that fails to comply with the American Declaration on the Rights and Duties of Man (American Declaration). In the case, *Jessica Gonzales and Others v. United States*, Case 1490–05, Inter-Am. C.H.R., O.E.A/ser. I./R./52/07 (2007), Gonzales alleged that government agencies in the United States failed to take appropriate measures to prevent the death of Gonzales' three young daughters at the hands of her husband. Despite two intimate partner violence restraining orders requiring her husband to stay away from her and her children with mandatory arrest provisions under state law, Ms. Gonzales' due process rights under the U.S. Constitution allegedly were violated because police agents failed to enforce the law. The claims were rejected by the U.S. Supreme Court in the case of *Town of Castle Rock v. Gonzales*, 545 U.S. 748 (2005).

Ms. Gonzales' petition before the Inter-American Commission, however, was successfully admitted for a hearing on the merits in 2007, when the Commission held that the deaths of Gonzales' daughters were preventable and that the harms suffered violated the right to life and personal security under Article I, the right to protection of private and family life under Article V, the right to protection of the family under Article VI, and the right to special protection for mothers and children under Article VII of the American Declaration. The Inter-American Commission further found that the United States failed to investigate Ms. Gonzales' complaints, and did not provide her an effective remedy and access to information regarding the circumstances of the death of her daughters in violation of her rights to resort to courts under Article XVIII and to petition the government and receive a prompt decision under Article XXIV of the American Declaration.

Jessica Gonzales's case has received additional international attention, having been brought to the U.N. Committee on the Elimination of Racial Discrimination because the case represents an example of the intersection between race and gender discrimination that women of color commonly face in the United States. Jessica Gonzales's case is cited as a compelling example of the manner in which Latinas and other women of color are underserved and disserved by the criminal justice system and the courts (*see, e.g.,* Coker 2001). It also is a case that has brought national and international pressure to bear on the United States to ratify and implement CEDAW and other international human rights treaties.

Although the United States has yet to ratify CEDAW, some municipal governments use CEDAW as a model to enact local laws that seek to provide the same or similar protections. In 1998, San Francisco's city government passed an ordinance implementing CEDAW at the local level. To this end, a task force was formed to work with the San Francisco Commission on the Status of Women and City Departments to identify discrimination against women and girls, and to implement the human rights principles found in international law. San Francisco also maintains a website (http://www.sfgov.org/site/cosw_index.asp?id=10848) dedicated to educating the public about CEDAW and its implementation.

See also: Part I essays: The U.S. War on Drugs and Latina/o Communities; Incarceration and Latinas/os in the United States; Gangs in the United States and Latina/o Communities. Part II entries: Chicanas/os; Civil Rights; Human Trafficking; International Human Rights; Slavery; Underrepresentation of Latinas/os in the Legal Profession; Victims.

Further Reading

Aguirre, Jr., Adalberto, and David Baker. 1988. A descriptive profile of the Hispanic penal population: Conceptual and reliability limitations in public use data. *Justice Professional* 3(3): 189–200.

American Civil Liberties Union. 2005 (March 15). *Caught in the net: The impact of drug policies on women and families*. New York: American Civil Liberties Union. http://www.aclu.org/files/images/asset_upload_file431_23513.pdf.

Amnesty International. 1999. "Not part of my sentence": Violations of the human rights of women in custody. http://www.amnesty.org/en/library/asset/AMR51/001/1999/en/ab8c7840-e363-11dd-937fa170d47c4a8d/amr510011999en.html.

Arboleda, Angela. 2002. Latinos and the federal criminal justice system. Washington, DC: National Council of La Raza. http://www.nclr.org/images/uploads/publications/1414_file_SB1_LatinosFederalJustice.pdf.

Bales, Kevin, and Steven Lize. 2007. Investigating human trafficking: Challenges, lessons learned, and best practices. *FBI Law Enforcement Bulletin* 76: 24–31.

Beijing Declaration and Platform for Action. 1995. Adopted at Fourth World Conference on Women. Report of the Fourth World Conference on Women. UN Document. A/CONF.177/20, 17.

Beltrán, Adriana, and Laurie Freeman. 2007. *Hidden in plain sight: Violence against women in Mexico and Guatemala.* Washington, DC: Washington Office on Latin America.

Bettinger-Lopez, Caroline. 2008. Domestic violence as a human rights violation. 40 *Colum. Hum. Rights Law Review* 19–77.

Bonczar, Thomas P. 2003. Prevalence of imprisonment in the U.S. population, 1974–2001, NCJ 197976. Washington, DC: Bureau of Justice Statistics.

Brown, Paulette, and Arina Reeves. 2006. *Visible invisibility: Women of color in law firms: Executive summary.* Chicago, IL: American Bar Association, Commission on Women in the Profession.

Bureau of Justice Assistance. 2001. Recruiting and retaining women: A self-assessment guide for law enforcement. *Bureau of Justice Assistance Bulletin.* Washington, DC: U.S. Department of Justice.

Bureau of Justice Statistics. 2008a. *Criminal victimization in the United States, 2006.* Washington DC: U.S. Department of Justice.

Bureau of Justice Statistics. 2008b. *Prisoners in 2007.* Washington, DC: U.S. Department of Justice.

Cardona, Felisa. 2010 (November 1). Federal sentencing guidelines change today for some drug crimes. *Denver Post.* http://www.denverpost.com/news/ci_16487678#ixzz142pjGyOt.

Child Welfare Information Gateway. 2009. Foster care statistics. http://www.childwelfare.gov/pubs/factsheets/foster.cfm#race. Accessed January 22, 1009.

Cohen, Thomas H., and Tracey Kyckelhahn. 2010. *Felony defendants in large urban counties, 2006.* NCJ 228944. Washington, DC: Bureau of Justice Statistics.

Coker, Donna. 2001. Crime control and feminist law reform in domestic violence law. *Buffalo Criminal Law Review* 4: 801–60.

Commission on Women in the Profession. 2006. *Visible invisibility: Women of color in law.* Washington, DC: American Bar Association. http://www.abanet.org/women/VisibleInvisibility-ExecSummary.pdf.

Constantino, Roselyn. 2006. Femicide, impunity, and citizenship: The old and new in the struggle for justice in Guatemala. *Chicana/Latina Studies* 6(1): 108–21.

Cruz, Jill L., and Melinda S. Molina (eds.). 2009. *Few and far between: The reality of Latina lawyers.* Washington, DC: National Hispanic Bar Association. http://www.hnba.com/publications/status-of-latinas-in-the-profession-report/. Accessed November 10, 2010.

Davison Aviles, Robert M., Manuel P. Guerrero, Heidi Barajas Howarth, and Glenn Thomas. 1999. Perceptions of Chicano/Latino students who have dropped out of school. *Journal of Counseling and Development* 77: 465–73.

Díaz-Cotto, Juanita. 2006. *Chicana lives and criminal justice*. Austin, TX: University of Texas Press.

Falcón, Angelo. 2002. *Opening the court house doors: The need for more Hispanic judges*. New York: Puerto Rican Legal Defense and Education Fund.

Fry, Richard. 2004. *Latino youth finishing college: The role of selective pathways*. Washington, DC: Pew Hispanic Center.

Fry, Richard, and Jeffrey S. Passel. 2009. *Latino children: A majority are U.S.–born offspring of immigrants*. Washington, DC: Pew Hispanic Center.

Garland, David (ed.). 2001. *Mass imprisonment: Social causes and consequences*. London: Sage Publications.

Gonzales, Felisa. 2008. *Hispanic women in the United States: 2007*. Washington DC: Pew Hispanic Center.

Guardians Association. 2007 (May/June). NYPD and their Counsel Bonita E. Zelman, Esq. *The Guardian*. http://nypdguardians.com/mayjunenewletter.pdf. Accessed November 14, 2010.

Hernández-Truyol, Berta Esperanza. 1997. Reconciling rights in collision: An international human rights strategy. In *Immigrants out! The new nativism and the anti-immigrant impulse in the United States*, edited by J. F. Perea, 254–76. New York: New York University Press.

Hudson, Lisa. 2003. *Racial/ethnic differences in the path to a postsecondary credential*. NCES. 2003–2005. Washington, DC: U.S. Department of Education.

Human Rights Immigrant Community Action Network. 2009. *Guilty by immigration status: A report on U.S. violations of the rights of immigrant families, workers and communities in 2008*. Oakland, CA: National Network for Immigrant and Refugee Rights.

Human Rights Watch. 2002. *Race and incarceration in the United States: Human Rights Watch briefing*. New York: Human Rights Watch.

Human Rights Watch. 2003 (April 28). *Incarcerated America: Human Rights Watch backgrounder*. New York: Human Rights Watch. http://www.hrw.org/en/reports/2003/04/28/incarcerated-america.

Human Rights Watch. 2009. United States ratification of international human rights treaties. http://www.hrw.org/en/news/2009/07/24/united-states-ratification-international-human-rights-treaties. Accessed November 9, 2009.

Kuh, George D., Jillian Kinzie, Jennifer A. Buckley, Brian K. Bridges, and John C. Hayek. 2006. *What matters to student success: A review of the literature*. Washington DC: National Postsecondary Educational Cooperative.

Ligiéro, Daniela. P., Ruth Fassinger, Moira McCauley, Jessica Moore, and Niina Lyyntinen. 2009. Childhood sexual abuse, culture, and coping: A qualitative study of Latinas. *Psychology of Women Quarterly* 33: 67–80.

Malaspina, Ann. [n.d.]. Wearing the badge: Latinas in law enforcement. *LatinaStyle*. www.latinastyle.com/currentissue/v11-4/f-wearing.html. Accessed October 1, 2009.

Mann, Coramae Richey. 1995. Women of color and the criminal justice system. In *The criminal justice system and women*. 2nd ed., edited by Barbara Raffel Price and Natalie J. Sokoloff, 118–35. New York: McGraw-Hill.

Mauer, Marc, and Ryan S. King. 2007. Uneven justice: State rates of incarceration by race and ethnicity. Washington, DC: The Sentencing Project.

Mauer, Marc, Cathy Potler, and Richard Wolf. 1999. *Gender and justice: Women, drugs, and sentencing policy*. Washington, DC: The Sentencing Project.

Merlo, Alida V., and Joycelyn M. Pollock. 2006. *Women, law and social control.* 2nd ed. Boston, MA: Pearson.

Molidor, Christian E. 1996. Female gang members: A profile of aggression and victimization. *Journal of Social Work* 41(3) 251–57.

Moore, Joan, and John Hagedorn. 2001. Female gangs: A focus on research. *Juvenile Justice Bulletin.* Washington DC: U. S. Department of Justice, Office of Justice Programs, Office of Juvenile Justice and Delinquency Prevention.

Morín, José Luis. 2009. *Latino/a rights and justice in the United States: Perspectives and approaches.* 2nd ed. Durham, NC: Carolina Academic Press.

National Center for Women & Policing. 2003. *Hiring and retaining more women: The advantages to law enforcement agencies.* Arlington, VA: Feminist Majority Foundation.

National Coalition of Hispanic Health and Human Services Organizations. 1999. *The state of Hispanic girls.* Washington, DC: COSSMHO Press.

National Latino Peace Officers Association. History. http://www.nlpoa.org/history.htm. Accessed December 5, 2009.

National Women's Law Center. 2009. *Women in the federal judiciary: Still a long way to go.* Washington DC: National Women's Law Center.

National Women's Law Center and Mexican American Legal Defense and Educational Fund. 2009. *Listening to Latinas: Barriers to high school graduation.* Washington, DC: National Women's Law Center.

New York Police Department Hispanic Society. [n.d.]. History. http://nypdhispanicsociety.org/history.asp. Accessed September 27, 2009.

Office of Juvenile Justice and Delinquency Prevention. 1998. Juvenile female offenders: A status of the states report. https://www.ncjrs.gov/pdffiles1/Digitization/174464NCJRS.pdf. Accessed October 23, 2015.

Porter, Nicole D. 2010. *The state of sentencing 2009: Developments in policy and practice.* Washington, DC: The Sentencing Project.

Ramirez, Rafael. 1999. Machismo. In *What it means to be a Puerto Rican man: Reflections on Puerto Rican masculinity.* New Brunswick, NJ: Rutgers University Press: 7–24.

Rivera, Jenny. 2002. The availability of domestic violence services for Latinas in New York State: Phase II Investigation. 21 *Buffalo Public Interest Law Journal*: 37–87.

Scalia, John. 2001. Federal drug offenders, 1999 with trends 1984–99. NCJ 187285. Washington, DC: Bureau of Justice Statistics. http://www.bjs.gov/content/pub/pdf/fdo99.pdf. Accessed October 22, 2015.

Schulz, Dorothy Moses. 1995. *From social worker to crime fighter: A history of women in the United States Policing.* Santa Barbara, CA: Praeger.

Sentencing Project, The. 2003. *Hispanic prisoners in the U.S.* Washington, DC: The Sentencing Project.

Sentencing Project, The. 2007. Women in the criminal justice system: Briefing sheets. http://www.sentencingproject.org/doc/publications/womenincj_total.pdf. Accessed November 14, 2010.

Smith, Erica L., and Donald J. Farole, Jr. 2009. *Profile of intimate partner violence cases in large urban counties.* NCJ 228193. Washington, DC: Bureau of Justice Statistics. http://bjs.ojp.usdoj.gov/content/pub/pdf/pipvcluc.pdf.

Smith, Selma Moidel. 1999. *A century of achievement: The centennial of the National Association of Women Lawyers.* Chicago: American Bar Association, Senior Lawyers Division.

Sorenson, Susan B., and Cynthia. A. Telles. 1991. Self-reports on spousal violence in a Mexican-American and non-Hispanic White population. *Violence and Victims* 6(1): 3–15.

Strum, Philippa, and Danielle Tarantolo (eds.). 2003. *Women immigrants in the United*

States. Washington, DC: Woodrow Wilson International Center for Scholars.

Telgen, Diane, and Jim Kamp (eds.). 1993. *Notable Hispanic American women, Book I.* Eagan, MN: Thomson-Gale.

UNiTE to End Violence against Women. 2008. *Fact Sheet: How widespread is violence against women?* New York: United Nations Department of Public Information, http://endviolence.un.org/docs/VAW.pdf.

United Nations. [n.d.]. CEDAW success stories. http://www.unifem.org/cedaw30/success_stories/#morocco. Accessed November 8, 2009.

United Nations. 1979. Convention on the Elimination of all Forms of Discrimination Against Women. Done at New York, Dec. 18, 1979. Entered into force, Sept. 3, 1981. U.N.G.A. Res. 34/180(XXXIV), 34 U.N. GAOR. Supp. (No. 46) 194, U.N. Doc. A/34/830 (1979), reprinted in 19 I.L.M. 33 (1980).

United Nations Office on Drugs and Crime. 2010. Human trafficking. http://www.unodc.org/unodc/en/human-trafficking/what-is-human-trafficking.html?ref=menuside.

University of New Brunswick. 2004. Researchers investigate the world of female corrections officers. *UNB Perspectives*. http://www.unb.ca/perspectives/view.php?=253.

U.S. Department of Justice. 2007. Guiding principles of the safe havens: Supervised visitation and safe exchange grant program. Washington DC: Office on Violence Against Women.

U.S. Department of State. 2010. *Trafficking in persons report, June 2010*. Washington DC: U.S. Department of State.

Valdez, Avelardo. 2007. *Mexican American girls and gang violence: Beyond risk*. New York: Palgrave Macmillan.

Velie, Karen. 2008 (July 23). Discrimination complaint filed against county. *Cal Coast News*. http://calcoastnews.com/2008/07/discrimination-complaint-filed-against-county/. Accessed November 14, 2010.

Violence Against Women Reauthorization Act of 2013. Public Law No. 113–4, 127 Stat. 54 (2013).

Walker, Nancy E., J. Michael Senger, Francisco A. Villarruel, and Angela M. Arboleda. 2004. *Lost opportunities: The reality of Latinos in the U.S. criminal justice system*. Washington, DC: National Council of La Raza.

Young Women's Christian Association. 2009. Violence and its impact on women's lives. http://www.ywca.org/site/pp.asp?c=djISI6PIKpG&b=281418.

Zarza, Maria J., Vicente Ponsoda, and Ricardo Carrillo. 2009. Predictors of violence and lethality among Latina immigrants: Implications for assessment and treatment. *Journal of Aggression, Maltreatment & Trauma* 18: 1–16.

Cases Cited

Bradwell v. State, 83 U.S. 16b Wall 130 (1873).

Gonzales v. United States, Case 1490–05, Inter-Am. C.H.R., O.E.A/ser. I./R./52/07 (2007).

Jessica Gonzales and Others v. United States, Case 1490–05, Inter-Am. C.H.R., O.E.A/ser. I./R./52/07 (2007).

Matter of G.Y., No. 02S05-0904-JV-146; 2009 Ind. LEXIS 484 (Ind. June 16, 2009).

Town of Castle Rock v. Gonzales, 545 U.S. 748 (2005).

Incarceration and Latinas/os in the United States

José Luis Morín, François Restrepo-Serrano, and Yolanda C. Martín

The United States today stands alone in the world for the vast number of persons it incarcerates. Latinas/os—along with other communities of color, most notably African Americans—are a population increasingly affected by high rates of imprisonment, a phenomenon referred to in the criminal justice literature as "**mass imprisonment**" or "mass incarceration." Many factors appear to converge to produce the increasing number of Latina/o prisoners. As is the case for African Americans, the construction of race in the United States provides fertile ground for the unequal treatment of Latinas/os within the criminal justice system. Although not identical, the Latina/o experience in the United States tends to mirror many patterns of domination and subordination endured by African Americans.

As with African Americans, Latinas/os have endured the indignities of **discrimination** throughout U.S. history. Today, African Americans and Latinas/os share the experience of hyper-incarceration stemming from myriad adverse policies, perceptions, and practices. Among the many factors contributing to their disproportionate rates of incarceration are the **war on drugs**, negative stereotypes and **media dipictions**, police practices and tactics, patterns of bias throughout the criminal justice system, and impediments related to immigrant status.

The formulation of public policy around the fear of crime, and the enormous role of media in driving crime policies based on fear are influential in producing incarceration rates skewed against African Americans and Latinas/os. Given that national data show a decline in the number of crimes committed since the 1990s, it appears that "crime rates themselves may not have driven the prison boom, but long-standing fears about crime and other social anxieties may form the backdrop for the growth in imprisonment" (Western 2006, 48). Moreover, since the 1960s, politics and policy making shifted from the "war on poverty" to the "war on crime" and the "**war on drugs**," often linking poverty with crime, especially poverty in "minority" communities (Beckett 1997). Notions about rehabilitation through the penal system gave way to a bourgeoning "culture of control," with fear-filled images of criminals as virtually irredeemable "'career criminals,' 'drug addicts,' 'thugs' and 'yobs'" (Garland 2001b, 135). Coupled with this imagery is a profoundly racialized victim—"not all **victims**, but primarily White, suburban, middle-class victims, whose exposure has driven waves of crime legislation" (Simon 2007, 76).

Modern crime legislation has come to represent victims in many powerfully symbolic ways, even when victims might not be referenced specifically in the legislation. Thus, even police officers themselves often are portrayed in such legislation as victims, not only of criminals, but of defense lawyers, soft-on-crime judges, misguided parole and probation officers, among others. Prison cells, meanwhile, are the purest expression of the public's embrace of and promise to protect the victims—and potential victims—of crime.

The construction of public policy around crime and the fear of crime, together with the role of the media in disseminating negative or incomplete images, has been influential in producing high incarceration rates that unfavorably affect persons of color. As many analysts point out, examining the conventional operation of the courts, law enforcement, and the criminal justice systems provides insights into the production of the racial and ethnic disparities evident in the penal system (*see, e.g.,* Beckett 1997; Garland 2001a, 2001b; Harris 2002; Haney López 2003). As is the case with African Americans, misconceptions associating Latinas/os with criminal behavior have been common; however, differences also exist. Most notably, Latinas/os often are the object of stereotypes that, according to research, erroneously link criminality to immigrant status. Scholars note that fear of crime as a driving force in criminal justice policy making, and persistent negative **media depictions** of Latinas/os and immigrants in relation to crime, pose formidable obstacles to the implementation of long-overdue, meaningful, and sensible changes in the prison and criminal justice systems and to reversing the trends in Latina/o incarceration in the United States.

Mass Imprisonment and Latinas/os

At the end of 2005, a total of 2,320,359 persons were incarcerated in the United States, a figure that includes persons held in federal and state prisons, territorial prisons, local jails, immigration facilities, military facilities, jails on Indian reservations, and juvenile detention facilities (Harrison & Beck 2006b, 1). Already the country with the highest rate of incarceration in the world, the United States has continued to steadily increase its prison population annually, despite a slowdown in the rate in recent years. One out of every 99.1 adults in the United States is incarcerated (Pew Center on the States 2008). Concomitant with the alarming expansion of the U.S. prison population is the issue that the increasing rates of imprisonment disproportionately affect communities of color, including Latinas/os.

Mass imprisonment is characterized by unprecedented high rates of incarceration that are "markedly above the historical and comparative norm for all societies of this type" and by "the systematic imprisonment of whole groups of the population" rather than of individuals (Garland 2001a, 1, 2). With rates 6 to 10 times greater, the United States far exceeds incarceration rates of comparable countries in Europe and Scandinavia (Garland 2001a, 1). Mass imprisonment in the United States also has not produced "racially uniform" results, and Latinas/os increasingly appear to meet the criterion of a group systematically subjected to disproportionately high levels of imprisonment (Simon 2007, 141).

During the 27-year period from 1974 to 2001, Latina/o imprisonment in state and federal facilities grew ten-fold (Bonczar 2003, 5). From 1985 to 1995, "the number of Hispanics in prison rose by 219%, with an average 12.3% increase each year," and by the 1990s, the Bureau of Justice Statistics declared that "Hispanics are the fastest growing group being imprisoned" (Mumola & Beck 1997, 9). Although Latinas/os represented 10.9 percent of all state and federal inmates in 1985, by 1995 the percentage had increased to 15.5 percent.

Since 1995, annual growth in the Latina/o prisoner population has continued. In 2001, approximately 7.7 percent of Latino males were current or former state or federal prisoners—nearly three (2.65) times the number of white males. Latino males, at 17.2 percent, are nearly three times as likely to go to prison within their lifetime as are white males (5.9 percent) (Bonczar 2003, 5, 8). In 2004, 60 percent of state and federal prisoners were African American and Latina/o (40.7 and 19.2 percent, respectively), with the rate of Latina/o incarceration in state and federal prisons being 2.6 times greater than for whites—1,220 per 100,000 compared to 463 per 100,000 (Harrison & Beck 2005, 8). Research has shown that "one in four federal prison inmates is Latino, even though fewer than one in eight U.S. residents is Latino" (Walker et al. 2004, 105). Recent data demonstrate a continuing increase in the number of Latinas/os held under state and federal jurisdiction, from 206,900 in 2000, to 303,500 in 2009 (West, Sabol & Greenman 2010).

When examining Latina incarceration rates for 2004, the Bureau of Justice Statistics finds that "female incarceration rates, though substantially lower than male incarceration rates at every age, reveal similar racial and ethnic disparities." Although African American women experienced an incarceration rate four times that of whites (170 per 100,000 as compared to 42 per 100,000, respectively), at 75 per 100,000, Latinas were not far behind at nearly twice the rate of white women (Harrison & Beck 2005, 8). For Latinas, imprisonment represents more than a temporary loss of personal liberty. An assessment of **Chicanas** in prison

Latinas/os and Racial/Ethnic Disparities in Incarceration

In a state-by-state look at Latina/o incarceration, the racial/ethnic disparities are glaring. Data compiled by Human Rights Watch summarizes the situation of Latinas/os as compared to whites in the early 2000s.

- In nine states, between 4 and nearly 8 percent of adult Latino men are incarcerated.
- In 12 states, between 2 and 4 percent of Hispanic adults (men and women) are incarcerated.
- In 10 states, Latino men are incarcerated at rates between five and nine times greater than those of White men.
- In eight states, Latina women are incarcerated at rates that are between four and seven times greater than those of White women.
- In four states, Hispanic youths under age 18 are incarcerated in adult facilities at rates between seven and 17 times greater than those of White youth (Human Rights Watch 2002).

Source: Human Rights Watch. 2002. Race and incarceration in the United States: Human Rights Watch briefing. New York: Human Rights Watch. https://www.hrw.org/backgrounder/usa/race/pdf/race-bck.pdf. Accessed November 13, 2015.

Contrasting the Incarceration of Latinas and White Women

In 2003, **The Sentencing Project** amassed the following data comparing the incarceration of Latinas to White women in the United States.

- In state prisons and jails, Hispanic females are incarcerated at almost twice the rate of White females (117 persons to 63 persons per 100,000 [persons in the] population).
- Hispanic women are three times as likely to go to prison in their lifetime as compared to White women (1.5 percent versus 0.5 percent).
- In the U.S. general population, 9.7 percent of women are Hispanic. In the U.S. prison population, 15 percent of women state prisoners and 32 percent of women federal prisoners are Hispanic.
- Between 1990 and 1996, the number of Hispanic female prisoners rose 71 percent.
- In New York, Hispanic women are 41 percent of the state's prison population but constitute 44 percent of women sentenced to prison for drug offenses (Sentencing Project 2003, 2).

Source: The Sentencing Project. 2003. *Hispanic prisoners in the United States.* Washington, DC: The Sentencing Project. http://www.sentencingproject.org/doc/publications/inc_hispanicprisoners.pdf. Accessed November 13, 2015.

discovered that Latinas often face discrimination, harassment, and abuse. Moreover, Latinas also must cope with the harmful effects of imprisonment on their children and their family life.

Race, Racial Profiling, and the War on Drugs

In the application of contemporary U.S. law and criminal justice policies and practices, Latinas/os most often continue to be relegated to a "racialized" status. The use of abusive language and racial and ethnic slurs by police officers, **racial profiling**, and the excessive use of physical and deadly force against Latinas/os and other people of color has been found to be a regular occurrence. Racial inequality in the penal system becomes most discernible when one considers how the ethnic composition of prisoners in the United States reverses dramatically, from 70 percent white circa mid-century to almost 70 percent black and Latina/o in the present—even though the ethnic paradigm of criminality did not change crucially during that period (Wacquant 2001).

Although illegal, racial profiling—the practice of using race in law enforcement—has proven to be an ongoing concern for its impact on disparities in the criminal justice system, including the composition of the incarcerated population. Its practice by New Jersey state troopers during the 1990s—in which at least 8 out of every 10 cars driven by Latinas/os and African Americans were singled out for searches on the New Jersey Turnpike—brought to the fore the systematic and institutionalized discrimination practiced in the day-to-day operations of the criminal justice system (Kocieniewski & Hanley 2000).

Reports issued by the New York State Attorney General and the United States Commission on Civil Rights (2000) have provided additional evidence that in New York City race frequently has been used as the sole criterion in the acts committed by law enforcement agents, making the problem of racial profiling as it affects Latinas/os ever more apparent. The New York City Police Department (NYPD) insisted that the reason Latinas/os and African Americans were stopped and frisked at greater rates was because they live in high crime–rate neighborhoods. A report by the state attorney general's office, however, found that even after accounting for differences in crime rates between communities of color and white communities, across all crime categories in New York City, Latinas/os were still "stopped" by police officers 39 percent more often than whites (Spitzer 1999, x).

Studies conducted in other cities reveal a similar pattern of illegal racial profiling by the police. In a study conducted in Chicago, 80 percent of African American high school students and 62 percent of Latina/o high school students reported being stopped by police, with 62 and 63 percent, respectively, reporting that, when stopped, they were treated disrespectfully by the police (Freidman & Hott 1995, 111). The pattern of racial profiling and "stops" by law enforcement officials strongly point to a continuation of longstanding stereotypes of Latinas/os and other people of color as a criminal element in society. This pattern—along with other aggressive police tactics, stricter sentencing laws, and the practice of **selective prosecution**—appears to play a part in elevating the number of Latinas/os and other people of color ending up in the prison system.

Many analysts note that current policies formulated on the fear of crime frequently produce racial or ethnic inequalities in the prison system. Get-tough antidrug strategies, commonly referred to as the "**war on drugs**," amount to "the single greatest force behind the growth of the prison population" (Human Rights Watch 2003, 1). Numerous researchers recognize that this "war" is being fought almost entirely in Latina/o and African American communities under the flawed premise that communities of color bear most of the responsibility for drug-related crime in the United States.

Contrary to such thinking, Latinas/os have not been shown to be any more inclined to engage in illegal drug activity than whites. Based on the 2002 National Survey on Drug Use and Health, the Office of National Drug Control Policy makes plain that "the lowest rate of lifetime illicit **drug use** was among Hispanics (38.9 percent) and Asians (25.6 percent)." Whites had a 54 percent rate of drug use over a lifetime, and African Americans had a rate of 43.8 percent. Moreover, the data show whites abusing certain **drugs** at greater levels. The Office of National Drug Control Policy also found that "of 12th graders, whites tended to have the highest rates of use for a number of drugs, including inhalants, hallucinogens, LSD, ecstasy, heroin without a needle, amphetamines, sedatives (barbiturates), tranquilizers, and narcotics other than heroin" (Office of National Drug Control Policy 2003, 1, 2).

These statistics notwithstanding, analysts indicate that the "**war on drugs**" waged in communities of color has had the "devastating" effect of escalating drug-related arrests and incarceration rates of Latinas/os and African Americans. Of a total of 23,784 federal offenders charged with drug trafficking in 2001, most were Latina/o (44.7 percent), only about a quarter (26.2 percent) were white, and 28.4 percent were African American (United States Sentencing Commission 2001, 14, table 4). For state prisons the statistics also are dismal. In 1996, 40 percent of Latinas/os sentenced to state prisons were convicted of drug-related crimes (Ditton & Wilson 1999, 6).

In the haste to combat the perceived drug problem in communities of color, studies point to growing evidence that racial profiling has become common, with Latinas/os and African Americans most often being singled out. There are documented instances in which law enforcement personnel have been trained to identify narcotics dealers by looking for "people wearing dreadlocks and cars with two Latino males traveling together." Further, a 1999 Drug Enforcement Agency (DEA) intelligence report identified major heroin traffickers as "Colombian, followed by **Dominicans**, Chinese, West African/Nigerian, Pakistani, Hispanic, and Indian. Midlevels are dominated by Dominicans, **Colombians**, **Puerto Ricans**, African Americans, and Nigerians" (Harris 2002, 49).

Drug-courier profiles used by federal agents at airports have included very long lists of seemingly odd and broadly defined categories, such as persons who "made a local call after deplaning . . . made a long-distance call after deplaning . . . carried a small bag . . . carried a medium-size bag . . . carried two bulky garment bags . . . dressed casually . . . left the airport by taxi" and anyone falling under the category of "Hispanics" (Cole 1999, 47–49). As one legal scholar notes, "racial profiling studies . . . make clear that the war on drugs has largely been a war on minorities. It is, after all, drug enforcement that motivates most racial profiling" (Cole 2001, 248).

Racial profiles appear not to correctly reflect the racial background of either illicit drug consumers or of traffickers. U.S. government data about drug use points to whites using illicit drugs at much the same or at higher rates than persons from other racial or ethnic groups. In 2001, "the rate among Blacks was 7.4 percent, whites 7.2 percent, and Hispanics 6.4 percent" (Substance Abuse and Mental Health Services Administration 2002, 1). Although precise data in this area is difficult to obtain, illicit drug users also report that they typically obtain drugs from persons of the same race, suggesting that whites are engaged in drug sales and exchanges at a greater rate than that of Latinas/os and African Americans (Riley 1997; Cole 2001, 247).

New York City serves as an example of the racial disparities in drug enforcement. In New York City in 1991, Latinas/os and African Americans comprised 92 percent of drug arrests (Donziger 1996, 116). A major study of marijuana arrests in New York City revealed that for more than a decade marijuana arrests have surged, with disproportionate outcomes for people of color. From 1977 to 1986, 33,000 persons were arrested in New York City for possession of marijuana, and from 1987 to 1996, 30,000 arrests were made. But from 1997 to 2006, arrests for marijuana possession increased to 353,000 (Levine & Small 2008, 9). Although national data consistently reveals higher percentages of marijuana use by white youth than by both Latina/o and African American youth (*e.g.*, Johnston et al. 2006, tables 4–9), from 1997 to 2007, whites made up only 15 percent of all marijuana arrests, even though they were 36 percent of New York City's population. By contrast, Latinas/os and African Americans comprised 83 percent of all marijuana arrests—31 percent and 52 percent, respectively—from 1997 to 2007, even though the percentages of the population in the city were 27 percent and 26 percent at the time (Levine & Small 2008, 9–13).

In addition to raising the specter of racial profiling, a recent investigation of police arrests of large numbers of Latina/o or African American youth for marijuana possession suggests that these arrests are being

Racial Disparities in Marijuana Arrests in New York City, 1997–2006

Race/Ethnicity	Percent of Arrests	Percentage of the City's Population
Latina/o	31%	27%
African American	52%	26%
White	15%	36%

Sources: New York State Division of Criminal Justice Services. 2008. Computerized Criminal History System, April 2008.

Levine, Harry G., and Deborah Peterson Small. 2008. *Marijuana arrest crusade: Racial bias and police policy in New York City, 1997–2007*. New York, NY: New York Civil Liberties Union, 9–13.

conducted in ways that violate the Fourth Amendment of the U.S. Constitution prohibiting unreasonable searches and seizures. Under New York law, possession of small quantities of marijuana is a violation subject to a fine, and it only becomes a misdemeanor criminal offense when the marijuana is smoked or exposed in a manner "open to public view." Reports suggest that police have been engaging in intrusive searches of Latina/o or African American youth without their consent on a systematic basis. Once that evidence is found by officers through an unlawful search, the youth is charged with having possession of marijuana in public view, even though it was originally hidden from view on the person. Powerless in the face of police officers able to contradict their claim of an unlawful search, many youth of color plead guilty rather than to face countless days in court for a lost cause.

The impact of the "**war on drugs**" also has adversely affected women generally, and Latinas in particular. As researchers in this field indicate, women in the United States have experienced a drastic increase in incarceration rates—nearly double the rate for men since 1980. "[D]rug offenses accounted for half (49 percent) of the rise in the number of women incarcerated in state prisons from 1986 to 1996, compared to one-third (32 percent) of the increase for men." The number of women imprisoned for drug offenses in state facilities increased by 888 percent from 1986 to 1996, and by 129 percent for nondrug offenses (Mauer, Potler & Wolf 1999, 1, 2, 3).

Prison Industrial Complex

The mass incarceration wave of African Americans and Latinas/os in the United States also is the product of corporate and private profiteering. The construction and tenancy of prisons is a lucrative machinery that has become a profoundly fixed part of the U.S. economic and political structure. Powerful entities and individuals—including political figures such as former Vice President Dick Cheney—have invested millions of dollars into private prisons. The relationship that exists between correctional communities, corporations, government, prison labor, incarceration, and the media is a phenomenon that has become known as the "**prison industrial complex**." This term also encompasses the notion that the construction and filling of prisons is motivated by an incentive that is both racist and profitable—as opposed to reflecting an actual increase in levels of crime (Davis 2003).

Prisons have become a vital source of economic development in many small rural communities that fall victim to unemployment but which nevertheless have available land and a workforce. Such communities at one time might have resisted the presence of prisons, but in recent years have become amenable to the construction of detention facilities in their jurisdictions. By 2003, the United States had spent a record $185 billion for "police protection, detention, judicial, and legal activities," and the justice system had employed about 2.4 million people with 58 percent at the local level and 31 percent at the state level. This means that "if four out of five people were released from prisons, far more than a million people could lose their jobs" (Alexander 2010, 218).

At the start of 2000, approximately 26 for-profit prison corporations in the United States operated 150 prisons or correctional facilities throughout 28 states, with Corrections Corporation of America and Wackenhut controlling about 76.4 percent of the global "private prison market" (Davis 2003, 97). Through its 2005 annual report to the Securities and Exchange Commission, the Corrections Corporation of America expressed the vested interests and concerns that enterprises of this nature have in the establishment and maintenance of prison facilities: "The demand for our facilities and services could be adversely affected by the relaxation of enforcement efforts, leniency in conviction and sentencing practices or through the decriminalization of certain activities that are currently proscribed by our criminal laws" (Alexander 2010, 218).

Prison-Based Gerrymandering and Felon Disenfranchisement

In combination with the prison industrial complex, prison-based gerrymandering has been a controversial practice that thrives on the high rate of incarceration of people of color in the United States. Prison-based gerrymandering occurs when state or local governments count, via the census, inmate populations who are not residents of that electoral district as constituents of the communities in which they are imprisoned. These inmates have become known as "phantom constituents," because their presence in a specific jail or prison is statistically manipulated to inflate the respective general population of the districts where the jails and prisons are located. Counting prisoners for purposes of population apportionment enables state or local governments to amass political power and influence not otherwise possible given the actual size of the country's or district's population.

Most states have constitutional provisions or laws that stipulate that a person does not lose or gain residency status as a result of being incarcerated, and a person's original residency status remains in effect for purposes of tax and court filings. It has been suggested that counting people of color from outside counties as being part of predominantly white counties where they are incarcerated has been viewed as reminiscent of the "three-fifths compromise" in the U.S. Constitution in which Southern States before the Civil War enhanced their political power by counting African American slaves among their constituents (National Association for the Advancement of Colored People Legal Defense and Education Fund 2010, 2).

Opponents of this practice have argued that prison-based gerrymandering subverts a fundamental principle of democracy—the concept of equal distribution of political power on the basis of population in accordance with the U.S. Constitution. Article I, section 2, requires an "actual enumeration" of the population every 10 years. Commonly referred to as the "One Person, One Vote" rule, this principle was recognized in the Supreme Court decision *Reynolds v. Sims,* 377 U.S. 533 (1963), in which the Court struck down an apportionment scheme for the Alabama state legislature that was based on counties and not population.

For many years, states with sizable Latina/o populations engaged in prison-based gerrymandering, including California, Pennsylvania, Connecticut, Illinois, and New York. Studies revealed that the impact of prison-based gerrymandering was considerable. In New York State, approximately 80 percent of New York's prisoners are African American or Latina/o, mostly from the New York City metropolitan area, but New York's prisons are located in overwhelmingly white upstate counties. One study estimated that New York City was losing 43,740 residents to the upstate prison towns through prison-based gerrymandering, diminishing political representation for downstate African American or Latina/o communities, and augmenting the political power of white upstate counties, in spite of a state constitutional mandate that imprisonment does not change a prisoner's place of residence (Prison Policy Initiative 2002). Similarly, in Connecticut, an estimated 72 percent of the state's prison population is African American or Latino. The state's prisons, however, are located in predominantly white, upper-middle class suburban or rural towns (such as Enfield or Cheshire) that have counted the prisoners as part of their population for apportionment purposes at the expense of urban centers (such as New Haven) (Yagla 2010).

Advocacy organizations and others have increased criticisms of prison-based gerrymandering, asserting that it undermines the "One Person, One Vote" principle and that it creates an incentive to continue supporting a prison industry in which certain groups and individuals with vested interests benefit from increasing the mass incarceration of persons of color. In response, some states recently have legislated reforms to prevent the use of census data for this purpose, among them Maryland, Delaware, and New York. Yet, despite the recent passage of legislation to prohibit this practice in New York State, the law did not deter New York State Senator Elizabeth Little, whose upstate district has 11 correctional facilities, a federal prison, and approximately 12,000 inmates, from filing a lawsuit to block the ban on prison-based gerrymandering, claiming that it is constitutionally permissible to count inmates as "residents" (*New York Times* 2011, A24).

As with prison-based gerrymandering, felon disenfranchisement has been viewed as another means through which political power is tipped in favor of whites at the expense of Latinas/os and African Americans. A 2003 study by the **Mexican American Legal Defense and Education Fund (MALDEF)** of 10 states with sizable Latina/o populations—Arizona, California, Florida, Nebraska, Nevada, New York, North Carolina, Texas, Virginia, and Washington—concluded that half a million Latina/o citizens could not vote and, together with other states that restrict the voting rights of felons, felony disenfranchisement laws were greatly diminishing the political power of Latina/o communities across the country. The study reveals that Latinas/os have disproportionately greater rates of disenfranchisement as compared with their presence in the voting-age population, and that the data suggest that whites are less likely to be affected by felony disenfranchisement laws than are African Americans or Latinas/os.

Felon disenfranchisement laws have been challenged in recent years. As a result of such efforts, from 1997 to 2010, 23 states have reformed felon disenfranchisement laws to lessen restrictions and increase voting eligibility. Latina/o and prison reform advocacy organizations continue to view prison-based gerrymandering and felon disenfranchisement as factors contributing to the mass incarceration of Latinas/os and African Americans, in addition to serving as means to politically and economically privilege white communities at the expense of communities of color. Consequently, legal and other advocacy work to contest prison-based gerrymandering and felon disenfranchisement continues. Felon disenfranchisement creates incentives for the mass imprisonment of Latinas/os and African Americans. By having and counting nonresident prisoners of color in prisons in their counties, white communities derive direct benefits from the political apportionment process and from the creation of employment opportunities.

The Role of the Media in the Incarceration of Latinas/os

A close look at Latinas/os and crime in the United States reveals that Latinas/os are not necessarily imprisoned at greater rates because they are more prone than whites to commit crimes. In a study of Latinas/os and the U.S. criminal justice system, it was found that Latinas/os generally are less likely to be involved in violent crime "than their non-Hispanic counterparts" (Walker et al. 2004, 4). The great majority of incarcerated Latinas/os are convicted of minor, nonviolent offenses, are first-time offenders, or both. Latinas/os also are more likely than whites to be arrested and charged for drug offenses even though they are no more likely than other groups to use illegal drugs and are less likely to use alcohol. Evidence in support of these facts notwithstanding, major news and entertainment media generally paint a very different picture of crime in the United States, frequently linking Latinas/os with criminal behavior. Invariably, such characterizations influence attitudes in favor of prison expansion as a solution to a perceived crime problem (Walker et al. 2004).

Although crime dropped by almost one-third between 1993 and 2000, it continues to dominate both the news and entertainment media. To the extent that the media's influence on public policy can be measured, it appears to "encourage punitive attitudes, especially when the offenders depicted are African American" (Beckett & Sasson 2004, 43, 100, 101). Hence, the power of the media lies not only in its ability to project fear but also in its capacity to convey a highly racialized picture of crime that tends to promote insecurity among whites.

Fear of violent crime has been a primary reason for adopting stiffer penalties that aim to incarcerate violent offenders. It generally has not been the case, however, that the vast majority of those imprisoned are there for committing violent offenses. In fact, the percentage of persons sentenced for nonviolent drug offenses constituted the largest group of federal prisoners in 2003 at 55 percent (Harrison & Beck 2006b, 10). Of the prisoners held in state facilities from 1995 to 2003, violent offenders most often have constituted only about half of those incarcerated: 46.5 percent in 1995, 49 percent in 2001, and 51.8 percent in 2003 (Harrison & Beck 2006b, 9).

Studies show that the major media tend to be saturated with stories that inaccurately represent Latinas/os. As reported by the National Association of Hispanic Journalists, 66 percent of network news stories about Latinas/os in 2002 focused exclusively on three topics: crime, **terrorism**, and illegal immigration. José Padilla, the suspected "dirty bomb" terrorist occupied "a central role in the coverage of Latinos . . . with 21 network stories or 18 percent of all stories aired on Latinos" (Méndez-Méndez & Alverio 2003, 3). Moreover, post–September 11 anti-immigrant sentiments and the politically opportunistic use of crime in election campaigns pose a formidable challenge to reversing the relentless drive to incarcerate. In spite of the facts that belie their portrayals by the media, Latina/o **youth** and Latina/o immigrants in particular are consistently and repeatedly associated with criminality conduct in the media.

Despite occasional spikes in violent crime, the United States has experienced a precipitous drop in violent crime—a decline of 58 percent from 1993 to 2005 (Catalano 2006, 1). As scholars have discovered, the National Crime Victimization Survey reported violent crime at its lowest in 25 years. Although evidence shows that whites actually are three times more likely to be victimized by other whites than by people of color, scholars found that media coverage has tended to present an exaggerated, unbalanced picture of crime: "while Blacks and Hispanics were overrepresented as violent offenders, Whites were underrepresented as violent offenders on the evening news" (Dorfman & Schiraldi 2001, 15).

Latina/o Immigrants and Incarceration

The popular belief that crime and high incarceration rates are the result of immigrants entering the country appears to persist as much in the present as it has in the past. Empirical data accumulated over three decennial censuses and by a myriad of scholars and studies over time demonstrate that there is no validity to this perception. Contrary to the conventional wisdom on the issue, studies suggest that immigrants to the United States—including **Mexicans** and **Central Americans** who comprise the greatest percentage of the unauthorized population in the country—are less prone to crime and incarceration and that immigration has been a factor in reducing crime rather than increasing it.

In the national media, one of the most effective and persistent in the proliferation of fear and false information about immigrants and incarceration rates has been CNN's Lou Dobbs. An exposé in the *New York Times* revealed that in 2003 Lou Dobbs had falsely reported on one of his broadcasts that "one-third of the inmates now serving time in federal prisons come from some other country—one-third" (Leonhardt 2007). Contrary to Dobbs's assertions, at midyear 2005, noncitizens actually comprise less than one-fifth (19 percent) of all prisoners in federal custody—well below one-third—and noncitizens in federal and state facilities combined comprised only 6.4 percent (Harrison & Beck 2006a, 5).

Research consistently indicates that immigrants to the United States actually have lower incarceration rates than other groups in the population. Although it is assumed that factors such as low education levels and low average wages would predispose immigrants to engage in criminal conduct, in the main, immigrants tend to come to the country highly motivated to use their skills to forge a better life and are not interested in run-ins with the law that would thwart this goal. Scholars find that immigrants typically are self-selecting and are not typical of the general population. Studies conducted specifically on Mexican immigrants reveal that they are less prone to commit crime than are native-born citizens and that their traditions, culture, and values serve as social and cultural capital that deter them from crime.

Census data and other scientific evidence also have shown repeatedly that immigrants—including undocumented and Latina/o immigrants—have lower rates of incarceration than those of natives. In 2000, the incarceration rate of native-born males age 18 to 39 years in the United States was five times *greater* than the incarceration rate of foreign-born men. Lower incarceration rates were found among every immigrant group, including Latinas/os. Among Latinas/os, native-born men were almost seven times more likely to be in prison than were foreign-born Latino men. Among whites, the incarceration rate of native-born white men was close to three times greater than that of foreign-born white men (Rumbaut & Ewing 2007).

It has been observed that as immigration—particularly unauthorized immigration—rose dramatically in the 1990s and into the 2000s, crime rates actually decreased considerably in border towns, such as San Diego and El Paso, as well as in major cities, such as Los Angeles, New York, Chicago, and Miami, where unauthorized immigration was at its highest. The **Uniform Crime Reports** of the Federal Bureau of Investigation (FBI) show that from 1994 to 2005 violent crime and property crime dropped at the same time that the foreign-born immigrant population grew.

Serious crimes committed by juveniles also declined and gun-related crimes leveled off. Many contemporary studies confirm this pattern of low criminality among immigrants, and even suggest that immigrants actually help reduce crime (e.g., Rumbaut & Ewing 2007; Sampson, Morenoff & Raudenbush 2005; Martínez, Lee, & Nielsen 2004; Lee, Martínez, & Rosenfeld 2001; Karmen 2000).

Popular misconceptions appear to override that which was studied and discovered in the early 20th century—there is no proof that immigrants are responsible for crime or high incarceration rates. The Industrial Commission of 1901, the [Dillingham] Immigration Commission of 1911, and the [Wickersham] National Commission on Law Observance and Enforcement of 1931 all studied the issue of immigrants and crime only to conclude that there is no evidence that demonstrates that increases in crime are due to immigration and that in fact it is possible that immigrants are less prone to crime than are native-born citizens. The presumed link between crime and immigrants from Latin America—and from Mexico specifically—has been shown to be unsubstantiated. As an empirical study of Mexican immigrants revealed, "it is currently the case that immigration and criminal justice policies which appear neutral in relation to Hispanic immigrants actually bias and distort public perceptions of immigration and crime by inflating Hispanic rates of imprisonment" (Hagan & Palloni 1999, 617).

Selective Prosecution and Bias in Sentencing

Contributing to disproportionate rates of incarceration of people of color are the problems of selective prosecution and bias in the functions of the criminal justice system. Noted scholars in the field have found evidence to corroborate the fact that a defendant's **race and ethnicity** can have an effect on decisions regarding bail and **plea bargaining**. This problem is compounded by the fact that many people of color are more likely than whites to not have a competent lawyer or to be detained before trial which, in turn, increases the chances of conviction and stricter sentences, and that "racially discriminatory charging decisions have similar 'spillover' effects at trial" (Walker, Spohn, & DeLone 2007, 194).

Research points to selectiveness in prosecutorial practices and other forms of unequal treatment in the courts producing disparate and unfair outcomes for Latinas/os and people of color generally in the justice system. A study conducted in Los Angeles revealed that Latino males were most likely to be prosecuted fully (42 percent), followed by African American (26 percent) and white males (39 percent) (Spohn, Gruhl, & Welch 1987). In another study, a similar pattern of prosecutorial decisions was discovered and attributed to indirect and subtle forms of discrimination against people of color. Other studies show that whites are more often given reduced sentences or plea bargains and more frequently are granted greater reductions of sentences than are people of color (e.g., Bernstein et al. 1977; Albonetti 1997; Maxfield & Kramer 1998).

Bail, Pretrial Detention, and Get-tough Sentencing

Other studies reveal that pretrial detention plays a role in producing racial and ethnic disparities in the justice system. Pretrial detentions have been found to increase the probability of a prison sentence after trial. Despite the fact that bail is extended to persons still under the presumption of innocence before trial, bail is less likely to be granted to Latinas/os than to whites, and although the absence of funds to make bail is a factor, research also reveals that race and ethnicity might influence judges' decisions regarding bail. The inability of Latinas/os to be granted bail or to make bail makes them susceptible to pretrial detention.

A range of "get-tough" sentencing laws also have contributed to the disproportionately high rate of incarceration of people of color. Strict mandatory minimum sentencing laws, "three-strikes" legislation, and so-called "truth in sentencing" laws, designed to replace indeterminate sentences with clearly defined penalties without the possibility of early release on parole, are among the laws most often criticized for their impact on incarceration rates. Whether stricter state and federal sentencing policies have had a discriminatory impact on people of color has been a subject of considerable study. Some prominent analysts for more than a decade have asserted that changes in sentencing guidelines might have worsened the racial divide within the criminal justice system (e.g., Tonry 1995). Others conclude that discrimination occurs and harsher penalties are imposed, but within certain contexts, such as when a person of color is accused of a crime against a white person as opposed to another person of color.

High rates of incarceration outcomes for Latina/o youth, in particular, have been linked to bias in the operation of the criminal justice system. National data reveal that Latina/o youth are charged with violent offenses at five times the rate of white youth and serve longer sentences than those of white youth—as much as 143 days longer for violent crimes. In Los Angeles, Latina/o youth are incarcerated at rates much higher than those of white youth—7.3 times as often from 1996 to 1998—and Latina/o youth are prosecuted as adults more often than are white youth—2.4 times as often from 1996 to 1998 (Villarruel et al. 2002, 2–3). **Gang** affiliation or involvement and stereotypes of Latina/o youth are typically cited as factors helping to produce disparities in rates of imprisonment.

Studies that specifically look at bias against Latinas/os in sentencing reveal a consistent pattern. In analyzing sentencing

Racial Disparities in Sentencing

In 2005, **The Sentencing Project** issued a review of the academic studies that had been conducted on racial disparities in sentencing in the United States. Below are a number of key findings as they relate to Latinas/os.

- Direct racial discrimination is evident against African Americans and Latina/o defendants in sentencing outcomes, with direct discrimination more prominent at the federal level than at the state level.
- At the state level, both Latinos and African Americans are extremely disadvantaged in decisions whether to incarcerate.
- Young African American and Latino males tend to be sentenced more severely than comparably situated white males.
- Whites receive a greater reduction in sentence time than African American and Latinas/os for providing "substantial assistance" to the prosecution.
- African Americans and Latinas/os with a more serious criminal record tend to be sentenced more severely than comparably situated whites.
- Whites are more likely to hire a private attorney than are Latinas/os or African Americans and thus most often receive less harsh sentences.
- Latinas/os and African Americans tend to be sentenced more harshly than whites for less-serious crimes, such as drug crimes and property crimes.
- Latinas/os and African Americans convicted of high-level drug offenses are more likely to be more severely sentenced than similarly situated whites.
- In most death penalty cases, the race of the victim tends to have an effect on the sentence outcome, and in cases involving a white victim, a death sentence is more likely.

Source: Sentencing Project. 2005. *Racial disparity in sentencing: A review of the literature.* Washington, DC: The Sentencing Project, 4–14.

data collected by the State Court Processing Statistics program of the Bureau of Justice Statistics for the years 1990, 1992, 1994, and 1996, investigators discovered that, "in general, Hispanic defendants were sentenced more similarly to Black defendants than White defendants. Both Black and Hispanic defendants tended to receive harsher sentences than White defendants" (Demuth & Steffensmeier 2004, 1008).

In an earlier study examining ethnicity as well as race as a factor in sentencing, using quantitative and qualitative data gathered on Pennsylvania sentencing practices, analysts revealed that Latinas/os are vulnerable to harsher penalties because of the prevalence of negative stereotypes and biases that associate Latinas/os with illegal drug activities, low intelligence, and the rise in neighborhood crime. Their qualitative data reinforces this conclusion, with one particular Pennsylvanian judge from a county with an expanding Latina/o population stating:

> We shouldn't kid ourselves. I have always prided myself for not being prejudiced but it is hard not to be affected by what is taking place. The whole area has changed with the influx of Hispanics and especially Puerto Ricans. You'd hardly recognize the downtown from what it was a few years ago. There's more dope, more crime, more people on welfare, more problems in school (Steffensmeier & Demuth 2001, 168).

A comprehensive review of bias in the courts confirms a familiar pattern—both Latinas/os and African Americans experience bias in sentencing practices and policies, and, as a result, they receive harsher sentences than whites. An examination of forty recent and methodologically sophisticated studies on the effects of race and ethnicity on sentencing—including thirty-two studies of state court decisions and eight studies of federal court decisions—concluded that

> Black and Hispanic offenders—and particularly those who are young, male, or unemployed—are more likely than their White counterparts to be sentenced to prison; they also may receive longer sentences than similarly situated White offenders. Other categories of racial minorities—those convicted of drug offenses, those who victimize Whites, those who accumulate more serious prior criminal records, or those who refuse to plead guilty or are unable to secure pretrial release, also may be singled out for more punitive treatment (Spohn 2000, 481–82).

The Sentencing Reform Act of 1984, which was designed to prevent "unwarranted sentencing disparity among defendants with similar records who had been found guilty of similar criminal conduct," appears not to have eliminated the influence on sentencing decisions of legally irrelevant factors, such as racial and ethnic characteristics and immigrant status (28 U.S.C. 991 [b][1][B]; Supp. 1993). Based on data on 14,189 defendants convicted of drug offenses, it is evident that in spite of the new federal sentencing guidelines adopted as a result of the Sentencing Reform Act of 1984, "judges impose significantly more severe sentences on defendants who are not U.S. citizens and on defendants who are Black or Hispanic" (Albonetti 1997, 817).

It is also important to note that biased sentencing is possible because federal judges can circumvent strict sentencing guidelines. "Although the federal sentencing guidelines severely constrain judges' discretion in deciding between prison and probation and in determining the length of the sentence, they place only minimal restrictions on the ability of judges (and prosecutors) to reduce sentences for substantial assistance or acceptance of responsibility. Mandatory minimum sentences also can be avoided through charge manipulation" (Walker, Spohn, & DeLone 2007, 273).

Studies on the effects of judicial and prosecutorial discretion on federal sentencing regularly show that African Americans and Latinas/os are treated more harshly in sentencing than whites. Most notably, researchers who examined federal court data gathered by the United States Sentencing Commission from 1993 to 1996 found that the ability under the federal sentencing statute to "depart downward" from the sentencing guidelines resulted in leniency toward white defendants and harsher sentences for Latina/o and African American defendants.

In studying the operations of the criminal courts and the treatment of Chicana/o rights movement members in Los Angeles in the late 1960s, it was posited that race often functions as a matter of "common sense" in the courts, as it does in the course of many day-to-day events. This study evidenced that white judges even unwittingly tended to privilege those of their own race and socioeconomic background, placing Mexicans at a disadvantage. By basing their decisions on a form of "common sense," judges accepted implicitly that white persons like themselves were generally worthy of opportunities, such as serving on a grand jury, above Mexicans. Thus, it was asserted that such "common sense" practices are illustrative of how, today, race is constructed on a daily basis and functions to the benefit of whites over Latinas/os and other people of color in the courts and in society at large (Haney López 2003).

Current Trends in Addressing Mass Imprisonment

The need to reverse the **mass imprisonment** phenomenon has increasingly gained support among a broad range of scholars, advocates, and policy makers at the local, state and national levels. There has been a considerable acknowledgement that mass incarceration has led to many inequitable outcomes, particularly for African Americans and Latinas/os. In addition, court orders to ameliorate overcrowded prisons and concern over the exorbitant costs of incarceration have led states to reassess and in some cases reduce rates of imprisonment. Scholars and advocates have also mounted efforts to call for the downsizing of the prison system as a solution to the prison population explosion and for the implementation of various cost-effective alternatives, such as sentencing reform, strategies to reduce recidivism rates, job placement, and increased community-based services.

Greater attention is now being given to the problems of recidivism and **prisoner reentry**. This effort includes a strong emphasis on creating or enhancing education opportunities and job training while in prison, the development of programs that help sustain and strengthen family and community ties during incarceration, and establishing projects that in other ways help enable incarcerated persons to become productive upon their release.

In relation to issues of reentry and recidivism, there is also emerging literature from legal scholars concerning the "collateral consequences" connected to criminal convictions in the United States under federal, state, and local regulatory or statutory schemes. In exploring the aftermath of convictions, this work uncovers the exclusion and hardship that individuals with criminal backgrounds encounter when attempting to access housing, public benefits, and employment. Among many post-conviction ramifications is the phenomenon of felon disenfranchisement that results in the ineligibility to vote. This literature and advocacy stress that harsh consequences are felt disproportionately by those convicted of drug offenses and by Latinas/os and African Americans.

Critical examinations of post-conviction issues also focus on the collateral costs and daunting reality about the ill effects that individuals with criminal backgrounds experience in becoming economically immobile and deficient. Scholars have discovered that criminal convictions often impede individuals from achieving economic mobility (the ability to move upwardly through the income ladder) for a lifetime and possibly for generations to come. Evidence shows that former African American and Latina/o prisoners earn less and work less yearly as a result of being formerly incarcerated. Although imprisonment is concentrated among men, the undereducated, and the young, it has been found that a vital segment of the male inmate population were once employed and served as the primary source of economic stability for their families before incarceration, suggesting that there is a critical need for providing former inmates with more promising alternatives upon reentering society to reduce their productivity loss and facilitate a lifestyle that would deter crime and provide a more prosperous future for their children and communities.

Recent studies of Latinas/os and the criminal justice system have examined measures that could help the criminal justice system rid itself of policies and practices that adversely and disproportionately impact people of color. Broader acknowledgement of the unfair impact of the criminal justice and correctional system on Latinas/os could be an important first step toward ending some of the most detrimental facets of the Latina/o experience within the criminal justice arena. Proposals to curtail racial profiling and other practices that lead to harsher and longer sentences for Latinas/os and other people of color, as compared to whites, are common in recent studies. Addressing longstanding inadequacies of the system that have negative consequences on Latinas/os—such as the lack of bilingual and culturally competent services—is also among the recommendations found in a number of analyses on Latinas/os and the criminal justice system.

With respect to policies and practices that disproportionately affect people of color, there are policy-driven initiatives that center on social investment and the nexus between low-income communities of color and the criminal justice system. Although the data produced from such efforts emphasize that poverty does not create crime, this type of research does highlight how people of color and low-income communities are disproportionately subjected to arrests and incarceration at alarming rates, in spite of decreasing crime indicators. More important, this research entails advocacy for changes in current policies, specifically as it pertains to access to affordable housing, quality education, and mental health and substance abuse treatment for Latinas/os and African Americans. These suggestions for policy reform are made with the objective of facilitating ways to reduce crime, improving public safety, and promoting community well-being.

Within the multifaceted criminal justice system in the United States, there is a vital need for reformation of the juvenile justice system. Recent investigations, such as in the State of New York, advocate for rehabilitating young people in ways that are more effective than the current punitive model. Although the focal point of this initiative was to examine what happens to juveniles after they had been adjudicated, this report also sheds light on very troubling and alarming data, including the fact that there is no fundamental and systematic standard in place for determining whether the youth in custody actually pose a threat of harm to public safety. Such information is essential when considering that as of 2007 a majority of the youth in custody had a misdemeanor as the most serious adjudicated offense, raising concern that the current system is harming children, endangering the public welfare, and wasting vast amounts of public funds. Among its many recommendations, the report strongly suggests downsizing the juvenile prison population, especially the representation of youth of color in custodial institutions (Task Force on Transforming Juvenile Justice 2009).

Although downscaling has been suggested for the incarcerated juvenile population, it has also become a matter of concern with respect to the general prison population in the United States. A recent study finds that the all-time high number of individuals in prison has created a hazardous effect on states' initiatives for public safety, fiscal budgeting, and community stability, particularly in a time of economic recession. As a result, certain states across the nation, such as New York, Michigan, New Jersey, and Kansas, have been implementing new policies to gradually reduce their respective prison populations. As the study emphasizes, the current modest wave of downscaling must be examined in the context of the mass incarceration phenomenon. More important, this study highlights the exemplary policies that have made such reductions possible, including policy reform, changes in sentencing guidelines, alternatives for "prison bound" individuals, parole release rates, and time reductions (The Sentencing Project 2010, 3).

Downscaling has also become a mechanism to alleviate overcrowding and the unsafe and unconstitutional conditions for prisoners, as in the case of the California prison system. Although a federal court assessed California's prison system in 2005, an inmate was dying each week as a result of the state's failure to provide the necessary adequate healthcare (*New York Times* 2010). By 2007, Governor Arnold Schwarzenegger had declared a state of emergency in regards to the overcrowding crisis, prompted in large part by lawsuits against the state. Although the governor signed legislation that included plans for construction of new facilities and for involuntary out-of-state transfers, progress toward a permanent solution has remained tenuous. In 2010, three judges in federal court issued an order to release 40,000 inmates by 2011 because they felt there was no other means of relief for persistent constitutional violations. In 2011, the U.S. Supreme Court in *Brown et al. v. Plata et al.*, 563 U.S. 493 (2011), affirmed the appeals court ruling to reduce California's prison population. The Supreme Court reasoned that the alarming conditions in the prison system jeopardized the health and safety of prisoners in violation of the constitutional right against cruel and inhuman punishment. Although reductions in the prison population have been underway, state officials have repeatedly sought additional time to fully comply with the court's order (Lovett 2014).

Currently there is debate among legal scholars and policy makers about the efficacy of the war on drugs, particularly in view of the negative impact of laws, such as New York State's **Rockefeller Drug Laws**. As more data is collected by various institutions and criminal justice scholars, the emerging consensus is that these laws have not necessarily improved public safety nor have they served as an effective deterrent to drug activity. Comprehensive analyses of the problem reveal a demographic map of urban enclaves severely harmed by these laws. It is a map that suggests an underlying racial and ethnic bias in drug policies. With the largest percentage of the population of felons arrested for drug-related offenses in New York State being African American or Latina/o, advocacy groups continue to fight for reforms claiming that current drug policies both hurt the integrity of the criminal justice system and have proven to be fiscally detrimental.

Comprehensive efforts to engage parents, youths, communities, law enforcement, and the political process have been promoted by scholars and advocates alike in recent years to provide a platform for effecting change in the prison and criminal justice system and to reverse the dangerous trend toward increased Latina/o imprisonment (e.g., Villarruel et al. 2002; Arya, et al. 2009). In the process of mobilizing communities and political support for achieving substantive change, greater dissemination of accurate information about the realities of Latinas/os in relation to the criminal justice and penal systems is believed to be indispensable.

See also: Part I essays: Latinas/os and the U.S. Criminal Justice System; Latina/o Immigrants, Crime, and Justice; The U.S. War on Drugs and Latina/o Communities; Latinas and the U.S. Criminal Justice System; Latina/o Youth and Criminal Justice. Part II entries: Central Americans; Chicanas/os; Colombians; Cultural Criminology; Death Penalty; Dominicans; Felon Disenfranchisement; Human Trafficking; International Human Rights; Media Depictions; Mexicans and Mexican Americans; Political Activist Groups; Salinas, Raúl R.; Segregation; Victims.

Further Reading

Acuña, Rodolfo. 2007. *Occupied America: A history of Chicanos*. 6th ed. New York, NY: Pearson Longman.

Albonetti, Celesta A. 1997. Sentencing under the federal sentencing guidelines: Effects of defendant characteristics, guilty pleas, and departures on sentence outcomes for drug offenses, 1991–1992. *Law & Society Review* 31(4): 789–822.

Alexander, Michelle. 2010. *The new Jim Crow: Mass incarceration in the age of colorblindness*. New York, NY: The New Press.

Amnesty International. 1998. *United States of America: Rights for all*. New York, NY: Amnesty International Publications.

Arya, Neelum, with Francisco Villarruel, Cassandra Villanueva, and Ian Augarten. 2009. *America's invisible children: Latino youth and the failure of justice*. Washington, DC: Campaign for Youth Justice and the National Council of La Raza.

Beck, Allen J., and Paige M. Harrison. 2001. *Prisoners in 2000*. NCJ 188207. Washington, DC: U.S. Department of Justice, Bureau of Justice Statistics.

Beckett, Katherine. 1997. *Making crime pay: Law and order in contemporary American politics*. Oxford: Oxford University Press.

Beckett, Katherine, and Theodore Sasson. 2004. *The politics of injustice: Crime and punishment in America*. Thousand Oaks, CA: Sage Publications.

Bender, Steven W. 2003. *Greasers and gringos: Latinos, law and the American imagination*. New York, NY: New York University Press.

Bernstein, Ilene Nagel, Edward Kick, Jan T. Leung, and Barbara Schultz. 1977. Charge reduction: An intermediary state in the process of labeling criminal defendants. *Social Forces* 56: 362–84.

Bonczar, Thomas P. 2003. *Prevalence of imprisonment in the U.S. population, 1974–2001*. NCJ 197976. Washington, DC: U.S. Department of Justice, Bureau of Justice Statistics.

Bureau of Justice Statistics. 2000. *Sourcebook of criminal justice statistics, 1999*. Washington, DC: U.S. Department of Justice.

Butcher, Kristin F., and Anne Morrison Piehl. 2005. *Why are immigrants' incarceration rates so low? Evidence on selective immigration, deterrence, and deportation*. Chicago, IL: Federal Reserve Bank of Chicago. http://www.chicagofed.org/publications/workingpapers/wp2005_19.pdf.

Catalano, Shannan M. 2006. *Criminal victimization, 2005: National crime victimization survey*. NCJ 2146644. Washington, DC: U.S. Department of Justice, Bureau of Justice Statistics.

Chang, Ailsa. 2011a (April 26). Alleged illegal searches by NYPD may be increasing marijuana arrests. *WNYC News*. http://www.wnyc.org/articles/wnyc-news/2011/apr/26/marijuana-arrests/.

Chang, Ailsa. 2011b (April 27). Alleged illegal searches by NYPD rarely challenged in marijuana cases. *WNYC News*. http://www.wnyc.org/articles/wnyc-news/2011/apr/27/alleged-illegal-searches/.

Cole, David. 1999. *No equal justice: Race and class in the American criminal justice system*. New York, NY: New Press.

Cole, David. 2001. Formalism, realism, and the war on drugs. *Suffolk University Law Review* 35: 241–55.

Crutchfield, Robert, Joseph G. Weis, Rodney L. Engen, and Randy R. Gainey. 1995. *Racial and ethnic disparities in the prosecution of felony cases in King County*. Olympia, WA: Washington State Minority and Justice Commission.

Davis, Angela Y. 2003. *Are prisons obsolete?* New York, NY: Seven Stories Press.

Demuth, Stephen, and Darrell Steffensmeier. 2004. Ethnicity effects on sentencing outcomes in large urban courts: Comparisons among white, black and Hispanic defendants. *Social Science Quarterly* 85: 994–1011.

Díaz-Cotto, Juanita. 2006. *Chicana lives and criminal justice: Voices from el barrio*. Austin, TX: University of Texas Press.

Ditton, Paula M., and Doris James Wilson. 1999. *Truth in sentencing in state prisons: Bureau of Justice Statistics special report (January 1999)*. NCJ 170032. Washington, DC: U.S. Department of Justice, Bureau of Justice Statistics.

Donziger, Steven R. (ed.). 1996. *The real war on crime: The report of the National Criminal Justice Commission*. New York, NY: Harper Perennial.

Dorfman, Lori, and Vincent Schiraldi. 2001. *Off balance: Youth, race and crime in the news*. Washington, DC: Building Blocks for Youth.

Dow, Mark. 2004. *American gulag: Inside U.S. immigration prisons*. Berkeley, CA: University of California Press.

Ellis, Edwin. 1993. *The non-traditional approach to criminal justice and social justice*. Harlem, NY: Community Justice Center.

Escobar, Edward J. 1999. *Race, police, and the making of a political identity: Mexican Americans and the Los Angeles Police Department 1900–1945*. Berkeley, CA: University of California Press.

Federal Bureau of Investigation. 2006. *Preliminary semiannual uniform crime report, January-June 2006*. Washington, DC: U.S. Department of Justice.

Freidman, Warren, and Martha Hott. 1995. *Young people and the police: Respect, fear and the future of community policing in Chicago*. Chicago, IL: Chicago Alliance for Neighborhood Safety.

Garland, David (ed.). 2001a. *Mass imprisonment: Social causes and consequences*. London: Sage.

Garland, David. 2001b. *The culture of control: Crime and social order in contemporary society*. Chicago, IL: University of Chicago Press.

Hagan, John, and Alberto Palloni. 1999. Sociological criminology and the mythology of Hispanic immigration and crime. *Social Problems* 46(4): 617–32.

Hall, Kermit L., William M. Wiecek, and Paul Finkelman. 1996. *American legal history: Cases and materials*. 2nd ed. New York, NY: Oxford University Press.

Haney López, Ian F. 1996. *White by law: The legal construction of race*. New York, NY: New York University Press.

Haney López, Ian. 2003. *Racism on trial: The Chicano fight for justice*. Cambridge, MA: Belknap/Harvard University Press.

Harris, David A. 2002. *Profiles in injustice: Why racial profiling cannot work*. New York, NY: New Press.

Harrison, Paige M., and Allen J. Beck. 2002. *Prisoners in 2001*. NCJ 195189. Washington, DC: U.S. Department of Justice, Bureau of Justice Statistics.

Harrison, Paige M., and Allen J. Beck. 2005. *Prisoners in 2004*. NCJ 210677. Washington, DC: U.S. Department of Justice, Bureau of Justice Statistics.

Harrison, Paige M., and Allen J. Beck. 2006a. *Prison and jail inmates at midyear 2005*. NCJ 213133. Washington, DC: U.S. Department of Justice, Bureau of Justice Statistics.

Harrison, Paige M., and Allen J. Beck. 2006b. *Prisoners in 2005*. NCJ 215092. Washington, DC: U.S. Department of Justice, Bureau of Justice Statistics.

Healey, Joseph F. 2007. *Race, ethnicity, gender, and class in the United States: Inequality, group conflict, and power*. 4th ed. Thousand Oaks, CA: Pine Forge Press.

Hood, Roger. 1992. *Race and sentencing*. Oxford, England: Clarendon.

Horsman, Reginald. 1981. *Race and manifest destiny: Origins of American racial Anglo-Saxonism*. Cambridge, MA: Harvard University Press.

Human Rights Watch. 2002. *Race and incarceration in the United States: Human Rights Watch briefing*. New York: Human Rights Watch. http://www.hrw.org/backgrounder/usa/race/pdf/race-bck.pdf. Accessed November 13, 2015.

Human Rights Watch. 2003. *Incarcerated America: Human rights watch backgrounder*. New York, NY: Human Rights Watch.

Jacobson, Michael. 2005. *Downsizing prisons: How to reduce crime and end mass incarceration*. New York, NY: New York University Press.

Johnson, Kevin R. 2003. The case for African American and Latina/o cooperation in challenging racial profiling in law enforcement. *Florida Law Review* 55: 341–62.

Johnston, Lloyd D., Patrick. M. O'Malley, Jerald G. Bachman, and John E. Schulenberg (2006). *Monitoring the future: National survey results on drug use, 1975–2005: Volume I, Secondary school students*. NIH Publication No. 06-5883. Bethesda, MD: National Institute on Drug Abuse. http://www.monitoringthefuture.org/pubs/monographs/vol1_2005.pdf.

Kajstura, Aleks, and Peter Wagner. 2010. Importing constituents: Prisoners and political clout in California. Northampton, MA: Prison Policy Initiative. http://www.prisonersofthecensus.org/ca/report.html.

Kamasaki, Charles. 2002. Testimony on drug sentencing and its effects on the Latino community, February 25, 2002. Presented before the United States Sentencing Commission, Washington DC.

Karmen, Andrew. 2000. *New York murder mystery: The true story behind the crime crash of the 1990s*. New York, NY: New York University Press.

Kocieniewski, David, and Robert Hanley. 2000. Racial profiling was routine. *New York Times*, November 28.

LaFree, Gary, K. Drass, and P. O'Day. 1992. Race and crime in post-war America: Determinants of African American and white rates, 1957–1988. *Criminology* 30: 157–88.

Lee, Matthew T., Ramiro Martínez, Jr., and Richard B. Rosenfeld. 2001. Does immigration increase homicide? Negative evidence from three border cities. *Sociological Quarterly* 42(4): 559–80.

Leonhardt, David. 2007 (May 30). Immigrants and prison. *New York Times*. http://www.nytimes.com/2007/05/30/business/30leonside.html?ex=1184299200&en=e350a7f3a7435f38&ei=5070.

Levine, Harry G., and Deborah Peterson Small. 2008. *Marijuana arrest crusade: Racial bias and police policy in New York City, 1997–2007*. New York, NY: New York Civil Liberties Union.

Lovett, Ian. 2014 (February 10). Court gives California more time to ease prison crowding. *New York Times*. http://www.nytimes.com/2014/02/11/us/court-gives-california-more-time-to-ease-prison-crowding.html?_r=0.

Lyons, Sarah, and Nastassia Walsh. 2010. *Money well spent: how positive social investments will reduce incarceration rates, improve public safety, and promote the well-being of communities*. Washington, DC: Justice Policy Institute.

Martínez, Elizabeth. 1993. Beyond black/white: The racisms of our time. *Social Justice* 20(1–2): 22–34.

Martínez, Jr., Ramiro, Matthew T. Lee, and A. L. Nielsen. 2004. Segmented assimilation, local context and determinants of drug violence in Miami and San Diego: Does ethnicity and immigration matter? *International Migration Review* 38(1): 131–57.

Mauer, Marc. 1999. *Race to incarcerate*. New York, NY: The New Press.

Mauer, Marc, Cathy Potler, and Richard Wolf. 1999. *Gender and justice: Women, drugs, and sentencing policy*. Washington, DC: The Sentencing Project.

Maxfield, Linda Drazga, and John H. Kramer. 1998. *Substantial assistance: An empirical yardstick gauging equity in current federal policy and practice*. Washington, DC: U.S. Sentencing Commission.

McWilliams, Carey. 1948/1990. *North from Mexico: The Spanish-speaking people of the United States*. New York, NY: Praeger.

Méndez-Méndez, Serafín, and Diana Alverio. 2003. *Network brownout 2003: The portrayal of Latinos in network television news, 2002*. Washington, DC: National Association of Hispanic Journalists.

Mexican American Legal Defense and Education Fund. 2003. *Diminished voting power in the Latino community: The impact of felony disenfranchisement laws in ten targeted states*. Los Angeles, CA: Mexican American Legal Defense and Education Fund.

Mirandé, Alfredo. 1987. *Gringo justice*. Notre Dame, IN: University of Notre Dame Press.

Moran, Rachel F. 1997. Neither black nor white. *Harvard Latino Law Review* 2: 61–99.

Morín, José Luis. 2008. Latinas/os and U.S. prisons: Trends and challenges. *Latino Studies* 6: 11–34.

Morín, José Luis. 2009. *Latina/o rights and justice in the United States: Perspectives and approaches*. 2nd ed. Durham, NC: Carolina Academic Press.

Mumola, Christopher J., and Allen J. Beck. 1997. *Prisoners in 1996*. NCJ 164619. Washington, DC: U.S. Department of Justice, Bureau of Justice Statistics.

National Association for the Advancement of Colored People (NAACP) Legal Defense and Education Fund. 2010. *Captive constituents: Prison-based gerrymandering and the distortion of our democracy*. New York, NY: National Association for the Advancement of Colored People Legal Defense and Education Fund.

New York Civil Liberties Union. 2009. *The Rockefeller drug laws: Unjust, irrational, ineffective*. New York, NY: New York Civil Liberties Union.

New York State Division of Criminal Justice Services. 2008 (April). Computerized Criminal History System, 2008.

New York Times. 2010 (December 7). The crime of punishment. Editorial.

New York Times. 2011 (April 19). Real prisoners, phantom residents. Editorial.

Office of National Drug Control Policy. 2003. *Minorities and drugs*. Washington, DC: Office of National Drug Control Policy.

Olivas, Michael A. (ed.). 2006. *"Colored men" and "*hombres aquí*":* Hernandez v. Texas *and the emergence of Mexican-American lawyering*. Houston, TX: Arte Público Press.

Oquendo, Angel. 1996. Colloquium proceeding: Comments by Angel Oquendo. *La Raza Law Journal* 9: 43–47.

Pastor, Manuel, Jr. 1993. *Latinos and the L.A. uprising*. Los Angeles, CA: Tomas Rivera Center Study.

Perea, Juan F., Richard Delgado, Angela P. Harris, and Stephanie M. Wildman. 2000. *Race and races: Cases and resources for a diverse America*. St. Paul, MN: West Group.

Petersilia, Joan, and Susan Turner. 1986. *Prison versus probation in California*. Santa Monica, CA: Rand.

Pew Center on the States. 2008. *One in 100: Behind bars in America 2008*. Washington, DC: The Pew Charitable Trusts.

Pew Charitable Trusts. 2010. *Collateral costs: Incarceration's effect on economic mobility*. Washington, DC: The Pew Charitable Trusts.

Pinard, Michael. 2010. Collateral consequences of criminal convictions: Confronting issues of race and dignity. *New York University Law Review*: 85: 457–534.

Porter, Nicole D. 2010. *Expanding the vote: State felony disenfranchisement reform, 1997–2010*. Washington, DC: The Sentencing Project.

Pratt, Travis C. 2009. *Addicted to incarceration: Corrections policy and the politics of misinformation in the United States*. Thousand Oaks, CA: Sage Publications.

Press, Eyal. 2006 (December 3). Do immigrants make us safer? *New York Times Magazine*. http://www.nytimes.com/2006/12/03/magazine/03wwln_idealab.html.

Prison Policy Initiative. 2002. *Importing constituents: Prisoners and political clout in New York*. http://www.prisonpolicy.org/importing/importing.html. Accessed November 12, 2015.

Rennison, Callie Marie, and Michael R. Rand. 2003. *Criminal victimization, 2002: Bureau of Justice Statistics National Crime Victimization Survey (August 2003)*. NCJ 199994. Washington, DC: U.S. Department of Justice, Bureau of Justice Statistics.

Riley, K. Jack. 1997. *Crack, powder cocaine, and heroin: Drug purchase and use patterns in six U.S. cities*. Washington, DC: U.S. Department of Justice, National Institute of Justice.

Rivera Ramos, Efrén. 2001. *The legal construction of identity: The judicial and social legacy of American colonialism in Puerto Rico*. Washington, DC: American Psychological Association.

Rothfeld, Michael. 2010 (January 13). Judges OK Schwarzenegger plan to reduce prison crowding. *Los Angeles Times*.

Rumbaut, Rubén G., and Walter A. Ewing. 2007. *The myth of immigrant criminality and the paradox of assimilation: Incarceration rates among native and foreign-born men*. Washington, DC: Immigration Policy Center.

Rumbaut, Rubén, Roberto G. Gonzales, Golnaz Komaie, Charlie V. Morgan, and Rosaura Tafoya-Estrada. 2006. Immigration and incarceration: Patterns and predictors of imprisonment among first- and second-generation young adults. In *Immigration and crime: Race, ethnicity, and violence*, edited by R. Martínez, Jr. and A. Valenzuela, Jr., 64–89. New York, NY: New York University Press.

Sampson, Robert J., and Janet L. Lauritsen. 1997. Racial and ethnic disparities in crime and criminal justice in the United States. In *Ethnicity, crime, and immigration: Comparative and cross-national perspectives*, edited by Michael Tonry, 311–74. Chicago, IL: University of Chicago Press.

Sampson, Robert J., Jeffrey D. Morenoff, and Stephen Raudenbush. 2005. Social anatomy of racial and ethnic disparities in violence. *American Journal of Public Health* 95(2): 224–32.

Sentencing Project, The. 2003. *Hispanic prisoners in the United States*. Washington, DC: The Sentencing Project. http://www.sentencingproject.org/doc/publications/inc_hispanicprisoners.pdf. Accessed November 13, 2015.

Sentencing Project, The. 2005. *Racial disparity in sentencing: A review of the literature*. Washington, DC: The Sentencing Project. http://www.sentencingproject.org/doc/publications/rd_sentencing_review.pdf.

Sentencing Project, The. 2010. *Downscaling prisons: Lessons from four states*. Washington, DC: The Sentencing Project. http://www.sentencingproject.org/doc/publications/publications/inc_DownscalingPrisons2010.pdf.

Simon, Jonathan. 2007. *Governing through crime: How the war on crime transformed American democracy and created a culture of fear*. Oxford: Oxford University Press.

Spitzer, Elliot. 1999. *The New York City Police Department's "stop and frisk" practices: A report to the people of the state of New York from the attorney general*. New York, NY: Civil Rights Bureau.

Spohn, Cassia C. 2000. Thirty years of sentencing reform: The quest for a racially neutral sentencing process. In *Criminal justice 2000: Policies, processes, and decisions of the criminal justice system,* Vol. 3, 427–80. Washington, DC: National Institute of Justice.

Spohn, Cassia, John Gruhl, and Susan Welch. 1987. The impact of the ethnicity and gender of defendants on the decision to reject or dismiss felony charges. *Criminology* 25: 175–91.

States News Service. 2010. Briefing report: Prison overcrowding crisis—AB 900 three years later. http://cssrc.us/content/briefing-report-prison-overcrowding-crisis-ab-900-three-years-later. Accessed November 12, 2015.

Steffensmeier, Darrell, and Stephen Demuth. 2000. Ethnicity and sentencing in U.S. federal courts: Who is punished more harshly? *American Sociological Review* 65: 705–29.

Steffensmeier, Darrell, and Stephen Demuth. 2001. Ethnicity and judges' sentencing decisions: Hispanic-black-white comparisons. *Criminology* 39: 145–78.

Stephanson, Anders. 1995. *Manifest destiny: American expansion and the empire of right*. New York, NY: Hill and Wang.

Substance Abuse and Mental Health Services Administration. 2002. *Results from the 2001 national household survey on drug abuse: Volume 1. Summary of national findings*. No. SMA 02-3758. Rockville, MD: Department of Health and Human Services, Office of Applied Studies.

Task Force on Transforming Juvenile Justice. 2009. *Charting a new course: A blueprint for transforming juvenile justice in New York State*. New York, NY: Task Force on Transforming Juvenile Justice.

Tonry, Michael. 1995. *Maligned neglect: Race, crime and punishment in America*. New York, NY: Oxford University Press.

Travis, Jeremy. 2005. *But they all come back: Facing the challenges of prisoner reentry*. Washington, DC: Urban Institute Press.

United States Commission on Civil Rights. 2000. *Police practices and civil rights in New York City: A report of the United States Commission on Civil Rights*. Washington, DC: U.S. Commission on Civil Rights.

United States Sentencing Commission. 2001. *2001 sourcebook of federal sentencing statistics*. Washington, DC: United States Sentencing Commission.

Villarruel, Francisco A., and Nancy E. Walker, with Pamela Minifree, Omara Rivera-Vázquez, Susan Peterson, and Kristen Perry. 2002. *¿Dónde está la justicia? A call to action on behalf of Latino and Latina youth in the U.S. justice system*. Washington, DC: Michigan State University/Building Blocks for Youth.

Wacquant, Loïc. 2001. Deadly symbiosis: When ghetto and prison meet and mesh. In *Mass imprisonment: Social causes and consequences*, edited by David Garland, 82–120. London: Sage.

Walker, Nancy, E., J. Michael Senger, Francisco A. Villarruel, and Angela M. Arboleda. 2004. *Lost opportunities: The reality of Latinos in the U.S. criminal justice system*. Washington, DC: National Council of La Raza.

Walker, Samuel, Cassia Spohn, and Miriam DeLone. 2007. *The color of justice: Race, ethnicity, and crime in America*. 4th ed. Belmont, CA: Thomson/Wadsworth.

West, Heather C., William J. Sabol, and Sarah J. Greenman. 2010. *Prisoners in 2009*. NCJ 231675. Washington, DC: U.S. Department of Justice, Bureau of Justice Statistics.

Western, Bruce. 2006. *Punishment and inequality in America*. New York, NY: Russell Sage Foundation.

Yagla, Betsy. 2010 (March 31). Why the state should stop "prison gerrymandering." *New Haven Advocate.* http://www.newhavenadvocate.com/featured-news/phantom-voters.

Zatz, Marjorie S., and Richard P. Krecker, Jr. 2003. Anti-gang initiatives as racialized policy. In *Crime control and social justice: The delicate balance,* edited by D. F. Hawkins, S. L. Meyers, Jr., and R. N. Stone, 173–96. Westport, CT: Greenwood Press.

Cases Cited

Brown et al. v. Plata et al., 563 U.S. 493 (2011).

Reynolds v. Sims, 377 U.S. 533 (1963).

Gangs in the United States and Latina/o Communities

Louis Kontos and Luis Barrios

There is much speculation about the nature and extent of the gang phenomenon in the United States. Problems with regard to measurement include the fact that the term "gang" is vague. Researchers still debate the question of what constitutes a gang. Law enforcement agencies have simply adopted definitions that suit practical purposes, without maintaining consistency across jurisdictions. National surveys that rely on **police** respondents indicate an extraordinary increase in the number of **gangs** and gang members, particularly Latina/o gang members, over the last few decades; yet they do not correlate with arrest data. Surveys also typically exclude hate groups, bikers, and other types of gangs that are mostly white. Matters are further complicated by a popular culture which has developed a fascination with Latina/o gangs and gang members. Social policy debate about how to reduce **youth** involvement in gangs in Latina/o communities and throughout the United States has been distorted historically by ethnic and racial stereotypes and by a lack of information and conceptual clarity.

History of Latina/o "Gangs" in the United States

The first Latina/o gangs in the United States were Mexican. They appeared in the 1920s, together with the first sustained wave of Mexican immigration. **Mexicans** came from mostly poor, rural parts of their home country to work in the United States as *braceros* (field workers), railway workers, and miners, and in other low-paying, unstable jobs. As Vigil (1990) describes, the people in this early group of Mexican immigrants settled in both rural and urban locations in California; in each case apart from other ethnic groups. Those who settled in urban "enclaves" had readier access to the dominant culture. Vigil estimated that 10 to 20 percent of the latter became "street socialized." Traditional forms of social control in the community broke down as young people turned away from ritualized hard work and sacrifice for meager outcomes. Gangs—for the second generation and beyond—provided an alternative form of community where members could live with relative freedom from adult constraints and simultaneously gain protection, economic opportunity, recognition, and respect.

It does not seem that there was much concern with Latina/o gangs among whites until the 1940s. The **Sleepy Lagoon** murder brought Mexican youth into the public consciousness as a dangerous and potentially subversive group. The event took place on August 2, 1942, when police found the body of a Mexican young man, José Díaz, in the Sleepy Lagoon reservoir in Southeast Los Angeles. Twenty-two Chicano youths were charged with this crime and subsequently endured a trial full of irregularities, with a jury composed exclusively of white people. The trial served as a catalyst for what later in 1943 would be known as the "**Zoot Suit Riots**." Acting under the belief that Mexican Americans were not cooperating in the war effort, hundreds of GIs decided to carry out raids against youth who wore zoot suits. The zoot suit consisted of a long coat jacket with wide lapels and baggy pants with narrow cuffs. Young Mexican Americans wore the popular zoot suit fashion as an expression of Mexican American youth culture and identity. Nevertheless, this distinctive form of dress was used by the media and law enforcement to single out Mexican American youth as a criminal element.

Anti-Mexican sentiment, fueled by sensationalist media reports about the Sleepy Lagoon murder, spread widely. Many violations against the Mexican community took place and most of them were not prosecuted by government agencies. When the rioting ended, the City Council of Los Angeles passed an ordinance banning zoot suits, with a sentence of 30 days in jail for those found guilty. The manner of dress and talk associated with **pachuco** subculture became the central criteria for labeling someone as a dangerous and criminal gang member.

The 1950s proved to be a stable period for Mexican American gangs, with returning GIs in Mexican American neighborhoods gaining all the benefits of the GI Bill and bringing a great deal of order to the *barrio*. The 1960s transformed these groups in various ways. The War on Poverty brought not only opportunity and hope, but also rising expectations. The Vietnam War provoked outrage and rebellion within an increasingly militant youth counterculture, which included "street socialized" Mexican American youth, now in its third and fourth generations. Mexican American gangs turned for the worse dramatically in the 1980s when industrialized cities experienced a massive exodus of well-paying, low-skilled jobs and the criminal justice system became the primary solution for dealing with surplus populations, including the start of the currently popular policy of **deportation**. Mexican American gang culture has diffused throughout major urban centers in Mexico that account for much of the current immigration from Mexico to the United States. As a result, many of the "new" Mexican immigrants require very little in the way of "street socialization" to join gangs in the United States.

Puerto Rican gangs, which appeared later, followed a similar pattern. Puerto Rican immigration began in the 1830s. Few changes occurred with regard to immigration in 1898 when Puerto Rico became a colony of the United States. Much changed a few decades later, however, in 1917 when the Jones Act provided Puerto Ricans with U.S. citizenship, and in 1921 when the Johnson Act restricted European immigration. During this period the peso had been significantly devalued, creating a strong incentive for Puerto Ricans to head for the mainland. Almost all the newcomers settled in New York City—East (Spanish) Harlem to be exact. In the 1950s, New York City experienced moral panic over perceived increases in "**juvenile delinquency**," with young Puerto Ricans as the face of the problem. It is doubtful that delinquency rates actually increased, at least not substantially and also doubtful that Puerto Rican rates of offending were substantially greater than other ethnic groups. Sensational incidents did, however, catch the public eye. One such instance was the "Capeman" case of 1959, in which **Salvador Agron**, a 16-year-old member of the Vampires gang who was known for wearing a cape, stabbed two white teenagers in New York's Hell's Kitchen. During a well-publicized trial, Agron not only showed no remorse but threatened to kill the prosecutor.

Puerto Rican migration to Chicago began in a sustained way in the 1950s, as a result of the dramatic effort to industrialize the island that came with the renaming of the colonial relationship with the United States under the label of "Commonwealth." The inability to create a sufficient number of industrial jobs for the island's population forced many people to leave Puerto Rico in search of employment in the continental United States. Puerto Rican migrants largely settled in major cities, such as New York and Chicago. One of the earliest documented Puerto Rican gangs in Chicago was La Hacha Vega, composed of adult males from the South side of the city. Unlike the South side, the North side of Chicago was composed of large apartment buildings, where residents faced less discrimination and established greater unity. In turn, they experienced animosity from other ethnic groups in the area—especially the Italian and Irish communities—and dealt with discrimination by Chicago Police which seemed also to "collude" with these groups against the newcomers. The 1966 riots, sparked by **police brutality**, served to politicize many of the extant Puerto Rican gangs in Chicago, particularly the **Young Lords**.

Many older Latina/o gangs that have survived every attempt to suppress them have become quasi-institutional in nature. They are patterned around rules, modes of interaction, and goals that provide a basis for reproduction of the same gangs past the first generation of members. They are no longer merely "interstitial," or in-between childhood and adulthood, as Thrasher (1927) said of gangs in general. Institutional gangs are also trans-local and, in certain cases, **transnational**. They spread as subcultures. Among the largest and most organized gangs, subculture is not merely an extension or distorted appropriation of ethnic culture (as when Italian gangs would call themselves Romans, for example), but also an assemblage of symbols, concepts, and ideologies from disparate sources. It also is not uncommon today to find gang literature that draws ideas and phrases from religious and political texts. These elements of subculture provide a basis for the construction of identity more intensely than what previous gang formations had accomplished.

Established gangs offer their members more in the way of culture (a style of life) and a sense of belonging and purpose, and they demand much more in return than did the gangs formed by second-generation immigrants which, for the most part, dissolved naturally with the aging-out of members. By contrast, the newer gangs that are composed of recent immigrants from Central America are less organized and provide less in the way of subculture. Because a great amount of **violence** and crime appears to be associated with **Central American** gangs, it is necessary to identify and dispel a few of the most egregious myths surrounding them. To start, such gangs did not originate in Central America. They formed in the United States. They also do not represent international criminal conspiracies, but are a locally based agglomerate of hybrid groups. Generally, they are more turf oriented, or territorial, than the established Latina/o gangs.

Sustained waves of immigration from Central America began in the 1980s. The newcomers fled from civil war, political persecution, and extreme poverty. In fact, with the exception of the end of the civil war in El Salvador—which left 75,000 dead and 8,000 missing—the conditions that force or "push" a population to emigrate still exist with virtually the same intensity. One-third of the Latin American population now lives in poverty. Of the 200 million teenagers and children living in Latin America and the Caribbean, half live in poverty. In El Salvador most youths are not educated beyond fourth grade, according to UNICEF (Valdez 2008). In the 1980s, Central American immigrants gravitated to places with large Latina/o populations and cheap housing. Mayan groups fled villages in the Guatemalan highlands and settled in the area northeast of MacArthur Park. Salvadorians settled in the Pico Union area of Westlake, Los Angeles. Some then moved to South Central Los Angeles, displacing part of the African American population in the process. As economic conditions worsened in Westlake in the 1980s, some Salvadorian youth were recruited into gangs, particularly 18th Street, and others formed their own gangs, among which **Mara Salvatrucha**, or MS-13, has become the most notable.

In 1996, changes in U.S. immigration law made it easier to deport unauthorized (and, in some cases, authorized) immigrants with felony criminal records to their Central American countries of origin. An endless stream of deportation, however, seems to have produced inadvertent consequences. The current murder rate in El Salvador is approaching the casualty rate of the country's civil war, most of that attributed by official sources to the *maras* (gangs), the largest being MS-13. There is reason to be skeptical regarding official accounts, however. Between 2003 and 2007, for instance, only 12 percent of murders in El Salvador were attributed to gangs by the Institute of Legal Medicine (IMC), whereas El Salvador's National Civil Police put the figure at 40 to 60 percent. Jeannette Aguilar, head of the Central American University Institute of Public Opinion (IUDOP-UCA), sides with the IMC after having conducted several research projects involving *maras*. Aguilar opines that many intransigent problems in El Salvador, including burgeoning organized crime syndicates and corrupt police officers that serve and protect it, have been overshadowed by the public hysteria stirred up by the National Civil Police over *maras* (Jutersonke et al. 2009).

Misperceptions of "Gangs"

One of the myths perpetuated by popular culture and media is that "gangs" are an exclusive Latino or African American phenomenon. Instead, gang membership reflects the ethnic composition of the communities where gangs are located. As communities change, so do their problems, including the problem of gangs. Ethnicity is relevant only in the context of place. Multi-ethnic gangs appear in multi-ethnic communities. If a gang develops in a rural white community, its members most likely will be white. According to the 2004 National Youth Gang Survey (NYGS), 49 percent of gang members in the United States were Latina/o, though they comprised only 17 percent of the 12- to 24-year-old population. The rest of the breakdown is as follows: 35 percent African-American, 9 percent white, and 7 percent other race/ethnicity (Egley, Howell, & Major 2006).

The NYGS is distributed annually to all law enforcement agencies in urban and suburban areas having more than 50,000 residents. It also includes a random sample of police departments in smaller areas. Respondents are instructed to exclude motorcycle gangs, prison gangs, ideological groups, hate groups, and adult gangs. This stipulation perhaps accounts for some of the variance between the ethnic make-up of gangs that appears in the NYGS and what appears via other surveys. The National Longitudinal Survey of Youth (NLSY) provides a significant contrast. The first round of the survey took place in 1997 with 9,000 youth born between 1980 and 1984. The sample was representative of a cross section of the population of youth in the United States. Respondents were re-interviewed annually over a four-year period. Applying NLSY prevalence rates to the 12- to 16-year-old population from the 2000 Census, Greene and Pranis (2007, 37) estimated that Latinos account for approximately 25 percent of gang members; whites comprise about 40 percent, African Americans 25 percent, and the remainder is composed of other racial groups.

The most comprehensive account of gang "trends" from law enforcement sources can be found in the *National Gang Threat Assessment, 2009*, a report prepared by The National Gang Intelligence Center (NGIC), "a multi-agency effort that integrates the gang intelligence assets of federal, state, and local law enforcement entities to serve as a centralized intelligence resource for gang information and analytical support." According to the NGIC,

> Gang members are increasingly migrating from urban to suburban areas and are responsible for a growing percentage of crime and violence in many communities. . . . Additionally, a rising number of U.S.-based gangs are seemingly intent on developing working relationships with United States and foreign-based **drug trafficking** organizations (DTOs) and other criminal organizations to gain direct access to foreign sources of illicit **drugs**.

It should be noted that that these conclusions were drawn from surveys similar to the NYGS rather than from arrest statistics or other objective data. Therefore, the claim that (Latina/o) gangs are developing into international criminal conspiracies amounts to speculation.

This fact is easily lost by virtue of the prestige of the Federal Bureau of Investigation (FBI), Justice Department, and other agencies which produced the report under the auspices of NGIC. Several newspapers around the country, for instance, including *USA Today*, printed the claim that, based on the NGIC report, 80 percent of crime in the United States is gang related, with Latina/o gangs playing the major role. The stories did not bother to mention that the report referred only to some unspecified, anomalous areas with this problem. The report actually states, "According to local law enforcement information, gang members are responsible for as much as 80 percent of the crime in some locations" (National Gang Intelligence Center 2009, 8). No mention is made as to which locations or how "local law enforcement" gathered the information.

The 2009 Gang Threat Assessment Report provides strong support for current policy initiatives, including legislation that intensifies deportation campaigns, militarized policing, and for broadening the net of the criminal justice system. Such initiatives are controversial because they entail a diversion of resources from social programs that benefit poor communities and from the institutions of civil society, including education, and because they serve to further criminalize entire sections of the population. Scholarly research appears increasingly at odds with official political discourse about gangs, notwithstanding the fact that researchers have been increasingly preoccupied with gang-related crime and violence.

The Problem of Defining Gangs

Aside from the fact that NGIC has existed for only four years and that the agencies that provide it with data employ disparate methods inconsistently, there is a glaring contradiction in its admission of a definitional problem and its willingness to generalize and further speculate upon sketchy facts. The definitional problem is framed in the report in terms of "lack of uniform definition of a gang" among various reporting agencies, and as "one of the greatest impediments to the collection of accurate gang-related data" (National Gang Intelligence Center 2009, 3). The problem is seemingly resolved through its selection "for the purposes of this assessment" of a single definition, the one used by the National Alliance of Gang Investigators (NAGIA): "A gang is a group or association of three or more persons with a common identifying sign, symbol, or name who individually or collectively engage in criminal activity that creates an atmosphere of fear or intimidation" (National Gang Intelligence Center 2009, 3). The report does not state how this definition was incorporated into the data before it was reported; for instance, whether any groups that previously were labeled as gangs by the relevant agencies were now omitted or whether new ones were added. Notice that—as with any definition of gangs—seemingly objective, legalistic language is mixed together with colloquial terms, such that maximum leeway is provided for the labeling of groups as gangs. Indeed, plenty of legitimate groups with odd and distinct signs, symbols, and names—including college fraternities—engage periodically, "individually and collectively" in criminal activity. Plenty of groups that are not normally labeled gangs create "an atmosphere of fear" for some part of the population, including groups of police officers. But none of this seems to matter.

The definitional problem also is encountered in academic gang research. That is to say, there is nothing resembling professional consensus among researchers regarding any aspect of the topic, including what constitutes a gang. There literally are dozens of attempts within the academic literature to define gangs. The most successful of these attempts can be found in the work of Klein (1971, 13), where the gang is defined as

> any denotable adolescent group of youngsters who (a) are generally perceived as a distinct aggregation by others in their neighborhood, (b) recognize themselves as a denotable group (almost invariably with a group name), and (c) have been involved in a sufficient number of delinquent incidents to call forth a consistent negative response from neighborhood residents and/or law enforcement agencies.

Despite the seemingly objective language in this definition (e.g., "denotable adolescent group," "distinct aggregation") it leaves much to be desired. What happens when there is disagreement about particular groups within or between the community and among law enforcement agencies? What is added to analyses of disparate groups that engage in delinquent acts by referring to them by the same name: gangs? Does the label capture something intrinsic about any group? Klein's answer is that a group becomes a gang when it acts like a gang. In which case there is no reason to exclude skinheads or biker gangs from the study of "gangs"; nor is there reason to focus exclusively on gangs in the inner-city. If gang researchers applied Klein's (or any) definition of gangs consistently and without the exclusion of large numbers of white kids who join delinquent groups, then the ethnic composition of gangs would be different from what is included in their work.

To be sure, valid information about gangs is difficult to find regardless of whether it is sought by researchers or law enforcement agents. Gangs are secretive organizations. Infiltrating them always has been difficult because members generally know each other from the neighborhood. Information from members themselves—particularly members who turn against the group or choose to cooperate with the police for whatever reason, whose motives are thereby suspect—is always only of relative value. It is worth mentioning, however, that the reasons that members provide for joining gangs remain relatively constant from the very earliest self-reports until now; the reasons being social rather than criminal in nature (*see* Kontos, Brotherton, & Barrios 2003). Very few members within any large organization know much about the organization itself, beyond what takes place in their immediate surroundings. With regard to such features as the size of the gang, its toughness, its commitment to violence, and the nature and extent of criminality within the gang, the observed tendency—and here it is possible to generalize—has been toward exaggeration rather than understatement. Membership in a gang generally involves overstatement and what Katz and Jackson-Jacobs (2004) call "myth making." The practice is in keeping with the logic of gang symbols, rituals, folklore, even gang names and monikers (e.g., Lord, Disciple, King).

Debunking Myths About Gangs

A basic principle of social research is that it should be possible to compare the "findings" of researchers across time and place (*see* Durkheim 1982). This task becomes difficult when the data that provide a basis for comparison are produced through widely disparate methods. In the case of gangs, this problem is especially pronounced because research, for the most part until very recently, has not been systematic; with an entire decade (1965–1975) of virtually nothing in the way of scholarly research and publications about gangs. Unless the focus is strictly on crime and how to prevent it, it is never clear what motivates researchers to take up the topic of gangs. Yet motivating interests, in this regard, can be discerned in part from the choice of methods. For instance, observations of group dynamics tend to humanize the gang, whereas large, structured surveys transform disparate groups into a mere aggregate which yields a closed system of variables, within which causal sequences, ratios, and rates of relevant phenomena can be discerned. As Horowitz (1990) puts it, the motivating interests and choice of methods of gang researchers oftentimes reflect ideological trends in the larger society.

It is worth noting that gang research began with the Chicago School in the 1920s, and that its members were empathetic toward gangs in a straightforward way. Thrasher (1927), in particular, appeared fond of the "gang boys" that he studied. He described their problems in empathetic terms, even though he did little to underplay the problems they caused to others in their community, or the fact that one-quarter of them (in his estimation) became involved in organized crime. It seemed to Thrasher that gangs should not be needed in a modern, industrial society such as the United States. Whatever functions the gang provided—protection, entertainment, acculturation, camaraderie, ways of making money—corresponded to legitimate entitlements and expectations. The society could ameliorate, if not eliminate, the gang problem in this view by providing "immediate substitutions" for the functions of gangs. Other approaches, such as social work or law enforcement, could achieve results, but nothing that would get to the root of the problem, namely that poor, disenfranchised young people (especially immigrants) in the United States were/are left to fend for themselves through a maze of dysfunctional institutions, dangerous neighborhoods, and sporadic or nonexistent employment opportunities; as if they live in the wilderness rather than urban society. Thrasher, perhaps, had a point when he likened gang members to "pioneers" and "frontiersmen."

Presently, the sociological study of gangs, generally speaking, is more narrowly criminological in its focus than was the case throughout most of its history. To the same extent, it more closely embraces the concerns of outsiders, including people who have left the city for the suburbs, the returning gentry and, most importantly, the business sector—their concerns being virtually interchangeable and their voices (grievances, demands) virtually indistinguishable. In the neighborhoods where gangs have a strong presence, the gang members are not a singular entity. Some are deemed innocuous, others dangerous. Even the "same" gang can gain and lose support of the locals, depending upon, among other reasons, changes within the gang itself. There usually is at least some degree of ambivalence associated with gangs in communities where a large number of members have past gang experience, or fear the police, or have witnessed a deteriorating local political economy with no remedy in sight.

Gangs in Latina/o Communities

It appears that the same places that have experienced the sharpest increases in gangs—including New York, California, Virginia, and the Carolinas—have experienced significant growth in immigration from Latin America. Because immigration historically has been associated with gangs, the criminalization and demonization of Latina/o youths is not surprising. The more important difference appears to be between newer and older generations of Latina/o immigrants, specifically Mexican and Puerto Rican immigrants versus Salvadorian, Colombian, and Guatemalan immigrants. The latter are forming gangs without waiting for the second. Unlike European immigrants throughout the early part of the 20th century, they already have been introduced to American styles of life, including American gangsterism, through popular representations and through the process of deportation (of immigrants who have committed felonies, a process that moved into high gear with the Immigration Act of 1996), which ensures that a steady stream of deported gang members will find contact with young men and women living in the poorest sections of Latin America. Deported gang members bring back home whatever version of gang culture they picked up in places such as New York, Chicago, and Los Angeles. They bring gang culture with them, recycling gang culture through massive, endless streams of deportation—a phenomenon that is not well understood but has provoked fear. The immigrant populations from Latin America lack the resources to counter a public image constructed for them by journalists, politicians, and often lack even the resources of established Latino communities.

It is difficult to separate the current wave of anti-immigrant reaction from legitimate concerns about what appears to be a growing street gang problem experienced in Latina/o communities. Some have framed the issue as "an immigrant gang plague" (Mac Donald 2004) or characterize a series of crimes associated with Mara Salvatrucha (MS-13), 18th Street, and the Latin Kings (Chicago) as the making of the next American mafia. In contrast, scholars and public interest groups—such as the Justice Policy

Institute—point to the empirical evidence that show that gangs actually account for a minor share of crime in most jurisdictions and that Latina/o immigrants are less prone to criminality than are full U.S. citizens.

Failed Policies

The logic of gang suppression has become increasingly difficult to refute, not because any particular suppression policy has been spectacularly effective—indeed, there is a long history of failed attempts to suppress gangs through increased penalties for gang-related crime, police sting operations, injunctions, and more recently the increased participation of the FBI and the development and expansion of "gang units" in urban areas across the country. Rather, the argument in support of increased suppression is that gangs today are qualitatively worse in almost every respect than their predecessors, and therefore there is a greater need to defend against them. The dramatic growth of gangs that law enforcement agencies across the country have been reporting to the FBI in recent years does not contradict the argument on behalf of suppression; the problem might be even more spectacular with less suppression. Inadvertent outcomes, such as the spread of gangs through the prison system, which happened in a big way in the 1980s, are never part of this discourse. Nevertheless, the majority of Americans appear to realize that suppression is not the answer. According to **public opinion** surveys, there is great support for the idea of "getting tough" on gangs, but not in the absence of intervention, **prevention**, and rehabilitation. The problem in this respect is that the voting public rarely is offered meaningful alternatives to punitive justice.

The historic crime drop that occurred over the last two decades has made the idea of punitive justice seem credible against the backdrop of failed experiments with alternatives. At the same time, tight municipal budgets make it difficult to justify any expenditure on alternatives to punitive justice on a scale that might make a difference. In contrast, the political environment of the 1930s and 1960s was more conducive to sociologically formulated solutions to the gang problem. An array of programs for gang members and other problematic youth materialized; the two most notable are the Chicago Area Project (CAP) and the Mobilization for Youth. They are notable not only for their range of services, but also because they were developed around theories that embodied a critique of American culture, society, and political economy.

CAP was developed around the work of Chicago school sociologists and took their claim that gangs were a natural response to "social disorganization" seriously. In this view, place was what mattered most of all. The gang was broadly understood to serve various functions that overburdened and dysfunctional local institutions failed to provide. CAP provided recreation and advocacy before school officials and within the criminal justice system. It was started by Clifford Shaw in 1934 in South Chicago in areas with the highest crime rates. Local residents were organized to help released offenders find jobs or attend school. Community leaders were expected to work directly with gangs, not only with individual members; for example to mediate gang disputes. In 1944, Shaw produced an equivocal evaluation of the program. He believed that it helped reduce "juvenile delinquency," but also stated that no causal connection could be made. The program remains popular today (Schlossman & Sedlak 1983).

The Mobilization for Youth (MFY) program is the most comprehensive and expensive to date. It was conceived in 1957 and funded in 1961. More than 50 million dollars was spent dealing with the problem of juvenile delinquency and gangs through this program. Attorney General Robert Kennedy, impressed by the book *Delinquency and Opportunity*, asked its co-author Lloyd Ohlin to help develop federal policy regarding delinquency. The Juvenile Delinquency Prevention and Control Act of 1961 was the result. Its focus on job creation, community organization, social services, and improvement of schools, made it a precursor to the War on Poverty. Cloward and Ohlin's (1969) argument that delinquent and conflict-oriented youth subcultures tend to develop in the absence of legitimate "opportunity structures" became the basis for the MFY. Much like CAP, the MFY drew on influential members of the community as a resource, regardless of criminal record or past gang affiliations. The MFY organized residents of New York City to take action against dysfunctional institutions, including the schools, welfare agencies, and the police. Confrontational tactics such as rent strikes and school boycotts made the MFY controversial. Its organizers routinely were accused of being communists and blamed for urban unrest. Nixon ended the program in 1968 when he was elected president.

The problems that faced the MFY, including the inability to show results significant enough to justify its cost and offset ideological attacks, today confronts virtually any organization that seeks to deal directly with active gang members. The most controversial of these organizations is **Homies Unidos**. Homies was founded in 1996 in El Salvador after a meeting of more than 20 rival gang members, most of whom recently had been deported from the United States. Its founder, Magdeleno Rose-Avila is recognized internationally as a human rights advocate. In 1997, Homies was co-founded in Los Angeles by **Alex Sánchez**, a former member of MS-13. Its board of directors includes former members of rival gangs. Homies is controversial in part because it does not require gang members to become former members, rather only to demonstrate commitment to peace. It seeks ostensibly to transform gang culture from within by redirecting many of the functional attributes of gangs—such as loyalty and solidarity—into positive societal goals. Homies provides a range of services, including vocational workshops, tattoo removal, arts and culture programs, assistance to gang members that are returning from prison, and family counseling services.

In 1999, Sánchez helped expose the notorious Los Angeles police corruption and abuse scandal, commonly referred to at the **Rampart Scandal,** by testifying before a State Senate Committee. Dozens of LAPD officers were eventually found guilty of criminal activities that included beating suspects and planting evidence. In 2000, Sánchez was arrested by LAPD officers on an Immigration and Naturalization Service warrant—even though the LAPD is explicitly barred from engaging in this practice. LAPD officials claimed that Homies was nothing more than a ruse that enabled Sánchez to engage in criminal activity. An outpouring of support from the community stopped the deportation proceedings. In 2009, Sánchez was again arrested, now accused of being a secret "shot caller" of MS-13 and of ordering the assassination of a rival member in El Salvador. In Senator Tom Hayden's (2009) words "The indictment of Alex Sánchez, a revered gangbanger-turned-peacemaker, raises new doubts about whether the Los Angeles police department has reformed sufficiently to be released from a federal court order." He continues by saying that this indictment "brings back strong memories in Los Angeles *barrios* of the Sleepy Lagoon case during war hysteria in 1942, when the LAPD and media helped railroad three young Mexican men into long murder sentences."

The endless controversy around Homies speaks to the question of how the gang problem should be understood—whether it is thought of as strictly a law enforcement problem or instead as a social problem with deep structural causes. A related question is what it means for any program that deals with gangs to be successful. The project Blueprints for Violence Prevention, developed in 1996 by the Center for the Study and Prevention of Violence (CSPV) at the University of Colorado at Boulder, for instance, appears successful with regard to reductions in gang crime and violence, but not in dissolving gangs or convincing members to leave them. It involves a model of intervention in the family life of gang members, called Functional Family Therapy, which has been replicated in hundreds of places throughout the country. Similarly, the Comprehensive Gang Program Model, developed in the mid-1990s in Chicago's Little Village Neighborhoods provides services ranging from family counseling to job referrals. The youth that participated in the program experienced a decrease in "gang-related drug arrests" even as such arrests in the neighborhood increased by 1,000 percent in the mid-1990s. There is no evidence that the program produced the result of fewer gangs or gang members, however. Inasmuch as the conditions that produce gangs continue to exist, the success of any program or policy directed at gangs legitimately only can be measured in terms of the actual types of assistance provided to gang members as people in need. Intuitively, this humanistic logic works to ameliorate the gang problem within a set of conditions that work against it.

Latina/o Gangs: Current and Future Challenges

Any objective account of the history and current social reality of Latina/o gangs makes evident the need to move toward a different set of public-policy objectives. Scholars argue that the logic of authoritarianism and punitive justice makes little sense with regard to gangs because, after several decades' worth of policies that embody this logic, the number of gangs and gang members has risen astronomically—at least according to the FBI—and because gang members are not foreign enemies but, for the most part, are members of distressed communities across the country. Latinas/os have been in the United States in significant numbers since at least 1848; they have and will continue to comprise a significant portion of the U.S. population into the future. The persistence of poverty and marginalization of this largely young population raises grave questions about how society will meet the socioeconomic needs and well-being of its future generations.

In the current political environment, academics and policy advocates appear compromised. Not much can be expected if seemingly every public-policy initiative targeting gangs not only fails to address the root causes of the gang problem, but also ignores predictable inadvertent consequences of the militarized policing of urban areas and the **mass incarceration** of young people. Though it is common nowadays to talk of the "failure" of alternatives to punitive justice, it bears repeating that the entire criminal justice system also has failed, in a spectacular way, particularly with regard to the objective of ameliorating the gang problem. It also should be noted that this failure is not something new. Recognition of the fact that the police and the courts are inadequate as a solution to the gang problem was integral to the thinking of organizers of the MFY in the 1960s. It is integral today to the thinking of progressive academic gang researchers and policy advocates.

See also: Part I essays: The U.S. War on Drugs and Latina/o Communities; Latinas and the U.S. Criminal Justice System; Incarceration and Latinas/os in the United States; Latina/o Youth and Criminal Justice. Part II entries: Central Americans; Deportation; Mexicans and Mexican Americans; Political Activist Groups; Transnational Crime.

Further Reading

Ball, Richard A., and G. David Curry. 1995. The logic of definition in criminology: Purposes and methods for defining "gangs." *Criminology* 33(2): 225–45.

Cloward, Richard A., and Lloyd E. Ohlin. 1969. *Delinquency and opportunity: A theory of delinquent gangs*. Glencoe, IL: Free Press.

Diaz, Tom. 2009. *No boundaries: Transnational Latino gangs and American law enforcement*. Ann Arbor, MI: University of Michigan Press.

Durkheim, Emile. 1982. *Rules of sociological method*. Glencoe, IL: Free Press.

Egley, Arlen Jr., James C. Howell, and Aline K. Major. 2006. National Youth Gang Survey: 1999–2001. Washington, DC: U.S. Department of Justice, Office of Juvenile Justice and Delinquency Prevention.

Escobar, Edward J. 1999. *Race, police, and the making of a political identity: Mexican Americans and the Los Angeles Police Department, 1900–1945*. Berkeley, CA: University of California Press.

Federal Bureau of Investigation. 2006. *Intelligence bulletin no. 198*. http://info.publicintelligence.net/streetgangs.pdf. Accessed November 2, 2015.

Federal Bureau of Investigation Los Angeles. 2009. "Twenty-four defendant indictment names members and leaders of notorious MS-13 gang, alleging federal racketeering violations, including multiple murders." https://www.fbi.gov/losangeles/press-releases/2009/la062409-1.htm. Accessed November 2, 2015.

García, Michelle. 2005. N.Y. using terrorism law to prosecute street gang: Critics say post-9/11 legislation is being applied too broadly. http://www.washingtonpost.com/wpdyn/articles/A52504-2005Jan31.html.

Gonzalez, Juan. 2000. *Harvest of empire: A history of Latinos in America*. New York, NY: Penguin Books.

Government Accountability Office. 2009. Combating gangs. Better coordination and performance measurement would help clarify roles of federal agencies and strengthen assessment of efforts. Report to the Ranking Committee member, Committee on Oversight and Government Reform, House of Representatives. Washington DC: Government Accountability Office.

Greene, Judith, and Kevin Pranis. 2007. *Gang wars: The failure of enforcement tactics and the need for effective public safety strategies*. Washington DC: Justice Policy Institute.

Gutiérrez, David G. (ed.). 2004. *The Columbia history of Latinos in the United States since 1960*. New York, NY: Columbia University Press.

Hagedorn, John M. (ed.). 2007. *Gangs in the global city: Alternatives to traditional criminology*. Chicago, IL: University of Illinois Press.

Hayden, Tom. 2009. Alex Sanchez's arrest. *The Nation*. June 29. http://www.thenation.com/doc/20090713/hayden.

Helfgot, Joseph H. 1981. *Professional reforming: Mobilization for youth and the failure of social science*. Lanham, MD: Lexington Books.

Hogan, Michael. 2009. *Savage capitalism and the myth of democracy*. Booklocker.com.

Horowitz, Ruth. 1990. Sociological perspectives on gangs: Conflicting definitions and concepts. In *Gangs in America*, edited by R. Huff, 37–54. Thousand Oaks, CA: Sage Publications.

Jutersonke, Oliver, Robert Muggah, and Dennis Rodgers. 2009. Gangs and violence reduction in Central America. *Security Dialogue* 40(4–5): 1–25.

Katz, Jack, and Curtis Jackson-Jacobs. 2004. The criminologist's gang. *The Blackwell companion to criminology,* edited by C. Summer, 91–124. Malden, MA: Blackwell.

Klein, Malcolm W. 1971. *Street gangs and street workers.* Englewood Cliffs, NJ: Prentice-Hall.

Klein, Malcolm W. 1995. *The American street gang: In nature, prevalence and control.* New York, NY: Oxford University Press.

Knox, George W. 2000. Gang profile: The Latin Kings. National Gang Crime Research Center. http://www.ngcrc.com/ngcrc/page15.htm.

Kontos, Louis, David C. Brotherton, and Luis Barrios (eds.). 2003. *Gangs and society: Alternative perspectives.* New York: Columbia University Press.

Mac Donald, Heather. 2004. The immigrant gang plague. *City Journal.* http://www.city-journal.org/html/14_3_immigrant_gang.html. Accessed November 2, 2015.

Mazon, Mauricio. 1984. *The Zoot-Suit Riots: The psychology of symbolic annihilation.* Austin, TX: University of Texas Press.

Mendez, Mervin. 2002. The Young Lords and early Chicago Puerto Rican gangs. http://libcom.org/history/young-lords-early-chicago-puerto-rican-gangs. Accessed November 2, 2015.

Miller, Walter B. 1990. Why the United States has failed to solve its youth gang problem. In *Gangs in America,* edited by C. R. Huff, 263–89. Thousand Oaks, CA: Sage Publications.

Minority Staff of the Committee on Homeland Security. U.S. House of Representatives. 2005. *The U.S. border patrol: Failure of the administration to deliver a comprehensive land border strategy leaves our nation's borders vulnerable.* http://homeland.house.gov/SiteDocuments/20060912174839-94357.pdf.

Muñoz, Jr., Carlos. 2007. *Youth, identity, power: The Chicano movement.* New York, NY: Verso.

National Gang Intelligence Center. 2009. National gang threat assessment 2009. https://www.fbi.gov/stats-services/publications/national-gang-threat-assessment-2009-pdf. Accessed November 2, 2015.

National Youth Gang Center. 2009. *The national youth gang survey analysis.* Accessed November 2, 2015.

Raikhlin, Raddai. 2003. *Civil war, terrorism and gangs.* BookSurge Publishing.

Sanchez, George J. 1923. *Becoming Mexican American: Ethnicity, culture, and identity in Chicano Los Angeles, 1900–1945.* New York, NY: Oxford University Press.

Schlossman, Steven, and Michael Sedlak. 1983. *The Chicago area project revisited.* Santa Monica, CA: The Rand Corporation.

Schneider, Eric C. 1999.*Vampires, dragons, and Egyptian kings: Youth gangs in postwar New York.* Princeton, NJ: Princeton University Press.

Semple, Kirk. 2008 (January 23). Padilla gets 17-year term for role in conspiracy. *New York Times.*

Short, Jr., James. 2007. Challenges of gangs in global contexts. In *Gangs in the global city: Alternatives to traditional criminology,* edited by J. Hagedorn, 319–43. Chicago, IL: University of Illinois Press.

Thrasher, Frederic. 1927. *The gang: A study of 1313 gangs in Chicago.* Chicago, IL: University of Chicago Press.

U.S. Department of Education. [n.d.]. http://www2.ed.gov/admins/lead/safety/training/gangs/index.html. Accessed November 2, 2015.

Walker, Samuel, Cassia Spohn, and Miriam DeLone. 2007. *The color of justice: Race, ethnicity, and crime in America.* 4th ed. Belmont, CA: Thomson/Wadsworth.

Williams, Paul L. 2005. *The Al Qaeda connection: International terrorism, organized crime, and the coming apocalypse.* Amherst, NY: Prometheus Books.

Williams, Timothy. 2007 (November 1). Gang member is convicted under terror law. *New York Times*. http://www.nytimes.com/2007/11/01/nyregion/01terror.html?_r=1&em&ex=1194062400&en=47fe558002f7a97f&ei=5087.

Valdez, Al. 2008. *Gangs and Central America. Maras, security and development in Central America task force*. Sept.-Nov. 2007. Miami, FL: Center for Hemispheric Policy, University of Miami.

Venkatesh, Sudhir Alladi. 1996. The gang in the community. In *Gangs in America*, edited by C. R. Huff, 242–55. Thousand Oaks, CA: Sage Publications.

Vigil, Diego. 1990. Cholos and gangs: Culture change and street youth in Los Angeles. In *Gangs in America*, edited by C. R. Huff, 116–28. Thousand Oaks, CA: Sage Publications.

Vigil, Diego. 1993. The established gang. In *Gangs: The origins and impact of contemporary youth gangs in the United States*, edited by S. Cummings and D. J. Monti, 95–112. New York, NY: University of New York Press.

VOA-News.com. 2005 (July 22). Latino street gangs a major law issue in U.S. http://www1.voanews.com/english/news/a-13-2005-07-22-voa45-66389682.html. Accessed November 2, 2015.

Crime and the U.S.-Mexican Border

Isabel Martínez

The U.S.-Mexican border has long been characterized as a site of unlawfulness across which criminal activity occurs. Beginning with its inception after the U.S.-Mexican war, the U.S.-Mexico border has suffered a history wrought with conflict, contention, and multiple calls for its closing due to the overflow of illegal activity caused by both countries. Although much attention has been paid to the criminal activities originating in Mexico, the complicity of United States policies and practices to this flow of illegality—including, in the 21st century, the smuggling of arms into Mexico—has been understated. As a result, frustration has been abundant on both sides of the border, with each country's government citing insufficient action by the other to curb criminal activity.

Extending this characterization into the 21st century, government, academic, and nongovernmental actors name crime organizations as the primary threat from Mexico to U.S. security. The administration of former Mexican President Felipe Calderon, however, repeatedly pointed to the United States' complicity in this phenomenon, criticizing the unwillingness of United States to reform lax gun-control laws that have fueled much of these crime organizations' activities. In the United States, however, discourse about the U.S.-Mexico border has focused predominantly on Mexican activities, in addition to the criminalization of immigration, and its potential as a portal for terrorism. These ideas have dictated contemporary discourses about the U.S.-Mexican border and the type of policies developing to control it.

The issue of whether the 1,959 mile U.S.-Mexican border should be open or closed has long been controversial and U.S. policy toward the border has appeared at times to be contradictory. Whereas the United States has implemented exclusionary border policies preventing unauthorized activities such as human and drug trafficking from crossing into the United States from Mexico, the United States has also implemented policies—most notably the North American Free Trade Agreement (NAFTA)—that promote the liberalization of the flow of goods across the U.S.-Mexico border. Prior to its passage, support for this agreement hinged on its ability to stem unauthorized immigration from Mexico to the United States. These economic policies have contributed to unauthorized immigration by increasing poverty in rural southern areas of Mexico. Left with few economic opportunities in Mexico, these former Mexican farmers have sought economic opportunities in the United States.

This paradox has had several negative effects on the U.S.-Mexican border and border crossers, authorized and unauthorized. For one, Mexican immigrants have become increasingly demonized and their acts of border crossing deemed "criminal." Secondly, residents have witnessed border law enforcement escalating, with billions of federal monies dedicated to the militarization of the border. Lastly, the militarization of the border, as well as the violence associated with this militarization and illegal activities, such as trafficking—both human and drug—has expanded to include **femicide**, kidnapping, and drug turf wars, endangering the daily lives of innocent border residents who have long engaged in ordinary binational and transnational activities.

Historical Context

The criminalization of the U.S.-Mexican border has its origin in the unauthorized settlement of Anglos in former Spanish, and then Mexican, territories. In 1810, Mexican *independistas* fought for liberation from the Spanish crown, and were victorious by 1821. This victory would include a transfer of lands stretching into current-day United States, including California, Arizona, and Texas. Under Spanish policies, Anglo settlers had been allowed to reside in these Spanish territories, as long as Spanish law was followed, and Mexican officials continued this hospitality after their independence. Unknown at the time, however, was the settlers' and the United States' ideological positions to extend its reach beyond its current territorial holdings.

Referred to as "**Manifest Destiny,**" Anglo-Saxon leaders of the United States believed that it was their God-given right to engage in territorial conquest for national expansion. Central to this ideology were notions that white Anglo-Saxon Protestants were the superior race, and that other races—including the "Mexican race"—were apt for domination. Additionally, the Mexican government abolished slavery in Mexico but Anglo settlers had minimal interest in ending this practice. These ideological differences would lead to a protracted struggle over Mexican lands, first with Texas, followed by the conquest of the current-day Southwest. These lands became flooded by Anglo-American *filibusteros* (freebooters) and other authorized and unauthorized Anglos. The settlers soon outnumbered native Mexicans in the area, and embarked on a campaign to annex from Mexico the territory today known as Texas. Considered a hostile act by the Mexican government, the annexation—backed by U.S. government funds—succeeded in 1845. The United States declared 251,579,800 acres of land as the Republic of Texas, with explicit boundaries drawn demarcating Texas territories and Mexican territories. Although the Mexican government subsequently recognized the Nueces River as being the southern border of Texas, the U.S. government viewed the Rio Grande River as the state's southern border (Martinez 2006).

In 1846, President James Polk, an avid proponent of Manifest Destiny, illegally sent troops beyond the Nueces River into the Mexican territories extending to the Rio Grande River. The Mexican government ordered a military response, resulting in both Mexican and U.S. casualties. Deliberately characterizing the military response as a Mexican military provocation rather than the United States' disregard for territorial jurisdiction, President Polk declared war on Mexico. The war ended with the signing of the Treaty of Guadalupe-Hidalgo on February 2, 1848, an agreement ceding roughly half of Mexico's territory to the United States. The signing of the Treaty of Guadalupe-Hidalgo would officially recognize the Rio Grande River as the border with Texas and mandate the United States' acquisition of the current states of California, New Mexico, Nevada, Colorado,

Arizona, and Utah. After the signing, however, the United States continued attempts to extend its borders further, offering varying amounts of money for the northern states of Mexico, including Chihuahua and Baja California. In the end, the Gadsen Purchase in 1853 and the Chamizal Treaty of 1963 resulted in only a minimal addition of Mexican lands, including a southern strip of contemporary New Mexico, Mesilla, and contested areas resulting from the shifting Rio Grande River. Although official United States history characterizes these land acquisitions as the results of legal treaties, these acquisitions were wrought with criminal activities.

Origins of Border Violence

With a racialized conquest of Mexican territories, racial, ethnic, and cultural tensions continued to shape social relations between Anglo Americans and Mexican Americans positioned along the U.S.-Mexico border. The earliest border violence actually was a result of conflicts over unauthorized immigration occurring from North to South (the United States to Mexico). At this time, Anglo settlers were unlawful immigrants. This became such a problem that the Mexican government, through the Mexican Decree of 1830, was forced to prohibit immigration from the United States into Mexico and militarized its border with the United States to monitor unauthorized immigration. After the annexation of Texas and the U.S.-Mexico war, however, Anglo settlers began a campaign of lawlessness and discrimination, using both legal and extralegal institutions and actors to commit acts of violence against Mexican settlers. Most common were violations of property rights and the subsequent responses, including Anglos encroaching upon the land of approximately 2,000 native New Mexicans in the early 1850s, and the Salt War in 1877 (Anglo takeover of El Paso salt deposits). Such actions prompted resistance by Mexicans.

Racially profiling Mexicans and Mexican Americans, Texans characterized them as lawless "*bandidos*" and ruthless outlaws, and filed complaints with the U.S. government to investigate their activities. Anglos established an American Presidential Commission, and the Mexican government also launched an independent investigation of the complaints filed by Texans against Mexican Americans in the border region. In 1873, the Mexican Border Commission concluded that many of the allegations made by Texans were unfounded and that, instead, Indians and Texans disguised as Indians and Mexicans were committing many of the crimes, including cattle stealing, horse theft, and other illegal acts. Framing innocent Mexicans for these acts, Anglo settlers then committed systematic violence against so-called bandits, including the violation of Mexican American citizens' civil liberties, lynching, engaging in physical abuse, imprisonment, and deportation.

Vigilantism and Lynching

Following the annexation of Texas and the subsequent colonization of the southwestern states, Anglo settlers engaged in inhumane treatment and acts of terrorism against Mexicans living on their own lands. **Vigilantism**—both state-sanctioned and unsanctioned—were rampant along the U.S.-Mexico border. Most often, vigilantes first incited Mexican Americans, then "reacted" oppressively to Mexican resistance to illegal and unfair laws and enforcement. Incidences of vigilante justice cited by scholars clearly document how vigilantes agitated Mexican Americans and then acted violently against them, claiming self-defense. **Lynching** became a common practice in these cases and, between 1848 and 1928, more than 600 Mexicans were lynched by vigilantes (Walker 2007). Although most lynching victims were men, women also were lynched, most often after resisting the sexual advances of Anglo settlers (Delgado 2009).

Informally organized in the beginning, vigilantism soon became politically institutionalized. Anglo settlers formed vigilante organizations, some of which operated under the auspices of the state government. One widely controversial legal organization, the **Texas Rangers**, eventually gained state authority from the state of Texas and continues to exist today. Although organized during the Texas revolt in 1835 as an unofficial state militia, the Texas Rangers were approved as a state-sanctioned organization in 1861, and were responsible for protecting the Texas frontier from both violent Indian uprisings and criminal Mexicans. The Texas Rangers, otherwise known as *los rinches*, is a paramilitary law enforcement group that was well-known for committing acts of violence against Mexicans. (For further discussion, see "Vigilantism" elsewhere in this entry and in this volume.)

Resistance

For years after 1848, a double standard of justice existed in the border area; acts against Anglo Americans by Mexicans invoked severe consequences but violence against Mexicans by Anglos rarely, if ever, earned any consequences. In response to injustice and impunity granted to Anglo Americans who engaged in violence, some Mexicans utilized armed resistance against Anglo Americans. Occurring both individually and collectively, these acts sometimes resulted in extended periods of protracted conflict between Anglos and Mexicans.

Key Mexican American figures in Texas challenging Anglo American racism and violence in the border areas include: Gregorio Cortez, a Mexican acting in self-defense when he shot a Texas Ranger and eluded capture; Catarino Garza, who hoped to organize other Mexicans in an uprising against Anglo rule; and Juan Cortina, a Mexican landowner who in 1859 shot and killed an Anglo lawman after witnessing the pistol-whipping of a Mexican prisoner in Brownsville, Texas. Soon after, Brownsville was taken under siege as Anglo residents of the city began a "reign of terror" against Mexicans and Cortina organized Mexicans to retaliate.

Other border states such as New Mexico and California experienced less-intense violence and interethnic conflict, due to the preservation of Mexican communities and the sheer outnumbering of Anglos by Mexican Americans. In New Mexico, collective acts of resistance included those of *Las Gorras Blancas*, a group of masked riders who sought to resist Anglo violence through acts of their own subversion, such as disrupting the railroad and communication industries, as well as private ranches. Ultimately these acts of resistance did little to prevent Anglo colonization in these areas. An absence of class unity among Mexicans and Mexican Americans in these border states prevented authentic, long-term resistance.

Cross-Border Criminal Organizations

In recent years, cross-border criminal organizations have gained international prominence for their roles in engaging in cross-border multi-billion-dollar drug, human, and arms trafficking. Among these syndicates are: the Tijuana Cartel, operating in the Baja California-California area; the Sinaloa Cartel, whose reach extends from Baja, California, to Jalisco, Mexico; the Gulf Cartel, operating predominantly along the Texas-Tamaulipas border; the Arellano Felix Cartel, located along the California–

Baja, California, border; and the Juarez Cartel, with major operations in 21 Mexican states including Sinaloa and Nuevo Leon, and more than 231 cities in the United States.

Fueled by the demand for drugs in the United States, cartels engaged in activities that include drug production in the United States. Although previous efforts were located primarily in California, their reach has extended throughout the United States, including the Pacific Northwest, the Midwest, and areas of the Eastern seaboard. In the United States, distribution also has been facilitated through increased partnerships with U.S.–based street and prison gangs.

Criminal organizations also utilize enforcer **gangs**, or *sicarios*, including Los Zetas, Beltran Leyva, and Los Negros. These paramilitary groups are composed of former and current federal, state, and local Mexican law enforcement officials, military, and civilians, and largely are utilized for physical protection of goods and key cartel figures. These groups engage in activities such as kidnapping, extortion, payment collection, and protection of goods along drug smuggling routes. Once limited only to Mexico, more recent acts have spilled over onto the U.S. side of the border, in cities such as Laredo, Texas, and in the Rio Grande Valley area. Reports of *sicario* activities in South Texas have included posting bounties of up to $50,000 for the assassination of United States law enforcement agents interfering with drug-smuggling efforts. *Sicario* members also increasingly have filled voids left in the wake of arrests of key cartel figures by the Mexican government.

Illicit Smuggling of Drugs, Humans, and Firearms

Drug Smuggling

Once considered merely an entry point for South and Central American illicit drugs, Mexico rapidly has become the main producer and distributor of major illicit drugs. This increase in regional prominence has led to the proliferation of infighting for control of the drug industry and, as a result, intensified violence along the U.S.-Mexico border. Cities such as Tijuana, Ciudad Juarez, Reynosa, and Matamoros have experienced spikes in violent crimes linked to drug smuggling, along with an increase in civilian fatalities and victimization. More recently, Mexican cartels have approved spillover violence, or attacks in the United States, but border cities have not exhibited simultaneous spikes in violent crime. Whereas Washington, DC, reported 186 homicides in 2008, Texas border cities such as Laredo, Brownsville, and McAllen experienced 11, 9, and 3 homicides respectively (Del Bosque 2009). Violent crimes appear to be occurring on the southern (Mexican) side of the border rather than the northern (U.S.) side.

Much of the violence in Mexico has been attributed not only to turf wars and the consolidation of cartels, but also to the increased tightening of the U.S.-Mexico border and increased government efforts in combating narco-trafficking in Mexico. As the United States at the federal, state, and local levels has increased border enforcement and the current Mexican government has restated its commitment to combating drug smuggling, the U.S.-Mexico border has become more prone to violence. Not only has the Mexico side of the border witnessed an increase in violent crime, but the brutality of violent crimes also has escalated.

Experts and law enforcement officials point to a handful of Mexican drug cartels responsible for the increased violence and criminal activities in Mexico. The most powerful drug cartels along the U.S.-Mexico border have included Tijuana's dominant drug cartel, the Arellano Felix Cartel, the Gulf Cartel and its paramilitary cell, the

Zetas, and the Juarez Cartel. Current drug enforcement strategies have included capturing cartel heads, and several leaders have been arrested and extradited to the United States for trial. Leaving a void in power and leadership, however, in many cases has led to increased violence, as those left in these crime organizations fight for internal control of the organization. Other cartels, detecting vulnerability, exploit the disruption in rival leadership and gain control of previously determined rival turf. One such case has occurred between the Sinaloa Cartel and the Gulf Cartel, with the capture of the head of the Gulf Cartel, Osiel Cardenas. Conflicts between the two cartels have made the Mexican state of Tamaulipas one of the bloodiest sites in a struggle for control over the drug industry. These violent struggles have occurred within border towns, oftentimes in public spaces.

Trade liberalization has contributed to the increased production and distribution of drugs across borders. It not only has obliterated the livelihoods of many rural Mexicans who now might turn to drug production for income, but trade liberalization also has created the opportunity for drugs to be more easily mixed with other goods destined for the United States via trailers and trucks. In addition, narco-tunnels, or underground smuggling passages spanning across the U.S.-Mexico border also have been utilized to smuggle drugs across the national borders.

As drug enforcement measures have increased, so have the battles over control of secure smuggling routes. Increased security measures have heightened the costs and difficulties associated with smuggling contraband across the border. As costs associated with moving illegal goods across the border have increased, the economic value of the smuggled goods also has increased. This has resulted in intensified hijacking and stealing of rival organizations' illicit goods as well as increased costs associated with protecting these illegal goods as they cross the border. Drug enforcement efforts have intensified on both sides of the border, prompting both organized crime syndicates and criminals to increasingly engage in stealing contraband goods (such as drugs), robbing unauthorized immigrants, and kidnapping unauthorized immigrants to extort money from their families.

Human Smuggling

In response to increased economic liberalization, a more competitive market for **human trafficking** has emerged in recent years. In fiscal year (FY) 2004, approximately 1,139,282 apprehensions of immigrants resulting in arrests occurred along the U.S.-Mexico border, with the most occurring in California and Texas. This marked an increase of almost 25 percent since FY 2003, with 905,065 apprehensions. Approximately 43 percent of all apprehensions occurred along the Tucson, Arizona, border region, followed by San Diego County, in which approximately 12 percent of all apprehensions occurred (Nuñez-Neto 2005; Wu 2006). The increased militarization of the border after 9/11 has made border crossing more difficult, but it has not necessarily deterred immigration. Rather, the increased difficulties of crossing the border have made unauthorized immigrants more vulnerable to severe victimization. They incur greater financial costs associated with human smuggling; they are forced to cross in more dangerous areas; and they face heightened risks of discrimination and violence from human traffickers and the **Border Patrol**.

The enhanced border enforcement along the Arizona-Mexico border also has led to an increase in migrant deaths along this region, as unauthorized immigrants are crossing in more remote and dangerous areas of the Arizona desert. Between 2004 and 2005, migrant deaths along the U.S. border increased by 43 percent, rising from 330 deaths in FY 2004 to 473 deaths to FY 2005. Various sources reported that the increases in deaths are attributed to the hazards and violence associated with border crossing when security efforts increased after 9/11. In May 2003, one of the nation's most horrific cases of death due to human trafficking occurred in Victoria, Texas, more than 200 miles from the U.S.-Mexico border. Resulting in 19 deaths from asphyxiation, dehydration, and other heat-related causes, more than 70 unauthorized immigrants were found trapped in a milk truck where temperatures reached as high as 173 degrees Fahrenheit. Human smuggler and legal Jamaican immigrant Tyrone Williams currently is serving a sentence of life in prison with no possibility for parole for his role in the smuggling deaths (Associated Press 2007; Cornelius 2001).

Firearms Smuggling

Whereas most discussions of smuggling are of South to North flows of illegal goods, less-oft discussed is the North-South flow of guns that has fueled drug cartel violence. Approximately 95 percent of firearms seized at sites of drug violence in Mexico can be traced back to the United States, with the majority of gun sales originating in the state of Texas (Grimaldi & Horwitz 2010; McKinley, Jr. 2009; Sullivan & Castillo 2009). Difficult to purchase legally in Mexico, arms are being purchased from gun dealers in the United States and brought into Mexico, where they are used in killings not only of rival cartel members, but also of Mexican police officers. Through "straw purchases" (illegal third-party sales), Mexican drug cartels have been able to fund, purchase, and smuggle high-power assault weapons from the United States to Mexico. These purchases have armed drug cartels, enabling them to outgun Mexican police officers, as drug cartel arms are oftentimes much more powerful than those utilized by Mexican police. Over a four-year period alone, Mexico has confiscated more than 110,000 weapons, including 50,000 assault rifles, 11,000 grenades, more than 150 high-powered sniper rifles, and 10 million rounds of ammunition—85 percent of which could be traced back to the United States (Grimaldi 2011).

Linked to efforts to prevent drug smuggling and spillover violence in the United States, Mexican authorities teamed with the United States Bureau of Alcohol, Tobacco, Firearms, and Explosives and border governors to combat this challenge. "Project Gunrunner" formally was launched by the United States Bureau of Alcohol, Tobacco, Firearms, and Explosives (ATF) to assist in tracing and confiscating guns headed to Mexico from the United States, as well as to prosecute illegal gun smugglers. Through Project Gunrunner, the ATF has committed to redirect its investigative, intelligence, and training resources to curb the flow of weapons from the United States to Mexico and, by default, lessen violence on both sides of the border. More than 100 special agents were assigned to this initiative on the southwest border, and by 2009 more than 650 cases had been referred for prosecution. Critical components of Project Gunrunner include e-trace (the tracing of arms, their purchase, and smuggling routes, and the sharing of this information across U.S. consulates in Mexico), and trainings with federal firearms licensees to identify "straw purchasers" and educate licensees about gun trafficking (FBI 2009).

In 2011, Project Gunrunner came under intense scrutiny for its failed strategies allowing traceable arms to be sold to drug cartel members. The shooting death of border patrol agent Brian Terry revealed missteps in ATF strategies. Terry was shot with a traceable AK-47 assault rifle which had been purchased with the intent to then deliver it to drug cartel members in Mexico. Dubbed "Operation Fast and Furious," ATF officials allowed some arms dealers to sell arms to straw purchasers who then smuggled them across the U.S.-Mexico border to sell and deliver the arms to cartels. This strategy allowed approximately 2,500 guns to be "walked" across the borders and put into the hands of cartels so that ATF officials could gather mass intelligence to indict not only minor gun smugglers, but also the more important cartel members (Attkisson 2011; Grimaldi & Horwitz 2011).

According to then-Mexican President Calderon, what could be most effective in slowing the flow of firearms into Mexico is a renewed ban on assault weapons in the United States. President Calderon attributed the increase in the flow of firearms across the border into Mexico to the expiration of the ban in the United States in 2004, and lobbied both former U.S. President George W. Bush, and President Barack H. Obama, to promote and pass more restrictive gun control legislation. President Obama has shown reluctance in entering into this debate, as political opposition to restricting the rights of gun owners is severe. A more feasible approach that has been proposed might be the ratification of an inter-American arms treaty which could effectively limit arms smuggling into Mexico from the United States.

Femicide

International attention has been drawn to femicide—or the mass murder of women simply because of their gender—occurring along the U.S.-Mexico border, particularly along the Texas-Chihuahua border. Since 1993, more than 400 women have been reported murdered or missing in Ciudad Juarez and Chihuahua, many of whom are *maquiladora* workers (workers in free trade zone factories) (Falcon 2001; National Organization for Women 2011). These acts of violence against women have been among the most brutal and heinous committed. Many of the women attacked were sexually assaulted, subjected to torture, and ultimately strangled or beaten to death.

Much criticism has been weighed against the state government of Chihuahua and the Mexican federal government for the systemic gross mishandling of investigations of these crimes, slow action regarding perpetrators, and overall continuous failure to protect Mexican women from violence. In response to public outcry over this mishandling, the Special Prosecutor's Office for the Investigation of Murders of Women was established in 1998. Upon review of 205 cases, the special federal prosecutor found that more than 177 state officials were culpable or possibly liable for negligence or omission in the original investigations, but few officials have been reprimanded (Economic Commission for Latin America and the Caribbean 2007). Although arrests have been made, the killings have been attributed to various sources, including organized crime syndicates, state and local law enforcement officials, and gangs.

The Mexican federal government took steps in 2003 to begin to protect and defend women against violence in Ciudad Juarez, however critics argue that more widespread protection that would cover the entire state of Juarez was not implemented. The United States, in a symbolic act of condemnation and under pressure from international and national feminist and human rights organizations, passed a resolution in January 2007 condemning these acts of violence against women in Chihuahua and promised support in the resolution of this violence.

Border Patrol

Originally formed in 1924 to monitor unauthorized Chinese immigration, the United States **Border Patrol** (formerly known as the "Mounted Inspectors") currently focuses most of its efforts on limiting unauthorized entry into the United States from Mexico. Within the past 30 years, the Border Patrol has dramatically increased in size, with the greatest growth occurring between 1992 and 1999, when the number of agents doubled from 3,651 to 7,982. As of 2010, 17,535 Border Patrol agents were assigned to the southwest border area, comprising more than 85% of the total national Border Patrol staff. Additionally, the time that agents spent patrolling the border increased from 1.9 million hours in 1985 to 8.6 million in 1999. Additionally, since 1970, the percentage of the federal budget allocated as enforcement funds has increased by 338 percent (U.S. Customs and Border Protection 2011).

Attributed to increased efforts to secure the U.S.-Mexico border against both unauthorized immigration and criminal smuggling, the number of assaults on Border Patrol agents has more than doubled in recent years. During FY 2007, the U.S. Border Patrol reported 987 assaults against Border Patrol agents, an increase of 31% from the previous year and the highest number of assaults ever reported since record keeping began in the late 1990s. One out of every four assaults has occurred in the San Diego sector, an area of 66 miles (Marosi 2008). Little discussed however, are the cases of assaults committed by INS agents against Mexican immigrants, including women.

A dramatic shift towards increased policing of the U.S.-Mexico border emerged during the Clinton Administration. Purposefully coinciding with the start of NAFTA, "Operation Gatekeeper" was enacted in 1994 to increase the number of Border Patrol agents, fencing, and lighting along the border. Abuse allegations occurred in the midst of Operation Gatekeeper, however, with the San Diego Mexican consulate reporting physical attacks committed against immigrants by Border Patrol agents, including some attacks so severe that hospitalization was required.

Implemented in 2005, "Operation Streamline" is an initiative targeting particular high-crossing areas along the U.S.-Mexico border, including Del Rio, Laredo, and Brownsville, Texas, and Tucson, Arizona. Uniting federal, state, and local agencies, this collaborative effort focuses on arresting, prosecuting, and jailing unauthorized immigrants who are caught crossing the US-Mexico border. Targeting high-traffic smuggling corridors along the 205 miles of the Rio Grande River resulted in a 76% reduction in the crime rate since the initiative's inception and the fewest number of reported border crossings since 1972. Under Streamline, detainees face unprecedented swiftness in arrest, arraignment, counseling, pleading, convictions, and (many times) deportation. Although touted as successful, the program has come under widespread criticism and scrutiny by legal and human rights activists for sacrificing the due process rights of immigrant detainees to achieve expeditiousness and convictions (Robbins 2010).

Part of President George W. Bush's $760 million package to improve border security, "Operation Jumpstart" was another border initiative targeting unauthorized immigration and terrorist activities occurring along the U.S.-Mexico border. Signed into effect in June 2006 by the four border-state (Arizona, New Mexico, Texas, and California) governors and the U.S. Department of the Defense, Operation Jumpstart deploys

National Guard troops along the border to assist in preventing unauthorized crossings. The assistance provided includes building roads and fences, adding cameras and sensors, alerting Border Patrol agents to illicit crossings, and providing medical aid and communication support. Designed to support—not replace—Border Patrol efforts, this operation provided up to 6,000 National Guard troops at various points along the U.S.-Mexico border and the Border Patrol doubled its size to 18,000 agents. Operation Jumpstart efforts officially ended on July 15, 2008, and the National Guard troops vacated their posts along the U.S.-Mexico border. Touted as a success in all states, in New Mexico, 6,300 illegal immigrant apprehensions, the seizure of 7,500 pounds of marijuana and nearly three pounds of cocaine, and the construction of 5.6 miles of vehicle barriers along the New Mexico-Mexico border are attributed to Operation Jumpstart. By June 2008, actual Operation Jumpstart activities had ended (Holstege 2008).

Although several of the aforementioned initiatives were implemented in response to unprecedented levels of unauthorized immigration, after the September 11, 2001 attacks on the United States, the U.S.-Mexico border became viewed not only as a site for unauthorized economic immigration, but also of terrorist entry. Arguably, the borderlands always have been perceived as a war site, but with the events of 9/11, the U.S.-Mexico border was hyper-constructed as a site of potential war, across which major security breaches could occur. Instead, the U.S.-Mexican border rapidly became characterized as a site where not only unauthorized immigration and illicit goods could cross, but also conceivably where another distinctly racialized group—Arabs—could arrive unnoticed to launch another catastrophic act of terrorism against the United States.

Announced in **Fall** 2005 by President Bush and the U.S. Department of Homeland Security (DHS), the "Secure Border Initiative" (SBI) is a $12.14 million initiative addressing issues of terrorism, unauthorized immigration, and national security. Several components of the initiative included developing and utilizing technology to effectively control entries into the United States, replacing "catch and release" programs with increased detention of unauthorized immigrants, improving existing infrastructure to decrease illicit entries, and improving worksite enforcement. Included in this initiative was "SBInet," a multi-billion-dollar comprehensive program integrating technology and infrastructure to control unauthorized immigration. Targeting 6,000 miles of border, SBInet utilized advanced technology such as radars and sensors, as well as increased fencing and personnel, to detect, identify, and classify cross-border entries, followed by proper response by law enforcement officials, including the Border Patrol (U.S. Department of Homeland Security 2006). Part of SBInet plans was the construction of a virtual fence to run along the length of the U.S.-Mexico border. Costing more than $1 billion, only 53 miles of border were covered by the virtual fence. Fraught with technical difficulties from its inception, Department of Homeland Security Secretary Napolitano ordered the initiative's cancellation in 2011, and the replacement of these plans with new technologies tailored to border regions' particular needs (Lipowicz 2011).

Border-enforcement efforts also have included the enactment of the 2006 Secure Fence Act, the $1.2 billion legislation including the construction of a 700-foot-long double-layered fence along the U.S.-Mexico border, as well as the aforementioned virtual fencing and other forms of barriers to prevent unauthorized crossing. Although the bill was reintroduced in 2008, the legislation died in Congress. By 2009, approximately 600 feet of physical fence and vehicle barriers had been constructed along the border, mostly in California and Texas (Wood 2008).

Billions of dollars have been poured into the border region in the name of national security, but some suggest that border enforcement has "never been a particularly effective or efficient deterrent against drugs and illegal immigrants" (Andreas 2000). Instead, the border has been—and is—a political stage on which the perception of success, the detention of immigrants and drugs, and the securing of the border from unlawful elements is more important than the actual success rate. Whereas the expressive function of law enforcement (assuring citizens that the border is secure) is being achieved through careful media manipulation and policy, the instrumental function or the actual defense of the border might not be.

Another indicator of these expensive policies' instrumental failures that has garnered much criticism has been a relatively new component of the Border Safety Initiative sponsored by the Department of Homeland Security. Capitalizing on the popularity of Mexican *corridos* (ballads), and more specifically, *narcocorridos*, which are ballads describing the exploits of different drug cartels, in 2009, the Department of Homeland Security contracted a Washington, DC–based advertising company to write, record, and distribute a CD of "*migracorridos*," to Mexican radio stations. A play on the slang word for the Border Patrol, *la migra*, this latest anti-immigration initiative is part of Border Patrol's most recent **prevention** campaign, *"No Mas Cruces La Frontera,"* or alternately "no more crossings on the border" and "no more crosses on the border." The Border Patrol has purchased television and radio airtime in Mexico for public service announcements cautioning Mexicans against immigrating. Employing Mexico's own radio stations to deter unauthorized immigration, the Department of Homeland Security distributed these *migracorridos* to 25 Mexican radio stations in high outmigration states for airplay. Although written and recorded by Mexican nationals living in Washington, DC, and New York, many Mexicans have thought that the CDs source is their own government. This latest anti-immigration initiative also has been seen by some Mexican nationals as the latest in United States' propaganda tactics—this time it is occurring in their own country. Future plans include an additional recording and broader distribution, including to Central America (LeBron 2009; Surdin 2009).

Although less popular, other proposals have focused on the legalization and decriminalization of unauthorized workers, including temporary worker programs, pathways to citizenship, and amnesty. Proposals such as legalizing and regularizing the movement of workers across the U.S.-Mexican borders would enhance national security and reduce crime, enabling Border Patrol and other border enforcement workers to focus on potential breaches of national security and crime rather than the unlawful entry of low-wage Mexican and Central American workers.

Binational Efforts Against Border Crime

Since 9/11, several binational initiatives have been signed by the United States and Mexico to combat criminal activities and violence occurring across the U.S.-Mexico border. The 2002 Smart Border Agreement, or U.S.-Mexico Border Partnership and Action Plan, was drafted to reduce human trafficking, to improve the screening of third-country nationals, and to monitor point-of-entry operations. The 2003 Mexican initiative, "Operation Centinela," also focused on reducing organized crime and human smuggling along the border. In 2004, both countries signed a Memo of Understanding which outlined each country's responsibilities in protecting the human rights of unauthorized immigrants and managing migration. In 2005, both countries expanded these efforts through OASISS (Operation Against Smugglers (and Traffickers) Initiative on Safety and Security) and the Permanent Program Against Human Smuggling, focusing on preventing human smuggling, as well as providing victim's assistance and information. Additionally, the United States, Canada, and Mexico are engaged in the Security and Prosperity Partnership aimed at increasing security and ensuring trilateral trade, economic cooperation, and cross-border movement.

In June 2008, the United States Congress approved the Merida initiative, a $1.4 billion aid package, modeled after their counter-narcoterrorism initiatives in Colombia. Included in this multiyear proposal are plans to increase the use of non-intrusive inspection equipment to detect drugs, arms, and human trafficking; to develop more effective communications systems for the creation and sharing of criminal information; to increase training and consulting for the strengthening of law enforcement and justice institutions; and to purchase surveillance aircrafts. This agreement emphasizes shared responsibilities and cooperation in the war on transnational/cross-border criminal activities, bringing both Mexico and Central American countries into partnership with the United States to combat crime spanning across national borders. After four years, however, the Mexican government has remained frustrated as it only has received 60 percent of the aid promised by both the Bush and Obama administrations to fight the war on drug violence (Powell 2011).

The United States government has publicly acknowledged complicity in transnational criminal activities. On her first trip to Mexico as Secretary of State, Hillary R. Clinton admitted that "America's insatiable demand" for illegal drugs and the flow of weapons from the United States to Mexico was fueling violence in Mexico. Initially, changes in border policies included a 10 percent increase in inspection of vehicles traveling from North to South, as well as increased inspection of vehicles returning to the United States and the sharing of a ballistic database tracking firearms traveling between the two nation-states.

With fears of South to North spillover violence and criticism from the Mexican government mounting, the United States has intensified collaborative efforts to combat narcotrafficking. Not only have United States law enforcement agents trained thousands of Mexican troops and police officers and worked with Mexican security forces, the United States Drug Enforcement Agency—with silent consent of the Mexican government—has engaged in eavesdropping on suspected narcotraffickers in Mexico and is upgrading Mexican security equipment and technology. Less known, as of March 2011, the United States and Mexico had opened two counternarcotics "fusion" centers in Mexico in which Mexican and American drug enforcement agents have been working together to share intelligence and combat drug trafficking. Most controversial has been the flying of Pentagon-ordered unarmed drones, first over the U.S.-Mexico border, and now deep into Mexico, to collect intelligence for Mexican anti-narcotics agencies. Excluding extreme circumstances, the Mexican Constitution specifically bars such foreign military and law enforcement interventions, and several Mexican scholars question the allowance of and lawfulness of such aid from the United States, including permitting U.S. agents to carry weapons, a violation of Mexico's laws. Various actors have raised concerns regarding the United States' long history of sovereignty violations, but U.S. officials have insisted all was done at the behest of the Calderon administration.

Despite these cross-national efforts, much frustration remains in the United States' inability to curb the firearms smuggling that is fueling much of the drug violence in Mexico. After the most recent Mexico-U.S. summit in March 2011, reports of Calderon's frustration with the United States Congress and President Obama's failure to stop the smuggling of firearms and cash across the border into the United States surfaced. Although the Mexican government repeatedly called for President Obama to honor his campaign promise to reinstate the assault rifle ban in the United States—a law that expired in 2004—gun lobbyists such as the National Rifle Association have been able to stymie attempts to strengthen these gun laws, expand investigative powers, and modernize tracing capabilities. Additionally, infrastructure to trace firearms purchases is reportedly outdated, with few efforts reported to modernize it. Without U.S. commitment to the modernization of these capabilities, however, capabilities to curb firearms smuggling into Mexico will remain weak.

"Spillover Violence" and Facts about Crime in U.S. Border States

Heightened fears that violence originating south of the U.S. border with Mexico has become part of the political rhetoric in support of tougher immigration laws, including Arizona's controversial Senate Bill 1070. The bill's most controversial provisions include the expansion of the power of local and state law enforcement agents to stop and detain suspected undocumented immigrants. Despite a court action brought by the U.S. Justice Department which barred implementation of the most controversial aspects of S.B. 1070 based on, among other things, the attempt to supersede the federal government's authority to regulate immigration under the U.S. Constitution, other states—including Arkansas, Colorado, Georgia, Oklahoma, Texas, and Utah—have sought to enact similar measures premised on the perceived threat that unauthorized immigrants pose to their states.

Although anecdotal and individual instances of undocumented persons having committed crimes often receive significant publicity, actual data and empirical research on crime in U.S. states that border Mexico belie the notion that crime is "spilling over" into the United States or that unauthorized immigrants are more prone to criminality and therefore stricter laws need to be passed to target undocumented persons. "High immigration" states—many of which are located along the U.S.-Mexico border—have some of the lowest crime rates of all states in the union (Immigration Policy Center 2010).

Based on the Federal Bureau of Investigation's Unified Crime Reports, which document annual rates of violent and total crime committed, crime overall has been lower in high-immigration states and the data show violent and non-violent crime as declining at a faster rate in high-immigration states than in the rest of the country.

Arizona, a state at the epicenter of the U.S. immigration debate, actually saw an overall drop in both violent and property crime from 2000 to 2008, even in years when the influx of immigrants to the state were high. Bureau of Justice Statistics reports indicate that the rate of violent crime (including murder, assault, and rape) in Arizona fell from 512 per 100,000 people in 2005 to 447 per 100,000 people in 2008, and property crime fell from 5,850 per 100,000 people in 2005 to 4,291 per 100,000 people in 2008 (Immigration Policy Center 2010).

California—the state with the highest proportion of immigrants than any other state and a state that has experienced one of the fastest increases in its immigrant population since 1970 (Johnson 2011; Public Policy Institute of California 2008)—is a state that also has witnessed a dramatic drop in crime. Research studies show that immigrants nevertheless are significantly underrepresented in California prisons. Specifically, it has been found that U.S.-born men are incarcerated at a rate 10 times greater than are foreign-born men (Butcher & Piehl 2008, 2).

The empirical evidence out of Arizona, California, and other states with significant immigrant populations reinforces what the social science research repeatedly points out:

- Immigrants—including those from Latin American countries, such as Mexico—are less prone to criminal conduct than are U.S.-born citizens;
- Immigrants tend to have lower incarceration rates than those of U.S.-born citizens;
- Immigration generally does not cause crime rates to rise; and
- Immigration appears to actually have a stabilizing effect, helping to reduce crime because immigrants tend to stimulate economic activity and revitalize communities (*see* Hagan & Palloni 1999; Martinez 2006; Lee 2003; Butcher & Piehl 2005; Myers & Pitkin 2010).

Free Trade and Border Crossings

The North American Free Trade Agreement (NAFTA) went into effect on January 1, 1994, much to the protest of Mexico's indigenous communities. This trade agreement facilitated increased capital mobility between the United States, Mexico, and Canada, but gave little thought to the issue of worker mobility. Transforming the U.S.-Mexican border zones into sites of integrated economies and capital production, NAFTA has resulted in the employment of more than a million Mexican workers, coinciding with the increase of U.S.-owned *maquiladoras* (factories) along the U.S.-Mexican border. Currently, approximately 26,000 U.S.-based companies provide Mexican *maquiladoras* with raw materials and components to be assembled into products that, once complete, are returned to U.S. border cities. Once assembled and sent back across the border, United States border cities then become distribution points for the rest of the country.

One of the most evident effects of NAFTA is increased economic hardships put upon Mexican farmers. NAFTA policies include the privatization of collective farms and the elimination of agricultural subsidies for small farm owners. As a result, millions of farmers who had relied on a more favorable market and government assistance for their goods have seen their generations-old farms unable to compete with U.S. farming.

Framed as a panacea to Mexico's economic woes and as a strategy to minimize unauthorized immigration through the creation of increased employment opportunities, NAFTA instead has increased not only unauthorized immigration to the United States, but also internal migration to the border area and more permanent settlement across the border in the United States. Although within the first three years of NAFTA, *maquiladora* employment along the border increased by

86 percent, little infrastructure was developed to absorb the influx of migrants from central and southern Mexico. Instead, an absence of thoughtful urban planning, in addition to internal migration, has led to severe overcrowding and undesirable living conditions in border towns. Increased employment opportunities in the *maquiladoras*, along with the collapse of sustenance farming, has led to increased migration to border towns from central and southern Mexico. People are migrating northward not only to live along the border, but also to cross into the United States and stay.

Discussed in detail in the following sections, the enhanced efforts by the United States to secure the border coincided with—and intensified with—the passage of NAFTA. NAFTA's success partially has been tied to the United States and Mexican governments' ability to ensure the safety of American *maquiladora* owners and workers, as well as the capital flowing across borders. Paired with increasingly restrictive immigration policies which are meant to deter more frequent crossings, shrinking opportunities for economic livelihood in Mexico have led to more permanent immigrant settlement on the U.S. side of the border, as risks—including deaths and sexual assaults—and costs (human smuggling fees) associated with crossing have increased. Paradoxically, these neoliberal economic policies, along with restrictive immigration policies have accelerated cross-border criminal activities.

Border Enforcement and Racial Profiling

Since their inception, the **Border Patrol** and other border enforcement entities have engaged in racial profiling to manage the U.S.-Mexico border. Originally targeting unauthorized Chinese immigrants, the United States Border Patrol has a long history of racially profiling Latinos, with practices intensifying after 9/11 in the name of counterterrorism. Scholars and advocates argue that Supreme Court cases, including ***United States v. Brignoni-Ponce* (1975)** and ***United States v. Martinez-Fuerte* (1976)** have opened the door to Border Patrol tactics that have been characterized as racial profiling.

Drawing limits to the protections of the Fourth Amendment, the aforementioned U.S. Supreme Court cases allow the U.S. Border Patrol to operate under what Alfredo Mirandé (2003) refers to as the "Mexican Exception." In *United States v. Brignoni-Ponce*, 422 U.S. 873 (1975), the Supreme Court ruled that Border Patrol agents were legally authorized to stop individuals based on similar appearances to particular groups of interest. On March 11, 1973, on the Interstate Highway in San Clemente, California, two Border Patrol officers halted a passing car based on the grounds that the three individuals in the car appeared to be of Mexican descent. Upon stopping, it was determined that the three individuals were unauthorized, but at trial, the nature of the stop, the conditions under which the individuals' immigration status were obtained, and the extent of the Border Patrol's powers were brought into question. In their own interpretation of the Fourth Amendment, a majority of Court justices ruled that Border Patrol agents were not held to the "probable cause" standard outlined in the Fourth Amendment, but, rather, could halt and question individuals and vehicles deemed unauthorized or thought to be transporting unauthorized immigrants on the basis of specific facts and inferences based on facts, including "appearing similar to a particular group of persons," or in this case, appearing to be (unauthorized) Mexicans. The U.S. Supreme Court ruled that "governmental interest in the prevention of entry of unauthorized immigrants" is sufficient to justify roving Border Patrol agents' authority to stop and question individuals at or near the U.S.-Mexican border about their citizenship and immigration status. Appeals drew from a previous case, *Almeida-Sanchez v. United States*, 413 U.S. 266 (1973), in which a legal Mexican immigrant was stopped and his car was searched without a warrant. In the case of *United States v. Brignoni-Ponce*, 422 U.S. 873 (1975), Court justices ruled in favor of the United States government because the Border Patrol only questioned people about their immigration status and had not conducted a search, thus committing no civil rights violations. Only their immigration status was brought into question, an act well within the authority of the enforcement agency. Unaddressed, however, was the primary basis upon which the individuals were stopped—namely the issue of racial profiling.

The following year, the Court again reinforced and extended Border Patrol authorization to operate racially motivated stops. In *United States v. Martinez-Fuerte*, 428 U.S. 543 (1976), Justice Powell delivered a majority opinion ruling that randomly stopping vehicles at permanent border checkpoints did not violate the Fourth Amendment, regardless of whether reasonable suspicion of the presence of unauthorized immigrants existed. In this case, three different defendants were stopped along the California Interstate 5 corridor, between San Diego and Los Angeles, and questioned on three different occasions about their citizenship and immigration status. Upon questioning, each of the defendants was arrested on various charges including human smuggling and unlawful entry into the United States. Upon the cases' consolidation for appeal in the Court of Appeals for the Ninth Circuit, the Court of Appeals ruled that arrests in these cases were unconstitutional. The Court of Appeals held that stops only would be constitutional if the Border Patrol "reasonably suspects" the presence of unauthorized immigrants on the premise of concrete facts. Upon the hearing in the Supreme Court, this decision was overturned (7 to 2) and the Court ruled that the Border Patrol was not in violation of the Fourth Amendment in its stopping of vehicles at permanent checkpoints, regardless of whether reasonable suspicion existed (*United States v. Martinez-Fuerte,* 428 U.S. 543 (1976)).

Critics of the Supreme Court's decisions in the *Brignoni-Ponce* and *Martinez-Fuerte* cases raise concerns that these cases have paved the way for racial profiling at the U.S.-Mexico border and inland checkpoints by enabling the Border Patrol to engage in practices that violate the civil rights of people of Mexican descent, immigrant or otherwise, targeting anyone it chooses largely based on phenotype. Critics point to Justice William Brennan's dissent in the *Martinez-Fuerte* case which warned that, from that day forward,

> [e]very American citizen of Mexican ancestry and every Mexican alien lawfully in this country must know after today's decision that he travels the fixed checkpoint highways at the risk of being subjected not only to a stop, but also to detention and interrogation, both prolonged and to an extent far more than for non-Mexican appearing motorists.

Justice Brennan noted that those persons stopped and detained would be subject to arbitrariness and humiliation likely to rouse resentment and feelings of unjust discrimination. Brennan further notes that relying on the Border Patrol's good faith or the practice of not relying solely on Mexican ancestry is insufficient and inconsistent with the Fourth Amendment's safeguards of personal liberty (428 U.S. 543, 573 [1976], n 4).

The U.S. Supreme Court further limited the Fourth Amendment protections of undocumented immigrants later in ***INS v. Lopez-Mendoza et al.***, 468 U.S. 1032 (1984). In that case, the Court held in a 5-to-4 decision that Fourth Amendment protections against illegal searches and seizures do not apply in deportation hearings because such proceedings are for civil actions and not criminal cases (468 U.S. 1032, 1040–1045). In disagreeing with this decision, the dissent opined that "[t]he Government of the United States bears an obligation to obey the Fourth Amendment; that obligation is not lifted simply because the law enforcement officers were agents of the Immigration and Naturalization Service, nor because the evidence obtained by those officers was to be used in civil deportation proceedings" (468 U.S. 1032, 1052; *see also* Hing 2004, 139–44).

Contemporary Vigilantism

Contemporary vigilantism largely can be attributed to two 21st-century phenomena: 9/11 and the perceived heightened threat to national security, and the large influx of unauthorized immigrants from Mexico and Central America. In spite of the United States' government's costly militarization of the border, contemporary vigilante groups have deemed these efforts ineffective in keeping foreign intruders out of the country, and have taken up border security themselves. More than 150 years after its demarcation, both state-sanctioned and unauthorized vigilantism continue to plague the U.S.-Mexican border. Among the most publicized vigilante groups and individuals are the Minuteman Project and Arizona Sheriff Joe Arpaio.

Founded in October 2004 by Jim Gilchrist, the Minuteman Project is a group of private citizens who patrol the U.S.-Mexico border in an effort to enforce immigration laws and secure the border. Although the group itself purports to be neither racist nor violent, it has been linked financially to Aryan Nation and to acts of violence against Mexican immigrants. The group's potency is on the decline, with increased infighting and allegations of financial mismanagement made against Gilchrist. These crises have led to the group's division into other border-monitoring groups, including the Texas Border Volunteers and the California Minutemen. More recently, the indictment of Minutemen members for the murder of a young Mexican girl and her family have further tarnished their legitimacy.

Sheriff Arpaio, known as "America's Toughest Sheriff," also has experienced his share of legal troubles and a decline in popularity. His "reign of terror" against Latinos in small Arizona towns included searching for unauthorized Latina/o immigrants to turn over to **Immigration and Customs Enforcement**. During raids, the Sheriff's Department racially profiled residents, and stopped and asked Latina/o residents for identification to prove their citizenship. Rather than arresting large numbers of unauthorized immigrants, however, Arpaio is responsible for conducting sweeps in areas in which he had no jurisdiction, disrupting town business, intimidating legal Latina/o residents into staying inside their homes, creating dangerous situations for his and the town's law enforcement, and neglecting his own jurisdiction's criminal activities. Sheriff Arpaio was stripped of his authority to conduct street patrols in search of unauthorized immigrants and a federal investigation for conducting unconstitutional raids was opened.

Contemporary vigilantism utilizes the Internet to increase the potential for reckless civilian practices along the border. Individual vigilante groups have utilized social media and the Internet to promote their message and organize calls to action. Referred to as "virtual vigilance," individual vigilante groups such as the American Border Patrol (ABP) have launched operations such as "Operation BEEF" (Border Enforcement Evaluation Force). Glenn Spencer, ABP founder, set up remote-control Internet cameras along the Arizona-Mexico border to pressure the U.S. government to further militarize the border. Using taxpayer dollars, even state governments have fueled the call for vigilantism by sponsoring websites that promote the civilian protection of the U.S.-Mexico Border. In November 2008, the Texas Border Sheriff's Coalition, funded by Texas Governor Rick Perry's criminal justice office, established the $4 million Texas Virtual Border Watch Program. This program enabled people from around the world to monitor the border via the Internet. More than 100,000 people from around the world had registered on www.blueservo.net to become "virtual deputies." These individuals watched the Texas-Mexico border through live feeds from 21 hidden surveillance cameras, 24 hours a day, 7 days a week. Upon viewing suspicious activities, the individual then could send an instant message to on-duty sheriffs. The site was shut down in 2011, stating that it was due to financial reasons.

In 2011, Texas Agricultural Commissioner Todd Staples launched the website www.protectyourtexasborder.com to allow border ranchers and farmers to share stories, pictures and videos that "document their daily struggles with drug cartels." Framed as a way that "Texas is taking matters into its own hands" to protect its food supply, the website acts not only as a critique of the federal government's handling of border security, but also has provided for calls to vigilantism (Aguilar 2011).

The Militarization of the Border and Human Rights Violations

Increased militarization practices along the border have also resulted in ongoing **police brutality** and harassment, including rape, unjustified shootings, excessive use of force, and beatings, committed by United States Border Patrol agents and National Guard troops against immigrants. More recent documentation of such abuses has gone largely neglected by government officials, with impunity most often granted to officials.

Changes in guidelines, as well as inadequate training regarding the apprehension and detention of immigrant border crossers during the 1980s arguably has led to increased human rights violations along the U.S.-Mexico border. Broader arrest authority has led to the creation of a "Wild West" culture that has only bred abuses by Border Patrol agents. In 1980, a report entitled, "The Tarnished Golden Door: Civil Rights Issues in Immigration" was released by the United States Commission on Civil Rights in which human rights violations and flawed reporting and investigative procedures of the Immigration and Naturalization Services were outlined.

Ten years later, dozens of cases of abuse were documented in the Human Rights Watch report, "Frontier Injustice," including the case of Border Patrol agent Michael Elmer, who shot fleeing immigrant Dario Miranda Valenzuela in his back, killing him. Upon investigation, numerous other abuses committed by Elmer were discovered, including shooting at a group of immigrants. Main grievances against Border Patrol agents and INS inspectors that persist include excessive use of force, shootings resulting in death and injuries, beatings and sexual assaults, as well as failure to provide adequate and timely medical attention. Additionally, National Guard troops placed along the border in the mid-1990s also have been cited as terrorizing not only unauthorized immigrants, but U.S. citizens as well. These troops, sent only to provide support to the Border Patrol, have been documented as detaining—and in some cases firing at—unauthorized immigrants.

Border Patrol agents have recently received increased attention for their facilitation of criminal activity along the border. Numerous accounts of corruption committed by Border Patrol agents have emerged, largely in the aiding of human smuggling by accepting bribes, and by acting as scouts for both human and drug smugglers. More than 200 cases of border law enforcement corruption have been opened with the numbers of cases increasing over time. Cases range from aiding and abetting human and drug smuggling to gun smuggling (Archibold 2008).

Additionally, a significant number of sexual assault cases have been brought against Border Patrol agents. Women have reported that Border Patrol agents have guaranteed border crossing without apprehension or deportation as well as the return of confiscated documents in exchange for sexual intercourse. Human Rights Watch reports and the Office of the Inspector General's semiannual reports to Congress have documented numerous violations and charges brought against Border Patrol agents by unauthorized Mexican women attempting to cross the border. Official estimates of such occurrences are unreliable due to the gross underreporting of such incidences by Mexican immigrant women. To bring charges against an INS officer, these women are confronting not only the agents, but also a large and powerful system at the risk of endangering their own presence in this country.

The United States' militaristic border strategies and Mexico's passive responses to immigrant deaths and abuses make the two countries culpable for human rights violations. Between 1994 and the present, or since the year Operation Gatekeeper was launched, more than 5,500 immigrants were reported dead and missing along the U.S.-Mexico border. More recently, although human smuggling has declined, the death rate has not followed suit. Between October 1, 2008, and September 20, 2009, 416 deaths were reported by the Border Patrol, a figure greater than that reported during the same period the previous year (*La Opinion* 2009). Attributed to increasingly stringent immigration policies and border enforcement, as well as the emergence of criminal organizations devoted to human trafficking efforts, the number of such deaths has increased. More severe border enforcement also has led to the formalization of an illicit human-smuggling industry, in which smugglers are charging more for crossing, are undertaking more perilous routes, are taking more risks with their human cargo, and are exposing immigrants to increased violence and death. Analysts and activists alike point out that the United States and Mexico have been accomplices in these violent acts against immigrants and in their deaths, as the tightening of the United States–Mexico border inadvertently has led to these tragedies.

See also: Part I essays: Policing and Latina/o Communities; Latinas and the U.S. Criminal Justice System. Part II entries: Civil Rights; Deportation; Hate Crimes; *Immigration and Naturalization Service (INS) v. Lopez-Mendoza et al.*, 468 U.S. 1032, (1984); Lesbian, Gay, Bisexual, and Transgender (LGBT); Lynching; Texas Rangers; *United States v. Brignoni-*

Ponce, 422 U.S. 873 (1975); *United States v. Martinez-Fuerte,* 428 U.S. 543 (1976); Vigilantism.

Further Reading

Aguilar, Julian. 2011 (March 9). On state website, calls for vigilante justice. *The Texas Tribune*.

Andreas, Peter. 2000. *Border games*. Ithaca, NY: Cornell University Press.

Archibold, Randal C. 2008 (September 11). Border fence is not likely to be done by year's end. *New York Times*.

Archibold, Randal C. 2009 (March 22). Mexican drug cartel violence spills over, alarming US. *New York Times*.

Archibold, Randal C., and Andrew Becker. 2008 (May 27). Border agents, lured by the other side. *New York Times*.

Associated Press. 2007 (January 18). Immigrant smuggler faulted in 19 deaths sentenced to life in prison.

Attkisson, Sharyl. 2011 (February 23). Gunrunning scandal uncovered at the ATF. *CBS News*. http://www.cbsnews.com/stories/2011/02/23/eveningnews/main20035609.shtml?source=related_story.

Butcher, Kristen F., and Anne Morrison Piehl. 2005. "Why are immigrants' incarceration rates so low? Evidence on selective immigration deterrence, and deportation." Working Papers 2005–19. Chicago: Federal Reserve Bank of Chicago. http://www.chicagofed.org/publications/workingpapers/wp2005_19.pdf. Accessed June 17, 2007.

Butcher, Kristin F., and Anne Morrison Piehl. 2008 (February). Crime, corrections, and California: What does immigration have to do with it? *California Counts: Population Trends and Profiles* 9 (3).

Chivvis, Dana. 2010 (September 7). Report: 90% of drug war guns originate in the United States," *AOL News*. http://www.aolnews.com/2010/09/07/report-90-percent-of-mexican-drug-war-guns-originate-in-u-s/.

Cornelius, Wayne. 2001. Death at the border: Efficacy and unintended consequences of US Immigration Control Policy. *Population and Development Review* 27(4): 661–85.

Del Bosque, Melissa. 2009 (April 16). Lights! Cameras! Mayhem: The national media invades El Paso and gets the story wrong. *The Texas Observer*.

Delgado, Richard. 2009. The law of the noose: A history of Latino lynching. *Harvard Civil Rights-Civil Liberties Law Review* 44(2): 297–312.

Delgado, Richard, Juan F. Perea, and Jean Stefancic. 2008. *Latinos and the law: Cases and materials*. St. Paul, MN: Thomson/West.

Economic Commission for Latin America and the Caribbean. 2007. No More! The right of women to live a life free of violence in Latin America and the Caribbean. Economic Commission for Latin America and the Caribbean. http://www.eclac.org/publicaciones/xml/7/31407/Nomore.pdf. Accessed March 13, 2010.

Falcon, Sylvanna. 2001. Rape as a weapon of war: Advancing human rights at the US-Mexico border. *Social Justice* 28(2): 31–50.

Federal Bureau of Investigation (FBI). 2009. Fact Sheet: Department of Justice efforts to combat Mexican drug cartels. Federal Bureau of Investigation. http://www.fbi.gov/news/pressrel/press-releases/fact-sheet-department-of-justice-efforts-to-combat-mexican-drug-cartels. Accessed May 23, 2010.

Fernandez-Kelly, M. Patricia, and Douglas Massey. 2007. Borders for whom? The role of NAFTA in Mexico-US migration. *The ANNALS of the American Academy of Political and Social Science*s 610: 98–118.

Finnegan, William. 2009 (July 20). Sheriff Joe. *The New Yorker*.

Geis, Sonya. 2007 (March 12). Minuteman project in turmoil over financial allegations. *Washington Post*.

Gonzalez, Juan. 2011. *Harvest of empire: A history of Latinos in America, revised edition.* New York: Penguin.

Grado, Gary. 2009 (October 6). Feds strip Arpaio of immigration authority. *East Valley Tribune.*

Griffin, Drew, and John Murgatroyd. 2008 (March 26). Smugglers' deadly cargo: Cop-killing guns. *CNN News.* http://articles.cnn.com/2008-03-26/world/gun.smuggling_1_gun-shops-mexican-police-gun-range?_s=PM:WORLD.

Grimaldi, James V. 2011 (March 9). ATF's tactics to end gun trafficking face a federal review. *Washington* Post.

Grimaldi, James V., and Sari Horowitz. 2010 (December 15). As Mexico drug violence runs rampant, U.S. guns tied to crime south of the border. *Washington Post.*

Grimaldi, James V., and Sari Horowitz. 2011 (February 1). ATF Gunrunning probe strategy scrutinized after death of Border Patrol agent. *Washington Post.*

Hagan, John, and Alberto Palloni. 1999. "Sociological criminology and the mythology of Hispanic immigration and crime." *Social Problems* 46(4): 617–32.

Harvard Law Review. 2004. Law, race and the border: The El Paso Salt War of 1877. *Harvard Law Review* 117 (3): 941–63.

Herzog, Lawrence A. 1990. *Where North meets South: Cities, space and politics on the US-Mexico Border.* Austin: University of Texas Press.

Hing, Bill Ong. 2004. *Defining America through immigration policy.* Philadelphia: Temple University Press.

Holstege, Sean. 2008 (June 12). National Guard wrapping up its US-Mexico border duty. *The Arizona Republic.*

Horowitz, Sari, and James V. Grimaldi. 2010 (December 17). White House delayed rule meant to stop gun flow to Mexico. *Washington Post.*

Hossain, Farhana, and G. V. Xarquin. 2009 (March 22). The reach of Mexico's drug cartels. *The New York Times.*

Human Rights Watch. 1993. Frontier injustice: Human rights abuses along the US border persist amid climate of impunity 5(4): 1–46.

Human Rights Watch.1995. Crossing the line: Human rights abuses along the US border persist amid climate of impunity. Human Rights Online. http://www.hrw.org/en/reports/1995/04/01/crossing-line. Accessed September 24, 2010.

Immigration Policy Center. 2010. Arizona's punishment doesn't fit the crime: Studies show decrease in Arizona crime rates over time. Washington, DC: American Immigration Council. http://www.immigrationpolicy.org/just-facts/arizona%E2%80%99s-punishment-doesn%E2%80%99t-fit-crime-studies-show-decrease-arizona-crime-rates.

Johnson, Hans. 2011. *Just the facts: Immigrants in California.* San Francisco: Public Policy Institute of California.

Johnson, Kevin. 1996–1997. Colloquium Proceedings: panel 1: Aliens and the immigration laws: The social and legal construction of non-persons. *University of Miami Inter-American Law Review* 263 (28).

Johnson, Kevin. 2003. Open borders? *UCLA Law Review* 263 (51): 193–266.

Johnson, Kevin. 2007. *Opening the floodgates: Why America needs to rethink its borders and immigration laws.* New York: New York University Press.

Karman, Andrew. 2000. *New York murder mystery: The true story behind the crime crash of the 1990s.* New York: New York University Press.

Kil, Sang Hea, and Cecilia Menjívar. 2006. The "war on the border": Criminalizing immigrants and militarizing the US-Mexico border. In *Immigration and Crime: Race, Ethnicity and Violence*, edited by R. Martínez, Jr., and A. Valenzuela, Jr., 164–88. New York: New York University Press.

La Opinion. 2009 (October 1). Border deaths increase despite fewer crossers.

Lacey, Marc. 2009 (March 30). In drug war, Mexico fights cartel and itself. *The New York Times.*

LeBron, Marisol. 2009 (March 17). *Migracorridos*: Another failed anti-immigration campaign. *NACLA*.

Lee, Matthew. 2003. *Crime on the border: Immigration and homicide in urban communities*. New York: LFB Scholarly Publishing.

Lipowicz, Alice. 2011. Boeing's SBInet contract gets the axe. *Washington Technology*. http://washingtontechnology.com/articles/2011/01/14/dhs-cancels-rest-of-sbinet-and-plans-mix-of-new-technologies-at-border.aspx. Accessed March 4, 2011.

Madhani, Aamer. 2011 (March 3). Mexico president balks at arming U.S. agents. *National Journal*.

Marosi, Richard. 2008 (January 21). Border Patrol attacks rising. *Los Angeles Times*.

Martinez, Oscar J. 2006. *Troublesome border*. Phoenix, AZ: University of Arizona Press.

Martínez, Ramiro, Jr. 2002. *Latino homicide: Immigration, violence and community*. New York: Routledge.

McKinley, James C., Jr. 2009 (February 26). US is arms bazaar for Mexican cartels. *The New York Times*.

McKinley, Jesse, and Malia Wollan. 2009 (June 26). New Border Fear: Violence by Rogue Militia. *The New York Times*.

Meneses, Guillermo A. 2003. Human rights and unauthorized migration along the Mexican-US border. *UCLA Law Review* (51)1: 267–82.

Migration Policy Institute. 2006 (June 1). *The US-Mexico border*. Washington, DC: Migration Policy Institute.

Mirandé, Alfredo. 1987. *Gringo justice*. Notre Dame, IN: University of Notre Dame Press.

Mirandé, Alfredo. 2003. Is there a "Mexican exception" to the Fourth Amendment? *Florida Law Review* 55: 365–89.

Morín, José Luis. 2009. *Latina/o rights and justice in the United States: Perspectives and approaches*, 2nd ed. Durham, NC: Carolina Academic Press.

Myers, Dowell, and John Pitkin. 2010. Assimilation today: New evidence shows the latest immigrants to America are following in our history's footsteps. Washington, DC: Center for American Progress.

NACLA Report on the Americas. Border vigilantes, Part II: Virtual vigilance. https://nacla.org/node/5382. Accessed March 10, 2011.

National Organization of Women. National Organization of Women, Femicides of Juarez fact sheet. http://www.now.org/issues/global/juarez/femicide.html. Accessed June 9, 2009.

Nevins, Joseph. 2002. *Operation Gatekeeper: The rise of the "illegal alien" and the making of the U.S.-Mexico boundary*. New York: Routledge.

Nevins, Joseph, and Timothy Dunn. 2008 (November 14). Barricading the border: A history of the US-Mexico border fence. *NACLA Report on the Americas* 41(6): 21–25.

No More Deaths. 2008. *Crossing the line: Human rights abuses of migrants in short-term custody on the Arizona-Sonora border*. Tucson, AZ: No More Deaths.

Nuñez-Neto, Blas. 2005. *Border security: The role of the U.S. border patrol*. Congressional Research Service: The Library of Congress.

Paget-Clarke, Nic. 1997. Interview with Roberto Martinez. *In Motion Magazine*, http://www.inmotionmagazine.com/border.html. Accessed November 9, 2010.

Paredes, Americo. 1958. *With his pistol in his hands*, Austin: University of Texas Press.

Powell, Stewart. 2011 (May 24). Three years later, U.S. still hasn't delivered 40% of promised drug war aid to Mexico. *Houston Chronicle*.

Prentice, Claire. 2009. Armchair deputies patrol US border, *BBC News*, http://news.bbc.co.uk/2/hi/americas/8412603.stm. Accessed April 11, 2010.

Public Policy Institute of California. 2008. Just the facts: Immigrants and crime. San Francisco: Public Policy Institute of California.

Robbins, Ted. 2010. Border Patrol program raises due process concerns. *National Public Radio.* http://www.npr.org/templates/story/story.php?storyId=129780261. Accessed October 1, 2010.

Rodriguez, Nestor P. 1997. Chapter 12: The social construction of the US-Mexican border. In *Immigrants Out! The New Nativism and the Anti-Immigrant Impulse in the United States*, edited by J. F. Perea, 223–43. New York, NY: New York University Press.

Samora, Julian, Joe Bernal, and Albert Pena. 1979. *Gunpowder justice: A reassessment of the Texas Rangers*. Notre Dame, IN: University of Notre Dame Press.

Schaefer, Agnes G., Benjamin Bahney, and K. Jack Riley. 2009. *Security in Mexico: Implications for U.S. policy options*. Santa Monica, CA: Rand Corporation.

Scott, Robert E., Carlos Salas, and Bruce Campbell. 2006. *Revisiting NAFTA: Still not working for North America's workers* (Briefing Paper No. 173). Washington, DC: Economic Policy Institute.

Soltero, Carlos R. 2006. *Latinos and American law: Landmark Supreme Court cases*. Austin: University of Texas Press.

Southern Poverty Law Center. [n.d.]. Glenn Spencer. http://www.splcenter.org/get-informed/intelligence-files/profiles/glenn-spencer. Accessed November 12, 2015.

Southern Poverty Law Center. 2005. Intelligence report: Arizona showdown. Southern Poverty Law Center. http://www.splcenter.org/intel/intelreport/article.jsp?pid=915.

Stolberg, Sheryl Gay. 2009 (April 17). In Mexico, Obama seeks curbs on arms sales to thwart drug cartels. *The New York Times*.

Sullivan, Eileen, and E. Eduardo Castillo. 2009 (April 2). US, Mexico work together to fight drug cartels. *Associated Press*.

Surdin, Ashley. 2009 (March 15). Crossover appeal: South of the border, popular ballads about the perils of illegal immigration have a surprising heritage: Made in—and by—the United States of America. *Washington Post*.

Texas State Historical Association. [n.d.]. *Handbook of Texas Online*, http://www.tshaonline.org/handbook/online/articles/PP/gzp2.html. Accessed November 10, 2009.

Thompson, Ginger, and Mark Mazzetti. 2011 (March 16). U.S. drones fly deep into Mexico to fight drugs. *The New York Times*.

United States Commission on Civil Rights. 1980. *The tarnished golden door: Civil rights issues on immigration: A report of the United States Commission on Civil Rights*, Washington, DC: United States Commission on Civil Rights.

U.S. Customs and Border Protection. 2011. U.S. Border Patrol fiscal year staffing statistics.

U.S. Customs and Border Protection. http://www.cbp.gov/linkhandler/cgov/border_security/border_patrol/usbp_statistics/staffing_92_10.ctt/staffing_92_10.pdf.

U.S. Department of Homeland Security. 2006. SBInet: Securing the U.S. borders fact sheet, United States Department of Homeland Security. http://www.dhs.gov/xlibrary/assets/sbinetfactsheet.pdf. Accessed November 27, 2010.

Villarreal, M. Angeles. 2011. *U.S.-Mexico economic relations: Trends, issues and implications*. Washington, DC: Congressional Research Service.

Walker, Christopher J. 2007. Border vigilantism and comprehensive immigration reform. *Harvard Latino Law Review* 10: 135–74.

Washington Office on Latin America. *Resolution on violence against women in Ciudad Juarez and Chihuahua*. Washington, DC: Washington Office on Latin America. http://www.wola.org/index.php?option=com_content&task=viewp&id=400&Itemid=2. Accessed February 26, 2009.

Washington Post. 2011. Mexico's Frustration with U.S. Drug Policy [Editorial]. March 5.

Waslin, Michele. 2003. The new meaning of the border: US-Mexico migration since

9/11. *National Council of La Raza*. Working Paper, Washington, DC: NCLR.

Wood, Daniel B. 2008 (April 1). Where U.S.-Mexico border fence is tall, border crossings fall. *The Christian Science Monitor*. http://www.csmonitor.com/USA/2008/0401/p01s05-usgn.html.

Wu, Amy. 2006. Border apprehensions: 2005. Washington, DC: Office of Immigration Statistics, Department of Homeland Security.

Yardley, Jim. 2000 (January 26). Some Texans say that border patrol singles out too many blameless Hispanics. *The New York Times*.

Zaitchik, Alexander. 2011 (Summer). Upending the Constitution. *Intelligence Report*.

Cases Cited

Almeida-Sanchez v. United States, 413 U.S. 266 (1973).

Immigration and Naturalization Service (INS) v. Lopez-Mendoza et al., 468 U.S. 1032 (1984).

United States v. Brignoni-Ponce, 422 U.S. 873 (1975).

United States v. Martinez-Fuerte, 428 U.S. 543 (1976).

Latina/o Youth and Criminal Justice

Victor M. Rios, Melissa Guzman, and José Luis Morín

Academic research and literature on the topic of Latina/o **youth** in the U.S. criminal justice system has, in general, been wanting. Notwithstanding deficiencies in the literature about Latina/o youth, sufficient data has been amassed to expose patterns of disparities in the treatment of Latina/o youth by law enforcement and throughout the criminal justice system. Similar to African American youth, Latina/o youth have been a part of the "**mass imprisonment** phenomenon," filling the prisons nationally at rates disproportionate to their population. As with African American youth, Latina/o youth also are subject to harsher sentences as compared to white youth accused of similar offenses. Race, criminal justice policies, law enforcement strategies, and **media depictions** repeatedly surface as factors contributing to a broad range of disparities and inequities in relation to Latina/o youth and the U.S. criminal justice system. "Get-tough" policies—such as the "**war on drugs**," aggressive anti-gang tactics, and the over-policing of schools—and the overrepresentation of youth of color in the media as criminals buttress what has come to be known as "the **schools-to-prison pipeline**." Independent studies confirm that the lack of sensible juvenile detention practices (which too often are inhumane) has had disproportionately negative consequences for Latina/o and African American youth. Disparate outcomes for Latina/o youth have resulted in calls for the implementation of more evidence-based policies and best practices, as well as for the adoption of major reforms in juvenile and criminal justice systems across the country.

Overrepresentation of Latina/o Youth in the Criminal Justice System

The dearth of information specifically about Latina/o youth in relation to the criminal justice system is attributable, in part, to the common practice of most criminologists considering the study of race and criminal justice synonymous with the study of African American/white crime and punishment. Further hampering the ability to accurately document the Latina/o experience in the criminal justice is the categorization by federal and other government agencies of "Hispanics" as an "ethnic" group that can be of any race, often leading to the exclusion of Latinas/os in data collected about race and crime. Latinas/os have been and still very frequently are classified as "whites" even though the criminal justice system most typically considers Latinas/os as being racially "other" and not as part of the dominant white society.

Despite the absence of extensive research on Latina/o youth, studies that have managed to isolate their experiences in the criminal justice system point out that Latina/o youth, similar to African American youth, face a crisis in the criminal justice system. These studies indicate that Latinas/os are overrepresented in the criminal justice system. When compared to whites, Latina/o youth are more likely to be arrested, charged with more severe crimes, detained before trial, represented by overworked public defenders, incarcerated more often, sentenced to longer prison terms for similar crimes, and subjected to **racial profiling**.

A 2002 groundbreaking report issued by academics and community-based organizations entitled *¿Dónde está la justicia?* presents a sobering picture of the inequities and racial and ethnic disparities experienced by Latina/o youth in relation to the U.S. criminal justice system. The presence of Latina/o juveniles in detention facilities nationally increased markedly between 1983 and 1991, with the number of Latina/o youth in public detention centers growing by 84 percent, although the number of white youth in detention increased only 8 percent and the number of youth in general increased by 46 percent. Latina/o youth are incarcerated in jails and prisons at rates two to three times those of white youth in nine states, three to six times the rates of white youth in eight states, and seven to seventeen times the rates of white youth in four states (Villarruel et al. 2002).

On average, Latina/o youth experience longer sentences in state public facilities than any other racial or ethnic group in all offense categories. Latina/o youths charged with violent crimes spend about 143 more days (nearly 5 months) incarcerated than do white youth convicted for the same offenses. Latina/o youth charged with property offenses were incarcerated an average of 45 days longer than white youth convicted of similar charges. For drug offenses, Latina/o youth were found to be incarcerated for more than twice the amount of time (306 days) than were white youth (144 days). Even minor violations of public order (such as gambling) result in disproportionately harsher sentences for Latina/o youth than for white youth—typically 220 days as compared to 147 days for white youths—equating to roughly 50 percent longer sentences (Villarruel et al. 2002).

Latinas/os have seen their presence among the incarcerated grow exponentially. From 1985 to 1995, "the number of Hispanics in prison rose by 219 percent, with an average 12.3 percent increase each year" (Mumola & Beck 1997, 9). The annual growth in the Latina/o prisoner population has continued. By year-end 2004, the total percentage of Latina/o prisoners in state and federal jurisdictions had grown to 19.2 percent (Harrison & Beck 2005, 8). Despite a recent reduction in the rate of incarceration nationwide, Bureau of Justice Statistics estimates show a continuing increase in the rate of Latinas/os under state and federal jurisdiction being sentenced to prison—from 295,800 in 2008, to 303,500 in 2009 (West, Sabol, & Greenman 2010, 27, Table 12).

For Latinas/os, **racial and ethnic discrimination** and prejudice in the courts appear to be constant factors in the meting out of unequal justice. As one study in Los Angeles found, Latino males regularly were prosecuted to the fullest extent, with African American males, white males, and women of all ethnicities following in descending order (Spohn, Gruhl, & Welch 1987). A 2004 report sponsored by the **National Council of La Raza (NCLR)** similarly found that "Latinos are overrepresented and unfairly treated at every stage of the criminal justice system" (Walker et al. 2004). As further evidence of the impact of a criminal justice system prone to intentional and unintentional racial and ethnic discrimination, a major study conducted by Michigan State University–Building Blocks for Youth suggests that bias in the criminal justice system is a key factor in the high rates of incarceration among Latina/o youth. National data reveal that, as a result, Latina/o youth are charged with violent offenses at a rate five times greater than for white youth and serve longer sentences than do white youth. In Los Angeles, Latina/o youth are incarcerated at rates much higher than those for white youth—7.3 times as often from 1996 to 1998—and Latina/o youth are prosecuted as adults more often than are white youth—2.4 times as often from 1996 to 1998 (Villarruel et al. 2002, 2–3).

Mass Imprisonment and the Prison Industrial Complex

Academics define mass imprisonment as unprecedented high rates of incarceration "markedly above the historical and comparative norm for all societies of this type" and as "the systematic imprisonment of whole groups of the population" (Garland 2001, 1–2). Consistent with this definition, Latinas/os—especially young Latinas/os—fall within the category of persons prone to systematic and disproportionate rates of imprisonment. Latinas/os largely are a young group within the U.S. population (U.S. Census Bureau 2003), and nearly three-quarters of all Latina/o jail and prison inmates in the United States are between 20 and 39 years old. At mid-year 2005, 3.9 percent of Latinas/os in their late twenties were incarcerated compared to 1.5 percent of whites in the same age range (Harrison & Beck 2006, 10). Scholars have maintained that since the 1970s, mass incarceration has become a "major and apparently indispensable element of social order" (Garland 2001, 3), and that mass imprisonment in the United States has been used as a system for regulating the poor. More than two million people living in the United States are in prisons or jails and almost three-quarters of them are people of color and are poor (Parenti 2000).

Being both a group living in the United States which is viewed and treated as racially "other," and a population that is disproportionately poor, Latina/o youth meet the criterion of a population vulnerable to encounters with the criminal justice system and its policies and practices. In 2008, nearly three out of five Latinas/os in the United States were born here and two of five were foreign-born Latinas/os (Pew Hispanic Center 2010a, Table 1). Yet, misperceptions of Latinas/os as being primarily a foreign-born population endure, and the persistence of negative racial and ethnic stereotypes frequently have resulted in xenophobic and discriminatory treatment towards Latinas/os (Delgado & Stefancic 2011; Morín 2009). With respect to criminal justice policies and practices specifically, disproportionately poor populations—including Latina/o communities in the United States—are the most susceptible to law enforcement policies and "get-tough" activities. In 2008, poverty among Latinas/os younger than 18 years of age was 26.8 percent, as compared to 10 percent for white youth (Pew Hispanic Center 2010a, Table 37).

Studies point to many examples throughout the United States in which youth of color, including Latinas/os, are overrepresented in the criminal justice system. A 1996 national report found that youth of color living in California comprised 53.4 percent of the youth population statewide but represented 59 percent of all juveniles arrested, nearly 64 percent of juveniles held in secure detention, and 70 percent of the juveniles placed in secure corrections. Ohio's youth of color comprised 14.3 percent of the youth population statewide, but represented 30 percent of the juveniles arrested and 43 percent of the juveniles placed in secure corrections. In Texas, youth of color comprised 50 percent of the youth populations statewide, but represented 65 percent of the juveniles held in secure detention, 80 percent of the juveniles placed in secure corrections, and represented 100 percent of the juveniles held in adult jails (Hamparian & Leiber 1997). As for Latina/o youth specifically, a national survey revealed that, for every 100,000 Latina/o youth in the general population, there were 515 incarcerated (Snyder & Sickmund 1999, 197).

Political gain and financial profits increasingly have been implicated in the expansion of prisons in the United States. A penal system in which government officials and private businesses have interests and benefit directly or indirectly in the construction and maintenance of prisons has come to be commonly referred to as "the **prison industrial complex**." Some scholars argue that the prison industrial complex generates profits by turning imprisoned bodies into profits and sources of consumption and production (Davis 2003; Alexander 2010). (For more information on the "prison industrial complex" see "Incarceration and Latinas/os in the United States" in this volume.)

Other scholars view the prison industrial complex to be a system of economic drain because it "drains" vital resources away from more productive or needed areas for the economic benefit of private business and the political gain of government officials. They point out that massive expenditures on prison construction and maintenance have depleted the resources for social services and education spending. In California, a teacher's average salary is $36,000 per year and a prison guard's average salary is $78,000; spending per pupil is $8,000 and spending per juvenile in detention is $216,000 (Hirschfield 2008). In New York State, detaining youths far exceeds the costs for educating them. The average annual detention cost per bed in fiscal year 2009 was $226,320 as opposed to the $15,371 annual average expense per student in a New York City public high school (Correctional Association of New York 2010).

Similar problems exist nationwide. States spend approximately $5.7 billion every year to detain roughly 93,000 youths—a majority of whom are held for nonviolent offenses—in largely ineffective facilities (Justice Policy Institute 2009). Scholars assert that vast disparities between funding for education and funding in the criminal justice system have resulted in the establishment of a "school-to-prison pipeline" that disproportionately affects many poor Latina/o and black youth and sets them on a trajectory that prepares them for prison rather than for a lifetime as productive members of society.

Crime Trends: Punitive Policies, "Superpredators," the War on Drugs, and Stops and Frisks

Although the United States witnessed a fourfold increase in incarceration rates from 1997 to 2007, prominent scholars attribute **mass incarceration** as having played only a small role in the surprising and precipitous drop in the national crime rate over the same period (Barker 2010, 498–99). Major violent and property crime rates continued at historically low levels from 2000 to 2009, with violent-crime rates overall declining by 39 percent (Truman & Rand 2010, 3). Yet, despite this historic downward trend in crime rates, punitive crime-control policies and practices intensified into the new millennium. Analysts point out that "get-tough-on-crime" policies, increased funding for corrections and correctional facilities, and passage of "mandatory minimum" sentencing and "three-strikes" laws account for the equally historic increase in the U.S. prison population. As a result, even though serious violent crime levels have declined by 50 percent in the United States since 1993, arrests for violent crimes have nearly doubled (Walker et al. 2004, 40–41).

Youths As "Superpredators"

Many of the punitive policies and practices specifically target juveniles, including the application of adult sentencing laws to youths under 18 years of age, the implementation of enhanced **gang** and gun sentences for juveniles, and the conversion of crimes typically committed by juveniles—such as vandalism and property offenses—into felony offenses. During the 1990s, the prediction that the country was facing a new and more dangerous type of youthful offenders, known as "superpredators," was popularly promoted as well as the notion that without more stringent laws society would soon be in great jeopardy (e.g., DiIulio 1995). This prediction never came to fruition. In fact, the leading proponent of the mass incarceration of youths regretted ever becoming "the 1990s intellectual pillar for putting violent juveniles in prison and condemning them as 'superpredators,' conceding that 'If I knew then what I know now, I would have shouted for prevention of crimes'" (Becker 2001, A19). This fact notwithstanding, get-tough policies targeting youths have remained popular over the years among law enforcement, politicians, and the public—policies that account for the high rates of youth imprisonment today.

As of 2008, roughly 93,000 youth were confined to juvenile justice facilities in the United States—at great expense. It is estimated that 70 percent of these youth were detained in a state-funded, post-adjudication residential facility at a cost averaging $240.99 per day per youth or about $88,000 a year per youth. In total, states spent approximately $5.7 billion each year to incarcerate youth, most of whom were nonviolent offenders. California, for instance, spent $604,555.05 per day based on the total population of juvenile detainees (Justice Policy Institute 2009). Yet, despite this tremendous expense and in the face of decreasing crime rates, scholars have found only a modest correlation between increasing prison populations and reduced crime rates. Major studies on the decline in the crime rate in the United States since the 1980s show that—overall—only 10 percent to 20 percent of the decline can be attributed to the increase in incarceration rates (Barker 2010, 498).

Data show that states which increased the number of youth in juvenile justice facilities did not necessarily see a greater drop in crime than that of states which reduced juvenile correctional populations. Additionally, a critical assessment of the last decade of data on incarceration and crime trends shows no direct correspondence between states that increase the number of youth in juvenile facilities and crime rates. Conversely, states that significantly reduced the number of youth incarcerated were more likely to experience drops in crime than those states which increased their correctional populations. Despite diminishing rates of violent crime, Latina/o youth continually are introduced into the criminal justice system at high rates. Scholars have noted that, although youth of color represented just 34 percent of the U.S. population, they constituted 62 percent of the youth in detention facilities, and 67 percent of youth in state institutions (Poe-Yamagata & Jones 2000).

The "War on Drugs" and Its Impact on Racial and Ethnic Disparities

Until recently, sentencing laws required a mandatory five-year sentence for possession of five grams or more of crack cocaine versus the five-year mandatory sentence for possession of 500 grams or more of powder cocaine. The discrepancy lies in that young, poor inner-city African Americans and Latinas/os were more likely to be caught with crack because of its cheaper value and receive more severe sentences than white people, who were more likely to be caught with powder cocaine (*see* Parenti 2000). Although these policies focused on a specific drug and not on a race of people, the fact that specific racialized populations have been affected by specific drug markets caused a disparity in arrests and led to sentencing along racial lines.

Scholars have argued that racism in the criminal justice system has been "coded" by laws that target specific behaviors or objects found in many poor communities—such as gang activity, cheap **drugs**, and misdemeanor street offenses—that only become visible because of heavy police surveillance and the lack of public and private venues to conduct leisure activity (Parenti 2000; Rios 2008). As discussed elsewhere in this volume (*see* "The U.S. War on Drugs and Latina/o Communities"), politicians and the public were captivated by the demonization of crack in the 1980s and the misperception linking it to certain racial and ethnic groups. The result was a concentrated drug-enforcement effort in African American and Latina/o communities that resulted in great disparities in arrests and incarceration rates in comparison to those for whites.

The growth in incarceration rates in the United States has been greatly affected by the rise in arrests for drug-related offenses since the 1970s (New York Civil Liberties Union [NYCLU] 2009b). In 1973, New York Governor Nelson Rockefeller began his crusade to execute the nation's "toughest" and inflexible drug sentencing statutes. The **Rockefeller Drug Laws** required a mandatory prison sentence for anyone convicted of unlawful possession or sale of controlled substances. Culpability was decided upon the drug involved and possession of even the slightest amount mandated a harsh prison term—terms that often exceed sentences for violent crimes. In practice, this law substantially increased trial rates, slowed down the courts, and produced severe injustices, as nonviolent drug offenders were the ones increasingly punished under mandatory prison sentences. Many states followed suit by enacting similar laws.

The Rockefeller Drug Laws have played a significant role in sending large numbers of African American and Latino men to prison in New York State. In the past decade, approximately 40 percent of prison admissions have been for drug offenses. In 1980, 886 people were incarcerated for drug offenses, of which 32 percent were white, 38 percent African American, and 29 percent Latina/o. In 1992—a year in which the state reported the greatest number of incarcerations for drug offenses, 5 percent were white, 50 percent African American, and 44 percent Latina/o. The demographics for those serving drug-related sentences from 1992 to 2000 remained relatively the same. In 2000, of the 8,227 people who were incarcerated for drug offenses, whites comprised 6 percent, 53 percent were African American, and 40 percent were Latina/o. Since 2003, roughly 9 out of 10 of persons imprisoned for drug offenses have been African American or Latina/o (NYCLU 2009b).

The racial and ethnic disparities among those persons incarcerated for drug offenses in New York have not corresponded with actual rates of illicit **drug use** in New York State. Government data from 2001 showed that, out of a total of 1.8 million adults in New York—approximately 13 percent of the total adult population—who reported using illegal drugs in the preceding year, 1.3 million (72 percent) were white. Research also suggests that trafficking in drugs is greater in white communities, but **drug trafficking** in white communities often fails to expose whites to law enforcement risks because exchanges typically take place behind closed doors rather than in public places (NYCLU 2009b; Council, Shi, & Hourani 2005; Riley 1997). Some scholars argue that the much higher arrest and conviction rates for drug-related charges among Latinas/os and blacks are not related to greater levels of crime. Rather, they can be explained by other factors, including racial discrimination. For this reason, evaluating drug sentencing laws and, more generally, the "war on drugs" requires analyzing the ways in which race works in law enforcement and judicial procedures. The war on drugs is yet another trend that has had a disparate impact on Latinas/os and other communities of color.

In New York and in states around the country, the number of individuals imprisoned for drug offenses only recently has begun to decline, to some extent due to the passage of reforms to the Rockefeller Drug Laws and other efforts to reduce the costs that states incur as a result of mass imprisonment. Nevertheless, the number of persons imprisoned remains historically high, and Latina/o and African American youth continue to be vulnerable to law enforcement tactics, such as **stops and frisks.**

Stop-and-Frisk Tactics

Despite recent reforms to the Rockefeller Drug Laws, concerns continue to mount about the impact of police stops of young people of color in urban centers. Given the disclosure of data about police **stops and frisks**—resulting from a freedom of information lawsuit brought against New York City—the city has become the most visible example of the disproportionate and arguably discriminatory impact of police stop-and-frisk tactics on African Americans and Latinas/os. In 2010, a record 600,601 persons were stopped by police in New York City, of which 87 percent were African American or Latina/o (Center for Constitutional Rights [CCR] 2011). This represented an increase from 2009, a year in which 576,394 people were stopped and 84 percent of those stopped were African American or Latina/o. Respectively, African Americans and Latinas/os represented 53 percent and 31 percent of New York City's total population in 2009. In previous years (2005 to 2008), 80 percent of persons stopped were African American or Latina/o.

Recent data on racial and ethnic disparities in police stops is consistent with a long record of concerns about police tactics applied in communities of color. Although the New York City Police Department insisted that Latinas/os and African Americans were stopped and frisked at greater rates because they live in neighborhoods with high crime rates, a 1999 New York State Attorney General's report found that—even after accounting for differences in crime rates in communities of color and white communities—in New York City, across all crime categories, Latinas/os still were stopped by police officers 39 percent more often than were whites (Spitzer 1999, x). The State Attorney General's report on **policing** in New York City and a 2000 U.S. Commission on Civil Rights report both point to race as frequently being used as a sole criterion in the actions of law enforcement agents.

Research studies of other major urban centers point to a nationwide pattern in which stops and frisks have a disproportionate and adverse impact on Latinas/os and African American youth. In Chicago, 80 percent of African American high school students and 62 percent of Latina/o high school students reported being stopped by police, with 62 percent and 63 percent reporting, respectively, that they were treated disrespectfully by the police when stopped (Freidman & Hott 1995, 111). Policing and police practices, including stop-and-frisk tactics, are discussed further in this volume (*see* **Policing and Latina/o Communities**).

The School-to-Prison Pipeline

Throughout the United States, public schools have expanded the use of metal detectors, police presence, and harsh disciplinary policies. Beginning in the 1990s, schools began adopting strict "zero tolerance" policies—a term for school or district policies that require a predetermined punishment for particular infractions—creating a penal environment in schools. Roughly 74 percent to 94 percent of schools have adopted zero tolerance policies. Although widely accepted, legal professionals and public health experts have criticized such policies. The American Bar Association has recommended an end to these policies because they inappropriately require automatic expulsion or referral to juvenile court without full consideration of the individual circumstances. The American Academy of Pediatrics also has cautioned against use of zero tolerance because suspensions and expulsions could "exacerbate academic deterioration, and when students are provided with no immediate educational alternative, student alienation, delinquency, crime, and substance abuse may ensue" (American Academy of Pediatrics 2003, 1206). Students least likely to have supervision at home—typically poor families, and youth of color—are the most susceptible to harsh school disciplinary policies that not only are ineffective as corrective measures, but which also can be unhealthy and detrimental to the child's academic progress (American Academy of Pediatrics 2003). Moreover, harsh zero tolerance policies frequently are associated with the "school-to-prison pipeline"—measures that enhance the chance that a young person will be incarcerated rather than successfully complete school.

The growing presence of police in New York City's public education system—a school system with a predominantly African American and Latina/o student population—has drawn considerable attention in recent years. In 1998, Mayor Rudolph Giuliani transferred school security from the Board of Education to the New York Police Department (NYPD). As a result, police personnel in schools increased by 62 percent, from 3,200 to 5,200. The NYPD has used regular law enforcement tactics and procedures to handle noncriminal violations within the school setting. More than 5,000 School Safety Officers and NYPD employees are assigned to the city's public schools, including nearly 200 armed police officers. This overwhelming police presence makes the NYPD's School Safety Division the nation's fifth largest police force—a police force that is bigger than those found in Baltimore, Boston, Dallas, Detroit, Las Vegas, Phoenix, San Francisco, San Diego, and Washington, DC (NYCLU 2007, 4).

Along with this marked police presence in schools has been an increase in the number of reported cases of police abuse. From 2002 to 2007, the NYPD Internal Affairs Bureau received 2,670 complaints against the School Safety Officers, averaging approximately 500 per year (NYCLU 2010). Complaints range from the use of derogatory language, intrusive searches, and various forms of harassment, to physical and other forms of abuse by police personnel. The students most affected are disproportionately poor, African American, and Latina/o, and are more likely to be confronted by police about "non-criminal" matters. Among the cases that have drawn public notice is the case of a 12 year old handcuffed and detained at the local police precinct for doodling on her desk using an erasable marker.

Many parents and civil liberties groups charge that the heightened levels of police personnel in school criminalizes young people—especially African American and Latina/o youth in schools where police presence tends to be most concentrated—and that it is emblematic of the school-to-prison pipeline in which youth of color are targeted by law enforcement at a very early age, and thus accumulate a record as a juvenile offender, or worse. Recent research has lent credibility to the hypothesis that youth of color pose a perceived "racial threat" to society and, as a result, schools with greater numbers of students of color have responded using more punitive disciplinary measures.

Although New York City officials assert that police presence in schools is not designed to target young men and women of color but rather to reduce crime, studies from Fordham and New York University suggest the opposite. As indicated in a study of 2004–2005 data, the impact of police in New York City public schools is felt most acutely in poorly funded and resource-poor schools with large numbers of students of color. At these schools, police interventions for the "non-criminal" activity can be as much as 77 percent (NYCLU 2007, 19–20).

Numerous scholars have come to regard these poorly resourced institutions as "dropout factories" where low student success rates are common, particularly among Latina/o and African American youth (Balfanz & Legters 2006; Losen 2006). New York State Education Department data for 2006 revealed a 43.5 percent graduation rate for New York City public schools (Losen 2006). Nationally, "some 41% of Hispanics ages 20 and older in the United States do not have a regular high school diploma, versus 23% of comparably aged blacks and 14% of whites" (Fry 2010, ii). In describing the vulnerability of students of color in poor neighborhoods and in poorly resourced schools to the criminal justice system, scholars—including those at the Harvard University Civil Rights Project—speak of a "school-to-prison pipeline" in which high dropout rates parallel high rates of incarceration (Wald & Losen 2003).

In New York City, where the youth who were less than 16 years of age accounted for less than 4 percent of arrests for major felonies, the City has continued to incarcerate large numbers of juveniles, with African Americans and Latinas/os comprising 95 percent of youth entering juvenile detention centers. By comparison, white youth—who comprise 26 percent of the city's children—only make up 4 percent of detainees in juvenile detention centers (Correctional Association of New York 2010). Moreover, New York State youth detention facilities have been cited by the Civil Rights Division of the U.S. Department of Justice for inadequately protecting youths from harm, including the use of excessive force, inappropriate restraints, lack of appropriate mental health care, and other serious forms of abuse.

School discipline correlates with higher chances of contact with police and increased potential for incarceration. The school-to-prison pipeline typically begins with disciplinary actions taken in the school that stigmatize youth. This stigma often follows poor, racialized students into the community where they are subject to systematic police surveillance and often face harassment as well. Acts of deviance committed in school by poor Latina/o youth often are symbolically converted into criminal acts by teachers, administrators, and school-based police officers—even in students' early elementary years. Eventually, the smallest of transgressions lead this population into a first arrest. Probation becomes a key to the school-to-prison pipeline. Violating probation for curfew and statutory offenses often leads to a severe sentence.

Shaped by their daily experiences of discipline at school and in the community, Latina/o youths' attitudes about schooling and policing become adversarial. These young people consequently believe they have become members of a group that is uniquely targeted by school discipline and police harassment.

Scholars also have discerned a convergence of many factors—distressed economic conditions, high unemployment, mass imprisonment of African Americans and Latinas/os, and hard fiscal times in public education—as contributing structurally to the implementation of harsh school disciplinary policies and practices, and to perceptions of poor students of color as being "on a criminal justice 'track'" (Hirschfield 2008, 92). According to some, the implementation of an "Impact Schools" initiative in New York targeting ostensible high crime rate schools for tougher **policing** policies has transformed entire schools into pipelines to prison. Low test scores and high suspension rates in already poorly funded schools often lead to heightened police surveillance and police treating students as though they were criminals. Sending students to the precinct rather than to the principal's office, instead of calling the parents, becomes routine even for noncriminal conduct.

The Criminalization of Latina/o Youth in the Criminal Justice System and in the Media

The criminalization of Latina/o youth is not a recent phenomenon. Systematic cultural and historical mechanisms of socialization and control have labeled Latina/o youth as deviant, criminal, and threatening for more than 150 years (Miranda 1994). A system of "racialized social control" has existed as a way of creating and perpetuating a racial order to regulate poor African American and Latina/o youth (Ward 2009). Despite a significant decline in violent crime nationally—54 percent from 1993 to 2002 (Rennison & Rand 2003, 1)—polls indicate an increase in the fear of **youth crime** and an upsurge in media coverage of crime. Even though whites actually are three times more likely to be victimized by whites than by minorities, the media coverage of crime continues to further fear of young people of color in relation to crime. In evening news coverage, Latina/o and African American youth are overrepresented as violent criminals, and whites are underrepresented as violent offenders (Dorfman & Schiraldi 2001, 3–4, 15).

The media's role in portraying Latina/o youth as criminals cannot be overlooked. Studies of popular entertainment and news media show a consistent pattern of overrepresenting Latina/o youth as criminals, and underrepresenting crimes committed by white youth. In the realm of popular entertainment, the long history of films such as *Tony the Greaser* (1911), *West Side Story* (1961), *Scarface* (1983), *Carlito's Way* (1993), and many others have ingrained the stereotype of Latinas/os as inherently prone to **violence** and criminality into the psyches of generations of movie-goers.

Research studies also show that television news media often inaccurately represent alleged criminal conduct by Latina/o and African American youth. Seventy-five percent of the studies on local television news overrepresented Latina/o and African American youth as perpetrators of crime, with Latinas/os 14 percent more likely to be portrayed committing violent crimes versus nonviolent crime even though Latinas/os were only 7 percent more likely to be arrested for a violent crime than a nonviolent crime. By comparison, whites were 31 percent more often to be shown committing a nonviolent crime than a violent crime, even though whites were only 7 percent more likely to be arrested for a nonviolent crime. Overall, the studies point to Latinas/os and African Americans being overrepresented as violent offenders and whites underrepresented as violent offenders on evening television news (Dorfman & Schiraldi 2001, 13, 15).

The National Association of Hispanic Journalists (NAHJ), which monitors Latina/o representation in major network news, also regularly has reported that the news stories of Latinas/os in the United States are almost exclusively negative. In 2003, NAHJ reported that 66 percent of network news stories about Latinas/os in 2002 focused exclusively on three topics: crime, **terrorism**, or illegal immigration. **José Padilla**—the suspected "dirty bomb" terrorist in 2002—occupied "a central role in the coverage of Latinos . . . with 21 network stories or 18 percent of all stories aired on Latinos" (Méndez-Méndez & Alverio 2003, 3).

NAHJ's study of Latinas/os in the major network news coverage in 2005, including *ABC World News*, *CBS Evening News*, and *NBC Nightly News*, continued to point out the absence of Latinas/os in news stories. Although Latinas/os comprised 14.5 percent of the U.S. population, less than 1 percent of stories on the network evening news were about Latinas/os. For 2004, NAHJ reported that Latinas/os most often were found in crime stories in which they were perpetrators and not **victims** (Montalvo 2006, 4–5).

The Youth Control Complex, Gangs, and the Criminalization of Latina/o Youth

Some scholars argue that in the late 20th century and into the new millennium, the criminal justice system had become central in maintaining racial inequality (*see, e.g.,* Wacquant 2006). It also has been asserted that the conflation of race and crime in political discourse and in laws and policies has led to unequal racial/ethnic outcomes in the operation of the criminal justice system, and serves as a form of social control of African American and Latina/o populations. The criminalization of youth becomes racialized through systematic practices of social control that are embedded in nurturing institutions such as schools, community centers, and families. These institutions have become penetrated and influenced by punitive institutions—police, probation, and prisons to form what scholars have called the "youth control complex" (Rios 2006). Many poor young Latinas/os are growing up in hyper-policed neighborhoods and under hyper-supervision. They experience ubiquitous criminalization from various institutions, including those historically intended to nurture young people. As the nurturing arm of the state continues to collapse with decreases in spending on poor families and community-development programs, the punitive arm of the state and the criminal justice system increases its power through prison construction, more police, and stricter laws. Young people face criminalization at school, home, and community centers where **family issues** become rooted and are affected by crime control discourses and practices.

California's ballot initiative, Proposition 21, is an instance of how recent "get tough" legislation racializes youth crime and criminalizes youth of color (Rios 2008). Proposition 21 and other anti-gang laws enacted in other states convert a broad range of youth offenses—including misdemeanors—into adult felony charges. The result is that many Latina/o youth around the country—only some of whom actually are gang members—

have received harsher treatment by police, detention center personnel, prosecutors, and judges. A mere allegation of gang-related activity under California's Proposition 21 empowers prosecutors to charge someone as young as 14 years old as an adult in court (Villarruel et al. 2002, 62).

As with the bold zoot suits worn by male Latino youths in the 1940s, law enforcement officers too often view the hip-hop fashions, tattoos, and other forms of expression currently in vogue among young Latina/o youth—regardless of whether a youth actually belongs to a gang—as being synonymous with crime. Thus, as was the case in the early 1940s, Latina/o youths in the main continue to be a racialized group of criminal "others" who

> may be penalized for suspected gang involvement based on appearance, neighborhood, clothing, or other factors not related to alleged unlawful behavior. . . . Latino/a and other youth of color who merely have a tattoo, wear hip-hop clothing or live in low income, high crime neighborhoods are sometimes presumed to be "gang affiliated" by police and, therefore, stopped, questioned, and physically threatened or assaulted (Villarruel et al. 2002, 7–8).

Proposition 21 was designed by politicians to systematically deal with the California youth violence and gang "crisis." Arguments for the proposition invoked racial fear of Latina/o and African American youth and racial solidarity among middle-class white voters by depicting racialized juvenile delinquents as "superpredators," "predatory gang members," "immoral criminals," "rapists," "gang murderers," and "blood-thirsty killers" (Rios 2008). Studies have found that, like their African American neighbors, poor young urban Latinas/os face criminalization in their communities daily, law enforcement policies and practices consistently and disproportionately affect them, the media portrays them negatively as gang members or as being prone to criminality, and schools create zero tolerance policies that shame, exclude, and criminalize them.

Evidence of systematic police harassment is evident in the academic literature. In Chicago, young Latinas/os report experiencing more injustice from police than do whites or blacks. The breakdown in confidence in the criminal justice system felt by Latina/o youth has dire consequences. Scholars have argued that "if [youth of color] perceive that police do not protect the community, then law enforcement becomes one more symbol of inequality, and the police will lack the ability to gain information needed to address crimes" (Solis, Portillos, & Brunson 2009, 46).

Arrests, convictions, and sentencing based on racialized interpretations of Latina/o youth as criminals are often preserved through daily encounters in local neighborhoods, schools, businesses, and homes. This phenomenon—where crime control discourses and practices are embedded in non–criminal justice institutions—is a result of what Jonathan Simon (2008) has called "governing through crime." The collapse of traditional institutions of governance, such as the welfare state, labor market, and education has led the state to govern its population through crime. Poor young Latinas/os face dilapidated schools, an ever-shrinking job market, and an ever-expanding criminal justice system. These crises of governance create a cultural and political "coming of age crisis" for Latina/o youth (Rios 2006).

Latina/o delinquency and crime often is linked to gang activity by the media, law enforcement agencies, and politicians. Like mandatory sentencing drug laws, many states have passed "gang enhancement laws" that provide added sentences for crimes committed in support of a gang. Many young Latinas/os are sentenced under these gang enhancements simply for having grown up in a gang community or for being labeled by a police officer as a gang member for having a nickname—even if it is from a person's childhood. Sophisticated state-level gang databases that connect with the Department of Homeland Security are utilized by local police officers to track children in Latina/o communities the minute that they are seen associating with known gang members, wearing baggy clothes, or drawing graffiti on their school binders.

In the face of falling youth violence rates at the end of the 1990s, gang membership estimates were near their all-time high. Increasing gang membership rates, however, do not correlate with national statistics of who commits crime and local research findings suggest that gang members are responsible for "fewer than one in 10 **homicides**; fewer than one in 16 violent offenses; and fewer than one in 20 serious (index) crimes," with a serious crime consisting of one of the following: aggravated assault, arson, burglary, larceny, murder, rape, robbery, and theft of a motor vehicle (Greene & Pranis 2007, 4). Gang members play a relatively small role in the crime problem. Some scholars argue that the problem of gang crime is underscored by law enforcement and media reports partly because gang-affiliated youth share a culture of highly visible graffiti, colors, hand signs, and dramatic rivalries. Law enforcement and the media also fuel our cultural imaginations regarding gang crime by equating all gang activity with criminal activity and by associating all gangs and members with the worst crimes committed by any individual gang member.

Scholars also have pointed out that young men of color are disproportionately identified as gang members and targeted for surveillance, arrest, and incarceration, but whites—who make up a significant share of gang members—rarely appear in accounts of gang enforcement efforts. African Americans and Latinas/os were approximately 15 times more likely than whites to be identified by police as gang members, and Latinas/os accounted for nearly half (49 percent) of the estimated youth gang population in 2004, according to the National Youth Gang Survey, despite the fact that they make up only 17 percent of the U.S. population of 12 to 24 year olds (Greene & Pranis 2007, 36; Egley, Howell, & Major 2006).

Studies of the phenomenon of youth violence in Los Angeles and Chicago during the rampant "supergang" myths of the 1990s have shown that newspapers reported increased fears about impending gang-related crime waves. Police reports, however, clearly showed that serious violent crime was declining, before and long after such a crime wave. This apparent spread of youth gang activity was not related to an increase of serious youth criminal activity. Moreover, most delinquent acts attributed to gang members were committed by youth who are not gang members. There is little to no correlation between law enforcement gang population estimates and overall crime trends.

One of the central stereotypes by which Latina/o youth are netted into the criminal justice pipeline is "gang member." In studying Arizona, scholars found that police-granted court referrals for **Chicana/o** youth were greatly disproportionate in comparison to their representation in the general population, and that they were referred to court for similar offenses regardless of their label as "gang members." Chicana/o youths were also increasingly prone to be arrested and referred to court for fighting than were youth who were not affiliated with gangs. As one criminologist explains,

> the fact that gang boys fought amongst themselves was threatening to the police. The police, as agents of the state, are the only group authorized to use force, yet the gang members acted as though they also controlled the right to use force within their communities. The very existence of this disagreement contradicts and threatens the authority of the state, and may have enhanced the perceived threat of disorder from within the barrios (Zatz 1987, 143).

Studies have found that police think that they should be the only group with the authority to use force. This might be a reason why poor young Latinas/os consistently are harassed and brutalized by police. The public and politicians appreciate and support aggressive policing because, from their perspective, this maintains control of a population that might commit more crime and violence.

Data suggests that police over-surveillance of Chicana/o youth leads to increased court referrals. Most Chicana/o youth who are arrested are taken into custody for fighting and property offenses and not for violent offenses that supposedly threatened the surrounding community. Research also suggests that powerful groups within society enforce and maintain their control over less-powerful groups by attaching to them definitions of deviance and punitively enforcing transgressions caused by this deviance. Scholars contend that instead of interpreting the experiences of poor Chicana/o youths as harassment, the public tends to only see the legitimate use of state apparatuses for controlling troublesome behavior as well as the enactment of more intricate forms of social control by a police force that only grows in its legitimacy.

In spite of the vast sums of money invested in aggressive anti-gang tactics, "get-tough" policies have not proven to be effective. Los Angeles—a city with a reputation for strict anti-gang enforcement—has become a case study in the shortcomings of these harsher strategies. Studies on the massive outlay of funds and other resources over many decades for more police, prisons, and tougher sentences in Los Angeles reveal that such spending had not necessarily produced a decrease in the number of gangs. In fact, during a period of such heightened expenditures a six-fold increase in the number of gangs had occurred along with a near doubling of the number of gang members in the region (Greene & Pranis 2007, 3).

Sentencing Latina/o Youth As Adults

Comparative data on the sentences of Latina/o youth versus white youth show clear disparity in treatment. Latina/o youth are 43 percent more likely than white youth to be waived to the adult criminal justice system, and 40 percent more likely to be committed to adult prison (Arya et al. 2009, 6). A recent review of the literature on the impact of prosecuting juveniles as adults reveals that the goals of the modern juvenile justice system to serve the best interests of the child, taking into consideration the differences in needs of youths from adults, no longer operate and cast serious doubt on fundamental questions of fairness and justice in the present-day functions of the criminal justice system (UCLA School of Law Juvenile Justice Project 2010).

Most studies conclude that youth transfers to adult courts have a disproportionate and adverse impact on youth of color. These transfers have multiple negative outcomes: they result in high rates of pretrial detention, conviction, and imprisonment; adult courts often sentence youth more harshly than juvenile courts and many youth are sentenced to adult prisons; and youth in adult facilities often experience assaults and physical and psychological abuse. Moreover, the adult criminal justice system is incapable of addressing the needs of youth offenders at every stage of the process—trial, sentencing, and incarceration. The overwhelming number of studies point to a system that is forcing juveniles into a system not designed for them, often worsening rather than resolving the problem (UCLA School of Law Juvenile Justice Project 2010).

As noted in U.S. Department of Justice publications, empirical evidence shows that transfer laws have negligible or no deterrent effect. The transfer of juveniles for trial and sentencing in adult criminal court has actually produced an increase, not decrease, in recidivism, especially of violent offenders. A number of factors contribute to the high recidivism rate, including: the stigmatization and labeling of youth as adult felons, feelings of resentment and unfairness about being punished as an adult; the experience of learning from and adopting adult criminal behavior in prison; and the lack of emphasis on rehabilitation and family support in adult institutions. The consequence is a system that produces life-long criminals, and not a system in which the juvenile courts provide a calibrated response to youth offenders to be adequately effective but not excessively harsh (Redding 2010).

Addressing Youth Violence and the Needs of Latina/o Youth

According to researchers, many traditional "get-tough" law enforcement efforts have not proven to have long-term effectiveness at stemming gang violence. Studies have found that many national gang and drug suppression programs have failed in their objective to halt drug use and prevent youth violence. Highly publicized programs, such as Nancy Reagan's D.A.R.E. (Drug Awareness, Resistance, and Education) have proven not to be successful. D.A.R.E. and similar national programs (e.g., G.R.E.A.T., Gang Resistance, Education, and Training) like it have come to be considered failures because they attempt to apply conventional wisdom in the absence of empirical data that points to real-world effectiveness.

Although the literature on addressing youth violence does not offer a clear and definitive solution, certain best practices appear to surface. Scholars argue that one way of reducing youth violence is to promote community safety, not the aggressive eradication of gangs. Generally, the literature suggests steering away from failed "get-tough" policies in favor of more positive public safety measures that emphasize the use of evidenced-based practices to reduce youth crime—that is practices that have been shown empirically to be successful at producing positive results. Other approaches include the development of programs and strategies that promote employment, education, healthy communities, and re-entry into society, and the allocation and redirection of resources from failed law enforcement tactics to more effective public safety strategies that provide youths with skills and opportunities (Greene & Pranis 2007).

Unhealthy social and economic conditions render many youth of color—especially young men of color—a vulnerable group to encounters with the criminal justice system. Nationally, extreme poverty and harsh social conditions affect communities of color in many ways: almost half of African American and Latina/o fourth graders attend impoverished schools; Latino male adults and adolescents run a risk of contracting HIV or AIDS 3.1 times higher than for whites; Latinas/os are 2.5 times more likely to have limited access to health care and 4.8 times more likely to lack health insurance; Latino boys and young men are 4.1 times more likely to suffer from post-traumatic stress disorder than white men and boys; and **residential segregation** and poverty contribute to lack of access to educational and other opportunities (California Endowment 2010). Compared to whites, Latinas/os with depression are less likely to receive counseling or treatment (National Center for Health Statistics 2007, 88).

The unhealthy and unsafe conditions in which young Latinas/os and African Americans live make them susceptible to violence and crime as well as to law enforcement policies and practices that have had a disproportionate impact on youth of color. Nationally, "Latino children are more than 3 times more likely than white children to have a parent in prison, which increases the chances of those children suffering from low self-esteem and depression and exhibiting inappropriate or disruptive behavior" (California Endowment 2010, 7). In contrast to young white men, young Latino men have homicide death rates that are 5 times higher, and in California, homicide is the seventh-leading cause of death among young Latino men. Latina/o communities experience high levels of residential segregation and poverty which have been found to contribute to lack of access to educational and other opportunities and provide fertile ground for exposure to violence and trauma. Given the dire social and economic conditions found in many Latina/o communities across the United States, addressing the unhealthy socioeconomic conditions of many Latinas/os has become a recurring need identified by analysts, academics, and activists as part of a comprehensive approach to resolve the challenges faced by Latina/o youth in relation to the criminal justice system.

Special initiatives have sought to have an impact on the disparities and other problems encountered by Latina/o youth with respect to the criminal justice system. In 2002, *¿Dónde está la justicia? A Call to Action on Behalf of Latino and Latina Youth in the U.S. Justice System,* the first national examination of Latina/o youth and the justice system, was published. The National Council of La Raza (NCLR) subsequently released *Lost Opportunities: The Reality of Latinos in the U.S. Criminal Justice System*, followed by a joint effort by the Campaign for Youth Justice and NCLR to compile the most recent data on Latinas/os in the criminal justice system. In each case, these studies posited a range of public policy strategies and proposals for actions at the local, state, and national levels.

Among the recurring themes of the most recent literature on Latina/o youth and the criminal justice system is the need to institute culturally competent approaches to services and in all aspects of the criminal justice system. Understanding that most evidence-based programs have focused disparities between whites and African Americans and not Latinas/os, these recent studies identify the need for evidence-based programs developed for Latina/o communities and that address the linguistic and cultural differences that can produce positive outcomes. **Cultural competency** refers to an institution's "ability to have attitudes, behaviors, policies, practices, procedures, and fiscal and personnel resources that enable them to work effectively in cross-cultural situations" (Arya et al. 2009, 55). As such, it is not simply the capacity to translate documents or providing services in another language. Instead, a truly culturally competent agency values diversity;

it engages in regular self-assessment of its services to ensure that it is meeting its goals of serving a culturally diverse population and it integrates and institutionalizes the lessons and knowledge gained from self-assessment to improve its cultural competency. It also adapts services to the communities served, institutionalizing and integrating policies and developing new or improved service delivery mechanisms, structures, attitudes, and behaviors to effectively navigate cultural differences.

A range of other approaches are recommended in the recent analyses on the topic of Latina/o youth and the U.S. criminal justice system which include, but are not limited to: reducing the negative impact of transfer laws on Latina/o youth; ensuring equitable investment in the development of evidence-based programs designed to meet the needs of Latina/o youth and families; improving data collection systems to keep better track of youth in the adult criminal system; disaggregating criminal justice data by **race and ethnicity**; ensuring due process protection and access to quality legal assistance for youths arrested and detained, including those detained in the course of immigration enforcement actions; and improving re-entry services for youth and facilitating the reintegration of youth convicted in the adult system into the community. The detrimental and counterproductive effects of processing and convicting youths using the adult criminal system has also drawn the attention of numerous academic and advocacy groups that have engaged in efforts to keep youth out of the adult system (e.g., Children's Action Alliance 2010; Arya et al. 2009; Villarruel et al. 2002).

Analysts have also made the point that racial profiling and other law enforcement tactics must be addressed at the local, state and national levels. In this regard, a reassessment and reform of practices related to racial and ethnic profiling, law enforcement policies and tactics (e.g., stops and frisks and anti-gang strategies, such as gang injunctions and gang databases) and certain immigration enforcement actions that negatively affect Latina/o communities have gained support among those examining these issues from Latina/o communities perspectives (e.g., Walker et al. 2004; Arya et al. 2009).

On a national scale, programs have been developed that have sought to promote strategies to reduce rates of youth confinement, change the federal guidelines for states to participate in the Juvenile Justice Delinquency Prevention Formula Grant Program which required that states assess levels of minority youth confinement, and implement strategies to reduce minority overrepresentation. This overrepresentation was called Disproportionate Minority Confinement (DMC). Besides keeping track of the overrepresentation of minorities in juvenile justice, the system needs to implement practices that prevent this imbalance. With the inclusion of the DMC provision to the Juvenile Justice and Delinquency Prevention Act (JJDPA) in 1988, some progress has been reported in those jurisdictions that have made a commitment to reducing racial and ethnic disparities, and strengthening these types of national programs and reforming JJDPA to prevent youth charged as adults to be held in adult jails are among the proposals that have been made that could have positive results on Latina/o youth.

For youth who have been involved in the juvenile justice system, **early intervention** and **violence prevention** programs founded on punishment have been found ineffective. Since youth ultimately have little control over the structural mechanisms that lead them to committing delinquency and being labeled as criminals, punitive corrective strategies imposed by the criminal justice system often backfire, leading young people deeper into the school-to-prison pipeline. In an effort to stem the use of punitive measures that buttress the school-to-prison pipeline, scholars, lawyers, and community members have called for a "dismantling of the school-to-prison pipeline." In Tallulah, Louisiana, for example, a juvenile detention facility was converted into a community college and education center where troubled youth are sent for rehabilitation rather than being sent to juvenile justice facilities or adult jails (NAACP Legal Defense and Educational Fund 2005).

The construction of effective programs cannot rely on assumptions of definitive solutions, since in the juvenile justice system, changes in policies or practices in one part may affect subsequent parts of the system. Therefore, different approaches are taken by intervention and **prevention** programs that may provide education to help youth gain a sense of cultural identity; become involved in political activism; and promote individual development—making kids do well in school and learn the tools to succeed in the job market, for instance. Around the United States there have been community-based organizations established to work with Latina/o youth, and recent literature on the subject has highlighted some of the programs that have had promising results (e.g., Arya et al. 2009; Villarruel et al. 2002).

Providing equal access to achievement opportunities and educational quality within educational settings has been found to assist in the prevention of violence at school. Analyses focusing on Latina/o youth and the justice system overwhelmingly emphasize the need for expanding educational and economic opportunities for them and the communities in which they live (*see, e.g.*, California Endowment 2010; Morín 2009).

For Latinas/os, culture plays a key role in rehabilitation and social mobility. Latina girls caught in the net of the juvenile legal system, for example, transformed their language and culture into an advantage: "claiming Latina/o culture, tradition, and language generated positive feelings of being special and as having something to which to belong . . . system-involved Latinas held on to an identity that was separate from that of 'criminal'" (Schaffner 2008, 130). Scholars have noted that the juvenile justice system might be able to play a role in reinforcing positive cultural projects to which Latina/o youth can actively belong and help them feel that they are agents with the power to make positive choices. To this end, the system would have to be involved in making positive connections between young Latinas/os and police, and to reform policy and create better **community policing** strategies for dealing with youth. It also is posited that a shift toward community policing strategies premised on forging police and community partnerships working cooperatively toward resolving problems could be more constructive and productive than traditional approaches that have worked to the detriment of Latinas/os and other persons of color.

See also: Part I essays: Policing and Latina/o Communities; The U.S. War on Drugs and Latina/o Communities; Incarceration and Latinas/os in the United States; Gangs in the United States and Latina/o Communities. Part II entries: Chicanas/os; Homicide; Media Depictions; Victims.

Further Reading

Advancement Project and The Civil Rights Project at Harvard University. 2000. *Opportunities suspended: The devastating consequences of zero tolerance and school discipline policies.* Washington, DC: The Civil Rights Project and the Advancement Project. http://civilrightsproject.ucla.edu/research/k-12-education/school-discipline

/opportunities-suspended-the-devastating-consequences-of-zero-tolerance-and-school-discipline-policies/crp-opportunities-suspended-zero-tolerance-2000.pdf.

Akiba, Motoko, Gerald K. LeTendre, David P. Baker, and Brian Goesling. 2002. Student victimization: National and school system effects on school violence in 37 nations. *American Educational Research Journal* 39(4): 829–53.

Alexander, Michelle. 2010. *The new Jim Crow: Mass incarceration in the age of colorblindness*. New York, NY: The New Press.

American Academy of Pediatrics. 2003. Policy statement: Out-of-school suspension and expulsion. *Pediatrics* 112(5): 1206–08.

Arya, Neelum, Francisco Villarruel, Cassandra Villanueva, and Ian Augarten. 2009. *America's invisible children: Latino youth and the failure of justice*. Washington, DC: Campaign for Youth Justice and National Council of La Raza.

Balfanz, Robert, and Nettie Legters. 2006 (July 12). The graduation rate crisis we know and what can be done about it. *Education Week* [Commentary]. http://web.jhu.edu/bin/a/b/Crisis_Commentary.pdf.

Barker, Vanessa. 2010. Explaining the great American crime decline: A review of Blumstein and Wallman, Goldberger and Rosenfeld, and Zimring. *Law and Society Inquiry* 35: 489–511.

Becker, Elizabeth. 2001 (February 9). As ex-theorist on young "superpredators," Bush aide has regrets. *New York Times*.

Berg, Charles Ramírez. 2002. *Latino images in film: Stereotypes, subversion, resistance*. Austin, TX: University of Texas Press.

California Endowment. 2010. *Health communities matter: The importance of place to the health of boys of color*, http://www.calendow.org/Article.aspx?id=4494. Accessed September 29, 2010.

Center for Constitutional Rights. [n.d.]. NYPD stop-and-frisk statistics: 2009 and 2010. New York, NY: Center for Constitutional Rights. http://www.ccrjustice.org/files/CCR_Stop_and_Frisk_Fact_Sheet_0.pdf.

Center for Constitutional Rights. 2011. Stop-and-frisks of New Yorkers in 2010 hit all-time high at 600,601; 87 percent of those stopped Black and Latino. New York, NY: Center for Constitutional Rights. http://ccrjustice.org/newsroom/press-releases/stop-and-frisks-of-new-yorkers-2010-hit-all-time-high-600%2C601%3B-87-percent-of. Accessed March 3, 2011.

Children's Action Alliance. 2010. Improving public safety by keeping youth out of the adult criminal system. Phoenix, AZ: Children's Action Alliance.

Correctional Association of New York. 2010. *Juvenile detention in New York City*. New York, NY: Correctional Association of New York. http://www.correctionalassociation.org/publications/download/jjp/factsheets/detention_fact_sheet_2010.pdf.

Council, Carol L., Weihua Shi, and Laurel L. Hourani. 2005. *Substance abuse and mental health in New York, 2001*. Washington, DC: U.S. Department of Health and Human Services, Substance Abuse and Mental Health Services Administration.

Davis, Angela Y. 2003. *Are prisons obsolete?* New York, NY: Seven Stories Press.

Delgado, Melvin. 2000. *New arenas for community social work practice with urban youth*. New York, NY: Columbia University Press.

Delgado, Richard, and Jean Stefancic (eds.). 2011. *The Latino/a condition: A critical reader*, 2nd ed. New York, NY: New York University Press.

DiIulio, John. 1995. *How to stop the coming crime wave*. New York, NY: Manhattan Institute.

Dorfman, Lori, and Vincent Schiraldi. 2001. *Off balance: Youth, race and crime in the news*. Washington, DC: Building Blocks for Youth.

Durán, Robert J. 2009. Over-inclusive gang enforcement and urban resistance: A comparison between two cities. *Social Justice:*

A Journal of Crime, Conflict and World Order 36(1): 82–101.

Durán, Robert J. 2009. The core ideals of the Mexican American gang: Living the presentation of defiance. *Aztlán: A Journal of Chicano Studies* 34(2): 99–134.

Durán, Robert J. 2009. Legitimated oppression: Inner-city Mexican American experiences with police gang enforcement. *Journal of Contemporary Ethnography* 38 (April): 143–68.

Egley, Arlen, Jr., James C. Howell, and Aline K. Major. 2006. *National Youth Gang Survey: 1999–2001*. Washington, DC: Office of Juvenile Justice and Delinquency Prevention.

Ferguson, Ann Arnett. 2001. *Bad boys: Public schools in the making of black masculinity*. Ann Arbor, MI: University of Michigan Press.

Finley, Laura L. 2007. *Encyclopedia of Juvenile Violence*. Westport, CT: Greenwood Publishing Group.

Freidman, Warren, and Martha Hott. 1995. *Young people and the police: Respect, fear and the future of community policing in Chicago*. Chicago, IL: Chicago Alliance for Neighborhood Safety.

Fry, Richard. 2010. *Hispanics, high school dropouts and the GED*. Washington, DC: Pew Hispanic Center. http://pewhispanic.org/files/reports/122.pdf.

Garland, David (ed.). 2001. *Mass imprisonment: Social causes and consequences*. London: Sage.

Gendreau, Paul, and Claire E. Goggin. 1996. Principles of effective correctional programming. *Forum on Corrections Research* 8: 38–41.

Greene, Judith, and Marc Mauer. 2010. Downscaling prisons: Lessons from four states. Washington, DC: The Sentencing Project.

Greene, Judith, and Kevin Pranis. 2007. *Gang wars: The failure of enforcement tactics and the need for effective public safety strategies*. Washington, DC: Justice Policy Institute.

Hagan, John, Carla Shedd, and Monique R. Payne. 2005. Race, ethnicity, and youth perceptions of criminal injustice. *American Sociological Review* 70 (June): 381–407.

Hamparian, Donna, and M. Leiber. 1997. *Disproportionate confinement of minority juveniles in secure facilities: 1996 National Report*. Champaign, IL: Community Research Associates.

Harring, Sidney L. 1983. Policing a class society: The experience of American cities, 1865 to 1915. New Brunswick, NJ: Rutgers University Press.

Harrison, Paige M., and Allen J. Beck. 2005. *Prisoners in 2004*. NCJ 210677. Washington, DC: Bureau of Justice Statistics.

Harrison, Paige M., and Allen J. Beck. 2006. *Prison and jail inmates at midyear 2005*. NCJ 213133. Washington, DC: Bureau of Justice Statistics.

Harrison, Paige M., and Jennifer C. Karberg. 2004. *Prison and jail inmates at midyear 2003*. Princeton, NJ: Princeton University, Industrial Relations Section Working papers: No. 494, 2004.

Hirschfield, Paul J. 2008. Preparing for prison? The criminalization of school discipline in the USA. *Theoretical Criminology* 12(1): 79–101.

Howell, James C. 2003. *Preventing & reducing juvenile delinquency*. Thousand Oaks, CA: Sage Publications.

Human Rights Watch. 2002. *Race and incarceration in the United States: Human Rights Watch Press Backgrounder, February 27, 2002*. http://www.hrw.org/legacy/backgrounder/usa/race/.

Jones-Brown, Delores. 2004. Changing the image of the "symbolic assailant." In *Policing and minority communities: Bridging the gap,* edited by D. Jones-Brown and K. Terry, 204–09. Upper Saddle River, N.J.: Pearson/Prentice Hall.

Jones-Brown, Delores. 2007. Forever the symbolic assailant: The more things change, the more they remain the same. *Criminology and Public Policy* 6: 103–21.

Justice Policy Institute. 2009. *The costs of confinement: Why good juvenile justice policies make good fiscal sense, May 2009*. Washington, DC: Justice Police Institute. http://www.justicepolicy.org/images/upload/09_05_REP_CostsofConfinement_JJ_PS.pdf.

King, Loretta. 2009. Investigation of the Lansing Residential Center, Louis Gossett, Jr. Residential Center, Tryon Residential Center, and Tryon Girls Center. Letter to Governor David Paterson, August 14, 2009. Washington DC: Civil Rights Division of the U.S. Department of Justice. http://www.justice.gov/crt/about/spl/documents/NY_juvenile_facilities_findlet_08-14-2009.pdf.

Klein, Malcolm W., and Cheryl L. Maxson. 2006. *Street gang patterns and policies*. New York, NY: Oxford University Press.

Krisberg, Barry. 2005. *Juvenile justice: Redeeming our children*. Thousand Oaks, CA: Sage Publications.

Losen, Daniel J. 2006 (March 20). Behind the dropout rate. *Gotham Gazette*. http://www.gothamgazette.com/article//20060320/202/1792.

Martínez, Ramiro, Jr. 2002. *Latino homicide: Immigration, violence and community*. New York, NY: Routledge.

Martínez, Ramiro, Jr. 2007. Incorporating Latinos and immigrants into policing research. *Criminology and Public Policy* 6: 57–64.

Mauer, Marc. 2004. Lessons of the "get tough" movement in the United States. Washington, DC: The Sentencing Project. http://www.sentencingproject.org/doc/publications/inc_lessonsofgettough.pdf.

Mauer, Marc, and Meda Chesney-Lind (eds.). 2002. *Invisible punishment: The collateral consequences of mass imprisonment*. New York, NY: New Press.

Méndez-Méndez, Serafín, and Diana Alverio. 2003. *Network brownout 2003: The portrayal of Latinos in network television news, 2002*. Washington, DC: National Association of Hispanic Journalists.

Michalowski, R. J. 1985. *Order, law and crime*. New York, NY: Random House.

Miller, Jody. 1995. Struggles over the symbolic: Gang style and the meanings of social control. In *Cultural Criminology*, edited by J. Ferrell and C. Sanders, 213–34. Boston, MA: Northeastern University Press.

Miranda, Rowan. 1994. Governments or markets? The privatization of municipal services. *Research in Governmental and Nonprofit Accounting* 8: 235–64.

Montalvo, Daniela. 2006. *Network brownout 2006: The portrayal of Latinos and Latino issues on network television news, 2005*. Washington, DC: National Association of Hispanic Journalists. http://www.nahj.org/resources/2006Brownout.pdf. Accessed July 14, 2007.

Morín, José Luis. 2009. *Latino/a rights and justice in the United States: Perspectives and approaches*. 2nd ed. Durham, NC: Carolina Academic Press.

Mumola, Christopher J., and Allen J. Beck. 1997. *Prisoners in 1996*. NCJ 164619. Washington, DC: Bureau of Justice Statistics, U.S. Department of Justice.

NAACP Legal Defense and Educational Fund. 2005. Dismantling the school-to-prison pipeline. New York, NY: NAACP Legal Defense and Educational Fund. http://naacpldf.org/publication/dismantling-school-prison-pipeline.

National Center for Health Statistics. 2007. Health, United States. Hayattsille, MD: U.S. Department of Health and Human Services.

New York Civil Liberties Union. 2007. *Criminalizing the classroom: The overpolicing of New York City schools*. New York, NY: New York Civil Liberties Union.

New York Civil Liberties Union. 2009a. *Safety with dignity: Alternatives to the over-policing of schools*. New York, NY: New York Civil Liberties Union. http://www.nyclu.org/files/Safety-with-Dignity-072909.pdf.

New York Civil Liberties Union. 2009b. The Rockefeller drug laws: Unjust, irrational, ineffective—A call for a public health approach to drug policy. New York, NY: New York Civil Liberties Union. http://www.nyclu.org/files/Rock.pdf. Accessed March 4, 2011.

New York Civil Liberties Union. 2010. *2 weeks after class action lawsuit filed over police in NYC schools, another child arrested for desk doodling*. New York, NY: New York Civil Liberties Union. http://www.nyclu.org/news/2-weeks-after-class-action-lawsuit-filed-over-police-nyc-schools-another-child-arrested-desk-do. Accessed May 20, 2010.

Parenti, Christian. 2000. *Lockdown America: Police and prisons in the age of crisis*. London: Verso.

Peguero, Anthony A. 2009. Victimizing the children of immigrants: Latino and Asian American student victimization. *Youth & Society* 41(2): 186–208.

Pew Hispanic Center. 2010a. *Statistical portrait of Hispanics in the United States, 2008*. Washington, DC: Pew Hispanic Center. http://pewhispanic.org/factsheets/factsheet.php?FactsheetID=58.

Pew Hispanic Center. 2010b. *Statistical portrait of the foreign-born population in the United States, 2008*. Washington, DC: Pew Hispanic Center. http://pewhispanic.org/factsheets/factsheet.php?FactsheetID=59.

Poe-Yamagata, E., and Jones, M. 2000. *And justice for some: Differential treatment of minority youth in the justice system*. Washington, DC: Building Blocks for Youth.

Reiman, Jeffrey, and Paul Leighton. 2010. *The rich get richer and the poor get prison*, 9th ed. Boston, MA: Allyn & Bacon.

Rennison, Callie Marie, and Michael R. Rand. 2003. *Criminal victimization, 2002: Bureau of Justice Statistics National Crime Victimization Survey (August 2003)*. NCJ 199994. Washington, DC: Bureau of Justice Statistics, U.S. Department of Justice.

Riley, K. Jack. 1997. Crack, powder cocaine, and heroin: Drug purchase and use patterns in six U.S. cities. Washington, DC: National Institute of Justice and the Office of National Drug Control Policy.

Rios, Victor M. 2006. The hyper-criminalization of black and Chicano youth in the era of mass incarceration. *Souls* 8: 40–54.

Rios, Victor M. 2008. The racial politics of youth crime. In *Behind Bars: Latino/as and Prison in the United States*, edited by Suzanne Oboler. New York, NY: Palgrave Macmillan.

Rios, Victor M. 2009. The consequences of the criminal justice pipeline on black and Latino masculinity. *The Annals of the American Academy of Political and Social Sciences* 623(1): 150–62.

Schaffner, Laurie. 2008. Latinas in U.S. juvenile detention: Turning adversity into advantage. *Latino Studies* 6(1–2): 116–36.

Simon, Jonathan. 2008. *Governing through crime: How the war on crime transformed American democracy and created a culture of fear*. Oxford: Oxford University Press.

Snyder, Howard N., and Melissa Sickmund. 1999. Juvenile offenders and victims: 1999 national report. Washington, DC: Office of Juvenile Justice and Delinquency Prevention, Department of Justice.

Solis, Carmen, Edwardo L. Portillos, and Rod K. Brunson. 2009. Latino youths' experiences with and perceptions of involuntary police encounters. *The Annals of the American Academy of Political and Social Science* 623(1): 39–51.

Spitzer, Eliot. 1999. *The New York City Police Department's "stop and frisk" practices: A report to the people of the State of New York from the Attorney General*. New York, NY: New York State Attorney General's Office, Civil Rights Bureau.

Spohn, Cassia, John Gruhl, and Susan Welch. 1987. The impact of the ethnicity and gender of defendants on the decision to reject or dismiss felony charges. *Criminology* 25: 175–91.

Truman, Jennifer L., and Michael R. Rand. 2010. *Criminal victimization, 2009*. NCJ 231327. Washington, DC: Bureau of Justice Statistics.

UCLA School of Law Juvenile Justice Project. 2010. *The impact of prosecuting youth in the adult criminal justice system: A review of the literature*. Los Angeles, CA: UCLA School of Law. http://www.campaignforyouthjustice.org/documents/UCLA-Literature-Review.pdf.

U.S. Census Bureau. 2003. *Young, diverse, urban: Hispanic population reaches all-time high of 38.8 million, new Census Bureau estimates show*. Press Release No. CB03-100. Washington, DC: Public Information Office, B. Bernstein and M. Bergman.

U.S. Commission on Civil Rights. 2000. *Police practices and civil rights in New York City: A report of the United States Commission on Civil Rights*, Washington, DC: Department of Justice.

Villarruel, Francisco A., and Nancy E. Walker, with Pamela Minifree, Omara Rivera-Vázquez, Susan Peterson, and Kristen Perry. 2002. *¿Dónde está la justicia? A call to action on behalf of Latino and Latina youth in the U.S. justice system*. Washington, DC: Michigan State University/Building Blocks for Youth. http://www.cclp.org/documents/BBY/Donde.pdf.

Wacquant, Loïc. 2006. *Punishing the poor: The new government of social insecurity*. Durham, NC: Duke University Press.

Wald, Johanna, and Daniel J. Losen. 2003. Defining and redirecting the school-to-prison pipeline. *New Directions for Youth Development: Deconstructing the School to Prison Pipeline* 99: 9–15.

Walker, Nancy, E., J. Michael Senger, Francisco A. Villarruel, and Angela M. Arboleda. 2004. *Lost opportunities: The reality of Latinos in the U.S. criminal justice system*. Washington, DC: National Council of La Raza. http://www.nclr.org/content/publications/detail/27567/.

Ward, Geoff. 2009. The "other" child-savers: Racial politics of the parental state. In *The child savers: The invention of delinquency*, edited by A. M. Platt. Piscataway, NJ: Rutgers University Press.

Welch, Kelly, and Allison Ann Payne. 2010. Racial threat and punitive school discipline. *Social Problems* 57(1): 25–48.

West, Heather C., William J. Sabol, and Sarah J. Greenman. 2010. *Prisoners in 2009*. NCJ 231675. Washington, DC: Bureau of Justice Statistics.

Wilkinson, Deanna L., Chauncey C. Beaty, and Regina M. Lurry. 2009. Youth violence: Crime or self-help? Marginalized urban males' perspectives on the limited efficacy of the criminal justice system to stop youth violence. *The Annals of the American Academy of Political and Social Science* 623: 25–38.

Zatz, Marjorie S. 1987. Chicano youth gangs and crime: The creation of a moral panic. *Contemporary Crises* 11: 129–58.

Part II

A to Z Entries on Latinas/os and Criminal Justice and Cross References

A

Agron, Salvador (1943–1986) (a.k.a. Capeman). *See* Part I essays: Latinas/os and the U.S. Criminal Justice System; Policing and Latina/o Communities; Latinas and the U.S. Criminal Justice System; Gangs in the United States and Latina/o Communities. Part II entry: Media Depictions; Puerto Ricans.

Arzu, Fermin. *See* Part I essay: Policing and Latina/o Communities; Civilian Oversight of Police.

B

Báez, Anthony. *See* Part I essay: Latinas/os and the U.S. Criminal Justice System; Policing and Latina/o Communities. Part II entries: Political Activist Groups; Civilian Oversight of Police; Puerto Ricans.

Báez, Iris. *See* Part I essay: Policing and Latina/o Communities. Part II entry: Political Activist Groups; Puerto Ricans.

Black/White Binary Paradigm. *See* Part I essay: Latinas/os and the U.S. Criminal Justice System. Part II entries: Felon Disenfranchisement; *Hernandez v. Texas*, 347 U.S. 475 (1954); Language Rights in the Courts; LatCrit: Latina & Latino Critical Legal Theory, Inc.

Border Crime. *See* Part I essay: Crime and the U.S.-Mexican Border; Latina/o Immigrants, Crime, and Justice. Part II entries: Hate Crimes; Immigration and Customs Enforcement (ICE); Vigilantism.

Border Patrol. *See* Part I essays: Latina/o Immigrants, Crime, and Justice; Crime and the U.S.-Mexican Border. Part II entries: Civil Rights; Deportation; Hate Crimes; Immigration and Customs Enforcement (ICE); Vigilantism.

Brown Berets. *See* Part II entries: Chicanas/os; Civilian Oversight of Police; Community-Based Latina/o Advocacy Organizations; Political Activist Groups.

C

Capeman. *See* Part I essays: Gangs in the United States and Latina/o Communities; Latinas/os and the U.S. Criminal Justice System; Policing and Latina/o Communities. Part II entries: Media Depictions; Puerto Ricans.

Central Americans

Maria Swimm

Central America comprises the series of countries located geographically south of Mexico, including, most broadly, Guatemala, Belize, Honduras, El Salvador, Nicaragua, Costa Rica, and Panama. A mountainous region with numerous active volcanoes and an array of tropical rainforests, Central America is a complex territory with varied and rich cultural traditions that have endured extensive political crises and economic downfalls. Over a 30-year period, these events have directly attributed to the massive increase in Central American migration to the United States. Although Mexicans still constitute the largest group of Latina/o immigrants nationwide, Salvadorans, Guatemalans, and other Central Americans that make up the nation's Latino community are among the fastest-growing populations in the United States.

Since the late 1970s, destabilizing armed conflicts throughout Central America—including the Nicaraguan Sandinista Revolution, the Salvadoran and Guatemalan Civil Wars, and the guerilla movement in Honduras—have accounted for the substantial influx of Central American migration to the United States. Many citizens were forced to abandon their homes and cross international borders to seek a safe haven for their families in regions with seemingly reduced economic and social degradation. Many people relocated to adjacent Central American countries, and others settled in established refugee camps in southern Mexico. A number of immigrants have since returned to their homelands, but a significant number have created vibrant communities in the leading destination of choice: the United States.

In 2013, there were approximately 4.8 million persons of Central American descent residing in the United States; of that number, more than 1.5 million were foreign-born Central Americans (Pew Research Center Hispanic Trends 2015). The actual number most likely is significantly greater, as undercounting among Latino populations in the United States is a consistent problem. Salvadorans over time have comprised the largest group of Central American immigrants living in the United States, at 1.9 million persons (Pew Research Center Hispanic Trends 2015). Only 37 percent of Latinas/os in the United States are foreign born, but of those Latinas/os who are foreign born, Guatemalans and Hondurans have the highest percentage of foreign born (67 percent each) (Motel & Patten 2012). Across the United States, Central Americans tend to reside in metropolitan areas rather than in rural districts or those outside central cities. According to the 2000 census these immigrants are generally of working age—between the ages of 18 and 65—although the distribution varies between countries of origin (Larsen 2004).

Salvadoran and Guatemalan migrants largely are representative of their home countries' class structures with respect to educational attainment and family income. Central Americans are not only the least likely of immigrants from Latin America to graduate from high school, but are the least likely among all immigrants, no matter what ethnicity. Their poverty rates are 2.5 times the rate of non-Central Americans, with the disparity in individual earnings being even more distinct. According to the 2000 census, approximately one-fifth of Guatemalan, Salvadoran, and Nicaraguan families in the United States live at standards below the poverty line. One compensatory fact is that because Central American households on average are larger, they have a greater number of wage earners in the household (Lopez et al.1996). Among foreign-born family households, "the proportion with five or more people was 39.3 percent when the householder was Central American" (Larsen 2004, 4).

As many are undocumented or have minimal formally attained skills, work opportunities for Central Americans are limited and typically are for low-wage jobs. Minimal knowledge of the English language combined with uncompetitive educational backgrounds do not allow for many individuals seeking employment to find adequate, stable work with desirable hours or sufficient pay. Many Central American men must gain employment in the textile, transportation, food service, and landscaping industries or in the informal workforce as day laborers working construction and other short-term projects. Women often find work as child care workers, domestic workers, or hotel maids. Low-paying, unskilled work leaves this population vulnerable to inadequate health and safety protections and to possible labor exploitation. Central Americans have come to play an important role in the economic stabilization of their home countries, with many sending weekly or monthly remittances home to support their relatives in their homelands. Transfers of funds from Central Americans living abroad "have become extremely significant to families' survival and to regional reconstruction and economic development in the post-war era" (Mahler & Ugrina 2006).

Although Spanish is the first language for the majority of Central Americans, the linguistic traditions of this population are numerous and diverse. Guatemalans are from Mayan descent and could speak one or more of the various Mayan languages (21 in total). Hondurans might speak Garifuna and Nicaraguans Mesquito (Menjívar 2006).

Spanish-only speakers many times experience difficulty in seeking out legal assistance and the services of law enforcement when needed, thus the opportunity for many Central Americans who speak native languages other than Spanish to communicate needs and requests for assistance can be especially problematic, if not nonexistent. Recognition of the multilingual and **cultural competency** needs of Guatemalans, Salvadorans, Hondurans, and others is an issue that should be attended to as much as possible, particularly in regions that have pockets of Central American neighborhoods. Also important is the development of culturally appropriate social services and community programs that consider the needs of Central Americans, particularly the indigenous population whose mores and social standards are in many ways different than those non-indigenous peoples from nearby regions.

Among the issues at the forefront of the international human rights agenda of Latina/o activists, researchers, and supporters is the **femicide** of women in Guatemala that has devastated the region since 2000. Femicide, commonly defined as the gender-motivated murder of women, remains the most extreme and disconcerting crime suffered by Latina **victims**. The eruption of murders has been attributed by some groups to be a direct result of the historical perception of women as weapons of war. The tactic of raping, torturing, and killing a woman has long been one used by the Guatemalan army, paramilitary, and even law enforcement "to destroy not only the individual woman, but to dishonor her family, her community, and her national and ethnic identity" (Guatemalan Human Rights Commission 2009, 3). Femicide in the region also has been attributed to **violence** perpetrated by gang activity, **drug trafficking**, and a misogynistic society that continually has tolerated violence against women in all facets of their lives.

The precise number of women killed in Guatemala is uncertain due to the lack of reliable data and because of differences among the criteria used by various agencies to compile numbers. Available police statistics from 2008, however, indicate that more than 4,000 women have been violently killed in Guatemala since 2000. As in Mexico, victims habitually are raped and tortured before their death, disfigured beyond recognition, and often are discarded in empty lots within city limits or in remote mountainous areas. Also, as is the case in Juarez, although abductions of victims are immediately reported to authorities by family members, a delayed response by law enforcement results in the ever-increasing number of young lives taken. Corrupt, ill-equipped authorities historically have done little to investigate or prosecute those responsible for the murders, and have been known to extract confessions from scapegoats through unlawful methods. Many cases have been inadequately investigated as law enforcement and judicial institutions remain shrouded by gender biases, resulting in a blatant failure to prosecute and punish those responsible and further contributing to a climate of impunity. In April 2008, the Law against Femicide and other Forms of Violence was passed by the Guatemalan Congress, officially acknowledging femicide as a punishable offense. The methodical murder of Guatemalan women, however, still remains a pervasive problem to date and must be given the legal and societal attention it so urgently requires, both within and outside of Central America. Crime and poverty form the basis for the continuing migration of Central Americans to the United States in search of better lives.

Another criminal justice matter to plague impoverished areas throughout Central America is that of *maras*, or youth **gangs**. The spread of U.S.-born gangs such as **Mara Salvatrucha**—also known as MS and MS-13—and its rival, 18th Street, to Guatemala, Honduras, and principally El Salvador has remained a consistent problem that has left Central American communities burdened with an influx of gang-related crime. This intensification of gang activity is a direct result of the continued **deportation** of gang-involved individuals to the region from the United States. Many deportees have little to no connection to their home countries, identifying first and foremost as young Americans after having been raised in the United States, and are made to choose between attempting to survive on their own or grouping together with other deported gang members for much-needed security. Such connections often contribute to street violence, directly promoting the organization of sub-groups or cliques of MS and Eighteenth Street. Others still focus on their return to the United States through illegal means so that they can return to the lifestyles, language, and relationships they are accustomed to in what truly is their home country. Contrary to the misconception that Latina/o immigrants bring crime into the United States, the U.S. immigration policy, ironically, has created and adopted as standard procedure the alarming trend of exporting gang crime and culture to Central America—not the other way around.

The development of federally funded initiatives, such as the Violent Gang Task Force in 1992, and the creation and implementation of various laws thereafter aimed at deporting criminal offenders, have managed to fan anti-immigrant sentiment across the nation. Papachristos (2005) has written that the movement of gang members overseas "not only spreads gang culture but also helps to establish links between gang members in different countries," thereby creating a means for international criminal networks to flourish (Papachristos 2005, 53). The surge in street violence in Central America as a result of mass deportation has directly increased the homicide rate in affected countries to a level that surpassed that experienced during the many years of civil war and political unrest. Those countries inundated with deportees usually are poorly equipped to manage the great number of gang-involved individuals it receives each year; this has resulted in the recognition of **youth** gangs as a national security problem.

Although the increase in homicides has been attributed to gang activity, human rights activists have estimated that most result from the *mano dura* or strong-arm tactics adopted by the government, namely the use of anti-gang death squads, organized to exterminate confirmed gang members as well as those merely suspected of gang involvement. Such ill-conceived methods have resulted in the continued repression of Central Americans in their homelands that only further endorses delinquency of the youth population, leading them to seek out the power and influence offered by the U.S.-bred gangs that have infiltrated their communities.

Central Americans have been referred to as the "invisible Latinos," unseen and unheard, often mistaken for Mexicans or "passing" as whites, all while serving as an integral part of the Latin American makeup in the United States. The political and economic struggles and victimization of Central Americans, both within and outside of the United States warrant consistent attention and will remain issues important to understanding the Latina/o experience within the larger U.S. society. Although not a new phenomenon, the influx of unaccompanied minors particularly from the countries of El Salvador, Guatemala, and Honduras underscores the ongoing social and economic crisis in these countries and the plight of children and families who are often seeking to escape violence. As highlighted in its 2014 study of the situation, the United Nations High Commissioner for Refugees (UNHCR) recommends full implementation of international legal protections to ensure the safety and well-being of unaccompanied children from Central America and Mexico seeking refugee status or political asylum in the United States.

See also: Part I essays: Latina/o Immigrants, Crime, and Justice; The U.S. War on Drugs and Latina/o Communities; Incarceration and Latinas/os in the United States; Latinas/os and the U.S. Criminal Justice System; Gangs in the United States and Latina/o Communities. Part II entries: Human Trafficking; Slavery; Victims; Vigilantism.

Further Reading

Bermúdez, Manuel. 2005. Central America: Gang violence and anti-death squads. http://ipsnews.net/news.asp?idnews=30163. Accessed November 12, 2015.

Center for Gender and Refugee Studies. University of California, Hastings College of the Law. http://cgrs.uchastings.edu/.

Decesare, Donna. 2003. From civil war to gang war: The tragedy of Edgar Bolanos. In *Gangs and society: Alternative perspectives,* edited by L. Kontos, D. Brotherton, and L. Barrios, 283–313. New York, NY: Columbia University Press.

Guatemalan Human Rights Commission. 2009. *Guatemala's femicide law: Progress against impunity?* Washington, DC: Guatemalan Human Rights Commission.

Larsen, Luke J. 2004. *The foreign-born population in the United States: 2003.* Current Population Reports, P20–551. Washington, DC: U.S. Census Bureau.

Lopez, David E., Eric Popkin, and Edward Telles. 1996. Central Americans: At the bottom, struggling to get ahead. In *Ethnic Los Angeles,* edited by R. D. Waldinger and M. Bozorgmehr, 279–304. New York, NY: Russell Sage Foundation.

Mahler, Sarah J., and Dusan Urgina. 2006. Central America: Crossroads of the Americas. http://www.migrationpolicy.org/article/central-america-crossroads-americas/. Accessed November 12, 2015.

Mejia, Thelma. 2006. Central America: Soaring violent crime threatens democracy. http://www.ipsnews.net/2006/09/central-america-soaring-violent-crime-threatens-democracy/. Accessed November 12, 2015.

Menjívar, Cecilia. 2006. Global processes and local lives: Guatemalan women's work and gender relations at home and abroad. *International Labor and Working-Class History* 70: 86–105.

Motel, Seth, and Eileen Patten. 2012. The 10 largest Hispanic origin groups: Characteristics, rankings, top counties. Washington, DC: Pew Hispanic Center. http://www.pewhispanic.org/2012/06/27/the-10-largest-hispanic-origin-groups-characteristics-rankings-top-counties/.

Papachristos, Andrew. (March/April 2005). Gang world. *Foreign Policy.*

Pew Research Center Hispanic Trends. 2015. Statistical Portrait of Hispanics in the United States, 1980–2013. Washington, DC: The Pew Charitable Trusts. http://www.pewhispanic.org/2015/05/12/statistical-portrait-of-hispanics-in-the-united-states-1980-2013/.

United Nations High Commissioner for Refugees. 2014. *Unaccompanied children leaving Central America and Mexico and the need for international protection.* Washington, DC: UNHCR. http://www.unhcrwashington.org/sites/default/files/1_UAC_Children%20on%20the%20Run_Full%20Report.pdf.

U.S. Census Bureau. 2006. *U.S. Hispanic Population: 2006.* Washington, D.C. http://www.census.gov/population/socdemo/hispanic/cps2006/CPS_Powerpoint_2006.pdf.

Chicanas/os

Brian Montes

The term Chicana/o reflects a political and cultural movement intimately tied to the history of **Mexican Americans**, U.S. citizens of Mexican origin living in the United States of America. Rooted in the political and social conquest of Mexico and its people by the United States, the term Chicana/o is characterized by a sense of cultural pride and political resistance. It is the assertion of Mexican cultural citizenship within an Anglo-American social, political, and legal system that privileges white Anglos as the only "real" and legal U.S. citizens.

The etymology of the term "Chicana/o" is unknown. Several folk theories exist regarding its conception, however. One theory suggests that the term Chicana/o is a derivative of the term "*chicamo*"—a pejorative term used to describe the Mexican poor and working class throughout the Southwest. Another popular folk theory links the term Chicana/o to the Nahuatl language of Mexico. It is believed that the term is an evolved form of the word "*Mesheecano*"; the Nahuatl word used to identify the Meshica people, a pre-Colombian tribe after which Mexico is named. As a result of the linguistic differences between the indigenous pre-Colombian tribes and the Spanish, specifically with regards to the pronunciation of the Spanish "x," it is believed that the term "*Mesheecano*" evolved throughout the years into the words "*Mechicano*" and, lastly, Chicana/o.

Used mostly by Mexicans living in the West and Southwestern portions of the United States, the term Chicana/o differs greatly from other labels used to identify Americans of Mexican origin. Principally, Chicana/o is a term of self-identification largely used by Mexican American political and cultural activists. Unlike the terms "Hispanic" and "Mexican American" (with or without the hyphen), which historically have promoted the Americanization and assimilation of Mexicans, the term Chicana/o promotes a sense of American "Mexicanization" with an emphasis on biculturation or strategic acculturation. A Chicana/o, as stated by Chicano journalist **Rúben Salazar** (1970) is "a Mexican American with a non-Anglo image of self."

Gaining prominence during the U.S. **civil rights** movement of the 1960s, the term Chicana/o placed an emphasis on challenging Anglo educational, cultural, and political supremacy, as well as institutional and legalized racism, through a non-white, non-Anglo Mexican American identity politic movement. The various struggles by Mexican American communities on separate fronts eventually would lead to the cultivation of what would be known as the Chicana/o movement. The emphasis of this movement was and is on political self-determination and cultural rights in the defense and expression of Chicanismo; a historical and communal consciousness tied to the history of Mesoamerica and the "source of political unity and strength" (Garcia 1997, 3). The participants of this movement identified themselves as Chicanas/os.

The Chicano Movement/*El Movimiento*

The movement for Mexican American civil, political, and human rights in the United States dates back to as early as the mid-19th century with the annexation of Mexico's Northwestern territories by the United States. It was during this period that approximately 75,000 Mexicans became, without consent, second-class citizens of the United States. These new Americans, and the subsequent generations after, suffered from discriminatory policies that viewed them as a "mongrel" race (Horsman 1981, 210). According to Cynthia E. Orozco (2009, 27), "Mexican Americans were racialized and excluded from the category of 'American,' " resulting in increased **segregation** and marginalization from Anglo American society. Although U.S. federal policy had incorporated Mexicans into the United States as early as 1848 with the signing of the Treaty of Guadalupe Hidalgo—a treaty that was supposed to safeguard newly annexed Mexicans, their civil liberties, and land rights—Anglo American society continued to view Mexicans and Mexican Americans as foreign invaders. Mexican Americans oftentimes were denied land rights, prohibited from attending public school, denied voting rights, arrested and tried without due process, and forced to work menial jobs. Most Mexican men worked as laborers for low wages. Women, if they worked, occupied domestic positions.

Mexican Americans also suffered from **residential segregation**. In addition to having their lands illegitimately repossessed and appropriated by Anglo ranchers following the Mexican American War, Mexican Americans were forced to live, through discriminatory real estate policies, in *barrios* or *colonias*. The alienation and discrimination towards Mexican Americans is evident in the United States' legal policy towards them. Legislative programs such as the **Greaser Act** of 1855 (an anti-loitering law in the state of California applied to people of Spanish and Indian descent, commonly known as "**Greasers**" (Haney-López 1996, 145), Mexican Repatriation 1929–1939 (which resulted in thousands of Mexican American citizens to be deported without due process), **Operation Wetback** (1954 operation designed to search for and deport Mexicans suspected of being unauthorized in the country), and the National Origins Act of 1924 sought to criminalize these new Americans as illegal. The purpose of these laws was to limit not only the number of Mexicans residing in the United States but also to limit political access and social opportunities for Mexican Americans and to continue to consolidate the hegemony of white Anglo America.

The resistance of Mexican Americans towards this volatile and discriminatory treatment became a dynamic and diverse social movement—one that existed simultaneously in separate states with multiple leaders and numerous organizations. Organizations such *as Alianza Hispano Americana*, *Las Gorras Blancas, La Hermana Mexicana Nacionál*, **League of United Latin American Citizens (LULAC)**, and *La Liga Protectora* became early components of the Mexican American movement for civil rights. This movement was localized and focused on social and political integration. Discourse for the majority of these organizations, with the exception of *Las Gorras Blancas*, centered on a Eurocentric Anglo-American racial identity that privileged a "white" racial identity. Mexican Americans throughout the Southwest and West coast were encouraged to assimilate and privilege their own European (Spanish), or "white" ancestry.

Despite the success of these organizations, Mexican Americans—even those who had claimed a white racial identity—continued to suffer from discriminatory policies and remained unprotected by the Equal Protection Clause of the Fourteenth Amendment to the U.S. Constitution (García 2009, 7). Mexican Americans became victims of a racial hierarchy in the United States, discriminated against either because they were racialized as non-white or "Indian." As a result, the movement for Mexican American rights began to develop a more antagonistic and radical attitude rooted not only in political and civil liberties but also in the development of a cultural identity and racial consciousness. Once local, this movement began to transcend states' borders, empowering thousands of Mexican Americans to fight for what the previous generation could not or did not care to achieve—a civil and socio-political movement with a Mexican American political body at the national level. Inspired by the larger movement for civil rights in the United States, Mexican American workers, organizers, students, and war veterans began fighting for their rights not just as Mexicans who were American but as working-class and poor Americans of Mexican origin. The catalysts for this movement were the **Zoot Suit Riots** (1943), the farmworkers' movement, the battle for land grants in New Mexico, and the 1968 student walkouts.

Pachucos, Sleepy Lagoon, the Zoot Suit Riots, and *Chola/os*

The rise of McCarthyism and American **nativism** during World War II resulted in

Mexican Americans in California becoming heavily targeted for suspicion of criminal activity and for what was considered anti-American behavior. A subset of this population, known as ***pachucos***, were discriminately targeted for speaking Caló, a form of Mexican American Spanish slang, and for wearing zoot suits, an outfit that consisted of a long coat, baggy pegged pants, and shoes. These young Mexican Americans, generalized as delinquents, gang members, and anti-American hoodlums, often were harassed and persecuted by **police** officers.

In 1942, in an attempt to address what was considered in California as the "Mexican Problem," the Los Angeles police department "launched a much publicized war" on *pachucos,* arresting more than 600 young men and women (Pagán 2003, 3). What gained particular notoriety was the arrest of 22 young Mexican Americans, 17 of whom were charged with assault and first-degree murder. Those arrested were tried and convicted without any substantial evidence or due process. Known as the **Sleepy Lagoon** murder case, the prejudiced conviction intensified an already volatile relationship between Mexican Americans and Anglos, sparking the 1943 **Zoot Suit Riots**.

In 1943, U.S. servicemen and police officers, as a result of pro-American sentiment, began attacking, beating, stripping, and arresting Mexican American **youths** (*pachucos*) dressed in zoot suits. The act of beating a *pachuco* in his zoot suit and then stripping him naked was not only an act of physical abuse but also a symbolic act. Authorities were stripping young Mexican American males of their cultural identity, a manifestation of a "vulgar anti-Mexican racism" (Muñoz 2007, 51). It is estimated that hundreds of Mexican Americans were beaten, arrested, and stripped during these riots. Mexican Americans, in protest of the **police brutality**, started to retaliate, sparking intense rioting. It was, as Rodolfo Acuña states (1998), "a natural response to 120 years of political, economic, and cultural suppression" (Acuña 1998, 1–5).

In 1944, a year after the riots, the conviction against the Sleepy Lagoon defendants was overturned by the California Court of Appeals. The trial was considered racially biased, partial, and an affront to the civil and legal rights of Mexican Americans. Despite the court's appeal, however, Mexican Americans remained marginalized by the racism and conservatism underlying McCarthyism, discriminated socially as unlawful, repressed politically as subversives, and exploited economically in the labor force.

Similar to the term, "*pachuco*," "***cholo,***" or "*chola*" originated as a pejorative expression for "low life." *Chola/o* later became synonymous with a Mexican street youth whose style of dress and speech resembled that of a *pachuco*. The significance of terms such as *chola/o* or *pachuco* resonates today with the manner in which Mexican youths are stereotyped or racially profiled—lessons that analysts have drawn from the events dating back to the 1940s.

The *Bracero* Program and Farmworkers Struggles

It was during World War II that Mexican nationals were contracted as cheap laborers by the United States under the *Bracero* program (1942–1964). The purpose for hiring Mexican nationals as cheap labor was to help subsidize U.S. companies, many of which had lost their employees to the war. The hiring of foreign nationals at low wages, however, hindered unionization efforts by U.S. farmworkers, many of whom were Mexican Americans working for low wages and in unsanitary working conditions. The mistreatment of domestic Mexican farmworkers and the efforts to exploit foreign Mexican nationals resulted in the farmworkers movement.

Led by César Chavez and the United Farm Workers, the emphasis of the movement initially was placed on the rights of U.S. farmworkers. In fact, the United Farm Workers—born from the union between the Agricultural Workers Organizing Committee (AWOC), led by Filipino organizer Larry Itliong, and the National Farm Workers Association (NFWA), led by Chavez and Delores Huerta—initially advocated for an anti-immigration policy. Its goals were to help improve labor laws for domestic farmworkers by limiting the amount of foreign nationals used as cheap labor. There was no disguising, however, that the exploitation and poor working conditions of U.S. farmworkers was racially motivated and directly associated to the exploitation of Mexican workers. Mexican nationals and Mexican Americans were consolidated into a cheap labor source and both were discriminated against equally. As a result, the farmworkers movement developed into a movement for all farmworkers and a symbol of resistance for young Mexican Americans who had become embittered by a society that exerted and institutionalized economic discrimination towards Mexican, domestic and foreign born, workers. Scholars have noted that "Chavez and the farmworkers movement transcended their fight for justice in California's fields and came to embody the era's struggles against racism and poverty" (Shaw 2008, 2).

The Battle to Restore Land Grants

In New Mexico, Reies "The Tiger" Lopez Tijerina, leader of the *Alianza de las Mercedes*, an organization that fought for the restoration of land rights, declared a legal battle to reinstate land grants guaranteed to Mexican Americans living in New Mexico. It must be noted that following the Mexican-American War, the United States Congress guaranteed that newly annexed Mexican Americans would retain rights to their lands. Despite this decree, however, many Mexican Americans—as a result of a United States ruling that regarded communal lands (known as "*ejidos*" in Spanish) as inconsistent with the rights of individual property—had their lands either seized by the United States National Forest or purchased through what could be considered illegal sales by Anglo ranchers. After researching the status of New Mexico land grants, Tijerina decided that Mexican Americans needed to re-acquire what he believed were stolen lands.

The most infamous of these attempts to re-acquire land took place in 1967 after Tijerina and the *Alianza* occupied Echo Amphitheater Park in New Mexico. After learning that the park had once been a part of the *San Joaquín del Río de Chama* land grant, Tijerina occupied and declared the park the Republic of San Joaquin. When Tijerina and other members of the *Alianza* attempted to meet again, state authorities arrested the group on several counts of sedition. This prompted Tijerina, who had escaped arrest, to raid the Rio Arriba County courthouse in Tierra Amarilla, New Mexico, and free those imprisoned. The raid garnered national attention and Tijerina and Chavez became the leaders of a national social movement for the economic, political, and legal rights of Mexican nationals living in the United States and Mexican Americans.

On October 21, 1967, Tijerina set out a call for young Mexican American activists to meet with each other in Albuquerque, New Mexico, to discuss the current plight of Mexican Americans. This event eventually transformed the political landscape of a Mexican American civil rights movement transfixed on social integration with a new movement focused on cultural citizenship.

Among those present at this meeting were Mexican American activists from the Mexican American Youth Organization (MAYO) of Texas, Rodolfo "Corky" Gonzales; and from the Crusade for Justice of Denver, Moctezuma Esparza and Carlos Montes—both of whom would later become members of the Young Citizens for Community Action. Known also as the **Brown Berets**, the Young Citizens for Community Action contributed to the militarization of the Chicana/o movement and participated along with high-school teacher Sal Castro in the notorious East Los Angeles High School walkouts.

Walkouts/Blowouts and the Chicana/o Movement

The East Los Angeles High School walkouts, or the "Blowouts" as they were known, called political attention to the discrimination endured by Mexican Americans attending high schools throughout East Los Angeles. Although the U.S. Court of Appeals for the Ninth Circuit in *Mendez v. Westminster School District of Orange County* (1947) held that the segregation of Mexican and Mexican American students into separate "Mexican schools" was unconstitutional, Mexican Americans continued to suffer from severe segregation within the education system. Schools attended by Mexican Americans were run down, lacked sufficient funding, lacked adequate resources, and suffered from "gross overcrowding, hostile teaching, and prison-like environments that consistently produced nothing but high dropout rates" (Haney-López 2003, 1). During the spring of 1968, thousands of high school students throughout the Los Angeles area walked out of their high schools in protest of these abysmal conditions.

One year later, in 1969, Rodolfo "Corky" Gonzalez, co-chair of the Mexican American contingent of the Poor People's March and founder of the Crusade for Justice, an organization which had protested the conditions of the working poor, called for the first National Chicano Liberation Youth Conference in Denver. It was at this conference that *El Plan Esprituál de Atzlán* was developed. The plan advocated for Chicana/o nationalism and the reappropriation of *Atzlán*, the land of the American Southwest and birthplace of the Chicana/o people. According to the manifesto, "we the Chicano inhabitants and civilizers of the northern land of Aztlán from whence came our forefathers, reclaim the land of their birth" (Rosales 2000, 361). In reclaiming the United States Southwest as their homeland, Mexican Americans were also claiming the civil and legal rights accorded to all U.S. citizens.

A month after the Denver conference, students at the University of California at Santa Barbara—many of whom had attended the National Chicano Liberation Youth Conference—developed *El Plan de Santa Barbara*. The plan was designed to implement Chicano/Mexican American studies into the California State University and University of California curriculum. Benefiting from the G.I. Bill and other educational opportunity programs, Mexican Americans were attending college at an unprecedented rate. It was imperative, these students argued, that Mexican Americans be given the opportunity to learn about the true history of Mexican Americans and that Mexican American students play a role in the development of its curriculum. It was at the U.C. Santa Barbara conference that *El Movimiento Estudiantíl Chicano de Atzlán* (MEChA) was created. The purpose of MEChA, according to the plan was to "bring to the mind of every young Chicana and Chicano . . . the liberation of her/his people from prejudice and oppression" (Muñoz 2007, 239).

Chicanas/os, *Pintas/os*, and the Criminal Justice System

Following the blowouts, a handful of Chicana/o students and community activists, many of whom were inspired by Tijerina, Sal Castro, and the Brown Berets, were promptly arrested, charged, and detained for possession of subversive literature, conspiracy, disturbing the peace, failing to disperse, and trespassing. Bail initially was set at $10,000, a "sum that exceeded normal bail amounts; it represented 10 times the bail usually imposed on those charged with burglary and twice the sum typically required in cases of assault with a deadly weapon" (Haney-López 2003, 27). The charges violated First Amendment rights and characterized the overt racism of the U.S. legal system. The absence of Mexicans on the indictment grand jury also violated the Equal Protection Clause of the Fourteenth Amendment of the U.S. Constitution.

As marginalized citizens, Chicanas/os have had a tumultuous history with law enforcement officials, oftentimes becoming the victims of harsh and biased laws and corruptive police practices. It was racism towards Mexican American youths that sparked the **Zoot Suit Riots** and it was in August 1970, at the National Chicano Moratorium, where the infamous and tragic death of **Rúben Salazar**, a prominent Mexican American journalist, occurred at the hands of law enforcement officials. Chicanas/os were knowingly targeted by law enforcement officials. According to Joseph Words, the LAPD during this time "was a bastion of white supremacy" (Haney-López 2003, 137). Police harassment towards Chicanas/os was rampant and deliberate. There was also an unwarranted increase of police presence within the Chicana/o community resulting in greater numbers of arrests.

Chicanas/os continue to suffer from discriminatory law enforcement practices and discourses and constitute a disproportionate and increasing number of prisoners in both state and federal prisons. Just as they were during the heyday of McCarthyism, Chicana/o youth still are criminalized as vagrants, gang members, and aliens or foreigners, and suffer from harsh criminal justice policies. From punitive "three-strikes" legislation to "get tough" legislation to post–September 11, 2001, immigration laws that transferred authority of the Immigration and Naturalization Services (INS) to the division of homeland security, many in the Chicana/o community have become victims of what has been noted as "the racialized and gendered nature of criminalization" (Olguín 2010, ix). As racialized subjects of a discriminatory criminal justice system Olguín believes that Chicana/o prisoner and incarceration rates must be understood and addressed within a larger international context of racism, the war on terrorism, and the violation of basic human rights of Chicanas/os (Olguín 2010, 261–81). Just as *pachucos* were labeled criminals and linked to anti-American sentiment during World War II, Chicana/o youths today have become victims of a racist post–September 11, 2001, environment, targeted, and subject to the **prison industrial complex**.

Identified as having a *pinta/o* (prison) prisoner identity, incarcerated Chicanas/os have established a revolutionary and counter-hegemonic prisoner subculture that links the criminalization of Chicana/o youths to the establishment of Anglo imperialism. As one scholar notes, "*la pinta* introduces an alternative global Chicana/o prisoner theory of crime and punishment as well as power and counter-power" linking the criminalization of Chicanas/os to U.S. capitalistic imperialism (Olguín 2010, 25). Critical in the construction of a *pinta/o* prisoner subjectivity is the experience of marginalization, a consciousness of resistance, the development of a linguistic discourse of resistance, and cultural symbols of brown pride including artwork, black-ink tattoos, and dress (notably khakis and t-shirts). Their experience of marginalization, negative encounters with the U.S. criminal justice system, as well as their societal anti-conformity, theoretically situates Chicanas/os, identified as *cholas/os* and understood as the modern day *pachuca/o*, as protagonists in a larger fight against U.S. capitalist imperialism and white supremacy.

Chicanas

Another major facet of the Chicano movement was the development and articulation of a feminist philosophy that had as its core the same principles and beliefs in social justice. Known as the Chicana movement, Mexican American women challenged the prevailing white feminist discourse that had centered, as the antagonist, on white Euro-American male patriarchy. As poor or working-class women of color, Chicanas challenged the masculine (*machista*) patriarchy of Chicanos who through customs and traditions engendered the oppression of Mexican American women. Chicanas agreed that the U.S. women's movement as well as the Chicano movement neglected their unique experiences as racialized women. By speaking through their subjective experiences of marginalization, Chicanas not only challenged Euro-American sexism but also challenged Chicano patriarchy by seeking gender, sex, ethnic, and racial equality. Chicanas transformed the Chicano movement from a movement focused on race to a movement that addressed the social inequalities of gendered people. Some of the issues addressed within the Chicana movement have included sexism, homophobia, single motherhood, sterilization, **domestic violence**, drug abuse, the prison experience of Chicanas and its effect on the family, and academic seclusion. Of particular interest is the manner in which Chicanas have been affected by the criminal justice system. As noted by a scholar on the subject, "most researchers ignore how discrimination based on social class, race/ethnicity, age, and gender determine why and how certain groups are disproportionately labeled criminal, arrested, and incarcerated" (Díaz-Cotto 2006, 1). How women are affected by discriminatory policies of the criminal justice system reflect "the racialized and gendered nature of criminalization" (Olguín 2010, ix).

The Political and Cultural Legacy of Chicanismo

In addition to the successes and accomplishments of Chavez and United Farm Workers, Reies Lopez Tijerina, the **Brown Berets**, MEChA, and numerous other individuals and organizations, the Chicana/o movement has also resulted in the creation of two national organizations committed to the political and social advancement of the Mexican American community: the *Partido Nacionál de La Raza Unida*, or La Raza Political Party (LRUP), and the **Mexican American Legal Defense and Education Fund (MALDEF)**. Organized by José Angel Gutiérrez in 1970, *La Raza Unida* grew out of the Mexican American Youth Organization in Texas to become a political party centered on the wants and needs of Mexican Americans. It was the first political party to have an overt, ethnically-based political platform and was responsible for the election of the first two Mexican American mayors of LaSalle County, Texas. Today, *La Raza Unida* is active throughout the Southwest and West coast.

Organized in 1967, MALDEF advocated for greater educational opportunities and won legal victories for Mexican Americans in lawsuits for educational equity and school funding. Some of the key legal victories for MALDEF include ***Plyler v. Doe* (1982)**, and *Edgewood Independent School District et al. v. Kirby et al.* (1989). In *Plyer vs. Doe* (1982), the Supreme Court held that unauthorized immigrant children were protected by the Fourteenth Amendment of the U.S. Constitution and thus had the right to an education without discrimination in the United States. *Edgewood Independent School District et al. v. Kirby et al.* (1989) improved educational funding for predominantly Mexican American educational institutions.

LRUP and MALDEF currently contribute to the defense and well-being of both the Mexican American and Latina/o communities—most recently contesting Legislation H.R. 4437, (2006) and Arizona's SB 1070 (2010), legislations that sought to persecute anyone who merely looked unauthorized (that is, "Mexican") and make a felon any unauthorized immigrant as well as anyone who helped unauthorized persons cross the border. Unlike early-20th century Mexican American activists who often side-stepped the plight of Mexican nationals and the unauthorized, the Chicana/o movement today has embraced the struggle of the unauthorized as its own.

Despite its focus on the political civil rights of Mexican Americans through aggressive protest and a militant ethos (García 1997), the attention to race and racism, gender, and focus on cultural citizenship and cultural nationalism also has made the Chicana/o movement a cultural movement of transformation and reclamation. Cultural expressions in the form of music, art, dance (*danza*), literature, and poetry introduced the Chicana/o, ***pachuca/o*** or ***chola/o*** as an American figure with a distinct socio-historical and cultural identity. At the core of the Chicana/o movement was *Chicanismo*, a movement of "cultural pride and a source of political unity and strength" that sought to make U.S. society more just (García 1997, 3). Notable figures who have participated in this socio-political movement have included scholars such as Américo Paredes, Gloria Anzaldúa, and Juan Gomez Quiñonez; artists Lalo Guerrero, Carlos Santana, Los Lobos, Harry Gamboa, Jr., Patssi Valdez, and Gronk; authors Cherríe Moraga, Ana Castillo, Rodolfo Anaya; and political activist **Raúl Salinas (raúlsalinas)**. Salinas, a pioneer of prisoner (*pinta/o*) poetry, became an advocate for prisoner rights and social justice, and a critical voice of dissent within what he believed was an unjust and racist penal system.

The term Chicana/o reflects a broader social movement that promotes the advancement of the Latina/o community. Through organization such as the MALDEF, LULAC, LRUP, and MEChA, the objectives of the Chicana/o movement remain the social and legal empowerment of those Mexican and Mexican American persons who remain marginalized and targeted by discriminatory policies and an unjust criminal justice system.

See also: Part I essays: Latinas/os and the U.S. Criminal Justice System; Latinas and the U.S. Criminal Justice System; Incarceration and Latinas/os in the United States; Latina/o Youth and Criminal Justice. Part II entries: Community-Based Latina/o Advocacy Organizations; Legal Advocacy Groups; Mexicans and Mexican Americans; Political Activist Groups; Segregation.

Further Reading

Acuña, Rodolfo. 1998. *Occupied America: A history of Chicanos*. New York, NY: Harper and Row.

Alaniz, Yolanda, and Megan Cornish. 2008. *Viva la raza: a history of Chicano Identity and resistance*. Seattle, WA: Red Letter Press.

Díaz-Cotto, Juanita. 2006. *Chicana lives and criminal justice: Voices from El Barrio*. Austin, TX: University of Texas Press.

Escobar, Edward J. 1999. *Race, police, and the making of a political identity: Mexican Americans and the Los Angeles Police Department 1900–1945*. Berkeley: University of California Press.

Garcia, Alma M. 1997. *Chicana feminist thought: The basic historical writings*. New York: Routledge.

García, Ignacio M. 1997. *Chicanismo: The forging of a militant ethos among Mexican Americans*. Tucson, AZ: University of Arizona Press.

García, Ignacio M. 2009. *White but not equal: Mexican Americans, jury discrimination, and the Supreme Court.* Tucson, AZ: University of Arizona Press.

Gómez-Quiñones, Juan. 1994. *Roots of Chicano politics, 1600–1940.* Albuquerque, NM: University of New Mexico Press.

Haney-López, Ian. F. 2003. *Racism on trial: The Chicano fight for justice*. Cambridge, MA: Harvard University Press.

Horsman, Reginald. 1981. *Race and manifest destiny: The origins of American racial Anglo Saxonism*. Cambridge, MA: Harvard University Press.

Mirandé, Alfredo. 1987. *Gringo justice*. Notre Dame, Indiana: University of Notre Dame Press.

Muñoz, Carlos, Jr. 2007. *Youth, identity, power: The Chicano movement*. New York, NY: Verso.

Olguín, Ben. V. 2005. Chicanos. In *Encyclopedia Latina: History, culture, and society in the United States*, edited by I. Stavans, and H. Augenbraum, 301–8. Danbury, CT: Grolier Academic.

Olguín, Ben. V. 2010. *La pinta: Chicana/o prisoner literature, culture, and politics*. Austin, TX: University of Texas Press.

Orozco, Cynthia. E. 2009. *No Mexicans, women, or dogs allowed: The rise of the Mexican American civil rights movement*. Austin, TX: University of Texas Press.

Pagán, Eduardo Obregón. 2003. *Murder at the Sleepy Lagoon: Zoot Suits, race and riot in wartime L.A*. Chapel Hill, NC: University of North Carolina Press.

Rosales, F. Arturo. 1997. *Chicano! History of the Mexican American civil rights movement*. Houston, TX: Arte Público Press.

Rosales, F. Arturo. 2000. Testimonio; *A documentary history of the Mexican American struggle for civil rights*. Houston, TX: Arte Público Press.

Salazar, Rúben. 1970 (February 6). Who is a Chicano? And what is it the Chicanos want? *Los Angeles Times*.

Shaw, Randy. 2008. *Beyond the fields: Cesar Chavez, the UFW, and the struggle for justice in the 21st century*. Berkeley, CA: University of California Press.

Cases Cited

Plyler v. Doe, 457 U.S. 202 (1982).

Edgewood Independent School District et al. v. Kirby et al., 777 S.W.2d 391 (TX 1989).

Mendez v. Westminster School District of Orange County, 64 F. Supp. 544, 549 (S.D. Cal. 1946), *aff'd* 161 F.2d 774 (9th Cir. 1947).

Chola/o. **See also:** Part I essay: Gangs in the United States and Latina/o Communities. Part II entries: Chicanas/os; Mexicans and Mexican Americans.

Civil Rights

Sandra Del Valle

Latina/o involvement in civil rights litigation spans decades. As early as 1946, when the Mendez family sued the Westminster School District in Texas for forcing **Mexican American** students into segregated schools,

Latinas/os have sued state and local policy makers, employers, and others over educational equity, **language rights**, voting rights, housing discrimination, and employment discrimination. In addition to seeking enforcement of state and federal constitutions, most often the Equal Protection Clause of the Fourteenth Amendment of the U.S. Constitution, litigation in these traditional areas of civil rights concern have been bolstered by the passage of specific civil rights statues, including Title VI and Title VII of the Civil Rights Act of 1964.

Civil rights organizations specifically dedicated to ensuring the civil rights of Latinos, such as the **Mexican American Legal Defense and Education Fund (MALDEF)** and the **Puerto Rican Legal Defense and Education Fund** (now known as **LatinoJustice/PRLDEF**), were established in the late 1960s and early 1970s to bring systemic reform cases in federal courts. Over time, these organizations secured education, voting, housing, and employment rights for Latinas/os.

Section 1983 of the Civil Rights Act of 1871

Litigation challenging **police** practices, in particular cases involving law enforcement's use of excessive force, do not fit under the above-mentioned traditional civil rights mechanisms for redress. Instead, criminal justice civil rights cases generally are brought under Section 1983 of the Civil Rights Act of 1871. Section 1983 is a historic civil rights act with its origins in the Reconstruction era as part of the federal effort to guarantee former African American slaves the right of citizenship. Congress had passed the Thirteenth, Fourteenth, and Fifteenth Amendments to free the slaves, securing for them the equal protection of the laws and the right to vote. The states, however, could not be entrusted with protecting the rights of the former slaves and they had become adept at finding ways to undermine federal constitutional rights. Indeed, the southern states condoned the terrorist acts of the Ku Klux Klan against African Americans. Local and state courts were ineffective, as prosecutors, judges, and juries—all white—were sympathetic to the Klan and its members, or were subject to intimidation.

To quell the Klan's **violence** and secure the constitutional rights of the freed slaves, Congress passed the Civil Rights Acts of 1871. One of the Acts, called the Ku Klux Klan Act, was codified as 42 U.S.C. §1983. It provided that any person who, "under color of" state or local law, "subjects" or "causes" a citizen of the United States or other person within the jurisdiction of the United States to be subjected to a deprivation of a federal legal or constitutional right, "shall be liable to the party injured" in law, equity, or "other proper proceeding for redress."

Section 1983 authorizes courts to grant relief when a party's federally protected rights have been violated by a state or local official or other person who acted under "color of law," that is, with a state's imprimatur of authority. It contains tort-like remedies for injured individuals so that plaintiffs can recover monetary damages (*Imbler v. Pachtman*, 424 U.S. 409 (1976)). It also provides for equitable, or non-monetary, relief as well so that courts can fashion broad remedies. Equitable remedies that courts have ordered in the past include school desegregation (*United States v. City of Yonkers*, 96 F.3d 600 (2nd Cir. 1996)), restructuring of state mental health facilities (*Wyatt v. Stickney*, 344 F. Supp. 373 (M.D. Ala. 1972)), and restructuring of prisons (*Hutto v. Finney*, 437 U.S. 678 (1978)). Court orders for equitable relief usually also appoint special masters charged with providing ongoing oversight of its orders.

The statute, however, does not confer additional substantive rights but is used as a vehicle for the enforcement of rights already found in the law. It was primarily seen as the vehicle for enforcing the Fourteenth Amendment against private individuals and states. Since those early intentions, however, § 1983 has been viewed expansively and has been used to enforce many federal laws (*Monroe v. Pape*, 365 U.S. 167 (1961); *Maine v. Thiboutout*, 448 U.S. 1 (1980)).

One of the most extensive uses of § 1983 has been in the criminal justice context. The law is used regularly to challenge police officers' use of excessive force (commonly referred to as **police brutality** cases) and discriminatory policies and practices of police departments (*Saucier v. Katz*, 533 U.S. 194 (2001)). To bring a § 1983 claim, a plaintiff must show that he or she was denied a federal right by an individual acting under the "color" of state law (*Gomez v. Toledo*, 446 U.S. 635 (1980)).

The Challenges of Civil Rights Litigation

Achieving victory under § 1983, however, is not simple. The U.S. Supreme Court has added layers of technical requirements to limit the types of claims that can be brought. It has created categories of individuals that are immune from suit (*Harlow v. Fitzgerald*, 457 U.S. 800 (1982); *Forrester v. White*, 484 U.S. 219 (1988)), and has limited the liability of states and supervisors for the unlawful acts of employees (*Will v. Michigan Department of State Police*, 491 U.S. 58 (1989); *Monell v. Department of Social Services*, 36 U.S. 658 (1978); *City of Canton, Ohio v. Harris*, 489 U.S. 378 (1989)). The Supreme Court has also developed a set of complex factors for determining which federal laws actually give rise to enforceable rights (*Anderson v. Creighton*, 483 U.S. 635 (1987); *Saucier v. Katz*, 533 U.S. 194 (2001)).

Still, over the last several decades plaintiffs have brought a series of cases challenging police departments across the country for **racial profiling** and for selective enforcement of laws and traffic regulations. Both types of practices hinge on the use of racial or other impermissible criteria to determine whom to target for law enforcement efforts. Racial profiling grabbed the nation's attention in the mid- to late-1990s and has held it into the 21st century, as the extent of the practice became widely known. In 2013, in the case, *Floyd et al. v. City of New York,* a federal district court judge found the New York City police to have engaged in "indirect racial profiling." The case was brought by plaintiffs who challenged the NYPD's **stop-and-frisk** practices. Evidence in the case pointed to officers being ordered to comply with what was, in essence, a quota system of summons and arrests. To reach their quotas, officers were encouraged to target "the right people." As a result, the court found that the police had been implementing stops and frisks in a manner inconsistent with the Fourth and Fourteenth Amendments of the U.S. Constitution. The City has since consented to the court's remedial actions, which include the appointment of an independent monitor to oversee the changes ordered by the court.

In 1993, African American and Latino men challenged a township for using pretextual traffic stops along Interstate 95 (*Wilson v. Tinicum Township*, No. CIV.A 92-6617, 1993 WL 280205 (E.D. Pa. July 20, 1993)). The men asserted that their race or national origin was the true reason for the stops. Using Section 1983, they brought challenges under the Equal Protection Clause and the Fourth Amendment and demanded both monetary and equitable relief. The court certified two classes of plaintiffs: those African American and Latino men who had not yet been stopped but could suffer the effects of the stops if the policy was not suspended. For them, equitable relief would be available. The other class, those who already had been denied their constitutional rights because of the unlawful policy, could be entitled to damages. Although the only decision available is the one on class certification, the case shows the type of broad relief that is available under a constitutional torts theory of Section 1983.

Concerns about racial profiling took on great urgency in 1998, when New Jersey State police officers fired 11 bullets into a van carrying three African American men and one Latino man while driving on the New Jersey Turnpike (Kifner 1998). Two of the men were seriously injured. The shooting came on the heels of a 1996 case in which 17 criminal defendants brought motions to suppress evidence in drug-related cases. The men charged that the evidence was seized in violation of the Fourteenth Amendment and the Fourth Amendment (*State v. Soto*, 324 N.J. Super. 66 (N.J. Super. Law Div. 1996)). All were African American men driving on the same portion of the New Jersey Turnpike; all had been stopped by New Jersey State Troopers. The men argued that they were the victims of selective enforcement of traffic violations and charged the state with **institutional racism**. The defendants used statistical evidence to argue that African American drivers on the N.J. Turnpike were more likely to be stopped and searched than were white drivers. The evidence revealed that although 98 percent of all the drivers exceeded the speed limit when driving along a specific stretch of the Turnpike—giving the police latitude to stop virtually anyone—only 13.5 percent of the drivers using the particular stretch of freeway were African American, yet 46 percent of those halted by the police over a 40-month period were African American. In granting the motions to suppress, the New Jersey Superior Court found the statistics "stark," and said that the lack of oversight by the department as a whole gave the practice a luster of authority.

The Supreme Court had been limiting rights under the Fourth Amendment since its decision in ***Terry v. Ohio***, 398 U.S. 1 (1968), and the prevalence of racial profiling practices can be laid at the door of the decision in that case. Indeed, within three months of the New Jersey decision, the Supreme Court in *Whren v. United States*, 517 U.S. 806 (1996) decided that an officer's use of traffic violations as a pretext for a racially motivated stop was not unconstitutional under the Fourth Amendment. The Court, however, did say that such complaints could be challenged under the Equal Protection Clause.

Although the Supreme Court has narrowly interpreted the Equal Protection Clause to prohibit only intentional acts of discrimination as opposed to policies or practices that have a disparate negative impact, it has found significant statistical disparities probative of discrimination (*Village of Arlington Heights v. Metropolitan Housing Corp.*, 429 U.S. 252 (1977); *Washington v. Davis*, 426 U.S. 229 (1976)).

Further, racial profiling cases could be indicative of the very type of discriminatory intent that can support an Equal Protection violation. (*See also National Congress for Puerto Rican Rights v. City of New York*, 191 F.R.D. 52 (S.D.N.Y. 1999); *United States v. Bell*, 86 F.3d 820, 823 (8th Cir.) *cert. denied*, 519 U.S. 955 (1996); *United States v. Anderson*, 923 F.2d 450, 453–54 (6th Cir.) *cert. denied*, 499 U.S. 980, and 500 U.S. 936 (1991); *Gardenhire v. Schubert*, 205 F.3d

303 (6th Cir. 2000); *United States v. Montero-Camargo*, 208 F.3d 1122, 1135 (9th Cir.) *cert. denied*, 531 U.S. 889 (2000); *Chavez v. Illinois State Police*, 251 F.3d 612 (7th Cir. 2001).) Indeed, in one § 1983 case, Latino men sued the Ohio State Highway Patrol for its conceded practice of selectively enforcing criminal laws (*Farm Labor Organizing Committee v. Ohio State Highway Patrol*, 308 F.3d 523 (6th Cir. 2002)). After pulling over motorists on routine traffic stops along the highway, the officers only questioned Latino drivers about their immigration status, requested proof, and even seized lawful immigration documents. Although the State Highway Patrol was part of a **drug**-interdiction team, it had begun to take an active role in immigration enforcement. Plaintiffs alleged violations of the Equal Protection Clause and the Fourth Amendment. After officers testified that they would only question individuals who looked Latino or spoke Spanish-accented English about their immigration status, the court ruled that the practice violated both the Equal Protection Clause and the Fourth Amendment.

Latino involvement in these racial profiling and selective enforcement cases is significant. A growing jurisprudence on racial, ethnic, and linguistic profiling is growing in the context of U.S. **border** enforcement that implicates vital civil rights issues for Latinos. The availability of § 1983 to pursue civil remedies for civil rights violations serves as an important tool in defending against discriminatory criminal justice practices.

See also: Part I essays: Latinas/os and the U.S. Criminal Justice System; Policing and Latina/o Communities; Incarceration and Latinas/os in the United States. Part II entries: Chicanas/os; Community-Based Latina/o Advocacy Organizations; Deportation; Hate Crimes; Language Rights in the Courts; Legal Advocacy Groups; Mexicans and Mexican Americans; Segregation.

Further Reading

Delgado, Richard, Juan F. Perea, and Jean Stefancic (eds.). 2008. *Latinos and the law: Case and materials*. St. Paul: Thomson West.

Kifner, John. 1998 (May 10). Van shooting revives charges of racial "profiling" by New Jersey State Police. *New York Times*. http://www.nytimes.com/1998/05/10/nyregion/van-shooting-revives-charges-of-racial-profiling-by-new-jersey-state-police.html.

Cases Cited

Anderson v. Creighton, 483 U.S. 635 (1987)

Chavez v. Illinois State Police, 251 F.3d 612 (7th Cir. 2001)

City of Canton, Ohio v. Harris, 489 U.S. 378 (1989)

Farm Labor Organizing Committee v. Ohio State Highway Patrol, 308 F.3d 523 (6th Cir. 2002)

Floyd et al. v. City of New York, 959 F. Supp. 2d 540 (2013).

Forrester v. White, 484 U.S. 219 (1988)

Gardenhire v. Schubert, 205 F.3d 303 (6th Cir. 2000)

Gomez v. Toledo, 446 U.S. 635 (1980)

Harlow v. Fitzgerald, 457 U.S. 800 (1982)

Hutto v. Finney, 437 U.S. 678 (1978)

Imbler v. Pachtman, 424 U.S. 409 (1976)

Maine v. Thiboutout, 448 U.S. 1 (1980)

Monell v. Department of Social Services, 36 U.S. 658 (1978)

Monroe v. Pape, 365 U.S. 167 (1961)

National Congress for Puerto Rican Rights v. City of New York, 191 F.R.D. 52 (S.D.N.Y. 1999)

Saucier v. Katz, 533 U.S. 194 (2001)

State v. Soto, 324 N.J. Super. 66 (N.J. Super. Law Div. 1996)

Terry v. Ohio, 398 U.S. 1 (1968)

United States v. Anderson, 923 F.2d 450, 453–54 (6th Cir.), *cert. denied*, 499 U.S. 980, and 500 U.S. 936 (1991)

United States v. Bell, 86 F.3d 820, 823 (8th Cir.), *cert. denied*, 519 U.S. 955 (1996).

United States v. City of Yonkers, 96 F.3d 600 (2nd Cir. 1996)

United States v. Montero-Camargo, 208 F.3d 1122, 1135 (9th Cir.) *cert. denied*, 531, U.S. 889 (2000)

Village of Arlington Heights v. Metropolitan Housing Corp., 429 U.S. 252 (1977)

Washington v. Davis, 426 U.S. 229 (1976)

Whren v. United States, 517 U.S. 806 (1996)

Will v. Michigan Department of State Police, 491 U.S. 58 (1989)

Wilson v. Tinicum Township, No. CIV.A 92-6617, 1993 WL 280205 (E.D. Pa. July 20, 1993)

Wyatt v. Stickney, 344 F. Supp. 373 (M.D. Ala. 1972)

Civilian Oversight of Police

Hector W. Soto, Marco Fernando Navarro, and José Luis Morín

Civilian oversight of policing refers to the idea that the public not only is the beneficiary of the police service, the public also oversees and assesses that service. Some interpretations of civilian oversight include complete control of that service. The idea of civilian oversight can be traced to the rules of policing developed by Sir Robert Peel for the guidance and training of members of what is considered the first modern-day police department, the London Metropolitan Police Force established in 1829. For his rules and other contributions to the founding of London's police department, Sir Robert Peel is recognized as the "Father of Modern Western Policing." United States policing and police departments—especially in northeastern cities—reflect the influence of Peel's rules as well as his conceptualization of policing. Indeed, New York City Police Commissioner Bill Bratton in 2014 disclosed to the *New York Times* that he keeps a copy of Peel's rules with him and considers it his "bible."

Taken together, Peel's rules present a vision of civil society policing as an extension of the responsibility to prevent crime and disorder that every member of civil society had and continued to have notwithstanding that there would be established a governmental entity, the police department, the members of which would be paid to fulfill that responsibility as a governmental employee on a daily basis. Peel's seventh rule summarizes his vision of policing well: "the police are the public and the public are the police" (*New York Times* 2014). There can be little doubt that imbedded in Peel's ideas about policing was the principle that the police not only would be the people, but at all times would be accountable to the people.

Today, the principle of civilian oversight of police flows from our civil governmental structure and its operations. In the United States, police departments are agencies typically under the control and direction of a mayor (or chief executive officer (CEO) of a particular city or town). This person usually is a civilian who was elected by the general populace of the jurisdiction. As the chief executive officer, he or she ultimately is responsible for the enforcement of laws within that jurisdiction. The police department is one of many administrative agencies for which the mayor/CEO selects the commissioner (or chief) to be responsible for the day-to-day enforcement of the criminal law and procedure within the jurisdiction. The mayor/CEO as the principal representative of the people of his or her jurisdiction, however, also is responsible—as a civilian—for the oversight and control of the police department.

Civilian oversight of policing often is inferred from the history, language, and operation of the Fourth Amendment of the U.S. Constitution. The Fourth Amendment protects people's liberty and privacy from unwarranted governmental interference and intrusion. Although applicable to any governmental action, the Fourth Amendment from its inception has been linked closely to the operations of law enforcement. Actions taken by law enforcement against civilians and subsequently found by a court to be in contravention of the Fourth Amendment are subject to censure, and any evidence of liberty and privacy rights seized by police could be deemed inadmissible and cannot be used in a court of law against a defendant. By implication, if not operation, the Fourth Amendment serves as a form of civilian oversight and control over police practices.

Presently, civilian oversight generally refers to the established processes of investigating alleged police officer misconduct that seemingly is independent—or at least beyond the direct influence—of that officer's police department or local politics. These processes have been created as a means of fostering law enforcement accountability to the communities it serves. Accountability, especially for communities of color that have a long history of poor relations with police agencies around the country, has been a central aspect in the development of civilian oversight mechanisms.

Current civilian oversight usually is directed or conducted by governmental entities or agencies, including auditors, inspector general offices, police complaint processes or oversight boards of various types. Nongovernmental organizations—such as the American Civil Liberties Union, Human Rights Watch, Amnesty International, and a variety of local civic organizations, including the Citizens Union of New York—conduct their own studies or investigations of alleged police misconduct, policies, and practices independent of police department or governmental influence, and can be considered a form of civilian oversight of police. These organizations might lack official governmental authority, but their findings and recommendations often are perceived and accepted by the public as being more credible and actionable than governmental agencies that might be viewed as partial to or in a conflict of interest with police departments.

Since the 1960s, demands for greater police accountability and civilian oversight or control over local policing have led to the development of two principal types of oversight entities within the United States: the independent monitor-auditor and the oversight or review board. These forms supplement the traditional accountability mechanisms of internal police review (that is, Internal Affairs or Integrity offices within police departments); state, federal, or special criminal prosecutions or civil rights violation litigation; or private-party civil court remedial actions.

The most prevalent type of civilian oversight is the independent monitor or auditor (sometimes called an "inspector general"). The independent monitor or auditor usually is a member of the police department or a city employee(s), and most often is hired with the knowledge and approval of the local police department. The monitor-auditor uses privileged access to departmental records, statistics, and personnel to assess and publicly report on issues, such as use of force, bias and discrimination, the disciplinary system, police-community relations, or any other subject that might be topical or of concern to the department or the community.

The monitor-auditor position generally is considered to be an internal police department managerial tool, although its findings and reports customarily are made public. The monitor-auditor model is attractive to local government in part because of its relatively low cost and its direct employee relationship with the police department or city. These factors provide the police department or appointing official with some measure of leverage, if not control, as well as measured outcomes and responses. Auditors should not be confused with monitors appointed as a result of a court judgment or settlement, or as a result of a federal U.S. Department of Justice study. A monitor engages in activities similar to those of an auditor, and any results or reports even could be made public. The scope and duration of a monitor's office, however, usually is limited. In New York City, for example, a legal action challenged the New York City Police Department's **stop-and-frisk** tactics in the case of *Floyd et al. v. City of New York* (2013). The case resulted in a federal court decision finding that the NYPD acted unconstitutionally and an order for independent monitoring of the department. The City of New York later settled the case, agreeing to an independent monitor and other reforms.

The Los Angeles Police Department has a unique monitoring office known as the Board of Police Commissioners which is composed of five independent civilians (non-police) appointed by the mayor. The Board of Police Commissioners reviews LAPD shootings and other serious uses of force. The Board reports both to the mayor and the public (Los Angeles Police [n.d.]).

The City of Philadelphia had an independent Integrity and Accountability Office (IAO) with a director who was appointed by the mayor and who reported to the mayor and the Police Commissioner. The IAO monitored the Philadelphia Police Department, studied policies and practices on departmental integrity and the use of force, and prepared reports. In 2005, the IAO was disbanded. Since 1993, in accordance with a Mayoral Executive Order, Philadelphia has had an oversight agency—the Police Advisory Commission (PAC)—whose primary mission is to improve police-community relations. As part of its processes, the PAC accepts complaints from the public concerning specific types of police misconduct. The PAC conducts independent investigation of complaints including (as necessary) a public administrative hearing on the charges after which an opinion is prepared citing findings on the allegations and such recommendations as are necessary. The PAC also accepts nominations from the public for police officer commendations and can issue such commendations of its own accord.

The indictment of six Philadelphia police officers on July 30, 2014, on charges of federal conspiracy, robbery, extortion, kidnapping, and drug dealing gave rise to renewed calls for the creation of a more permanent and independent police oversight board. Rampant misconduct and corruption by officers has led to a loss of confidence in the Philadelphia Police Department, and has incurred great expense in the form of civil rights litigation and damages against the city. The proposed oversight body not only would investigate complaints against police officers and make recommendations for disciplinary action, it also would have subpoena power.

Civilian oversight boards (such as Philadelphia's PAC) are the second most common form of police oversight. The National Association of Civilian Oversight of Law Enforcement (NACOLE), a nonprofit organization dedicated to establishing or improving police oversight in the United States, lists more than

130 such civilian oversight agencies throughout the country. Each monitor-auditor or oversight-review board has a locally based history that has shaped and continues to impact the department's operations and effectiveness. Civilian oversight organizations generally present findings and recommendations to the public in the form of periodic or special reports.

In theory, the oversight or review board is supposed to be representative of the community that the department serves, and hence the department would be accountable to the community. The composition of board members and the number of board members vary from jurisdiction to jurisdiction but, for the most part, members are civilians who are not police department or governmental employees. They might be retired law enforcement personnel, however. Not only are board members intended to be representative of the community served, but board member composition generally is expected to reflect the demographic composition of the community. Moreover, the implication is that board members will bring to the table the knowledge, experiences, and sensitivities of the community. It is understood that the board's task is to convey those perspectives to the police department for its consideration in the formulation or review of policies and practices.

Civilian oversight or review board members usually are appointed by the mayor, City Council, or other governing executive or legislative body of a jurisdiction. Most boards are composed of members who are unpaid volunteers. They serve for a fixed term of years during which time the member cannot be removed except for cause. Some boards, like New York City's Civilian Complaint Review Board (CCRB), have multiple recommending entities: the mayor recommends five members, including the board chair; the City Council recommends five other members; and the police commissioner recommends three members (who should have law enforcement experience). The mayor has the power to make all official board appointments, providing him or her with an unchallengeable authority. Board members of the CCRB serve three-year terms and are paid per session, but some opt to serve pro bono.

The functions and responsibilities of oversight boards (and board members) varies significantly from jurisdiction to jurisdiction although all are limited in the scope of their ability to investigate police conduct, especially as it concerns the disciplining of individual officers. Some boards, such as New York City's CCRB, only are authorized to receive complaints from the public against police officers concerning limited types of allegations—those involving the "use of unnecessary or excessive force, abuse of authority, discourtesy, offensive language" (New York City Civilian Complaint Review Board 2014a).

Prior to 2012, if the CCRB substantiated a complaint and determined that an officer committed misconduct, then the case was sent to the NYPD, usually with a recommendation for disciplinary action. The CCRB only can investigate complaints and issue findings of misconduct, and—by law—only the police commissioner can decide on disciplinary action. Pursuant to a 2012 Memorandum of Understanding (MOU) between the NYPD and the CCRB, through its Administrative Prosecution Unit (APU) the CCRB now can bring substantiated cases before an administrative law judge or NYPD deputy commissioner for trials. If culpable, the officer could receive "a warning and admonishment, loss of vacation days, suspension without pay, a dismissal probation, or termination from the NYPD," but it is the police commissioner who decides the level of punishment (New York City Civilian Complaint Review Board 2014b).

To date, there does not exist in the United States a civilian police oversight board or agency that has the authority to fully prosecute officers that it has found to have engaged in police misconduct, and then have the determinations of the presiding judge or hearing officer be the actual discipline imposed. As with the CCRB in NYC, the legal authority and power to discipline the police lies with the department's chief executive officer.

Since its transition from an internal police department sub-unit to its current all-civilian, non-NYPD standing in 1993, New York City's Civilian Complaint Review Board has been criticized as lacking the adequate authority and resources to handle its caseload and impact on the levels of police misconduct. There have been numerous investigations into the New York City Police Department's interaction with civilian communities and the CCRB. Two reports in 1999—one by then–Public Advocate, Mark Green, and the other by then–Attorney General, Eliot Spitzer—were issued following up on allegations of police misconduct and abuses related to NYPD's stop, question, and frisk policy and practices. The Public Advocate's report found that only 2 percent of officers who had substantiated CCRB complaints were disciplined in 1996. More disturbingly, the report noted that in approximately 90 percent of the cases the NYPD failed to discipline officers—even after the CCRB concluded that there was sufficient evidence of misconduct—without offering an explanation to the CCRB, the victim, or the public as to why it reached the opposite conclusion (Green 1999). As part of the MOU, permitting the CCRB to litigate some of its substantiated investigations before an administrative law judge or Deputy Commissioner of Trials, the police commissioner is supposed to provide a written explanation for why he or she is not following the CCRB's recommended level of discipline or recommended penalty.

The 1999 New York Attorney General's report provided statistical data revealing stark disparities between the treatment of whites and persons of color in the implementation of the NYPD's **stop-and-frisk** tactics. The report contradicted the NYPD's reasoning that Latinas/os and African Americans are stopped and frisked at greater rates than other groups because they live in high–crime rate areas. In fact, after accounting for differences in crime rates found in various communities, the study showed that Latinas/os still were being stopped 39 percent more often than whites in the city across all crime categories (Spitzer 1999). As noted in the Public Advocate's report, the need for greater police oversight and accountability was a core theme.

In 2009, the Citizen's Union of New York, an independent, nonpartisan civic organization that promotes governmental reform in New York City and New York State, presented testimony on the 2007 Annual Report of the Civilian Complaint Review Board before the New York City Council Committee on Public Safety. Based on data that showed that complaints of police abuse remained high and disciplinary action appeared to be declining, the Citizen's Union recommended that prosecutorial powers be transferred to the CCRB so that it could adjudicate substantiated cases. The Citizen's Union also urged that the range of penalties available to the Police Commissioner be expanded; that a policy of zero tolerance for false statements under oath ("testalying") to the CCRB by police officers be restored; that CCRB be given the power to prosecute officers found guilty of lying during CCRB investigations; and that a permanent and more robust Commission to Combat Police Corruption be established. More recently, the Citizens Union has advocated for greater transparency and public accountability by the police commissioner whenever the CCRB's recommendations are not followed.

Notwithstanding the 2012 MOU that provided the CCRB with the ability to try substantiated cases through its Administrative Prosecution Unit, the controversy regarding the CCRB's effectiveness continue. The sustained use of chokeholds by NYPD officers has raised concerns about the CCRB's capacity to rein in this practice (which is prohibited under departmental rules). Although the CCRB substantiated nine complaints of illegal chokeholds occurring from 2009 to 2013, and recommended the toughest penalty in each case, in all but one of the cases the police commissioner—who has the final say regarding disciplinary action—failed to discipline the officers or levied the most lenient punishment (a review of the rules). The death of Eric Garner, an African American man, caused by an apparent chokehold has renewed concern about the CCRB's efficacy (Goodman 2014, A13).

The issue of police oversight and accountability often has taken center stage during election seasons. In 1965, New York City mayoral candidate John Lindsay ran on a platform that included adding civilians to the "panel" that reviewed complaints of police officers. Lindsay sought to spearhead reforms that his predecessor, Mayor Robert F. Wagner, Jr., was unable to realize. Lindsay's proposed reforms were bitterly opposed by the police unions. Historians note that although Mayor Wagner succeeded in creating a board that was seemingly more interested in civil liberties and community complaints than were past boards, little actually was done to address the problem of police misconduct and brutality (Cannato 2012, 156).

When running for the position of Public Advocate in 2009, then–New York City Councilman Bill de Blasio proposed legislation that would have further empowered the civilian oversight board. As mayor of New York City, Mayor de Blasio already has had to face the conundrum of how to address calls for increased police accountability without seeming to sacrifice public safety. The police involvement in the homicide of Eric Garner on Staten Island as well as the subsequent failure of the Staten Island District Attorney to get an indictment, followed soon thereafter by the seemingly random murder of two police officers by a deranged gunman in Brooklyn, brought all the relevant issues and parties to the fore in bright relief. The persistence and complexity of the issue—improved police oversight and accountability and assuring that public safety is maintained—is not unique to New York City.

The series of fatal police shootings of people of color since the death of 18-year-old Michael Brown in Ferguson, Missouri, has renewed attention to the issue of police misuse of deadly force, **racial profiling**, and civilian oversight of police officers. In jurisdictions with existing civilian review processes, discussions have ensued about strengthening the way police can be monitored and held accountable. In jurisdictions without civilian compliant boards, calls for establishing civilian review processes have become increasingly vocal.

History Citing the Need for Civilian Oversight Agencies in Jurisdictions with Large Latina/o Populations

Calls for respectful policing and police accountability developed over time in response to longstanding community concerns over police abuse, misconduct, and excessive use of force—commonly referred to as **police brutality**. Communities of color—particularly African American and Latina/o communities—have been the most vociferous about the need for civilian oversight of police. Among those adversely affected by policing abuse, Latinas/os in the United States historically have been active in the effort to establish civilian oversight agencies. The two largest groups of Latinas/os—**Mexicans**, who comprise 64.6 percent of the total U.S. Latina/o population, and **Puerto Ricans**, who comprise 9.5 percent of the total population of Latinas/os in the United States (Lopez, Gonzalez-Barrera, & Cuddington 2013, 3)—have an especially long history of encountering police abuse and of addressing the issue of police oversight and accountability. It should be noted that these two groups of Latinas/os experienced forms of direct colonization by the United States. Mexicans living on lands that presently comprise much of the western and southwestern United States lost many of their civil and political rights as well as their claims to land and property after the U.S. war with Mexico. The U.S.-Mexican War ended in 1848 and culminated in U.S. conquests of territories that were once part of the sovereign nation of Mexico. With the end of the U.S. war with Spain in 1898, Puerto Ricans also came under U.S. domination and authority with restriction of their civil and political rights.

Scholars and theorists have posited that in relation to U.S. law and dominant-subordinate group relations Mexicans, Puerto Ricans, and other Latinas/os in the United States resemble an internal colonized group. That is, Latinas/os have endured disadvantages in many spheres of U.S. society—including discrimination in housing, education, voting rights, and health care—that are analogous to that of peoples who live as colonial subjects. As in other aspects of life in the United States, Latinas/os have endured disadvantages in their interaction with and experience of the U.S. criminal justice system. More specifically, there is a long history of strained relations between Latina/o communities and law enforcement, based on the treatment that Latinas/os have received at the hands of police officers, and prompting numerous grievances and calls for police oversight and accountability over the years and into the present.

Civilian Oversight of Police and Latinas/os: A Brief History

In the 1920s and 1930s in Los Angeles, conflicts between the police and the Mexican community resulted in mounting outcries for justice. From 1926 to 1939, the number of Mexicans arrested by the Los Angeles Police Department (LAPD) increased by approximately 79 percent. Complaints of police misconduct against the Mexican Community rose during this time period, with sexual harassment, indiscriminate searches, verbal abuse, unwarranted arrests, and the use of excessive force among the forms of misconduct that most aggrieved the Mexican community (Escobar 1999, 134–35, 172).

Tensions between the Mexican community and the LAPD became especially acute in the early 1930s with the questionable suicide of **Juan Reyna**. Juan Reyna, who claimed to have fatally shot a police officer and wounded another out of self-defense while in police custody on May 11, 1930, was cleared of the most serious charges by a jury and found guilty of manslaughter and assault with a deadly weapon. While imprisoned in the San Quentin Correctional Facility, however, Reyna on May 2, 1931, was found dead in his cell, reportedly from a self-inflicted wound.

Many in the Mexican community of Los Angeles believed that Juan Reyna had been killed by someone in law enforcement. Through the investigative work of *La Opinion*, Los Angeles' largest Spanish-language newspaper, many discrepancies were uncovered. Questions were raised about the autopsy results, the removal of organs, the severity of the self-inflicted wound, Juan Reyna's character, and the suicide note that surfaced six days after his death. The incident electrified the Mexican community. Protests ensued, and there were demands for action by the *Partido Liberal Méxicano*, of which Reyna was a member, and the *Confederación de Uniones Obreras Mexicanas*. Reyna's funeral became a community event attended by more than 5,000 people. The calls for just investigations into the death of Juan Reyna were stymied, however, when San Quentin warden James Holohan ended the official inquiry, stating that there was no need for any further investigation.

In 1934, the LAPD successfully petitioned to amend the Los Angeles City Charter to give officers a vested right to their jobs and handed over total control of internal disciplinary procedures to the police department. The charter, as amended, also set in place a one-year statute of limitations on all claims of police misconduct. By 1938, the LAPD successfully gained control over all internal disciplinary actions. The lack of civilian oversight of the police served to further exacerbate tensions between the LAPD and the Mexican community.

The homicide of **José Díaz** on August 2, 1942, at the **Sleepy Lagoon** reservoir in Los Angeles would turn into an affair that would justify the LAPD's crackdown on young Mexican American men. Police were especially keen on targeting those who dressed in the flashy attire popular among Mexican American youth at the time and known as the "zoot suit." Following anti-Mexican hysteria perpetuated by William Randolph Hearst in the *Los Angeles Evening Herald Express* and the *Los Angeles Examiner*, public support for police action grew. In the aftermath of José Díaz's death, police arbitrarily rounded up numerous Mexican Americans, and the press sensationalized and stirred up public sentiment against Mexicans. Eventually, 24 young men, mostly of Mexican descent who had attended the party where Díaz was murdered, were arrested and indicted on charges of felony murder. In a trial characterized by gross misconduct, Los Angeles Superior Court Judge Charles Frickle forbade the defendants from changing their clothes or cutting their hair, ensuring that the young Mexican defendants would be publicly seen in the worst possible light. Of the 24 suspects, 17 were found guilty, 9 of them on murder charges.

The Sleepy Lagoon case helped reinforce within the law enforcement community and the news media the notion that Mexican youth posed an inherent and dangerous criminal threat to society. By contrast, that 17 Mexican youths were convicted without proof that they had even assaulted the deceased victim caused outrage in the Mexican American community, leading them to organize the Sleepy Lagoon Defense Committee that worked to bring to light the pervasiveness of anti-Mexican bias within the LAPD and the criminal justice system.

Growing tensions between the LAPD and the Mexican-American community stemming from the Sleepy Lagoon case set the stage for the **Zoot Suit Riots**. In June of 1943, altercations between Mexican Americans and U.S. sailors developed into a full-scale riot. With the tacit approval of the police, sailors marched into the Mexican *barrio* under the guise of pursuing young Mexican American men in zoot suits, which in the mind of these servicemen and law enforcement authorities represented clothing only worn by criminals. Police stood back as servicemen brutalized not only Mexicans in zoot suits but Mexican American males and females as well as an African American who happened to be in the area, and police only intervened to arrest or further abuse Mexicans.

Although the committee established by California Governor Earl Warren to investigate the Zoot Suit Riots called for all responsible parties to be held accountable and for improvements in police training, in particular, training regarding law enforcement in Mexican American communities, the committee's report essentially was disregarded. The idea that race played a role in the riots was categorically denied by Los Angeles Mayor Fletcher Bowron, dismissing concerns of Mexican Americans that police and the criminal justice system regularly functioned in a racially discriminatory manner towards their community.

Typecast as innately criminal, Mexican Americans continued to have strained relations with the police in Los Angeles and elsewhere. Public demands for civilian oversight and police accountability reemerged in the political organizing activities of the **Brown Berets** in the 1960s. A group of young Latinas/os known as the United Mexican American Students (UMAS) along with Latina/o high school students who had organized into the Young Citizens for Community Action (YCCA), chose to follow a militant political activist agenda similar to the Black Panthers and formed the Brown Berets. Grounded in dignity and pride for their Mexican ancestry, the Brown Berets sought to address the social, political, and economic inequities faced by the Mexican community, including unfair and discriminatory treatment by the police and by the criminal justice system. With respect to matters related to criminal justice, the Brown Berets' 1968 "Ten Point Program" not only demanded the creation of a Civilian Police Review Board it also called for a board completely composed of community residents who would screen officers before the officers were assigned to the community, and it stipulated that police officers must reside in the community and be able to speak Spanish. The use of excessive force by police (i.e., **police brutality**) was a paramount concern and a focal point for political activism and lawsuits for many decades.

Similar outcries for an end to police brutality and for racial justice in the criminal justice system were heard from Puerto Rican and Latina/o populations in a number of major U.S. cities. Founded in the late 1960s by young Puerto Ricans, the **Young Lords** organized a movement that was successful in publicizing the plight of Puerto Ricans in major U.S. cities, such as Chicago, Philadelphia, and New York City. As with the Brown Berets and Black Panthers, the Young Lords were dedicated to community organizing and activism around issues of social, political, and economic inequality and fairness. Ending police brutality against Puerto Ricans and communities of color was a major concern. To rein in police abuses, the Young Lords advocated for complete community control of the police, as found in point five of the group's 13-point Program and Platform.

Despite a long history of community activism, commission investigations, and lawsuits in pursuit of greater police accountability, the impact of police abuse and brutality on Latina/o and other communities of color has a long trajectory in cities such as New York (*see, e.g.*, Johnson 2003). In the face of mounting allegations of police corruption, New York City Mayor David Dinkins convened a commission in the early

1990s to be headed by former judge Milton Mollen to investigate. Over the course of two years, the Mollen Commission uncovered numerous instances of police misconduct and brutality, including **vigilantism**, the planting of guns on suspects, the use of lead-filled gloves to beat victims, and different forms of torture tactics, such as the application of ammonia on the face of a detainee. The hearings confirmed that Latina/o and African American communities were particularly vulnerable to police brutality. The hearings also brought to the public's attention the need for major institutional reforms to root out abuse and corruption.

In response to the Mollen Commission report, Walter Mack, a well-regarded civilian deputy commissioner of internal affairs, advocated for establishing a 24-hour special anti-brutality unit, but by 1995 Mack was forced out by Police Commissioner William Bratton, a move criticized by those calling for heightened police oversight. After ending their work, some Mollen Commission staff members voiced concerns about a return to the status quo ante, as had occurred following the famous Knapp Commission corruption hearings of the early 1970s, which also found corruption deeply entrenched in the NYPD. Concerns that police misconduct would reemerge were justified, as cases of police brutality and abuse directed at Latinas/os and communities of color across the country have recurred.

Cases of "Driving While Black" or "**Driving While Brown**"—referring to African Americans or Latinas/os who are subject to racial profiling by law enforcement officers while in an automobile—also have prompted demands for police oversight and accountability. One such case that attracted national attention involved New Jersey state troopers John Hogan and James Kenna. The troopers stopped a van driven by an African American male, age 20, and his three passengers—two African American males and one Latino male—on April 23, 1998, allegedly for speeding while driving through Gloucester County on the New Jersey Turnpike. After further investigation of the incident, it was revealed that troopers Hogan and Kenna were not equipped with radar on the day of the incident, although the officers' report stated that their radar detected speeding. Additionally, the accounts of Juan Polk, a witness to the incident, did not coincide with the state troopers' account. During the stop three of the young men were shot. One of them, Danny Reyes, was shot four times and subsequently was hospitalized and in critical condition. The ensuing civil case against the New Jersey state troopers resulted in a $12.95 million settlement for the four men. As part of the settlement, New Jersey Attorney General John J. Farmer, Jr. also dismissed the charges against 128 other defendants who claimed their arrests had been racially motivated and, in a stunning move, reinstated criminal charges against state troopers John Hogan and James Kenna that had been dropped in a lower court.

Over time, incessant and blatant examples of police misconduct and excessive use of force—particularly by white police officers against members of other racial, ethnic, or national-origin groups—have reinforced ongoing suspicions and stirred allegations of a lack of police accountability. For communities of color who have borne the brunt of tough policing policies and practices in New York City, the numerous atrocities promoted and justified under various theories and tactics—most notably "broken-windows," "zero tolerance," and "quality of life"—have left an indelible mark on those communities and have sparked many protests and calls for justice. Among the most notorious historical examples of police brutality committed against persons of color are the 1994 police chokehold killing of **Anthony Báez**; the 1995 shooting death of a 16-year-old Chinese youth, Yong Xin Huang; the brutal torture and sodomizing of Haitian immigrant Abner Louima in a Brooklyn police precinct in 1997; the 1999 death of African immigrant Amadou Diallo, killed in a hailstorm of 41 bullets fired by NYPD officers; the police shooting of African American Sean Bell in 2006, and the death of Honduran immigrant **Fermin Arzu**, who was shot by police in 2007.

As has been demonstrated in New York, Latinas/os and other communities of color in cities throughout the United States also have experienced their share of police abuse and brutality. These experiences have prompted efforts to strengthen oversight of the police and enhance access to remedies to address massive civil rights violations suffered by victims. The Los Angeles Police Department's **Rampart Scandal** of the late 1990s, for instance, which implicated police officers in illegal drug activity, brutality, and the planting of evidence to cover up their crimes, among other serious violations of the law, led to an examination of the operations of the LAPD. The Los Angeles Board of Inquiry Report concluded that the department's internal review process of police misconduct was meaningless, justifying the need for civilian oversight of the LAPD. In the aftermath of the Rampart Scandal, in which more than 100 criminal convictions were overturned and more than a dozen officers were either reassigned or terminated, the city of Los Angeles settled the outstanding cases for approximately $70 million.

The Rampart Scandal represented an almost complete breakdown of relations between the Latina/o community and the police. Countless numbers of Latinos were framed and physically brutalized as part of the police scheme to profit from illicit drug dealing and other illegal activities. To restore confidence in law enforcement, greater police transparency and accountability as well as civilian control and supervision was demanded. As in many other similar cases around the country, a foremost concern for communities has been the issue of impunity—that is, the inability to hold police officers accountable for violence and misconduct. Thus, calls for enhanced civilian and community oversight of local policing typically have been accompanied by recommendations for a community voice, if not control, over when and how police are disciplined.

In recent years, aggressive police policies and practices—including **stop-and-frisk** tactics—have eroded confidence in the police, particularly in communities of color, and have sparked protests and demands for improved oversight and accountability. With the succession of deaths of persons of color at the hands of police in recent years, the issue of civilian oversight of police not only has been revived it is more likely than not to remain an issue for Latina/o and African American communities well into the foreseeable future.

See also: Part I essays: Latinas/os and the U.S. Criminal Justice System; Policing and Latina/o Communities; Latinas and the U.S. Criminal Justice System. Part II entry: Civil Rights.

Further Reading

Acuña, Rodolfo. 2011. *Occupied America: A history of Chicanos*. 7th ed. New York: Longman.

Amnesty International. 1998. *United States of America: Rights for all*. New York: Amnesty International Publications.

Blauner, Robert. 1972. *Racial oppression in America*. New York: Harper & Row.

Broder, John. 2005 (April 1). Los Angeles paying victims $70 million for police graft. *New York Times*.

Cannato, Vincent. 2002. *The ungovernable city.* New York: Basic Books.

Citizens Union of the City of New York. 2009. Testimony of Citizens Union of the City of New York on the 2007 annual report of the Civilian Complaint Review Board before the New York City Council Committee on Public Safety, January 29, 2009. http://www.citizensunion.org/www/cu/site/hosting/Testimony/1_29_09_CCRB_Hearing_Testimony.pdf.

Cruz, Wil. 2009 (August 4). Watchdog agency that oversees NYPD has no bite, officials say. *Daily News.* http://www.nydailynews.com/news/crime/watchdog-agency-oversees-nypd-bite-officials-article-1.398307#ixzz0TKCnWFBj.

Delgado, Richard, Juan F. Perea, and Jean Stefancic (eds.). 2008. *Latinos and the law: Case and materials.* St. Paul: Thomson West.

Democracy Now. 2009. "Influential Puerto Rican activist group the Young Lords marks 40th anniversary" (transcript), broadcast aired August 21, 2009. http://www.democracynow.org/2009/8/21/young_lords.

Escobar, Edward J. 1999. *Race, police, and the making of a political identity: Mexican Americans and the Los Angeles Police Department, 1900–1945.* Los Angeles: University of California Press.

Fernandez, Manny. 2007 (May 27). Remembrance, and protest, for a man slain by an officer. *New York Times.*

Goldstein, Joseph, and J. David Goodman. 2014 (April 15). A London guide for 1 Police Plaza. *New York Times.* http://www.nytimes.com/2014/04/16/nyregion/a-london-guide-for-1-police-plaza.html?_r=0.

Gonzales, Manuel. 2009. *Mexicanos: A history of Mexicans in the United States*, 2nd ed. Bloomington, IN: Indiana University Press.

Goodman, J. David. 2014 (July 21). In 9 cases of police chokeholds, punishment was rare, review board says. *New York Times.*

Green, Mark. 1999. *Investigation of the New York City Police Department's response to civilian complains of police misconduct: Interim report.* New York: Office of the Public Advocate.

Haney-López, Ian F. 2003. *Racism on trial: The Chicano fight for justice.* Cambridge, MA: Belknap/Harvard University Press.

Human Rights Watch. 1998. *Shielded from justice: Police brutality and accountability in the United States.* New York: Human Rights Watch.

Johnson, Marilynn S. 2003. *Street justice: A history of police violence in New York City.* Boston: Beacon Press.

Kifner, John, and David M. Herszenhorn. 1998 (May 8). Racial "profiling" at crux of inquiry into shooting by troopers. *New York Times.*

Krauss, Clifford. 1994 (July 23). Mollen Commission ends, but life goes on for staff. *New York Times.*

Krauss, Clifford. 1995 (January 29). Bratton assailed on ouster of top official. *New York Times.*

Lopez, Mark Hugo, Ana Gonzalez-Barrera, and Danielle Cuddington. 2013. *Diverse origins: The nation's 14 largest Hispanic-origin groups.* Washington, DC: Pew Hispanic Center.

Los Angeles Police. [n.d.]. The function and role of the Board of Police Commissioners. http://www.lapdonline.org/police_commission/content_basic_view/900. November 12, 2015.

Mathis, Joel. 2014a (July 30). Update: Philly cops charged with robbing, extorting drug dealers. http://www.phillymag.com/news/2014/07/30/report-six-philly-cops-arrested-feds-mug-shots/. November 12, 2015.

Mathis, Joel. 2014b (July 31). Committee of seventy calls for police oversight board. *Philadelphia.* http://www.phillymag.com/news/2014/07/31/committee-seventy-calls-police-oversight-board/. November 12, 2015.

McArdle, Andrea, and Tanya Erzen (eds.). 2001. *Zero tolerance: Quality of life and the new police brutality in New York City.* New York: New York University Press.

Morín, José Luis. 2009. *Latino/a rights and justice in the United States: Perspectives and approaches,* 2nd ed. Durham, NC: Carolina Academic Press.

National Association for Civilian Oversight of Law Enforcement. 2014. Oversight agencies; Tucson, AZ. NACOLE. http://nacole.org/.

New York City Civilian Complaint Review Board. 2014a. About CCRB. http://www.nyc.gov/html/ccrb/html/about/about.shtml. November 12, 2015.

New York City Civilian Complaint Review Board. 2014b. APU and police discipline http://www.nyc.gov/html/ccrb/html/police/police.shtml. November 12, 2015.

New York City Civilian Complaint Review Board. 2014c. The Board. http://www.nyc.gov/html/ccrb/html/about/board.shtml. November 12, 2015.

New York Times. 2014 (April 15). Sir Robert Peel's nine principles of policing. http://www.nytimes.com/2014/04/16/nyregion/sir-robert-peels-nine-principles-of-policing.html?_r=0. November 12, 2015.

Pagán, Eduardo Obregón. 2003. *Murder at the Sleepy Lagoon: Zoot suits, race, and riot in wartime L.A.* Chapel Hill, NC: University of North Carolina Press.

Pérez-Peña, Richard. 2015 (April 8). Fatal police shootings: Accounts since Ferguson. *New York Times*. http://www.nytimes.com/interactive/2015/04/08/us/fatal-police-shooting-accounts.html.

Peterson, Iver, and David M. Halbfinger. 2001 (February 3). New Jersey agrees to pay $13 million in profiling suit. *New York Times*.

Rosales, F. Arturo. 1999. *¡Pobre raza! Violence, justice, and mobilization among México lindo immigrants, 1900–1936.* Austin, TX: University of Texas Press.

Sanchez, George J. 1995. *Becoming Mexican American: Ethnicity, culture, and identity in Chicano Los Angeles, 1900–1945.* New York: Oxford University Press.

Spitzer, Eliot. 1999. *The New York City Police Department's "stop and frisk" practices: A report to the people of the State of New York from the Attorney General.* New York: Civil Rights Bureau.

The Sixties Project. 1993. "Young Lords Party 13-point program and platform." Charlottesville, VA: Institute of Advanced Technology in the Humanities at the University of Virginia. http://www2.iath.virginia.edu/sixties/HTML_docs/Resources/Primary/Manifestos/Young_Lords_platform.html.

Urbina, Martin G. 2003. *Capital punishment and Latino offenders: Racial and ethnic differences in death sentences.* New York: LFB Scholarly Publishing.

Urbina, Martin G. (ed.). 2012. *Hispanics in the U.S. criminal justice system: The new American demography.* Springfield, IL: Charles C. Thomas.

Walker, Samuel. 2005. *The new world of police accountability.* Thousand Oaks, CA: Sage Publications.

Witkin, Richard. 1965 (May 21). Lindsay proposes adding civilians to police board. *New York Times*.

Cases Cited

Floyd et al. v. City of New York, 959 F. Supp. 2d 540 (S.D.N.Y. 2013).

Code of Silence. *See* Part I essay: Policing and Latina/o Communities.

Colombians

Hernando A. Estévez

Four significant conditions characterize Colombian communities' understanding of the criminal justice system in the United States: immigration, "the **war on drugs**," extradition, and **racial/ethnic profiling**. These conditions not only reveal the basis upon which Colombian communities relate to the United

States criminal justice system, but they also help explain the way the United States criminal justice system perceives Colombian communities.

Colombians and Immigration

An estimated 989,000 persons of Colombian origin—immigrants from Colombia or persons who trace their ancestry to Colombia—live in the United States. As such, they constitute the seventh-largest Latina/o group in the country, as compared to Mexicans, who make up the single largest group of Latinas/os with a population of 33.5 million (Lopez, Gonzalez-Barrera, & Cuddington 2013). Overall, 69.5 percent of persons of Colombian origin are U.S. citizens by birth or naturalization (Pew Hispanic Center 2011).

An undeclared war comprising paramilitarism, drug-related **violence**, economic instability, considerable guerrilla activity, and widespread corruption in the Colombian government has caused tens of thousands of Colombian citizens to flee rural areas. Many of these rural residents are relocating to small cities or to the margins of Colombia's most industrialized cities. Others are escaping to neighboring countries, and some wealthy Colombians are immigrating to the United States. Major motives for immigrating to the United States include fear of the general violence in Colombia, a sense of feeling protected in the United States, and prospects of economic opportunities.

Colombian immigration to the United States falls into four periods. The first wave of "traditional immigrants" was from 1918 to 1948. The years after World War I marked the first entry of a small number of highly qualified Colombian professionals. Most of them were students attending universities in the United States who decided to stay after completing their studies, along with other professionals with some technical education who arrived legally and eventually became permanent residents and citizens. This first wave of immigrants is considered traditional because their experiences and motives for traveling to the United States are similar to those of European immigrants.

The second wave was incited by a period of civil conflict between traditional Colombian political parties—Conservative and Liberal—known as "La Violencia" (1948 to 1958). Armed insurrection, as well as some guerrilla presence in rural areas, precipitated the immigration of people from the lower and lower-middle classes seeking better and safer living conditions and economic opportunities. The third wave began in the 1970s and continued until the late 1990s. Colombians who left during this period mainly were escaping economic crisis and increasing drug-related violence, as well as other security threats. They came to the United States in search of economic prosperity and professional opportunities, but many also were "risk takers" looking for adventure.

The second and third waves of immigration to the United States mentioned above occurred while the Act of Immigration of 1965 was in place, which eased immigration requirements. The fourth wave of Colombian immigration began in the late 1990s and continues to the present. This latest wave is characterized by an increase in the number of upper–middle-class and upper-class professionals and entrepreneurs seeking to escape violence, extortion, kidnapping, and murder by paramilitary groups and guerrillas, as well as government security forces. Unique to the third and fourth waves of immigration was the increased presence of Colombians associated with the **drug** trade and drug consumption throughout the United States. This trend has resulted in the negative stereotyping of all Colombians as drug producers and **traffickers** and the emergence of discrimination on racial and ethnic grounds. This stereotyping adversely affects other Colombians looking to immigrate and skews the decisions made about Colombians during criminal justice processes.

Colombians often are more likely than other Latinas/os to be stopped and searched by immigration officers when other prejudices based on nationality, age, gender, and behavior that could create suspicion of trafficking drugs are taken into account. The development of this stereotype about Colombians has been the result of the mass production and distribution of illegal drugs by criminal organizations—cartels—in Colombia, whose primary purpose is the promotion and control of drug trafficking routes and operations. The Medellin and Cali cartels grew in response to a worldwide demand for drugs during the 1960s and 1970s which, in turn, produced a new social and economic class that influenced most aspects of both civil and political Colombian life. Although laws prohibiting and prosecuting drug activities ranging from production to consumption were implemented in Colombia as well as in the United States and Europe, the impact of the significant scale of production and processing as well as trafficking already had created negative effects in society at large. Even if these stereotypes only have a material influence in the process of immigration to the United States, being Colombian might call up different standards of interrogation, process, and judgment in the legal system.

Colombians and the "War on Drugs"

The phrase "drug war" refers specifically to those policies and actions that are characterized by the U.S. approach to drug control aimed at eradicating the production and supply, distribution, and consumption of illegal drugs from source countries. For countries in Latin America—such as Bolivia, Colombia, and Peru—the metaphorical "**war on drugs**" became a battlefield that required training civilian forces in military operations and strategies. By the mid-1990s, Colombia became the world's largest producer of cocaine and a major producer of opium poppies. As a result, the U.S. public generally associates Colombia—more than any other country in the region—with the '"war on drugs."

In the mid-1980s, the increase of drug-related violence in the United States propelled U.S. drug-control policies that are still in effect today. President Ronald Reagan first declared illicit drugs a national security threat. Later, President George H. W. Bush responded to the threat of drugs with the Andean Counterdrug Initiative and intensified the drug war. The presumption of this initiative is that reducing the production and supply of drugs will result in higher trading costs and ultimately discourage the buying and, consequently, the use of illicit drugs. The aim of the Andean Counterdrug Initiative was to empower Latin American **police** and military to carry out counter-drug initiatives and, most importantly, to target the primary links of the grower-to-user chain: cultivation, processing, and transit.

Since the Andean Counterdrug Initiative was launched in 1989, its effectiveness is questionable precisely because of the flaws endemic to a supply-demand approach to the war on drugs and the lack of attention to the extreme poverty in the region and the weak civilian institutions in charge of societal problems. By 2000, Colombia supplied an estimated 80 percent of the cocaine consumed in the United States. The war on drugs, however, suggests that the U.S. drug-control agencies as well as the criminal justice system must take into consideration the complex social and economic roots of illegal drug production, consumption, and trading. In that sense, the U.S. criminal justice system has developed a joint effort focused on both the prevention and criminalization of **drug use** and production.

The United States Drug Enforcement Administration (DEA) has sought to reduce the supply of drugs by limiting drug production and confiscating shipments en route. The Colombian and United States governments have developed both internal and international policies and strategies to control, criminalize, and reduce the production, trade, and consumption of illicit drugs. Among these tactics, the extradition treaty and Plan Colombia are considered to be the most effective. These programs were developed in conjunction with U.S. policy on drug control, the DEA, the U.S. criminal justice system, and the Colombian government, military, and police institutions.

Colombians and Extradition

Extradition, the legal process by which a state hands over an accused or convicted person to the authorities of another country, has been touted as an essential judicial tool of the U.S. criminal justice system to ensure a victory in the war on drugs. The administration of President Jimmy Carter (1977–1981) urged Colombian authorities to eliminate the cultivation and production of illegal drugs and to pursue drug traffickers within a criminal law enforcement that included extradition of Colombian traffickers to the United States. Although the implementation and use of extradition between Colombia and the United States is controversial because of its lack of success in reducing drug production and trafficking, its impact on the relations between the U.S. criminal justice system and the Colombian government has been to shift decisively toward a more aggressive approach to the war on drugs. Extradition agreements have undergone a series of stages. In 1979, Colombian President Julio Cesar Turbay (1978–1981) signed an extradition treaty with the United States government that went into effect in 1982. Although by February 1990 more than 14 extraditions had taken place, they had no effect in reducing either drug production or drug trafficking. In 1991, Colombia adopted a new constitution stating extradition was prohibited.

During the 1990s the United States implemented a new legal procedure by which countries would be recognized or certified as cooperators in the war on drugs. This procedure would associate or certify countries and their political leaders and officially recognize their commitment to the United States government and its policies on drug control. During the presidency of Cesar Gaviria (1990–1994), the Colombian Congress ratified a proposal in which traffickers who turned themselves in and confessed to a crime would be spared extradition. The year 1996 marked a crisis in United States–Colombian relations due to allegations that drug cartels had financed the presidency of Ernesto Samper (1994–1998). The United States canceled Samper's visa and decertified Colombia for neglecting cooperation in drug control. A year later, however, in seeking to improve diplomatic relations with the United States, the Colombian Congress amended the 1991 constitution to restore the extradition treaty. By the end of 1996, Colombia became the primary beneficiary of counter-drug aid from the United States. Andres Pastrana was elected president in 1998 on a political campaign that pledged total control over the drug trade and a peace treaty with guerrilla movements. Pastrana's administration designed Plan Colombia, a plan to not only considerably reduce coca production by aerial eradication, but to invest in social capital, infrastructure, and productive projects.

Although the original Plan Colombia did not include counterinsurgency and military aid, in July 2000 the U.S. Congress approved a special supplement of $1.3 billion for the initiative, shifting the focus of the plan to more military and police enforcement by the training and formation of a Counternarcotics Brigade within the Colombian army. Plan Colombia continues to be widely used to refer to the U.S. aid package to Colombia, but its aim is to support the Andean Counterdrug Initiative and to assist neighboring countries. The events of September 11, 2001, and the beginning of the war on **terrorism** facilitated this shift of Plan Colombia by expanding its goals. Former Colombian president Alvaro Uribe (2002–2010) embraced the language and logic of counterterrorism, making Plan Colombia a strategy for achieving national security. However, the institutional and judicial system has not fully overcome the legacy of military autonomy and impunity. Colombia's government and the U.S. criminal justice system continue to use extradition as part of Plan Colombia's initiative in the war on drugs and on the war on terrorism. Currently, the Colombian government not only extradites drug lords, but also criminals associated with the trade and production of illicit drugs, paramilitaries, and guerrilla fighters.

Colombians and Racial/Ethnic Profiling

The experience of Colombians in the United States has been affected by the stereotypes created as a result of the war on drugs, the desire and need to immigrate to the United States, and the history of illicit drug production and trade. These events have considerably shaped the perception of Colombians within the U.S. criminal justice system. In the 1980s, the Drug Enforcement Administration (DEA) and customs agents elaborated and advanced profiles of individuals belonging to U.S. national and international distribution networks by observing how drugs moved out of source countries and through borders. The DEA instructed state and local police to look for a variety of physical and behavioral characteristics making race and—in the case of Colombians—nationality part of the equation. Although all Latinas/os are subject to ethnic and **racial profiling** as developed by the U.S. criminal justice system, Colombians continue to be prone to searches in airports both when leaving Colombia and arriving in other countries.

The direct impact of the "war on drugs" on Colombians is seen in what has been called "the **drug-courier profile**." This specific form of racial and ethnic profiling not only contributes to guiding U.S. law enforcement officials in deciding who to target, it also relies on the officer's limited experience, which in turn reinforces the use of stereotypes when dealing with Colombians. Although federal drug law enforcement agents in the DEA and state and local police departments regularly deny the direct use of ethnic and racial profiling, extensive evidence shows that its use is a common practice, especially when training police officers and federal agents. "Operation Pipeline," in fact, was controversial and well-known for identifying particular groups of people based on their age, ethnic groups, and race in conducting stops, frisks, and arrests. As "the war on drugs" has unfolded, to be Colombian became the "racial" characteristic that give rise to a set of unsubstantiated assertions—assertions that imply connection to illegal drug-related activity. Profiling of this type has prompted decisions at different stages of the U.S. criminal justice process that, in turn, increased the probability of misguided and biased judgments based on stereotypes. Relying on racial and national characteristics in making law enforcement and judicial decisions can undermine constitutional rights. In the case of Colombians, racial and ethnic profiling combined with a history of immigration to the United States have rendered them vulnerable to the questionable practices and policies within law enforcement and the criminal justice system.

See also: Part I essays: The U.S. War on Drugs and Latina/o Communities; Incarceration and Latinas/os in the United States. Part II entry: Media Depictions.

Further Reading

Anderson, Benedict. 1983. *Imagined communities*. London: Verso Press.

Bergquist, Charles, Ricardo Peñaranda, and Gonzalo Sánchez (eds.). 2001. *Violence in Colombia, 1990–2000: Waging war and negotiating peace*. Wilmington, DE: Scholarly Resources Books.

Caulkins, Jonathan P. 2005. *How goes the War on Drugs: An assessment of U.S. drug problems and policy*. Santa Monica, CA: RAND Corporation.

Cole, David. 1999. *No equal justice: Race and class in the American criminal justice system*. New York, NY: The New Press.

Crandall, Russell. 2002. *Driven by drugs. U.S. policy toward Colombia*. London: Lynne Rienner Publishers.

Harris, David A. 2002. *Profiles in injustice: Why racial profiling cannot work*. New York, NY: New Press.

Livingstone, Grace. 2004. *Inside Colombia: Drugs, democracy, and war*. Piscataway, NJ: Rutgers University Press.

Lopez, Mark Hugo, Ana Gonzalez-Barrera, and Danielle Cuddington. 2013. Diverse origins: The Nation's 14 largest Hispanic-origin groups. Washington, DC: Pew Research Center/Hispanic Trends. http://www.pewhispanic.org/2013/06/19/diverse-origins-the-nations-14-largest-hispanic-origin-groups/.

Pew Hispanic Center. 2010. Fact sheet: Hispanics of Colombian origin in the United States. http://pewhispanic.org/files/factsheets/64.pdf.

Pew Hispanic Center. 2011. Country of origin profiles. http://pewhispanic.org/data/origins.

Portes, Alejandro, Luis E. Guarnizo, and Patricia Landolt. 1999. The study of transnationalism: Pitfalls and promise of an emergent research field. *Ethnic and Racial Studies* 22(2): 217–37.

Thoumi, Francisco. 1995. *The political economy and illegal drugs in Colombia*. Boulder, CO: Lynne Rienner Press.

Weitzer, Ronald, and Steven Tuch. 2006. *Race and policing in America: Conflict and reform*. New York, NY: Cambridge University Press.

Community-Based Latina/o Advocacy Organizations

Rosa Maria Gonzalez-Guarda

A community-based organization (CBO) is a type of non-governmental, non-for-profit organization composed of a group of people that come together to accomplish a common goal relating to the well-being of a particular community of interest (Duke University Libraries [n.d.]). Community-based organizations provide advocacy, legal representation, and other social and health services to communities composed of individuals who share a common characteristic such as a racial/ethnic identity, culture, neighborhood, shared interest, or need. Such organizations usually are created when members of a community identify a pressing need that is not adequately being addressed by the current array of existing community resources. In this way, CBOs are driven by the needs, talents, and resources of the communities they are designed to target (i.e., grassroots). They also usually are directed by members of the targeted community, often with the support of other agencies and organizations, businesses, and community leaders (e.g., community activists, political leaders). As they address important needs and interests, CBOs often become major advocates for their members and clients, as well as the general communities they represent. The focus of this entry is on CBOs that provide advocacy for Latina/o communities. Legal advocacy organizations are described in another section (*see* **Legal Advocacy Groups**).

Latina/o CBOs and advocacy groups in the U.S. began to emerge in the late 1800s after the Civil War, when Mexicans began moving into Texas and New Mexico in greater numbers and large waves of Anglo-American farmers settled in areas of Texas that previously were inhabited by Mexicans. During this time, Anglo-Mexican relations became increasingly antagonistic as the Mexican elite in Texas lost power and the Mexican working class was exploited. In response to concerns regarding segregation, racism, and economic and educational inequities, Mexicans began to develop community-based mutual aid groups which they called *mutualistas*. The primary focus of *mutualistas* was to provide health care, education, legal representation, advocacy, and a cultural refuge for Mexican immigrants and Mexican Americans in the United States. Additional CBOs and advocacy groups emerged in the early 1900s as Mexicans began to comprise a larger segment of the working-class in the Southwest region of the United States. To respond to the exploitation experienced by the Mexican working class and the failure of current labor unions to include Mexicans in their efforts, Mexican labor unions, farmworker organizations, and additional *mutualistas* were formed.

Immigration of Mexicans to other areas of the United States (e.g., the Midwest), the Great Depression, and World War II inflamed racism towards Mexicans during the first half of the 20th century as Euro-Americans aimed to push them out of the labor market. To respond to the **civil rights** struggles of both foreign-born and U.S.-born Mexicans, more formalized CBOs and national advocacy organizations emerged, such as the **League of United Latin American Citizens (LULAC)**, developed to represent middle-class Mexican Americans, and the American G.I. Forum, developed to address the discrimination encountered by Latina/o servicemen. Today LULAC is the oldest Latino organization in the United States and implements 700 community-based educational, economic, health, political, and civil rights programs throughout the United States. In implementing these, LULAC spends more than one million dollars a year to provide scholarships to Latino students, develop low-income housing and leadership programs at the community level, encourage citizen and voter registration, and empower Latinos to serve as leaders at the national level.

Additional CBOs and advocacy organizations at the local and national level were formed in the latter portion of the 20th century in response to the needs that were uncovered by Latina/o communities during the Civil Rights and Chicano Movements of the 1960s. These included organizations that provided legal advocacy, political representation, and social programs for Latinas/os. For example, the **National Council of La Raza (NCLR)** emerged during this period as a result of a need for Mexican Americans, Puerto Ricans, and other Latinas/os to come together as a unified voice, gain national visibility, and fight for their civil rights. Today the NCLR is the largest civil rights and advocacy national organization for Latinos in the United States. Through NCLR's network of approximately 300 CBOs, educational, employment, economic, health, and legal opportunities are provided for Latinas/os throughout the nation.

Other politically and socially active Latina/o groups also emerged through grassroots efforts to represent the specific needs and interest of Latina/o subgroups. For example, the **Brown Berets** (composed of Mexican Americans) and the **Young Lords** (composed of Puerto Ricans) were formed during the 1960s and 1970s to address the lack of political representation of their communities and important issues such as police harassment, inadequate housing, unemployment, and unequal opportunities for education, health care, and employment that were specific to the communities and *barrios* of the sub-groups. The National Farmwork Association (NFWA), which later became the United Farmworker Union, also emerged during this period to champion the rights of migrant and farm workers. Legal advocacy also emerged at the national level to represent the specific needs of Latina/o subgroups. The most notable of these included the **Mexican American Legal Defense and Education Fund** (MALDEF) and the **Puerto Rican Legal Defense and Education Fund** (PRLDEF) (now LatinoJustice PRLDEF). Groups such as ASPIRA also were organized at the national and local levels to address the educational and cultural needs of Latina/o youth and to encourage their empowerment.

Today there continues to be a plethora of CBOs and advocacy organizations serving the needs and interests of Latinas/os in the United States, some which still exist from the early 1900s and others which recently have been created to address new and emerging issues for Latinas/os. Many of the newer CBOs and advocacy groups were created to address pressing criminal justice issues affecting the Latina/o population, such as **gang** violence. For example, **Homies Unidos** and Homeboy Industries, two CBOs that primarily focus on the prevention of gang violence among Latinas/os in Los Angeles, have received national recognition for the important work they are doing to create peace in high-crime neighborhoods. These programs provide placement for youth looking for a way out of gang life, mediation between gang members, case management, legal services, tattoo removal, twelve-step meetings, and prison-to-community transition.

Another example of a CBO that has received national attention is the Chicago Project and CeaseFire. This program is housed under the School of Public Health at the University of Chicago and includes a partnership between various community-based organizations and government agencies. The major goal of CeaseFire is to prevent and reduce violence in the city through conflict mediation between gangs, and to promote alternatives to violence. Community outreach workers, faith leaders, and other community members play an important role in accomplishing this. A study funded by the U.S. Department of Justice documented significant reductions in shootings and killings in areas in Chicago that were targeted by the organization.

As can be noted by examining the context in which CBOs and advocacy groups focusing on Latina/o issues have emerged and the needs they address, it is clear that they have played—and continue to play—a vital role in addressing the needs of vulnerable and marginalized communities. Latinos in the United States are one of the most vulnerable of these groups, as they face a host of barriers that impede them from accessing quality and equitable social services from governmental agencies, academic institutions, and private organizations and businesses. Among the most noted of these barriers are the lack of linguistically and **culturally competent** services, economic barriers, legal barriers (especially among non-documented Latinos), and a general sense of mistrust among Latinos towards organizations and institutions, especially the criminal justice system.

In 2002, the groundbreaking report, *Donde esta la justicia? A call to action on behalf of Latino and Latina youth in the U.S. justice system*, documented systematic biases in the criminal justice system that result in the overrepresentation of Latinas/os in jails and prisons (e.g., harsher sentencing as compared to whites, ethnic stereotypes related to gang membership), the lack of bilingual services and cultural competency among criminal justice personnel, and policies that promote harsher consequences among Latinas/os (e.g., immigration and anti-gang laws). In this report, the organization of local communities and grassroots efforts, the expansion of community-based programs for at-risk youth, and the creation of Latino advocacy groups to guide policy all were identified as being essential in addressing the injustice that Latinas/os experience in the U.S. criminal justice system. Key Latina/o CBOs and advocacy groups were identified in the report as potential resources and agents of change to help eliminate these injustices. The groups that were mentioned include:

- ASPIRA Association,
- Chicano/Latino Youth Leadership Project,
- Hispanic Federation,
- Hispanic National Bar Association (HNBA),
- JobLatino, Latino Issues Forum,
- Latino Social Workers Organization (LSWO),
- League of United Latin American Citizens (LULAC),
- Mexican American Legal Defense and Education Fund (MALDEF),
- National Alliance for Hispanic Health,
- National Association for the Advancement of Hispanic People (NAAHP),
- National Community for Latino Leadership, Inc. (NCLL),
- National Hispanic Institute,
- National Latino Children's Institute,
- National Council of La Raza (NCLR),
- Prison Moratorium Project (PMP), and
- Puerto Rican Legal Defense and Education Fund (PRLDEF), now known as Latino Justice PRLDEF.

The criminal justice system increasingly is encouraged to partner with CBOs, advocacy groups, and other community organizations (e.g., faith-based organizations) to prevent and reduce crimes within high-risk communities. The Centers for Disease Control and Prevention (2001) has identified various important factors that can be utilized to support these partnerships. First, collaborating parties must recognize that many of the issues (e.g., drug abuse, violence) that they will be addressing together cut across sectors, disciplines, professions, and foci. In the case of partnerships between health focused CBOs and the criminal justice system, for example, the focus could vary from public health to public safety issues. Nevertheless, participant organizations must recognize that their areas of concern have tremendous overlap. In addition to being able to recognize commonalities, participating collaborators also must be aware of each other's cultures, approaches, and expertise, and be able to navigate within these different worlds. For example, CBOs must be aware that the primary role and expertise of the criminal justice system is control and security. Therefore, the programs developed in these settings must be able to be run within these more "controlled" settings.

Similarly, the criminal justice system also must be aware of the expertise that CBOs have in working closely with communities and having access to hard-to-reach populations. Programs implemented in these settings that include the criminal justice system must be able to work in a less-controlling and more trusting environment. Another important factor identified by the CDC (2001) is the importance of CBOs and criminal justice systems to recognize that that the issues being addressed are complex and thus require a great deal of dedicated time and effort.

Controversial police practices and deaths at the hands of law enforcement officers in recent years have given rise to many community-based groups interested in educating, organizing, and mobilizing communities of color. In New York City, for example, the **Justice Committee**—an organization spearheaded by Latinas/os—has been actively engaged in education, leadership development, and movement building around the issue of police violence and racial justice. As tensions between police/policing and communities of color persist, it is likely that organizations such as the Justice Committee will develop in Latina/o communities around the country.

See also: Part I essays: Latinas/os and the U.S. Criminal Justice System; Policing and Latina/o Communities. Part II entries: Chicanas/os; Civil Rights; Hate Crimes; Legal Advocacy Groups; Political Activist Groups.

Further Reading

Acuña, Rodolfo F. 1988. *Occupied America: A history of Chicanos,* 3rd ed. Philadelphia, PA: Harper & Row Publishers.

American Public Health Association (APHA). 2005. "Community based organizations." http://depts.washington.edu/ccph/pdf_files/NCBONFactSheet%2010-2805%5B1%5D_docupdated.pdf.

ASPIRA. 2013. Our history. http://www.aspira.org/manuals/our-history. Accessed October 22, 2015.

CeaseFire. 2009. "CeaseFire is an evidence-based approach to reducing violence." http://www.ceasefirechicago.org/.

Centers for Disease Control and Prevention, CDC. 2001. Working with the criminal justice system. http://www.cdc.gov/idu/facts/cj-workingwith.pdf. Accessed October 22, 2015.

Duke University Libraries. [n.d.]. Non-Governmental Organizations (NGO) guide. http://guides.library.duke.edu/ngo_guide. Accessed October 22, 2015.

Homeboy Industries. [n.d.]. "Programs." http://homeboyindustries.org/. Accessed October 22, 2015.

Homies Unidos. [n.d.]. "Programs." http://homiesunidos.org/programs/. Accessed October 22, 2015.

Israel, Barbara A., Eugenia Eng, Amy Schulz, and Edith A. Parker. 2005. "Introduction to methods in community-based participatory research for health." In *Methods in community-based participatory research for health,* edited by Barbara A. Israel, Eugenia Eng, Amy J. Schultz, and Edith A. Parker. San Francisco, CA: Jossey-Bass.

Justice Committee 2013. http://www.justicecommittee.org/. Accessed October 22, 2015.

Kaplowitz, Craig A. 2005. *LULAC, Mexican Americans and national policy*. College Station, TX: Texas A&M University Press.

Latino Justice PRLDEF 2015. Four decades of protecting Latino civil rights. http://latinojustice.org/about/history/. Accessed November 13, 2015.

League of the United Latin American Citizens (LULAC). 2015. "About LULAC." http://www.lulac.org/about/. Accessed November 13, 2015.

Meléndez, Miguel. 2003. *We took the streets: Fighting for Latino rights with the Young Lords*. New York: St. Martin's Press.

Mexican American Legal Defense and Education Fund (MALDEF). 2009. "Leadership programs." http://maldef.org/leadership/. Accessed November 13, 2015.

National Council of La Raza (NCLR). [n.d.]. "About NCLR." http://www.nclr.org/about-us/. Accessed November 12, 2015.

Pew Hispanic Center. 2009. Hispanics and the criminal justice system: Low confidence, high exposure. http://pewhispanic.org/files/reports/106.pdf. http://www.nclr.org/about-us/. Accessed November 13, 2015.

Skogan, Wesley G., Susan M. Hartnett, Natalie Bump, and Jill Dubois. 2009. Evaluation of CeaseFire-Chicago. Washington, DC: U.S. Department of Justice. https://www.ncjrs.gov/pdffiles1/nij/grants/227181.pdf. Accessed November 13, 2015.

Tatum, Charles M. 2001. *Chicano popular culture: Que hable el pueblo*. Tucson, AZ: University of Arizona Press.

Torres, Andrés, and Velázquez, José E. 1998. *The Puerto Rican movement: Voices from the diaspora*. Philadelphia, PA: Temple University Press.

Villarruel, Francisco A., and Nancy E. Walker, with Pamela Minifree, Omara Rivera-Vázquez, Susan Peterson, and Kristen Perry. 2002. *¿Dónde está la justicia? A call to action on behalf of Latino and Latina youth in the U.S. justice system*. Washington, DC: Michigan State University/Building Blocks for Youth.

Walker, Nancy E., J. Michael Senger, Francisco A. Villarruel, and Angela M. Arboleda. 2004. *Lost Opportunities: The reality of Latinos in the U.S. criminal justice system*. Washington, DC: National Council of La Raza.

Community Policing. *See* Part I essays: Latinas/os and the U.S. Criminal Justice System; Policing and Latina/o Communities; Latina/o Youth and Criminal Justice. Part II entry: Segregation.

Crimmigration. See Part I essay: Latina/o Immigrants, Crime, and Justice. Part II entries: *Immigration and Naturalization Service (INS) v. Lopez-Mendoza et al.*; The Innocence Project.

Critical Race Theory. See Part I essay: Latinas/os and the U.S. Criminal Justice System. Part II entries: Cultural Criminology; LatCrit: Latina & Latino Critical Legal Theory, Inc.

Cubans

Lisandro Pérez

The 2009 American Community Survey conducted by the U.S. Bureau of the Census placed the number of persons in the United States who are of Cuban origin or descent at nearly1.7 million—less than 4 percent of the total Latino U.S. population. Cuban Americans, however, have a more conspicuous presence in the U.S. political and economic landscape than what is suggested by their relatively modest numbers, largely because of their concentration in southern Florida, where a majority of the Cuban-origin population of this country now lives. That concentration has made it possible for Cuban Americans to maximize the strength of their numbers by becoming the largest single ethnic group in Miami, the foremost city in an important electoral state and America's gateway to Latin America and the Caribbean. In metropolitan Miami, Cubans not have only created an economically strong community, but they have also occupied most of the leadership positions in the area's political, economic, educational, and cultural institutions.

Another factor that bolsters the visibility of Cuban Americans is the political context of their migration to the United States. The bulk of the contemporary Cuban American population is composed of the migrants who have left Cuba since the rise of the Cuban Revolution in 1959 (more than 70 percent of the Cuban-origin population is Cuban-born). Despite spanning nearly five decades, that migration has occurred in a political climate marked by an enduring hostility in the relations between the two countries, and—at least initially—a favorable and even welcoming reception in the United States for those who left the island. That migration context produced a Cuban American population in which the ethos of exile continues to be a powerful force. That ethos involves an uncompromising opposition to the island's government. The national visibility of Cuban Americans is due at least in part to their success in influencing, even determining, the continuation of a hostile United States stance towards Cuba, playing a role—as few immigrant groups have been able to do—in the formulation of U.S. foreign policy. Consequently, most Americans have an image of Cubans in the United States as not only an economically successful group, but also as an influential, conservative force whose politics are still rooted in the Cold War.

There have been five major migration waves from Cuba to the United States since the rise of the present Cuban government in 1959, all the result of a protracted international conflict in which migration has been used as a political tool. A climate of hostility and an absence of normal relations between the two countries, combined with the geographic fact that Cuba is an island, have made migration difficult and generally unavailable except when the two governments unilaterally or bilaterally have allowed migration to take place.

Waves of Cuban Migration to the United States and the Migration Process

The first wave of Cuban migration to the United States occurred from 1959 to October 1962. The approximately 200,000 persons that composed this wave were automatically granted refugee status by the U.S. government, placing them outside the restrictions normally imposed. A federal program was established in 1961 to assist in the resettlement and economic adjustment of the new arrivals. In this wave, Cuba's displaced elite class was disproportionately represented. The contentious transition to socialism affected first and foremost, although not exclusively, the upper sectors of Cuban society.

The second wave started in the fall of 1965 when the Cuban and U.S. governments agreed to establish an orderly airlift of twice-daily flights to Miami. Thus far it has been the largest of all the waves, with some 260,500 persons arriving until both governments agreed to end the airlift in 1973. During the airlift, the Cuban government favored the departure of women and the elderly and excluded males of military age, resulting in a demographic profile hardly typical of international migrants. In its first few years, the airlift brought the remnants of Cuba's upper classes, especially the elderly parents of those who arrived in the earlier wave. In the late 1960s, however, the airlift started including those in the middle sectors of the island's class structure, such as small business owners, clerical workers, and blue-collar workers. As with the earlier wave, the airlift arrivals were automatically granted refugee visas, facilitating their entry into the United States.

Looking to once again defuse tensions in the island, in 1980 the Cuban government opened a port, Mariel, to allow unrestricted emigration. What became known as the "Mariel boatlift" lasted for six months and brought more than 125,000 Cubans to the United States. It was a disorganized exodus on private vessels that went to Cuba from Florida to pick up relatives of persons already living in the United States. More than just relatives were placed on the boats, however, resulting in a wave with a profile that is closest to the Cuban population itself, with significant representation from Cuba's lower socioeconomic and nonwhite sectors, as well as writers, artists, professionals, and even government officials. Also arriving in the boatlift were convicted felons and inmates of mental institutions, who were placed on the boats by the Cuban government.

The fourth wave, in 1994, faced barriers to entering the United States that were unprecedented in the history of Cuban immigration. During the 1980s and the early 1990s, relatively few Cubans were admitted each year through the issuance of visas by the U.S. consulate in Havana. On August 11, 1994, responding to an alarming rise in unauthorized, and even violent, departures from the island, the Cuban government stopped detaining anyone trying to leave on a raft or in other vessels, thus initiating the fourth wave. Remembering the Mariel experience, however, the Clinton administration was unwilling to hold the door open for Cubans. Rescued rafters were sent to camps set up at the U.S. Naval Base in Guantánamo with the expectation that they would never be admitted into the United States. The Coast Guard rescued nearly 37,000 Cubans and most were interned at the base. Eventually the United States admitted the "rafters" into the country, however, given the lack of alternative destinations for them as well as the deteriorating conditions in the camps.

What became known as the Rafter Crisis of 1994 was halted after only a month when the two governments negotiated an agreement. The United States committed itself to admit at least 20,000 Cubans a year through a regular visa process. In turn, the Cuban government agreed to accept the return of any future unauthorized migrants interdicted by the Coast Guard before reaching U.S. shores. This has become known as the "wet-foot, dry-foot policy." Because of the 1966 Cuban Refugee Adjustment Act, which granted any Cuban already in the United States the right to apply for permanent residence in the United States, those Cubans arriving and stepping on U.S. soil (dry foot) are allowed to remain even if they entered in an unauthorized manner. If the Coast Guard interdicts them at sea, even a few feet from shore ("wet foot"), however, then these Cubans are placed on a Coast Guard vessel and returned to the island in accordance with the 1995 agreement with the Cuban government.

The 1995 agreement continues to govern United States–Cuba migratory relations. Some 20,000 Cubans still arrive each year through a normal visa process. Additionally, a limited number of unauthorized migrants continue to enter, usually doing so with the help of smugglers with powerboats who bring them across the Strait of Florida and deposit them directly on U.S. soil. The rickety vessels and rafts that previously had brought Cubans to the United States are no longer effective, because now the migrants need to elude not only the Cuban authorities but the U.S. Coast Guard as well.

Cubans and the U.S. Criminal Justice System

The changing conditions under which Cuban emigrants arrived in the United States have largely shaped their relationship to the justice system in the United States. Two particular features of that migration are of special importance in shaping the relationship. One is the privileged immigration status that Cubans have enjoyed as a result of the Cuban Refugee Adjustment Act (CRAA) of 1966. The intent of Congress in enacting it was to normalize the status of Cubans in the United States by granting them an immigrant visa one year and one day after their arrival. The CRAA was necessary because by 1966 a large number of Cubans lived in the United States with only a refugee visa, which is a temporary status. The Act stipulated that all Cubans already in the United States could qualify to have their status adjusted to a permanent residence visa, placing them on the road to citizenship. The CRAA still is in effect and is a major reason for the "wet-foot, dry-foot" policy that resulted from the 1994–1995 migration accords, because Cubans who arrive on U.S. soil cannot be denied entry and, eventually, permanent residence. What this has meant is that, by definition, Cubans are not illegally in the United States, even if they entered in an unauthorized fashion. Therefore, in effect, Cubans do not face criminalization due to immigration status.

Another important feature of the migration process from Cuba that has shaped the relationship of Cubans to the U.S. criminal justice system was the attention the Mariel boatlift received in the United States, especially through the media. The focus of that attention inordinately was placed on those who had evidently been inmates of penal or mental institutions, despite the fact that they represented a small minority of all Mariel arrivals. The newspaper and television outlets in southern Florida tended to give extensive coverage to any crime committed by a Mariel entrant, always noting that it had been committed by a "*marielito*." The criminal stereotyping of this group of Cubans even found its way to the movie screen, with a remake of the classic gangster movie *Scarface,* featuring Al Pacino playing a pathological murderer and drug lord who had arrived through the boatlift. The negative stereotyping of Mariel Cubans no doubt was further abetted by the fact that this was the first wave of Cubans to the United States with a significant representation of Afro-Cubans and persons from the lower socioeconomic sectors of Cuban society.

In the end, only about 2,800 of the 125,000 persons who arrived during the boatlift were deemed "excludable" by the U.S. government. Nearly 1,400 of these people eventually were deported to Cuba under an agreement with the Cuban government. In 2006, about 600 "excludables" still were in prison. After more than 25 years, the "excludables," regardless of whether they are detained, still are subject to **deportation** to Cuba whenever the next opportunity arises to send them back. They have never been legally admitted to the United States.

The Mariel boatlift was a dramatic migration and represented the first time that Cuban Americans became associated with criminality in the minds of many Americans. It was an unfair characterization. Data on all crimes and homicides in southern Florida in the period following the boatlift showed no significant increase in crime rates. The bulk of the *marielitos* made successful and productive adjustments to life in this country. After the boatlift finally was halted, however, it was clear that the "welcome mat" that always had been extended to Cubans had worn thin.

See also: Part I essays: Latinas/os and the U.S. Criminal Justice System; Latina/o Immigrants, Crime, and Justice; The U.S. War on Drugs and Latina/o Communities. Part II entries: Deportation; Media Depictions.

Further Reading

Grenier, Guillermo, and Lisandro Pérez. 2003. *The legacy of exile: Cubans in the United States*. Boston, MA: Allyn and Bacon.

Martínez, Ramiro, Jr. 2002. *Latino homicide: Immigration, violence, and community*. New York, NY: Routledge.

Masud-Piloto, Félix Roberto. 1996. *From welcomed exiles to illegal immigrants: Cuban migration to the U.S., 1959–1995*. Lanham, MD: Rowman & Littlefield.

Pérez, Lisandro. 2007. "Cubans." In *The new Americans,* edited by M. C. Waters and R. Ueda, 386–98. Cambridge, MA: Harvard University Press.

Portes, Alejandro, and Alex Stepick. 1993. *City on the edge: The transformation of Miami*. Berkeley, CA: University of California Press.

Ramírez Berg, Charles. 2002. *Latino images in film: Stereotypes, subversion, resistance.* Austin: University of Texas Press.

U.S. Bureau of the Census. 2011. *2009 American community survey.* http://factfinder.census.gov. Accessed November 13, 2015.

Cultural Competency. *See* Part I essays: Latinas/os and the U.S. Criminal Justice System; Policing and Latina/o Communities; Latinas and the U.S. Criminal Justice System; Latina/o Youth and Criminal Justice. Part II entries: Central Americans; Community-Based Latina/o Advocacy Organizations; Latina/o Fraternal Law Enforcement Organizations.

Cultural Criminology

Louis Kontos

Cultural criminology encompasses a broad range of work that calls into question traditional understandings of the relation between culture and crime and between crime and the institutions of civil society. In the United States, cultural criminology originates as a branch of sociology and is integral to the development of the discipline in its earliest stage (1920s to 1930s) at the University of Chicago. Chicago School sociologists provided an empathetic understanding of the plight of immigrants even as they explored various problems associated with immigrant society, including a sprawling gangland. Heterogeneity was celebrated, but it also was feared. Massive waves of immigration were thought to loosen the social bond and foster the "spirit of competition" and "exploitation" among individuals who have no sentimental or emotional ties to one another (Wirth 1938). To counter "potential disorder," it was believed, formal social control would have to be better (and less corrupt) and there would have to be more of it.

By the 1950s, sociology no longer was celebrating heterogeneity, but instead was heralding a new age of enlightenment brought about through technological progress and advanced methodology (i.e., quantitative methods). The dominant mode of sociological theorizing was functionalist and the dominant mode of research was statistical analysis—which perfectly suited the functionalist paradigm. It now became possible to demonstrate—for instance through attitude surveys of the type pioneered by Stouffer and Lazarsfeld at Columbia University—that Americans from all walks of life held almost interchangeable "ultimate" values, none of which required the rejection of liberal-democracy, the idea of the melting-pot, or capitalism. It now also became possible to make claims about ideology that, in a few short years, would appear foolish—including the claim that the "grand" ideologies of the modern period, Marxism in particular, were no longer relevant to any progressive political movement. The preoccupation of the Chicago School with economic competition as a source of social problems and disorder ostensibly had dissipated. In its place it became a common feature of sociological discourse to isolate social problems (e.g., from trend data) and propose makeshift technical solutions.

With a few notable exceptions (particularly the Frankfurt School, which gained recognition throughout Europe but barely received any acknowledgment of its existence from American sociology), the discipline of sociology was unmoved by social movements until the 1960s. Thereupon it became necessary to deal with the question of disorder once again; but few illusions remained about the possibility of apolitical solutions to the problem, or about the prospects of social engineering more generally. Sociology now was immersed in ideological battles with no way out. Because much of the perceived disorder of the 1960s was bound up with movements and resistance to movements, the idea of *conflict* was broadened beyond the notion of cultural conflict. Hence, it was broadened beyond the work of the Chicago School which, in the process, lost its relevance in sociology; save for the concept of *social disorganization*, which remains a source of explanation in the sociology of deviance and social problems. In retrospect, the social scientific project of the 1950s was ungrounded; the celebratory claims were illusory. The cultural and ideological antagonisms and contradictions that exploded in the 1960s were already there, ready to explode. There was a need for sociology to take sides; alternatively, to involve itself more forcefully in a raging public political debate.

Sociology of Deviance and Cultural Criminology

The sociological study of deviance and crime is a controversial field because it has taken form around ethnographic observations that humanize the putative deviant, and explanatory concepts that draw attention to conditions that push or pull ordinary people into wayward routines and styles of life; that also provide the basis for recommendations regarding the development or augmentation of effective, humane, rational modes of social control. Much of it has been reductive, especially around the topic of culture. Unlike the work of the Chicago School—which theorized and examined culture as a dimension of social action, including crime—the sociology of deviance since the 1950s generally has pathologized the culture of putative deviants, for instance around the idea of middle-class envy or values like ***machismo***. By the same token, there does not appear to be much concern outside the growing sociological field of cultural criminology with understanding the deviant as responsive to social conditions and not merely reactive to them, not merely a puppet of larger forces.

In that regard, cultural criminology has revived the concern of the Chicago School with empathetic understanding together with its focus on ethnic and class conflict. It rejects the approach of bringing normalcy into view alongside putative deviants as an innocuous backdrop and standard of judgment. This rejection is appropriate on political as well as scientific grounds, toward a proper basis for comparison—the essential principle of any method of investigation that purports to be objective or scientific. By contrast, within the sociology of deviance, **gangs** generally are compared with other gangs, as instances of various types, and not with **youth** groups and subcultures generally. Cults are compared with other cults, not with mainstream sects or denominations of established religion. Radical political groups (e.g., black and Puerto Rican Nationalists) are compared with other groups that are labeled radical or extremist, though such groups are hard-pressed to say or do anything more extreme than talk-radio hosts or politicians who are labeled populist. In the process, the sociology of deviance and sociological criminology serve an ideological purpose: reinforcing the illusion of moral consensus in a society that is pluralistic, multicultural, and sharply divided along the lines of race and class.

The cultural backdrop of cultural criminology constantly is in flux. There currently is not a single town in the United States without a legal framework that prohibits discrimination against people because of the color of their skin. Nor does this society require people to own property to vote. It does not put debtors in prison or indenture them as servants. It has come a long way, indeed. Yet it is approaching a level of wealth concentration that evokes comparisons with the Gilded Age.

The United States warehouses more than one-quarter of the world's prison population, more than 2,300,000 people—20 percent of them Latino. The majority of inmates is composed of the uneducated, the poor, and members of minority groups. Such people occasionally provoke sympathy, or pity, as when conditions of incarceration are manifest in the public eye, or when someone is found innocent of charges for which he or she was incarcerated over a prolonged period. But rarely does there appear any need for empathy or any type of understanding that brings the relation between deviance and normalcy into view, or that warrants self-reflection.

Ideology Critique in Cultural Criminology

Since the 1970s, cultural criminology has branched out into many areas, including media analysis, political economy, and social psychology. It now is strongly associated with the idea, popularized by members of the Birmingham School, that ideological consensus broke down after World War II, and that "subcultures" began to reflect ideological contradictions and to manifest resistance to the machinery of ideological indoctrination in spectacular ways; interrupting and potentially subverting the process of "normalization" (Hebdige 1981, 18). Subcultural *style* becomes important to study, then, as a mode of articulation of counter-hegemonic attitudes and values, and disarticulation of conventional expectations and judgments. Its messages are inscribed in code as well as overt. The endless transformations of youth subculture, in particular, problematize the distinction between political (ideological) and ordinary deviance. Subcultures that emerge from marginalized populations typically manifest the strongest and least ambiguous forms of resistance to dominant ideology, commercial culture, and aesthetics of social control.

Subcultural style becomes a process through which identity is reclaimed and labels are contested. Several dimensions of this process have drawn significant attention from cultural criminologists, including the way discursive spaces are constructed, and the way that the distinction between normalcy and deviance is disarticulated and rearticulated. As compared to the work of the Chicago School, contemporary cultural criminologists do not assume that assimilation is an inevitable result of acculturation over time; rather that stereotyping and labeling are parallel self-serving processes for members of the dominant (i.e., European) group, whose ever-increasing ontological insecurity manifests itself routinely in such reactionary forms as anti-immigration hysteria and scapegoating, as well as in the demand for greater scrutiny and control of marginalized populations. Jock Young presents an incisive analysis of such dynamics. According to Young, the marginalized are over-immersed in the allure of the material trappings of the dominant culture and simultaneously are denied its fruits—they are both included and excluded in what he refers to as "bulimic" society.

Ontological insecurity can be seen most clearly as a feature of the phenomenon of **racial profiling**. Whereas profiling has been featured in mainstream academic and political discourse with regard to police behavior, cultural criminology also is concerned with the ways in which labels are naturalized, such that profiling appears as a necessary and appropriate response to fear of crime, job loss, or any number of existential dilemmas that provoke ontological insecurity.

The Significance of Cultural Criminology to Latinas/os

Racial profiling can be seen wherever stereotyping is coupled with a need to respond to disorder by scrutinizing, surveilling, and controlling a subset of the population. For the Latina/o population of the United States profiling is nothing new; it was a factor during the **Sleepy Lagoon** murder trial in 1942 and the subsequent **Zoot Suit Riots** in 1943. The ***pachuco***, an "especially visible symbol of cultural autonomy and resistance" (Mirandé 1985, 179), became a feared and despised figure. The criminality associated with *pachuco* subculture was wildly exaggerated and the claim that its members were anti-American—which circulated in the mainstream press—was not exceptionally hysterical by historical standards; whereas now exaggerations and hysterical sentiments about putative deviance are more carefully constructed throughout popular media, generally speaking. Profiling is a factor now as crime-control (especially anti-gang) policies increasingly are merged, and based as they are on unsubstantiated depictions of international Latin American criminal conspiracies spreading wildly across urban America. It is also a factor throughout anti-immigrant campaigns, such as California's Proposition 187, "which profiled all Mexican-origin persons in California as immigrants seeking to deprive White persons of social and economic opportunity" (Aguirre 2004, 933). The backlash against Latina/o immigrants has given a political dimension to even the most careful and innocuous scholarly accounts of the relation between Latino/as and deviance, crime, and disorder. Cultural criminology makes this problem explicit.

Backlash rarely takes place without resistance on the part of its **victims**. Responses to anti-immigrant campaigns have taken many forms, including organized social movements and subcultures. The 2003 Freedom Ride could be understood as an instance of both, because it emulated the event of 1961, and because participants were doing something more than drawing attention to a cause—they were drawing attention to themselves as subjects who experience fear, insecurity, and *disorder*, and whose experience implicates reactionary public policy as part of the problem rather than the solution; rather than mere objects which other people fear or about which other people have opinions. "In this insubordinate act of making themselves visible, calling attention to the mere corporeal fact of their deportable presence, the migrant Freedom Riders held themselves up as potential targets for the state's recriminations" (De Genova 2009, 450). For Latina/o immigrants, both legal and otherwise, the struggle for recognition is a constant feature of daily life. The topics of immigration, deviance, crime, and disorder concern the entire Latina/o population in the United States because this population has been invisible within the mainstream culture throughout the 20th century, except for spectacular events and media spectacles related to crime and disorder.

Cultural criminology is relevant to the study of Latina/o criminality because it supports a discourse about crime and social control that does not rely on stereotype and which does not accept profiling as a means to an end. In this view, end and means cannot be separated when it comes to social control. Cultural criminology is also *critical* in that it refuses to separate questions related to criminal justice from the topic of social justice. It takes for granted that structural inequality and injustice are sources of crime as well as oppositional politics, therefore it does not belabor the issue of *causality*; it rather seeks methods of critical engagement with parallel and relational social processes and phenomena, including deviance, crime, disorder, and social control. Cultural criminology seeks further to problematize the relation between the criminal and the political, especially with regard to claims about crime and disorder that serve to delegitimize political demands or that provide support for discriminatory and authoritarian policies, including profiling.

See also: Part I essays: Latinas/os and the U.S. Criminal Justice System; Incarceration and Latinas/os in the United States; Gangs in the United States and Latina/o Communities. Part II entries: LatCrit: Latina & Latino Critical Legal Theory, Inc.; Political Activist Groups; Victims.

Further Reading

Aguirre, Jr., Adalberto. 2004. Profiling Mexican American identity: Issues and concerns. *American Behavioral Scientist* 47: 928–42.

Bell, Daniel. 1962. *The end of ideology*. Glencoe, IL: The Free Press.

Cohen, Stanley. 1992. *Against criminology*. Piscataway, NY: Transaction Publishers.

De Genova, Nicholas. 2008. "American" abjection: "Chicanos," gangs, and Mexican/migrant transnationality in Chicago. *Aztlan: A Journal of Chicago Studies* 33(2): 141–74.

De Genova, Nicholas. 2009. Conflicts of mobility, and the mobility of conflict: Rightlessness, presence, subjectivity, freedom. *Subjectivity* 1629: 445–66.

Ferrell, Jeff. 1999. Cultural criminology. *Annual Review of Sociology* 25: 395–418.

Hebdige, Dick. 1981. *Subculture: The meaning of style*. New York, NY: Routledge.

Lazarsfeld, Paul, and Elihu Katz. 2005. *Personal influence*. Piscataway, NJ: Transaction Publishers.

Mirandé, Alfredo. 1985. The Chicano experience: An alternative perspective. Notre Dame, IN: University of Notre Dame Press.

Park, Robert E. 1915. The city: Suggestions for the investigation of human behavior in the city environment. *American Journal of Sociology* 20: 577–612.

Park, Robert E., and Ernest Burgess. 1921. *Introduction to the science of sociology*. Chicago, IL: University of Chicago Press.

Riesman, David. 1953. *The lonely crowd*. New Haven, CT: Yale University Press.

Shaw, Clifford, and Henry D. McKay. 1842. *Juvenile delinquency in urban areas*. Chicago, IL: University of Chicago Press.

Stouffer, Samuel A. 1953. Measurement in sociology. *American Sociological Review* 18(6): 591–97.

Thomas, William, and Florian Znaniecki. 1918. *The Polish peasant in Europe and America: Monograph of an immigrant group,* Volumes 1 and 2. Chicago, IL: University of Chicago Press.

Thomas, William, and Florian Znaniecki. 1919. *The Polish peasant in Europe and America: Monograph of an immigrant group.* Volume 3. Boston, MA: Gorham Press.

Thomas, William, and Florian Znaniecki. 1920. *The Polish peasant in Europe and America: Monograph of an immigrant group*. Volumes 4 and 5. Boston, MA: Gorham Press.

Thrasher, Frederic. 1927. *The gang: A study of 1313 gangs in Chicago*. Chicago, IL: University of Chicago Press.

Wirth, Louis. 1938. Urbanism as a way of life. *American Journal of Sociology* 44: 1–24.

Young, Jock. 1999. *The exclusive society: Social exclusion, crime and difference in late modernity*. Thousand Oaks, CA: Sage Publications.

Young, Jock. 2007. *The vertigo of late modernity*. Thousand Oaks, CA: Sage Publications.

D

De Facto Segregation. *See* Part I essays: Latinas/os and the U.S. Criminal Justice System. Part II entries: International Human Rights; Segregation.

De Jure Segregation. *See* Part I essays: Latinas/os and the U.S. Criminal Justice System. Part II entries: International Human Rights; Segregation.

Death Penalty

José Luis Morín

Growing concerns that capital punishment represents an affront to human rights has resulted in a global movement to end the use of the death penalty. International human rights law has moved in the direction toward the abolition of the death penalty worldwide, and most countries in the world have banned its use. Amnesty International (2015) reports that 98 countries have abolished the death penalty for all crimes, 7 countries have abolished capital punishment for ordinary crimes only, and 35 countries in practice have ended executions. A total of 140 countries prohibited capital punishment as a matter of law or in practice, and 58 countries, including the United States, preserve the death penalty.

In addition to the global trend to abolish the death penalty on human rights grounds, numerous studies have shown that capital punishment does not effectively deter crime. States that do not have capital punishment have consistently lower murder rates (Death Penalty Information Center 2010). A 2009 survey of leading criminologists found an "overwhelming consensus among these criminologists that the empirical research conducted on the deterrence question strongly supports the conclusion that the death penalty does not add deterrent effects to those already achieved by long imprisonment" (Radelet & Lacock 2009, 489). Nevertheless, the United States is the only developed nation in the world that maintains a system of capital punishment.

In 2014, a minimum of 607 people were executed in 22 countries, and at least 2,466 people were sentenced to be executed in 22 countries. Five countries—the United States, China, Saudi Arabia, Iran, and Iraq—carried out most of the executions around the globe. For being among the five countries with the greatest number of executions and for the ongoing controversies surrounding its system of capital punishment, the United States of America continues to receive severe criticism for falling outside acceptable human rights standards.

Latinas/os and the Death Penalty

At the center of much of the death penalty controversy in the United States is the issue of **race and ethnicity**, particularly as it concerns the disproportionate numbers of persons of color sentenced to death. A person of color is more likely to be sentenced to death for killing a white person than a white person is for having murdered a person of color (Death Penalty Information Center 2010;

Amnesty International 1998). Overall, in cases where executions are carried out, more than 77 percent of murder **victims** are white, despite the fact that only 50 percent of victims of murder are white (Death Penalty Information Center 2010).

In relation to the application of the death penalty in the United States, Latinas/os generally have not experienced as disproportionately high numbers as have African Americans, but nevertheless they represent a group that has been susceptible to significant disparities in treatment in the criminal justice system as compared to whites. As noted by **The Sentencing Project**'s review of the literature on racial disparities in the U.S. system of capital punishment, the race of the victim in most cases has a significant effect on death penalty sentence. Specifically, the death penalty is more likely when a victim is white. Additionally, in many cases—especially in the federal system—if the defendant is a person of color then the death penalty also is more likely to be the outcome.

The increase in the number of Latinas/os subject to the death penalty from 2007 to 2008 could signal a worsening situation for Latinas/os with respect to capital punishment. In proportion to their numbers within the U.S. population at year end 2008, African Americans continued to be grossly overrepresented on death row at 41 percent of prisoners under sentence of death whereas whites were at 56 percent of prisoners on death row. In contrast, on December 31, 2007, there were 361 Latinas/os under death sentence and as of December 31, 2008, that number had risen to 373. At the end of 2008, Latinas/os represented 13.2 percent of prisoners under sentence of death out of a total of 3,207 persons on death row, but of those admitted to death sentences for 2008, Latinas/os comprised 19.8 percent (Snell 2009, Table 5 & Table 6), more than their percentage of the U.S. population (15.4 percent) in 2008 (Pew Hispanic Center 2008). As incarceration rates of Latinas/os have risen in recent decades, it will be important to continue to track the number of Latinas/os under capital punishment.

As a group, Latinas/os in the criminal justice literature are considered vulnerable to racial and ethnic bias in the criminal justice system and harsher sentences when compared to those of whites. It would follow,

Table 1 Prisoners under Death Sentence in 2008 by Hispanic/Latino Origin, Race, and Gender

Characteristic	Year end	Admissions
Total inmates	3,207	111
Hispanic/Latino Origin		
Hispanic	13.2%	19.8%
Race		
White	56.1%	58.6%
Black	41.7	39.6
All other races	2.2	1.8
Gender		
Male	98.2%	97.3%
Female	1.8	2.7

Note: The U.S. Department of Justice's Bureau of Justice Statistics uses the term "Hispanic" to indicate ethnicity, not race, and therefore Hispanics could be placed into any of the three racial categories—"White," "Black," or "All other races"—and are represented in each of the categories.

Source: Snell, Tracy L. 2009. *Capital Punishment, 2008—Statistical Tables, December 2009*, NCJ 228662. Washington, DC: Bureau of Justice Statistics, U.S. Department of Justice (Table 5). http://bjs.ojp.usdoj.gov/content/pub/pdf/cp08st.pdf. Accessed March 21, 2010.

then, that disparities could become more prominent for Latinas/os with regard to the death penalty as they have in other areas of criminal justice. As "the fastest growing minority group being imprisoned" according to the Bureau of Justice Statistics (1997, 9), Latinas/os might become increasingly susceptible to greater numbers of death sentences. Current anti-immigrant sentiments in the United States also could contribute to Latina/o vulnerability to harsher sentences and the death penalty in the future. The growing number of persons on death row who have been exonerated raises serious doubts about the fairness of the U.S. system of capital punishment. Between 1973 and 1999 there was an average of 3.1 death row inmates exonerated per year; from 2000 to 2007, an average of 5 per year were exonerated (Death Penalty Information Center 2010). Opponents of the death penalty point to the growing number of persons on death row who have been exonerated as proof that the system is fundamentally flawed because in the United States innocent people are sentenced to death every year.

Consistent with many criminological studies about bias against and the lack of fair treatment of Latinas/os in relation to the criminal justice system, concern exists about fairness of the application of the death penalty in the case of Latinas/os. One death penalty study found that Latinas/os "do not receive the same type of treatment by the criminal justice system" (Urbina 2003, 233). The study showed that, from 1975 to 1995, Latinas/os encountered many difficulties in California, Florida, and Texas in their efforts to have their death sentences reversed or declared unconstitutional. Language barriers, financial constraints, and the ability to retain adequate counsel were among the many impediments Latinas/os faced in securing a fair hearing.

A study of Latinos executed in the United States from 1997 to 2010 yielded several key characteristics: Most of the persons executed were of Mexican origin. Contrary to the popularly held fear and misperception that Latinos prey on whites, most of the victims were Latino. Many of those executed had prolonged stays in prison prior to their execution, raising doubts about the efficacy of the entire system. Most were young at the time of the commission of the crime, were poorly educated, and had extremely low income. Other common characteristics of executed Latinos included questionable mental capacity or competency to stand trial—including some considered "mildly mentally retarded" or having endured "severe brain impairment"; long histories of substance abuse; the absence of an expression of remorse, which might have contributed to the decision to execute; several who claimed complete innocence to the end; and many who appeared to lack adequate counsel and were convicted by juries that had no persons of color (Peña & Urbina 2012, 275). These characteristics, as the analysts assert, raise doubt about the fairness of the legal process. Particularly when the defendant was a Mexican national, rather than a U.S. citizen, questions have been raised whether "Mexico itself was being scapegoated" (Peña & Urbina 2012, 290).

Nationals from Latin American countries facing the death penalty in the United States have experienced a specific form of vulnerability, because on many occasions the United States has been unwilling to abide by the Vienna Convention on Consular Relations. Many human rights organizations—including Amnesty International (1998)—continue to denounce the U.S. government's failure to allow non-citizens sentenced to death to consult with their country's consular officials, as required by the Convention.

In spite of an International Court of Justice (ICJ) decision and a presidential directive from George W. Bush ordering compliance with the ICJ ruling, Texas refused to review the case of Mexican national, José Medellín, who was executed in 2008. As Amnesty International points out, Medellín was executed in 2008 for his role in the murder of two teenage girls committed when he was barely 18 years old. The death sentences of his two co-defendants were commuted following the U.S. Supreme Court decision in *Roper v. Simmons* (2005), which barred the execution of minors. Medellín was assigned a court-appointed lawyer who had been suspended from practicing law for six months for unethical conduct in another case during the investigation and prosecution of Medellín's case. The Mexican Consulate only learned of the case almost four years after Medellín's arrest, when the first appeals court decision affirming his conviction and death sentence already had been handed down. Amnesty International further cites that the Mexican Consulate could have secured appropriate expert and legal assistance to present potentially mitigating circumstances in court—including Medellín's difficult upbringing and battles with depression, suicidal behavior, and alcohol dependency. The Consulate's involvement was also too late to point out or correct the inadequate legal representation Medellín had received.

See also: Part I essay: Incarceration and Latinas/os in the United States. Part II entries: International Human Rights; Victims.

Further Reading

Amnesty International. 1998. *United States of America: Rights for all*. New York: Amnesty International Publications.

Amnesty International. 2009. *United States of America: Too much cruelty, too little clemency: Texas nears 200th execution under current governor*. AMR 51/057/2009. New York: Amnesty International Publications.

Amnesty International. 2010. *Abolitionist and retentionist countries*. http://www.amnesty.org/en/death-penalty/abolitionist-and-retentionist-countries#allcrimes. Accessed March 21, 2010.

Amnesty International. 2015. *Death sentences and executions in 2014*. http.//www.amnesty.org.uk/sites/default/files/death_sentence_and_executions_2014_en.pdf. Accessed January 8, 2016.

Bureau of Justice Statistics. 1997. *Prisoners in 1996*. NCJ 164619. Washington, DC: U.S. Department of Justice.

Death Penalty Information Center. 2010. Deterrence: States without the death penalty have had consistently lower murder rates. http://www.deathpenaltyinfo.org/deterrence-states-without-death-penalty-have-had-consistently-lower-murder-rates. Accessed March 21, 2010.

Human Rights Watch. 2009. World report 2009: United States. http://www.hrw.org/en/world-report-2009/united-states. Accessed March 20, 2010.

Morín, José Luis. 2009. *Latino/a rights and justice in the United States: Perspectives and approaches*, 2nd ed. Durham, NC: Carolina Academic Press.

Peña, Ilse Aglaé, and Martin Guevara Urbina. 2012. The legacy of capital punishment: Executing Latinas and Latinos. In *Hispanics in the U.S. criminal justice system: The new American demography,* edited by Martin G. Urbina, 261–90. Springfield, IL: Charles C. Thomas.

Pew Hispanic Center. 2008. Statistical portrait of Hispanics in the United States, 2008. http://pewhispanic.org/files/factsheets/hispanics2008/Table 1.pdf.

Radelet, Michael L., and Traci L Lacock. 2009. Do executions lower homicide rates? The views of leading criminologists. *Journal of Criminal Law & Criminology* 99(2): 489–508.

Sentencing Project, The. 2005. *Racial disparity in sentencing: A review of the literature.* Washington, DC: The Sentencing Project.

Snell, Tracy L. 2009. *Capital Punishment, 2008—Statistical Tables, December 2009*, NCJ 228662. Washington, DC: Bureau of Justice Statistics, U.S. Department of Justice. http://bjs.ojp.usdoj.gov/content/pub/pdf/cp08st.pdf. Accessed March 21, 2010.

Urbina, Martin G. 2003. *Capital punishment and Latino offenders: Racial and ethnic differences in death sentences.* New York: LFB Scholarly Publishing.

Urbina, Martin G. 2012. *Capital punishment in America: Race and the death penalty over time.* El Paso, TX: LFB Scholarly Publishing.

Urbina, Martin G. (ed.). 2012. *Hispanics in the U.S. criminal justice system: The new American demography.* Springfield, IL: Charles C. Thomas.

U.S. Census Bureau. 2006. U.S. Hispanic population: 2006. http://www.census.gov/population/socdemo/hispanic/cps2006/CPS_Powerpoint 2006.pdf. Accessed March 20, 2010.

Cases Cited

Roper v. Simmons, 543 U.S. 551 (2005).

Deportation

Louis Kontos and Luis Barrios

Latinas/os are subjected to deportation in far greater numbers than are other immigrants. They also comprise the largest population of undocumented immigrants; 78 percent of the total 12 million undocumented immigrants in American society are Latinas/os. More than half are **Mexican** (Passel & Cohn 2009).

Often overlooked is that deportation policies in the United States originated with anti-Mexican sentiment. During the Great Depression, President Hoover ordered the deportation of all undocumented immigrants. More than 2 million Mexicans were deported—60 percent of them U.S. citizens (Koch 2006). After WWII, President Truman addressed the problem of unemployment among returning G.I.'s by ordering the deportation of unauthorized Mexican immigrants and by unsuccessfully seeking congressional approval for measures to crack down on their employers. During the Truman administration, 3.4 million Mexicans were deported or left voluntarily under threat of deportation. The largest deportation effort in American history, **Operation Wetback**, took place in 1954. It resulted in a "round up" of 3.7 million Latinos, tens of thousands of them citizens (Gutiérrez 1995). Most recently, deportation has become the central policy option for dealing with unauthorized immigrants, particularly immigrants from Mexico and Central and South America.

Immigration Law in Historical and Sociological Perspectives

In the current political environment, it is easy to forget that the United States always has been a "nation of immigrants," and that immigration throughout U.S. history has been encouraged with little concern as to cultural or structural assimilation. Until the Immigration Act of 1891, the United States lacked a single immigration policy. The issue had been left to the states without coordination or oversight from the federal government. The Immigration Act created the Office of the Superintendent of Immigration under the Treasury Department. Pursuant to the Act, 24 inspection centers were opened, including Ellis Island in New York. In 1895, the Bureau of Immigration replaced the Office of the Superintendent, and consolidated immigration services and oversight procedures. In 1903, it was transferred to the Department of Commerce and

Labor. In 1906 Congress passed the Basic Naturalization Act, establishing the Bureau of Immigration and Naturalization in the Commerce Department. The Bureau standardized the naturalization process.

The Bureau was renamed the Immigration and Naturalization Service (INS) in 1933. In 1940, the INS was transferred to the Department of Justice. In 1952, Congress passed the Immigration and Nationality Act, which consolidated immigration and naturalization laws into a single body of text. The INS subsequently turned its focus to illegal aliens and to the problem of assimilating European refugees. The Immigration and Nationality Act of 1965 replaced national-origin quotas with a system that encouraged more family members and skilled workers to immigrate. The immigrant population doubled between 1965 and 1970. Additionally, the ethnic make-up of American society changed dramatically, as the unlimited number of visas for family reunification authorized by the Act resulted in a heavy influx of Asian immigrants, a group whose ability to immigrate had previously been restricted. Additional laws in the 1980s and 1990s established the basis for the current high rates of deportation.

Table 2. Immigration Laws

Title	Year	Purpose
Immigration Reform and Control Act	1986	This law represented the first attempt to significantly amend the Immigration and Nationality Act of 1952 to improve immigration control.
Personal Responsibility and Work Opportunity Reconciliation Act	1996	Also known as the "Welfare Reform Act of 1996," this law "contained unprecedented new measures restricting immigrant access to federal means-tested social programs, primarily including welfare–cash assistance, Social Security disability benefits, food stamps, and public housing and rent vouchers."
Antiterrorism and Effective Death Penalty Act	1996	This act "limited the application of habeas corpus for federal prisoners, foreshadowing the broader habeas corpus restrictions introduced by the REAL ID [Act]."
Illegal Immigration Reform and Immigrant Responsibility Act (IIRAIRA)	1996	IIRAIRA provided "the most sweeping changes to immigration enforcement since the 1952 Immigration and Naturalization Act, far outpacing the Immigration Reform and Control Act and the Immigration Reform Act of 1900."
Enhance Border Security and Visa Entry Reform Act	2001	This act "continued the increase in spending on the immigration enforcement arm of the Department of Homeland Security (DHS, formerly the Immigration and Naturalization Service) that was initiated by the Immigration Reform and Control Act (but was increased most dramatically by the Illegal Immigration Reform and Immigrant Responsibility Act [IIRAIRA])."

USA PATRIOT Act	2001	The USA PATRIOT Act did not provide any major immigration-related provisions, but "its antiterrorism measures reinforced many of the same priorities introduced by the Antiterrorism and Effective Death Penalty Act and greatly expanded the ability of the government to monitor all U.S. residents, including non-citizens."
REAL ID Act	2005	This law "intensified many of the measures that were introduced by the Illegal Immigration Reform and Immigrant Responsibility Act (IIRAIRA). Unlike IIRAIRA, however, it focused primarily on restricting legal options for noncitizens in the immigration court and criminal court systems. Among other things, it further limited judicial review options for noncitizens facing deportation (in particular, for noncitizens being deported because of criminal convictions), expanded the grounds of inadmissibility and deportability for terrorism-related charges, and introduced even more rigorous criteria for asylum claims."
Secure Fence Act	2006	The Secure Fence Act augmented spending on border-control measures including the expanded use of technology and the funding for extending the fence along the U.S.-Mexico border as well as increasing the number of border-control agents.

Source: Compiled from Brotherton, David C., and Philip Kretsedemas. 2008. *Keeping out the other: A critical introduction to immigration enforcement today.* New York, NY: Columbia Univ. Press, 375–79.

Aggravated Felonies

In 1980, Congress passed an immigration law that mandated deportation for people convicted of "aggravated felonies." The term was defined by Congress in 1990 as "any" crime of **violence** that is punishable by a sentence of at least five years. At the same time, several other deportable offenses were added, including marrying to evade immigration laws, voting in a federal election as a noncitizen, and falsely claiming citizenship to secure employment. The list of nonviolent felonies and non-felony offenses grew in the mid-1990s. Aggravated felony was redefined as any violent felony punishable by a sentence of at least one year. In addition, the Anti-**Terrorism** and Effective Death Penalty Act of 1996 invented a new deportable offense—that of "moral turpitude"—when added to any criminal conviction. Arguably, there are few types of crimes that truly warrant this distinction, whereas the label "moral turpitude" routinely is applied in deportation cases (*see, e.g., Chu v. Cornell* (1957)).

The government's burden of proof in deportation cases is not the same as in criminal trials, as the criterion of adjudication is "clear and convincing evidence" rather than "beyond a reasonable doubt." Prior conviction in a criminal court, even just arrest or admission of guilt—under whatever circumstances—usually is enough to meet that standard.

The case of Andre R. provides an illustration of the way in which immigrants are deportable by mistakenly pleading to an "aggravated felony." Andre arrived in the United States at age five and lived in the United States as a legal permanent resident for 36 years. Never asked about his status when he enlisted, he nevertheless applied for citizenship after leaving the army. He reports that he never received notice of his citizenship hearing, and consequently it was determined that he failed to appear. In 1995, he pled guilty to an aggravated felony that made him deportable in 1996 when the immigration laws changed. His explanation for pleading guilty was his belief that "it was the best for me so I could go to work and not miss any time . . . I should be able to be home with my family working and doing what a man is to do to take care of his children." He further explained: "I have paid tax all my life to this country until DHS detained me. . . . All I ask for is a fair chance to fight for what is right and that is my family and my right to be in a country that I fought for in the military" (Human Rights Watch 2007, 76).

The pace of deportation has increased considerably since Congress passed the USA PATRIOT Act of 2002, which virtually eliminated burden of proof as an obstacle to detention by authorizing the Attorney General to detain non-citizens for seven days without charges. Much longer detentions became typical. The administrative rule that detainees could be held indefinitely under "extraordinary circumstances," initially formulated as a response to perceived terrorist threats, now routinely is applied to deportable immigrants. Thus, endless detention has become a mechanism through which the government coerces potential deportees to "voluntarily" repatriate to gain release. As stated by the United Nation's Working Group on Arbitrary Detention, such a practice ostensibly violates Article 9 of the International Convention on Civil and Political Rights (ICCPR), which prohibits "arbitrary" detention. The United States became a party to the ICCPR in 1992.

In its first year, the Obama administration set a record in the **removal** of unauthorized immigrants. A total of 387,790 unauthorized immigrants were removed forcibly or voluntarily from the country in the year ending September 30, 2009, in contrast to 369,221 in 2008, representing a 5 percent increase. Of those forcibly deported by ICE, the total increase was 13 percent—from 264,541 in 2008, to 298,401 in 2009 (Hsu & Aizenman 2010). Although worksite raids dropped from 2008 to 2010—765 undocumented immigrants were arrested at places of work in the first half of the fiscal year 2010, as compared with 5,100 in 2008—company audits related to the employment of undocumented workers quadrupled (Slevin 2010).

The U.S. Supreme Court and Aggravated Felonies

Recent decisions by the U.S. Supreme Court—in particular *Lopez v. Gonzales* (2006)—are likely to have an impact on the way the government applies the category "aggravated felony" to deport people automatically. Lopez was convicted of a crime that was a felony in South Dakota but not under federal law. The Supreme Court ruled that the conviction was not a basis for deporting him. Lopez entered the United States in 1986 and became a legal permanent resident in 1990. In 1997, he pled guilty to aiding and abetting in the possession of cocaine, a crime for which he served 15 months in prison. Upon his release, the INS attempted to deport him, claiming that he had been convicted of an aggravated felony controlled substance violation. The immigration court ordered his deportation. The Board of Immigration Appeals upheld the decision. Lopez petitioned for review to the 8th Circuit Court but was denied. The Supreme Court agreed to hear the case based on what it perceived to be conflict in the federal courts of appeals on how to classify such crimes. In *Lopez*, the Supreme Court ruled that unless a state offense is punishable as a federal felony it does not count as "aggravated felony."

More recently, the Supreme Court ruled that a second possession offense might not be interpreted as an aggravated felony when the state conviction is for a misdemeanor, even if "hypothetically" the charge could have been based on a prior conviction and thus qualified as a felony (*Carachuri-Rosendo v. Holder* [2010]). José Angel Carachuri-Rosendo, a legal permanent resident, lived in the United States since 1993. He was sentenced in Texas to 20 days for a misdemeanor marijuana charge in 2004 and, a year later, served 10 days for the misdemeanor charge of possession of Xanax without a prescription.

Whereas *Lopez* and *Carachuri-Rosendo* work to the benefit of immigrants who are convicted of relatively minor crimes, other recent decisions do not. In *Nijhawan v. Holder* (2009), the Supreme Court found that the immigration court was correct in looking at the underlying facts of a state fraud conviction to determine whether it qualified as an aggravated felony aside from what was established by the conviction itself. The traditional "categorical" approach provides that the government is bound by what is established by the prior conviction and cannot "go beyond" the record of conviction. As a legal basis for establishing exceptions to the categorical approach, *Nijhawan* likely will prove relevant to future policy debates about deportation (*see* Immigration Defense Project 2009).

Immigration and Customs Enforcement (ICE)

Pursuant to the Homeland Security Act of 2002, the Department of Homeland Security (DHS) was created. The **Immigration and Customs Enforcement** Agency is the largest investigative branch of the DHS. It has replaced INS, the Customs Service, and the Federal Protective Service. The ICE is composed of the following law enforcement divisions: The Office of Investigations (OI), which investigates a wide variety of crimes, including human rights violations and financial crimes; the Office of Intelligence—Field Intelligence Groups (FIGs), which are responsible for providing information about terrorist groups to other departments of DHS; the Office of Intelligence and the Office of Detention and Removal (DRO), which detains and removes unauthorized aliens; and the Office of International Affairs (OIA), which investigates organized crime networks and works with local law enforcement agencies throughout the world to investigate terrorist activity. The ICE is charged with enforcement of more than 400 federal statutes dealing with the maintenance and security of the nation's borders. It maintains more than 400 offices throughout the world (U.S. Immigration and Customs Enforcement [n.d.]).

The ICE now is at the center of public debate regarding immigration and deportation. Human rights organizations and advocacy groups have been concerned with the fact that ICE routinely targets immigrants who have broken no laws and who have committed minor offenses, and that ICE appears to be assuming a law-enforcement function contrary to its stated mission. Conversely, there are notable politicians and pundits who would like to see the ICE become even more aggressive in its operations. Disgruntled employees and former employees of ICE now have gained a voice in this debate by claiming that they have been restricted by unspecified pro-immigrant policies of the Obama administration, and that they were instructed to not detain unauthorized immigrants unless these immigrants have committed crimes. In August 2010, the union representing immigration officers issued a vote of no confidence in ICE director John Morton for what it perceived as his commitment to "amnesty." Agents, according to their union, would like to be able to detain anyone not authorized to be in the United States, including by making "street arrests" (Picket 2010). The problem with this scenario is that street arrests in the absence of criminal conduct violate the strictures of the ICCPR. It also is problematic with regard to the First, Fourth, Fifth, Sixth, Eighth, and Fourteenth Amendments to the Constitution, which apply to "everybody" living in the United States.

High-profile ICE sting operations have made the agency especially controversial. They include Operation Cross Check (targeting industries that employ high numbers of undocumented immigrants), Operation Community Shield (targeting immigrant **gang** members), and Operation Predator (targeting immigrant sex offenders). These operations generally proceed with administrative warrants in place of judicial warrants. Such warrants are not directed toward uncovering crime but only furthering compliance with health, safety, and welfare regulations; therefore they can be obtained without demonstrating "probable cause," which is the standard for searches and seizures under the Fourth Amendment to the U.S. Constitution. The great majority of arrests through ICE operations appears not to be arrests of targeted offenders but rather are collateral arrests of civil immigration status violations. It further appears that, according to a recent study, in more than three-quarters of cases involving arrests in private residences, ICE agents have entered without informed consent, in violation of extant law and the ICE's own stated policies.

Immigration Enforcement

Since 2003, when it was made part of the Office of Detention and Removal (DRO) within ICE, the National Fugitive Operation Program (NFOP) has received a 23-fold increase in funding, from 9 million dollars in fiscal year 2003 to 218 million dollars in FY 2008. It has expanded its staffing over the same period by 1,300 percent. Thus, it has grown far more than any other immigration enforcement program. The official mission of this program is the detainment and removal of *dangerous* fugitives. "Fugitive" is defined by NFOP as any person that has been ordered deported or excluded but has not left the country, or that has not reported to DHS

Table 3 Total Funding for Fugitive Operation, FY 2003 to FY 2008

FY	Amount
2008	$218,945,000
2007	$183,200,000
2006	$121,852,000
2005	$79,049,000
2004	$12,683,962
2003	$9,333,519

Source: United States Immigration and Customs Enforcement (ICE) budget sheets; DHS Office of Inspector General Report (March 2007), An Assessment of United Sates Immigration and Customs Enforcement's Fugitive Operation Teams. http://dhs.gov/xoig/assets/mgmtrpts/OIG_07-34Mar07.pdf.

Table 4 Aliens Removed or Returned: Fiscal Years 1998 to 2008

Year	Removals[1]	Returns[2]
1998	174,813	1,570,127
1999	183,114	1,574,863
2000	188,467	1,675,876
2001	189,026	1,349,371
2002	165,168	1,012,116
2003	211,098	945,294
2004	240,665	1,166,576
2005	246,431	1,096,920
2006	280,974	1,043,381
2007	319,382	891,390
2008	358,886	811,263
Total	**2,558,024**	**13,137,177**

1. Removals are the compulsory and confirmed movement of an inadmissible or deportable alien out of the United States based on an order of removal. An alien who is removed has administrative or criminal consequences placed on subsequent reentry owing to the fact of the removal.

2. Returns are the confirmed movement of an inadmissible or deportable alien out of the United States not based on an order of removal. Most of the voluntary returns are of Mexican nationals who have been apprehended by the U.S. Border Patrol and are returned to Mexico.

Source: U.S. Department of Homeland Security. 2009. *2008 yearbook of immigration statistics—Homeland Security.* Washington, DC: U.S. Department of Homeland Security.

when required to do so (Mendelson, Strom, & Wishnie 2009). NFOP is an especially aggressive program. It dispatches Fugitive Operations Teams (FOTs) across the country to arrest fugitives. In fiscal year 2008, FOTs arrested 96,000 immigrants, yet 73 percent of arrestees had no criminal convictions whatsoever (Mendelson, Strom, & Wishnie 2009). (See Table 3 titled "Total Funding for Fugitive Operation, FY 2003 to FY 2008.")

Deportations on Criminal Charges

Since 1998, a total of 15,695,201 immigrants have been deported. Unlike what takes place within the criminal justice system, the process of deportation guarantees neither the right to legal counsel nor the opportunity to obtain the same by paying out of pocket. Non-citizens deported for crimes typically receive their deportation orders after appearing before an immigration judge without adequate legal representation. A study of deportation hearings in 2005 found that 65 percent of immigrants had no legal representation whatsoever (Brulliard 2007). Table 5 titled "Criminal Sentences Contrasted with Penalty of Deportation" describes the disproportionate nature of sentences when they involve immigration consequences.

Table 6 titled "Deportable Aliens Located by Region of Nationality" gives a distribution of deportable aliens for the year 2008; 791,568 people were labeled deportable by ICE. The DHS defines "deportable aliens located" as unauthorized immigrants who have been apprehended by **border patrol** agents or subject to "administrative" arrest by ICE. Most non-citizens who were deported from the United States cannot apply to return lawfully for a period of 5 to 20 years, depending on their circumstances. When an "aggravated felony" is involved, the immigrant usually is barred permanently from reentering the United States. Table 7 titled "Deportable Aliens Located by Latin American Countries: Fiscal Year 2008" lists the Latin American countries from which the "deportable aliens" originate.

Table 5 Criminal Sentences Contrasted with Penalty of Deportation

Criminal Offense	Immigration Consequence	Examples of Likely Federal or State (NY Law Used) Sentence
Shoplifting offenses	Mandatory detention and deportation.	For first conviction individual could receive sentence to several days of community service. For second conviction, individual could receive a sentence of up to six months imprisonment.
Tax evasion, causing loss of more than $10,000	Mandatory detention and deportation.	Fine equaling tax loss plus zero to six months' imprisonment.
Possessing stolen property within five years of entry to the United States	Mandatory detention and deportation.	Restitution of property, plus one year's imprisonment.
Possession with intent to sell of 35 grams or more of marijuana	Mandatory detention and deportation.	Between 15 days and up to 1 year of imprisonment.

Source: Compiled from Human Rights Watch. 2007. *Forced apart: Families separated and immigrants harmed by United States deportation policy.* New York: Human Rights Watch. http://www.hrw.org/en/reports/2007/07/16/forced-apart. Accessed November 28, 2015.

Collateral Damage

There is very little recognition of the **civil rights** of undocumented immigrants within the current public political discourse about immigration and deportation, thus there is little chance of including any consideration of the idea of human rights as outlined by the Universal Declaration of Human Rights and the International Covenant on Civil and Political Rights. Sensational accounts of crimes committed by unauthorized immigrants now are commonplace; notwithstanding the fact that immigrants—legal and illegal—are responsible for less crime than citizen counterparts. At the same time, compelling reports from human rights organizations regarding deportation in the United States receive little attention in the mainstream media. The demonization of immigrants is nothing new in American society. It is, however, especially common during times of economic contraction.

At this moment, there are approximately 11 million unauthorized immigrants in the United States, comprising more than 5 percent of the entire U.S. labor force. Repatriation on a mass scale, especially for anything less than serious offenses (e.g., punishable by 5 years or more in jail), defies logic. Yet

Table 6 Deportable Aliens Located by Region of Nationality: Fiscal Year 2008

Region and country of nationality	Number
Africa	2,932
Asia	7,740
Europe	2,922
North America	769,266
Oceania	191
South America	8,456
Unknown	61
Total	791,568

Source: U.S. Department of Homeland Security. 2009. *2008 yearbook of immigration statistics—Homeland Security*. Washington, DC: U.S. Department of Homeland Security, Table 34.

Table 7 Deportable Aliens Located by Latin American Countries: Fiscal Year 2008

Country	Numbers
Argentina	187
Bolivia	180
Brazil	2,649
Chile	132
Costa Rica	22
Dominican Republic	1,934
Ecuador	2,322
El Salvador	17,911
Guatemala	22,670
Honduras	23,789
Mexico	693,592
Nicaragua	1,862
Panama	135
Peru	949
Uruguay	96
Venezuela	303
Total	**769,033**

Source: U.S. Department of Homeland Security. 2009. *2008 yearbook of immigration statistics—Homeland Security*. Washington, DC: U.S. Department of Homeland Security, Table 34.

that is the current policy, even extending to people with "green cards."

Families Torn Apart

Of the total number of non-citizens who were deported between 1997 and 2005, 672,593 were deported for criminal offenses, mostly nonviolent crimes such as **drug** convictions and larceny, and most of them had families that were "torn apart." Human rights organizations that have examined this problem report that there is no certainty as to how many of the 672,593 non-citizens were lawfully in the United States (permanent residents or with other legal authority) and how many were unauthorized or documented. Although very little data exists about their family relationships, based on the 2000 U.S. Census an estimated 1.6 million spouses and children in the United States were separated from their parent or spouse as a result of these deportations (Human Rights Watch 2007).

The impact of deportations on families is significant when considering the thousands of children who are U.S. citizens by birth, but whose parents are not citizens. During the 10-year period of 1997 to 2007, nearly

Table 8 Number of Non-U.S. Citizens Held in State or Federal Prisons, June 30, 2000–2007

Year	Total	Male	Female
2000	89,676	86,130	3,546
2001	87,917	84,196	3,721
2002	88,677	84,931	3,746
2003	90,568	86,751	3,817
2004	91,815	88,013	3,802
2005	91,089	87,430	3,659
2006[a]	91,053	87,353	3,700
2006[b]	93,267	89,485	3,782
2007[a]	87,226	83,657	3,569
2007[b]	96,703	92,739	3,964
Average Annual Change 2000–2006	0.3%	0.2%	0.7%

a. Totals based on numbers reported by states.

b. Totals estimated. Nevada and Virginia did not provided data on non-U.S. citizens in custody at midyear 2006. Florida, Illinois, and Oregon did not provide data on non-citizens in custody at midyear 2007.

Source: Couture, Heather, and William J. Sabol. 2007. Prison inmates at midyear 2007. Bureau of Justice Statistics. http://bjs.ojp.usdoj.gov/index.cfm?ty=pbdetail&iid=840. Accessed November 28, 2015.

2.2 million immigrants were deported, and of those an estimated 100,000 were the parents of children who are U.S. citizens as a result of being born in the country. Because it is difficult to ascertain the precise number of children deportees had, the number of children who are U.S. citizens affected by deportations could be greater (Falcone 2009).

According to the Urban Institute, one citizen child is affected for every two adults arrested by ICE. Immigrant children separated by their parents as a result of ICE enforcement activities are known to undergo anxiety, depression, sleep and eating problems, and symptoms associated with Post Traumatic Stress Disorder, often with very few or no family, friends, or social services to assist them.

Deportation in the United States: Ongoing Concerns

The United States during President Barak Obama's term as president has been deporting record numbers of immigrants. Yet DHS has not been required to provide detailed and timely information about the operations of its various agencies, nor about the people that it deports. No public information is provided by DHS regarding criminal convictions of deportees. Nor does DHS publish information regarding the immigration status, work history, or family relations of deportees. Such information is needed if public debate about immigration and deportation is to be meaningful.

See also: Part I essays: Latina/o Immigrants, Crime, and Justice; The U.S. War on Drugs and Latina/o Communities; Latinas/os and the U.S. Criminal Justice System; Crime and the U.S.-Mexican Border. Part II entries: Civil Rights; Deportation Laws; Hate Crimes; Immigration and Customs Enforcement (ICE); Mexicans and Mexican Americans.

Further Reading

American Civil Liberties Union. [n.d.]. ACLU sues State Department for passport requirement discrimination. http://www.aclu.org/racialjustice/gen/passports.html.

Arboleda, Angela. 2007 (Summer). Latinos and incarceration: Prisons, jails, and immigration detention. *Justice matters*. http://www.safetyandjustice.org/node/1122.

Becker, Andrew. 2010 (August 27). Tension over Obama policies within Immigration and Customs Enforcement. *Washington Post*. http://www.washingtonpost.com/wp-dyn/content/article/2010/08/26/AR2010082606561.html.

Brotherton, David C. 2008. Exiling New Yorkers. In *Keeping out the other: A critical introduction to immigration enforcement today*, edited by D. C. Brotherton and P. Kretsedemas, 161–78. New York, NY: Columbia University Press.

Brotherton, David C., and Luis Barrios. 2009. Displacement and stigma: The social-psychological crisis of the deportee. *Crime, Media, Culture* 5(1): 29–55.

Brotherton, David C., and Philip Kretsedemas. 2008. *Keeping out the other: A critical introduction to immigration enforcement today*. New York, NY: Columbia University Press.

Brulliard, Karin. 2007 (January 8). Battling deportation often a solitary journey. *The Washington Post*.

Bureau of Justice Statistics. 2008 (June). Prison inmates at midyear 2007. *Bureau of Justice Statistics Bulletin*. Washington, DC: U.S. Department of Justice.

Carrasco, Gilbert Paul. 1997. Latinos in the United States. In *Immigrants out! The new nativism and the anti-immigrant impulse in the United States*, edited by J. F. Perea, 190–204. New York, NY: New York University Press.

Chiu, Bess, Lynly Egyes, Peter L. Markowitz, and Jaya Vasandani. 2009. *Constitution on ICE: A report on immigration home raid operations*. New York, NY: Cardozo Immigration Justice Clinic.

Chomsky, Aviva. 2007. *They take our jobs! and 20 myths about immigration*. Boston, MA: Beacon Press.

Couture, Heather, and William J. Sabol. 2007. Prison inmates at midyear 2007. Bureau of Justice Statistics. http://bjs.ojp.usdoj.gov/index.cfm?ty=pbdetail&iid=840.

Department of Homeland Security. Yearbook of immigration statistics: 2009. http://www.dhs.gov/publication/yearbook-immigration-statistics-2009-immigrants. Accessed November 12, 2015.

DeSapio, Louis, and Rodolfo O. de la Garza. 1998. *Marking Americans, remaking America: Immigration and immigration policy*. Boulder, CO: Westview Press.

Ewing, Walter. 2012. How deportations devastate families and communities. American Immigration Council. http://immigrationimpact.com/2012/08/20/how-deportations-devastate-families-and-communities/. Accessed November 3, 2015.

Factcheck.org. 2010. http://www.factcheck.org/2010/07/hoover-truman-ike-mass-deporters. Accessed December 15, 2010.

Falcone, Michael. 2009 (February 14). 100,000 parents of citizens were deported over 10 years. *New York Times*.

Gutiérrez, David G. 1995. *Walls and mirrors: Mexican Americans, Mexican immigrants, and the politics of ethnicity*. Berkeley, CA: University of California Press.

Horowitz, Carl F. 2001. An examination of U.S. immigration policy and serious crime. *Center for Immigration Studies*. http://www.cis.org/articles/2001/crime/toc.html. Accessed November 12, 2015.

Hsu, Spencer S., and N. C. Aizenman. 2010 (March 8). DHS corrects report that overstated ICE deportations under Obama. *Washington Post*. http://voices.washingtonpost.com/44/2010/03/dhs-corrects-report-that-overs.html.

Human Rights Watch. 2007. *Forced apart: Families separated and immigrants harmed by United States deportation policy*. New York, NY: Human Rights Watch. http://www.hrw.org/en/reports/2007/07/16/forced-apart.

Human Rights Watch. 2009. Discrimination, denial, and deportation. http://www.hrw.org/en/node/83651/section/2. Accessed September 15, 2010.

Illinois Coalition for Immigrant and Refugee Rights. 2009. Immigration enforcement: Realities and reforms. http://icirr.org/sites

/default/files/fact%20sheet-immigration%20enforcement.pdf. Accessed November 12, 2015.

Immigration Defense Project. 2009. *The impact of* Nijhawan v. Holder *on application of the categorical approach to aggravated felony determinations*. http://www.nilc.org/dc_conf/flashdrive09/Immigration-Law-and-Enforcement/imm-201_Nijhawanpractice advisory-NIP-NLG-IDP.pdf. Accessed June 24, 2009.

Jewkes, Yvonne. 2004. *Media and crime*. Thousand Oaks, CA: Sage Publications.

Kanstroom, Daniel. 2007. *Deportation nation: Outsiders in American history*. London: Harvard University Press.

Koch, Wendy. 2006 (April 5). U.S. urged to apologize for 1930s deportations. *USA Today*. http://www.usatoday.com/news/nation/2006-04-04-1930s-deportees-cover_x.htm.

Kurzban, Ira J. 2008. Democracy and immigration. In *Keeping out the other: A critical introduction to immigration enforcement today*, edited by D. C. Brotherton and P. Kretsedemas, 63–78. New York, NY: Columbia University Press.

Mendelson, Margot, Shayna Strom, and Michael Wishnie. 2009. *Collateral damage: An examination of ICE's fugitive operation program*. Washington, DC: Migration Policy Institute. http://www.migrationpolicy.org/pubs/NFOP_Feb09.pdf.

Morín, José Luis. 2009. *Latino/a rights and justice in the United States: Perspectives and approaches*. 2nd ed. Durham, NC: Carolina Academic Press.

Office of the United Nations High Commissioner for Human Rights. 2015. Ratification of 18 International Human Rights Treaties. http://www2.ohchr.org/english/. November 12, 2015.

Passel, Jeffrey, and D'Vera Cohn. 2009. Mexican immigrants: How many come? How many leave? http://pewhispanic.org/reports/report.php?ReportID=112. November 12, 2015.

Picket, Kerry. 2010. Ice union employees: Ice Director won't let us enforce U.S. immigration laws. *The Washington Times*. August 5. http://www.washingtontimes.com/blog/watercooler/2010/aug/5/ice-union-employees-leadership-wont-let-us-enforce. Accessed December 5, 2010.

Slevin, Peter. 2010 (July 26). Deportation of illegal immigrants under Obama administration. *Washington Post*. http://www.washingtonpost.com/wp-dyn/content/article/2010/07/25/AR2010072501790.html. Accessed December 12, 2010.

U.S. Department of Homeland Security. 2007. ICE budget sheets and DHS Office of Inspector General report. An assessment of United States Immigration and Customs Enforcement's fugitive operation teams. https://www.oig.dhs.gov/assets/Mgmt/OIG_07-34_Mar07.pdf. Accessed November 12, 2015.

U.S. Department of Homeland Security. 2009. *2008 yearbook of immigration statistics-Homeland Security*. Washington, DC: U.S. Department of Homeland Security.

U.S. Immigration and Customs Enforcement. [n.d.]. www.ice.gov. Accessed September 15, 2010.

Walker, Nancy E., J. Michael Senger, Francisco A. Villarruel, and Angela M. Arboleda. 2004. *Lost opportunities: The reality of Latinos in the U.S. criminal justice system*. Washington, DC: National Council of La Raza.

Waslin, Michelle. 2009. Citizen children neglected and deserted in wake of immigration raids. American immigration Council. http://immigrationimpact.com/2009/03/26/children-immigration-raids-urban-institute/. Accessed November 12, 2015.

Cases Cited

Carachuri-Rosendo v. Holder, 560 U.S. 563 (2010).

Chu v. Cornell, 247 F.2d 929 (9th Cir. 1957), *cert. denied*, 355 U.S. 892 (1957).

Lopez v. Gonzalez, 549 U.S. 47 (2006).

Nijhawan v. Holder, 557 U.S. 29 (2009).

Deportation Laws

Manuel D. Vargas

Persons who are not nationals of the United States, even if they are lawfully admitted immigrants, may be subject to **deportation** for engaging in criminal conduct. Under U.S. deportation laws, immigrants may be deported based on a conviction or, in some cases, based on an admission or other evidence of certain categories of criminal conduct. These laws, which were greatly expanded by Congress in 1996, have led to the deportation of hundreds of thousands of immigrants since 1996 and have had a disproportionate impact on Latina/o immigrants residing in the United States.

According to Department of Homeland Security (DHS) statistics, in the 10 years after the new criminal deportation laws were enacted in 1996, 763,897 persons were removed from the United States based on a criminal charge or criminal conviction. Of the people deported, 592,895 were nationals of Mexico (about 77.6 percent of the total), 64,774 were nationals of Central American countries (about 8.5 percent), 26,978 were nationals of South American countries (about 3.5 percent), and 21,887 were nationals of the Dominican Republic (about 2.9 percent). Thus, more than 90 percent of nationals from other countries removed from the United States since the new 1996 deportation laws were enacted were of Latin American origin (U.S. Department of Homeland Security 1997–2009).

Up until 1996, a long-term lawful permanent resident immigrant who became deportable based on a criminal conviction or conduct was usually eligible to apply to an immigration judge for a waiver of deportation known as a 212(c) waiver (based on the former Immigration and Nationality Act statutory citation for this waiver). An immigration judge had the discretion to grant a 212(c) waiver if the immigrant could demonstrate equities such as long residence in the United States, having a close family with lawful status in the United States, evidence of hardship to the individual and family if deportation occurred, service in the armed forces, history of employment, existence of property or business ties in the United States, evidence of value and service to the community, and proof of genuine rehabilitation.

After the 1996 amendments to the immigration laws, however, many lawful permanent residents rendered deportable based on criminal convictions or conduct are no longer eligible to have such equities considered by an immigration judge prior to entry of a **removal** order. This is primarily due to two congressional enactments in 1996: the Antiterrorism and Effective Death Penalty Act (AEDPA), which came into effect on April 24, 1996, and the Illegal Immigration Reform and Immigrant Responsibility Act (IIRIRA), which generally came into effect on April 1, 1997. These new enactments expanded the types of crimes and dispositions that trigger deportability and, at the same time, dramatically cut back on immigrant eligibility for relief from deportation. Additionally, agency and court interpretations of the law have further extended the negative impact of the new laws for immigrants.

Criminal Deportation Grounds

The immigration statute subjects a lawful permanent resident immigrant to removal based on a long list of criminal offenses triggering deportability. As amended by AEDPA and IIRIRA, the deportability grounds, listed in the federal code at 8 U.S.C. 1227(a), now include the following:

- Conviction of an *aggravated felony*. The immigration law "aggravated felony" ground in particular was significantly expanded by AEPDA and IIRIRA and earlier amendments so that the category now includes not only crimes such as murder and illicit **drug** or firearm trafficking, but any crime of **violence**, theft or burglary offense, or obstruction of justice offense for which an individual is sentenced to imprisonment for one year or more, any fraud or deceit offense where the loss to the victim(s) exceeds $10,000, as well as many other offenses. Despite its name, the "aggravated felony" term has been deemed to include even misdemeanors that are found to come within the immigration law definition of the term (*see, e.g., United States v. Graham*, 169 F.3d 787 (3d Cir. 1999)). Not only has the aggravated felony deportation ground been significantly expanded by statute, but federal government lawyers have sought to apply broad interpretations of its reach. For many years, for example, the federal government argued that the portion of the aggravated felony definition covering "**drug trafficking** crimes" could include even many low-level simple possession offenses. This interpretation of the statute was rejected 8 to 1 and 9 to 0 as overly broad in two decisions of the U.S. Supreme Court (*see Lopez v. Gonzales*, 549 U.S. 47 (2006) (finding 8 to 1 that the petitioner's single state drug simple possession offense could not be deemed a drug-trafficking aggravated felony) and *Carachuri-Rosendo v. Holde*r, 560 U.S. 563 (2010) (finding 9 to 0 that the petitioner's second or subsequent drug simple possession offense could not be deemed a drug-trafficking felony). The Court observed that "ordinarily 'trafficking' means some sort of commercial dealing" and stated that the government's broad interpretation of the immigration statute nevertheless would turn simple possession into trafficking, "just what the English language tells us not to expect" (*Lopez* at 54).
- Conviction of a *crime involving moral turpitude committed within five years of admission to the United States and punishable by a year in prison*. The "crime involving moral turpitude" immigration law term includes crimes in many different criminal-offense categories; for example, crimes in which either an intent to steal or to defraud is an element (such as theft and forgery offenses); crimes in which bodily harm is caused or threatened by an intentional or willful act, or serious bodily harm is caused or threatened by an act of recklessness (such as murder, rape, and certain manslaughter and assault offenses); and most sex offenses. In most states, many misdemeanors as well as felonies are punishable by a year so the offenses could, if deemed to involve moral turpitude, make an immigrant deportable if he or she committed the offense within five years after admission to the United States.
- Conviction of two crimes involving moral turpitude, whether felony or misdemeanor, committed at any time and regardless of actual or potential sentence.
- Conviction of any controlled substance offense (other than a single offense of simple possession of 30 grams or less of marijuana), whether felony or misdemeanor.
- Conviction of a firearm or destructive device offense, whether felony or misdemeanor.

- Conviction of a crime of **domestic violence**, stalking, or child abuse, neglect, or abandonment, whether felony or misdemeanor.

Further expanding the reach of these criminal grounds for deportation, Congress, in the 1996 IIRIRA amendments, expanded the types of criminal case dispositions that now can be considered convictions for immigration purposes. Congress defined "conviction" for immigration purposes to include not only formal judgments of guilt, but also dispositions where adjudication of guilt is "withheld" but where the following two requirements are met: (1) a judge or jury has found the alien guilty or the alien has entered a **plea** of guilty or *nolo contendere* or has admitted sufficient facts to warrant a finding of guilt; and (2) the judge has ordered some form of punishment, penalty, or restraint on the alien's liberty to be imposed (8 U.S.C. 1101(a) (48)(A)). The United States Justice Department has taken a very broad view of the reach of this new statutory definition. As a result, many state criminal dispositions that are not convictions for any other purpose under state law now will be considered convictions triggering deportation.

In a 1999 decision, for example, the Justice Department's Board of Immigration Appeals found that an immigrant who'd had his guilty plea to the offense of possession of a controlled substance vacated and his case dismissed upon termination of his probation under the criminal laws of the State of Idaho nevertheless was deemed to have a conviction for immigration purposes. Going further than necessary to decide the case at hand, the board stated:

> We . . . interpret the new definition to provide that an alien is considered convicted for immigration purposes upon the initial satisfaction of the requirements of [the statutory definition], and that he remains convicted notwithstanding a subsequent state action purporting to erase all evidence of the original determination of guilt through a rehabilitative procedure (*see Matter of Roldan-Santoyo*, 22 I&N Dec. 512, 523 [BIA 1999]).

Criminal Inadmissibility Grounds

In addition to the grounds of deportability, the immigration statute also contains separate grounds for inadmissibility. Although the grounds apply principally to individuals who have not been lawfully admitted to the United States, they also may be applied to lawfully admitted individuals when such individuals travel abroad and seek readmission. Thus, although a lawful permanent resident immigrant generally should be concerned primarily with the deportability grounds, he or she also might need to be concerned with the inadmissibility grounds if he or she travels outside the United States.

The inadmissibility grounds, listed at 8 U.S.C. 1182(a), include the following.

- Conviction or admitted commission of any controlled substance offense, whether felony or misdemeanor (with no exception for one-time possession of less than 30 grams of marijuana), or DHS reason to believe that the individual is a drug trafficker.
- Conviction or admitted commission of a crime involving moral turpitude, whether felony or misdemeanor (subject to a petty offense exception).
- Conviction of *two or more offenses of any type with aggregate sentences to imprisonment of at least five years.*
- Prostitution and commercialized vice.

The importance for a lawful permanent resident immigrant of considering the inadmissibility as well as the deportation grounds is demonstrated by the example of an immigrant pleading guilty to possession of a small amount of marijuana. Such a conviction should not make the immigrant deportable if it does not involve possession of more than 30 grams of marijuana. Nonetheless, if this individual takes a trip outside the country, he or she could be detained and placed in removal proceedings based on the drug inadmissibility ground, which does not have an exception for the possession of a small amount of marijuana.

Removal Proceedings Based on Criminal Grounds

Removal proceedings involving criminal grounds are to take place expeditiously, generally either in the penal institution where the immigrant is serving a sentence of imprisonment, or in a DHS detention facility or DHS contract facility. Since 1998, IIRIRA has required that federal immigration authorities detain most foreign nationals convicted of offenses triggering removability, even those who are lawful permanent residents, when the individual is released from criminal custody. There is no longer any statutory right to release on bond pending completion of removal proceedings. Thus, when an immigrant becomes removable from the United States, he or she will be subject to the issuance of a DHS detainer on the penal custodian and DHS detention upon completion of prison time. If the immigrant is not sentenced to prison time, he or she is subject to immediate DHS arrest and detention. Under the statute, an immigrant could be released pending completion of removal proceedings only if release "is necessary to provide protection to a witness, a potential witness, a person cooperating with an investigation into major criminal activity, or an immediate family member or close associate of a witness, potential witness, or person cooperating with such an investigation" (8 U.S.C. 1226(c)).

IIRIRA also provides that, if an immigrant is convicted of certain offenses or receives a jail sentence of a certain length, he or she not only is rendered deportable or inadmissible but also is unable to ask the immigration judge for virtually any form of relief from deportation that might have been available in the past. For example, a lawful permanent resident immigrant is eligible to seek cancellation of removal—the discretionary form of relief currently in the statute to replace the 212(c) waiver—if the individual has been a permanent resident for at least five years at the time of his or her removal hearing, and the individual can show that he or she has resided in the United States continuously for more than seven years after lawful admission in any status (8 U.S.C. 1229 b (a)). The clock for the seven-years residence requirement stops at the time of commission of an offense triggering deportability or inadmissibility; however, it does so only if the offense is one of those "referred to" in the INA 212(a)(2) crime-related grounds of inadmissibility (*see* 8 U.S.C. 1229b (d) (1)). Finally—and significantly—the individual must not have been convicted of an aggravated felony, an ever-expanding category of crimes. Thus, if the disposition of a criminal case not only makes the immigrant deportable or inadmissible but also ineligible for any relief, removal will be mandatory regardless of U.S. family ties or other equities.

The immigration statute now requires that the DHS remove a foreign national with a final order of removal from the United States within 90 days (8 U.S.C. 1231(a)(1)(A)). If the individual is incarcerated when the removal order becomes final, the 90-day period begins on the date the individual completes his or her criminal imprisonment and is released to DHS custody (8 U.S.C. 1231(a)(1)(B)). Once the removal order is final and the DHS has taken custody, the DHS is required to detain the individual during the 90-day period (8 U.S.C. 1231(a)(2)). Under the statute, if the person is removable for crime-related reasons, the DHS can detain the individual for a reasonable period beyond the 90-day period until removal is accomplished (8 U.S.C. 1231(a)(6)).

Consequences of Removal Based on Criminal Grounds

If an immigrant is removed from the United States, the reality in many cases, if not most, is that the individual never will be able to return to the United States, at least not for permanent residence. In the case of an immigrant removed on the basis of virtually any drug offense, the drug offense makes the individual permanently inadmissible. For admission as a permanent resident after removal, a possibility of a waiver exists only for a single offense of simple possession—for one's own use—of 30 grams or less of marijuana (*see* 8 U.S.C. 1182(a)(2)(A)(i)(II), and (C); 8 U.S.C. 1182(h)). A more general waiver exists for admission as a temporary visitor, but this waiver is difficult to obtain and will not allow the individual to reestablish any lawful residence that he or she previously had in the United States (*see* 8 U.S.C. 1182(d)(3)).

An immigrant who is removed on the basis of conviction of an aggravated felony also is made permanently inadmissible (8 U.S.C. 1182(a)(9)(A)). Although there is an exception to this ground of inadmissibility if the individual obtains the consent of the attorney general prior to reapplying for admission (8 U.S.C. 1182(a)(9)(A)(iii)), such consent is difficult to obtain.

Lastly, even if the immigrant does not fall within the drug-related grounds of inadmissibility, or is not removed on the basis of an aggravated felony conviction, he or she could be barred from future admission after removal for 5 years (in the case of a first removal based on inadmissibility), 10 years (in the case of a first removal based on deportability), or 20 years (in the case of a second or subsequent removal) (8 U.S.C. 1182(a)(9)(A)). Additionally, the individual should not be under the impression that he or she automatically will be able to return once the period of 5, 10, or 20 years has passed. Although the bar on admission based on the prior removal no longer will be present, the individual still must otherwise establish eligibility for an immigrant visa. This very well might not be a possibility.

If the immigrant attempts unauthorized reentry after being removed, then he or she is subject to federal prosecution under federal immigration criminal laws for lengthy federal prison sentences. These laws now provide for a sentence of up to 20 years if the individual had been removed subsequent to conviction of an aggravated felony; up to 10 years if the individual had been removed subsequent to conviction of any felony other than an aggravated felony, or three or more misdemeanors involving drugs or crimes against the person; and up to 2 years in other cases (8 U.S.C. 1326). In recent years, U.S. attorneys' offices across the country have dramatically stepped up enforcement of these criminal provisions.

See also: Part I essays: Latina/o Immigrants, Crime, and Justice; The U.S. War on Drugs and Latina/o Communities; Incarceration and Latinas/os in the United States; Crime and the U.S.-Mexican Border. Part II entries: Deportation; Immigrant Detention Centers; Immigration and Customs Enforcement (ICE); Mexicans and Mexican-Americans.

Further Reading

Brady, Katherine, and Dan Kesselbrenner. 2008. *Grounds of deportability and inadmissibility related to crimes*. http://nationalimmigrationproject.org/resources/deportation/General%20Information/Grounds%20of%20Deportability%20and%20Admissibility.pdf. Accessed November 13, 2015.

Families for Freedom and NYSDA Immigrant Defense Project. 2008. *Deportation 101: Detention, deportation, and the criminal justice system*. http://familiesforfreedom.org/sites/default/files/documents/NYCAreaDeportation101.pdf. Accessed November 13, 2015.

Transactional Records Access Clearinghouse. 2006. *Aggravated felonies and deportation*. http://www.trac.syr.edu/immigration/reports/155/. Accessed October 22, 2015.

Transactional Records Access Clearinghouse. 2008. *Immigration overshadows all other administration enforcement efforts*. http://www.trac.syr.edu/whatsnew/email.080716.html. Accessed October 22, 2015.

U.S. Department of Homeland Security. 1997–2009. *Yearbook of immigration statistics*. http://www.dhs.gov/sites/default/files/publications/ois_yb_2009.pdf. Accessed November 12, 2015.

Vargas, Manuel D. 1999 (July 12). Immigration consequences of conviction: Noncitizens may face mandatory removal. *New York Law Journal*.

Vargas, Manuel D. 2006. Immigration consequences of guilty pleas or convictions. *NYU Review of Law and Social Change* 30: 701–16.

Cases Cited

Carachuri-Rosendo v. Holder, 560 U.S. 563 (2010).

Lopez v. Gonzales, 549 U.S. 47 (2006).

Matter of Roldan-Santoyo, 22 I&N Dec. 512, 523 (BIA 1999).

United States v. Graham, 169 F.3d 787 (3d Cir. March 5, 1999).

Díaz, José. *See* Part I essay: Gangs in the United States and Latina/o Communities. Part II entry: Civilian Oversight of Police.

Domestic Violence. *See* Part II entry: Intimate Partner Violence/Domestic Violence.

Dominicans

Charles R. Venator-Santiago

Not enough has been written about the experience of Dominicans with the U.S. criminal justice system. However, it is known that Dominicans have disproportionately high levels of incarceration and **deportation** rates. Those interested in the study of the relationship between Dominicans and the United States criminal justice system are encouraged to look at various dimensions of the criminal justice system and the role of legal actors such as judges, juries, clerks, and case managers. More importantly, it is also crucial to explore both behavioral and structural questions related to the status of Dominicans within the U.S. criminal justice system.

A recent demographic profile of Dominicans in the United States by Pew Research Center/Hispanic Trends, based on the American Community Survey, indicate that Dominicans are the fifth largest population of Latinos living in the United States. An estimated 1.5 million Dominicans reside in the United States, accounting for upwards of 3.0 percent of the overall Latina/o population in the country. Although almost six out of every ten Dominicans residing in the United States was born in the Dominican Republic (57 percent), a majority (70 percent) of Dominicans in the United States are U.S. citizens. The Dominican population is a fairly young population with an approximate median age of 29 in 2010. The largest portion of the

Dominican community in the United States lives in the Northeast with the greatest number in New York State, and the county with the most Dominicans is the county of the Bronx, New York. Dominicans have a slightly lower level of educational attainment than the overall U.S. population of 28 percent, with about 26 percent of the Dominican population in the United States 25 years of age and older having earned at least a bachelor's degree. The rate of poverty among Dominicans at 26 percent, however, was greater than the general U.S. population at 15 percent, and slightly lower than Hondurans, Puerto Ricans, and Mexicans, respectively, at 27 percent (Motel & Patten 2012).

Researchers often use demographic data to understand the social context of a particular group within the criminal justice system. Demographic data can help us better understand some of the underlying socio-economic conditions that could be influencing individual behaviors as well as the structural context that shapes the relationship between a particular population and the criminal justice system. It is known, for example, that as immigrants and migrants establish roots in the United States they tend to acculturate and incorporate some of the cultural norms of their new home environment.

In the case of Dominicans, the high proportion of migration and transnational connections between the U.S. and the Dominican Republic suggests that Dominicans' attitudes towards the U.S. criminal justice system might be highly informed by their experiences—or the experiences of friends and relatives—with the Dominican criminal justice system. Some research suggests that Dominican perceptions and responses to the criminal justice system are informed by cultural interpretations that are rooted in both the island cultural experiences and the U.S. mainland experiences. Another example can be drawn from research on the relationship between youth and high levels of criminal activity within a community. Mainstream criminal justice research suggests that most offenders tend to be younger and that patterns of crime within a community could be explained by demographic cycles within a particular group. Some researchers would correlate high levels of crime within Dominican communities to high levels of youth and poverty within this particular population. Of course, other ongoing research also suggests that the increasing number of penalties that are ascribed to immigrants by changes in immigration law actually could be contributing to the inflation of the statistics of Dominicans who are accused of committing felonies. The point, however, is to consider how demographic patterns can provide insights into developing a more comprehensive understanding of the relationship between Dominicans and the criminal justice system.

Dominicans, like other immigrant groups in the United States, have long been subject to **racial profiling** and to disproportionate detentions by law enforcement. Research and polls suggest that Dominican perceptions of the police are fairly negative. These perceptions have been informed by consistent abuses committed by law enforcement officers towards Dominicans and other Latinos. The killing of **José "Kiko" Garcia** in 1992 by members of the New York Police Department (NYPD) is emblematic of the interactions and resulting perceptions of the relationship between the police and Dominicans in the United States. According to public accounts, an NYPD officer shot Mr. Garcia at point blank while seeking to arrest him for the alleged possession of a gun in the entryway of an apartment building located in Washington Heights. Witnesses described how Mr. Garcia had been harassed by police officers and subsequently shot at close range without provocation. After a Grand Jury refused to indict the police officers responsible for the death of Mr. Garcia, Dominican residents of Washington Heights and other surrounding areas took to the streets for several days to protest the criminal justice system's failure to provide justice to Mr. Garcia. Mr. Garcia's case, like other cases of police brutality, came to symbolize abusive treatment of Dominicans by the police and the criminal justice system.

As a result of these and other widespread experiences with police abuse and discrimination, Dominicans (like other Latinas/os and persons of color) tend to be distrusting of the police. Research also suggests that Dominican immigrants and migrants, like other groups, are more likely to have had negative experiences with the police in their country of origin. Additionally, the lack of appropriate Spanish-language and **culturally competent** services tends to discourage Dominicans from reporting crimes. Notwithstanding the prevalence of general distrust towards policing entities, some available research suggests that when Dominicans do report crimes, they are more likely to report property offenses and violent crimes over drug-related crimes. Despite the fact that Dominicans are more likely to be arrested and subsequently convicted on drug-related offenses, property crimes such as home break-ins and burglaries are perceived as more shameful culturally. Dominicans both on the island and in the United States are twice as likely to report burglaries and other violent offenses as they are to report drug-related crimes.

A report by the Northern Manhattan Coalition for Immigrant Rights (NMICR) suggests that the combination of overpolicing Dominican neighborhoods, racial profiling, lack of job opportunities, and increasingly punitive laws have led to a disproportionately high rate of incarceration of Dominicans. Most Dominicans who are prosecuted face drug-related charges. Many state correctional systems coordinate with the federal government to notify immigration agents once they identify an undocumented immigrant. Special agreements between the United States and Dominican governments also facilitate the deportation of Dominicans, which in turn account for a disproportionate number of Dominican deportations from the United States.

Deportations have sharply defined another dimension of the relationship between Dominicans and the criminal justice system. Dominicans historically have been deported in disproportionally high numbers. According to the NMICR, in 2007 Dominicans had the highest proportion of criminal deportees. The deportation process has created a number of challenges for most Dominicans residing in the United States. It is estimated that every Dominican family has either a family member or a friend who has been deported to the Dominican Republic.

The U.S. deportation process is mired with policies and practices that can run counter to basic human and **civil rights**. Deportees have been subject to ex post facto sentencing and basic due process violations. Because the courts have established that migrants are not entitled to the same civil rights as citizens and because the U.S. government refuses to become a party to key human-rights conventions, challenging the policies and practices of U.S. government agencies has been difficult. The case of *Duarnis Perez v. United States* (2006) provides a glimpse into the often unjust deportation policies.

In 1988, Duarnis Perez unknowingly became a citizen through the naturalization of his mother. On July 5, 1996, Mr. Perez was convicted for the manufacture and sale of heroin. He promptly was deported to the Dominican Republic. In 2000, Mr. Perez was arrested in New York and charged with illegal reentry. After serving the full term of his imprisonment, and while discussing the terms of his release, Mr. Perez met with an **Immigration and Customs Enforcement** (ICE) official who informed him that he had been a U.S. citizen since 1988. Mr. Perez demanded to be released on account that he had been improperly sentenced for an immigration violation even though he was a citizen at the time. The U.S. government refused and Mr. Perez sued in federal court, where the court ruled that the government had violated his right to due process under the U.S. Constitution for wrongfully deporting and incarcerating, knowing that he was, in fact, a U.S. citizen yet prosecuting him for illegal reentry into the country. What made this case so egregious is that the U.S. government continued to challenge Mr. Perez in court, even though the evidence of the ICE agent's violation of Mr. Perez's civil rights was incontrovertible.

The study of the relationship between Dominicans and the criminal justice system begs a more concerted focus on the disproportionate application of the law on the Dominican population in the United States. The relationship between the Dominican community and policing as well as questions of human and civil rights as they pertain to the criminal prosecution deserve particular attention.

See also: Part I essays: Latinas/os and the U.S. Criminal Justice System; Incarceration and Latinas/os in the United States; Part II entries: Civil Rights; Deportation; Deportation Laws.

Further Reading

Brotherton, David C., and Philip Kretsedemas (eds.). 2008. *Keeping out the other: A critical introduction to immigration enforcement today.* Columbia University Press.

Davis, Robert C., and Nicole J. Henderson. 2003. Willingness to report crimes: The role of ethnic group membership and community efficacy. *Crime & Delinquency* 49: 564–80.

Dow, Mark. 2004. *American gulag, inside U.S. Immigration prisons.* Berkeley: University of California Press.

Hernández, Ramona, and Silvio Torres-Saillant. 1996. Dominicans in New York: Men, women, and prospects. In *Latinos in New York: Communities in transition,* edited by Gabriel Haslip-Viera, and Sherrie. L. Baver, 30–56. Notre Dame, Indiana: Notre Dame University Press.

Jackall, Robert. 1997. *Wild cowboys, urban marauders and other forces of order.* Cambridge: Harvard University Press.

Motel, Seth, and Eileen Patten. 2012. The 10 Largest Hispanic-origin groups: Characteristics, rankings, top counties. Washington, DC: Pew Research Center/Hispanic Trends. http://www.pewhispanic.org/2012/06/27/the-10-largest-hispanic-origin-groups-characteristics-rankings-top-counties/.

Northern Manhattan Coalition for Immigrant Rights. 2009. Deportado, Dominicano y humano: The realities of Dominican deportations and related policy recommendations. New York: Northern Manhattan Coalition for Immigrant Rights. http://nmcir.org/Deportado%20Dominicano%20y%20Humano.pdf.

Cases Cited

Duarnis Perez v. United States, 502 F. Supp. 2d 301 (N.D.N.Y. 2006).

Driving While Brown. *See* Part I essays: Latinas/os and the U.S. Criminal Justice System; Policing and Latina/o Communities. Part II entries: Civil Rights; Civilian Oversight of Police.

Drug Trafficking. *See* Part I essays: The U.S. War on Drugs and Latina/o Communities; Latinas and the U.S. Criminal Justice

System; Incarceration and Latinas/os in the United States; Gangs in the United States and Latina/o Communities; Crime and the U.S.-Mexican Border; Latina/o Youth and Criminal Justice. Part II entries: Colombians; Deportation Laws.

Drug Treatment. *See* Part I essays: The U.S. War on Drugs and Latina/o Communities; Policing and Latina/o Communities; Latinas and the U.S. Criminal Justice System.

Drug Use. *See* Part I essays: The U.S. War on Drugs and Latina/o Communities; Policing and Latina/o Communities; Latinas and the U.S. Criminal Justice System; Incarceration and Latinas/os in the United States; Latina/o Youth and Criminal Justice. Part II entries: Chicanas/os; Cultural Criminology; Colombians; Felon Disenfranchisement.

Drug User/Courier Profile. *See* Part I essays: Incarceration and Latinas/os in the United States; Latinas/os and the U.S. Criminal Justice System; The U.S. War on Drugs and Latina/o Communities; Latinas and the U.S. Criminal Justice System. Part II entries: Colombians; *Immigration and Naturalization Service (INS) v. Lopez-Mendoza et al.*, 468 U.S. 1032 (1984).

Drugs. *See* Part I essays: Latinas/os and the U.S. Criminal Justice System; Latina/o Immigrants, Crime, and Justice; The U.S. War on Drugs and Latina/o Communities; Policing and Latina/o Communities; Latinas and the U.S. Criminal Justice System; Incarceration and Latinas/os in the United States; Gangs in the United States and Latina/o Communities; Latina/o Youth and Criminal Justice. Part II entries: Civil Rights; Colombians; Deportation; Deportation Laws; Language Rights in the Courts.

E

Early Intervention. *See* Part I essays: Latinas/os and the U.S. Criminal Justice System; Latina/o Youth and Criminal Justice.

F

Family Issues. *See* Part I essays: Latinas/os and the U.S. Criminal Justice System; Gangs in the United States and Latina/o Communities; Crime and the U.S.-Mexican Border; Latina/o Youth and Criminal Justice. Part II entries: Deportation; Segregation.

Felon Disenfranchisement

Juan Cartagena

Felon disfranchisement is the amalgamation of laws that in some states go back hundreds of years and remove the basic badge of citizenship—the franchise—from a segment of our population. Presumably still citizens, persons with felony convictions become even more invisible by these laws. Civil death, as recognized in Anglo-Saxon jurisprudence, removed political rights and even property from those guilty of serious crimes and also was reflected in the societal norms of Greek and Roman civilizations that removed political rights from those who committed transgressions against customary law. After the Revolutionary War, the newly independent states maintained the civil disabilities that accompanied the commission of "infamous" crimes, creating the foundation of today's felon disfranchisement. Currently, 48 states engage in some combination of eliminating the franchise to prisoners, probationers, and parolees or, in the case of 11 states, permanently disfranchise any citizen convicted of a felony. Only Maine and Vermont allow prisoners to vote from their cells, as do Canada and Puerto Rico. In 2015, approximately 5.85 million people across the United States were unable to vote as a result of laws that ban the exercise of the franchise for persons with felony convictions (The Sentencing Project 2015).

The United States has the highest rate of incarceration in the world—716 out of 100,000 residents in 2011 and, in total, 2.2 million people in the nation's prisons or jails in 2012 (The Sentencing Project 2014). When viewed from the prism of adults only, the rate of incarceration for whites is one in 194, for African Americans is one in 29, and for Latinos is one in 64 (Pew Center on the States 2008). This national data obscures the effects of **mass incarceration** at the state level, where white incarceration never surpasses the national average but in Pennsylvania, Idaho, Connecticut, Massachusetts, Arizona, New Hampshire, and Colorado the incarceration rates for Latinos are well above average at more than 1,000 for every 100,000 Latino residents. Similarly, North Dakota, Montana, Utah, Texas, Oklahoma, California, New York, Iowa, Kentucky, and Nebraska have rates for Latinos that exceed the national average (Paige & Beck 2006).

The effects of the use of mass incarceration as a social tool cannot be measured solely by the harms caused to the individual prisoners or the disruption and dislocation produced for families, as important as those might be. The "punishment industry," as Angela Davis (2003) calls it, also suppresses the political voice of prisoners and former prisoners, renders voiceless the home communities from which they came and where they still reside, and dilutes the collective voting strength of Latinos as a whole.

Recent developments in the courts—especially foreign courts—have condemned this practice, but felon disfranchisement nonetheless is common in the Americas. Recently, the highest courts in Canada, South Africa, Israel, and the European Court of Human Rights have decisively and eloquently outlawed incarceration disfranchisement. Legal cases addressing this issue include the Canadian case of *Suave v. Canada* (*Chief Electoral Officer*), 3 S.C.R. 519, 2002 SCC 68 (2002); the South African case of *Minister of Home Affairs v. National Institute for Crime Prevention and Reintegration of Offenders* (CCT 03/04, 2004); the Israeli case of *Hilla Alrai v. Minister of the Interior*, HC 2757/96 (1996); and, in Europe, the *Hirst v. United Kingdom*, (*Hirst No. 2*) [2005] ECHR 681) case.

In Canada, Chief Justice McLachlin wrote, "Denial of the right to vote to penitentiary inmates undermines the legitimacy of government. . . . It is more likely to erode the respect for the rule of law than to enhance it, and more likely to undermine sentencing goals of deterrence and rehabilitation than to further them" (*Suave v. Canada* (*Chief Electoral Officer*), 3 S.C.R. 519, 2002 SCC 68, para. 58 [2002]). Similarly, in Puerto Rico, voting is extended to all duly qualified prisoners since 1980 and their votes are pivotal in close elections (*Partido Socialista Puertorriqueño v. Comisión Estatal de Elecciones y Administrador General de Elecciones,* 80 JTS 92 [at 1738], citing 16 L.P.R.A. 3052 to 3242, as amended by Ley Núm. 3 of September 8, 1980; Rivera Vargas 2004).

Puerto Rico, however, clearly is the exception within Latin America and the Caribbean. No other country in the Americas—indeed, in the world—is as punitive and retrogressive in its felon disfranchisement policies as is the United States, further marginalizing U.S. election systems as models of inequality. The United States is the only country in the Americas that permanently disfranchises its citizens across broad categories of crimes. Incarceration disfranchisement is the most common form of disfranchisement in the Americas, but a number of countries follow the U.S. practice of extending the period of disfranchisement, including Chile, Costa Rica, Cuba, Dominican Republic, Mexico, and Uruguay. Conversely, the Latin American nations that have limited the practice to incarceration disfranchisement are Panama, Paraguay, Peru, and Venezuela.

Felon disfranchisement reform focuses primarily on America's black community—and rightfully so, because blacks remain disproportionately found among the prison and parolee population in numbers that are inconsistent with propensity for crime, in general, or propensity for illegal **drug use** and trade, in particular. Latinas and Latinos also are disproportionately saddled with these disabilities but because their numbers are not as stark as African Americans, or because data collection is woefully inadequate and mired in a **black-white binary**, or because Latino civil rights and advocacy organizations have yet to fully understand the effects of a discriminatory criminal justice system on Latino community life, the debate has not fully incorporated Latino voices of concern.

This is not true in the courts, however, where Latino prisoners have been in the forefront as catalysts to legal challenges to the discriminatory felon disfranchisement laws. In the 1970s, Mr. Abran Ramirez, a former prisoner in California, brought an Equal Protection Clause constitutional challenge to felon disfranchisement that went all the way to the U.S. Supreme Court and lost. His case, *Richardson v. Ramirez* (1974), was brought by formerly incarcerated Latinos before the

Supreme Court which rejected the constitutional challenge by noting that felon disfranchisement is sanctioned by the Fourteenth Amendment of the Constitution, thereby converting a section of that amendment meant to politically penalize states that came into the Union after the Civil War that insisted on disqualifying former slaves, into a sword against full black and Latino political empowerment. Not until the passage of the Fifteenth Amendment were states directly prohibited from denying the vote on the basis of race.

Following this lead, Latino prisoners were major players in four out of the five major lawsuits filed since then, with the only exception being *Johnson v. Governor of Fla.,* 2005 WL 832357 (11th Cir. April 12, 2005) (en banc), which was brought only on behalf of African American voters in Florida. *Farrakhan v. Washington* (2009), a Voting Rights Act challenge to the discriminatory nature of felon disfranchisement in Washington State, was brought by black, Latino, and Native American prisoners. *Hayden v. Pataki* (2006), a constitutional law challenge to New York's felon disfranchisement laws, was brought by black and Latino prisoners and parolees. In Massachusetts, where prisoners were able to vote from their cells as recently as the 2000 election, Pedro Valentin was one of three prisoners who sued to restore the vote to prisoners in the case of *Simmons v. Galvin* (2009). Although keeping open the possibility of other types of claims under the Voting Rights Act, the court in the *Simmons* case ruled that, based on its reading of the history and language of the Voting Rights Act, Congress never intended section 2 of the Act to bar states from disenfranchising felons that currently are incarcerated.

Lastly, *New Jersey State Conference NAACP v. Harvey* (2005) was an unsuccessful state constitutional law challenge in New Jersey to felon disfranchisement and its effects on black and Latino parolees. The fact that three of these court challenges to felon disfranchisement were prisoner-led distinguishes these efforts in the courts from Latino advocacy efforts in general. In Washington, New York, and Massachusetts, prisoners acting as their own attorneys pro se, filed the actions and subsequently public interest law attorneys followed the call.

What these prisoners are reclaiming, in large part and often with no response, are the number of lost votes in Latino communities in a handful of critical states. The states of California, Texas, New York, and Florida each rank among the top four states with the largest Latino populations and also among the top four states with the largest number of prisoners in the country. The negative effects of felon disfranchisement on Latino political strength result in California potentially losing 100,000 Latino votes in 2003 due to felon disfranchisement; Texas losing 156,000 Latino votes in 2003; New York losing 43,000 Latino votes in 2003; and Florida losing 119,000 Latino votes in 2002 (Demeo & Ochoa 2003; Cartagena 2008). Even when adjusting these numbers for citizenship, the number of lost votes is significant. An estimated half a million Latino votes are lost because of felon disfranchisement in the states of Arizona, California, Florida, Nebraska, Nevada, New York, North Carolina, Texas, Virginia, and Washington alone.

Every state that sanctions felon disfranchisement conditions the qualifications for the franchise on the operation of its own criminal justice system. When the latter produces discriminatory and biased outcomes the State then operates, manages, and establishes both arms of governmental activity implicated in felon disfranchisement. Advocates argue that when states delegate defining who is disqualified from voting to their criminal courts, they must be held accountable for the discriminatory results of felon disfranchisement. They assert that assessing Latino collective political strength requires a look at the "punishment industry" and its legacy in our streets today, and that to ignore the intersection of criminal justice and Latino political power is to ignore a major obstacle in the struggle for social justice.

See Part I essays: Latinas/os and the U.S. Criminal Justice System; Incarceration and Latinas/os in the United States. Part II entries: Civil Rights; International Human Rights; Segregation.

Further Reading

Cartagena, Juan. 2008. Lost votes, body counts and joblessness: The effects of felon disfranchisement on Latino civic engagement. *Latino Studies* 6: 192–200. doi:10.1057/lst.2008.12.

Davis, Angela Y. 2003. *Are prisons obsolete?* New York: Seven Stories Press.

Demeo, Marisa J., and Steven A. Ochoa. 2003. *Diminished voting power in the Latino community: The impact of felony disenfranchisement in ten targeted states*. Washington, DC: Mexican American Legal Defense and Education Fund.

Paige, Harrison M., and Allen J. Beck. 2006. *Prison and jail inmates at midyear, 2005* (NCJ 213133). Washington, DC: U.S. Department of Justice, Bureau of Justice Statistics.

Pettus, Katherine Irene. 2005. *Felony disfranchisement in America: Historical origins, institutional racism, and modern consequences*. New York: LFB Scholarly Publishing.

Pew Center on the States. 2008. One in 100: Behind bars in America 2008. Washington, DC: The Pew Charitable Trusts. http://www.pewtrusts.org/~/media/legacy/uploadedfiles/wwwpewtrustsorg/reports/sentencing_and_corrections/onein100pdf.pdf.

Rivera Vargas, Daniel. 2004 (December 21). "A contar votos de presos." *El Nuevo Día*.

Sentencing Project, The. 2014. Facts about prisons and people in prison. Washington, DC: The Sentencing Project. http://sentencingproject.org/doc/publications/inc_Facts%20About%20Prisons.pdf. Accessed November 25, 2015.

Sentencing Project, The. 2015. Felony disenfranchisement restriction by state, 2015. Washington, DC: The Sentencing Project. http://sentencingproject.org/template/page.cfm?id=133. Accessed November 25, 2015.

Sentencing Project, The, and International Human Rights Clinic, Washington College of Law, American University. 2007. Barriers to democracy: A petition to the Inter-American Commission on Human Rights for a thematic hearing on felony disenfranchisement practices in the United States and the Americas. Washington, DC: The Sentencing Project. http://www.sentencingproject.org/doc/publications/fd_PETITION%20TO%20IACHR_final_formatted.pdf. Accessed November 25, 2015.

Walker, Nancy E., J. Michael Senger, Francisco A. Villarruel, and Angela M. Arboleda. 2004. *Lost Opportunities: The reality of Latinos in the U.S. criminal justice system*. Washington, DC: National Council of La Raza.

Cases Cited

Farrakhan v. Washington, 338 F.3d 1009 (9th Cir. 2003).

Hayden v. Pataki, 449 F.3d 305 (2006).

Hilla Alrai v. Minister of the Interior, HC 2757/96 (1996).

Hirst v. United Kingdom, (*Hirst No. 2*) [2005] ECHR 681.

Johnson v. Governor of Florida, 2005 WL 832357 (11th Cir. April 12, 2005) (en banc).

Minister of Home Affairs v. National Institute for Crime Prevention and Reintegration of Offenders (CCT 03/04, 2004).

New Jersey State Conference NAACP v. Harvey, 885 A.2d 445 (N.J. Super. A.D. 2005).

Partido Socialista Puertorriqueño v. Comisión Estatal de Elecciones y Administrador

General de Elecciones, 80 JTS 92 [p. 1738], citing 16 L.P.R.A. 3052 to 3242, as amended by Ley Núm. 3 of September 8, 1980.

Richardson v. Ramirez, 418 U.S. 24 (1974).

Simmons v. Galvin, 575 F.3d 24 (2009).

Suave v. Canada (*Chief Electoral Officer*), 3 S.C.R. 519, 2002 SCC 68 (2002).

Femicide. *See* Part I essay: Latinas and the U.S. Criminal Justice System; Crime and the U.S.-Mexican Border. Part II entry: Central Americans.

Flores, Enrique Funes. *See* Part I essay: Policing and Latina/o Communities.

G

Gangs/Street Organizations. *See* Part I essays: Latinas and the U.S. Criminal Justice System; The U.S. War on Drugs and Latina/o Communities; Latinas and the U.S. Criminal Justice System; Incarceration and Latinas/os in the United States; Crime and the U.S.-Mexican Border; Gangs in the United States and Latina/o Communities; Latina/o Youth and Criminal Justice. Part II entries: Central Americans; Chicanas/os; Community-Based Latina/o Advocacy Organizations; Cubans; Cultural Criminology; Deportation; Homicide; Human Trafficking; Immigrant Detention Centers; International Human Rights; LatCrit: Latina & Latino Critical Legal Theory, Inc.; Political Activist Groups; Puerto Ricans; Salinas, Raúl R. (raúlrsalinas) (1934–2008); Segregation; Transnational Crime.

García, José "Kiko" (1968–1992). *See* Part I essay: Policing and Latina/o Communities. Part II entry: Dominicans.

Gender Issues. *See* Part I essays: Latinas/os and the U.S. Criminal Justice System; Latinas and the U.S. Criminal Justice System. Part II entries: Lesbian, Gay, Bisexual, and Transgender (LGBT); Slavery.

Gonzalez, Leticia. *See* Part I essay: Policing and Latina/o Communities.

***Gonzalez v. United States*, 33 F.3d 1047 (9th Cir. 1994).** *See* Part II entries: Language Rights in the Courts; International Human Rights.

Greaser. *See* Part I essays: Latinas/os and the U.S. Criminal Justice System; Policing and Latina/o Communities; Latina/o Youth and Criminal Justice. Part II entries: Chicanas/os; LatCrit: Latina & Latino Critical Legal Theory, Inc.; Media Depictions; Mexicans and Mexican Americans.

Greaser Act. *See* Part I essays: Latinas/os and the U.S. Criminal Justice System; Policing and Latina/o Communities; Gangs in the United States and Latina/o Communities. Part II entries: Chicanas/os; Mexicans and Mexican Americans.

H

Halo Effect. *See* Part I essay: Policing and Latina/o Communities.

Hate Crimes

Maria Swimm

Hate crimes are those criminal acts in which a person, institution, business, or other group is intimidated, physically attacked, or otherwise harmed and the motivation on the part of the offender is based—in whole or in part—on prejudice towards the victim's perceived race, ethnicity, sexual orientation, or religious affiliation. In 2009, the federal hate crime law was expanded to include protections against crimes based on actual or perceived gender, gender identity, sexual orientation, and disability. Some state hate crime protections have been extended to **victims** violated on the basis of their age, political affiliation, socioeconomic standing, or perceived status of citizenship. Current legal standards assert that for a criminal incident to be categorized as a hate crime, physical **violence**, intimidation, verbal threat, or vandalism based on hate must be present. Further categorization includes the display of hate symbols and the vocalization of insults by the perpetrator during the incident that are rooted in racial, ethnic, religious, or homosexual prejudice. Additionally, responding law enforcement personnel must confirm the crime was indeed an act of hate.

Although legal definitions can vary between jurisdictions, the common denominator in incidents categorized as hate crimes is that they are provoked by great intolerance, abhorrence, or fear. Also referred to as "bias crime" and "ethno-violence," hate crimes are those acts viewed as elements of intimidation and control that seek to dehumanize the victim, where violence is motivated purely by hatred of the "other."

Latina/o Lynching and Early Hate Crimes

Although the categorization of a crime as a hate act is a modern-day development, hate crimes long have been a part of U.S. history. Centuries of African enslavement, the near-genocide of the Native American, and the internment of the Japanese during World War II are examples of racial bias propelled by economic interests within the United States that resulted in a culture of hate—one that continues to fester in the country's foundation today. Accounts of Latinas/os as victims of hate crimes date back to the mid-19th century, when men and women of Mexican origin were abducted and lynched in the Southwest over the course of a 50-year period. Mostly members of the impoverished working class, Mexicans were criminalized by white **vigilante** groups that labeled them as inferior and undesirable, and who claimed to murder in the interest of justice and the common good. Hanged, shot, burned, and even mutilated, victims were targets of an insatiable hate that law enforcement authorities not only condoned, but also often actively participated in—with very few officers ever being made to stand trial for their criminal exploits. Latina women were victims of **lynching** as a result of having dismissed the sexual advances of white men. The mere act of speaking Spanish also was cause for a hanging death for those among the Mexican population during this time. Although some people attempt to discount this history as an extreme and remote example of ethnic intolerance, many of the elements represented in the lynching murders of **Mexicans** are readily apparent in modern-day hate crime incidents involving Latina/o victims.

Contemporary Hate Crimes

The official recording of hate crimes is a fairly recent practice in the United States. In 1990, Congress passed the Hate Crime Statistics Act which charges the Federal Bureau of Investigation (FBI) with collecting and disseminating hate crime information. Since 1992, an annual report of hate crime data collected from law enforcement agencies nationwide is published and made available to the public. Although the number of participating agencies has increased exponentially since the initial 1992 effort, reporting practices in many jurisdictions remain inadequate. As is the case with other personal crimes, such as sexual assault and **domestic violence**, many incidents are not reported to police and therefore are not counted in official records. As a result, the true volume and gravity of hate crimes in the United States remains unknown.

The range of hate crimes statistics has averaged from 6,000 to 10,000 annually since 1992. The most recent hate crimes statistics available from the FBI are from 2009, in which 6,604 hate crime incidents were recorded involving 7,789 offenses, 8,322 victims, and 6,219 offenders (Federal Bureau of Investigation 2009). Overall, national estimates of the number of hate groups in the United States show a steady increase—from 602 in the year 2000 to more than 1,000 in 2010, with the anti-government "patriot" movement organizations and radical right-wing organizations experiencing the largest growth over that period (Potok 2011, 41).

Table 9 The Rise in Hate Groups from 2000 to 2010

Year	Number of Hate Groups Nationally
2010	1002
2009	932
2008	926
2007	888
2006	844
2005	803
2004	762
2003	751
2002	708
2001	676
2000	602

Source: Compiled from Potok, Mark. 2011. U.S. hate groups top 1,000. *Intelligence Report*. Montgomery, AL: Southern Poverty Law Center. http://www.splcenter.org/get-informed/news/us-hate-groups-top-1000.

Over time, racial bias has continued to be the most prominent source of hate crimes, with African Americans and Latinas/os steadily remaining the principal targets. Religion and sexual orientation are the secondary and tertiary bases for bias crimes, with the ethnicity/national origin category following thereafter. From 2003 to 2007, anti-Latina/o hate crimes, specifically, increased by 40 percent (Potok 2008).

Because of the significant likelihood that targets of hate crimes do not report their victimization, the Department of Justice's Bureau of Justice Statistics analyzed data from

Table 10 Incidents of Anti-Latina/o Hate Crimes, 2003–2007

Year	Number of Incidents
2007	595
2006	576
2005	522
2004	475
2003	426

Source: Compiled from Potok, Mark. 2008. *Anti-Latino hate crimes rise for fourth year in a row.* Montgomery, AL: Southern Poverty Law Center. http://www.splcenter.org/blog/2008/10/29/anti-latino-hate-crimes-rise-for-fourth-year/.

the National Crime Victimization Survey (NCVS) of 2005 which uncovered an average of 191,000 hate crime incidents. Of these hate crimes, more than 75 percent were violent personal crimes, including aggravated assault, simple assault, robbery, or threats without injury. Perhaps an even more revealing result of the 2005 report was that more than 50 percent of hate crime victimizations were found to have never been reported to police. This problem is exacerbated in the unauthorized immigrant community, whose members typically are apprehensive about reporting crimes to law enforcement, fearing such interaction will result in **deportation**. According to the analysis, Latinas/os were victimized at a rate of 0.9 per 1,000 individuals, with a majority of crimes originating from ethnic bias, as compared to 0.9 victims per 1,000 whites, and 0.7 victims per 1,000 blacks (Wolf Harlow 2005, 1).

Victims of hate crimes based on sexual orientation have been a focal point in the anti-bias movement since the heinous murder of Matthew Shepard in 1998. A college student at the University of Wyoming, Shepard was targeted in a bar by two men because of his homosexuality and was lured, robbed, pistol-whipped, and tied to a fence, left to die alone in a remote field. Although hate crimes involving Latinas/os and based on sexual orientation or gender identity may not always be as prevalent as those based on ethnicity, the level of violence and humiliation employed by perpetrators in these incidences is comparably disconcerting. Bias crimes rooted in homosexual and transgender intolerance often involve more than one offender, are more likely to occur in the home as compared to other bias types, and, in number, are the most lethal of all hate acts. The number of **lesbian, gay, bisexual, and transgender** people killed in bias-motivated incidents increased by 20 percent from 2007 to 2008 (Leadership Conference on Civil Rights 2009).

As anti-Latina/o violence steadily increases, the Southern Poverty Law Center (SPLC), a non-profit organization that specializes in litigation and education combating discrimination and intolerance, reported a 48 percent swell in hate groups between 2000 and 2007 (Potok 2008). The increase is directly attributed to the anti-nativist focus of some hate groups based in areas with substantial Latina/o immigrant populations. The widespread tolerance of nativist propaganda and the unrelenting vilification of Latinas/os, including the persistent labeling of immigrants as "illegal aliens," remains a deep-seated problem within mainstream society nationwide.

Nativism and Nativist Extremist Groups

Nativism is the severe hostility toward certain groups perceived to be foreigners and "un-American," along with a strong preference for those considered "true Americans," typically white Anglos (Perea 1997, 1). The Southern Poverty Law Center characterizes "nativist extremist" groups as "organizations that do not limit themselves to pushing for legislative change or more border patrols, but rather target suspected undocumented immigrants at work sites or when they cross the border" (Beirich 2011, 35). Nativist extremist groups are those racial extremist organizations whose militaristic anti-immigration agenda specifically has targeted the unauthorized Latina/o population. Although the nativist movement has long been a source of concern for immigrant **civil rights** groups, it has gone "mainstream" since 2009, having gained political power by expanding alliances with other far-right collectives such as anti-government "patriot" groups. Since its creation in 2005, **The Minuteman Project**—a major nativist extremist group—specifically has remained a dominant threat to those individuals attempting to cross United States borders. Its citizen patrols actively engage in hate-driven violent criminal behavior, upholding the nativist doctrine that demands the "protection" of American society and its ideals from foreign influence.

Table 11 Increases in the Number of Nativist Extremist Groups in the United States, 2007–2010

Year	Number of Incidents
2010	319
2009	309
2008	173
2007	144

Source: Compiled from Beirich, Heidi. 2011 (Spring). The year in nativism, 2010. *Intelligence Report*, 35. http://www.splcenter.org/get-informed-intelligence-report/browse-all-issues/2011/spring/the-year-in-nativism. Accessed November 28, 2015.

The SPLC's best estimates are that the number of nativist extremist groups from 2007 to 2008 increased by 20 percent, from 144 to 173. Between 2008 and 2009, these groups increased nearly 80 percent, from 173 to 309. Numbering around 319 in 2010, these groups are believed to have been emboldened by the signing of Arizona's S.B. 1070, a harsh immigration law (Beirich 2011).

Although anti-Latina/o hate crimes certainly are not isolated incidents geographically, the state of New York has been an area of focus since the November 2008 stabbing murder of Ecuadorean immigrant **Marcelo Lucero** in the Long Island village of Patchogue. Law enforcement conjectured the killing was the culmination of a year-long series of anti-Latina/o attacks by local teenagers who called themselves the "Caucasian Crew" and engaged in an activity which they termed "beaner hopping." The incident caused great protest by Latina/o residents who stated that police efforts to protect the targeted population were insufficient and that unrelated hate crime events reported prior to the murder never were appropriately investigated or were neglected entirely. In May 2009, a jury found two of the seven teenage defendants guilty of simple assault despite mounting evidence of a hate-driven and violent attack. In May 2010, Jeffrey Conroy, the individual alleged to have killed Mr. Lucero, was sentenced to 25 years in prison after having been acquitted of the most serious charge against him—murder as a hate crime. The Patchogue hate crime came only months after the beating death of **Luis Ramirez** in Shenandoah,

Pennsylvania, by teenagers who yelled racial epithets while kicking the victim in the head.

In December 2010, **José Osvaldo Sucuzhañay** was stabbed and beaten to death after he and his brother were savagely attacked when walking arm in arm in the streets of Brooklyn, NY. Hit in the head with a bottle and beaten with an aluminum baseball bat while being taunted with anti-Latina/o and anti-gay slurs, the Sucuzhañay hate crime remains fresh in the minds of Latina/o residents, activists, and leaders who struggle to move past obvious sentiments of the hate they must deal with every day. The nonrandom, degrading acts of intimidation, threats of physical injury, and incidents of violence and robbery suffered by Latina/o immigrants require urgent action on the part of criminal justice authorities and legislators—who have remained complacent for much too long.

Latina/o advocacy groups such as the **Mexican American Legal Defense and Education Fund (MALDEF)** have made it a priority to work aggressively to prevent and organize against hate crimes and to punish perpetrators to the full extent of the law. **LatinoJustice PRLDEF** (Puerto Rican Legal Defense and Education Fund), a nonprofit organization organized in the early 1970s, launched a campaign to have a formal inquiry into the practices of the police department in Suffolk County, New York, where Marcelo Lucero was killed. LatinoJustice argued that the police department failed to satisfactorily protect the county's Latina/o residents and maintained a practice of asking victims about their citizenship status when reporting crimes.

In 2009, the SPLC launched its own comprehensive investigation into the anti-Latina/o hate movement in Suffolk County, examining the practices of local law enforcement when interacting with immigrant victims, and learning more about the hate incidents that go unreported and the extent to which anti-immigrant sentiment among county officials has contributed in maintaining an intolerant atmosphere. In the SPLC report titled *Climate of Fear: Latino Immigrants in Suffolk County, N.Y.* (2009), immigrant victims gave researchers firsthand accounts of the physical, psychological, and verbal abuse they endured daily by local nativists. Those who reported their victimization to police stated that they believed they were not taken seriously and often were subjected to illegal searches and seizure and even were blamed for their own victimization. Researchers put forward several measures to be taken by county officials to help correct mistakes, including a call for strict maintenance of precise hate-crime statistics, the promotion of educational programs on racial and ethnic tolerance in public schools, and the directive that those who in positions to serve and protect hate-crime victims at all levels of the criminal justice system not inquire about the victim's immigration status at any point in the investigation or legal proceedings.

Racially motivated violence often intersects with homophobia and anti-transgender animus. Over the years, the use of excessive force by police against lesbian, gay, bisexual, and transgender (LGBT) Latinas/os and African Americans has become an increasingly common and recognized phenomenon. Recent studies have sought to divulge the extent to which excessive police force, unjust arrests, and other forms of police misconduct against LGBT persons of color are substantial throughout the United States. In certain cities, such as Los Angeles and New York, Latina/o survivors of anti-LGBT hate violence make up the largest percentages of victims of such hate crimes, more than other racial and ethnic groups.

The Southern Poverty Law Center, respected for its national monitoring of hate crimes, has declared that "LGBTQ people are more victimized than any other minority. But within that world, trans women of color face the worst of all" (Terry 2015, 27). A recent survey by the National Center for Transgender Equality and the National Gay and Lesbian Task Force, reveals the "devastating" impact that "the combination of anti-transgender bias and persistent, structural racism" is having, with people of color faring worse than whites overall. As one example, 61 percent of transgender victims of physical assault report having attempted suicide, as compared to a rate of 1.6 percent for the U.S. general population (Grant et al. 2011, 2).

Legislative action in response to hate crimes in the United States was first initiated in 1994 with the passing of the Violent Crime Control and Law Enforcement Act—a measure that increased penalties for perpetrators of hate crimes committed on the basis of perceived race, religion, ethnicity, or gender. The introduction of the Local Law Enforcement Hate Crimes **Prevention** Act of 2007, more commonly referred to as the Matthew Shepard and James Byrd, Jr. Hate Crime Prevention Act, enhanced the existing federal law by eradicating the condition that the victim must be participating in a federally protected activity, such as when serving as a juror, as a student at a private college or public school or college, or as a state or private employee, when the incident occurred. On October 28, 2009, President Barack Obama signed the Act into law, extending federal protections to victims of hate acts based on sexual orientation, gender, gender identity, or disability and removing the requirement that the victim be taking part in a federally protected activity for the perpetrator to be prosecuted. In addition to these centralized measures, 46 states and the District of Columbia have enacted statutes known commonly as "hate crime laws," many of which vary from one jurisdiction to the next in terms of inclusiveness and local law enforcement responsibility.

Another development in the struggle to control bias crime is the creation of hate crime units in jurisdictions across the country where police officers are specially trained in hate crime identification and victim assistance. Although the effectiveness of these specialized units is unknown in most areas, their formation is a good first step in ensuring members of local law enforcement are knowledgeable about the distinct crime types that fall under the hate crime umbrella and the individualized needs of its victims. Improvements in record keeping and the consequential production of more accurate hate-crime statistics are expected benefits resulting from the promotion of such law enforcement efforts.

Several recommendations have been proposed by advocates and researchers in the criminal justice arena to further address the distinct problems that hate crimes present both within and outside of the Latina/o community. Law enforcement officials nationwide must train responding officers to appropriately engage hate crime victims and witnesses by not inquiring about immigration status and maintaining an unbiased, culturally sensitive approach when interviewing Latinas/os about victimization episodes.

Advocates for reform also have called for criminal justice authorities at all levels to take hate crime reports seriously and to employ responsible and sufficient investigatory methods to ensure the effective adjudication of perpetrators to deter future incidents. As has been the case in Suffolk County on Long Island, New York, the Latinas/os have complained not just of the hate crimes committed against members of their community, they also have been critical of the inaction of the Suffolk County police for failing to adequately investigate hate crimes against Latinas/os. Even under an agreement with the Justice Department to address discriminatory police practices, in 2014 the Suffolk County police were implicated in racially profiling Latina/o immigrants and robbing them, furthering distrust between Latinas/os and law enforcement officers. As a result, community activists and advocates have urged for comprehensive change that includes police accountability to safeguard community safety both from hate crimes and police abuse. The creation of multilingual community and government-based educational and outreach programs that promote tolerance and diversity also have been supported as a public service effort, as well as improvements in the collection of hate-crime data by law enforcement bodies at the local and national levels.

On June 17, 2015, a young white man shot and killed six African American women and three African American men in a historically prominent church in Charleston, South Carolina. The gunman was reported to have said that "You rape our women. And you're taking over our country. And you have to go," insinuating that he was justified because African American men rape white women (Carroll 2015). The shooting rampage, ostensibly motivated by racial hatred, came one day after billionaire real estate mogul Donald Trump remarked at his event announcing his candidacy for president that Mexico is "sending people [to the United States] that have lots of problems, and they are bringing those problems to us. They are bringing drugs, and bringing crime, and their rapists" (Neate & Stafford 2015). The massacre at Charleston and Trump's statements sparked condemnation by many but has also raised concerns about how far the country still needs to go in resolving the problem of racial and ethnic bigotry and hatred and forms of hate expressed through violence.

See also: Part I essays: Latinas/os and the U.S. Criminal Justice System; Policing and Latina/o Communities; Crime and the U.S.-Mexican Border. Part II entries: Civil Rights; Community-Based Latina/o Advocacy Organizations; Deportation; Legal Advocacy Groups; Lesbian, Gay, Bisexual, and Transgender (LGBT); Mexicans and Mexican Americans; Victims; Vigilantism.

Further Reading

Beirich, Heidi. 2009. *The nativist lobby: Three faces of intolerance.* Montgomery, AL: Southern Poverty Law Center.

Beirich, Heidi. 2011 (Spring). The year in nativism, 2010. *Intelligence Report,* 35. http://www.splcenter.org/get-informed/intelligence-report/browse-all-issues/2011/spring/the-year-in-nativism, Accessed November 28, 2015.

Carrigan, William D., and Clive Webb. 2009. Repression and resistance: The lynching of persons of Mexican origin in the United States, 1848–1928. In *How the United States racializes Latinos: White hegemony and its consequences,* edited by J. A. Cobas, J. Duany, and J. R. Feagin, 68–86. Boulder, CO: Paradigm Publishers.

Carrigan, William D., and Clive Webb. 2013. *Forgotten dead: Mob violence against Mexicans in the United States, 1848–1928.* Oxford: Oxford University Press.

Carroll, Rebecca. 2015 (June 18). The Charleston shooter killed mostly black women. This wasn't about "rape." *The Guardian.* http://www.theguardian.com/commentisfree/2015/jun/18/charleston-shooter-black-women-white-women-rape.

Delgado, Richard. (2009). The law of the noose: A history of Latino lynching. *Harvard Civil Rights and Civil Liberties Review* 44: 297–312.

Federal Bureau of Investigation. [n.d.]. Hate crimes—overview. Washington, DC:

Department of Justice, Federal Bureau of Investigation. http://www.fbi.gov/about-us/investigate/civilrights/hate_crimes/overview.

Federal Bureau of Investigation. 2009. Hate crimes statistics, 2009. Washington, DC: Department of Justice, Federal Bureau of Investigation. http://www2.fbi.gov/ucr/hc/2009/abouthcs.html.

Fernandez, Manny. 2010 (May 26). L.I. man gets 25-year term in killing of immigrant. *New York Times*. http://www.nytimes.com/2010/05/27/nyregion/27patchogue.html?_r=1&ref=marcelo_lucero.

Gonzales-Day, Ken. 2006. *Lynching in the West: 1850–1935*. Durham, NC: Duke University Press.

Grant, Jaime M., Lisa A. Mottet, Justin Tanis, Jack Harrison, Jody L. Herman, and Mara Keisling. 2011. *Injustice at every turn: A report of the National Transgender Discrimination Survey*. Washington, DC: National Center for Transgender Equality and the National Gay and Lesbian Task Force. http://www.thetaskforce.org/static_html/downloads/reports/reports/ntds_full.pdf.

Leadership Conference on Civil Rights. 2009. Confronting the new faces of hate: Hate crimes in America, 2009. http://www.civilrights.org/publications/hatecrimes/. Accessed October 22, 2015.

Matthew Shepard Foundation. 2007. http://www.matthewshepard.org/.

Mexican American Legal Defense and Education Fund. 2009. http://www.maldef.org/. Accessed October 22, 2015.

National Coalition of Anti-Violence Programs. 2014. Lesbian, gay, bisexual, transgender, queer, and HIV-affected hate violence in 2013. New York: NCAVP.

Neate, Rupert, and Zach Stafford. 2015 (June 29). Donald Trump dropped by NBC over candidate's comments about Mexico. *The Guardian*. http://www.theguardian.com/us-news/2015/jun/29/donald-trump-dropped-nbc-mexico.

Perea, Juan (ed.). 1997. *Immigrants out! The new nativism and the anti-immigrant impulse in the United States*. New York, NY: New York University Press.

Perry, Barbara. 2001. *In the name of hate: Understanding hate crimes*. New York, NY: Routledge.

Perry, Barbara. 2003. *Hate and bias crime: A reader*. New York, NY: Routledge.

Potok, Mark. 2008. Anti-Latino hate crimes rise for fourth year in a row. Montgomery, AL: Southern Poverty Law Center. http://www.splcenter.org/blog/2008/10/29/anti-latino-hate-crimes-rise-for-fourth-year/.

Potok, Mark. 2011. U.S. hate groups top 1,000. *Intelligence Report*. Montgomery, AL: Southern Poverty Law Center. http://www.splcenter.org/get-informed/news/us-hate-groups-top-1000. Accessed October 22, 2015.

Semple, Kirk. 2104 (March 2). Latino drivers report thefts by officers." *New York Times*. http://www.nytimes.com/2014/03/03/nyregion/latino-drivers-report-thefts-by-officers.html?_r=0. Accessed October 22, 2015.

Southern Poverty Law Center. 2009. *Climate of fear: Latino immigrants in Suffolk County, N.Y.* http://www.splcenter.org/news/item.jsp?aid=395.

Terry, Don. 2015 (Summer). In the crosshairs. *Intelligence Report*, 158.

Walker, Samuel, Cassia Spohn, and Miriam DeLone. 2007. *The color of justice: Race, ethnicity, and crime in America*. 4th ed. Belmont, CA: Wadsworth.

Wolf Harlow, Caroline. 2005. *Hate crimes reported by victims and police, Bureau of Justice Statistics special report*. Washington, DC: U.S. Department of Justice, Office of Justice Programs.

Hernandez v. New York, 500 U.S. 352 (1991)

Jenny Rivera

The Equal Protection Clause (Section 1 of the Fourteenth Amendment to the Constitution) provides that no state shall "deny to any person within its jurisdiction the equal protection of the laws." The prosecutor's exclusion of prospective jurors on the basis of race, ethnicity, or sex violates the Equal Protection Clause. In 1991, the U.S. Supreme Court decided *Hernandez v. New York* (1991), a case which involved the exclusion of Latinas/os from jury service. The challengers claimed that the prosecutor intentionally excluded Latinas/os because they were bilingual and understood Spanish, and that this exclusion of Latinas/os violated their rights under the Equal Protection Clause of the United States Constitution. The Court concluded that the exclusion of bilingual Latino jurors was not unconstitutional.

One mechanism for excluding prospective jurors is through the use of peremptory challenges, which allow the parties in a case to request that a prospective juror be kept from serving on the jury. The prosecutor and the defendant in a criminal prosecution each has available a set number of challenges. Once a peremptory challenge is asserted, with one exception, the party exercising the challenge does not have to explain why they are excluding the prospective juror. According to *Batson v. Kentucky* (1986), a party cannot use peremptory challenges to exclude prospective jurors based on the juror's race or ethnicity. The defendant in *Hernandez v. New York* argued that the prosecutor had used the peremptory challenges to exclude Latinas/os because of their **race and ethnicity**.

New York State successfully prosecuted Dionisio Hernandez for attempted murder and criminal possession of a weapon. Mr. Hernandez shot at Charlene Calloway and her mother Ada Saline. Ms. Calloway suffered three gunshot wounds. The remaining shots missed Ms. Saline and hit two men in a nearby restaurant. All of the victims survived. All of the witnesses were scheduled to testify in Spanish at the trial, and a court interpreter would then repeat their testimony in English, on the record. The jurors were required to follow only the English interpretation of the testimony.

During the jury selection the prosecutor exercised four peremptory challenges to exclude Latino prospective jurors. The defendant challenged the use of the peremptories claiming that the prosecutor intentionally had sought to exclude Latinas/os from the jury. The prosecutor argued that he had no motive to exclude Latinas/os because all of the complainants and the witnesses were Latino. The prosecutor excluded two Latino prospective jurors because they had brothers convicted of crimes and one had been prosecuted by the same district attorney's office that was prosecuting Hernandez. With respect to the other two prospective jurors, the prosecutor argued that—based on his observation of the prospective jurors and their responses to questions posed by the prosecutor and the judge—he was uncertain that the prospective jurors would adhere to the official interpretation of the live witness testimony. The trial court denied the defendant's motion for a mistrial and concluded that the prosecutor did not act improperly.

On appeal, the New York state appellate court affirmed the trial court, concluding that the prosecutor offered a legitimate basis for striking the prospective jurors. Two judges on the state's highest court dissented, concluding that the prosecutor's exclusion of the Latino bilingual prospective jurors violated state constitutional law.

The **Puerto Rican Legal Defense and Education Fund** (presently known as **LatinoJustice PRLDEF**), a nonprofit **civil rights** organization whose mission is to promote the rights of Latinas/os, argued the case before the Supreme Court. Counsel for PRLDEF argued that the prosecutor had violated the Equal Protection Clause and did not provide a race-neutral basis for the peremptories because Spanish-language ability is closely related to ethnicity and, thus, striking a Latino juror based on language violates the Equal Protection Clause. Also, allowing prosecutors to exclude based on bilingualism will have a disparate impact on Latinas/os, thus converting the peremptory challenge practice into one that ensures Latinas/os will not be represented fairly on juries.

The U.S. Supreme Court accepted the case on *writ of certiorari*. The Court applied the test it had set forth previously in *Batson v. Kentucky* (1986), to determine whether the prosecutor's use of peremptory challenges to exclude bilingual Latino jurors violated the Equal Protection Clause. Under the *Batson* three-part test, the defendant must establish a *prima facie* showing that the prosecutor exercised the peremptory challenge based on race. If the defendant satisfies this first step, then the burden shifts to the prosecutor to provide a race-neutral explanation for striking the prospective juror. The trial court then determines whether the prosecutor has discriminated based on race in violation of the Equal Protection Clause.

In *Hernandez v. New York*, the Supreme Court held that because an equal protection violation requires intentional discrimination and because the prosecutor had based his peremptory challenges on a race-neutral reason—specifically that the prospective jurors would not follow the official interpreter's version of the Spanish-language testimony—the prosecutor did not exclude the prospective jurors because of race. The Court distinguished between intentional discrimination and prosecutorial conduct that has a disproportionate impact on one group over another. The Court stated that the prosecutor had distinguished between prospective jurors whose conduct suggested to the prosecutor that they would not be able to accept the interpreter's version of the testimony and those prospective jurors whose conduct did not raise such a concern. Because each category includes Latinas/os and non-Latinas/os, the fact that Latinas/os would be disproportionately impacted was not alone a basis to conclude that the prosecutor violated the Constitution.

According to the Court, the prosecutor did not violate the Equal Protection Clause because he did not exclude prospective Latino jurors because they are Latino or because of some stereotype about Latino jurors, but rather because of his concern regarding their ability to accept the interpreter's version of the testimony. Thus, the prosecutor did not rely solely on the language ability of the prospective jurors, but rather on their conduct during the jury selection process.

The Supreme Court did not decide under what circumstances discrimination against Latinas/os based on language acquisition and language status constitutes unlawful discrimination based on race or ethnicity. The Court, however, suggested that language indeed might constitute a characteristic sufficiently significant to a group (such as Latinas/os) that to discriminate based on language is akin to discrimination based on race. In the words of the Supreme Court, "It may well be, for certain ethnic groups and in some communities, that proficiency in a particular language, like skin color, should be treated as a surrogate for race under an equal protection analysis" (*Hernandez v. New York*, 500 U.S. 352, 371 (1991)).

Three Justices (Blackmun, J., Stevens, J., and Marshall, J.) dissented, concluding that disparate impact can sufficiently establish discriminatory purpose. The dissenters noted that when the prosecutor's concern can be accommodated, the reason cannot justify the exclusion. The dissenters suggested that, as is the case in other states, the jury could have been properly instructed to follow the official interpretation of the testimony; bilingual jurors could have been permitted to raise with the judge any disagreements with the interpreter; and the jury could have been allowed to hear only the English-language interpretation of the testimony.

Historically, Latinas/os initially were openly excluded from participation on juries. In ***Hernandez v. Texas*** (1954), the petitioner challenged a more subtle practice, which the petitioner argued had the result of reducing the number of potential Latino jurors. The *Hernandez v. New York* decision is important because it allowed the lawful exclusion of Latinas/os from juries in criminal cases based on language acquisition. Given the large numbers of Latinas/os who are bilingual or sufficiently proficient in Spanish, so as to be excludable from jury service under the reasoning of *Hernandez v. New York*, the case provides legal justification for the underrepresentation of Latinas/os on juries. The decision does nothing less than endanger the constitutional right to a jury of "one's peers" and lay the foundation for a system rejected in *Hernandez v. Texas*, in which Latinas/os are absent from juries, and Latina/o defendants are tried in a system that neither represents them nor understands them. This exclusion of Latinas/os based on language calls into question the fairness of the criminal justice system and the United States democratic system of government.

The *Hernandez v. New York* decision failed to recognize the moral and legal imperative for accurate translation and interpretation of proceedings in the criminal justice system. Rather than focus on the accuracy of communication in the courtroom, the linguistic paradigm accepted by the Court allows for inaccuracies, miscommunications, and potential factual errors in criminal cases. By providing for the exclusion of bilingual jurors who could bring potential errors in translation to the court's attention, the Supreme Court has elevated form over substance and justice in the courts.

The Court in *Hernandez v. New York* recognized that different treatment based on language acquisition and skill could serve as a basis for unconstitutional discrimination based on national origin. The Court, however, disregarded the significance of language to Latinas/os and its position as a cultural marker with deep connections to ethnicity and national origin, rather than solely as a mode of communication. Language serves as a way to identify with a national origin or ethnic group, and can be central to identity. Having failed to understand this role of language, the Court was unable to appreciate the constitutional violation inherent in a criminal justice system which mandates the separation of language from identity and national origin.

See also: Part II entries: Civil Rights; *Hernandez v. Texas*, 347 U.S. 475 (1954); International Human Rights; Language Rights in the Courts; Segregation.

Further Reading

Dressler, Joshua, and Alan C. Michaels. 2006. *Understanding criminal procedure: Adjudication.* 4th ed., vol. 2. Albany, NY: Matthew Bender & Co.

Mendez, Miguel A. 1993. *Hernandez:* The wrong message at the wrong time. *Stanford Law & Policy Review* 4: 193–202.

Mirandé, Alfredo. 1996. Now that I speak English, no me dejan hablar ("I'm not allowed to speak"): The implications of *Hernandez v. New York*. 18 *Chicano-Latino Law Review* 18: 115–49.

Morín, José Luis. 2009. *Latino/a rights and justice in the United States: Perspectives and approaches*. 2nd ed. Durham, NC: Carolina Academic Press.

Olivas, Michael A. 2006. *"Colored men" and "hombres aquí": Hernandez v. Texas and the emergence of Mexican-American lawyering*. Houston, TX: Arte Público Press.

Perea, Juan. 1992. *Hernandez v. New York*: Courts, prosecutors and the fear of Spanish. 21 *Hofstra Law Review* 21: 1–61.

Ramirez, Roberto R. 2004. *We the people: Hispanics in the United States*. U.S. Bureau of the Census Special Report. Washington DC: U.S. Bureau of the Census.

Rivera, Jenny. 2007. An equal protection standard for national origin subclassifications: The context that matters. *Washington Law Review* 82: 897–965.

Sandrino-Glasser, Gloria.1998. Los confundidos: De-conflating Latinos/as' race and ethnicity. *Chicano-Latino Law Review* 19: 69–161.

Soltero, Carlos R. 2006. *Latinos and American law: Landmark Supreme Court cases*. Austin, TX: University of Texas Press.

U.S. Constitution, Fourteenth Amendment.

Cases Cited

Batson v. Kentucky, 476 U.S. 79 (1986).

Hernandez v. New York, 500 U.S. 352 (1991).

Hernandez v. Texas, 347 U.S. 475 (1954).

Hernandez v. Texas, 347 U.S. 475 (1954)

François Restrepo-Serrano

Hernandez v. Texas, 347 U.S. 475 (1954), decided approximately two weeks before *Brown v. Board of Education*, is a landmark Supreme Court ruling within the context of Latinas/os in the criminal justice system and their **civil rights**. Although the holding in this case had a significant impact on other forms of **segregation** of Latinas/os, the Supreme Court's opinion in *Hernandez* had a more crucial impact on Latinos in the U.S. legal system. *Hernandez* involved the exclusion of Mexican-Americans from serving as jurors in trials, in a nation where jury trials are a hallmark of its legal system and an equitable manner of administering the law. Serving on a jury is a privilege, right, and duty of being a U.S. citizen; however, Mexican Americans—and by extension all Latinas/os—were being denied a basic right to be judged by a jury of one's own peers, a pillar of equity in the U.S. criminal justice system.

This case was a first in many ways. It was the first time that the U.S. Supreme court extended protections to Mexican Americans/Latinos under the Equal Protection Clause of the Fourteenth Amendment. As a predecessor to *Brown v. Board of Education* (1954), *Hernandez v. Texas* represented a phenomenal and critical development in constitutional and civil rights and within the realm of the U.S. criminal justice system. It also signified a major step forward for Latinas/os in breaking through the limited **black/white binary paradigm** that had for so long dominated questions about race, ethnicity, and civil rights in the United States. It addressed the **invisibility** of Latinas/os at a national level, particularly with regard to the systematic deprivation of Latina/o civil rights, and it also was the first time that Mexican American attorneys argued a case before the U.S. Supreme Court.

Pete Hernandez was convicted and sentenced to life imprisonment for the murder of Joe Espinoza in Jackson County, Texas. Hernandez repeatedly tried to quash the indictment and the jury panel, claiming that U.S. citizens of Mexican descent in Jackson County were systematically prevented from performing such civic duties as jury commissioners, grand jurors, and petit jurors.

Although potential Latina/o jurors were U.S. citizens fully qualified to serve in these respective capacities in Jackson County, this case brought to light the deeply entrenched and institutionalized forms of discrimination and exclusion to which Latinas/os were subjected to in the state of Texas. In fact, the courts in Texas affirmed the sentence and conviction, declaring that there had been no discrimination in the exclusion of Mexican Americans on the jury. As an institution of justice and law, Texas' highest criminal court reasoned that Mexicans "are not a separate race but are white people of Spanish descent" and because other whites had served on juries, the lack of jurors from Mexican descent did not violate the law or equal protection.

Before the Supreme Court, attorneys for Hernandez asserted that Mexican Americans were members of an excluded class and that, as a result, they systematically were being excluded as jurors, thereby denying Pete Hernandez equal protection of the law as guaranteed by the Fourteenth Amendment of the Constitution. Hernandez asserted that those administering the system of jury selection in Texas were doing so in a manner that was unfair and discriminatory. Chief Justice Earl Warren, in delivering the Supreme Court's unanimous opinion, affirmed this assertion by noting that such a system was "susceptible to abuse" and discriminatory practices. Chief Justice Warren made it known that the Supreme Court had previously held that a denial of equal protection under the Fourteenth Amendment occurs when a person of a particular race or color is tried as a result of an indictment that was issued by a jury, grand or petit, "from which all persons of [the defendant's] race or color have, solely because of that race or color, been excluded by the State, whether acting through its legislator, courts, or its administrative officers." Chief Justice Warren further stated that the Supreme Court did not agree with the State of Texas' view that with respect to considering the application of the Fourteenth Amendment there are only two classes to consider: "white and Negro."

After determining the scope of the Fourteenth Amendment, the Supreme Court then considered a much more vexing issue: whether Mexican-Americans constituted a class separate from whites. The protection of the Fourteenth Amendment substantially weighed on whether Hernandez could prove, among other things, that he was a member of an existing class. Chief Justice Warren posited that

> from time to time other differences from the community norm may define other groups which need the same protection. Whether such a group exists within a community is a question of fact. When the existence of a distinct class is demonstrated, and it is further shown that the laws, as written or as applied, single out that class for different treatment not based on some reasonable classification, the guarantees of the Constitution have been violated.

To determine and ascertain whether "persons of Mexican descent" constituted a separate class in Jackson County, the Court assessed the community's attitudes. In conducting such a review, the court listened to testimony from the county's officials and citizens who admitted that members of this community, in fact, did distinguish between being Mexican and white.

In the *Hernandez* case, the Supreme Court reviewed the evidence pointing to the exclusion and discrimination of Mexican Americans/Latinos as a distinct protected class. The court considered the lack of Mexican representation in local businesses and groups; the forced segregation of Mexican children in the first four grades of school; and overt forms of segregation in public places, including restaurant signs that read "No Mexicans Served" or bathroom signs that read "Colored Men" and "*Hombres Aqui*" ("Men Here")—signs that were found even on the Texas courthouse grounds.

After establishing the existence of a class, Hernandez then had to prove that there was actual discrimination. Hernandez proved that 14 percent of Jackson County's population was composed of people who had surnames of Mexican or Latina/o descent, and that 11 percent of males older than 21 years "bore such names." In assessing the county's tax records regarding property interests, Hernandez proved that 6 or 7 percent of such interests were held by individuals of Mexican ancestry. This evidence was considered in light of the shocking revelation that Mexican Americans/Latinos in Jackson County, Texas, had not served on a jury commission or grand or petit jury in 25 years.

Once the Supreme Court determined that Hernandez had satisfied his burden of proof, the State of Texas had to attempt to overcome Hernandez's case. It sought to do so by claiming that the "only objective had been to select those whom they thought were best qualified." The Court was not persuaded and found that based on the facts and evidence presented it was not "mere chance" that Mexican Americans had been excluded from a group of more than 6,000 jurors who previously had been called to serve. In ruling in favor of Hernandez, the Court stated that the result of such conduct "bespeaks discrimination."

At the heart of mainstream civil rights discourse as it pertains to the pursuit of justice in direct relation to the U.S. legal system, the presence and contribution of the Latina/o experience has vacillated between invisibility and neglect. Traditionally, the discourse and thought have been couched in limited notions of exclusive black-white relations. This black-white binary paradigm of race has served as an additional barrier for Latinas/os to confront social injustices in the United States. Because conventional civil rights thought had been limited to blacks and whites, other groups, such as Latinos/as or Asian Americans, only have been able to enter into this discourse to the extent that their experiences can be successfully analogized to the experiences of blacks or whites. Although Latinos/as and African Americans mutually benefit from the camaraderie and solidarity that has come about from their respective plights, the American consciousness suffers from the limitations of a black-white paradigm in which Latino/a identity and experiences can be relegated to invisibility. The ramifications of such a dilemma can be harmful, as injuries or violations against Latinas/os might not ever be recognized and, worst, relief might not be achieved.

On the day that *Hernandez* was litigated before the Supreme Court, one of Hernandez's attorneys, Carlos Cadena, made his opening statements by declaring, "your petitioner is an American citizen of Mexican descent," one of the justices responded to this statement of fact by asking, "What is that?" (Sandoval 2009). Although the Supreme Court struggled with categorizing Latinas/os, the *Hernandez* case finally made it possible for Latinas/os to be recognized as a distinct and separate class within the context of assessing the application of the U.S. Constitution to matters of race and discrimination in the criminal justice system. Moreover, this case made visible the effects that **racialization** had on Latinas/os as subjects of a legal system that was structured within a "dominant racist frame" that could be traced as far back as "the momentous U.S. Supreme

Court decision in *Plessy v. Ferguson* (1896)" (Cobas, Duany & Feagin 2009, 3).

As a "class apart," Latinas/os had achieved protection under the color of law in *Hernandez*, but such protection has not been fully secured as Latinas/os are still susceptible to systematic abuse. In 1991, the U.S. Supreme Court, in ***Hernandez v. New York***, in fact, handed down a decision mired in controversy. In its ruling the Court let stand the prosecutor's use of peremptory challenges to exclude prospective Spanish-speaking Latino jurors for fear that they would not adhere to the official interpreter's translation of the proceedings. It did so by stating that it was not racial or ethnic discrimination to exclude potential jurors, as anyone, regardless of race and ethnicity, could be fluent in Spanish, disregarding the centrality of language to Latinas/os as a cultural marker rooted in ethnicity and national origin. Moreover, *Hernandez v. New York*, which still stands as the law today, is viewed by many legal analysts as a setback for Latinas/os. Particularly in localities such as New York City, with sizable Latina/o populations that potentially can be in the jury pool, Latinas/os are the most susceptible to be subject to peremptory challenges that exclude them from juries based on language ability. A Spanish-speaking defendant can find himself or herself tried by a jury in which all Latinas/os had been excluded based on their knowledge of Spanish. *Hernandez v. New York* continues to cause concern that the courthouse doors that were supposed to have opened for Latina/o jurors with the 1954 *Hernandez v. Texas* decision now might have closed for many Latinas/os as a result of the Supreme Court's 1991 *Hernandez v. New York* ruling.

See also: Part I essay: Latinas/os and the U.S. Criminal Justice System. Part II entries: Civil Rights; *Hernandez v. New York*, 500 U.S. 352 (1991); Language Rights in the Courts; LatCrit: Latina & Latino Critical Legal Theory, Inc.; Segregation.

Further Reading

Bender, Steven W., Raquel Adana, Gilbert Paul Carrasco, and Joaquin G. Avila. 2008. *Everyday law for Latino/as*. Boulder, CO: Paradigm Publishers.

Cobas, José A., Jorge Duany, and Joe R. Feagin (eds.). 2009. *How the United States racializes Latinos: White hegemony and its consequence*. Boulder, CO: Paradigm Publishers.

Delgado, Richard, Juan F. Perea, and Jean Stefancic. 2008. *Latinos and the law: Cases and materials*. St. Paul, MN: Thomson/West.

Garcia, Ignacio M. 2009. *White but not equal: Mexican Americans, jury discrimination, and the Supreme Court*. Tucson, AZ: University of Arizona Press.

Morín, José Luis. 2009. *Latino/a rights and justice in the United States: Perspectives and approaches*. 2nd ed. Durham, NC: Carolina Academic Press.

Olivas, Michael A. 2006. *"Colored Men" and "Hombres Aqui": Hernandez v. Texas and the emergence of Mexican-American lawyering*. Houston, TX: Arte Publico Press.

Sandoval, Carlos (writer, producer, and director), and Peter Miller (producer and director). 2009. *A class apart: A Mexican American civil rights story*. PBS Home Video, motion picture. DVD Video. AMx62104. Approx. 60 minutes.

Soltero, Carlos R. 2006. *Latinos and American law: Landmark Supreme Court cases*. Austin, TX: University of Texas Press.

Valencia, Reynaldo Anaya, Henry Flores, Sonia R. García, and José Roberto Juárez, Jr. 2004. *Mexican Americans and the law*. Tucson, AZ: University of Arizona Press.

Cases Cited

Brown v. Board of Education, 347 U.S. 483 (1954).

Hernandez v. New York, 500 U.S. 352 (1991).

Hernandez v. Texas, 347 U.S. 475 (1954).
Plessy v. Ferguson, 163 U.S. 537 (1896).

Hispanic Society of the New York City Police Department. *See* Part I essay: Latinas/os and the U.S. Criminal Justice System; Policing and Latina/o Communities. Part II entries: Latina/o Fraternal Law Enforcement Organizations; Legal Advocacy Groups; Puerto Ricans.

Hispanics/Latinas/os. *See* Introduction; Part I essay: Latinas/os and the U.S. Criminal Justice System.

Homicide

Ramiro Martínez, Jr.

The study of ethnicity and homicide usually involves research on racial and ethnic differences in crime patterns or the overrepresentation of racial and ethnic minorities, including Latinas/os, in violent crime. Despite recognition that racial and ethnic variations in crime and justice exist, our knowledge on the sources and consequences of the Latina/o and homicide linkage is incomplete. In part, this is because the categories of **race and ethnicity** are evolving. Also, some of the racial and ethnic categories reported by criminal justice agencies are limited or require refinement. For example, some criminal justice agencies do not always use the same racial and ethnic categories, particularly with respect to Latinas/os, and code **victims** or offenders as white or black. Nevertheless, although current knowledge is limited, there is still a large body of research on the relationship among ethnicity and homicide.

Criminologists tend to favor examining the impact of racial or ethnic composition or percent Latinas/os, net of other social and economic factors, on violent crimes such as homicide across cities or to examine racial or ethnic specific outcomes across communities. However one chooses to examine Latinas/os and homicide, there are considerable racial and ethnic disparities across the nation concerning this topic. Therefore, there are good reasons for anticipating a positive association between levels of Latinas/os and homicide.

Latinas/os have high levels of poverty, are heavily immigrant, and are assumed to have high levels of homicide. Although some studies have called into question the "more immigrants means more crime" thesis, and even classic works failed to find a consistent empirical link between immigration and crime, scholarship that directly investigates the contemporary immigration/crime link currently is in short supply and is just beginning to emerge. Nevertheless, existing research unrelated to crime offers substantial indirect support of the counter-claim that immigrants are not generating social upheaval in urban areas. Martinez (2014), for example, found that rather than creating chaotic conditions, immigrant Latinas/os revitalized communities by stopping population flight, and stabilized economic and cultural institutions. The implication is that Latina/o communities actually might be strengthened by immigration, an image that is at odds with traditional criminological theory. In fact, some scholars have long argued against the myth that residents of impoverished urban Latina/o areas are poor and victimized by criminals, which contributes to high crime rates because they are disorganized in the sense that they lack common values or strong ties to each other.

The study of Latina/o homicide centers heavily on empirical topics related to racial/ethnic variations in homicide or the impact of immigration on homicide. Much of the current scholarship in this area is quantitative in nature and many examine the impact of immigration on homicide at the census place, city, census tract, or community level (*see* Feldmeyer & Steffensmeier 2009; Graif & Sampson 2009; Stowell & Martinez 2009). This is important to note because Latinas/os comprise more than one-quarter of the population in large Southwestern states such as California and Texas, as well as form major percentages in various cities across the nation given substantial increases from the previous decennial census in the Latina/o population.

Yet, research findings on Latina/o homicide in very different settings have similar findings. In a recent article it was reported that immigration did not mean more homicide offending in 328 census-defined places (e.g., cities, towns, and villages) across the state of California (Feldmeyer & Steffensmeier 2009). That is, the percent of immigration had no impact on total and Latina/o-specific arrests and arrests for white and black homicide were lower in places with more immigrants across California.

The Southwestern United States, however, long has been a primary entry point for those of Mexican origin, the largest Latina/o group, and there are studies on Latina/o homicide outside of this traditional destination. A recent study investigated levels of criminal involvement for homicide and other violent crimes in the Orlando, Florida, area. In this case, the authors made an important contribution to the literature by examining citizenship arrest data (i.e., arrest rates by native-born, foreign-born, naturalized citizens, and non-citizens) and reiterate that arrest rates for non-citizens—who were primarily Latina/o in this study—usually are lower than those for the native-born. Yet again, immigrant concentration has no impact on native-born and foreign-born arrest rates at the census-tract level.

The effect of immigration influences on race- and ethnic-specific violent deaths, including homicide, recently was reported in the city of Miami, Florida. The results demonstrate that Latina/o immigrants are not disrupting communities, increasing homicide, or undermining social integration in a city populated primarily by the foreign born. Like other homicide researchers, the authors emphasize the importance of considering immigration for understanding white- , black- , and Latina/o-specific lethal **violence** and encourage others to examine the community contexts in which both important types of violent death tend to occur among Latinas/os in urban America. Still, others focus on the degree to which the impact of immigration operates differentially as a product of ethnicity in the city of Miami. Using community-level data, some find that homicides occur more often in Miami census tracts with fewer immigrant Cubans, Hondurans, and Nicaraguans, a finding consistent with the expectations of the "Latina/o Paradox," which is the notion that Latinas/os have a lower level of crime and other health problems than expected given high levels of poverty or economic disadvantage, which typically means more homicide, not less.

Homicide researchers long have conducted studies in the city of Chicago. Some note that neighborhood characteristics vary in their effects across neighborhood space. For example, researchers emphasize the importance of this finding because neighborhood characteristics in Chicago vary significantly in predicting homicide and, in some cases, show countervailing effects depending on spatial location. They also find that immigrant concentration is either unrelated or inversely related to homicide, whereas places with more language diversity were consistently associated with lower homicide rates. This finding sheds more light on how language diversity, assimilation, and immigration influence homicide.

Others also draw from Chicago in their analysis of homicides in general and Latina/o homicides specifically. Some demonstrate that stable and consistent growth in the total foreign-born population is not associated with neighborhood trends in violence, whereas increases in recent immigrants occur only in the most stable neighborhoods with the lowest levels of violence. Some highlight how an interaction between recent immigrant composition and neighborhood disadvantage influence homicide. That is, extremely disadvantaged neighborhoods are better off in terms of lethal violence as the percent of recent arrivals increases.

Much of the contemporary homicide research in this area has drawn from archival sources. There is no doubt that data sources on patterns and trends in ethnicity and homicide are limited because the Latina/o population has just reemerged as an important research topic. The data usually are found in two major types: special data compiled by various criminal agencies including police, or injury and death statistics from public health agencies, such as the U.S. Centers for Disease Control and **Prevention** (Web-Based Injury Statistics Query and Reporting System). In some cases, Latina/o ethnicity information is available. Researchers generally regard data as more reliable when similar patterns and trends are established across data sources.

Yet, some researchers have contributed to the growing Latina/o research agenda in creative ways. The complexity of street **gang** homicides within disadvantaged minority communities in San Antonio, Texas, for example, recently was explored by Valdez, Cepeda, and Kaplan (2009). This topic is difficult to research because gang members as a group are hard to find and difficult to interview. In this case, the data was derived from a series of scenario questions that addressed the last time the subject saw someone get killed. (The authors avoid having the subject admit to participating in a homicide.) This paper is also important because the absence of immigrant **youth** involvement in these types of violent crimes is noted by the authors, which suggests that more immigrants do not translate to more gang homicides, even in a large predominantly Latina/o city.

The study of Latinas/os and homicide is increasing and now is connected to the study of violent crime, race, and ethnicity at the community and individual levels. More work is necessary, including linking micro- and macro-level approaches to race, ethnicity, and violence. Little exists for those interested in the study of gender, race, and ethnicity, or studies which explore inter- and intragroup homicides.

See also: Part I essays: Latinas/os and the U.S. Criminal Justice System; Latina/o Immigrants, Crime, and Justice; Latina/o Youth and Criminal Justice. Part II entry: Victims.

Further Reading

Chavez, Jorge M., and Elizabeth Griffiths. 2009. Neighborhood dynamics of urban violence: Understanding the immigration connection. *Homicide Studies* 13: 261–73.

Feldmeyer, Ben, and Darrell Steffensmeier. 2009. Immigration effects on homicide offending for total and race/ethnicity-disaggregated populations (White, Black, and Latino). *Homicide Studies* 13: 211–26.

Graif, Corina, and Robert J. Sampson. 2009. Spatial heterogeneity in the effects of immigration and diversity on neighborhood homicide rates. *Homicide Studies* 13: 242–60.

Martínez, Ramiro, Jr. 2014. *Latino homicide: Immigration, violence and community*. 2nd edition. New York: Routledge.

Nielsen, Amie L., and Ramiro Martínez, Jr. 2009. The role of immigration for violent deaths. *Homicide Studies* 13: 274–87.

Olson, Christa Polczynski, Minna K. Laurikkala, Lin Huff-Corzine, and Jay Corzine. 2009. Immigration and violent crime: Citizenship status and social disorganization. *Homicide Studies* 13: 227–41.

Stowell, Jacob I., and Ramiro Martínez, Jr. 2009. Incorporating ethnic-specific measures of immigration in the study of lethal violence. *Homicide Studies* 13: 315–24.

Valdez, Avelardo, Alice Cepeda, and Charles Kaplan. 2009. Homicidal events among Mexican American street gangs: A situational analysis. *Homicide Studies* 13: 288–306.

Vélez, María B. 2009. Contextualizing the immigration and crime effect: An analysis of homicide in Chicago neighborhoods. *Homicide Studies* 13: 325–35.

Homies Unidos. *See* Part I essays: Latinas/os and the U.S. Criminal Justice System; Gangs in the United States and Latina/o Communities. Part II entries: Community-Based Latina/o Advocacy Organizations; Political Activist Groups.

Human Trafficking

Maria Swimm

Human trafficking generally is defined as the coerced transporting or harboring of a vulnerable person for the purpose of exploitative activities. The flow of trafficking is often from poverty-stricken regions to more prosperous countries where labor prospects are believed to be more promising and overall living conditions are superior. Although adult men and women are sometimes transported willingly from one country to another so as to enter into legitimate jobs, they are categorized as **victims** of trafficking when they are transported under false pretenses and forced to work under exploitative, dangerous conditions—conditions that further intensify their vulnerabilities. Following narcotics and weapons, trafficking in human beings is among the most lucrative global criminal activities, bringing in worldwide profits of tens of billions of dollars annually. Impoverished or insolvent with little prospect to support themselves and their families, persons from Latin America are particularly vulnerable to forms of modern-day **slavery**.

Traffickers minister to their contemptible trade as a genuine business. Many have built an elaborate, well-orchestrated network of agents who support day-to-day operations, including shippers, truckers, and establishment owners who participate in the recruitment and transportation process. Those men and women desperate to improve their financial situations might rely on transport by way of a *coyote*, a human smuggler who facilitates migration throughout Latin America to the United States for a sizeable fee. All too often does this misplaced trust result in weeks, months, or even a lifetime of coerced forced labor or sex work for ill-fated victims. Individuals trafficked across international borders can be transported by land, air, or sea, depending on the distance between their region of origin and destination country. It is not at all uncommon for stops to occur along trafficking routes so that victims can earn money for their custodian before moving on to more lucrative locations.

Individuals can be trafficked in groups or individually and oftentimes must endure transport conditions that are potentially dangerous or even life-threatening. Some victims are given fake documents upon reaching their new place of living. In reality, falsified identification makes traveling easier only for the trafficker. Victims many times must unwillingly pay for these documents and are made to work off the debt as soon as they arrive to the destination country.

Latin Americans frequently are trafficked from the Caribbean and South and Central America to Europe and Asia, but a significant number are transported into the United States each year. Once in the United States, they become part of a segment of the Latina/o population that is undocumented and extremely susceptible to exploitation and abuse. Although human trafficking can include the involuntary removal of organs for trade on the black market, it is most often that individuals are trafficked into the United States and Europe for the purpose of labor exploitation and sexual abuse. Latino men are often the victims of forced labor, made to work in manufacturing plants, construction sites, farming fields, mining and logging sectors, and factories in unsafe conditions for excessive hours with little to no compensation and without adequate health care. In addition to labor exploitation, specifically domestic servitude, apparel assembly, and other forced factory work, women are the victims of sexual exploitation, threatened and coerced into working in all facets of the sex trade, risking their lives by engaging in unwanted and unsafe sexual activities without regard for their physical or emotional health.

Although the situation involving adults as victims of human trafficking is nothing less than severe, children, unfortunately, are viewed to be the most profitable and compliant of trafficking victims. Children as young as five years of age have been reported to be working as domestic servants or as laborers in textile sweatshops, recruited as child soldiers in war-torn countries, forced into child marriage, made to work as panhandlers, rock breakers, or mules to smuggle illicit **drugs**, and sold into prostitution. **Violence**, sex crimes such as rape, and other extreme hazards are among the chronic perils that young victims face, suffering psychological and physical devastation beyond their years. It is estimated by the U.S. government that of the 800,000 persons trafficked worldwide in 2006, approximately half were younger than 18 years old (Rodriguez Pizarro 2008).

Just as in adult trafficking, child trafficking can originate through coercion, abduction, or personal and familial arrangements, as well as through highly organized international criminal networks. Oftentimes youngsters and adolescents are sold by hopeless families seeking a better life for the children they are unable to care for, unknowingly selling them into a life of slavery with no chance for escape. The psychological and physical harms to young victims are especially damaging, leaving them isolated and extremely vulnerable after having been torn from their families and communities. The ease of transporting children across borders, coupled with the great demand-supply dynamic of the sex and exploitative labor industries worldwide allow child trafficking to remain an ever-expanding global industry that leaves no country untouched.

The number of trafficking victims is difficult to confirm due to its secretive nature. Various efforts have been made, however, to accurately measure the problem. Inconsistencies in defining human trafficking across nations, distinguishing trafficking from voluntary migration, a resistance for individuals to identify as trafficking victims, and failure on the part of various foreign governments to adequately acknowledge the urgency of the issue are just a few of the problems nongovernmental organizations and advocacy groups must confront when attempting to collect data so that appropriate initiatives to combat human trafficking can be developed. The Trafficking in Persons Protection Act (TVPA) of 2000 was enacted in the United

States, mandating various federal agencies to issue reports on the status of conditions globally as well as to ensure traffickers are effectively punished and victims are adequately served.

The Trafficking Victims Reauthorization Act of 2003 "added to the original law a new requirement that foreign governments provide the United States Department of State with data on trafficking investigations, prosecutions, convictions, and sentences in order to be considered in full compliance with the Act's minimum standards for the elimination of trafficking" in persons (U.S. Department of State 2010, 45).

Asian and African countries comprise a majority of Tier 3 and Tier 2-WL designees. Most Latin American countries, on average, rank Tier 2. Legislation to combat trafficking in persons has passed within a wide range of Central and South American countries and in Mexico within the last five years, although certain statutes in some regions are not all-inclusive and focus only on one form of trafficking, more often trafficking for the purpose of sexual exploitation. Mexico, Guatemala, and Colombia steadily remain the countries of focus for trafficking in persons in all its forms in the Latin American world, as does the mountainous tri-border

The U.S. Department of State Tier System

The development of tier rankings was established to indicate the extent of compliance among nations. Tier assignments are published annually in the *Trafficking in Persons* report submitted to Congress by the Department of State (2010, 22) and are categorized as follows.

Tier 1: Countries whose governments fully comply with the Trafficking in Persons Protection Act's (TVPA) minimum standards.

Tier 2: Countries whose governments do not fully comply with the TVPA's minimum standards, but are making significant efforts to bring themselves into compliance with those standards.

Tier 2 Watch List (WL): Countries whose governments do not fully comply with the TVPA's minimum standards, but are making significant efforts to bring themselves into compliance with those standards and:

- The absolute number of victims of severe forms of trafficking is very significant or is significantly increasing; or
- There is a failure to provide evidence of increasing efforts to combat severe forms of trafficking in persons from the previous year; or
- The determination that a country is making significant efforts to bring themselves into compliance with minimum standards was based on commitments by the country to take additional future steps over the next year.

Tier 3: Countries whose governments do not fully comply with the minimum standards and are not making significant efforts to do so.

Source: U.S. Department of State. 2010. *Trafficking in persons report, June 2010*. Washington DC: Department of State.

area of Paraguay, Argentina, and Brazil, where child sex tourism is rampant.

In addition to creating new forced labor and sex-trafficking criminal offenses for perpetrators, the TVPA seeks to provide federal and state assistance to trafficked persons and protect victims so that they can attempt to rebuild their lives. Victims of human trafficking might be able to receive benefits and special services through the TVPA similar to those extended to refugees, as well as link to appropriate social service providers and legal aid so that they can apply for a stay of **deportation** or "T immigrant" visa.

Because of their distrust of police in their home countries and the fear of an unfamiliar criminal justice system, gaining the cooperation of those who have been trafficked can be difficult for law enforcement agents. Additionally, trafficked persons oftentimes do not readily identify as victims, making it difficult for police to distinguish victims from their perpetrators. As a result, trafficked persons often are treated like criminals, resulting in the incarceration and **deportation** of innocent victims. A compassionate approach by well-informed federal and local police is an effective first step in adequately protecting and assisting trafficked persons.

Although the issue of human trafficking continues to gain much-needed attention internationally, further advancements must be made. The combination of cultural, political, and socio-economic factors that keep populations marginalized and vulnerable to trafficking must be confronted head on, specifically in **border** areas and along international routes where trafficking often is concentrated. Collaborative efforts to control poverty and promote the worth of women and children worldwide also would contribute to a decline in trafficking activity. Additionally, the acknowledgement of trafficked individuals as victims rather than solely undocumented persons must be a shared response across nations so that adequate services can help victims reintegrate into society and the probability of their being retrafficked can be weakened. Concomitantly, traffickers and consumers of sexual exploitation and cheap labor must be adequately punished and brought to justice so as to promote a unified, global stance that human trafficking, in all its forms, will not be tolerated.

See also: Part I essays: Latinas/os and the U.S. Criminal Justice System; Incarceration and Latinas/os in the United States; Crime and the U.S.-Mexican Border. Part II entries: Deportation; Slavery; Transnational Crime; Victims.

Further Reading

Bales, Kevin. 2004. *Disposable people: New slavery in the global economy.* Revised edition. Berkeley, CA: University of California Press.

Bales, Kevin, and Steven Lize. 2007. Investigating human trafficking: Challenges, lessons learned, and best practices. *FBI Law Enforcement Bulletin* 76: 24–31.

Bechard, Raymond. 2006. *Unspeakable: The hidden facts behind the world's fastest growing crime.* New York, NY: Compel Publishing.

DeStefano, Anthony. 2007. *The War on human trafficking: U.S. policy assessed.* New Brunswick, NJ: Rutgers University Press.

Langberg, Laura. 2005. A review of recent OAS research on human trafficking in the Latin American and Caribbean region. *International Migration* 1: 129–39.

Rodriguez Pizarro, G. 2008. Human trafficking in Latin America in the context of international migration. In *Trafficking in humans: Social, cultural, and political dimensions*, edited by S. Cameron and E. Newman, 206–23. New York, NY: United Nations University Press.

U.S. Department of State. 2010. *Trafficking in persons report, June 2010.* Washington DC: Department of State.

I

Immigrant Detention Centers

David Manuel Hernández

It is well-known that the United States imprisons more persons than any other nation. Skyrocketing statistics regarding African American and Latino men have become the norm in the U.S. prison system. Additionally, rapid prison construction and increased popular fear of crime (when crime is decreasing nationally) dominate contemporary discussions of the U.S. "**prison industrial complex**." The public, however, knows very little about the government's capacity to jail its noncitizens, especially in immigrant detention centers, even though immigrant detention has been called the "fastest-growing form of incarceration" in the United States (Bernstein 2007, A1). Immigrant detention centers in the United States instead are a hidden form of incarceration, often overlooked because of the enormity of the criminal justice system, the undefined "sentences" of immigrant detainees, and the "administrative" characterization of immigrants' incarceration as a process meant only to facilitate their removal from the United States. This capacity grew throughout the late 1990s, tripling in this period, and expanding dramatically after the September 11, 2001, terrorist attacks on New York City and Washington, DC. In 2014–2015, the federal government dramatically expanded its capacity for "family detention" by 350% in response to the influx of unaccompanied Central American minors and families traveling together to seek asylum in the United States (Hernández 2015). Importantly, the authority to incarcerate noncitizens in immigrant detention centers, although both separate and overlapping with federal, state, county, and municipal jail systems, is located outside the criminal court system and largely is unaddressed by prison literatures. The parameters and conditions of immigrant detainees' confinement, as a result, are obscured and legally ambiguous.

Detaining Noncitizens

In general terms, immigrant detention is the practice of incarcerating noncitizens that are apprehended at ports of entry or within the nation's interior. Detainees consist of undocumented immigrants, asylum-seekers, lawful permanent residents, and, at times, individual or particular groups of citizens. They are maintained in custody at federal immigrant detention centers, privately run facilities, or local public facilities contracting bed space to the federal government until they are released, bonded, and paroled, or deported from the United States. The government maintains that immigrant detention is an administrative process and not a punitive one, utilized pursuant to their **deportation** from the country. In practice, however, immigrant detention historically has been deployed as an additional tool of law enforcement and for other government priorities—for example, anti-terrorism, anti-**gang** efforts, and anti-labor-organizing. As witnessed after 9/11, the government utilized preventive detention and the immigration court system in its domestic anti-terrorism efforts because of the prosecutorial advantages (e.g., closed hearings, wide latitude in prosecutorial evidence, the authority to detain without charges, reduced access to counsel) that it affords the government. These practices have been widely bemoaned as "second-class justice" (Cave 2009).

The present authority to detain noncitizens derives from the Immigration and Nationality Act (INA) enacted in 1952 and amended to the present. According to the INA, the attorney general is authorized to detain noncitizens, including persons seeking asylum in the United States, pending their deportation or exclusion hearing before an immigration judge. Detention ensures that immigrants will attend deportation hearings by preventing their ability to abscond and it restricts mobility if the detainee is determined to be a danger to society. In 2004, there were more than 23,000 immigrants in detention daily within the United States, and more than 230,000 immigrants were detained during the fiscal year (U.S. Immigration and Customs Enforcement 2004). Even though length of stay can range from days to years, the average adult immigrant was detained for 37.6 days in 2007 at an average cost of $95 per day per bed. By 2013 the average cost was $119 (Zakaria 2013). It should be noted that the average stay in detention is skewed in two ways. Primarily, it is distorted downward by the large number of Mexicans apprehended, detained, and deported rapidly through a procedure called expedited removal. Secondly, it is skewed upward by the lengthy detentions, ironically, of those with the best legal chances of remaining in the United States, many who are detained for the duration of this adjudication process.

Beginning in 2009, however, Congress has required in its annual appropriations bill that a minimum number of beds be funded specifically for detaining immigrants at any given time. Presently, "the national detention bed quota," as it has become known, is 34,000. In fiscal year 2009, 383,524 persons were detained under the quota system, but by 2012 the number of people detained increased to 477,000. Over the last decade, the immigrant detention system grew 75 percent (Detention Watch Network & the Center for Constitutional Rights (DNW & CCR) 2015, 1). The national detention bed quota policy relies on the use of private contractors, such as the Corrections Corporation of America (CCA) and the GEO Group (GEO), to provide the facilities and services to maintain a quota system. Under this policy, the **Immigration and Customs Enforcement** (ICE), which oversees immigrant detentions, is pressed to round up sufficient numbers of immigrants and private corporations that maintain the detention centers are virtually guaranteed profits, with 62 percent of the detention beds being run by private companies (DNW & CCR 2015, 2). As a result, immigrant and human rights organizations have urged for the discontinuation of the minimum bed standard, greater transparency in the bidding process for detention facility contracts, and an end to the abuses that are associated with the national immigrant detention bed quota, such as contracting with corporations engaged in public policy lobbying to grow profits at the expense of taxpayers and immigrants' rights (DNW & CCR 2015).

Infrastructure and Conditions

Formerly managed by the Immigration and Naturalization Service (INS) under the Department of Justice (DOJ), custody of detainees is administered at present by Immigration and Customs Enforcement's (ICE) Office of Detention and Removal (DRO) within the Department of Homeland Security (DHS). Detainees are held in three types of detention facilities—federally owned and operated detention centers operated by ICE, denoted

"Service Processing Centers" (SPCs); privately contracted for-profit jails, called Contract Detention Facilities (CDFs); and municipal and county jails subcontracting bed space to federal authorities, or Intergovernmental Service Agreement facilities (IGSAs). There are seven SPCs holding 13 percent of detainees and an additional seven CDFs holding 17 percent of detainees. Two-thirds of detainees, or 67 percent, are held in IGSAs throughout the country, and an additional 3 percent of detainees are held in facilities run by the Bureau of Prisons (Tumlin, Joaquin, & Natarajan 2009). Three facilities—the Berks Family Residential Center in Pennsylvania run by Berks County, Karnes County Residential Center in Texas run by the GEO Group, and the South Texas Family Residential Center in Dilley, Texas, run by the Corrections Corporation of America—are noted for detaining families with children who are seeking asylum or are in deportation proceedings. These facilities demonstrate the wide-ranging capacity for immigrant detention, relying heavily on nonfederal sites spread throughout the nation.

Due to the imbalance in federal management of immigrant incarceration, privately contracted jails and local facilities holding 80 percent of detainees suffer a lack of federal oversight and evaluation which has resulted in a broad range of poor conditions for detainees, including 151 deaths "in ICE custody" since 2003, according to ICE's reporting (USICE 2015). One report noted that 18 of the reported deaths occurred in immigrant detention facilities privately run by the Corrections Corporation of America, the nation's largest prison contractor (Shahshahani 2009). "They get treatment that you might see in a Third World country, and it's really a stain on our system of justice to treat detainees this way," noted one immigration attorney (Fears 2007, A4). This situation is exacerbated by weak, unenforceable guidelines that fail to establish standardized detention conditions in nonfederal facilities. According to the Government Accounting Office, "The standards are not codified in law and thus represent guidelines rather than binding regulations" (GAO 2007, 9).

In 2015, **media** exposés, academic reports, and legal challenges have sought to contest what have been characterized as the harsh and inhumane conditions under which many immigrants are detained by the U.S. **Border Patrol**. The term, *hielera* (Spanish for "ice box"), has been used to describe the cold and punitive conditions of the "holding cells" used at Border Patrol Stations located at ports of entry and Forward Operating Bases. Reports by human rights groups contradict government statements that the detainees are held temporarily. The reports and a class-action lawsuit filed against the government, *Doe v. Johnson*, allege that women, men, and even very young children are kept for many days in overcrowded, unsanitary, and frigid conditions with inadequate food, water, and healthcare, often with no beds to sleep on and no blankets (Legal Action Center 2015).

Lack of Due Process

Detainees' experiences in immigrant detention centers are mediated by the poor conditions of incarceration in addition to the unequal treatment that noncitizens receive in the immigration court system in comparison with the criminal justice system. Noncitizens' detentions are governed by administrative rules and practices that affect detainees' access to counsel and visitation, the pace of legal proceedings, and the overall length of stay in detention. Due procedural rights are severely curtailed or infringed upon through numerous administrative mechanisms, including evidentiary standards, access to bond, and multiple transfers through the web of immigrant detention facilities. The distinct lack of legal rights and poor conditions of incarceration hinge on the categorization of detention as an administrative process separate from the criminal justice system, a determination made by the Supreme Court in the 19th century. The Court ruled in *Fong Yue Ting v. the United States* (1893) that "The order of deportation is not punishment for crime," and clarified the role of immigrant detention in *Wong Wing v. the United States* (1896) when it stated that "Detention . . . is not imprisonment in a legal sense."

These rulings remain consequential in the contemporary era. In one detention case, in which the government mistook a Latino U.S. citizen for an undocumented immigrant, immigration authorities held the citizen in detention for 13 months. The final five months of detention were the result of an appeal by immigration authorities after a judge determined the detainees' lawful citizenship status through parental, marriage, school, military, and Social Security records. Called a "nightmare" by the detainee, his immigration attorney stated, "You give up your citizenship at the prison door. . . . The system is set up so even if they believe you, you have to prove it in court. It could take six months to five years to prove it and you're detained in the meantime" (Hendricks 2009).

Latinas/os in Detention

When it comes to incarcerated persons in immigrant detention centers who hail from across the globe, Latinas/os predominate, representing more than 90 percent of detainees between 2011 and 2013 (Simanski 2014). The collective demographic profile of Latinas/os in the United States contributes to their high rates of confinement in immigrant detention facilities. Latinas' and Latinos' numerical size, in particular in migration categories, and their "societal construction as violent, foreign, criminal-minded, disloyal, and as overrunning the border" (Bender 2002, 1154) have contributed to the long history of Latina/o immigrant detention. Latinas/os represent the largest group of foreign-born, documented, and undocumented immigrants, border apprehensions and removals, criminal alien detainees, and the largest minority group in the United States. In 2005, for example, Latinas/os represented seven of the top-ten foreign-born groups in immigrant detention, and Mexicans comprised half of all detainees (Siskin 2007). Additionally, widespread beliefs about Latino criminality, especially as it relates to the widely bemoaned and sensationalized presence of "illegals" or undocumented immigrants, have led to the routine and popular conflation of Mexican nationals and other Latinas/os as "illegals." As a result, Latinas/os have euphemistically represented and epitomized "the illegal" as well as a preponderance of deportation and detention categories for many decades.

Historically, Latinas/os have been detained as a result of biological reasoning and fears of contagion, as part of nationally coordinated deportation campaigns in the 1930s and 1950s, for ideological motives as labor activists or refugees, or persistently as criminalized noncitizens. It is critical to recognize that episodes of racialized immigrant detention also include Chinese and Chinese Americans in the late-19th and early-20th centuries; Japanese and Japanese American citizen detainees during World War II; immigrant laborers detained during the early 20th century Red Scare and later in the Cold War; Haitian detainees since the 1970s; and, most recently, Arab, Muslim, and South Asian detainees after 9/11. These racialized episodes of immigrant detention are related directly and indirectly to contemporary Latina/o detention because they have created the enforcement patterns, legal precedents, diminished legal avenues for relief from incarceration, and the physical infrastructure of detention.

Post-9/11 Developments in Detention

In the new century, under the auspices of the domestic "war on terror," the Department of Homeland Security has expanded its detention capacity, ratcheted-up enforcement, and coordinated with local and state governments at levels not seen since "**Operation Wetback**" in the 1950s and the national Mexican repatriation effort during the Great Depression. For example, the Office of Detention and Removal's "Strategic Plan 2003–2012: Endgame," developed under the George W. Bush Administration, sought a "100% removal rate" of deportable immigrants, necessitating increased detention bed space (Tangeman 2003). The Obama Administration, although publicly committed to comprehensive immigration reform, modified some of the previous administration's policies, and sustained or expanded others. Immigrant detention, for example, continues its decades-long expansion. According to Janet Napolitano, the former Secretary of the Department of Homeland Security, "We are expanding enforcement, but I think in the right way" (Preston 2009, A1). Accordingly, immigration arrests and deportations in 2009 were double what they were two years prior, signaling a continued reliance on and expansion of immigrant detention.

Whereas noncitizens in the United States from all over the world are vulnerable to this process, Latinas/os remain the primary demographic among detainees. From lengthy and large-scale detention and deportation operations in the 20th century; to the detention of asylum seekers during the Cold War; to the collapsing of federal and local anti-drug, anti-crime, anti-immigrant, and anti-terrorism efforts today, expansions of the capacity to detain noncitizens substantially impacts Latina/o families and communities. For immigrant advocates, the conditions and legal rights for detainees are central goals for comprehensive immigration reform. Despite policy changes, however, including a major federal review of the detention system and the conversion of a private family-detention center in Texas to a women's immigrant facility in 2009, only to again expand "family detention" in 2014, the key policy left unchanged by the Obama Administration is its reliance on legally unenforceable guidelines for immigrant detention centers. Although the Department of Homeland Security has stated that enforceable rules "would be laborious, time consuming and less flexible" than the review process, advocacy groups are more concerned about the ongoing mistreatment and medical neglect throughout the detention system. One advocacy group stated, "The department has demonstrated a disturbing commitment to policies that have cost dozens of lives" (Bernstein 2009).

Tomorrow's Detainees

The majority of today's immigrant detainees are persons who committed deportable offenses and served their sentences in jails and prisons before being incarcerated in immigrant detention centers. As such, it is important to further explore the relationship between criminal and immigration enforcement, for both processes and institutions serve as feeder programs for one another. A 2009 report from the Pew Hispanic Center detailed an overrepresentation of Latinas/os among sentenced federal offenders—40 percent, in relation to Latinas/os' 13 percent share of the U.S. population. Among these Latina/o federal offenders, nearly three out of four were noncitizens. Also important, by 2007, immigration offenses accounted for one-quarter of all federal convictions, triple the number from 1991 (Lopez & Light 2009, i). Such figures indicate the significance of immigration enforcement in the federal prison system, and because many, if not all, federal convictions trigger the deportation process for noncitizens in federal prison, each enforcement system bolsters the other.

The expansion of bed space to accommodate these future detainees is central to the long-term growth of detention capacity and reflects the increased coordination of the criminal justice system, anti-terrorism initiatives, and the immigration court system. Leaders in the private prison industry view such growth as profitable for its investors. One corporate leader suggests "ICE will continue providing meaningful opportunity for the industry for the foreseeable future," and a second private prison executive stated, "My personal view is that Homeland Security and the detention beds necessary to detain illegal aliens will increasingly be seen as a national imperative to protect U.S. workers and their jobs" (Feltz & Baksh 2009). Dovetailing with continued criminal and immigration enforcement efforts, the incarceration of noncitizens in immigrant detention centers is thus related to their surveillance, punishment, and overall inequality in society, in addition to their value as commodities for the private-prison industry.

Immigrant detention—a central tool in the nation's expanded immigrant enforcement campaign—is not immune to the effects of popular sentiment and the media. These two factors converged with political gamesmanship immediately after 9/11 and during the domestic "war on terror" to shape the contours of the immigration debate, especially in terms of national security. Anti-immigrant sentiment is a powerful political tool in the contemporary crisis surrounding the severe economic downturn, impacting policy reform debates over economic stimulus packages, state and local budget cuts, and healthcare reform. Far more than a wedge issue to derail policy reform, anti-immigrant sentiment has led to denials of public benefits for lawful immigrants in addition to the unauthorized, as well as a 40 percent increase in hate crimes against all Latinas/os in the United States when the national average dropped overall (Hsu 2009). One report on media and immigration suggested "the cumulative effect of U.S. media coverage has distorted the underlying realities of immigration while conditioning audiences in ways that make it more difficult to forge policy compromises" (Suro 2008, viii). For immigrant detainees and the immigrant detention system, which are impacted by presumptions of guilt and "illegality" and a lack of forms of relief to challenge detention, the struggle for immigration reform is likely to be severely disputed by politicians, conservative populist sentiments, and a media that addresses immigration in the context of crisis.

See also: Part I essays: Latina/o Immigrants, Crime, and Justice; Crime and the U.S.-Mexican Border. Part II entries: Deportation, Deportation Laws, Immigration and Customs Enforcement (ICE).

Further Reading

Balderrama, Francisco, and Raymond Rodríguez, 1995. *Decade of betrayal: Mexican repatriation in the 1930s.* University of New Mexico Press.

Bender, Steven W. 2002. Sight, sound, and stereotype: The war on terrorism and its consequences for Latinas/os. *Oregon Law Review* 81: 1153–78.

Bernstein, Nina. 2007 (June 26). New scrutiny as immigrants die in custody. *New York Times*, A1.

Bernstein, Nina. 2009 (July 28). U.S. rejects changes in detainee rules. *New York Times*, A17.

Brookings Institution. 2008. *A report on the media and the immigration debate*. Washington, DC: Brookings Institution.

Cave, Damien. 2009 (June 4). Cleared of terror charges, but then a target for deportation. *New York Times*: A1/A4.

Chin, Gabriel J. 2005. Chae Chan Ping and Fong Yue Ting: The origins of plenary power. In *Immigration Stories,* edited by D. A. Martin and P. H. Schuck, 7–32. New York, NY: Foundation Press.

De Genova, Nicholas. 2004. The legal production of Mexican/migrant "illegality." *Latino Studies* 2: 160–85.

Detention Watch Network and the Center for Constitutional Rights. 2015. Banking on detention: Local lockup quotas and the immigrant dragnet. http://www.detentionwatchnetwork.org/sites/default/files/Banking_on_Detention_DWN.pdf. Accessed November 13, 2015.

Dow, Mark, 2004. *American gulag: Inside U.S. immigration prisons*. Berkeley: University of California Press.

Ehrenreich, Ben. 2008 (September). Death on Terminal Island. *Los Angeles Magazine*: 142–47, 235–39.

Fears, Darryl. 2007 (June 13). Illegal immigrants received poor care in jail, lawyers say. *Washington Post*: A4.

Feltz, Renee. 2008. A new migration policy: Producing felons for profit. *NACLA: Report on the Americas* 41(6): 26–30.

Feltz, Renee, and Stokely Baksh. 2009. Detention retention. *American Prospect*. http://prospect.org/cs/articles?article=detention_retention. Accessed November 13, 2015.

Gilmore, Ruth Wilson. 2007. Golden gulag: Prisons, surplus, crisis, and opposition in globalizing California. Berkeley, CA: University of California Press.

Government Accounting Office. 2007. Alien detention standards: Telephone access problems were pervasive at detention facilities; other deficiencies did not show a pattern of noncompliance. GAO-07-875, Washington, DC: Government Accounting Office.

Hendricks, Tyche. 2009 (July 27). U.S. citizens wrongfully detained, deported by ICE. *San Francisco Chronicle*. http://www.sfgate.com/cgibin/article.cgi?f=/c/a/2009/07/26/MNGQ17C8GC.DTL.

Hernández, David Manuel. 2008. Pursuant to deportation: Latinos and immigrant detention. *Latino Studies* 6: 35–63.

Hernández, David Manuel. 2015. Unaccompanied child migrants in "crisis": New surge or case of arrested development? *Harvard Journal of Hispanic Policy* 27: 11–17.

Hsu, Spencer S. 2009 (June 17). Immigration debate tied to rise in hate crimes. *Washington Post*.

Immigration and Nationality Act. 1952. INA § 236, 8 U.S.C. § 1226.

Legal Action Center. 2015. Border Patrol "Hieleras"—Background and Legal Action. Washington, DC: American Immigration Council. http://www.legalactioncenter.org/litigation/border-patrol-%E2%80%9Chieleras%E2%80%9D-background-and-legal-action. Accessed November 24, 2015.

Lopez, Mark Hugo, and Michael T. Light. 2009 (February 18). *A rising share: Hispanics and federal crime*. Washington, DC: Pew Hispanic Center. http://pewhispanic.org/files/reports/104.pdf. Accessed November 24, 2015.

Preston, Julia. 2009 (August 3). Firm stance on illegal immigrants remains policy. *New York Times*. http://www.nytimes.com/2009/08/04/us/politics/04immig.html.

Shahshahani, Azadeh. 2009 (June 11). Private prisons for immigrants lack accountability, oversight. ACLU.org. https://www.aclu.org/blog/speakeasy/private-prisons-immigrants-lack-accountability-oversight.

Simanski, John F. 2014 (September). Immigration and Enforcement Actions: 2013. *Annual Report of the Office of Immigration Statistics*. Department of Homeland Security.

Siskin, Alison. 2007. Immigration-related detention: Current legislative issues. CRS Report for Congress. Congressional Research Service, January 25.

Suro, Robert. 2008. A report on the media and the immigration debate. Washington, DC: Brookings Institute. http://www.brookings.edu/~/media/research/files/reports/2008/9/25-immigration-dionne/0925_immigration_dionne.pdf. Accessed November 13, 2015.

Tangeman, Anthony S. 2003. Memorandum for Deputy Assistant Director, Field of Operations Division and Field Office Directors: Office of Detention and Removal (ORO) Strategic Plan 2003–2012: Endgame. Office of Detention and Removal.

Tumlin, Karen, Linton Joaquin, and Ranjana Natarajan. 2009. A broken system: Confidential reports reveal failures in U.S. immigrant detention centers. http://www.nilc.org/brokensyspr.html. Accessed November 13, 2015.

U.S. Immigration and Customs Enforcement. 2004. Fact Sheet: ICE Office of Detention and Removal. May 4.

USICE. 2015. List of Deaths in ICE Custody: October 2003 to May 26, 2015. http://www.ice.gov/sites/default/files/documents/FOIA/2015/detaineedeaths2003-present.pdf. Accessed November 13, 2015.

Zakaria, Tabbasum. 2013 (Feb 28). U.S. agency says average cost of immigration detention $119 per day. *Reuters*. http://www.reuters.com/article/us-usa-fiscal-immigration-idUSBRE92001120130301. Accessed November 24, 2015.

Cases Cited

Fong Yue Ting v. the United States, 149 U.S. 698 (1893).

Wong Wing v. the United States, 163 U.S. 228 (1896).

Immigration and Customs Enforcement (ICE)

Nancy Guarneros

Immigration and Customs Enforcement (ICE) is a federal law enforcement agency that was established on March 1, 2003, as part of the newly created Department of Homeland Security (DHS) and the reorganization of the Immigration and Naturalization Service (INS). The ICE "enforces federal laws governing border control, customs, trade and immigration to promote homeland security and public safety" (Immigration and Customs Enforcement [n.d.]). With more than 20,000 employees, ICE is headquartered in Washington, DC, but has more than 400 offices in the United States and operates in 48 foreign countries. Its annual budget of roughly $6 billion is dedicated to operating two key directorates: Homeland Security Investigations (HSI) and Enforcement and Removal Operations (ERO). Its third directorate, Management and Administration (M&A), provides management and mission support to ICE (Immigration and Customs Enforcement [n.d.]). For fiscal year 2014, ICE reports having conducted 315,943 removals of person unauthorized to be in the United States, with 56 percent of all removals or 177,960 being persons previously convicted of a crime and the primary countries for removals being Mexico, Guatemala, Honduras, and El Salvador (Immigration and Customs Enforcement 2015).

Prior to the creation of the Department of Homeland Security in a massive bureaucratic reorganization following the September 11, 2001, terrorist attacks, the duties of ICE were performed by the INS within the Department of Justice. On March 1, 2003, several border and security agencies were reorganized and transferred into the U.S Department of Homeland Security. As a result, the INS "split" into three agencies: Immigration and Customs Enforcement (ICE), Customs and Immigration and Services (CIS), and Customs and Border Protection (CBP). As a consequence of the September 11, 2001, attacks, the federal government adopted aggressive enforcement practices in the name of "homeland security" to which ICE contributed. Border and interior immigration enforcement intensified resulting in increased arrests, detentions, and **deportations** of noncitizens. Along with aggressive enforcement also came years of criticisms by civil and human rights groups that various forms of **racial profiling** had reemerged as the strategy in the "war on terror." The concern that racial profiling was being used in criminal and immigration law enforcement grew among noncitizens and persons from immigrant families, alienating immigrants in many communities, especially in Arab, Muslim, and South Asian communities. Through an anti-terror lens, noncitizens were viewed as "national security threats" and special measures were taken in reaction to the perceived threats. In 2002, for example, then-Attorney General John Ashcroft introduced the New Security Entry-Exit Registration System, which imposed special registration requirements for noncitizens who were determined by the federal government to pose national security risks.

The formation of ICE and new enforcement initiatives—although initially targeted at persons suspected to be linked to terrorism domestically and internationally—also ensnared the broader immigrant populations in the United States, in particular Latin Americans and U.S. Latinas/os perceived to be noncitizens. Similar to the INS and the U.S. **Border Patrol**, ICE—or *la migra,* as it is commonly referred to in Latina/o communities—became the primary government agency overseeing deportations. Immigrant communities, employers, and advocates have noted the alarming growth and reach of ICE—most significantly, its presence beyond the **U.S-Mexican border** and its increased efforts to raid workplaces in search of undocumented persons. For many immigrants and immigrants' rights groups, ICE enforcement initiatives not only took a tough stance toward undocumented immigrants, it acted aggressively toward legal permanent residents and citizens perceived to be unauthorized immigrants. During the Bush administration, ICE utilized home raid operations to locate and apprehend individuals suspected of civil immigration law violations. With the evolution of ICE, militarized strategies targeting immigrants at the border and in the nation's interior were embraced and have continued to be a central approach to immigration control.

The new forms of immigration enforcement by ICE led to charges that the agency was engaged in patterns of misconduct and abuse. In 2009, the Cardozo Immigration Justice Clinic at Yeshiva University released a report that examined the evidence on the prevalence of constitutional violations occurring during ICE raids. The study concluded that certain patterns of misconduct were in fact discernible: ICE agents illegally entered homes without legal authority; ICE agents illegally seized individuals based solely on racial or ethnic appearance or limited English proficiency; and ICE agents readily took actions in violation of Fourth Amendment Constitutional protections against unreasonable searches and seizures. ICE's patterns of misconduct also tended to be arbitrary—arresting non-target, innocent persons; breaking into homes with no legal justification; and using physical force without legal authorization or justification. Consequently, many immigrants became victims of "collateral" arrests—they were arrested by ICE even though they had not committed a deportable offense.

ICE is an armed federal agency with the power to deport a variety of noncitizens to their countries of origin, including undocumented immigrants, legal permanent residents who have committed deportable crimes, and persons who have overstayed their visa. Under the agency's strategic plan, titled Endgame, ICE's goal was a "100%

removal rate," requiring a vast increase in resources and heightened coordination with local authorities (Tangeman 2003). Prior to 2006, ICE Fugitive Operations Teams (FOTs) had an annual quota of 125 fugitives—also known as absconders or persons who had been ordered deported but remained in the United States. With the 100% removal rate plan ICE increased each FOT's annual arrest quota to 1,000 arrests per year (Bess et al. 2009, 23). Although many have applauded ICE's efforts in deporting persons with criminal records, a chief collateral concern among affected communities has been the breakup of immigrant families who as a unit are often comprised of citizens and noncitizens.

Increases in anti-immigrant sentiment nationwide in recent years correlate with the negative experiences many Latina/o legal residents and U.S. citizens have had either with law enforcement agents, including those from ICE, or hostility or **hate crimes** based on racial/ethnic difference. In 2008, the Pew Hispanic Center reported that one in ten Latina/o adults—native-born U.S. citizens and immigrants alike—stated that in the past year the police or other authorities have stopped them to ask about their immigration status, and a majority of the Latinas/os surveyed (76 percent) said they disapproved of workplace raids by ICE (Lopez & Minushkin 2008). In addition to experiencing a rise in scrutiny and vulnerability to potential abuse by ICE and other law enforcement agents, Latinas/os—whether undocumented or authorized in the United States—have seen a jump in hate crimes against them. From 2003 to 2007, anti-Latina/o hate crimes, specifically, increased by 40 percent (Potok 2008; *see also* Leadership Conference on Civil Rights Education Fund 2009). The Southern Poverty Law Center also has documented that the number of nativist extremist groups—racial extremist organizations that adhere to a militaristic, anti-immigration agenda that often targets the unauthorized Latinas/os—expanded 20 percent from 2007 to 2008, from 144 to 173 nationally, and between 2008 and 2009, these groups increased nearly 80 percent across the country, from 173 to 309 (Beirich 2011).

During the Bush administration ICE adopted enforcement strategies with high-profile SWAT-style raids on homes and workplaces that targeted civil immigration violators. Additionally, under the Bush administration the 287(g) program was initiated—more formally known as Delegation of Immigration Authority under Section 287(g) of the Immigration and Nationality Act. This program allows state and local law enforcement agencies to partner with ICE, under a joint Memorandum of Agreement (MOA) that delegates to those state or local entities the authority to perforce certain immigration enforcement duties usually performed by ICE, such as identifying undocumented immigrants. This development has created a new set of legal and humanitarian concerns as to whether under the U.S. Constitution federal authority can or should be delegated to state and local law enforcement agents or whether local law enforcement agencies, as in the state of Arizona, are likely to abuse immigration enforcement powers to discriminate against Latinas/os and others suspected of being unauthorized in the country. Arizona presents one of the most glaring examples of local abuse of this authority, as the local sheriff's office, under the leadership of Sheriff Joe Arpaio, has been found by a federal court to have engaged in unconstitutional sweeps of Latina/o communities.

ICE's enforcement actions have affected Latina/o communities around the country. Concerns have grown over how removal and deportations have broken up families and how the rights of Latinas/os, including those legally in the country have been infringed. ICE's aggressive tactics and the blurring of the lines between police enforcement and immigration enforcement agents have been perceived by many Latinas/os as excessive and undue. Although officially it has been said that aggressive immigration law enforcement initiatives aim to root out criminals and "dangerous fugitives," these strategies have raised apprehension and fear in Latina/o and immigrant communities. Studies show that Latina/o communities are less confident in local law enforcement agents and in the justice system than are whites. Local police and ICE agents' interchangeably using immigration enforcement powers, instances of racial profiling, and invasions of persons' homes and workplaces, and the apprehension and deportation of persons who are not criminals has even caused Latina/o citizens and permanent residents to question law enforcement motives and actions.

Under President Barak Obama, deportations by ICE achieved unprecedented levels. By 2014, the number of persons deported under his administration reached the two million mark, more than the previous administration. It has done so utilizing many of the mechanisms established during the Bush administration, including the 287(g) program which enlists local law-enforcement agencies to identify "illegal" immigrants and "E-verify," a controversial online employment verification system used to check a person's eligibility to work.

Having set a target of 400,000 deportations a year, ICE has been taking strong steps during the Obama years to enforce immigration laws. But in spite of the administration's assertions that these measures are aimed at deporting dangerous criminals, a *New York Times* analysis reveals that two-thirds of the estimated two million deportations actually were for minor offenses, such as traffic violations, and some people had committed no criminal offenses. Only 20 percent (approximately 394,000) were deported for having been involved in serious crimes, which included drug offenses (Thompson & Cohen 2014). The Obama administration's removal policy has been perceived by Latina/o community leaders as draconian and unjust, as numerous families have been torn apart by removal proceedings. In an expression of disappointment similar to that being voiced by many community and civic leaders around the country, Janet Murguia, the president of the **National Council of La Raza**, the largest Latina/o civil rights organization in the United States, named President Obama the "deporter in chief" and called on him to safeguard immigrant families and children from harsh deportation actions. Since then, President Obama has sought to expand the Deferred Action for Childhood Arrivals (DACA) and create a new program called the Deferred Action for Parental Accountability (DAPA). Both programs seek to temporarily protect undocumented persons from deportation who meet certain criteria (e.g., they have not committed a serious criminal offense), but neither is a substitute for comprehensive immigration reform—something that requires Congressional action.

See also: Part I essays: Latina/o Immigrants, Crime, and Justice; Latinas and the U.S. Criminal Justice System; Crime and the U.S.-Mexican Border. Part II entries: Deportation; Deportation Laws; Hate Crimes; Immigrant Detention Centers.

Further Reading

Beirich, Heidi. 2011 (Spring). The year in nativism, 2010. *Intelligence Report*: 35. http://www.splcenter.org/get-informed/intelligence-report/browse-all-issues/2011/spring/the-year-in-nativism.

Bess Chiu, Lynly Egyes, Peter L. Markowitz, and Jaya Vasandani. 2009. Constitution on ICE: A report on immigration home raid operations. New York: Cardozo Immigration Justice Clinic. http://cw.routledge.com/textbooks/9780415996945/human-rights/cardozo.pdf.

Californians for Safety and Justice. 2014. *Latino voices: The Impacts of crime and criminal justice on Latinos*. Oakland, CA: Californians for Safety and Justice. http://libcloud.s3.amazonaws.com/211/04/1/430/LatinoReport_7.8.14v1.pdf.

Immigration and Customs Enforcement. [n.d.]. Who we are. http://www.ice.gov/about. Accessed November 13, 2015.

Immigration and Customs Enforcement. 2015. FY 2014 ICE Immigration Removals. http://www.ice.gov/removal-statistics.

Johnson, Kevin. 2004. The huddled masses: Myth, immigration and civil rights. Philadelphia: Temple University Press.

Leadership Conference on Civil Rights Education Fund. 2009. *Confronting the new faces of hate: Hate crimes in America*. Washington, DC: LCCREF. http://www.protectcivilrights.org/pdf/reports/hatecrimes/lccref_hate_crimes_report.pdf.

Lopez, Mark Hugo, and Gretchen Livingston. 2009. "Hispanics and the criminal justice system: Low confidence, high exposure." Pew Hispanic Center, Washington, DC.

Lopez, Mark Hugo, and Susan Minushkin. 2008. *National survey of Latinos: Hispanics see their situation in U.S. deteriorating; oppose key immigration enforcement measures*. Washington, DC: Pew Hispanic Center. http://pewhispanic.org/files/reports/93.pdf. Accessed November 13, 2015.

Potok, Mark. 2008. *Anti-Latino hate crimes rise for fourth year in a row*. Montgomery, AL: Southern Poverty Law Center. http://www.splcenter.org/blog/2008/10/29/anti-latino-hate-crimes-rise-for-fourth-year/.

Schwartz, David. 2014 (October 29). Judge orders Arizona Sheriff Joe Arpaio to undergo training to stop racial profiling. *Reuters*. http://www.huffingtonpost.com/2014/10/29/joe-arpaio-racial-profiling-training_n_6065792.html.

Tangeman, Anthony S. 2003 (June 27). "Memorandum for Deputy Assistant Director, Field Operations Division and Field Office of Detention ad Removal (DRO) Strategic Plan 2003–2012: Endgame." Office of Detention and Removal. http://www.endgameplan.info/Memorandum.html.

Thompson, Ginger, and Sarah Cohen. 2014 (April 6). More deportations follow minor crimes, records show. *New York Times*. http://www.nytimes.com/2014/04/07/us/more-deportations-follow-minor-crimes-data-shows.html?_r=0.

Immigration and Law Enforcement. *See* Part I essays: Latinas/os and the U.S. Criminal Justice System; Latina/o Immigrants, Crime, and Justice; Policing and Latina/o Communities; Latinas and the U.S. Criminal Justice System; Crime and the U.S.-Mexican Border. Part II entries: Deportation; Deportation Laws; Immigrant Detention Centers; Immigration and Customs Enforcement (ICE).

Immigration and Naturalization *Service (INS) v. Lopez-Mendoza et al.*, 468 U.S. 1032 (1984)

Evin R. Rodkey

Immigration and Naturalization Service (INS) v. Lopez-Mendoza et al. (1984) was a U.S. Supreme Court case that ruled the exclusionary rule of the U.S. Constitution does not necessarily apply to **deportation** proceedings. Decided on July 5, 1984, the ruling reversed two appeals court decisions that had ruled that evidence produced by the unlawful arrests of two Latino men would be excluded from admission. The decision was a narrow margin of five to four, with Justices O'Connor, Burger, Blackmun, Powell, and Rehnquist voting to reverse the decision of the appeals court. Justices Brennan, White, Marshall, and Stevens filed dissenting opinions. The Fourth Amendment protects defendants by excluding from admissible evidence anything obtained from an unlawful arrest. The decision determined that the exclusionary rule under Fourth Amendment protection does not apply to civil proceedings such as deportations. Though deportation was identified as a civil rather than criminal matter, this case represents a step in a trend that increasingly criminalizes matters pertaining to immigration, bearing significant consequences for Latino immigrants.

The decision held three main points regarding deportation hearings. First, the purpose of deportation trials are to uphold the law as it pertains to the violation of immigration laws, not to punish past transgressions. Second, a defendant's identity cannot itself be suppressed, even if produced by an unlawful arrest. An illegal arrest cannot mitigate the circumstances of a subsequent deportation hearing. The identity of the person is not in question, and the identity is the evidence of illegal presence in the United States. Third, the exclusionary rule of the Fourth Amendment does not apply in deportation hearings. Therefore admissions of illegal entry that follow unlawful arrests can be included as evidence at deportation hearings. The Court reasoned that applying the exclusionary rule in deportation proceedings would result in the release of detainees who would, by default, resume committing a crime with their unlawful presence in the United States.

The case of *INS v. Lopez-Mendoza et al.* was a response to two cases involving unlawful arrests of unauthorized immigrants. The first of these immigrants, Adan Lopez-Mendoza, was arrested in 1976 by INS agents on suspicion of unauthorized presence in the United States. Lopez-Mendoza was working at an automobile repair shop in San Mateo, California, when INS agents entered the facility, reportedly responding to a tip that the shop employed unauthorized immigrants. The owner of the shop refused the request of the agents to engage employees during working hours. Without a search or arrest warrant, one agent entered the shop and approached Lopez-Mendoza while the other agent spoke to the shop owner. Lopez-Mendoza gave his name and divulged that he was from Mexico. The questioning agent placed Lopez-Mendoza under arrest and transferred him to the INS office. Under further questioning, Lopez-Mendoza executed an affidavit confirming he was a Mexican citizen and was not authorized to enter into the United States. INS agents prepared the necessary documents to order the deportation of Lopez-Mendoza to Mexico.

Because Lopez-Mendoza's arrest was unlawful, his legal counsel motioned to terminate his deportation proceedings. The immigration judge ruled that the unlawful arrest proceedings were irrelevant to the deportation proceedings. With the evidence of Lopez-Mendoza's affidavit confirming his unauthorized presence in the United States, an immigration judge ordered Lopez-Mendoza deported with the option of voluntary departure. The Court of Appeals considered the circumstances of the arrest, as the officers entered Lopez-Mendoza's place of employment in defiance of the business owner and without a warrant for search or arrest. The appeals court vacated the deportation to determine whether Lopez-Mendoza's Fourth Amendment rights had been violated when he was arrested.

The second defendant, Elias Sandoval-Sanchez, was arrested in 1977 while entering the potato processing plant in Pasco, Washington, where he was employed. With permission from the plant's personnel manager, INS agents entered to investigate the presence of unauthorized immigrants. As INS officers covered the plant exits, two agents proceeded to the lunchroom. They identified themselves as immigration officers, and many of the employees in the room moved around or attempted to exit. Upon learning of the situation, others still working or on their way into the plant attempted to exit as well. The two officers proceeded to the main entrance and looked for employees who showed signs of avoiding detection, such as avoiding eye contact or hiding within the larger group. Passing employees who exhibited suspicious behavior were questioned in English, or if they could not understand, in Spanish, as to their status to legally reside in the United States. Sandoval-Sanchez was one of 37 employees whose behavior was deemed suspicious and he was taken to the county jail after being detained at the plant.

Although about one-third of those arrested opted for voluntary departure and were transported to Mexico, Sandoval-Sanchez exercised his right to a deportation hearing. Upon further questioning before his hearing, Sandoval-Sanchez admitted to being unauthorized to enter the United States. As with Lopez-Mendoza, however, Sandoval-Sanchez's counsel contested his arrest on grounds that it was unlawful, as Sandoval-Sanchez was not aware that he had the right to remain silent. Sandoval-Sanchez's case raised complex questions about the proper arrest procedures in raids that involve large groups of people and confusing circumstances. At his hearing, the immigration judge ruled that the unlawful arrest proceedings were irrelevant to the deportation hearing and ordered Sandoval-Sanchez deported with the option of voluntary departure. The court of appeals, however, reversed the decision after determining that the detention of Sandoval-Sanchez violated the Fourth Amendment. Evidence of his illegal presence was excluded, as he was not made aware of his rights in the arrest proceedings. Because the statements he made resulted from that detention, the exclusionary rule prevented their admission into a deportation hearing. The Supreme Court decision reversed the decision of the appeals court in both cases.

The application of *INS v. Lopez-Mendoza* and Sandoval-Sanchez to deportation hearings has important implications for the rights of unauthorized Latino immigrants. Under this ruling, unlawful arrest proceedings can be used to identify immigrants as unauthorized and deportable. This case shares similar implications with other Supreme Court rulings that weaken Fourth Amendment protection for immigrants. In ***U.S. v. Martinez-Fuerte* (1976)**, for example, the Court upheld (7 to 2) that searching vehicles for unauthorized immigrants at fixed checkpoints does not violate Fourth Amendment protection. In his dissenting opinion, Justice Brennan, joined by Justice Marshall, pointed out that the decision was inconsistent with ***U.S. v. Brignoni-Ponce* (1975)** decided one year prior, which upheld (9 to 0) that the Fourth Amendment would not allow roving stops of vehicles near the southern U.S. border on the basis of the passengers appearing to be of Mexican ancestry. The decision in *U.S. v. Martinez-Fuerte* allows full searches with no probable cause if the search takes place at a fixed checkpoint, which ultimately allows officials to search passengers based, at least in part, on appearing "Mexican." Similarly, the use of **drug**-courier profiles for searching suspected illicit drug traffickers in airports and other routes of passage threatens Fourth Amendment protection for Latinas/os. The use of drug-courier profiles to identify characteristics consistent with transporting illicit drugs has increased successful identifications and arrests of suspects. No standards for these profiles exist, however. Because various local law enforcement agencies use different means of profiling, race and ethnicity have been used by some, putting Latinas/os at a disadvantage. *INS v. Lopez-Mendoza et al.*, as well as other Court decisions and contemporary legal measures, contributes to the merging of criminal and immigration law, sometimes known as "**crimmigration**." Such proceedings stand to disproportionately affect Latinas/os and other people of color.

See also: Part I essays: Latinas/os and the U.S. Criminal Justice Systems; Latina/o Immigrants, Crime, and Justice; The U.S. War on Drugs and Latina/o Communities; Crime and the U.S.-Mexican Border. Part II entries: Deportation; Deportation Laws.

Further Reading

Dey, Irene. 1998. Drug courier profiles: An infringement on Fourth Amendment rights. *University of Baltimore Law Forum* (28): 3.

Mirandé, Alfredo. 2003. Is there a "Mexican Exception" to the Fourth Amendment? *Florida Law Review* 55: 365–89.

Morín, José Luis. 2009. *Latino/a rights and justice in the United States: Perspectives and approaches*. 2nd ed. Durham, NC: Carolina Academic Press.

Soltero, Carlos R. 2006. *Latinos and American law: Landmark Supreme Court cases*. Austin, TX: University of Texas Press.

Stumpf, Juliet. 2006. The crimmigration crisis: Immigrants, crime, and sovereign power. *American University Law Review* 56: 367–419.

Urbina, Martin G. (ed.). 2012. *Hispanics in the U.S. criminal justice system: The new American demography*. Springfield, IL: Charles C. Thomas.

Cases Cited

Immigration and Naturalization Service (INS) v. Lopez-Mendoza et al. 468 U.S. 1032 (1984).

United States v. Brignoni-Ponce 422 U.S. 873 (1975).

United States v. Martinez-Fuerte 428 U.S. 543 (1976).

Implicit Bias. *See* Part I essay: Latinas/os and the U.S. Criminal Justice System.

Innocence Project, The

Evin Rodkey

The Innocence Project is an American nonprofit legal clinic that works to exonerate wrongfully convicted inmates through DNA testing and to reform the criminal justice system to prevent such convictions. The Innocence Project was founded by Barry Scheck and Peter Neufeld in 1992 at the Benjamin N. Cardozo School of Law at Yeshiva University in New York City. The Project is now an independent nonprofit but remains closely affiliated with Yeshiva University's Cardozo School of Law. The mission of the Innocence Project is to free the wrongfully convicted and affect reform to the legal system that results in wrongful imprisonment. The Project holds that wrongful convictions are not isolated events but are embedded in a defective criminal justice system. Latinas/os represent the fastest growing segment of the U.S. prison population; as a case in point, Latino men are nearly four times as likely as are white men to face incarceration. The work of the Innocence Project therefore is crucial to the future of justice for Latinas/os.

Clients of The Innocence Project usually are inmates with no recourse left but DNA testing. Inmates must contact the Innocence Project and have their case reviewed before the Project will take their case. The Innocence Project handles only those cases in which DNA testing can be used. The Project, however, is a founding member of The Innocence Network, a group of law schools, journalism schools, and public defender offices that works to exonerate the innocent in cases without DNA testing. The Innocence Project also employs social workers who help the exonerated adjust after release. The documentary film, *After Innocence*, features seven exonerees assisted by the Innocence Project and profiles their adjustment after release from prison. The founders of the Innocence Project, Barry Scheck and Peter Neufeld, appear in the film.

The Innocence Project centers its work on what it identifies as the seven most common causes of wrongful conviction: (1) *Eyewitness Misidentification*: Misidentification by an eyewitness is the greatest cause of wrongful convictions and contributes to more than 75 percent of convictions overturned through DNA testing. The Innocence Project points out that this method has been under scrutiny as a reliable method for more than 100 years and supports reforms to its uses; (2) *Unreliable and Limited Science*: Due to the strength in DNA testing, the Innocence Project raises awareness of the lack of reliability in older forms of forensic science such as blood typing (serology) and hair comparisons that still are used in court cases; (3) *False Confessions*: Approximately 25 percent of those exonerated by DNA testing confessed to the crime or pled guilty in court. External influences such as coercion, mental impairment, and ignorance of the law contribute to false confessions. The Innocence Project has recommended mandatory recording of interrogations to increase the reliability of confessions; (4) *Forensic Science Misconduct*: False testimony, misleading statistics, and even fraud have led to wrongful convictions. Steps in handling forensic evidence, such as collecting, testing, and storing, sometimes lead to its destruction, rendering retesting impossible. The Innocence Project works to reform standards for the preservation and handling of evidence, such as imposing independent audits of lab work; (5) *Government Misconduct*: The Innocence Project notes that though most officials are honest, some take deliberate steps to ensure a conviction regardless of proof of guilt. Cases of DNA exonerations have exposed such misconduct as suggestiveness in identification procedures, withholding evidence from defense, and the use of unreliable informants or snitches. The Innocence Project works to establish criminal justice reform commissions to help safeguard against such misconduct; (6) *Informants / Snitches*: For more than 15 percent of wrongful conviction cases overturned by DNA testing, an informant or snitch testified against the defendant. In some cases informants were paid to testify or given commuted sentences in exchange for their testimony; and (7) *Bad Lawyering*: Cuts in funding for public defenders and court-appointed attorneys means overburdened or incompetent lawyers sometimes mishandle cases. Overworked lawyers could fail to fully investigate, arrange for witnesses, or adequately prepare for trial. In some cases, incompetent lawyers have failed to investigate alibis, slept during the trial, and have not shown up for court. The Innocence Project offers recommendations for improving the quality of defense for poor defendants. Because Latinas/os are more likely than whites to be poor, bad lawyering makes Latinas/os particularly vulnerable to wrongful conviction. Furthermore, the **underrepresentation** of Latina/o lawyers and judges has been raised as contributing to uneven justice for Latinas/os in the legal system.

In addition to identifying the key areas (Eyewitness Identification; False Confessions;

DNA Testing Access; Evidence Preservation; Forensic Oversight; Innocence Commissions; and Exoneree Compensation), the Innocence Project has developed model legislation for jurisdictions considering reforms to use. These models include post-conviction DNA testing, evidence preservation, eyewitness identification reform, false confessions, crime lab oversight, compensation, and criminal justice reform commissions (also known as Innocence Commissions).

The Innocence Project has assisted wrongfully convicted Latinos, both U.S. citizens and noncitizens. At the age of 16, Alejandro Dominguez of Mexico was convicted of rape in Illinois. Eyewitness misidentification by the victim and the procedure employed by the investigators was biased and highly suggestive. The victim testified that the lead detective had singled out Dominguez during the lineup. When reporting the crime to police, the victim's description of the attacker included a diamond earring and a tattoo. She also reported that the attacker spoke to her in English. Dominquez was found to have neither a pierced ear nor any tattoos, and he could speak only Spanish. The use of forensic evidence in the form of blood typing also was used to convict Dominguez. Upon requesting a semen sample from Dominquez, testing revealed that Dominquez could not be excluded as a match with the sample recovered from the victim. William Wilson, the forensic serologist from Northern Illinois Crime Laboratory who testified, however, did not disclose that 67 percent of all males would not be excluded as well. In 1990, Dominguez was convicted and served four years in jail. After his release, the Immigration and Naturalization Service threatened to deport him in 2001 for failing to register his conviction. At this point, Dominquez sought DNA testing that proved his innocence and exonerated him from the crime on April 26, 2002.

In another case, two Latino men forced a 14-year-old girl into a car in Houston, Texas, in 1987. The men drove the girl to a house where both men raped her. After raping her, the men drove the girl away from the house and left her at the side of a road. During the abduction, the victim claimed she heard one attacker call the other George. She also said she suspected this was a false name, as she had heard the attackers discuss not using their real names. Police knew of two brothers who lived together, Manuel and Uvaldo Beltran, who were associated with someone named George. Officers visited the Beltran home to investigate George Rodriguez as a suspect. Under questioning at the Beltran home, Uvaldo told police that he saw his brother Manuel and a man named Isidro Yanez, who had been named in a similar crime in the area, taking a girl to his bedroom. Manual Beltran then confessed to the abduction and rape of the 14-year-old girl with Yanez. Police went on to confirm that Yanez's car was used to abduct the victim. Rodriguez claimed that he was at work during the crime, which his work records confirmed.

Nonetheless, the victim had identified Rodriguez in a photo and later identified him in a lineup. She later testified that she had been able to view his face for only 3 or 4 seconds during the attack. Two months after the attack, the victim was shown a picture of Yanez, which was in a photo book along with a photo of Rodriguez. The victim picked out both Rodriguez and Yanez, noting their similarities. Eventually, she confirmed Rodriguez as the attacker. In addition, the Houston Police Department Crime Laboratory found a hair from the victim's underwear similar to a sample taken from Rodriguez. Jim Bolding, director of the crime lab, testified that Rodriguez could not be excluded and Yanez could not be included as contributors of the hair.

George Rodriguez was convicted and sentenced to 60 years in prison.

In 2003, retesting showed that both of the claims by Jim Bolding were false. DNA testing on the hair, rather than microscopic comparisons, showed that Rodriguez could not have left it. The testing also showed that Yanez could not be excluded. Further, a retesting of Yanez's blood type showed that the original test was mistaken and he could be included after all. In 2005, after 17 years in prison, George Rodriguez was released from prison and his record cleared.

Through the 1990s and into the current decade, crime in the United States has decreased dramatically. Nevertheless, news and entertainment **media** portray crime as if it is at record high levels, and media depictions correlate with increased fear of crime, overrepresenting Latinas/os and African Americans as perpetrators of crime. The pervasiveness of inaccurate and negative portrayals of Latinas/os as violent criminals throughout U.S. society makes it all the more possible that any given Latina/o could be wrongful convicted. This possibility makes the work of the Innocence Project relevant and important to Latinas/os, African Americans, the indigent, and all others who are vulnerable and least able to mount an adequate defense within the criminal justice system.

See also: Part I essays: Policing and Latina/o Communities; Incarceration and Latinas/os in the United States. Part II entries: Civil Rights; Death Penalty; International Human Rights.

Further Reading

Dorfman, Lori, and Vincent Schiraldi. 2001. *Off balance: Youth, race and crime in the news*. Washington, DC: Building Blocks for Youth.

The Innocence Project. [n.d.] http://www.innocenceproject.org/. Accessed November 12, 2015.

Morín, José Luis. 2009. *Latino/a rights and justice in the United States: Perspectives and approaches*. 2nd ed. Durham, NC: Carolina Academic Press.

Morín, José Luis. 2008. Latinas/os and U.S. prisons: Trends and challenges. *Latino Studies* 6(1–2): 11–34.

Sanders, Jessica (Director). 2005. *After Innocence*. (Feature Film Documentary). Produced by American Film Foundation and Showtime.

Walker, Samuel, Miriam DeLone, and Cassia Spohn. 2007. *The color of justice: Race, ethnicity, and crime in America*. 4th edition. Belmont, CA: Thomson/Wadsworth.

Institutional Racism. *See* Part I essays: Latinas/os and the U.S. Criminal Justice System; Latinas and the U.S. Criminal Justice System; Incarceration and Latinas/os in the United States. Part II entries: Civil Rights; International Human Rights; Slavery.

International Human Rights

José Luis Morín

Latina/o communities in the United States are increasingly looking to international human rights laws, norms, and principles in response to infringements of their rights in both the criminal justice and civil domains. Specifically in relation to the U.S. criminal justice system, international human rights laws, norms, and principles resonate with Latina/o communities because they reinforce existing **civil rights** protections. Equally significant, international human rights hold the potential for addressing economic, social, and cultural obstacles and challenges that Latinas/os encounter in securing rights through the criminal justice system. Contemporary international human rights laws and principles not only strengthen rights recognized under the U.S. Constitution and U.S. civil rights laws, but they also offer a broader concept of human rights that recognizes economic, social, and cultural rights, rights that advocates see as important to adopt as part of a comprehensive approach to improving criminal justice outcomes.

Global Human Rights Systems

International human rights law refers to the rules recognized and adopted as binding by nations around the globe to promote and protect certain individual and collective rights. Contemporary international human rights law largely is grounded in efforts by countries after the two world wars of the 20th century. Following the First World War, the League of Nations sought to protect ethnic, linguistic, and religious minorities left vulnerable by the transformation that occurred with the redrawing of parts of the geopolitical map of Europe. Although the League of Nations was short lived, it took significant steps toward establishing international respect and safeguards for ethnic, linguistic, and religious minority rights. With the formation of the United Nations in 1945 after the Second World War, a broad range of human rights standards and treaties were developed, and mechanisms to monitor and enforce human rights were established.

International human rights laws and instruments generally fall within two broad categories of rights: (1) political and civil rights; and (2) economic, social, and cultural rights. The Universal Declaration on Human Rights of 1948 acknowledges both. With respect to criminal justice policies, practices, and processes, the Universal Declaration affirms the right to be free from torture or cruel, inhuman, or degrading treatment or punishment (article 4); to protection from arbitrary arrests and detentions (article 9); to be accorded full equality to a fair and impartial tribunal (article 10); and to the presumption of innocence (article 11) as part of the civil rights protections that should be universal. The International Covenant on Civil and Political Rights (ICCPR) of 1966 contains these and other civil and political rights, including provisions that directly speak to criminal justice issues, such as the **death penalty** (article 6); torture or cruel, inhuman, or degrading treatment or punishment (article 7); freedom from arbitrary arrests and detention (article 9); and the right to a fair trial and the presumption of innocence (article 14), among other provisions.

As a treaty that has been ratified by many countries, states that have ratified the ICCPR are obligated to adhere to its principles, whereas declarations are not necessarily considered to contain binding obligations. The United States has ratified ICCPR, but with the reservation that additional federal laws must be passed to make it enforceable in U.S. courts. Thus, it cannot be used as a basis for a human rights claim in the courts of the United States, although as a matter of international law the United States has signed and ratified it and is supposed to fulfill its requirements.

The Universal Declaration on Human Rights also identifies certain economic, social, and cultural rights, including the right to adequate food, clothing, housing, and health care (article 25), the right to an education (article 26), and rights to cultural participation (article 27). These provisions are augmented by the International Covenant on Economic, Social and Cultural Rights (ICESCR) of 1966, which provides for such rights as the right to work (article 6), to fair wages and equal wages (article 7); and to an adequate standard of living, including adequate food, clothing, and housing (article 11).

The U.N. human rights system employs various means to enforce human rights standards. U.N. Charter–based human rights machinery include its Human Rights Council, which assesses human rights situations in U.N. member states; provides expertise and advice on thematic human rights issues; and receives complaints from individuals and organizations about human rights violations in member states. United Nations "treaty-based" mechanisms consist of committees and processes for human rights oversight and enforcement pursuant to treaties ratified by member states. Part IV of the 1966 International Covenant on Civil and Political Rights, for example, establishes the Human Rights Committee, a body of independent experts that monitors the treaty's implementation. As a result, the United States is subject to regular human rights scrutiny at the international level. In addition to reviewing a wide range of human rights matters in the United States, the Human Rights Committee has been examining the U.S. record on criminal justice and it has issued concerns and recommendations on such matters as racial disparities in the criminal justice system, **racial profiling**, **stop-and-frisk** police tactics, and continuing racial inequities associated with the death penalty (*see, e.g.*, Human Rights Committee 2014). As a member state of the United Nations, the United States undergoes human rights monitoring through the Universal Periodic Review process in which the U.N.'s Human Rights Council examines the human rights situation of every member state of the United Nations on a rotating basis.

Under the First Optional Protocol to the International Covenant on Civil and Political Rights of 1996, the Human Rights Committee also can receive complaints concerning states that have ratified the Protocol. Other treaties contain similar individual complaint procedures, such as the Convention on the Elimination of All Forms of Discrimination Against Women (CEDAW), and some require periodic compliance reports, as with the Convention on the Rights of the Child. The United States has not ratified the First Optional Protocol to the International Covenant on Civil and Political Rights, the Convention on the Elimination of All Forms of Discrimination Against Women (CEDAW), the Convention on the Rights of the Child, or most international human rights treaties. Although most counties of the world have ratified many more human rights treaties, as of June 2015, the United States has only ratified 5 of the 18 major U.N. human rights treaties: The International Covenant on Civil and Political Rights; the Convention against Torture and Other Cruel, Inhuman or Degrading Treatment or Punishment; the International Convention on the Elimination of All Forms of Racial Discrimination; the Optional Protocol to the Convention on the Rights of the Child on the Involvement of Children in Armed Conflict; and the Optional Protocol to the Convention on the Rights of the Child on the Sale of Children, Child Prostitution and Child Pornography.

That the United States has ratified very few international human rights treaties and that it has imposed reservations on their use in U.S. courts places severe limitations on human rights litigation and advocacy. Nevertheless, the underlying principles and provisions of these treaties are considered authoritative statements of universally recognized standards and rights that should be respected and observed by the United States. In fact, a 2002 research and advocacy report by Michigan State University and Building Blocks for Youth, *¿Dónde Está la Justicia? A Call to Action on behalf of Latino and Latina Youth in the U.S. Justice System*, cites the Convention on the Rights of the Child for its applicability to the situation of Latina/o **youth**, calling for the use of this U.N. convention "as a basis for including youth as active participants in the systems and decision processes that affect them" (Villarruel et al. 2002, 73).

Regional Human Rights Systems

Regional international organizations, such as the Organization of American States (OAS), composed of the 35 sovereign nations of the Americas, have established their own human rights system with standards and mechanisms for human rights protection and enforcement. The Inter-American Commission on Human Rights was established by the Protocol of Buenos Aires in an amendment to the OAS Charter of 1948, the OAS's founding document. That amendment, which entered into force in 1970, empowers the Inter-American Commission to act as a quasi-judicial body with the responsibility to promote and protect human rights. The Inter-American Commission is guided by the American Declaration of the Rights and Duties of Man of 1948, a normative and authoritative instrument protecting fundamental rights such as the right to life, the right to equality before the law, and other rights. The Inter-American Commission's functions include the ability to receive and render opinions on individual cases. Although lacking the power to enforce its decisions, the Inter-American Commission can seek settlements and bring cases to the attention of the OAS General Assembly.

Under the 1969 American Convention on Human Rights, the Inter-American Commission can also present cases to the Inter-American Court of Human Rights against a state that has ratified the American Convention. In such cases, the Court can issue orders to enforce its rulings. Among its other responsibilities, the Inter-American Commission conducts country studies and on-site investigations of the human rights situation in various OAS member states. The United States has not ratified the American Convention on Human Rights, preventing human rights claims against it from being brought before the Inter-American Court of Human Rights. Nevertheless, as an OAS member, the United States is subject to the jurisdiction of the Inter-American Commission on Human Rights, and it must abide by the obligations under 1948 American Declaration of the Rights and Duties of Man. It is before the Inter-American Commission on Human Rights that claims against the United States for human rights violations have been filed, including petitions on behalf of Latinas/os in the United States.

International Human Rights and the U.S. Criminal Justice System

As a body of law and principles that reinforce the protection of certain basic civil rights embodied in current U.S. law, international human rights have taken on increasing relevance for Latina/o communities in relation to the operations of the criminal justice system in the United States. Other developments in international human rights in the area of economic, social, and cultural rights, though not recognized by the United States, carry potential significance for protecting Latinas/os in relation to crime and the operations of the criminal justice system.

From the **Zoot Suit Riots** of the 1940s to more contemporary examples of police abuse, police misconduct and brutality have a long history in Latina/o communities. An array of international human rights documents have been developed on human rights issues in the context of the administration of justice and the protection of persons subjected to detention or imprisonment. The standards set forth in these documents seek to address the problem of police misconduct and abusive treatment and to provide guidelines for law enforcement personnel. One such document is the Code of Conduct for Law Enforcement Officials of 1979, which maintains that "law enforcement officials may use force only when strictly necessary and to the extent required for the performance of their duty" (art. 3). Additional guidance to law enforcement personnel is found under article 5 of the Code, which instructs that

> [n]o law enforcement official may inflict, instigate or tolerate any act of torture or other cruel, inhuman or degrading treatment or punishment, nor may any law enforcement official invoke superior orders or exceptional circumstances such as a state of war, threat to national security, internal political instability or any other public emergency as a justification of torture or other cruel, inhuman or degrading treatment or punishment.

As a matter of international law, torture, and cruel, inhuman, or degrading treatment or punishment are prohibited pursuant to many international human rights treaties, including the International Covenant on Civil and Political Rights of 1966 (article 4) and the Convention against Torture and other Cruel, Inhuman or Degrading Treatment or Punishment of 1984. Having ratified both treaties, the United States is obligated to observe the prohibition against torture. Reservations made by the United States when it ratified these treaties, however, render these documents non-self-executing—that is, they cannot be used to bring a claim in a U.S. court without an additional law passed by Congress that permits their use. Advocacy groups in the United States and around the world, including Human Rights Watch and Amnesty International, continue to campaign for the removal of U.S. reservations that impede the implementation and enforcement of these treaties.

International Human Rights and the Administration of Justice

The United Nations lists the following documents among the treaties and other documents that serve as legal obligations or guidelines to nations with respect to the administration of justice, with particular attention to the protection of persons subjected to detention or imprisonment.

- Standard Minimum Rules for the Treatment of Prisoners
- Basic Principles for the Treatment of Prisoners
- Body of Principles for the Protection of All Persons under Any Form of Detention or Imprisonment
- United Nations Rules for the Protection of Juveniles Deprived of their Liberty
- Declaration on the Protection of All Persons from Being Subjected to Torture and Other Cruel, Inhuman or Degrading Treatment or Punishment
- Convention against Torture and Other Cruel, Inhuman or Degrading Treatment or Punishment (CAT)
- Optional Protocol to the Convention against Torture and Other Cruel, Inhuman or Degrading Treatment or Punishment (OPCAT)

- Principles of Medical Ethics relevant to the Role of Health Personnel, particularly Physicians, in the Protection of Prisoners and Detainees against Torture and Other Cruel, Inhuman or Degrading Treatment or Punishment
- Principles on the Effective Investigation and Documentation of Torture and Other Cruel, Inhuman or Degrading Treatment or Punishment
- Safeguards guaranteeing protection of the rights of those facing the death penalty
- Code of Conduct for Law Enforcement Officials
- Basic Principles on the Use of Force and Firearms by Law Enforcement Officials
- United Nations Standard Minimum Rules for Non-custodial Measures (The Tokyo Rules)
- United Nations Standard Minimum Rules for the Administration of Juvenile Justice (The Beijing Rules)
- Guidelines for Action on Children in the Criminal Justice System
- United Nations Guidelines for the Prevention of **Juvenile Delinquency** (The Riyadh Guidelines)
- Declaration of Basic Principles of Justice for Victims of Crime and Abuse of Power
- Basic Principles on the Independence of the Judiciary
- Basic Principles on the Role of Lawyers
- Guidelines on the Role of Prosecutors
- Principles on the Effective Prevention and Investigation of Extra-legal, Arbitrary and Summary Executions
- Declaration on the Protection of All Persons from Enforced Disappearance
- Basic Principles and Guidelines on the Right to a Remedy and Reparation
- International Convention for the Protection of All Persons from Enforced Disappearance
- United Nations Rules for the Treatment of Women Prisoners and Non-custodial Measures for Women Offenders (the Bangkok Rules)
- Updated Set of principles for the protection and promotion of human rights through action to combat impunity

Source: Compiled from the Office of the United Nations High Commissioner for Human Rights. 2015. http://www.ohchr.org/EN/ProfessionalInterest/Pages/UniversalHumanRightsInstruments.aspx.

Under Article VI of the U.S. Constitution, "all Treaties [international law] . . . shall be the supreme Law of the Land." But in addition to treaties that bind the United States to observe and enforce particular rights, international law also recognizes certain human rights to be so fundamental as to be mandatory or a peremptory norm of international law ("*jus cogens*" in legal parlance), and, therefore, regardless of whether a country has ratified a treaty it is expected to comply with that particular obligation under international law. The prohibition against torture and **slavery** are examples of human rights obligations from which deviation is not allowed under any circumstance.

International Human Rights and U.S. Prisons

Numerous studies in recent years have exposed inhumane conditions and harsh treatment of prisoners and other persons in detention throughout the United States. Among the many well-documented studies of the conditions under which immigrants are detained is one by Mark Dow (2004) entitled *American Gulag: Inside U.S. Immigration Prisons*. Studies show that too often immigrant detainees are treated arbitrarily, beaten, and even sexually abused. A 2009 study of New York's juvenile detention system commissioned by Governor David Paterson revealed that there is ample "reason to believe that the current system is unfair. African American and Latino youth represent only 44 percent of New York's total youth population, yet they comprise more than 80 percent of all youth in the state's institutional placement facilities. Remarkably, this disparity never has been adequately investigated to understand its causes or consequences." Additionally, there is "compelling evidence" of psychological and physical maltreatment of young girls in two New York State institutional facilities and the repeated use of excessive force to restrain youths "for minor incidents, such as refusing to get dressed or slamming a door" and that this use of force has resulted in "concussions, broken bones, and lost teeth" (Task Force on Transforming Juvenile Justice 2009, 14, 15).

In California, as evidenced in the cases of *Plata v. Schwarzenegger* (2010) and *Coleman v. Schwarzenegger* (2010), courts have ruled that prison conditions—including overcrowding and the severe lack of adequate medical and mental health care—violate the U.S. Constitution's prohibition against cruel and unusual punishment and have ordered the state to reduce its prison population. As in New York and California, throughout the United States Latinas/os and other persons of color are cited among the most vulnerable populations to incarceration and abuse in prisons (*see also* Justice Policy Institute 2009; Amnesty International 1998; Dow 2004).

The shortcomings of the present system have led civil rights and human rights advocates to promote the adoption of international human rights laws or models to ensure that all persons held in detention have the basic protections of human dignity and human rights. One document frequently referenced as a "seminal guide for the treatment of incarcerated persons" is the "Basic Principles for the Treatment of Prisoners," adopted by U.N. General Assembly in resolution 45/111 of December 14, 1990. The resolution mandates that all prisoners "be treated with the respect due to their inherent dignity and value as human beings."

Bias in the Criminal Justice System

Racial profiling, harsher sentences, the excessive use of force by police, **felony disenfranchisement** laws that politically disempower communities of color, and stricter penalties for crack cocaine than powdered cocaine are just some of the controversial policies and practices often cited by Latinas/os and African Americans in the United States as examples of bias within the criminal justice system. In 1994, the United States ratified the International Convention on the Elimination of All Forms of Racial Discrimination of 1965. In accordance with article 2, all state parties to this treaty are required to take appropriate steps to eliminate racial discrimination, which includes reviewing all national and local policies and practices that have a discriminatory effect.

The International Convention on the Elimination of All Forms of Racial Discrimination covers discrimination against persons based on national or ethnic origin, not just race and, therefore, its provisions speak to the experience of Latinas/os in the United States, people who have a long history of experiencing discrimination based on race, ethnicity, and national origin. Hence,

Basic Principles for the Treatment of Prisoners

U.N. General Assembly Resolution 45/111 of 14 December 1990

(Excerpts)

1. All prisoners shall be treated with the respect due to their inherent dignity and value as human beings.
2. There shall be no discrimination on the grounds of race, colour, sex, language, religion, political or other opinion, national or social origin, property, birth or other status.

***

5. Except for those limitations that are demonstrably necessitated by the fact of incarceration, all prisoners shall retain the human rights and fundamental freedoms set out in the Universal Declaration of Human Rights, and, where the State concerned is a party, the International Covenant on Economic, Social and Cultural Rights, and the International Covenant on Civil and Political Rights and the Optional Protocol thereto, as well as such other rights as are set out in other United Nations covenants.

***

9. Prisoners shall have access to the health services available in the country without discrimination on the grounds of their legal situation.
10. With the participation and help of the community and social institutions, and with due regard to the interests of victims, favourable conditions shall be created for the reintegration of the ex-prisoner into society under the best possible conditions.

international human rights advocacy organizations regularly cite and call for the application of and compliance with this Convention with respect to Latinas/os (*see, e.g.,* Amnesty International 1998; Human Rights Watch 1998).

The Death Penalty

Contemporary international law embraces the goal of abolishing the death penalty worldwide. Consistent with the principle that all human beings have an "inherent right to life," article 6 of the International Covenant on Civil and Political Rights (ICCPR) of 1966 seeks to limit the use of capital punishment to only the most serious crimes and to prohibit its use against minors and pregnant women in those countries where it exists. Of the two protocols to the ICCPR—the Optional Protocol to the International Covenant on Civil and Political Rights of 1966 and the Second Optional Protocol to the International Covenant on Civil and Political Rights of 1989—the Second Optional Protocol is specifically dedicated to promoting the abolition of capital punishment.

Today, most countries of the world have abolished the use of the death penalty. The United States remains the only developed nation in the world that maintains a system of capital punishment. Its use in the United States has been mired in controversy, particularly because of the disproportionate numbers of persons of color sentenced to death. Studies have shown that a person of color is more likely to be sentenced to die for

International Convention on the Elimination of All Forms of Racial Discrimination U.N. General Assembly Resolution 2106 A (XX) of 21 December 1965

(Excerpts)

Article 1, Paragraph 1

In this Convention, the term "racial discrimination" shall mean "any distinction, exclusion, restriction or preference based on race, colour, descent, or national or ethnic origin which has the purpose or effect of nullifying or impairing the recognition, enjoyment or exercise, on an equal footing, of human rights and fundamental freedoms in the political, economic, social, cultural or any other field of public life."

***

Article 5

In compliance with the fundamental obligations laid down in article 2 of this Convention, States Parties undertake to prohibit and to eliminate racial discrimination in all its forms and to guarantee the right of everyone, without distinction as to race, colour, or national or ethnic origin, to equality before the law, notably in the enjoyment of the following rights.

(a) The right to equal treatment before the tribunals and all other organs administering justice;
(b) The right to security of person and protection by the State against violence or bodily harm, whether inflicted by government officials or by any individual group or institution.

killing a white person than a white person for having murdered a person of color (Death Penalty Information Center 2010; Amnesty International 1998).

Recent national data show that for cases in which executions are carried out, more than 77 percent of homicide **victims** were white, despite the fact that overall only 50 percent of homicide victims are white (Death Penalty Information Center 2010). In proportion to their size within the U.S. population at year-end 2008, African Americans continued to be overrepresented on death row at 41 percent of prisoners under sentence of death, and whites comprised 56 percent of prisoners on death row. Latinas/os represented 13.2 percent of prisoners under sentence of death out of a total of 3,207 persons on death row but, of those admitted to death sentences for 2008, Latinas/os were 19.8 percent (Snell 2009, Table 5 and 6), more than their percentage of the U.S. population (15.4 percent) in 2008 (Pew Hispanic Center 2008).

Although Latinas/os are not as disproportionally represented on death row as are African Americans, as a group generally viewed in the criminal justice literature as vulnerable to bias in the criminal justice system and harsher sentences when compared to whites, the death penalty could emerge as a more serious problem. As "the fastest growing minority group being imprisoned" according to the Bureau of Justice Statistics (1997, 9), Latinas/os might become an increasingly vulnerable group and current anti-immigrant trends in the United States could be a factor that contributes to Latina/o susceptibility to harsher sentences and the death penalty. The steady increase of persons sentenced to die who have been proven to have been wrongfully convicted has raised questions worldwide about the fairness of the application of capital punishment in the United States. Between 1973 and 1999 an average of 3.1 death row inmates were exonerated per year; from 2000 to 2007, an average of 5 per year were exonerated (Death Penalty Information Center 2010).

International Human Rights and Strengthening the Social Safety Net

Criminologists long have raised concerns about the correlation between social and economic inequality and the conditions under which crime can become prevalent. Indeed, poor health and low economic status have been linked to social alienation and greater levels of criminality (*see* Walker, DeLone, & Spohn 2007). Along with African Americans, Latinas/os have an extensive history of **de jure** and **de facto** school and **residential segregation**, unequal educational and employment opportunity, high rates of youth unemployment, soaring levels of hunger, and inadequate housing and health care. Indeed, the *Journal of the American Medical Association* has documented that Latino children suffer from high rates of tuberculosis (13 times greater than whites); half a million Latino children have asthma, with two-thirds being Puerto Rican; Latina/o youth have the greatest school dropout rate in the nation at 29 percent, in contrast to African Americans at 13 percent and whites at 7 percent; 36 percent of Latina/o children live in poverty; and Latina/o children are more at risk to be uninsured at 27 percent than is any other group of children in the United States (Flores et al. 2002, 83–88).

Whereas rights in the United States primarily have focused on the protection of civil and political rights, international human rights norms, principles, and laws recognize the right to health care, housing, education, and employment as fundamental to any society as civil and political rights. To this end, the International Covenant on Economic, Social and Cultural Rights of 1966 promotes the right to work, fair wages, adequate health care, education, and the maintenance of the linguistic and cultural traditions of all groups. As such, these rights serve as a social safety net and preventive measure against crime and other social problems. Although African Americans and Latinas/os are disproportionately poor, whites numerically constitute the largest single racial group in poverty. Specifically, the Bureau of the Census (2015, 13, Table 3) identifies 31,089,000 "White, not Hispanic" persons, 13,104,000 "Hispanics" and 10,755,000 "Blacks" living below the poverty level. Whites also comprise more than two-thirds of all persons arrested for all categories of crime annually (*see* Walker, DeLone, & Spohn 2007). Thus, it is argued that all racial and ethnic groups in the United States would be served by an expansion of the social safety net through the recognition of rights in the area of employment, housing, and health care. Consistent with this notion, the Justice Policy Institute's comprehensive study of **gangs** notes that research has shown that expansion of job and educational opportunities helps keep youth from joining gangs.

Some researchers have concluded that the future for children in the United States only can be improved by the expansion of the social safety net, including job creation and increased funding for education and programs for child care. These measures would be consistent with the Convention on the Rights of the Child—a document that addresses the social and economic needs of children and particular rights and protections children should be afforded in the criminal justice system, as found in article 40 of the Convention. Latinas/os also look to rights and protections recognized under the 1992 Declaration on the Rights of Persons Belonging to National or Ethnic, Religious and Linguistic Minorities, a document that calls for safeguarding the economic, social, and cultural rights of ethnic groups.

The Rights of Immigrants

As is the case for the International Covenant on Economic, Social and Cultural Rights of 1966, the United States also has not ratified the International Convention on the Protection of the Rights of All Migrant Workers and Members of their Families of 1990, a treaty that seeks to protect the health, conditions of employment, and overall well-being of all migrant workers and their families. This covenant is viewed as potentially having a positive impact on the situation of Latina/o migrant workers and their children.

Contrary to the common misimpression that immigrants threaten or burden the U.S. economy, immigrants from Latin America and the Caribbean who are in the United States legally and documented and undocumented immigrants alike contribute to the local and national economy and pay local sales and other taxes. Yet discrimination and acts of **violence** against immigrant workers persist. **Hate crimes**, such as the attacks on Latino day-laborers and the firebombing of a Latina/o immigrant family home in Farmingville, New York, are typical of the animosity and violence Latina/o immigrants have experienced in recent years. The International Convention on the Protection of the Rights of All Migrant Workers and Members of their Families of 1990 and the International Convention on the Elimination of All Forms of Racial Discrimination of 1965 are just two international human rights documents that seek to protect racial and ethnic groups from discrimination and violence.

Language Rights in the Courts

In the United States, there exists no national standard for court translations in state courts and no decision of the U.S. Supreme Court recognizing a constitutional right to have an interpreter in court. It has been common in civil or administrative court proceedings for interpreters to be rejected. Although the Court Interpreters Act, 28 U.S.C. §1827 (1994), grants the right to an interpreter in federal courts, it typically demands non-English speaking persons to secure an attorney to advocate vehemently for an interpreter. In ***United States ex rel. Negron v. New York***, 434 F.2d 386 (2d Cir. 1970), the Second Circuit Court of Appeals ruled that non-English-speaking defendants had a right to simultaneous interpreters at the government's expense, but if a defendant's lawyer is able to interpret, then courts have required the attorney to translate, placing an additional burden on the lawyer and possibly impairing the ability to offer the best advocacy and the ability to have simultaneous translation. Hence, Latinas/os not proficient in English can encounter tremendous language barriers to understanding charges, court proceedings, and testimony in U.S. courts.

When appropriate translation services are not provided in a court case, scholars cite ***Gonzalez v. United States*** (1994) as a case that exemplifies the harm that could result to a non-English-speaking party. In *Gonzalez*, the court's refusal to grant a proper interpreter service might have led the defendant to involuntarily plead guilty. In that case, the court denied a request for a certified interpreter and ruled that Gonzalez's wife could serve as an interpreter without proof that she could translate fairly and accurately, as required by the Court Interpreters Act.

A particularly precarious decision for Latinas/os in criminal proceedings is ***Hernandez v. New York*** (1991), in which the U.S. Supreme Court held that a criminal defendant's Fourteenth Amendment right to equal protection is not violated when a prosecutor excludes Spanish-speaking persons from a jury. In that case, Latinas/os in the jury pool were rejected through the use of a peremptory challenge on the basis that they could understand Spanish in a case involving a Spanish-speaking defendant on the suspicion that such a juror might not abide by the official translation given their knowledge of the language. Despite the potentially discriminatory impact that eliminating Spanish-speaking jurors would have on Latinas/os in New York—who comprise the vast majority of persons who speak Spanish in the region—the Court was not convinced that this was a denial of constitutional rights because the exclusion was based on the person's ability to speak Spanish, not on race or national origin. In his dissent in *Hernandez*, Justice Stevens makes the point that "the [prosecutor's] justification [for the use of the peremptory challenge] would inevitably result in a disproportionate disqualification of Spanish-speaking venire persons [prospective jurors]" and less drastic means are available to assuage the prosecutor's concerns (*Hernandez v. New York* at 379). The *Hernandez* case continues to be the law in the United States and remains a much-criticized decision among Latina/o studies scholars for its impact on Latinas/os, especially in the ways in which it can potentially be used to exclude Latinas/os from juries.

Although Latinas/os come from Latin American countries, linguistic differences exist in the meaning and nuances of words and expressions in the Spanish language which could be crucial in a court proceeding. Researchers and advocates have pointed out the harmful consequences of not providing **culturally competent** services in the criminal justice contexts and have urged for the proliferation of such services consistent with international human rights standards.

The Rights of Latinas

As detailed elsewhere in this volume, international human rights law, norms, and principles have been important for Latinas in particular. Latinas, as with other women in the United States, have and continue to face economic, social, and political inequalities and discrimination. In fact, they often experience inequalities and discrimination in ways disproportionate to white women. Latina girls are more at risk to drop out of school without graduating, with a rate of 26 percent, in contrast to 13 percent of African American girls, and 6.9 percent of white girls (Canedy 2001, 1). With respect to the criminal justice system, Latinas are incarcerated in state prisons at a rate that is almost double the rate of white women, and face three times at risk of going to prison in their lifetime as compared to white women (Sentencing Project 2003).

To address concerns about bias in the criminal justice system that result in these troubling disparities, the Convention on the Elimination of all Forms of Discrimination against Women of 1979 (CEDAW) envisions protecting women by requiring States that ratify this convention take affirmative steps to prohibit discrimination against women. If the United States were to ratify and observe CEDAW, one possible step that could be taken to address the unequal treatment of Latinas in the criminal justice system is the enactment of legislation in compliance with articles 1, 3, and 5 to advance the rights of Latinas in all areas of political, economic, social, and cultural life. CEDAW also seeks to fortify all aspects of family, employment, education, health, and security for women, leaving Latinas less vulnerable to being victims of crime or susceptible to engaging in criminal activity. As with other international human rights treaties, the CEDAW contains a procedure for individuals to file complaints, providing a means for enforcing the convention's provisions. CEDAW also requires that the state parties submit periodic compliance reports to a monitoring committee, in a manner similar to the Convention on the Rights of the Child and other human rights laws.

Utilizing International Human Rights Enforcement Mechanisms

Although the United States lags behind in ratifying many major international human rights treaties, advocacy groups in the United States increasingly are using international regional and global mechanisms to file human rights complaints against the United States for failing to comply with international human rights standards, as has been the practice elsewhere in the world, especially in the rest of the Americas and Europe.

In 2008, **LatinoJustice PRLDEF**, a national civil rights organization whose mission is to promote the rights of Latinos in the United States, filed a petition with the Inter-American Commission on Human Rights on behalf of **Marcelo Lucero** (Deceased), Angel Loja, Hector Sierra, Luis Eduardo Martinez (Deceased), **Romel Sucuzhañay, Josè Osvaldo Sucuzhañay** (Deceased), and other Latina/o victims of hate crimes targeting Latinos and undocumented immigrants. The petition asserts that "the United States is failing to meet its obligation to ensure the security of Latinos . . . being targeted, attacked, brutalized and murdered because of their **race and ethnicity**, and increasingly because of their perceived immigration status in incidents with rising frequency and severity throughout the United States." LatinoJustice PRLDEF claims that "the United States is doing nothing to prevent these attacks or to protect Latinos from these incidents of hate" and, as a result, the United States is in violation of its obligations under the American Declaration of the Rights and Duties of Man, including Article I, the Right to Life, Liberty and Personal Security; Article II, the Right to Equality before Law; Article V, the Right to Protection of Honor, Personal Reputation, and Private and Family Life; Article XVII, Right to Recognition of Juridical Personality and Civil Rights, and Article XVIII, the Right to Fair Trial. The petition describes brutal—and in some cases deadly—beatings of Latinos at the hands of whites. The petition contends that the United States' Federal Bureau of Investigation (FBI) has identified Latinas/os as "the No. 1 victim of hate crimes motivated by ethnicity or national origin, representing 62.8 percent of the victims of such crimes" and that "attacks on Hispanics grew 40 percent from 2003 to 2007" (LatinoJustice PRLDEF 2008, 2, 3).

Although the Inter-American Commission on Human Rights does not have the enforcement powers of a court, filing a case with the Commission brings international attention to a human rights issue. The Commission's decisions also are reported to the General Assembly of the Organization of American States which could decide to draw more attention to the matter. Moreover, LatinoJustice PRLDEF has generated support from many other rights groups in support of the petition before the Inter-American Commission.

Other cases and issues have been brought in international forums to address issues affecting Latinas/os. The case of *Jessica Gonzales v. United States of America*, filed in 2005, is an example of another complaint filed before the Inter-American Commission of Human Rights. The petition, which won admission before the Commission in 2007, alleges that the United States violated its duty to protect the human rights of the petitioner, Jessica Gonzales, and her children when the police failed to take action to prevent her estranged husband from seizing and murdering their three minor daughters (ages 7, 8, and 10) in breach of a restraining order against him. The *Gonzales* case has become emblematic of the problem of violence against Latinas, as further discussed in this volume.

Pursuant to Article 64 of the Rules of Procedure of the Inter-American Commission, the Lawyers' Committee for Civil Rights Under Law, **The Sentencing Project**, and the American Civil Liberties Union (three U.S.-based nongovernmental organizations (NGOs)), requested that the Inter-American Commission on Human Rights hold a hearing to examine the laws, policies, and practices of member states of the Organization of American States on the issue of felony disenfranchisement. These NGOs claim that countries that maintain a system of felony disenfranchisement are violating fundamental provisions of the American Declaration on the Rights and Duties of Man and the American Convention on Human Rights, including the right to vote and the right to be free from discrimination. The request points out the racially disparate impact of the felony disenfranchisement laws in the United States. As an issue that affects Latinas/os, the use of international human rights law in this manner could serve to influence laws and policies related to felony disenfranchisement.

See also: Part I essays: Latinas/os and the U.S. Criminal Justice System; Latinas and the Criminal Justice System; Incarceration and Latinas/os in the United States; Gangs in the United States and Latina/o Communities. Part II entries: Civil Rights; Death Penalty; Hate Crimes; *Hernandez v. New York*, 500 U.S. 352 (1991); Language Rights in the Courts; Segregation; Slavery; Victims.

Further Reading

Amnesty International. 1998. *United States of America: Rights for all*. New York, NY: Amnesty International Publications.

Baldus, David C., Charles Pulaski, and George Woodworth. 1983. Comparative review of death sentences: An empirical study of the Georgia experience. *Journal of Criminal Law and Criminology* 74(3): 661–753.

Bayefsky, Anne F. 2002. *How to complain to the U.N. human rights treaty system*. Ardsley, NY: Transnational Publishers.

Bureau of the Census. 2015. *Income and poverty in the United States: 2014*. Current Population Reports, P60–252. Prepared by Carmen DeNavas-Walt and Bernadette D. Proctor. Washington, D.C.: U.S. Department of Commerce, Economics, and Statistics Administration.

Bureau of Justice Statistics. 1997. *Prisoners in 1996*. NCJ 164619. Washington, DC: U.S. Department of Justice.

Canedy, Dana. 2001 (March 25). Troubling label for Hispanics: "Girls most likely to drop out." *New York Times*.

Death Penalty Information Center. 2010. *Facts*. http://www.deathpenaltyinfo.org/documents/FactSheet.pdf. Updated February 25, 2010.

Dow, Mark. 2004. *American Gulag: Inside U.S. immigration prisons*. Berkeley, CA: University of California Press.

Federal Bureau of Investigation. *Hate crime statistics*. Washington, DC: Department of Justice, http://www.fbi.gov/ucr/ucr.htm#hate.

Flores, Glenn et al. 2002. The health of Latino children: Urgent priorities, unanswered questions, and research agenda. *Journal of the American Medical Association* 288, 1 (July): 82–90.

Gootman, Elissa. 2003 (August 18). Old tensions over immigrants surface after firebombing. *New York Times*.

Greene, Judith, and Kevin Pranis. 2007. *Gang wars: The failure of enforcement tactics and the need for effective public safety strategies*. Washington, DC: Justice Policy Institute.

Human Rights Committee. 2014. *Concluding observations on the fourth periodic report of the United States of America*. CCPR/C/USA/CO/4 International Covenant on Civil and Political Rights, 23 April, 2014, United Nations.

Human Rights Watch. 1998. Shielded from justice: Police brutality and accountability in the United States. New York, NY: Human Rights Watch.

Justice Policy Institute. 2009. Factsheet: DOJ report on prisoners in 2008: Prisons are still growing and racial disparities persist, despite availability of cost-effective alternatives. http://www.justicepolicy.org/images/upload/09-12_FAC_Prisoners08_PS.pdf. Accessed March 20, 2010.

LatinoJustice PRLDEF. 2008. Inter-American Commission on Human Rights, Organization of American states petition alleging violations of the human rights of Latinos by the United States of America. http://latinojustice.org/civil_rights/PETITION ALLEGING VIOLATIONS OF THE HUMAN RIGHTS OF LATINOS BY THE UNITED STATES OF AMERICA.pdf. Accessed November 13, 2015.

LatinoJustice PRLDEF 2009. Rights groups join LatinoJustice PRLDEF in Human Rights petition against the United States. http://latinojustice.org/briefing_room/press_releases/rights_groups_join_latinojustice_prldef_in_human_rights/index.html. Accessed March 11, 2010.

Lawyers' Committee for Civil Rights Under Law, The Sentencing Project, and the American Civil Liberties Union. 2009. Request for a thematic hearing on the discriminatory effects of felony disenfranchisement laws, policies and practices in the Americas. https://www.aclu.org/legal-document/request-thematic-hearing-discriminatory-effects-felony-disenfranchisement-laws. Accessed November 13, 2015.

Lewis-Anthony, S., and M. Scheinin. 2004. Treaty-based procedures for making human rights complaints within the U.N. system. In Guide to international human rights practice, 4th ed., edited by H. Hannum, 43–64. Ardsley, NY: Transnational Publishers.

NAACP LDF. 2009. Death row, U.S.A http://www.naacpldf.org/death-row-usa. Accessed November 13, 2015.

Office of the United Nations High Commissioner for Human Rights. 2015. http://www.ohchr.org/EN/ProfessionalInterest/Pages/UniversalHumanRightsInstruments.aspx. Accessed November 13, 2015.

Pew Hispanic Center. 2008. Statistical portrait of Hispanics in the United States, 2008. http://pewhispanic.org/files/factsheets/hispanics2008/Table 1.pdf. Accessed March 20, 2010.

Rainwater, Lee, and Timothy M. Smeeding. 2003. *Poor kids in a rich country: America's children in comparative perspective*. New York: Russell Sage Foundation.

Reddy, Sumathi. 2008 (November 24). FBI finds attacks against Latinos on rise. *Seattle Times*. http://www.seattletimes.com/nation-world/attacks-against-latinos-increasing-fbi-reports/. Accessed November 13, 2015.

Sentencing Project, The. 2003. Hispanic prisoners in the United States. Washington, DC: The Sentencing Project.

Sentencing Project, The. 2005. Racial disparity in sentencing: A review of the literature. http://www.sentencingproject.org/doc/publications/rd_sentencing_review.pdf. Accessed February 28, 2010.

Snell, Tracy L. 2009. *Capital Punishment, 2008—Statistical Tables, December 2009*, NCJ 228662. Washington, DC: Bureau of Justice Statistics, U.S. Department of Justice. http://bjs.ojp.usdoj.gov/content/pub/pdf/cp08st.pdf. Accessed March 21, 2010.

Southern Poverty Law Center. 2008. Anti-Latino hate crimes rise for fourth year in a row. https://www.splcenter.org/hatewatch/2008/10/29/anti-latino-hate-crimes-rise-fourth-year-row. Accessed November 13, 2015.

Task Force on Transforming Juvenile Justice. 2009. Charting a new course: A blueprint for transforming juvenile justice in New York State. http://www.vera.org/paterson-task-force-juvenile-justic-report. Accessed November 24, 2015.

Thayer, Leah. 2004. Hidden hell: Women in prison. *Amnesty International Magazine*. http://www.amnestyusa.org/amnesty-magazine/fall-2004/hidden-hell-women-in-prison/page.do?id=1105165. Accessed March 10, 2010.

United Nations. 1948. Universal declaration of human rights. Adopted by the U.N. General Assembly, Dec. 10, 1948. U.N.G.A. Res. 217 A(III), U.N. A/810, at 71 (1948).

United Nations. 1965. International convention on the elimination of all forms of racial discrimination. Done at New York, Mar. 17, 1966. Entered into force, Jan. 4, 1969. 660 U.N.T.S. 195, reprinted in 5 I.L.M. 352 (1966).

United Nations. 1966. International covenant on civil and political rights. Done at New York, Dec. 16, 1966. Entered into force, Mar. 23, 1976. U.N.G.A. Res. 2200(XXI), 21 U.N. GAOR, Supp. (No. 16) 52, U.N. Doc. A/RES 11/6316 (1967), reprinted in 6 I.L.M. 368 (1967).

United Nations. 1966. International covenant on economic, social and cultural rights. Done at New York, Dec. 16, 1966. Entered into force, Jan. 3, 1976. U.N.G.A. Res. 2200(XXI), 21 U.N. GAOR, Supp. (No. 16) 49, U.N. Doc. A/RES/6316 (1967), reprinted in 6 I.L.M. 360 (1967).

United Nations. 1979. Code of conduct for law enforcement officials. Adopted December 7, 1979, G.A. Res. 34/169 (1979).

United Nations. 1979. Convention on the elimination of all forms of discrimination against women. Done at New York, Dec. 18, 1979.

United Nations. 1984. Convention against torture and other cruel, inhuman or degrading treatment or punishment. Done at New York, Dec. 10, 1984. Entered into force, June 26, 1987. U.N.G.A. Res. 39/46 Annex, 39 U.N. GAOR, Supp. (No. 51) 197, U.N. Doc. E/CN.4/1884/72, Annex (1984), *reprinted in* 23 I.L.M. 1027 (1984).

United Nations. 1989. Convention on the rights of the child. Done at New York, Nov. 20, 1989.121A/Res/44/25 (1989) reprinted in 28 I.L.M. 1457 (1989).

United Nations. 1990. International convention on the protection of the rights of all migrant workers and members of their families. Adopted 18 December 1990, G.A. Res. 45/158, (1990).

United Nations. 1992. Declaration on the rights of persons belonging to national or ethnic, religious and linguistic minorities. Adopted 18 Dec. 1992, G.A. Res. 47/135, reprinted in 32 ILM 911 (1993), 14 HRLJ 54 (1993).

United Nations. 2015a. Universal periodic review. http://www.ohchr.org/EN/HRBodies/UPR/Pages/UPRMain.aspx. Accessed November 13, 2015.

United Nations. 2015b. Status of Ratification. http://indicators.ohchr.org/. Accessed November 13, 2015.

U.S. Census Bureau. 2007. The American community—blacks: 2004: American community survey reports, ACS-04. U.S. Department of Commerce, Economics, and Statistics Administration. http://www.census.gov/prod/2007pubs/acs-04.pdf. Accessed February 28, 2010.

Vera Institute of Justice. 2009. Charting a new course: A blueprint for transforming juvenile justice in New York State. http://www.vera.org/pubs/charting-new-course-blueprint-transforming-juvenile-justice-new-york-state. Accessed November 13, 2015.

Villarruel, Francisco A., and Nancy E. Walker, with Pamela Minifree, Omara Rivera-Vázquez, Susan Peterson, and Kristen Perry. 2002. *¿Dónde está la justicia? A call to action on behalf of Latino and Latina youth in the U.S. justice system.* Washington, DC: Michigan State University/Building Blocks for Youth.

Walker, Samuel, Miriam DeLone, and Cassia Spohn. 2007. *The color of justice: Race, ethnicity, and crime in America.* 4th ed. Belmont, CA: Thomson/Wadsworth.

Cases Cited

Coleman v. Schwarzenegger, No. 90-0520, 2010 U.S. Dist. LEXIS 2711 (N.D. Cal. January 12, 2010).

Gonzales and Others v. United States, Case 1490–05 Inter-Am. C.H.R., O.E.A/ser. I./R./52/07 (2007).

Gonzalez v. United States, 33 F.3d 1047 (9th Cir. 1994).

Hernandez v. New York, 500 U.S. 352 (1991).

Plata v. Schwarzenegger, 603 F.3d 1088 (9th Cir. 2010).

United States ex rel. Negron v. New York, 434 F.2d 386 (2d Cir. 1970).

Intimate Partner Violence/ Domestic Violence

Jenny Rivera

Intimate partner violence—commonly referred to as **domestic violence**—includes physical, psychological, sexual, and economic abuse between current and former spouses and intimate partners. Although any person can be the victim of this **violence**, according to the Department of Justice approximately 86 percent of domestic violence **victims** are female. The human toll of this violence is devastating. The violence is potentially life-threatening to victims and life-altering for children, other family, and friends. It imposes significant economic stress on victims and their families, communities, and society. Interpersonal violence occurs regardless of race, ethnicity, national origin, and economic or immigration status. It is no less devastating to the lives of Latinas/os than it is to non-Latinas/os. Latina survivors, however, face challenges unique to them which affect their ability to fully benefit from legal reforms and social programs designed to address domestic violence.

Historically, society, law enforcement, and government officials ignored or condoned intimate partner violence. Over time, advocates secured legal reforms that significantly helped survivors. These reforms included criminalizing domestic violence, establishing social service programs for victims and their families, and gaining public financial support for survivors, community-based organizations, law enforcement training, and anti-violence education efforts. Existing federal and state legislation provides for criminal sanctions, civil remedies, temporary shelter, family counseling, and other social services. Some jurisdictions have established domestic violence courts to address more fully the range of legal issues raised in these cases, including divorce and custody matters. Another trend has been the inclusion of men in community-based strategies to end violence, and public support for rehabilitation programs for male batterers.

Criminal justice reforms are wide-ranging and include penal sanctions for abuse against current and former intimate partners, mandatory and pro-arrest policies, mandatory prosecution policies, and orders of protection. Each of these legal tools has had varying rates of success and comes with potential advantages and disadvantages for survivors and the advocates who seek to assist them.

The institutional social services system includes residential and non-residential programs, and federal and state domestic violence hotlines established to provide information, referrals, and social service assistance to victims. Another trend in the delivery of services is a holistic community-based system known as Family Violence Centers. Family Violence Centers provide a coordinated service delivery program at one location where a team of professionals working together provides assistance to family violence victims. Participants include victims' advocates, legal service providers, prosecutors, and other law enforcement personnel.

Latina survivors, along with other women, have benefited from these legal and social strategies implemented to address domestic violence. Latinas, however, could find it difficult to secure legal protection for themselves and their families, or to fully access the programs and services provided by public and private sources because of unique obstacles Latinas face based on ethnicity, culture, language, and socio-economic conditions, and—in the case of recent immigrant Latinas—on the basis of immigrant status.

The legal system's focus on criminalization, punishment, and separation from the batterer presents many challenges to survivors and, for some Latinas, can be at odds with cultural norms and social and economic realities within the Latino community and Latino families. The criminalization of domestic violence, although a necessary and positive aspect of legal reform, has its limits.

Many women, including Latinas, might be afraid to seek assistance from the police, might not wish to participate in the batterer's prosecution, or might want to avoid the imposition of criminal sanctions on the batterer. There are many possible reasons for women's inability or unwillingness to fully utilize the apparatus of the criminal justice system. Some women, for example, fear that the violence will get worse if they seek help or file a criminal complaint against the batterer. Data establishes that violence often escalates once a woman seeks to leave. Additionally, criminal prosecutions and orders of protection cannot always protect victims from the batterer. Economic dependence on the batterer also could be an obstacle for women who need financial support for themselves and their children.

The Latino community has had mixed experiences with law enforcement, and has complained of police bias, brutality, and inaction towards community demands, as well as the intermingling of state, local, and federal immigration enforcement policies, to the detriment of Latino immigrants. Thus, Latinas might be hesitant to contact police. They might fear that Latino batterers will face particularly severe treatment in the criminal justice system and view this as ultimately unacceptable for themselves, their families, and their communities. Increased risk of escalating violence, loss of economic support, fear of isolation, and concern about adverse consequences resulting from the intervention of law enforcement officials into their personal lives can present insurmountable obstacles to Latinas.

Latino immigrant communities also are particularly vulnerable to isolation and insularity. Although Latino immigrants have increased in number throughout the United States, in many communities they are a minority in a white majority population and face hostile and threatening behavior from the surrounding community. Some advocates complain that police do not respond to abuse against immigrants and do not treat violent acts against Latinos as **hate crimes**. For example, police might not investigate or could refuse to classify criminal acts against immigrants and Latinas as hate crimes but rather as assaults and vandalism. The dangerous environment and the avoidance and denial by the non-Latino community and by law enforcement officials of race- and ethnicity-based attacks have had an adverse chilling effect on Latinas' confidence in local law enforcement.

Other obstacles faced by Latina survivors include limited access—based on language and cultural barriers—to the courts and social service programs. Although a majority of Latinas in the United States speak and understand English, the shortage of bilingual and bicultural personnel is an ongoing problem for Latinas who need language assistance or who prefer speaking in Spanish. For recent immigrant women who are not sufficiently literate in English, the language barrier is almost insurmountable. Those women for whom language is not a practical impediment because they are fluent in English might find that the opportunity to speak with someone in Spanish provides a sense of comfort and assists in developing a level of trust critical to providing services to domestic violence victims.

Limited financial resources are a serious obstacle for Latina survivors. The lack of financial resources can be due to economic dependence on the batterer, the poverty status of the victim and her family, limited financial resources in neighborhoods where Latinas are concentrated, and limited opportunities for economic independence due to the discrimination and isolation of Latinos. Without access to necessary economic support, even those Latinas who seek to leave their batterers can find that leaving home and their neighborhoods is unrealistic.

Scholars have noted that, for some Latina survivors, leaving home and family is not an option because of their ties to community and family. The familiarity with their communities and the ethnic and family bonding associated with home and neighborhood is absent once they leave. Residential shelters that fail to provide a culturally welcoming environment also could feel alienating and thus reinforce a Latina's sense of powerlessness.

Women who have recently immigrated face additional obstacles, especially if they are unauthorized. Recent immigrants might lack familiarity with U.S. legal and social services systems and, thus, do not know how to seek assistance and might not realize that they are entitled to assistance—especially if they are undocumented. Immigrant women out of lawful status are particularly vulnerable to batterer threats that they will be turned over to immigration authorities, and their children taken from them and possibly left in the custody of the batterer. When assistance is available it might be located far from Latina/o communities and access could be difficult. Even if victims can get help, service providers and legal assistants could lack training on immigrant law–related issues relevant to immigrant survivors.

Domestic violence programs seek to provide much-needed assistance to survivors, including assistance with navigating the criminal justice system. Programs that are bilingual, bicultural, and designed to address the specific needs of Latina victims, however, have great potential to attract and assist Latina survivors. The national Latino roundtable on domestic violence, La Alianza Latina Naciónal para Erradicar la Violencia Domestica (Alliance for the Elimination of Domestic Violence), for example, provides educational materials and develops national policy on domestic violence in the Latino community. This organization along with state and locally based organizations that focus on Latinas help to provide expertise and assistance to Latina survivors, and have increased the visibility of intimate partner violence as it affects Latinas within the Latino community, the anti-violence movement, and the larger society.

Over the years, efforts to enact legislation to protect women from violence have had some success. On a national level, the 2013 reauthorization of the Violence Against Women Act (VAWA) was not only crucial to upholding protections and services in the original law, but it also extended safeguards and services. Among other things, VAWA now guarantees **lesbian, gay, bisexual, and**

transgender survivors access to the services; it provides victims in publicly subsidized housing the opportunity to transfer to different locations to stay safe; and it enhances protections available to college students. Additionally, international human rights principles, treaties, and mechanisms have become an avenue for redress, resulting in the evolution of legal standards created to protect victims of intimate partner violence around the globe. For additional information see the **International Human Rights** entry in this volume.

See also: Part I essay: Latinas and the U.S. Criminal Justice. Part II entries: Chicanas/os; Deportation Laws; Hate Crimes; International Human Rights; Lesbian, Gay, Bisexual, and Transgender (LGBT); Victims.

Further Reading

Aldarondo, Etiony. 2002. Evaluating the efficacy of interventions with men who batter. In *Programs for men who batter: Intervention and prevention strategies in a diverse society*, edited by E. Aldarondo and F. Mederos, 3–20. New York: Civic Research Institute.

Aldarondo, Etiony, Glenda Kaufman Kantor, and Jana L. Jasinski. 2002. A risk marker analysis of wife assault in Latino families. *Violence Against Women* 8(4): 429–54.

Alianza Latina Nacionál para Erradicar la Violencia Domestica. [n.d.]. Alianza fact sheet. Domestic violence affects families of all racial, ethnic and economic backgrounds. http://www.dvalianza.org/images/stories/ResourcePubs/fact_sheets/factsheet2010.pdf.

Anderson, Deborah K., and Daniel G. Saunders. 2003. Leaving an abusive partner: An empirical review of predictors, the process of leaving, and psychological well-being. *Trauma, Violence & Abuse* 4(2): 163–79.

Bell, Jeannine. 2007. Hate thy neighbor: Violent racial exclusion and the persistence of segregation. *Ohio State Journal of Criminal Law* 5: 47–77.

Department of Justice. 2007. Guiding principles of the safe havens: Supervised visitation and safe exchange grant program. Washington DC: Office on Violence Against Women.

Department of Justice. 2013. Celebrating reauthorization of the Violence Against Women Act. Washington, DC. http://www.justice.gov/ovw/blog/celebrating-reauthorization-violence-against-women-act. Accessed November 12, 2015.

Durose, Matthew R., Caroline Wolf Harlow, Patrick A. Langan, Mark Motivans, Ramona R. Rantala, Erica L. Smith, and Elizabeth Constantin. 2005. *Family violence statistics: Including statistics on strangers and acquaintances*. Washington, DC: U.S. Department of Justice.

Farole, Donald J., Jr., and Erica L. Smith. 2009. Bureau of Justice Statistics Crime Data Brief, Intimate Partner Violence. http://bjs.ojp.usdoj.gov/content/pub/pdf/pipvcluc.pdf. Accessed November 12, 2015.

Fiscal Policy Institute. 2007. Working for a better life: A profile of immigrants in the New York state economy. http://www.fiscalpolicy.org/publications2007/FPI_ImmReport_WorkingforaBetterLife.pdf. Accessed November 12, 2015.

Frank, Phyllis B. 2005. *NY model for batterer programs*. VCS Inc. Community Change Project. http://www.nymbp.org.

Frias, Sonia M., and Ronald J. Angel. 2005. The risk of partner violence among low-income Hispanic subgroups. *Journal of Marriage and Family* 67: 552–64.

Klevens, Joanne. 2007. An overview of intimate partner violence among Latinos. *Violence Against Women* 13(2): 111–22.

Rivera, Jenny. 1994. Domestic violence against Latinas by Latino males: An analysis of race, national origin, and gender differentials. *Boston College Third World Law Journal* 14(2): 231–57.

Rivera, Jenny. 1997–1998. Preliminary report: Availability of domestic violence services for Latina survivors in New York State. *Buffalo Journal of Public Interest Law* 16: 1–29.

Rivera, Jenny. 2003. The availability of domestic violence services for Latinas in New York State: Phase II investigation. *Buffalo Journal of Public Interest Law* 21: 37–86.

Tjaden, Patricia, and Nancy Thoennes. 2000. *Extent, nature, and consequences of intimate partner violence: Findings from the National Violence against Women Survey*. Washington, DC: U.S. Department of Justice.

Statutes

37 N.Y. Soc. Serv. L. § 459 (McKinney 1992 & Supp. 1997).

18 NYCRR §§ 452.2(e) (1), 452.9(a) (1), 453.1, 454.2, and 455.1 (2000).

McKinney's Family Court Act, Article 8, Family Offenses Proceedings, § 812. Procedures for family offense proceedings.

Violence Against Women Act, Pub. L. No. 103–322, 108 Stat. 1902 (1994).

Violence Against Women and Department of Justice Reauthorization Act of 2005, Pub. L. No. 109–162, 119 Stat. 2960 (2006).

Violence Against Women Reauthorization Act of 2013, Pub. L. No. 113–4, 127 Stat. 54 (2013).

Selected Intimate Partner Violence/Domestic Violence Service Providers

Alianza Latina Naciońal Para Erradicar La Violencia Domestica (National Latino Alliance for the Elimination of Domestic Violence). http://www.dvalianza.org/.

An Abuse, Rape and Domestic Violence Aid and Resource Collection. http://www.aardvarc.org/dv/sepviolence.shtml.

Dominican Women's Development Center. www.dwdc.org.

National Family Justice Center Alliance. http://www.familyjusticecenter.com/.

New York City Bar Association. http://www.nycbar.org.

New York City Mayor's Office to Combat Domestic Violence. http://www.nyc.gov/html/ocdv/html/home/home.shtml.

Violence Intervention Program. http://www.violenceinterventionprogram.org/.

J

Justice Committee. *See* Part I essays: Latinas/os and the Criminal Justice System; Policing and Latina/o Communities. Part II entries: Community-Based Latina/o Advocacy Organizations; Political Activist Groups; Puerto Ricans.

Juvenile Delinquency. *See* Part I essays: Gangs in the United States and Latina/o Communities; Latina/o Youth and Criminal Justice. Part II entries: Cultural Criminology; International Human Rights; LatCrit: Latina & Latino Critical Legal Theory, Inc.

L

Language Rights in the Courts

Juan Cartagena

The term "language rights" encompasses the right to be free from discrimination because of your language and the corollary right to have access to your home, community, and native language. Both principles are implicated whenever court systems adapt to the demands of a Spanish-speaking populace, or delineate spaces where English is required for participation in the courts.

Spanish has been treated as an identifying characteristic of Latinas/os, often used for singling them out for adverse treatment. Court challenges include ***Hernandez v. Texas* (1954)**, in which the U.S. Supreme Court ruled that the Fourteenth Amendment's Equal Protection Clause prohibited discrimination beyond the **black/white binary paradigm**. Although the important issue of language proficiency for jury service, outlined below, was not before the court, *Hernandez v. Texas*—which eventually outlawed the exclusion of Spanish-surname persons from jury service in a criminal trial—is perhaps one of the most critical U.S. Supreme Court cases affecting Latinos for two reasons: it applied the constitutional protections of nondiscrimination to Latinos for the first time in history, and it ushered in the advent of **Mexican American** lawyering.

Criminal courts in the United States were slow to prohibit the discrimination inherent in an English-only prosecution against limited-English defendants and avoid "the Kafkaesque specter of an incomprehensible ritual which may terminate in punishment" (*United States v. Mosquera*, Memorandum & Order 1993; Judge Jack Weinstein, at 13). As recently as the mid-20th century, the appointment of an interpreter to assist a criminal defendant never was mandatory and the refusal to appoint one—even when the defendant testified—was insufficient to reverse a conviction (*Perovich v. United States* (1907)). State courts were amenable to these concerns, as in the case of *State v. Vazquez* in 1942 in which the Utah Supreme Court reversed the conviction of a Mexican national whose request for an interpreter was denied. In 1948, in *Garcia v. State*, a Texas court did likewise noting that, along the Rio Grande, "our citizenship is comprised of Latin Americans who speak and understand only the Spanish language" (*Garcia* at 580). Arizona followed this trend acknowledging the state's significant minority population that could not communicate in English in *State v. Natividad* (1974).

All this changed in 1970 in New York when Rogelio Negrón, a Puerto Rican farm laborer, was charged with murder. A translator was hired to translate the Spanish testimony into English, but no direct translation was provided to Mr. Negron when testimony was given in English, and his attorney spoke no Spanish. In ***United States ex rel. Negron v. New York*** (1970), a federal appeals court definitively established the right of language-minority defendants to understand the nature of the proceedings against them. The court held that a defendant's Sixth Amendment right to confront witnesses and the right to counsel, as well as due process rights, require that non-English-speaking defendants be provided with a simultaneous interpretation of the proceedings at government expense: "Particularly inappropriate in this nation where many languages are spoken is a callousness to the crippling language handicap of a newcomer to its shores, whose life and freedom the state by the criminal processes chooses to put in jeopardy" (*Negron* at 390). The *Negron* case was a watershed and set the benchmark for all subsequent litigation. It became the "original impetus" for the first federal statutory entitlement to interpreters in federal courts via the 1978 Court Interpreters Act, 28 U.S.C. § 1827, et seq. (*see* H.R. Rep. No. 95-1687, 95th Cong. 2d Sess. 3, 3 (1978 U.S. Code, Cong. & Admin. News 4652)). Subsequently, Congress noted that 6 percent of all proceedings in federal courts required an interpreter and that by far, interpreters for Spanish-speaking defendants were the most in demand—more than 99 percent of all such proceedings—and yet only 292 certified interpreters existed nationwide (H.R. Rep. No. 100–889, 100th Cong. 2d Sess. 58, 58 (1988 U.S. Code, Cong. & Admin. News 5982)). Recent data confirm that the demand for interpreters in federal courts has not abated. District courts reported using interpreters in 282,721 incidents (up more than 14 percent from the previous year with Spanish interpreters being used nearly 96 percent of the time (U.S. Courts 2009)). Despite the importance of *Negron*, to date no United States Supreme Court decision has recognized a constitutional right to an interpreter and no national standards for interpreters in state courts exist.

Although the Court Interpreters Act allows for the appointment of "otherwise qualified interpreters" when certified interpreters are unavailable the system's inability, or indifference, to appreciate the distinction between social conversational English and the English inherent in a criminal court proceeding has created significant problems for witness testimony in criminal courts (Piatt 1990, 84). This phenomenon is made clear in the case of Miguel Ángel González whose plea of guilty to **drug** charges in a court in Oregon was upheld by a divided appeals panel in ***Gonzalez v. United States* (1994)**. Despite the defendant's protestations that he could not read the documents in English, and the court's acknowledgement that González had language difficulties but was able to answer simple yes or no questions in English, the court found that his right to an interpreter under the Court Interpreters Act only would come into effect if his language difficulties constituted a major problem.

This pattern also is seen in other cases. In Nebraska in 1986, a court upheld the denial to appoint an interpreter when the defendant was overheard conversing in jail in English (*State v. Topete* (1986)). In Texas, it has been reported that a court allowed a prosecutor to interpret for a prosecution witness. The National Center on State Courts regularly receives reports on the problems that frequently occur in state courts due to the use of improperly trained and unqualified court interpreters, and noted in 1992 that a majority of states codified minimum qualifications for interpreters for the deaf and hearing impaired but only five states had similar statutory regulations for court interpreters for non-English speakers. The artificiality of courtroom testimony where normal storytelling is subjected to the adversarial rigors of cross-examination and witnesses are expected to resist the suggestions of the cross-examiner poses additional problems to limited English-speaking witnesses who are forced to testify in English. Conversely, however, and reflecting this country's inconsistent patch-work of language policy, is *State v. Lopez* (1952), a case in which a court refused to overturn a conviction when it was convenient to allow a portion of the grand jury proceedings to proceed entirely in Spanish because the defendant testified in Spanish and every member of the grand jury understood Spanish.

Additionally, an English-proficiency requirement exists in most criminal courts for jury service—a policy that in Latino communities tests the maxim "defendants should be judged by a jury of their peers." Intentional legislative or administrative exclusion of protected groups from jury service, such as blacks (*Strauder v. West Virginia,* 1879) and Latinos (*Hernandez v. Texas*, 1954), clearly is unconstitutional. The presence of a federal district court in Puerto Rico, however, raises vexing issues regarding this English-proficiency requirement under statutory law (28 U.S.C. § 1865). In *United States v. Valentine* (1968) Puerto Rican Vietnam War draft resisters challenged the constitutionality of the juror qualification on the basis that it would exclude representation on juries from a cross-section of the island. The court repeatedly observed the unique nature of this legal challenge: No other federal court exists within a state or territory where the primary language of the majority of American citizens is a language other than English. It nonetheless upheld the English requirement for jurors and ruled that the cross-section requirement for jury pools was applicable only after the imposition of minimal qualifications for jury service. Ironically, in *Jackson v. Cintron Garcia* (1981) a federal court rejected a subsequent challenge by a non-Spanish-speaking defendant who was tried and convicted in Spanish in Puerto Rico's local courts, ruling that it would be an unwarranted federal intrusion into the island's local affairs to do otherwise.

Lastly, language rights protections also are implicated for bilingual Spanish-English jurors. In ***Hernandez v. New York* (1991)**, a rare pronouncement on language rights by the U.S. Supreme Court, the court recognized that discrimination based on proficiency in Spanish could rise to a pretext for unlawful, **racial discrimination**. Its discussion of the intersection between translated witness testimony in Spanish and bilingual jurors is an important chapter in understanding the role of language rights in criminal courts. The court, however, did not accept the defendant's arguments that striking bilingual jurors who hesitated at exclusively accepting—though not refusing to accept—translated testimony from the interpreter was tantamount to striking Latino jurors in a court sitting in Brooklyn, New York.

The prevalence of Spanish within Latino communities along with data on migration and immigration patterns warrants continued attention towards the language rights of Latinos in the judiciary. In numbers well above the national average, 75 percent of Latinos in the United States speak a language other than English at home, and equally important, the percentage of Latino persons who speak English less than "very well" and who speak Spanish at home nationally is more than 40 percent (Ramirez 2004). These language trends reflect Latino immigration patterns to the United States. From 1970 to 1996, the Latino foreign-born population grew from 1.8 million to more than 17 million. Simultaneously, the Latino share of the country's foreign-born population, during the same period, grew from 19 percent to 54 percent (U.S. Hispanic Leadership Institute 2008). Migration patterns among Puerto Ricans—who have been citizens of the United States since 1917—also support this phenomenon. Indeed, the language rights of Puerto Ricans within the United States occasionally receive favorable treatment as a result of the dominance of

Spanish on the island and the unrestricted travel to the United States as cogently observed in *United States v. County Board of Elections of Monroe County* (1965). Close to 40 percent of persons older than age five in Puerto Rico do not speak English at all (U.S. Census Bureau 2000) and contemporary Puerto Rican migration still is transient and bidirectional in flow.

See also: Part I essay: Latinas/os and the U.S. Criminal Justice System. Part II entries: *Hernandez v. New York*, 500 U.S. 352 (1991); *Hernandez v. Texas*, 347 U.S. 475 (1954); International Human Rights; LatCrit: Latina & Latino Critical Legal Theory, Inc.; Mexicans and Mexican Americans.

Further Reading

Duany, Jorge. 2002. *Puerto Rican nation on the move: Identities on the island and in the United States*. Chapel Hill, NC: University of North Carolina Press.

Hewitt, William E. 1995. *Court interpretation: Model guides for policy and practice in state courts*. Williamsburg, VA: National Center for State Courts. http://www.ncsconline.org.

Macias, Reynaldo F. 1979. Language choice and human rights in the United States. In *Georgetown University round table on languages and linguistics 1979: Language in public life*, edited by J. E. Alatis and G. R. Tucker, 86–101. Washington, DC: Georgetown University Press.

Mendez, Miguel A. 1997. Lawyers, linguists, storytellers and limited English-speaking witnesses. *New Mexico Law Review* 27: 77–99.

Morín, José Luis. 2009. *Latina/o rights and justice in the United States: Perspectives and approaches*. Durham, NC: Carolina Academic Press.

Norgen, Jill, and Serena Nanda. 1996. *American cultural pluralism and law*. Westport, CT: Praeger.

Olivas, Michael A. 2006. *"Colored men" and "hombres aquí": Hernandez v. Texas and the emergence of Mexican-American lawyering*. Houston, TX: Arte Público Press.

Piatt, Bill. 1990. *¿Only English? Law and language policy in the United States*. Albuquerque, NM: University of New Mexico Press.

Ramirez, Roberto R. 2004. *We the people: Hispanics in the United States*, 2000 Special Reports, December. Washington, DC: U.S. Census Bureau.

U.S. Census Bureau. 2000. Summary File 4 (SF4). Washington, DC. http://www.census.gov/census2000/SF4.html.

U.S. Courts. 2009. Court interpreting events increased in FY 2008, January 28, 2009. http://www.uscourts.gov/news/NewsView/09-01-8/Court_Interpreting_Events_Increased_in_FY_2008.aspx.

U.S. Hispanic Leadership Institute. 2008. *The almanac of Latino politics*. Chicago, IL: U.S. Hispanic Leadership Institute.

Cases Cited

Garcia v. State, 210 S.W.2d 574 (Ct. Crim. App. Tex. 1948).

Gonzalez v. United States, 33 F.3d 1047 (9th Cir. 1994).

Hernandez v. New York, 500 U.S. 352 (1991).

Hernandez v. Texas, 347 U.S. 475 (1954).

Jackson v. Cintron Garcia, 665 F.2d. 395 (1st Cir. 1981).

Perovich v. United States, 205 U.S. 722 (1907).

State v. Lopez, 252 S.W.2d 701 (Ct. Crim. App. Tex. 1952).

State v. Natividad, 111 Ariz. 191, 526 P.2d 730 (Sup. Ct. Ariz. 1974).

State v. Topete, 221 Neb. 771, 380 N.W.2d 635 (1986).

State v. Vazquez, 121 P.2d 903 (1942).

Strauder v. West Virginia, 100 U.S. 303 (1879).

United States v. County Board of Elections of Monroe County, 248 F. Supp. 316 (W.D.N.Y. 1965).

United States ex rel. Negron v. New York, 434 F.2d 386 (2d Cir. 1970).

United States v. Mosquera, Memorandum & Order, C.R. 92-1228; C.R. 93-0036 (U.S. Dist. Ct. E.D.N.Y., Mar. 16, 1993, Judge Jack Weinstein).

United States v. Valentine, 288 F. Supp. 957 (D.C. P.R. 1968).

LatCrit: Latina & Latino Critical Legal Theory, Inc.

Charles R. Venator-Santiago

The Latina & Latino Critical Legal Theory, Inc. (LatCrit) organization is part of a genre within the legal academy known as "outsider" or "outcrit" jurisprudence. Outcrits or legal thinkers from this tradition have written about the ways in which the law has been used to exploit, oppress, and subordinate various groups in society based on socially constructed identities. These forms of subordination draw upon socially constructed ideologies that are based on essentialist narratives of race, gender, class, nationality, and other identities. LatCrit emerged as an amorphous group of legal scholars that sought to offer an alternative to the **Critical Race Theory** Workshops, as well as a space for challenging some of the more oppressive dimensions of law and its institutions. LatCrit was formally organized in 1995 during a meeting of the Hispanic National Bar Association in San Juan, Puerto Rico. The organization was launched the following year as the result of both an internal challenge to subordinating effects essentialist or homogenizing ideologies within other leftist or progressive legal forums, and as a response to the external forms of exploitation being perpetuated by the law and legal actors such as judges, lawmakers, and the legal academy.

Central to the LatCrit organization have been two basic goals: (1) to develop a critical, activist, and inter-disciplinary discourse or way of describing the relationship between the law and policy towards Latinas/os; and (2) to foster both the development of coalitional theory and practice as well as the accessibility of this knowledge to agents of social and legal transformation. LatCrit scholars have pursued these goals by writing about and finding ways to encourage internal diversities within larger inter-group frameworks both locally and globally. This approach encourages a critical understanding of the intersections and multiple dimensions of exploitation and oppression that are present in the relationship between law and society.

Although LatCrit's early academic pursuits were anchored on the study of the anomalous relationship between Latinos and the law, LatCrit should not be confused with other ongoing critiques such as the Latinos and the Law or Latino Legal Studies initiatives. Many important Latino legal scholars, including Richard Delgado and Kevin R. Johnson, have participated in LatCrit meetings over the years, but they have also carved out a different critique that centers on the multiple dimensions of Latinos and the law. For example, Richard Delgado has offered a critique of LatCrit that centers on the need to rescue what he perceives to be a shift away from class and the material effects of law in society. Although early LatCrit colloquia gathered materials that are not centered on Latinos, it is possible to begin to see a decentering of Latinos within the LatCrit symposia by the Fourth Annual Conference. This is not to say that LatCrit does not address questions of Latinos and the law, but rather it is to suggest that LatCrit has become a more encompassing organization. This has been a conscious shift that seeks to create a broader coalition of critical scholars irrespective of race, gender, ethnicity, or other socially constructed identities. Presently, LatCrit provides an interdisciplinary space for scholars and activists to engage in critical reflections of the law and its subordinating practices.

Primarily remaining an organization of law professors within the United States, LatCrit, as an organization, continuously has endeavored to find ways to assist local, national, and global activists across disciplines. Presently the LatCrit community operates as a 501(c)(3) organization that raises funds for various educational purposes. The organization is managed by a diverse board of directors and project team members that carry out smaller projects. Although LatCrit generally is composed of law professors and other scholars, the organization welcomes and encourages participation from students, activists, policy makers, and other interested persons.

LatCrit and the Criminal Justice System

Scholars writing in LatCrit forums have approached the study of the relationship between Latinos and the criminal justice system in two ways, namely in a theoretical and in a practical interdisciplinary manner. A theoretical approach has used at least four conceptual lenses to criticize multiple and interconnected dimensions of the criminal justice system. These include a critique of legal remedies and responses that are based on essentialist identities; an emphasis on the intersection of multiple identities; a focus on the subordinating practices of the law; and a defense of egalitarian interpretations of the legal system. LatCrit scholars also have written about police violence, the juvenile justice system, the criminalization of immigration, the violation of **civil rights**, and the intersection of immigration, human rights, and terrorist laws and policies. The latter approach focuses more on the description of events using interdisciplinary and intersectional methods. These two approaches to the study of the criminal justice system constitute what LatCrit would describe as a form of critical praxis.

One example of the critique of essentialist identities, or identities that describe people in homogeneous and single-minded ways, can be discerned from the efforts to transcend the **black/white binary paradigm** of law. United States law traditionally has relied on essentialist or homogenizing conceptions of race to both criminalize Latinos and to offer remedies to the violence committed by the state and its legal actors (e.g., police or law enforcement agents, judges, prosecutors). Although most Latinos are likely to rely on ethnic or national identities to self-identify, the law often has used racial stereotypes to represent or describe Latinos. The criminal justice system more often than not has used racial stereotypes to profile, arrest, prosecute, and convict Latinos—often ignoring the nuances that are informed by different ethnic and nationalist identities. Likewise, civil rights law that has provided some relief to the abuses committed by the state and its legal actors traditionally has been framed in racial terms and limited to the experiences of black Americans. Immigration law and policy has also been framed to respond to the experiences of white immigrants. A LatCrit approach cautions us that the black/white paradigm might not take into account the particular experiences of Latinos, experiences that Latinos do not describe in racial terms. This is not to say that the criminal justice system has not used racialist categories to process Latinos, but rather to point to the limits of the use of these racial binaries to address the injustices that Latinos face in the United States.

LatCrit scholars such as Steven Bender and Juan Velasco also have written about the essentialist representation of Latinos as criminals in popular culture. For example, Hollywood historically has relied on pejorative or negative stereotypes of **Chicanas/os** or **Mexicans** to represent the criminal antagonists in popular films. Actors and films often used stereotypical language and depictions of the Chicana/o criminal or "**Greaser**" to describe Mexicans, and these essentialist or one-dimensional descriptions of Chicanas/os or Mexicans often entered the popular imagination of the average U.S. citizen. Police officers and other legal actors within the criminal justice system often assumed that media representations of the "Greaser" provided an accurate baseline or standard to understand the attitudes and behaviors of Chicanas/os, Mexicans, and Latinos more generally.

Intersectionality and multidimensionality describes how a Latina/o identity can be shaped by multiple intersecting identities. A Latino, for example, can be gendered as male, might be gay, and could be poor. The intersection of his physical, social, and economic experiences makes the Latino—or any person, for that matter—a complicated being. A LatCrit approach warns that the experience of the Latina/o with the criminal justice system should take into account the ways in which the intersection of multiple identities can shape how Latinas/os experience a criminal justice system that tries to treat him or her as a one-dimensional subject—a subordinated subject that is expected to experience and respond to the criminal justice system in stereotypical ways. LatCrit theory shines a spotlight on the ways that legal actors within the criminal justice system can choose to ignore the complex identities of Latinos. Police officers, for example, might neglect to consider cultural dimensions of gender and masculinity when arresting a Latino male suspect in front of his family and consequently eliciting more aggressive resistance from the suspect and causing a more punitive response by the courts. A focus on the intersecting dimensions of identity can assist legal actors throughout the enforcement and legal process by providing a more comprehensive understanding of the complexity of individual subjects.

LatCrit theory also emphasizes a focus on the role that law plays in oppressing or subordinating persons. LatCrit theory focuses on how legal actors, legal narratives, and legal institutions more generally enable the use of law to control subjects. A LatCrit approach, for example, would challenge the Patriot Act's provisions that enable the profiling of Latino immigrants and their subsequent criminalization for violating what otherwise would be considered a civil infraction.

A central tenet of LatCrit theory calls for a more egalitarian and democratic society. LatCrit theory highlights the ways in which the criminal justice system, and the law more generally, create anti-democratic and inegalitarian policies. A LatCrit focus hones in on the use of legal double-standards present in the criminal justice system. For example, there is ample evidence that demonstrates how the judges can issue disproportionate sentences to Latino offenders as compared to white offenders. LatCrit theory emphasizes the way in which the legal system or the ambiguities within the criminal justice system can make it possible for Latinos to experience an inferior or disparate form of justice.

Contributors to the LatCrit project also have engaged the practical dimensions of the criminal justice system. LatCrit's concern with social control and the disciplinary state has led some writers to focus on policy abuse and violence. More specifically, some scholars have criticized the use of racial profiling in Latino communities. Past and present participants in the LatCrit annual meetings have argued that police officers have used racist stereotypes to stop and search Latinos without probable cause or reasonable suspicion. They also challenge that a singular focus on racial paradigms that are based on the experience of African Americans often obscures the ways in which police officers use physical stereotypes to profile Latinos. The representation of the Latino "*bandido*" or **gang** member often has been used to profile bystanders in Latino enclaves or communities. A LatCrit approach requires expanding the understanding of the scope of racial profiling and becoming aware that although Latinos might not necessarily constitute a single race, the criminal system often uses racist profiles to ascribe a criminal identity to Latinos.

As Mary Romero and Marwa Serag remind us, the case of the Chandler Roundup in Arizona provides an important example of the ways the Immigration and Naturalization Service (renamed **Immigration and Customs Enforcement** (ICE)) and the local police's use of race, culture, and class profiles to capture and deport undocumented migrants led to various civil rights violations of Latinos residing in Arizona. The Chandler Roundup was part of a series of joint operations beginning in 1995 that sought to raid facilities and other public establishments that were identified as having a large presence of undocumented Mexican migrants in the city of Phoenix and its surrounding areas. LatCrit scholars point out that not only did the local police officers seek to enforce federal immigration laws, but they also relied on racial, cultural, and class profiles to harass Latino residents regardless of their citizenship status. A LatCrit approach can assist in exposing the intersection of class, race, culture, and other classifications that can be used to create a negative profile of Latinos and result in the violation of basic due process rights and civil liberties more generally. Some scholars have used a LatCrit approach to explain how these negative profiles have been used to ascribe a "foreign" or alien identity on Latinos regardless of their citizenship or immigration status.

Racial essentialism has also been used to ascribe Latino youth with a "gang member" identity that echoes the notion of the "superpredator." Again, as Mary Romero has written in her essay addressing the relationship between state violence and the criminalization of Latinos, the case of Julio Valerio, a 16 year-old former resident of Phoenix, Arizona, who was shot upwards of 25 times by 6 police officers, provides an important example of how scholars have used a LatCrit approach to describe state violence more generally towards Latinos. In this case, the mother of Julio Valerio phoned 911 after her son had left the house with a knife following a fight between her husband and Julio. She called the police in order to seek help with her son. Soon after, six police officers and upwards of eight patrol cars were called to an alley where Mr. Valerio was identified and subsequently was sprayed with mace. As Mr. Valerio sought to move away from where the police officer was spraying the mace, the other police officers opened fire on Mr. Valerio. A subsequent analysis of the media and related transcripts, however, revealed how the police had represented this young adult as a "dangerous superpredator" that posed a threat to the officers. A LatCrit analysis can help in discerning how the internalization of racist stereotypes might have contributed to the exacerbation of the police's response to the plea for help from a Latino mother that led to the overwhelming use of force to subdue a 16-year-old youth.

Scholars who have participated in LatCrit forums also have written about the overrepresentation of police officers in schools that have high percentages of minority students. The presence of police officers in school could contribute to an increase in the reliance on the criminal justice system to address behavioral issues rather than non-penal alternatives. Schools that are policed by law enforcement officers often can become an extension of the criminal justice system at the expense of parental and juvenile rights. LatCrit scholars have challenged the expansive encroachment of law enforcement in social areas at the increasing expense of family and individual rights. Because children and youth possess ambiguous legal rights they often are more vulnerable to police coercion and other forms of social control.

A significant number of LatCrit scholars also have written about various dimensions of the criminalization of immigration. LatCrit scholars have challenged the use of criminal laws to process immigration violations, which are civil in nature. They have challenged states' use of police officers to arrest and detain undocumented migrants and enforce federal immigrations laws. Because immigrants and undocumented migrants lack access to many of the rights and due process protections that citizens are entitled to, they find themselves in vulnerable positions within the criminal justice system. LatCrit scholars have sought to expose the inegalitarian treatment of noncitizens throughout the criminal justice system. Some of the clearest examples of this unjust treatment can be discerned from the experiences of Latino migrants who have been rounded up, prosecuted, and deported following collective immigration raids. In other instances, LatCrit scholars have documented how noncriminal migrants have been arrested and subsequently deported following arbitrary home inspections by police officers conducting unrelated investigations.

Notions such as intersectionality and multidimensionality have been used by LatCrit scholars to criticize the one-dimensional representations of crimes committed by migrants. Some migrants who are engaged in the "**drug**-trade," for example, often are acting in response to social, economic, and political pressures in their home countries. They are forced to find ways to sustain their families—who could be living in poverty or exploitative conditions in their original homes. A LatCrit approach challenges the criminal justice system to consider the whole picture rather than a simplistic characterization of an offender. In doing so, some LatCrit scholars argue, aggravating factors and questions of intent can be seen in a more critical and just manner.

Some early contributors to the LatCrit project also homed in on the ways that the use of the term "alien" ascribed a foreign status to individuals who otherwise should be entitled to the same civil and human rights that citizens of the United States enjoy. The classification of the alien as "illegal" facilitates the use of more punitive legal responses that deny the migrant civil rights that citizens take for granted. Following the 1996 immigration law reforms, for example, the U.S. government began to rely on immigration courts in which immigration judges were not bound to the rules of evidence required in Article III or constitutionally sanctioned courts. Immigration judges, who in many instances are not trained as legal actors, often imposed punitive sanctions that were disproportionate to the offenses committed by migrants. Imagine, for example, being permanently banished from your home community for failing to or being unable to renew a visa. **Deportations** often carry the weight of a permanent banishment and in some cases can be tantamount to a death sentence.

LatCrit scholars have written about the intersection of criminal punishments with immigration law. They highlight the increasingly oppressive nature of immigration laws such as the 1996 Anti-Terrorism and Effective **Death Penalty** Act and the Illegal Immigration and Immigrant Responsibility Act, which increased the number of offenses that could be treated as aggravated felonies and made it easier to permanently deport migrants for certain offenses. LatCrit scholars continue to denounce the legal double standards that immigration law imposes on immigrants and undocumented migrants, which in some instances violate basic due process and human rights. As has been noted by many, for instance, the 1996 immigration laws allowed for the retroactive or ex post facto application of punitive sanctions that could lead to deportation, regardless of whether the migrant already had paid his or her debt to society. In other words, imagine that an immigrant violated a law 20 years prior and he or she served time in a jail or prison. Under the 1996 laws if an individual commits a minimal offense, his or her prior record could be used to enable and expedite a deportation, even if the prior offense was not a deportable offense at the time.

Some LatCrit scholars have also questioned the use of "conspiracy" charges to legitimate the deportation of migrants. Under the terms of a conspiracy charge, knowledge of criminal activity would be sufficient grounds for deportation even if the person possessing that knowledge has not committed a crime or criminal offense. LatCrit scholars have denounced the practice of using conspiracy charges to pressure migrants to assist law enforcement officers in criminal investigations when migrants are not involved in criminal activity.

Additionally, LatCrit scholars have challenged the ways in which immigration law creates a vulnerable population that is afraid to use the law. "Battered" undocumented women who experience abuses, for example, are less likely to seek help for fear of deportation because of their undocumented status. In some instances, for a woman who gave birth to children of a U.S. citizen, reporting an abuse and exposing the mother's undocumented status can lead to the deportation and separation of the mother from children who could be vulnerable to further abuses by the father. LatCrit has challenged the criminal justice system to create more just ways that enable human beings—regardless of their legal status—to seek justice without fear of deportation.

LatCrit scholars also have pushed for the use of human rights standards instead of **civil rights** standards. Some writers argue that international standards provide more just and egalitarian legal protections than do civil rights. Scholars suggest that international or human rights standards could be used to rethink national civil rights laws and to provide more just legal protections and liberties.

LatCrit scholars have denounced the use of national security laws and anti-terrorism legislation to profile immigrants as potential terrorists. Many LatCrit scholars denounced post-September 11 legislation such as the Patriot Act, which enabled the indefinite detention or deportation of immigrants and undocumented migrants for mere immigration violations. LatCrit scholars denounced the use of national security and anti-terrorism logics to address immigration-related offenses. The use of a counterterrorist logic to address immigration issues, LatCrit scholars argue, creates anxieties and criminalized representations of the immigrant that are tantamount to earlier representations of aliens as "Greasers," "***pachucos***," or "*bandidos*."

Beyond Latina/o Essentialisms

Central to a LatCrit approach is a concern with intersections, essentialism, anti-subordination, and egalitarian or democratic conceptions of the relationship between law and the subject. Focusing on these concepts can provide resources for more complex and encompassing descriptions of events that shape the relationship between Latinas/os and various dimensions of the criminal justice system. LatCrit scholars draw upon these theoretical perspectives to offer different insights and explanations that otherwise might be neglected by traditional approaches to the study of the criminal justice system and the relationship between law and society more generally.

See also: Part I essays: Latinas/os and the U.S. Criminal Justice System; Latina/o Immigrants, Crime, and Justice; Policing and Latina/o Communities; The U.S. War on Drugs and Latina/o Communities; Gangs in the United States and Latina/o Communities; Crime and the U.S.-Mexican Border; Latina/o Youth and Criminal Justice;. Part II entries: Civil Rights; Cultural Criminology; Immigration and Customs Enforcement (ICE).

Further Reading

LatCrit publications are available at www.latcrit.org.

Bender, Steven W. 2003. *Greasers and Gringos: Latinos, law and the American imagination.* New York: New York University Press.

Romero, Mary. 2001. State violence and the social and legal construction of Latino criminality: From El Bandido to the gang member. *Denver University Law Review* 78: 1081–1118.

Romero, Mary, and Marwa Serag. 2005. Violations of Latino civil rights resulting from INS and local police's use of race, culture and class profiling: The case of the Chandler Roundup in Arizona. *Cleveland State Law Review* 52(1 & 2): 75–96.

Symposium: Latinos and Latinos at the epicenter of contemporary legal discourses. 2008. *Indiana Law Journal* 83(4): 1141–1588.

Valdes, Francisco, Jerome McCristal Culp, and Angela P. Harris (eds.). 2002. *Crossroads, directions and a new critical race theory.* Philadelphia: Temple University Press.

Valdez, Norberto, Marcia Fitzhorn, Cheryl Matsumoto, and Tracey Emslie. 2001. Police in schools: The struggle for student parental rights. *Denver University Law Review* 78: 1063–80.

Velasco, Juan. 2001. Making evil: Crime thrillers and Chicano cinema. *Denver University Law Review* 78: 1049–58.

Latina/o Fraternal Law Enforcement Organizations

Hector W. Soto and Marco Fernando Navarro

Fraternal law enforcement organizations generally refer to organizations whose membership consists of varying levels of uniformed, non-uniformed, and retired personnel from state, local, and national law enforcement agencies. These organizations were created with the purpose of supporting their members from unfair and exploitative departmental protocols, including advocating for fair wages, fair hours, and adequate retirement benefits for police personnel. Founded in 1915, the Fraternal Order of Police was the earliest of these fraternal organizations. Operating initially as a de facto union of police officers, the Fraternal Order of Police was the first organization of law enforcement personnel to advocate for the rights of, and file grievances on behalf of, officers. Today, fraternal law enforcement organizations often represent a particular group interest from within a department and most are organized based on a common group identity (e.g., religious, ethnic, racial, gender). Over time, local and national fraternal law enforcement organizations developed specifically to support and advocate on behalf of Latina/o law enforcement personnel.

Latina/o fraternal law enforcement organizations adopted the model of fraternal law enforcement organizations established around the turn of the 20th century by other national-origin, ethnic, cultural, and religious groups. Among the earliest of these organizations was the Shomrim Society founded in 1924 in New York City, and which still represents Jews on the police force. In 1943, the Guardians Association, a law enforcement organization that continues to be a voice for African American officers, was established in New York City. Due to the often contentious relationships between law enforcement agencies and fraternal law enforcement organizations, the Guardians Association was not officially recognized by the New York City Police Department until 1949.

Among the earliest Latina/o fraternal law enforcement organizations were those established in California, Illinois, New York, Texas, and Florida during the 1950s and 1960s. These organizations were created to foster a consensus among the increasing numbers of Latinas/os within local law enforcement departments, and to address the concerns of the growing numbers of Latinas/os in the United States. One of the oldest Latino/a fraternal law enforcement organizations is the Latin American Police Association (LAPA), founded in 1961 in Chicago, Illinois. The Latin American Police Association states as its purpose:

> to develop, promote and encourage a greater degree of understanding and cooperation between the Hispanic community, and local, state and federal law enforcement agencies. . . . [It] promotes and encourages a higher degree of professionalism, education and advancement among Hispanic law enforcement officers . . . [and] seeks to enhance the quality of life for both Hispanic law enforcement officers and for the Hispanic communities we serve (Latin American Police Association 2015).

These goals are similarly reflected in the mission statements of many Latina/o fraternal law enforcement organizations throughout the country today.

The Growth of Latina/o Fraternal Law Enforcement Organizations

Latina/o law enforcement officers have experienced a myriad of challenges—from being perceived as "sellouts" in their own communities to facing discrimination and bias that have prevented them from gaining admission into departments and obtaining promotions. Latino/o officers have been stereotyped as "lazy," denied opportunities for advancement, and shown to suffer high levels of posttraumatic stress disorder. In response, a number of Latina/o fraternal law enforcement organizations—such as the National Latino Peace Officers Association, founded in 1974 in California—placed recruitment and support of Latinas/os for advancement and promotion as high priorities in their work. Other organizations, including the Hispanic American Police Command Officers Association, the Hispanic National Law Enforcement Association, and the Federal Hispanic Law Enforcement Officers Association, have taken on similar efforts in support of Latina/o officers.

Latina/o fraternal law enforcement organizations also were created to increase the **cultural competency** of law enforcement agencies. But to do so requires adequate representation in police departments and law enforcement agencies. Hence, Latina/o fraternal law enforcement organizations have challenged discriminatory barriers to entry-level employment and their accessibility to promotion. They have gone beyond voicing concerns and have served as plaintiffs or witnesses in lawsuits. In 1980, the **Hispanic Society of the New York City Police Department**, represented by the **Puerto Rican Legal Defense and Education Fund (PRLDEF)**, in conjunction with the Guardians Association (the African American/black fraternal organization of the New York City Police Department) played a key a role as an advocate, plaintiff, and witness in a groundbreaking decision by a United States court of appeals in the case, *Guardians Association of New York City Police Department v. Civil Service Commission of City of New York* (1980), which upheld the lower court's finding that the police department's test to select entry-level officers discriminated against African Americans and Latinas/os.

In New York City, Latina/o fraternal law enforcement organizations gained ground in eliminating discriminatory practices in the police department by mounting legal actions. In 1984, Latina/o officers succeeded in winning a court-approved settlement challenging the discriminatory impact that the NYPD exam for promotions had on Latinas/os and African Americans. In describing the facts of the case on appeal before the U.S. Court of Appeals for the Second Circuit, the court noted that the "racial/ethnic composition of the group taking the exam was 79.0% white, 12.3% black, and 8.7% Hispanic; the breakdown of the eligible list derived from the test scores was 93.47% white, 2.31% black, and 4.23% Hispanic" (*Hispanic Society of New York City Police Department v. New York City Police Department*, 806 F.2d 1147, 1150 (2nd Cir. 1986)). Despite the evidence showing that the promotions examination was having a disparate impact on Latina/o and African American test takers and despite having a settlement already approved by a federal district court judge, the New York City Police Department, along with 350 white officers and fraternal law enforcement organizations representing white ethnic groups, such as the Columbia Society, the Emerald Society, and the Shomrim Society, appealed the case. They lost on appeal. As a result of this case and other lawsuits—including challenges to culturally biased civil service examinations and non-job related requirements, such as height requirements—employment in the NYPD and promotion within the higher ranks of the department became possible for Latinas/os and other persons of color in ways not previously conceivable.

The National Latino Officers Association of America (NLOA), through its predecessor organization, the NYPD-based Latino Officers Association, in conjunction with the Guardians Association, sued the New York City Police Department concerning discriminatory disciplinary practices and circumstances that created a hostile work environment for Latina/o and African Americans police officers. In 2004, the New York City Police Department, without conceding any wrongdoing, settled the lawsuit for $26.8 million. A year later, 576 Latina/o and African American officers received compensation ranging from $3,500 to $400,000, depending on the severity of the discrimination or hostility faced, especially in relation to the departmental disciplinary procedures (Fenner 2005).

Latina/o fraternal law enforcement organizations now have a presence in jurisdictions around the United Sates that have a significant Latina/o population. Some of the organizations, such as the Hispanic Society of the New York City Police Department and the Houston Police Organization of Spanish Speaking Officers, are local in scope and concern themselves primarily, if not strictly, with matters pertaining to their respective city's departmental impact on the local Latina/o community. Others, such as the National Latino Peace Officers Association, function through state or regional chapters and concern themselves with national, regional, and local law and policing issues that impact, or could impact, Latina/o law enforcement officers or the Latina/o community. Additionally, there are state-based Latina/o law enforcement fraternal organizations, such as the Latino Officers Association of Florida and the Hispanic Illinois State Law Enforcement Association, that concentrate primarily on state and local area issues.

The National Latino Officers Association (NLOA) is an example of a Latina/o fraternal law enforcement organization that has operated independently and without the sanction of the New York City Police Department or other police departments. **Anthony Miranda**, a retired New York City Police Department sergeant and head of NLOA, has stressed that NLOA's "mission is to promote racial and ethnic tolerance and equality and to end all forms of discrimination, sexual harassment, and retaliation against people of color in law enforcement agencies" (Morín 2009, 109). The NYPD's refusal to recognize or sanction the New York City Chapter of the Latino Officers Association over the years often is attributed to NLOA's zealous public advocacy and legal actions to contest NYPD practices that it believes have had a negative impact on Latina/o law enforcement officers and the Latino community (*see New York Times* 1999).

Latina/o fraternal law enforcement organizations maintain as a central facet of their mission or operations, the recruitment and advancement of Latinas/os within law enforcement agencies. As these organizations have grown both in number and political clout, they have expanded their ability to serve their members, providing emotional and personal support for individual members as well as legal representation for the group. Their importance in meeting the needs of Latinas/os in law enforcement could increase as their presence in law enforcement agencies across the United States increases. Given the post-Ferguson climate and the record reduction in crime nationally as the number of African American and Latina/o officers continues to grow, the role of Latina/o fraternal law enforcement organizations in matters related to police department politics and policies as well as police-community relations likely will be enhanced.

See Part I essays: Latinas/os and the U.S. Criminal Justice System; Policing and Latina/o Communities; Latinas and the U.S. Criminal Justice System. Part II entries: LatinoJustice PRLDEF; Puerto Rican Legal Defense and Education Fund (PRLDEF).

Further Reading

Crawford, Charles. 2012. The historical dynamics of ethnicity in law enforcement. In *Hispanics in the U.S. criminal justice system: The new American demography,* edited by Martin G. Urbina, 23–41. Springfield, IL: Charles C. Thomas.

Fenner, Austin. 2005 (November 22). 576 cops split $17m. *New York Daily News*. http://www.nydailynews.com/archives/news/576-cops-split-17m-article-1.586882.

Latin American Police Association. 2015. About us. http://www.lapa1961.com/htm/about/about_us.htm. Accessed November 12, 2015.

Morín, José Luis. 2009. *Latino/a rights and justice in the United States: Perspectives and approaches*. 2nd ed. Durham, NC: Carolina Academic Press.

Moynihan, Colin. 2004. Latino police officers and city settle suit. *New York Times*, February 1. http://www.nytimes.com/2004/02/01/nyregion/latino-police-officers-and-city-settle-suit.html

New York Times. 1999 (September 25). Safir defends rejection of Latino officers' group. http://www.nytimes.com/1999/09/25/nyregion/metro-news-briefs-new-york-safir-defends-rejection-of-latino-officers-group.html. Accessed November 25, 2015.

Urbina, Martin Guevara, and Sofía Espinoza Álvarez. 2015. *Latino police officers in the United States: An examination of emerging trends and issues*. Springfield, IL: Charles C. Thomas.

Cases Cited

Guardians Association of New York City Police Department v. Civil Service Commission of City of New York, 484 F. Supp. 785 (S.D.N.Y. 1980); 630 F.2d 79 (2nd Cir. 1980), *cert. denied*, 452 U.S. 940 (1981).

Hispanic Society of New York City Police Department v. New York City Police Department, 806 F.2d 1147 (2nd Cir. 1986).

Latina/o Invisibility. *See* Introduction; Part I essay: Latinas/os and the U.S. Criminal Justice System; Latinas and the U.S. Criminal Justice System. Part II entry: *Hernandez v. Texas*, 347 U.S. 475 (1954).

LatinoJustice PRLDEF/Puerto Rican Legal Defense and Education Fund. *See* Part I essay: Latinas/os and the U.S. Criminal Justice System. Part II entries: Civil Rights; Community-Based Latina/o Advocacy Organizations; Hate Crimes; International Human Rights; Legal Advocacy Groups; Lesbian, Gay, Bisexual, and Transgender (LGBT).

League of United Latin American Citizens (LULAC). *See* Part I essay: Latinas/os and the U.S. Criminal Justice System. Part II entries: Chicanas/os; Community-Based Latina/o Advocacy Organizations; *Hernandez v. Texas*, 347 U.S. 475 (1954); Legal Advocacy Groups; Mexicans and Mexican Americans.

Legal Advocacy Groups

Isabel Martínez

Although predecessor organizations existed before their founding, the social unrest at the middle of the 20th century brought about a different model of organizing and advocacy to address social inequalities and discrimination against Latinas/os, both in the Northeast and the Southwest. With the advent of **Mexican American Legal Defense and Education Fund (MALDEF)** and the **Puerto Rican Legal Defense and Education Fund (PRLDEF)** (now **LatinoJustice PRLDEF**) in the late 1960s and early 1970s, social justice struggles for Latina/o rights drew from integrationist models of the past as well as the era of radical politics. Drawing from both the legal defense model established by the National Association for the Advancement of Colored People, and predecessor organizations such as the League of Latin American Citizens, these organizations would lead the legal and educational charge against discrimination towards Latinas/os in the United States.

Predecessors to the Mexican American Legal Defense and Education Fund and the Puerto Rican Legal Defense and Education Fund: The League of United Latin American Citizens and the American GI Forum

A discussion of social justice organizations championing Latina/o civil rights would be incomplete without the mention of the **League of United Latin American Citizens (LULAC)**. In the face of social, economic, and political discrimination during the 1940s and the 1950s, Latinas/os in the Southwest turned to LULAC and the American GI Forum—an organization that played a particularly important role in supporting and advocating for the civil rights of Latinas/os returning from World War II. Acts of housing and educational segregation, political disenfranchisement, and labor discrimination were challenged by attorneys associated with LULAC and the American GI Forum. These two organizations and their affiliate attorneys argued cases of injustice at all levels of the judicial system—local, state, and federal. The breadth of cases, however, proved to be too much of a burden to be handled by individual attorneys. An umbrella organization had to be established to organize and fund challenges to the discriminatory status quo. The Mexican American Legal Defense and Education Fund (MALDEF) as well as the Puerto Rican Legal Defense and Education Fund (PRLDEF) (renamed LatinoJustice PRLDEF), were born of this need.

Mexican American Legal Defense and Education Fund

Anxious to engage in a more concerted effort to combat discrimination against Latinas/os and frustrated by piecemeal efforts to pool resources to defend the civil rights of Latinas/os, Pedro "Pete" Tijerina (1922–2003) and other interested colleagues and allies founded the Mexican American Legal Defense and Education Fund (MALDEF). Their intention was to create one central organization that could harness resources and file suits against public and private institutions that engaged in discriminatory practices against the Mexican American community and individuals. Tijerina, born in 1922 in Laredo, Texas, joined the military (air corps) in 1941 and served in the Pacific during World War II. Upon his return he completed both undergraduate studies and law school, passing the Texas legal bar exam in January 1952. His involvement with LULAC, however, would be influential in his social and political development. Tijerina belonged to a "traveling troupe" of attorneys and activists affiliated with LULAC who would enlist local attorneys to engage in the pro bono filing and arguing of court cases in local courts (Iber 2005).

To create a single entity with adequate resources to effectively challenge discriminatory practices, Tijerina in 1966 brought together fellow attorneys and activists. With the NAACP Legal Defense Fund and LULAC as models, Tijerina sought to create a new organization. Jack Greenberg, the acting director of the NAACP's Legal Defense Fund, was instrumental in helping to form MALDEF and served as a conduit between Tijerina and the Ford Foundation to jumpstart the financial viability of the organization. Attorneys from both the NAACP Legal Defense Fund and LULAC met to establish a blueprint for MALDEF. After much deliberation, they opted to establish the MALDEF headquarters in San Antonio, Texas.

The Ford Foundation was essential in MALDEF's inception, granting it more than $2 million to "file constitutionally significant cases" that would challenge discriminatory policies and practices in education, labor, and other civil rights. To emphasize the importance of education in the Mexican American community, the Ford Foundation provided additional funds for MALDEF to establish a scholarship for Spanish-surname students who were pursuing legal degrees (Iber 2005). Soon after Tijerina was named MALDEF's first executive director, and Mario Obledo—a former state director of LULAC—was named its first general counsel, Anglo political leaders complained of their "radical politics" and pressured the Ford Foundation to move the organization's location from San Antonio—the hub of Chicano/a political action. By 1970, MALDEF offices moved to San Francisco, California, and later to Washington, DC, to establish a national office. During these years, MALDEF, in the words of Obledo, would shift from being a "legal organization of militants" to becoming a "law firm for the Latino community."

Litigation

From its inception until the 1980s, MALDEF engaged in "impact" litigation—litigation which has the possibility of establishing legal precedent. At its origin, MALDEF's primary emphasis focused on education and voting rights. Among the MALDEF cases that have had a lasting impact are ***Plyler v. Doe*, 457 U.S. 202 (1982)** and *Edgewood Independent School District et al. v. Kirby et al.*, 777 S.W.2d 391 (TX 1989).

Plyler v. Doe (1982) and *Edgewood Independent School District v. Kirby* (1989) directly addressed far-reaching educational issues. *Plyler v. Doe* (1982) addressed the education of undocumented youth in the United States. Citing protection under the Equal Protection Clause of the Fourteenth Amendment, the opinion of the court struck down a Texas statute which effectively withheld state funds from school districts enrolling youth who were unable to demonstrate their lawful presence in the United States. Instead, the ruling asserts that states could not deny to any person within its jurisdiction the equal protection of law to citizens or noncitizens alike. In regards to the *Plyler* case, this ruling deemed that all persons residing within a state's boundaries, lawfully or not, can be afforded free access to public education from age 5 to age 21, or from Kindergarten to grade 12. These youth were in the United States without choice and thus were eligible for educational services. A 5-to-4 decision, the United States Supreme Court guaranteed equal protection and access to public education to undocumented youth.

In *Edgewood Independent School District v. Kirby* (1989), MALDEF challenged funding formulas for education in Texas. In a lawsuit against Texas Education Commissioner William Kirby, Edgewood ISD joined seven other poor school districts in Texas in charging that the existing system of school-tax distribution produced extreme funding disparities across Texas school districts. Despite higher tax rates, predominantly minority school districts—even with state and federal aid—were unable to match the per-pupil spending of wealthier school districts. In Texas, the wealthiest school districts were spending up to four times the amount spent per pupil by the poorest, predominantly minority school districts. To address these disparities, in a 9-to-0 ruling, the Texas Supreme Court ruled that Texas was violating the equal protection clause of the U.S. Constitution and ordered wealthier school districts to share their financial resources earned through property taxes to poorer, predominantly Latina/o and African American school districts. This plan would become known as the "Robin Hood plan."

After 1980, the focus of MALDEF moved from issues arising in the local Southwest to national and transnational concerns. MALDEF's services expanded to ensure justice in Latina/o communities by addressing legal, language, and immigration rights. Legal cases argued by MALDEF include challenges to Proposition 187 in California, which sought to prevent undocumented people from accessing a variety of public benefits, as well as a class action lawsuit against Maricopa County (Arizona) Sheriff Joe

Arpaio and the Maricopa County Sheriff's Office ("MCSO"), alleging that the sheriff had engaged in racially profiling Latinas/os. In *Ortega Melendres et al. v. Arpaio et al.* (2013), MALDEF, joined by other litigators including the American Civil Liberties Union, was successful in having a federal court judge rule that Sheriff Arpaio and MSCO had engaged in discriminatory and unlawful policies and practices in violation of the Fourth and Fourteenth Amendments to the U.S. Constitution, having unlawfully targeted and detained undocumented immigrants through practices of racially profiling Latinos. The court ordered, among other things, that such conduct cease.

Activism

Since 1968, MALDEF has engaged in a wide array of tactics to address discriminatory practices towards Latinas/os in the United States. These strategies predominantly addressed local education, voting rights, and labor rights. Under MALDEF's third president, Vilma Martinez, MALDEF extended its strategies beyond court challenges and acted to involve all actors in policy making. Citizens who were interested in promoting Latina/o interests were trained by MALDEF to fill various elected positions, including on school boards, resulting in the election of Latinas/os onto decision-making entities. One such program is the Parent School Partnership program which educates and trains parents regarding their rights in their children's school districts and prepares them to become leaders in their children's schools. Additionally, multi-pronged challenges to discriminatory voting practices would lead to the dissolution of at-large election systems in large, Latina/o-populated cities, including San Antonio. Such efforts were crucial to the election of Henry Cisneros to the San Antonio City Council, and later as mayor.

With an eye to the growing Latina/o immigrant population, MALDEF expanded its efforts to focus on the civil rights of Latina/o immigrants. Harsh immigration enforcement policies that emerged after the events of September 11, 2001, prompted MALDEF to actively work to ensure the rights of Latina/o immigrants. Its efforts have included pressing state and local governments to accept the Mexican *matricula consular* (the Mexican consular identification card) as well as fighting for the rights of day laborers. Correspondingly, MALDEF has opened offices into new locations where the Latina/o population is growing. MALDEF opened an office in Atlanta, Georgia, an area that has experienced tremendous Latina/o population growth.

Puerto Rican Legal Defense and Education Fund/LatinoJustice PRLDEF

Founded in 1972, the Puerto Rican Legal Defense and Education Fund (PRLDEF) joined other emerging race- and ethnicity-based civil rights organizations, such as the NAACP and MALDEF, during the late1960s and early 1970s to successfully challenge discrimination in education, voting, housing, and employment practices. In New York City, the Puerto Rican community began organizing against oppressive policies and practices which had led to its social and economic marginalization. Organizations such as the Puerto Rican Student Union and the **Young Lords** protested discriminatory practices by city institutions, including the City University of New York and the New York City Department of Sanitation, and needed legal representation. In response, individual Puerto Rican attorneys organized to represent these activist organizations fighting for social and economic change. The attorneys recognized the need for a well-organized and well-funded collective legal entity to specifically represent and fight for the civil rights of the Puerto Rican community. By 1968, three Puerto Rican attorneys, Jorge Batista, Victor Marrero, and Cesar Perales—all former staff members of New York City Mayor John Lindsay—joined together to create the Puerto Rican Legal Defense and Education Fund in New York City.

The PRLDEF outlined its objectives as "providing high-quality legal representation for the Puerto Rican community at large in order to secure fair and equal protection of the law and of the civil rights of Puerto Ricans" and "to promote legal education and information among Puerto Ricans in order to increase the number of Puerto Rican lawyers serving the community" (Research Collections in Latino Studies 2004). By February 1972, PRLDEF was granted nonprofit, tax-exempt status and was able to fundraise and organize for the Latina/o community, not only in the tri-state area, but nationally.

By the summer of 1972, PRLDEF opened its doors to the New York City Latina/o community. Cesar Perales was named the first executive director of the organization, and its first donors were the Ford Foundation, the Rockefeller Foundation, and the Carnegie Foundation. Through the years, the organization at times has struggled to maintain financial stability. By 1993, PRLDEF president and general counsel, Juan Figueroa, outlined six litigation areas that PRLDEF would emphasize: Education rights, Latina rights, voting rights, housing rights, employment rights, and criminal justice rights.

In 2008, after 37 years as the "Puerto Rican Legal Defense and Education Fund," the Board of Directors renamed the organization "LatinoJustice PRLDEF." Cesar Perales summarized the change as follows.

> In the end it was simple; we are a Latino organization that is committed to justice for our community. No matter our roots in Latin America, our success in this nation will be based on a common struggle. We are proud to be a pan-Latino civil rights organization with national impact and our name should communicate that (Garcia 2008).

To honor the Puerto Rican legacy and origins of the organization, the acronym "PRLDEF" was kept as part of the organization's new name.

Litigation

Many of PRLDEF's efforts emphasize "community lawyering," focusing on rectifying policies and practices that most affect the Puerto Rican community in New York City, the Northeast, and Chicago. In New York City, many of PRLDEF's initial court challenges emphasized the language rights of non–English speaking Puerto Ricans and other Latinas/os in New York City. Its first lawsuit, *ASPIRA v. Board of Education*, was filed in 1972 to ensure adequate services for non–English speaking students in the New York City public school district. Resolution of the case resulted in the establishment of a bilingual education program in New York City. By 1974, PRLDEF also fought to ensure voting rights for Puerto Rican citizens. In the case *Lopez v. Dinkins* (1975), PRLDEF argued New York City was violating the civil rights of non–English speaking Latinas/os by not providing bilingual ballots for school board elections.

Addressing employment discrimination, PRLDEF supported the Guardians Association and the **Hispanic Society of the New York City Police Department** in their lawsuit against the Civil Service Commission. Citing discriminatory practices in the New York Police Department entrance and promotional exams, PRLDEF was victorious in forcing the department to redesign its hiring practices to produce a more diverse police force. Not limited to the U.S. mainland, PRLDEF also was involved in a number of legal cases on behalf of Puerto Ricans who live on the island. PRLDEF successfully challenged the government of Puerto Rico for violation of the labor rights of Puerto Rican migrant farmworkers.

Activism

LatinoJustice PRLDEF has remained committed to being active in the areas of education, training, and the provision of social services. One of its primary goals has been to increase the number of Latinas/os in the legal profession, particularly in the public interest sector. To this end, LatinoJustice PRLDEF's Education Division has sponsored LSAT and law school application preparation programs, and has offered law school internships, opening up the opportunity for law students to gain experience in the field of civil rights. Additionally, as the impact of its work has increasingly benefited the broader Latina/o community beyond Puerto Ricans, the organization has sought to meet the needs of other Latinas/os and established *Proyecto Ayuda* after September 11, 2001. Providing case management and social services, *Proyecto Ayuda* protected and fought for the rights of Latina/o victims and families affected by 9/11. The PRLDEF provided case management, workshops, and advocacy to victims and families of 9/11 victims.

LatinoJustice PRLDEF's work also has included public policy analysis and advocacy, civic participation, and communication. For a brief period it had merged with the Institute for Puerto Rican Policy (now the National Institute for Latino Policy), to engage in public policy analyses and advance policy changes in support of Puerto Ricans and other Latinas/os. It continues to address public policy matters on a range of issues and is an outspoken advocate on such issues as immigrant rights and criminal justice reform.

LatinoJustice PRLDEF garnered national and international notoriety with the appointment process and confirmation of Supreme Court Justice Sonia Sotomayor. Characterized by senators including Orrin Hatch (R-Utah) and Lindsay Graham (R-TN) as an extremist organization, LatinoJustice PRLDEF and its practices suddenly were under scrutiny, as Justice Sotomayor had served on the organization's Board of Directors. Prior to Sotomayor's appointment, Tom Saenz, MALDEF's head of litigation, was under consideration to head Obama's Department of Justice Civil Rights Division. Saenz's litigation on behalf of immigrants and day laborers, however, proved too controversial and political for smooth appointment and he was disregarded. Paradoxically, Chief Justice Roberts and Justice Samuel Alito's affiliation with neoconservative organizations, such as the Federalist Society, drew no ire from the same individuals who criticized Sotomayor and Saenz. Analysts have made note of this ostensible double-standard and the irony that a nominee associated with organizations seeking to promote equality and civil rights for all would receive such intense scrutiny for governmental or legal appointments.

The Future of Latina/o Civil Rights Organizations

Organizations such as MALDEF and LatinoJustice PRLDEF remain highly relevant in the 21st century. Latinas/os, both native-born and immigrant, continue to endure discrimination in employment and housing and suffer severe disparities in the educational and criminal justice systems. Both MALDEF and LatinoJustice PRLDEF in the coming years likely will be concerned with **hate crimes** against Latinas/os and immigration rights issues.

The current climate of tensions between police and communities of color likely will mean that criminal justice matters—including police misconduct—will be at the top of the agenda for these groups as well. In April 2015, LatinoJustice PRLDEF, representing 21 Latinos on Long Island, filed a class action lawsuit charging that officers in the Suffolk County Police Department (SCPD) regularly stopped Latinos based on their race and ethnicity, and robbed them or gave them an unjustified traffic summons. The federal lawsuit also alleges that over a 10-year period SCPD engaged in "a crime spree that left local Latinos too afraid to drive their cars, leave their homes or interact with the police" (LatinoJustice PRLDEF 2015). The lawsuit comes in the aftermath of the arrest of SCPD Sergeant Scott Greene for having stolen money from a Latino driver while purportedly conducting a police operation. The SCPD has been under federal investigation stemming from a pattern of discriminatory practices, particularly in relation to its treatment of Latinas/os.

See also: Part I essays: Latinas/os and the U.S. Criminal Justice System; Policing and Latina/o Communities. Part II entries: Chicanas/os; Civil Rights; Community-Based Latina/o Advocacy Organizations; Hate Crimes; Lesbian, Gay, Bisexual, and Transgender (LGBT); Political Activist Groups.

Further Reading

Badillo, David A. 2005. MALDEF and the evolution of Latino civil rights. *Research Reports*. Volume 2005.2. Institute for Latino Studies, Notre Dame, IN: University of Notre Dame.

Centro de Estudios Puertorriqueños. 1991. Guide to the records of the Puerto Rican Legal Defense and Education Fund (PRLDEF): Archives of the Puerto Rican Diaspora. New York: Centro de Estudios Puertorriqueños.

Garcia, John. 2008 (October 6). "Puerto Rican Legal Defense and Education Fund is now LatinoJustice PRLDEF." Press Release, Latina/o Justice PRLDEF. http://latinojustice.org/briefing_room/press_releases/puerto_rican_legal_defense_and_education_fund_is_now/. Accessed October 16, 2015.

Gonzalez, Juan. 2011. *Harvest of empire: A history of Latinos in America*, revised edition. New York: Penguin.

Iber, Jorge. 2005. "Mexican American Legal Defense and Education Fund." In *The Oxford Encyclopedia of Latinos and Latinas in the United States*, Volume 3, edited by Suzanne Oboler and Deena J. Gonzalez, 117–21. London: Oxford University Press.

Johnson, Kevin. 2009. "An essay on the nomination and confirmation of the first Latina Justice on the U.S. Supreme Court: The 'high-tech lynching' of a 'wise Latina'?" *UC Davis Legal Studies Research Paper No. 188*: 1–49.

Kozol, Jonathan. 1991. *Savage inequalities: Children in America's schools*. New York: Broadway Books.

LatinoJustice PRLDEF. 2015. Press release: 21 Latinos charge Suffolk Police with condoning officers' 10-year crime spree against Latinos in federal class action lawsuit. http://latinojustice.org/civil_rights/21_Latinos_Charge_Suffolk_Police_Condoning_Officers_10_Year_Crime_Spree/.

Research Collections in Latino Studies. 2004. The Puerto Rican Legal Defense and Education Fund, Part 1: Executive and administrative records. Bethesda, MD: LexisNexis Academic & Library Solutions. http://cisupa.proquest.com/ksc_assets/catalog/100437.pdf.

Rivera, Jenny. 2005. "Puerto Rican Legal Defense and Education Fund." In *The Oxford Encyclopedia of Latinos and Latinas in the*

United States, Volume 3, edited by Suzanne Oboler and Deena J. Gonzalez, 496–98. London: Oxford University Press.

Cases Cited

Aspira of New York, Incorporated et al. v. Board of Education of the City of New York, et al. 72 Civ. 4002 S.D.N.Y. (MEF). Complaint, September 1972.

Edgewood Independent School District et al. v. Kirby et al., 777 S.W.2d 391 (TX 1989).

Lopez v. Dinkins, 73 Civ. 695 (S.D.N.Y. March 27, 1975).

Ortega Melendres et al. v. Arpaio et al. 989 F. Supp. 2d 822 (D.C. Ariz. 2013).

Plyler v. Doe, 457 U.S. 202 (1982).

Lesbian, Gay, Bisexual, and Transgender (LGBT)

Joshua G. Kellison

To condense the broad subject matter on lesbian, gay, bisexual, and transgender (LGBT) people of color, particularly in regard to the experience of LGBT Latinas/os, this entry places primary emphasis on the West and Southwest (borderlands) of the United States and on criminal justice and related immigration issues. Attempts by the United States to control both gender norms and sexuality at the **border** is a topic that invariably overlaps with issues of sexual orientation–motivated **hate crimes** and how these acts affect the lives and well-being of Latina/o LGBT people throughout the United States. These acts continue to be perpetrated by both law enforcement agencies and the general public. In fact, in recent times, increases in sexual orientation–related hate crimes have been reported. By including the Latina/o LGBT community, the diversity of the Latina/o experience in the criminal justice system is expanded. In doing so, it is important to acknowledge LGBT Latinas/os as a historically marginalized group not only in the United States, but also in their own countries of origin.

This entry uses the theoretical frameworks of "Queer Theory," "Border Theory" (Borderlands Theory), and "Gender Schema Theory" to examine the criminal justice issues and the experience of LGBT Latinas/os. Both Queer Theory and Gender Schema Theory arguably have been influenced by the semiotic work of Michel Foucault (1990) and his analyses of power relations where, he argues, normalization occurs. On the one hand, Gender Schema Theory is psychologically centered and depicts gender-role development as a culturally based socialization process. Similarly, Queer Theory focuses on issues of identity (including gender, ethnicity, sexuality, and race) and incorporates many disciplines to inform and create theoretical perspectives and empirical foci. On the other hand, Border/Borderlands Theory aids in the understanding of both the immigrant and national, and how the two intersect in a system of inequality and marginality, creating different power relations within and between each group. Consequently, the complicated dynamics of sexuality, race/ethnicity, gender, nationalism, and immigration status are defined as identity constructs informed through theories related to power relations and psychosocial idealizations.

"Homosexual" is the term used to describe individuals who are physically and emotionally attracted to people of their own sex. More specifically, "lesbian" is the preferred term for women who are primarily attracted to women and "gay" is the preferred term for men who are primarily attracted to men. The term "gay" at times also is used as a catch-all term for both male and female homosexuals and bisexuals. People who prefer the term "bisexual" are those that are physically and emotionally attracted to persons of both sexes. The term "transgender" historically has been used as a blanket term for those who challenge societal idealizations for men and women. Currently, transgender means those people who do not identify with the biological sex that they were prescribed at birth (e.g., born male and identify as female). Transgender people can include transsexuals (people who have had sex-reassignment surgery), people who feel that their gender is fluid or blended, and others who do not conform to the conventional gender binary. There are numerous biological and psychosocial causal theories regarding LGBT identities that go beyond the scope of this entry (e.g., Bockting 2014; Somerville 2000).

Gender and Sexuality at the Border

As early as 1917, laws have been in place to keep those with "abnormal sexual instincts" from coming into the country, and as late as 1990 lesbian immigrants still were deportable from the United States. Although the Senate Committee of the Judiciary recommended adding homosexuality to the list of undesirables, in 1952 the Immigration and Nationality Act (INA) did not explicitly mention homosexuals. The INA, however, followed a Public Health Service (PHS) suggestion to include homosexuality under the provision of "psychopathic personalities." In 1965, however, gays and lesbians were excluded from entry as "sexual deviants" (Somerville 2005).

One noteworthy case discussed by scholars was the 1960 case of Sara Harb Quiroz who, upon coming back from visiting family in Juarez, Mexico, was detained in El Paso, Texas, by an immigration agent who thought her to be a "psychopathic personality." Although no documents that detail the reasons for her detainment exist, Quiroz's lawyer believed it to be related to how Quiroz acted, spoke, and dressed (Luibheid 2002), and because she was perceived to be a sexual deviant. One explanation of this case is that the state "entwined" sexuality with the discourse of race and the inclusion of homosexuality in the 1952 INA at a time when explicit arguments of race were losing legitimacy (Somerville 2005). The ideologies of body differences that were used for race had now become a part of "diagnosing" homosexuality at the border.

Consequently, there were many opportunities for LGBT immigrants to be discovered by INS agents through third-party informants, visual body comportment strategies, gender norms, and medical checkpoints. Once an immigrant was labeled as LGBT he or she was given a Class A medical exclusion certificate by the PHS and was deported. For those who were caught in an act of homosexuality while in the United States, however, not only could they be deported, they also were criminalized and in some cases were sentenced to anywhere from one year to life in prison. Some suspected LGBT Latina/o detainees reported lengthy interrogations and humiliation under the hands of both racist and homophobic INS agents during secondary inspection. They also reported being asked to sign and agree to statements that they could not read or understand because the INS agent would not translate items into Spanish.

In 1973, the American Psychiatric Association (APA) voted to remove homosexuality as an illness. Subsequently, the PHS could no longer give Class A medical exclusion certificates. The INS, however, continued to place suspected homosexuals in secondary inspection where they were questioned and a decision for a hearing or **deportation** was made. Finally, in 1990 the U.S. Congress repealed immigration exclusion based on being labeled as a sexual deviant. More recently, however, HIV-AIDS has been added to the list of communicable diseases used to ban possible immigrants and, in a way, has justified the barring of gay men and people of color. Moreover, there are still INS agents who use "good moral character" judgments as a pretext to detain and deport Latina/o LGBT immigrants.

Hate Crimes

Hate crimes, also known as bias-related crimes, can involve such activities as physical **violence**, emotional abuse, and damage to property. These crimes are motivated by the perpetrator's hatred toward certain social groups of which they believe the victim is a member (e.g., nationality, sexual orientation, disability, race, ethnicity, age). It has been shown that in times of economic hardship and when people are under great amounts of psychological stress some commit such crimes. Furthermore, people in general under similar conditions believe and use stereotypes to make behavioral choices in social situations or to condone other people's commission of hate crimes.

Currently, U.S. federally protected groups include those for a person's race, color, religion, and nation of origin. Yet, since October of 2007, the U.S. Congress has been considering the Local Law Enforcement Hate Crimes Prevention Act (HCPA) (a.k.a. Matthew Shepard and James Byrd, Jr. Hate Crimes **Prevention** Act, in remembrance of the 1998 unrelated brutal murders of the 21-year-old University of Wyoming student and the 49-year-old African American in Jasper, Texas, respectively). The Act would add gender, gender identity, sexual orientation, and disability to the hate crime prevention list. On July 15, 2009, the Act was added as an amendment to the National Defense Authorization Act for Fiscal Year 2010 and passed by the Senate when the Defense bill passed on July 23, 2009. Difference and alteration arguments by congressional opponents who believed that the amendment would eliminate freedom of speech for religious organizations to express their beliefs kept the bill from being signed into law. In October 2009, the HCPA was passed in both the House and the Senate, and was signed into law by President Barack Obama.

In 2006, the Federal Bureau of Investigation's review of hate crimes statistics reported that anti-LGBT-motivated hate crimes accounted for 15 percent of U.S. total hate crimes, and in 2008 the data showed an increase in such crime to 16 percent (Federal Bureau of Investigation 2008). It has been argued that this increase is due, in part, to the increased LGBT visibility and activism, an increased willingness of **victims** to report these crimes, and the severe national economic downturn in recent years. Overall, hate crimes committed against Latinas/os increased 40 percent between 2003 and 2007 (Leadership Conference on Civil Rights 2009). Because hate crimes tend to correspond to periods of economic and psychological stress, the hated group is perceived as receiving lost resources or benefits. That is, hate crimes are directed at immigrant workers who often are mistakenly believed to be taking jobs away from "natives" or at LGBT people because it's believed that the LGBT community's desire for marriage equality undermines heterosexual privilege.

Multiple layers of hate can be directed toward LGBT Latinas/os. Hate can come in the form of perceived immigration status and **race and ethnicity**. It also can be rooted in the perception of their sexual identity. In either case, the intersectional nature of LGBT Latinas/os' identity as both sexual and racial minorities can create more socio-legal problems than either identity alone. Although anti-LGBT hate violence is a national phenomenon wherever sizable numbers of Latinas/os reside, as in Los Angeles and New York, some data suggest that LGBT Latinas/os are especially vulnerable because LGBT Latinas/os survivors of anti-LGBTQ hate violence tend to comprise a greater percentage of victims of such crimes than do other racial and ethnic groups.

In the case of hate crimes as reported by perpetrators, when the identities are combined, the amount of hate is increased more than either aspect alone, and the assaults tend to be more brutal. On December 7, 2008, in Brooklyn, New York, for example, Ecuadorean immigrant brothers **José** and **Romel Sucuzhañay** were attacked. Witnesses stated that anti-gay and anti-Latino slurs were shouted from the vehicle of the assailants before they chased and beat José Sucuzhañay with a baseball bat. He died six days later.

Another example involved Angie Zapata, an American trans-woman who, on July 17, 2008, in Greeley, Colorado, was beaten to death with a fire extinguisher after her assailant learned she was transgender. Her murderer, Allen Andrade, was later convicted of first-degree murder and for committing a biased-motivated crime. Andrade was the first in the nation to receive a conviction for committing a hate crime against a transgender victim.

LatinoJustice PRLDEF and other **civil rights legal advocacy groups** were outraged by these crimes and have formally stated that the United States is failing to protect Latinas/os. They believe that due to "celebrated" **vigilante** groups (e.g., the Minuteman Project) and agreements that allow local communities to deputize their police forces to carry out immigration law, Latinas/os can be attacked with impunity and that all Latinas/os can be treated as suspects of immigration violations. Such incidents arouse Latina/o community distrust of police and other law enforcement agencies. For some victims, lack of confidence in law enforcement and the criminal justice system prompts them to not report hate crime victimization. Furthermore, it has been argued that the current political climate and wave of vigilante activism enables perpetrators of hate crimes to feel justified in their actions and encourages onlookers to condone such behavior.

See also: Part I essays: Latinas/os and the U.S. Criminal Justice System; Crime and the U.S.-Mexican Border. Part II entries: Civil Rights; Deportation; Hate Crimes; Legal Advocacy Groups; Victims; Vigilantism.

Further Reading

Anzaldúa, Gloria. 2007. *Borderlands/La frontera: The new mestiza*. San Francisco, CA: Aunt Lute.

Ballard-Reisch, Deborah, and M. Elton. 1992. Gender orientation and the Bem Sex Role Inventory: A psychological construct revisited. *Sex Roles* 27: 291–306.

Bell, Jeannine. 2002. *Policing hatred: Law enforcement, civil rights, and hate crime*. New York, NY: New York University Press.

Bem, Sandra L. 1981. Gender Schema Theory: A cognitive account of sex typing. *Psychological Review* 88(4): 354–64.

Bem, Sandra L. 1983. Gender Schema Theory and its implications for child development: Raising gender-aschematic children in a gender-schematic society. *Signs* 8: 598–616.

Bem, Sandra L. 1993. *The lenses of gender: Transforming the debate on sexual inequality*. New Haven, CT: Yale University Press.

Bockting, Walter O. 2014. Transgender identity development. In *APA handbook of sexuality and psychology, Vol. 1: Person-based approaches*, edited by D. L. Tolman, L. M. Diamond, J. A. Bauermeister, W. H. George, J. G. Pfaus, and M. L. Ward, 739–58. Washington, DC: American Psychological Association.

Bussey, K., and Albert Bandura. 1999. Social Cognitive Theory of gender development and differentiation. *Psychological Review* 106: 676–713.

Butler, Judith. 1999. *Gender trouble: Feminism and the subversion of identity.* New York: Routledge.

Butler, Judith. 2004. *Undoing gender*. New York, NY: Routledge.

Cantu, Lionel. 2003. A place called home: A queer political economy of Mexican immigrant men's family experiences. In *Perspectivas on Las Américas: A reader in culture, history & representation,* edited by M. C. Gutmann, F. V. Matos Rodríguez, L. Stephen, and P. Zavella, 259–73. Malden, MA: Blackwell Publishing.

Castaneda, Antonia I. 1990. Gender, race, and culture: Spanish-Mexican women in the historiography of frontier California. *Frontiers: A Journal of Women Studies* 11: 8–19.

Cousins, Mark, and Athar Hussain. 1984. *Michel Foucault.* New York, NY: Macmillan.

Fahim, Kareem. 2010 (April 22). Witnesses detail beating of an immigrant. *New York Times.*

Federal Bureau of Investigation. 2008. Uniform Crime Reporting Program. http://www2.fbi.gov/ucr/hc2008/victims.html. Accessed October 22, 2015.

Foucault, Michel. 1990. *The history of sexuality: An introduction.* Translated by Robert Hurley. New York, NY: Pantheon Books.

Gruberg, Sharita. 2013. *Dignity denied: LGBT immigrants in U.S. Immigration detention* (Washington: Center for American Progress). http://www.americanprogress.org/wp-content/uploads/2013/11/ImmigrationEnforcement.pdf. Accessed October 22, 2015.

Harek, Gregory M., Jeanine C. Cogan, and J. Roy Gillis. 2002. Victim experiences in hate crimes based on sexual orientation. *Journal of Social Issues* 58: 319–39.

Jargose, Annmarie. 1996. *Queer theory: An introduction.* New York, NY: New York University Press.

Leadership Conference on Civil Rights. 2009. Hate against Hispanics. http://www.civil-rights.org/publications/hatecrimes/hispanics.html. Accessed October 22, 2015.

Luibheid, Eithne. 2002. *Entry denied: Controlling sexuality at the border.* Minneapolis, MN: University of Minnesota Press.

Luibheid, Eithne, and Lionel Cantu (eds.). 2005. *Queer migrations: Sexuality, U.S. citizenship, and border crossings.* Minneapolis, MN: University of Minnesota Press.

Michaelsen, Steven, and David E. Johnson. 1997. *Border theory: The limits of cultural politics.* Minneapolis, MN: University of Minnesota Press.

National Coalition of Anti-Violence Programs. 2014. Lesbian, gay, bisexual, transgender, queer, and HIV-affected hate violence in 2013. New York: NCAVP.

Slonim, Maureen B. 1991. *Children, culture, and ethnicity: Evaluating and understanding the impact.* New York, NY: Garland Publishing.

Somerville, Siobhan B. 2000. *Queering the color line: Race and the invention of homosexuality in American culture.* Durham, NC: Duke University Press.

Somerville, Siobhan B. 2005. Sexual aliens and the racialized state: A queer reading of the 1952 U.S. Immigration and Nationality Act. In *Queer migrations: Sexuality, U.S. citizenship, and border crossings,* edited by E. Luibheid and L. Cantu, 75–91. Minneapolis, MN: University of Minnesota Press.

Spellman, Jim. 2009. Transgender murder, hate crime conviction a first. *CNN.* http://www.cnn.com/2009/CRIME/04/22/transgender.slaying.trial/index.html. Accessed October 22, 2015.

Spence, Janet T., and Camille E. Bukner. 1995. Masculinity and femininity: Defining the undefinable. In *Gender, power and communication in human relationship,* edited by P. J. Kalbfleisch and M. J. Cody, 105–38. Hillsdale, NJ: Erlbaum.

Tabak, Shana, and Levitan, Rachel. 2014. LGBTI migrants in immigration detention: A global perspective. *Harvard Journal of Law and Gender* 37(1).

Lucero, Marcelo. *See* Part I essay: Policing and Latina/o Communities. Part II entries: Hate Crimes; International Human Rights.

Lynching. *See* Part I essays: Latinas/os and the U.S. Criminal Justice System; Policing and Latina/o Communities; Crime and the U.S.-Mexican Border. Part II entries: Hate Crimes; Media Depictions; Mexicans and Mexican Americans; Texas Rangers; Vigilantism.

M

Machismo. *See* Part I essay: Latinas and the U.S. Criminal Justice System. Part II entries: Cultural Criminology; Political Activist Groups.

Manifest Destiny. *See* Part I essays: Latinas/os and the U.S. Criminal Justice System; Policing and Latina/o Communities; Crime and the U.S.-Mexican Border. Part II entries: Chicanas/os; Mexicans and Mexican Americans; Texas Rangers; Vigilantism.

Mara Salvatrucha. *See* Part I essay: Gangs in the United States and Latina/o Communities. Part II entries: Central Americans; Transnational Crime.

Marianismo. *See* Part I essay: Latinas and the U.S. Criminal Justice System.

Mass Imprisonment/Mass Incarceration. *See* Part I essays: Latinas/os and the U.S. Criminal Justice System; Policing and Latina/o Communities; Incarceration and Latinas/os in the United States; Latinas and the Criminal Justice System; Latina/o Youth and Criminal Justice. Part II entries: Felon Disenfranchisement; Segregation.

Media Depictions

Manuel A. Huerta

All too often, the collective cultural imagination of the United States has propagated a largely misunderstood and dehumanized image of Latinas/os, which has led to general stereotypes, **racial profiling**, and ongoing injustices for Latinas/os in the criminal justice system. A long history of stereotypes and racism in literature, the news media, and films, and eventually on television and on the Internet, has rendered an image of Latinas/os as routinely being on the wrong side of the law. Throughout the history of the United States, these depictions have produced a direct and detrimental impact on the manner in which the criminal justice system views and treats Latinas/os.

Early Representations of Latinas/os and Crime in News Media and Literature

The literature, newspapers, and popular culture of the mid-19th century constructed an unfavorable view of Latinas/os, which affected their treatment as a people in the United States. One text that was particularly popular and widely read in the United States in the 1840s and thereafter was William H. Prescott's (1843) *History of the Conquest of Mexico*. In this historical text, Prescott wrote that **Mexicans**, and all other people with indigenous blood, were inherently indolent, savage, hot-blooded, barbaric, and treacherous. Shortly after Prescott's book was published and after the Mexican-American War ended in 1848, Mexicans increasingly became the **victims** of mob justice and **lynchings** without the benefit of judicial trials. Many lynchings took place as local authorities turned a blind eye. Some lynchings were documented in local newspapers or in editorials that attempted to justify and even rouse the citizenry towards additional extra-judicial killings. The vast majority of lynchings, however, are absent not only from primary sources, but also missing from past and current scholarship on this topic.

Latina/o Representations with the Advent of Film and Television

With the creation of the film medium as a powerful new tool for social communication in the early 1890s, Latinas/os faced an unprecedented rise in increasingly negative stereotypes and depictions of their culture. In the images created by the film industry, the nature of Latina/o culture was increasingly presented as one without morals; a culture and a people predisposed to criminal activity, vice, and—for Latinas in particular—wantonness. In 1894, one of the very first narrative films ever made was produced by Thomas Alva Edison and titled *Pedro Esquirel and Dionecio Gonzales: Mexican Duel*. The film depicted two Mexican men fighting each other with knives in an unlawful duel. This would be the start of the violent *bandido* and **Greaser** images that later would permeate Hollywood films and television ads, shaping the beliefs of U.S. audiences with regards to Mexicans and Latinas/os in light of these rigid stereotypes.

The 20th century brought an increase in dehumanized, criminalized images of Latinas/os in U.S. films, television, and the mass media. Beginning in 1908, with movies such as *The Greaser's Gauntlet*, the term "Greaser" became popularized in many American films. Films such as *Tony the Greaser* (1911), *The Girl and the Greaser* (1913), *The Greaser's Revenge* (1914), and *Bronco Billy and the Greaser* (1914) sustained and expanded the negative convention of Mexicans and Latinas/os as a people who instinctually murdered, robbed, raped, plundered, lied, and manifested every vice shown on screen. In these films, the law—in terms of both authority figures and vigilantes—always caught up to the Mexican criminals or, less often, the Mexicans would submit to the Anglo-Saxon protagonists and assimilate to their rules. The Greaser depictions were protested by Latinas/os in the United States and in other parts of the world, but they remained an explicit staple of films with Mexican or other brown-skinned characters until 1934, when these negative portrayals temporarily were restrained. Greaser images, however, eventually would make their way back onto the screen.

During the Second World War, the now infamous **Sleepy Lagoon** case of 1942 resulted in the arrest of more than 600 Latino **youth** in Los Angeles and the conviction of 12 of them for murder and 5 for assault without the right of due process (Escobar 1999). Racially biased articles and press hysteria published in the *Los Angeles Times* and the *Herald-Express* newspapers fueled these arrests, influenced the ensuing trial, and eventually led to a socio-political climate that catalyzed what became known as the **Zoot Suit Riots**. These media depictions also helped to spark a unified rage against Latinas/os, and particularly against all Mexicans in Los Angeles. During the Zoot Suit Riots biased news reports in the *Los Angeles Times* defended young, white soldiers—mostly navy men—after they brutally mobbed, beat, and humiliated urban Mexican and **Chicana/o** youth in Los Angeles and East L.A.

Similar press coverage demonized **Puerto Rican** youth in 1959 after Puerto Rican **gang** members, including **Salvador "Capeman" Agron**, committed a murder in New York City. The press sensationalized the murder then stereotyped and attacked the Puerto Rican community in general. Shortly after the Agron incident, one of the most critically acclaimed films of all time, "West Side Story," swept the Academy Awards. The film depicted Puerto Rican youth as the antagonistic members of a criminal gang who kill the seemingly irreproachable white leader of the Jets gang as they vie to take over the entire neighborhood with their stereotypical spitfire girlfriends. At the same time, Greaser images made a comeback in the 1960s with the film, "One Eyed Jacks." Once again, this film blew the door open for a new generation of films that essentialized Latinas/os as vile, dirty, criminal "Greasers."

With increasing **Cuban**, **Colombian**, and Mexican immigration to the United States during the 1970s and 1980s, Hollywood responded with wariness and alarm. One of the most notorious films that stereotyped Cubans specifically and all Latinas/os in general was Brian de Palma's *Scarface*. The main character, Tony Montana, chooses a life of petty crime then, later, organized crime, which leads him to sell and consume copious quantities of **drugs**. He also is depicted as an incorrigible gangster who resorts to lying, physical abuse, and murder while vying for control over the Miami drug trade in competition with Colombian counterparts. The Cuban community protested this depiction during the production of the film and also upon its release. It became a cult classic, however, and it still exerts much influence in popular culture today.

Latinas/os and the Media: The Late 1980s to the Present

In 1989, Fox Network premiered the television series "Cops," currently one of the longest running programs in the United States. "Cops" has received considerable criticism for its common overrepresentation of poor blacks and Latinas/os allegedly involved in criminal activity. It is important to note that the show also overrepresents white officers as the main enforcers of the law. These factors combined create a "docu-reality" that reinforces and creates new stereotypes and conventions that have real-world impact on **police** practices, including **racial profiling** and unequal sentencing for people of color.

Popular **media** representations of Latina/o culture as morally corrupt and prone to criminality influence the way that Latinas/os are stereotyped and treated by society. Twice as many white Americans hold the belief that they are much more likely to be victimized by a person of color than at the hands of a white person. This idea is perpetuated despite the fact that whites are three times more likely to be victimized by other whites than by people of color. Moreover, upwards of three-quarters of the general **public** says that they form opinions on crime based on what is read in the newspaper or what is seen on the TV news. The mainstream media still routinely skews depictions of Latinas/os as an ethnic group prone to acts of crime. The stereotype of violent Latino youth, in particular, is compounded by the fact that Latinos and blacks are roughly 15 times more likely to be identified by the police as gang members as compared to their white peers. These portrayals foster racial profiling of Latinas/os and inequitable treatment throughout the criminal justice system (Dorfman & Schiraldi 2001).

Even though Latinas/os often are depicted in a negative manner in the mass media, it is equally troubling that, altogether, Latinas/os and Latina/o issues rarely are covered in the media. Yet, when they are discussed, Latinas/os themselves often are excluded from the conversation. There are more than 50 million Latinas/os in the United States. Nonetheless, in 2006, out of more than 12,000 news stories from the 3 largest television networks, fewer than 1 percent of those stories were about Latinas/os or Latina/o issues. Within the sparse coverage that Latina/o issues get in the news, there often is a tendency to focus too much attention on one major issue, as occurred in 2004 when the network news stories focused 35 percent of their attention on the issue of immigration, to the detriment of other important issues affecting Latinas/os (National Association of Hispanic Journalists 2006). This has led to the stereotype of Latinas/os as a monolithic, one-dimensional group of people who are often seen as immigrants and not fully participating and contributing citizens of the United States.

Many conservative media pundits have jumped at the opportunity to exploit the consistently hot-button issue of immigration, but no one has pushed the issue front and center and added as much invective to the immigration debate in the mass media as has CNN's former host, Lou Dobbs, who resigned from his post in November 2009. Dobbs has been critiqued for making many false allegations against undocumented immigrants, and particularly against those of Latina/o origin. In 2003, on his nationally televised show Dobbs alleged that one-third of all inmates in federal prisons were immigrants. Later, Dobbs went further and falsely alleged that one-third of federal prisoners were "illegal immigrants." Experts on unauthorized immigrants have handily invalidated these assertions by confirming that they comprise significantly fewer than one-third of all federal inmates. Dobbs made additional false claims on his program, stating that Latina/o immigrants had created a new outbreak of leprosy in the United States and that the U.S. Hispanic Chamber of Commerce was commiserative with regard to Mexico's exportation of "illegal aliens" and narcotics into the United States. These claims also were proven false and Dobbs eventually apologized for having made those statements.

See also: Part I essays: Latinas/os and the U.S. Criminal Justice System; Policing and Latina/o Communities; Incarceration and Latinas/os in the United States; Latina/o Youth and Criminal Justice. Part II entries: Chicanas/os; Colombians; Cubans; Hate Crimes; Mexicans and Mexican Americans; Texas Rangers; Victims.

Further Reading

Bender, Steven. 2003. *Greasers and gringos: Latinos, law, and the American imagination.* New York: New York University Press.

Berg, Charles Ramírez. 2002. *Latino images in film: Stereotypes, subversion, resistance.* Austin, TX: University of Texas Press.

Carrigan, William D., and Clive Webb. 2003. The lynching of persons of Mexican origin or descent in the United States, 1848–1928, *Journal of Social History* 37: 411–38.

Delgado, Richard. (2009). The law of the noose: A history of Latino lynching. *Harvard Civil Rights and Civil Liberties Review* 44: 297–312.

Dorfman, Lori, and Vincent Schiraldi. 2001. Off balance: Youth, race & crime in the news. Building Blocks for Youth. http://www.cclp.org/documents/BBY/offbalance.pdf. Accessed November 13, 2015.

Doyle, Aaron. 2003. *Arresting images: Crime and policing in front of the television camera.* Toronto, Canada: University of Toronto Press.

Escobar, Edward J. 1999. *Race, police, and the making of a political identity: Mexican Americans and the Los Angeles Police Department, 1900–1945.* Los Angeles, CA: University of California Press.

Greene, Judith, and Kevin Pranis. 2007. *Gang wars: The failure of enforcement tactics and the need for effective public safety strategies.* Justice Policy Institute Report. http://www.justicepolicy.org/research/1961. Accessed November 13, 2015.

Keller, Gary D. (ed.). 1985. *Chicano cinema: Research, reviews, and resources.* Binghamton, NY: Bilingual Press.

Leonhardt, David. 2007 (May 30). Immigrants and prison. *New York Times*. http://www.nytimes.com/2007/05/30/business/301eonside.html?ex=1184299200&en=e350a7f3a7435f38&ei=5070. Accessed November 25, 2015.

Martínez, Ramiro, Jr. 2002. *Latino homicide: Immigration, violence, and community*. New York, NY: Routledge.

Morín, José Luis. 2009. *Latino/a rights and justice in the United States: Perspectives and approaches*. 2nd ed. Durham, NC: Carolina Academic Press.

National Association of Hispanic Journalists. 2006. Network brownout report: The portrayal of Latino and Latino issues on network television news, 2005. National Association of Hispanic Journalists. http://www.nahj.org/resources/2006Brownout.pdf.

Prescott, William H. 1843. *History of the conquest of Mexico*. New York, NY: Harper & Brothers.

Riera, Emilio G. 1987. *Mexico visto por el cine extranjero*. Guadalajara, Mexico: Universidad de Guadalajara Ediciones Era.

Rodríguez, Clara E. (ed.). 1997. *Latin looks: Images of Latinas and Latinos in the U.S. media*. Boulder, CO: Westview Press.

Rosales, F. Arturo. 1996. *Chicano: The history of the Mexican American civil rights movement*. Houston, TX: Arte Público Press.

Woll, Allen L. 1980. *The Latin image in American film*. Revised edition. Los Angeles, CA: UCLA Latin American Center Publications.

Mexican American Legal Defense and Education Fund (MALDEF).

See Part I essays: Incarceration and Latinas/os in the United States; Latinas and the U.S. Criminal Justice System; Policing and Latina/o Communities. Part II entries: Chicanas/os; Civil Rights; Community-Based Latina/o Advocacy Organizations; Hate Crimes; Legal Advocacy Groups; Segregation.

Mexicans and Mexican Americans

Isabel Martínez

Comprising approximately 67 percent of the nation's Latina/o population, Mexicans and Mexican Americans represent the largest Latina/o subgroup in the United States. Totaling 29.7 million, the vast majority of people of Mexican descent is native-born, with only 11.7 million being foreign born. The Mexican population continues to be predominantly concentrated in the United States Southwest, with numerous Mexican families boasting four and five generations of settlement (Telles & Ortiz 2008). New destinations for Mexican immigrant settlement in recent years, however, have included southern states such as Georgia and North Carolina, Midwestern states such as Ohio and Nebraska, and the Eastern seaboard, including New Jersey and New York.

Unlike any other population in the United States except for Native Americans, Mexicans can be considered original inhabitants of the United States, as the conquest of the northern territories of Mexico from 1836–1848 led to absorption of Mexicans into the United States. Overnight, Mexican citizenship changed to U.S. citizenship. Prior to the signing of the Treaty of Guadalupe-Hidalgo, Mexican residents living in current-day California, Arizona, New Mexico, Colorado, Utah, and Texas were Mexican citizens. After the treaty was signed, however, these residents were United States citizens—in other words, the "border crossed them, they did not cross the border." Despite this transfer of citizenship, however, people of Mexican descent in the United States continue to be viewed as foreigners in their own land, different from "true Americans," and as second-class citizens.

The Birth of the Mexican Population

Mexicans are people borne of violent conquest and colonization. Perhaps best characterized in the story of *La Malinche*, an indigenous woman who was raped by a Spanish conquistador, the Mexican identity is defined as a forced *mestizaje*, or the brutal mixing of European and indigenous ethnicities. In postcolonial times, however, indigenous peoples as well as those of African descent continue to be ignored and rendered invisible. Although it was once believed that Mexico's indigenous roots could be rendered obsolete through *mestizo* mating, currently, there are more than 10 million indigenous peoples in Mexico. It would take the 1994 Zapatista uprising to remind Mexicans and global citizens alike of this indigenous element of the Mexican identity.

Rarely discussed are other racial and ethnic groups' contribution to the heterogeneous identity of Mexico, namely the inclusion of African-descent peoples in the northern states of Coahuila, as well as the southern states of Oaxaca, Guerrero, and Veracruz. Africans arrived in Mexico primarily through two methods: as slaves, brought to New Spain by Spanish conquistadors, or as runaway slaves or slaves who had otherwise escaped the brutal conditions of the United States South. In spite of their presence since the 16th century, it would not be until 500 years after Mexico's independence that the Mexican government would officially acknowledge "African" as the third race of Mexico. Currently, black Mexican activists estimate the presence of approximately one million Afro-Mexicans in Mexico.

In the United States, Anglo-Saxon settlers established their racial superiority early and, as such, justified their increasingly aggressive settlement practices. Invoking "**Manifest Destiny**"—their God-given right to expand westward—Anglo-Saxon settlers began to emphasize their "white" heritage as pure and superior to Mexicans' *mestizaje*, or mixed-racial heritage. The Mexican race was marked as inferior and socially distant from the pure whiteness of Anglo-Saxons, and Mexicans were designated as the racial "other" (Martinez 1997; Mirandé 1987). Even prior to the annexation of Texas and the subsequent war with Mexico, Mexicans were characterized as lowly, inferior, barbaric, and cruel. Portraying Mexicans as such allowed Anglos to justify their own criminal activity and lawlessness, as they violated treaties and informal agreements with the government of Mexico. These characterizations formed the basis of Anglo-Saxon expansionism—albeit illegal—conducted against undeserving savages. Hence, the civilized, lawful Anglos were "rescuing" these lands from the backwards Mexicans.

Race-Based Colonization

Beginning in the 1830s, Anglo-Saxon racial superiority was framed by its contrast with the Mexican peoples' racial inferiority. Seeking explanations for their violent expansion, Anglo-Saxon settlers emphasized this and, as a result of racial inferiority, Mexico's inability to manage its lands. Instead, it was the racial purity and superiority of Anglo-Saxons that could best manage the current-day U.S. Southwest.

Although sometimes accepting of light-skinned elites, it was the mongrelization of Mexicans, darker-skinned *mestizos* and indigenous Mexicans who Anglo-Saxons most loathed and viewed as inferior. According to Anglo-Americans, racially mixed Mexicans were doubly despicable. Due to their miscegenation, *mestizos* were hostile in temperament, inheriting the most despised qualities of both Spaniards and Indians. Whereas the *mestizo's* Spanish's savagery was rooted in the Inquisition, the *mestizo* also possessed the indigenous cruelty coursing through his veins.

Compounding ideas about Mexicans' backwardness was Mexico's central religion: Catholicism. Similar to later depictions of the predominantly Catholic Irish and Italian immigrants in the Northeast, Anglo Protestants believed that Mexicans' adherences to Catholicism mixed with indigenous practices further proved their inferiority.

After the United States-Mexico War and Mexico's loss of more than 55 percent of its territory, Anglo violence continued against Mexicans, even those who were now considered citizens under the conditions outlined in the Treaty of Guadalupe-Hidalgo. Any Mexicans who had resided in territories obtained by the United States were granted U.S. citizenship. Despite this citizenship, however, Anglo settlers continued to harass and terrorize these residents. Whereas Anglos previously had separated the Mexican nationality from race, with their newfound citizenship and reignited hostilities, Anglos now conflated nationality and race, and began to pass legislation emphasizing the Mexican mixed race. In 1855, the California legislature passed the Vagrancy Act, more commonly known as the "**Greaser Act**." The anti-loitering law specifically targeted those of Spanish and Indian blood, or Mexicans, for vagrancy, criminalizing not only noncriminal behavior, but also Mexicans.

Looking to extend their racial domination beyond their victory, Anglo settlers also looked to evict individual Mexican (now U.S. citizen) landowners from lands that were rightfully theirs. Economic competition was the primary catalyst for employing intimidation and terror to force Mexicans to relinquish these lands, as they proved to be financially successful in both the agricultural and mining industries. Anglo settlers quickly passed new laws challenging their ownership, as well as crippling their economic advantages.

Some Mexican residents were successful in using the Treaty of Guadalupe-Hidalgo and Anglo courts to retain their legally entitled lands and industries, which they had acquired prior to the war. When legal avenues to acquire desired lands and industries failed, Anglo settlers often turned to extralegal means to intimidate and rid the United States southwest of Mexicans, and Mexicans of their lands and other property. Through violent tactics, as well as harassment and intimidation, Anglos began a campaign to confiscate land. Met with Mexican resistance, Anglos turned to systematic violence against so-called "bandits" that would last well into the 20th century. During this period, Anglos engaged in the violation of Mexican American citizens' civil liberties, and deportations, **lynchings**, imprisonment, and other forms of physical abuse—including the unprovoked killing of Mexicans—was common.

The desire to acquire lands and property from Mexicans led to wide-scale confrontations. One such conflict was the Salt War in 1877—an attempt the takeover of salt mines in New Mexico. Despite their status as citizens, Anglo settlers redefined Mexicans as foreigners and subjected them to discriminatory policies. Only enforced against Latin American miners, taxes often were imposed and if unpaid would become grounds for eviction and even violence.

In Texas, the newly hyphenated "Mexican-Americans" were **racially profiled** and characterized as lawless *bandidos* and ruthless outlaws. Complaints frequently were filed against them with the United States government to initiate investigations into their activities. In fact, an American Presidential Commission was established in Texas to file complaints against Mexican-Americans in the border region. The Mexican government, in turn, also conducted its own independent assessment of allegations against Mexican Americans. In 1873, the Mexican Border Commission concluded that many of the allegations made by Texans were unfounded, and that instead Indians and Texans disguised as Indians or Mexicans were committing many of the crimes—including cattle and horse theft. Anglo settlers used accusations of Mexican criminal behavior to justify acts against innocent Mexican and Mexican American citizens. **Vigilante** groups, including the **Texas Rangers**, went as far as violating international treaties to cross the United States-Mexico border to steal cattle and livestock in Mexican territories. When confronted, these vigilante groups argued that they were merely reconfiscating property that had been reported stolen from Anglo residents.

In spite of Anglo cruelty, narratives of Anglo-Mexican relations commonly emphasized the savagery of Mexican men. Mexican women, however, were not immune from stereotypical characterizations. In many instances, Mexican women were sexualized, describing them as the "Spanish maid, with eyes of fire," desirable to Anglo men, and Mexican male counterparts were described as being "sunk in sloth" (Horsman 1981, 233). In contrast, few accounts describe acts of violence by Anglos against Mexican women. In once such account, a Mexican woman, Chepita, is documented as the first woman executed in the state of Texas. Lynched in 1863, Chepita was charged with killing an Anglo man, despite little evidence linking her to the murder. Her execution only demonstrated the intolerance for Mexican on Anglo violence, regardless of gender.

Contemporary Criminalization of Mexicans and Mexican Americans

The beginning of the 20th century only reinforced the racialization and criminalization of Mexicans and Mexican Americans in the United States. The legal construction of race supported a **black/white binary paradigm** in which Mexicans, although legally deemed "white," were never granted equal rights as European, Anglo white citizens. Mexican Americans in the United States were considered "alien" citizens (born in the United States with formal citizenship, but viewed as foreigners), and thus they were subject to Jim Crow–type segregation and discrimination in the Southwest.

Challenges to institutionalized and systematic racism in the criminal justice system were not successful until midway through the 20th century. In ***Hernandez v. Texas***, a case decided by the U.S. Supreme Court in 1954, attorneys backed by the League of **United Latin American Citizens (LULAC)** successfully argued that Mexicans were eligible for protection under the Fourteenth Amendment, but had not been granted such in civil and criminal trials. Rather, Mexicans had been excluded from jury service, denying Mexicans their right to a trial by a jury of their peers. Legally categorized as "white," the courts had maintained that all-white juries were constitutional and that Mexicans did not constitute a separate group in need of special protection. Gus Garcia, a LULAC attorney, effectively asserted before the Supreme Court that Mexicans were perceived and treated as members of a separate class in their communities, and thus deserved jury representation. The Supreme Court ruling in favor of Mexican Americans in the *Hernandez* case would have widespread implications not only for the treatment of Mexicans in the criminal justice system, but in other areas in which the civil rights of Latinas/os were infringed.

Criminalization of Mexican Immigration

With the beginning of the 20th century also came increased immigration restrictions.

Although not the original target of exclusion or national quotas, Mexicans experienced restriction through immigration policies that were meant to address unauthorized Chinese and European immigration. By the end of the 1880s, visa requirements and border-control policies were implemented, including the head tax of 1882, the Contract Labor Law of 1885, and the literacy test of 1917. In times of labor shortages, these requirements were waived so that Mexican laborers could work in the United States agriculture industry. Over the next 50 years, Mexicans would be subject to policies promoting both authorized and unauthorized immigration. They also typically encountered harsh deportation policies during difficult economic times. The Great Depression created significant levels of unemployment. Consequently, foreign labor no longer was needed and was viewed as a threat to native workers. As a result, Mexicans as well as Mexican Americans were deported en masse. During World War II, as native workers were sent to fight, Mexican labor was needed once more, and the *Bracero* program was born. During these years, Mexico's position as the largest supplier of exploitable unskilled labor to the United States became institutionalized. From 1942 to 1964, the United States and Mexico coordinated this state-sanctioned and supervised labor program in which Mexican males were imported to work for low wages in poor conditions at predominantly unskilled, agricultural work sites. Over time, depending on economic circumstances in the United States, Mexicans were demonized as criminals and undesirables and deported, or were lured and encouraged to come to the United States as a source of cheap labor to be exploited for the benefit of U.S. business interests.

Despite efforts to regulate the immigration of Mexican workers, some formal policies created conditions in which Mexicans and employers felt no option but to engage in unauthorized immigration. For one, certain states were not granted *Bracero* contracts, including Texas. In response, Texas agricultural industry owners, competing with *Bracero* states, recruited and contracted non-*Bracero* Mexicans. Additionally, *Bracero* labor contracts and conditions oftentimes were unjust and dishonest, with many employers paying Mexican workers less than what was agreed upon, and preventing workers' departure. To avoid such exploitation, many Mexicans immigrated without authorization so that they could negotiate their own wages, move from work site to work site, and return home if needed. In light of these conditions, an unauthorized Mexican immigrant population began to grow. Nearly 25 years later, the Immigration Reform and Control Act of 1986 (IRCA) legalized many unauthorized Mexican workers. Families oftentimes were excluded, however, leading to the widespread unauthorized immigration of families not included in IRCA.

The Hyper-Criminalization of Mexican Immigrants

Following the trajectory of managing Mexican entry into the United States from the Department of Labor, to the Department of Justice, to (now), the Department of Homeland Security, Anglo perceptions of Mexicans—and especially of Mexican immigrants—have been transitioned from being surplus or competing labor to being criminals and drug smugglers, and to being potential terrorists. Only to accelerate in the post-September 11 era, immigration and criminal justice systems converged more explicitly during the Clinton Administration, with Mexican immigrants, in particular, becoming hyper-criminalized. The Illegal Immigration Reform and Immigrant Responsibility

Act of 1996 (IIRIRA) included provisions which criminalized not only entry into the United States without inspection, but efforts at family reunification, including the falsifying of information about children by immigrant parents, and the hiring of unauthorized immigrants. Other practices which have intensified since 9/11 have included the increased militarization of the U.S.-Mexico border, as well as increases in the number of workplace raids and deportations.

Immigration enforcement was respatialized, as enforcement was no longer maintained only at the U.S.-Mexico border but, increasingly, "interior immigration policing practices" were adopted, which included workplace raids and local law enforcement stops across the country. For example, section 287(g) of the Immigration and Nationality Act has allowed state and local law enforcement officials to engage in practices formerly controlled by federal immigration officials, such as identifying, arresting, and incarcerating immigrant offenders. Meant to target only serious criminals, immigrants with minor infractions—driving a car that has a broken taillight, for instance—have been criminalized and have resulted in deportation hearings. Section 287(g) has been associated with racial profiling and is considered by some analysts as disproportionately resulting in the incarceration and deportation of Mexican and Central American individuals who pose no serious criminal threat.

The country also has witnessed efforts to toughen immigration enforcement, particularly on the state level. On April 23, 2010, Arizona governor Jan Brewer signed SB 1070 into law, criminalizing the failure to produce immigration documents and providing local and state law enforcement with the power to identify and charge individuals deemed "reasonably suspicious" of being an unauthorized immigrant with criminal (illegal) trespassing. If unable to produce proper documentation, the individual could be transported to a federal immigration facility, be fined, detained for months, and eventually be deported. Many scholars and immigrant rights groups assert that the impetus for such laws comes largely from the conflation of Mexican immigrants with criminality.

It could be argued that laws such as 278(g) and SB 1070 hyper-criminalize all unauthorized immigrants. Another view is that the intersection of recent changes to immigration law and the longstanding and persistent racial hierarchy and bias in the United States tend to ensure that Mexicans and other Latin Americans are disproportionately affected by new immigration law enforcement measures. As recently found by a federal district court judge in the lawsuit against Maricopa County, Arizona, Sheriff Joe Arpaio in *Ortega Melendres et al. v. Arpaio et al.* (2013), immigration law enforcement practices have been abused and have resulted in violations of the constitutional rights of Mexican Americans, as they have been unlawfully targeted and detained through practices encouraged and carried out by the sheriff's office. In determining what is "reasonably suspicious," one's individual's physical appearance is not supposed to be the determining factor.

See also: Part I essays: Latinas/os and the U.S. Criminal Justice System; Latina/o Immigrants, Crime, and Justice; Incarceration and Latinas/os in the United States; Gangs in the United States and Latina/o Communities; Crime and the U.S.-Mexican Border. Part II entries: Chicanas/os; Civil Rights; Deportation; Hate Crimes; Language Rights in the Courts; Media Depictions.

Further Reading

Alcala, R. C. 2001. From Chingada to Chingona. *Aztlan* 26(2): 31–61.

Anzaldúa, Gloria. 1987. *Borderlands/La Frontera: The new mestizo.* San Francisco, CA: Aunt Lute Books.

Archibold, R. A. 2010 (April 24). Arizona enacts stringent law on immigration. *The New York Times*, at A.

Bender, Steven W. 2003. *Greasers and Gringos: Latinos, law and the American imagination.* New York: New York University Press.

Coleman, Matthew. 2007. Immigration geopolitics beyond the Mexico-U.S. border. *Antipode* 39 (1): 54–76. doi: 10.1111/j.1467-8330.2007.00506.x.

Cruz-Carretero, Sagrario. 2005. Yanga and the black origins of Mexico. *Review of Black Political Economy* 33 (1): 73–77.

Cruz-Carretero, Sagrario. 2006. *The African Presence in Mexico: From Yanga to the present.* Chicago, IL: Mexican Fine Arts Center Museum.

De Leon, Arnold. 1983. *They called them Greasers: Anglo attitudes towards Mexicans in Texas, 1821–1900.* Austin, TX: University of Texas Press.

Department of Homeland Security, Office of Immigration Statistics. 2008. *2008 yearbook of immigration statistics.* Washington, DC: Department of Homeland Security.

Gomez, Laura E. 2008. *Manifest destinies: The making of the Mexican American race.* New York: New York University Press.

Haney López, Ian. 1994. The social construction of race: Some observations on illusions, fabrication and choice. *Harvard Civil Rights-Civil Liberties Law Review* 1: 1–62.

Hing, Bill Ong. 1998. Immigrant as criminal: Punishing the dreamers. *Hastings Women Law Journal* 9(1): 70–97.

Horsman, Reginald. 1981. *Race and manifest destiny: The origins of American racial Anglo Saxonism.* Cambridge, MA: Harvard University Press.

Kil, Sang Hea, and Cecilia Menjívar. 2006. The "war on the border": Criminalizing immigrants and militarizing the U.S.-Mexico Border. In *Immigration and crime: Race, ethnicity and violence*, edited by Ramiro Martínez, Jr. and Abel Valenzuela, Jr., 164–88. New York: New York University Press.

Lewis, Laura A. 2001. Of ships and saints: History, memory and place in the making of Moreno Mexican identity. *Cultural Anthropology* 16(1): 62–82.

Lopez, Felipe H. 2002. The construction of Mexican identity. *Rutgers Law Review* 54: 989–98.

Martinez, George A. 1997. The legal construction of race: Mexican Americans and whiteness. *Harvard Latino Law Review* 2: 321–47.

Mirandé, Alfredo. 1987. *Gringo justice.* Notre Dame, Indiana: University of Notre Dame Press.

Munoz Ramirez, Gloria, and Hermann Bellinghausen. 2008. *El fuego y la palabra: Una historia del Movimiento Zapatista.* San Francisco, CA: City Lights Books.

Okeowo, Alexis. 2009 (September 15). Blacks in Mexico. *Time.* Online Edition.

Paz, Octavio. 1976. *El laberinto de la soledad.* 3rd edición. Distrito Federal: Fondo de Cultura Económica.

Pew Hispanic Center. September 2009. Hispanics of Mexican origin in the United States, 2007. Washington, DC: Pew Hispanic Center.

Sadowski-Smith, Claudia. 2008. Unskilled labor migration and the illegality spiral: Chinese, European and Mexican indocumentados in the United States, 1882–2007. *American Quarterly* 60(3): 779–804.

Samora, Julian. 1971. *Los Mojados: The Wetback story.* Notre Dame: University of Notre Dame Press.

Telles, Edward E., and Vilma Ortiz. 2008. *Generations of exclusion: Mexican Americans, assimilation and race.* New York: Russell Sage Foundation.

Vélez-Ibañez, Carlos. 1996. *Border visions: Mexican cultures of the Southwest United States.* Tucson, AZ: University of Arizona Press.

Webb, Walter Prescott. 1965. *The Texas Rangers: A century of frontier defense*. Austin: University of Texas Press.

Weber, David J. (ed.). 1973. *Foreigners in their native land: Historical roots of the Mexican Americans*. Albuquerque, NM: University of New Mexico Press.

Weissman, Deborah M., Rebecca C. Headen, and Karen Lewis Parker. 2009. The policies and politics of local immigration enforcement laws: 287g Program in North Carolina. Chapel Hill, NC: American Civil Liberties Union of North Carolina Legal Foundation and the Immigration & Human Rights Policy Clinic, University of North Carolina at Chapel Hill. http://www.law.unc.edu/documents/clinicalprograms/287gpolicyreview.pdf.

Wilbur-Cruce, Eva Antonia. 1987. A beautiful, cruel country. Tucson, AZ: University of Arizona Press.

Case Cited

Hernandez v. Texas, 347 U.S. 475 (1954).

Ortega Melendres et al. v. Arpaio et al. 989 F. Supp. 2d 822 (D.C. Ariz. 2013).

Minuteman Project, The. *See* Part I: essay: Crime and the U.S. Mexican Border. Part II entries: Hate Crimes; Vigilantism.

Miranda, Anthony. *See* Part I essay: Policing and Latina/o Communities. Part II entry: Latina/o Fraternal Law Enforcement Organizations.

Miranda v. Arizona, 384 U.S. 436 (1966)

Sandra Del Valle

An indigent Mexican American was the lead petitioner in *Miranda v. Arizona*, 384 U.S. 436 (1966), a consolidation of four criminal cases in which the Supreme Court first delineated the rights of suspects to Fifth Amendment protections before being questioned by **police**. In this landmark 5-to-4 decision, the Court decided that police officers must advise suspects in their custody of their right against self-incrimination before being questioned, and of their right to consult with counsel before and during questioning. Failure to advise suspects of what has come to be known as "*Miranda* rights" will render inadmissible any statement made by the suspect to the police. Further, the burden is on the prosecution to establish that defendants were indeed informed of these rights before any statement will be accepted into evidence.

Miranda, charged with rape, was described by the Court as "seriously disturbed" and having "pronounced sexual fantasies." He was taken into a special interrogation room and the police secured a confession. One of the salient and controversial features of the decision is that Miranda had not accused the police officers of using particularly coercive interrogation tactics. The Court was concerned with the ways in which an intimidating environment alone can overwhelm an individual's clear thinking. It stated that:

> [a]n individual swept from familiar surroundings into police custody, surrounded by antagonistic forces, and subjected to . . . techniques of persuasion . . . cannot be otherwise than under compulsion to speak. As a practical matter, the compulsion to speak in the isolated setting of the police station may well be greater than in courts or other official investigations, where there are often impartial observers to guard against intimidation or trickery.

The *Miranda* decision brought a nuanced psychological understanding to the interactions between police and the public. It created a model for mediating that relationship in way that serves law enforcement and maintains the integrity of the Fifth Amendment. As complex as the issue of self-incrimination is, it becomes moreso when linguistic and national origin issues are introduced. The scaffolding upon which the Fifth Amendment is built is language itself. As such, it is culturally based and sensitive to the linguistic varieties of experience. At a minimum, *Miranda* rights must be communicated in a language that the arrested person can understand. For those Latinos and other language minorities who are not fluent in English, critical questions arise as to whether *Miranda* rights were conveyed in the appropriate language, which can include questions of dialect, accent (as in *United States v. Martinez* (1979)), degrees of English, and, for recent immigrants, whether the foreignness of the culture generally contributed to an atmosphere of coercion or affected a suspect's knowledge of the U.S. criminal justice system (as in *United States v. Longoria* (2007)).

Language and culture present particularly complicated issues with which courts must contend. Although trial courts are tasked with weighing evidence and determining credibility, they most often operate within an Anglo and English-dominant context: the prosecution, defendants, witnesses, lawyers, and other ancillary players usually are English-fluent and Americanized even if within a minority culture. If *Miranda* issues arise, usually in the context of waiver of the rights, trial courts often find themselves treading through the waters of foreign lands. Often they must determine what level of English fluency a defendant possessed and whether it was sufficient for an understanding of *Miranda* warnings conveyed in English. The inquiry is critical because, to be valid, waivers must be knowing, intelligent, and voluntary. The waiver cannot be the product of coercion and the decision must have been made with a full awareness of both the nature of the rights being abandoned and the consequences of the decision to abandon them (*United States v. Barbour* (1995); *Miller v. Dugger* (1988); *United States v. Gonzalez* (1984); *United States v. Martinez* (1978)).

In *United States v. Longoria* (2007), one of the defendants, Juan Geraldo Arredondo, moved to suppress statements made after he waived his *Miranda* rights. Arredondo argued that the waiver was not valid because he was read the rights in English, and not in his native Spanish. In refusing to suppress the statement, the court found that Arredondo spoke fluent English. The court credited the police officer's testimony that Arredondo spoke to him only in English before and after his rights were read to him and never requested an interpreter. In *Valdez v. Ward* (2000), the appellate court upheld the trial court's decision that Valdez understood the *Miranda* rights read to him in English even though he used an interpreter intermittently throughout the trial. Other cases in this area of court decisions include *United States v. Todisco* (1981), in which the defendant's behavior in court supported the trial court's finding that he understood the *Miranda* rights read to him in his non-native language; *United States v. Sanchez-Valderuten* (1993), in the consensual search context in which the court had to distinguish between a defendant's "receptive English language skills" versus his proactive ability in speaking English; and *United States v. Corral* (1990), in the search context in which the court determined that the defendant had a "working knowledge" of English.

A waiver of *Miranda* rights is effective "[o]nly if the totality of the circumstances surrounding the interrogation reveal[s] both an uncoerced choice and the requisite level of comprehension" (*Moran v. Burbine* (1986)).

To determine whether a valid waiver had been obtained, a court "should consider all the circumstances surrounding the interrogation, including the defendant's age, experience, education, background and intelligence" (*United States v. Nakhoul* (1984); *Michigan v. Moseley* (1975)).

Reviewing the totality of the circumstances, the court in *United States v. Nakhoul* found that the defendant, a Lebanese national, probably did not understand the U.S. legal system sufficiently to realize the iconic status of *Miranda* rights in the United States such that the rights carried forward from the time of arrest to a later interrogation. The court found that although the first admission which was made in the police car soon after the rights were conveyed was admissible, a second admission made an hour and a half later, without the benefit of a re-reading, at headquarters was not (see also *United States v. Short* (1986), in which the court disallowed the use of a statement when the accused had only been living in the United States for three months, was socially isolated, and spoke only halting English). In *Thatsaphone v. Weber* (1998), the trial judge adopted the magistrate's recommendation that Thatsaphone's statements were involuntary because, given Thatsaphone's Laotian background, "merely summoning him to the police station, excluding him from his friend, and demanding information was sufficient coercion to overcome [his] resistance to confession" (*Thatsaphone* at 1046).

Providing *Miranda* rights in the suspect's native language through the use of a previously translated and printed card safeguards against attacks made against the confession on the basis of the quality of the translation. If a translation is attacked, however, it is the trial courts which must determine whether the translation was adequate. Trial courts are given great latitude and once a trial court has determined that a translation was adequate, an appellate court only will overturn that decision after a showing of abuse of discretion. One commentator has noted that to appeal a trial court's ruling on the adequacy of translations, a defendant would have to introduce evidence "of the questionable interpretation practices of the interpreter, the terms or legal concepts misused, or evidence demonstrating a defendant's lack of comprehension" (Cole & Maslow-Armand 1997, 204).

Miranda protections are not implicated unless a suspect has been taken into custody (see also *Beckwith v. United States* (1976)). The Supreme Court has held that whether a person is in custody is determined by reference to the "reasonable" person, an objective not a subjective standard. Under an objective standard, the officer's or suspect's own understanding of the situation is of no significance (*Berkemer v. McCarty* (1984)); *Stansbury v. California* (1994)). Whether the national origin or cultural background of a suspect could cause them to believe that they are in custody only was touched upon in *Thatsaphone*, and the lower court found that the defendant's cultural background could have caused him to believe that he was in custody when, in fact, he was free to leave. On appeal, the circuit court gave that argument short shrift, finding that not only was Thatsaphone's personal sense of no consequence, but that his English language skills were sufficient for him to understand the police officer's assurances that he was not in custody. The reasonable person standard, however, was developed with the U.S. citizen in mind. The nature of custody, control and freedom of movement, as well as the historical experience and attitude toward police officers generally all are culturally based and the U.S. model simply is inappropriate for many defendants.

Some of the issues raised by *Miranda* go to the very roots of language and culture, national origin, and national history. Trial and appellate courts, applying standards conceived and developed with Anglo-U.S. models, must respond to multifaceted factual scenarios with culturally appropriate norms. In some areas, applying current standards is a relatively easy matter, as when the record is quite clear that a defendant has lived in the country for decades or has a fluent command of English. Other times the scenario is much cloudier—the length of time an immigrant has lived in the country, his or her experience with law enforcement in their native land, and the extent of ease in using the English language are not issues that are subject to easy adjudication and the current norms might not always allow trial judges to consider all of these elements.

See also: Part I essay: Policing and Latina/o Communities. Part II entries: Civil Rights; Language Rights in the Courts.

Further Reading

Cole, Richard W., and Laura Maslow-Armand. 1997. The role of counsel and the courts in addressing foreign language and cultural barriers at different stages of a criminal proceeding. *Western New England Law* Review 19: 193–228.

Soltero, Carlos R. 2006. *Latinos and American law: Landmark Supreme Court cases*. Austin, TX: University of Texas Press.

Cases Cited

Beckwith v. United States, 425 U.S. 341 (1976).

Berkemer v. McCarty, 468 U.S. 420 (1984).

Michigan v. Moseley, 423 U.S. 96 (1975).

Miller v. Dugger, 838 F.2d 1530 (11th Cir. 1988).

Miranda v. Arizona, 384 U.S. 436 (1966).

Moran v. Burbine, 475 U.S. 412 (1986).

Stansbury v. California, 511 U.S. 318 (1994).

Thatsaphone v. Weber, 137 F.3d 1041 (8th Cir. 1998).

United States v. Barbour, 70 F.3d 580 (11th Cir. 1995).

United States v. Corral, 899 F.2d 991 (10th Cir. 1990).

United States v. Gonzales, 749 F.2d 1329 (9th Cir. 1984).

United States v. Longoria, 229 Fed. App. 885 (11th Cir. 2007).

United States v. Martinez, 588 F.2d 1227 (9th Cir. 1978).

United States v. Nakhoul, 596 F. Supp. 1398, 1401 (D. Mass. 1984), *aff'd sub. nom., United States v. El-Debeib*, 802 F.2d 442 (1st Cir. 1986).

United States v. Sanchez-Valderuten, 11 F.3d 985 (10th Cir.1993).

United States v. Short, 790 F.2d 464 (6th Cir. 1986).

United States v. Todisco, 667 F.2d 255 (2d Cir.1981).

Valdez v. Ward, 219 F.3d 1222 (10th Cir. 2000).

N

National Congress for Puerto Rican Rights (NCPRR). *See* Part I essay: Policing and Latina/o Communities. Part II entries: Civil Rights; Political Activist Groups; Puerto Ricans.

National Council of La Raza (NCLR). *See* Part I essays: Latinas/os and the U.S. Criminal Justice System; Policing and Latina/o Communities; Latina/o Youth and Criminal Justice. Part II entries: Community-Based Latina/o Advocacy Organizations; Immigration and Custom Enforcement (ICE); Legal Advocacy Groups; Political Activist Groups; Underrepresentation of Latinas/os in the Legal Profession.

Nativism. *See* Part II entries: Chicanas/os; Hate Crimes; Vigilantism.

O

Operation Wetback. *See* Part I essays: Latinas/os and the U.S. Criminal Justice System; Policing and Latina/o Communities. Part II entries: Chicanas/os; Deportation; Immigration Detention Centers.

P

Pachuco. *See* Part I essay: Gangs in the United States and Latina/o Communities. Part II entries: Chicanas/os; Cultural Criminology; LatCrit: Latina & Latino Critical Legal Theory, Inc.; Salinas, Raúl R. (raúlsalinas) (1934–2008).

Padilla, José (1970–). *See* Part I essays: Latina/o Youth and Criminal Justice; Incarceration and Latinas/os in the United States.

Pérez, Richie (1944–2004). *See* Part I essay: Policing and Latina/o Communities. Part II entries: Political Activist Groups; Puerto Ricans.

Plea/Plea Bargaining. *See* Part I essay: Incarceration and Latinas/os in the United States. Part II entries: Deportation; Deportation Laws; International Human Rights.

***Plyler v. Doe*, 457 U.S. 202 (1982).** *See* Part I essay: Latina/o Immigrants, Crime, and Justice. Part II entries: Chicanas/os; Legal Advocacy Groups.

Police Brutality. *See* Part I essays: Latinas/os and the U.S. Criminal Justice System; Latinas/o Immigrants, Crime, and Justice; Policing and Latina/o Communities; Gangs in the United States and Latina/o Communities; Crime and the U.S.-Mexican Border. Part II entries: Chicanas/os; Civil Rights; Civilian Oversight of Police; Political Activist Groups.

Policing and Latina/o Communities. *See* Part I essays: Latinas/os and the U.S. Criminal Justice System; Latina/o Immigrants, Crime, and Justice; Policing and Latina/o Communities; Latinas and the U.S. Criminal Justice System; Latina/o Youth and Criminal Justice. Part II entries: Civilian Oversight of Police; Colombians; Dominicans; Lesbian, Gay, Bisexual, and Transgender (LGBT); Mexicans and Mexican Americans; Texas Rangers; Vigilantism.

Policing and Race. *See* Part I essays: Latinas/os and the U.S. Criminal Justice System; Latina/o Immigrants, Crime, and Justice; Policing and Latina/o Communities; Latina/o Youth and Criminal Justice. Part II entries: Colombians; Mexicans and Mexican Americans; Texas Rangers; Vigilantism.

Policing/Law Enforcement. *See* Part I essays: Latinas/os and the U.S. Criminal Justice System; Latina/o Immigrants, Crime, and Justice; Policing and Latina/o Communities; The U.S. War on Drugs and Latina/o Communities; Latinas and the U.S. Criminal Justice System; Incarceration and Latinas/os in the United States; Gangs in the United States and Latina/o Communities; Latina/o Youth and Criminal Justice. Part II entries: Chicanas/os; Civil Rights; Civilian Oversight of Police; Colombians; Deportation; Dominicans; Latina/o Fraternal Law Enforcement Organizations; Media Depictions; Mexicans and Mexican Americans; Political Activist Groups; Vigilantism.

Policing Policy. *See* Part I essays: Latinas/os and the U.S. Criminal Justice System; Policing and Latina/o Communities; The U.S. War on Drugs and Latina/o Communities; Latina/o Youth and Criminal Justice. Part II entry: Civilian Oversight of Police.

Political Activist Groups

Louis Kontos

Latina/o political activism outside of the realms of electoral politics and **legal advocacy** has taken many forms. It often defies simple categorization and explanation. Certain recurring themes surface, however, in the work of various Latina/o groups to mobilize against injustice and empower their communities. Latina/o political activism frequently has combined the reaffirmation of culture and identity with efforts to contest government policies and practices on the federal, state, and local levels. Over the years, Latina/o groups have sought to organize around a broad range of causes, including reclaiming Mexican land grants; exerting the right to education, housing, and health care; protecting workers' rights; and ending **police brutality**.

Activism of the 1960s

The 1960s were a turning point. The Land Grants movement (1966–1969) began in New Mexico and Colorado centering on the issue of land tenure. It was organized by the Federal Alliance of Land Grants (La Alianza Federal de Mercedes). Pentecostal preacher Reies López Tijerina, founder of Alianza, argued that the 1848 Treaty of Guadalupe Hidalgo failed to protect the land rights of Mexicans from Anglo Americans who coveted those lands and that the Treaty merely "provided the appearance of fair treatment of Mexicans in compliance with international law" (Morín 2009, 52). Alianza sought the return of land in common to members of local communities who held Spanish and Mexican American Land Grants. Tijerina and his followers held protest marches in Albuquerque and Santa Fe, New Mexico, in July 1966. In October 1966, they occupied the Echo Amphitheater on the San Joaquin grant. In June 1967, Tijerina led a raid of the Rio Arriba Courthouse on the Tierra Amarilla grant, attempting to make a citizen's arrest of the district attorney. An armed struggle ensued and Tijerina fled. He eventually was captured and sentenced to three years in prison. The raid made Tijerina a legendary figure among young activists.

Another source of inspiration for Latina/o activist groups in the late 1960s and early 1970s came from Cesar Chavez. Born in Arizona, Chavez spent most of his early life working in California. He was recruited to a Community Service Organization (CSO) chapter in San Jose in 1952. The CSO—founded in 1947 by Fred Ross and Edward Roybal—started as a grassroots movement to organize Mexican American immigrants against labor exploitation, discrimination, and police brutality. Chavez learned organizing techniques from the CSO, and became its national director in 1958. He resigned in 1961, after being unable to convince the organization of the need to organize farm workers. A year later, Chavez, along with Dolores Huerta and Gilbert Padilla, organized grape pickers in California into the National Farm Workers Association (NFWA), which in 1973 was renamed United Farm Workers of America (UFWA). In 1965, the NFWA joined the grape strike started by the Filipino labor union Agricultural Workers Organizing Committee (AWOC). In 1966, AWOC merged with NFWA to become the Farm Workers Association Committee (UFWOC). The UFWOC / UFWA engaged in litigation and led boycotts and secondary boycotts that gained national attention and the support of clergy, university students, and **civil rights** groups. The philosophy of nonviolence of the UFW, inspired by Mahatma Gandhi and Martin Luther King, resonated with activists across a broad spectrum of movements at the time (Taylor 1975).

The Latina/o organizations that mobilized later had more radical demands and were more consistently militant in their tactics than were the Federal Alliance and the UFWA. The Mexican American Youth Organization (MAYO) became the avant-garde. It was formed in San Antonio in 1967 by a group of activists—José Angel Gutiérrez, Mario Compean, William "Willie" Velásquez, Juan Patlán, and Ignacio (Nacho) Pérez—who came to be known as "Los Cinco" (The Five). Los Cinco studied revolutionary theories and organizational models and met with movement leaders, including Reies López Tijerina. The politics of MAYO revolved around the **Chicana/o** movement and the idea of *Chicanismo*—cultural pride and rebirth—rejecting the idea of assimilation in favor of cultural pluralism. It published newspapers in San Antonio, Rio Grande Valley, Uvalde, and Kingsville. MAYO's educational agenda included bilingual teaching, hiring Chicana/o teachers, and including Mexican American courses in school curricula. It staged approximately 38 walkouts between 1967 and1972. Other forms of "direct action" included mass demonstrations and protests against segregation, police brutality, and inadequate education. In 1969, at the only national meeting of MAYO, activists decided to form La Raza Unida Party (RUP) as a third party. The RUP fielded candidates in South Texas for city council, school board, mayoral, and gubernatorial races. It won a total of 15 seats, including 2 mayoralties. MAYO eventually was integrated into RUP.

Among the most significant figures in the Chicana/o movement and RUP was Rodolfo "Corky" Gonzales. In 1969, he wrote the epic and inspirational poem, "I am Joaquin," which became a cornerstone of Chicano literature and identity. Gonzales gave the keynote address at the RUP's national convention in El Paso in 1972. In 1966, he resigned from the Democratic Party and founded Crusade for Justice. The Crusade sought to promote Chicano identity as distinct from Indian, European, and Mexican. It published the newspaper *El Gallo*, which contained coverage of current events, philosophical statements, news related to the organization, and poetry. The Crusade's members protested for better housing, educational opportunities, jobs, land reform, and in solidarity with striking workers. It is most well-known for organizing annual Chicano Youth Liberation conferences from 1969 to 1970. At the first of these conferences *El Plan Espiritual de Aztlán* was created.

The Chicano/a identity movement was galvanized by the Chicano poet Alurista (Alberto Baltaza Urista Heredia) who wrote the political manifesto, "*El Plan Espiritual de Aztlán*" (The Spiritual Plan of Aztlan). Alurista co-founded the San Diego State University (SDSU) chapter of *El Movimiento Estudiantil Chicano de Aztlán* (MEChA) and *Movimiento Estudiantil de Aztlán* (Chicano Student Movement of Aztlan). *El Plan Espiritual de Aztlán*, written in March of 1969 by Chicano activists who gathered at the Youth and Liberation Conference in Denver, Colorado, drew upon Aztec myth, the rhetoric of land grants in New Mexico, and political activism. It called for Chicanos to recognize themselves as a "new people," "bronze brothers," with a proud heritage and the need for unity and economic, social, and political self-determination.

In 1969, Chicana/o activists expanded the Plan's principles into the area of education reform. The Plan of Santa Barbara called for the University of California to establish a comprehensive Chicana/o Studies program that engaged the larger Chicana/o community. Education was identified as having particular significance because "without a strategic use of education, an education that places value on what we value, we will not realize our destiny. Chicanos [and Chicanas] recognize the central importance of institutions of higher learning to model progress, in this case, to the development of our community" (Movimiento Estudiantil Chicano de Aztlán [n.d.]). The Plan also called for consolidation of student groups into El Movimiento Estudiantil Chicano de Aztlán (the Chicano Student Movement of Aztlan). MEChA still is active on many campuses, particularly in the areas of civil rights, affirmative action, and immigration.

The Brown Berets

The Brown Berets originally called itself Young Citizens for Community Action (YCCA), and was founded in 1966 by six high school students from East L.A. The group participated in the Community Service Organization where they were introduced to Cesar Chavez. With financial support from Father John Luce, the group opened La Piranya, a coffeehouse where activists and civil rights leaders came to speak. In 1968, the YCCA adopted a uniform and became the **Brown Berets**. "Law enforcement abuses had transformed them from moderate reformers into visually distinctive and combative crusaders on behalf of justice for Chicanos" (Chavez 2002, 45). In 1969, the Brown Berets' newspaper, *La Causa*, reported that there were 28 chapters throughout the West and Midwest. The Brown Berets were actively involved with the UFW and the student movement, maintaining high visibility throughout. The group's tactics were confrontational and therefore controversial, and yet its political philosophy was not especially radical in historical context. Its "Ten Point Program" delineated its political philosophy and grievances, including with regard to the educational system, **policing** policies and tactics, and the justice system.

The "Ten Point Program" called for bilingual education and voting rights for non-English speakers as well as addressing the problems of housing and economic insecurity in Mexican American communities. It also made very specific demands to resolve problems Mexican Americans face involving policing and the criminal justice system. The Ten Point Program called for: a Civilian Police Review Board to be established and composed of people from the community, and be empowered to screen police officers prior to the officers being assigned to the communities; juries to be made composed of Mexican Americans only, if a Mexican American was being tried; police officers to be required to reside in the community and to know Spanish; and the use of the Second Amendment of the United States Constitution to protect their right to "bear arms to defend our communities against racist police" (Haney López 2003, 187).

Student Activism: Blowouts

The term "blowout" refers to a series of student walkouts that took place in East Los Angeles high schools in March 1968, involving more than 10,000 students at five schools. The first blowout happened on March 1, 1968, at Wilson High School to protest the cancellation of the student performance of the play, "Barefoot in the Park." On March 5, 1968, students walked out of Garfield High School. The number increased to 2,700 the next day. On March 8, students at Roosevelt, Garfield, Lincoln, and Wilson high schools walked out together and gathered for a rally at Hazard Park. Prior to the blowouts student activists at Garfield, Roosevelt, and Lincoln high schools had established strike committees and formulated demands, including smaller class sizes, better library facilities, hiring more Mexican American teachers, bilingual education, and community control of the school system. On the second day, police responded to the walkouts with **violence**. The Los Angeles police chief and Governor Reagan condemned the walkouts and blamed them on the Brown Berets. Criminal charges were filed against several Brown Beret ministers, the editor of *La Raza* newspaper, student leaders from UCLA and Sal Castro, and a faculty member from Lincoln High School who helped organize the walkouts. Together they came to be known as the "East L.A. 13." The indictments originally all were misdemeanors, and included disturbing the peace and trespassing on school grounds, but felony charges were added, including conspiracy to commit crimes. All charges were dropped in 1972.

Young Lords

Street organizations within Latina/o communities also were becoming politicized. The most notable among them was the **Young Lords**, which began as a "street **gang**" with seven members in Chicago in 1958–59. It reputedly took the name from Vice Lords of Chicago and Majestic Lords of New York. It renamed itself Young Lords Organization (YLO) to reflect its transformation. The 1966 Chicago riots—erupting in response to police brutality—politicized the group. According to General Secretary Cha Cha Jimenez (its last leader from the gang phase), it was at their convention in 1968 that the Young Lords decided to involve themselves in politics. Jimenez, the child of a migrant worker, recounted being personally and politically affected by encounters with Black Panther Fred Hampton and Chicano leader Corky Gonzalez.

The goals and methods of the Young Lords were spontaneous, unconventional, and controversial throughout. It established activist credentials by taking over a Community Conservation Council meeting in 1968, and a year later taking over the 18th District Chicago Avenue Police workshop meeting, which was held inside the police station. As YLO protests and activism continued, established rights groups joined the struggle, including the Latin American Defense Organization (LADO), the Latin American Student Organization (OLAS), and Mothers and Others (MAO).

The New York chapter of the Young Lords was founded on July 26, 1969, by a group of seven Puerto Rican **youth** who had formed a reading group at Queens College to study Puerto Rican and revolutionary texts. This group merged with another that had taken the name Young Lords in 1967. "Cha Cha was talking about revolution and socialism and the liberation of Puerto Rico and the right to self-determination," said Pablo "Yoruba" Guzmán, one of the founding members of the New York branch of the Young Lords Organization, in an interview. "That's what really got us started. That's all it was, man" (Herz 2009). Unlike its Chicago counterpart, this group of activists did not have a gang history. It made local news headlines by protesting the accumulation of garbage in East Harlem. It began the "garbage offense" by sweeping the neighborhood streets on Sundays. Community leaders joined. When the Sanitation Department refused a request for additional brooms, the group reacted by blocking the streets with uncollected garbage.

In the fall of 1960, the Lords moved to occupy the Methodist Church in East

Harlem. Felipe Luciano, the chairman, approached the altar to make the case to the congregation for a transformation of the church such that it could better serve the needs of the poor and the outcast. He was badly beaten by the New York City Police. The event was widely publicized and the Lords subsequently received an outpouring of community support. Three weeks later the group took over the building and named it "People's Church." The occupation, which lasted 11 days, was widely deemed a success.

In June 1970, the Lords "appropriated" a Health Department X-Ray truck to test community residents for tuberculosis. In the next month the group occupied Lincoln Hospital for more than 12 hours. It demanded greater services for the *barrio*; including maternity care, provisions for senior citizens, and drug-addiction treatment. During this time, organizational differences led to a break with the Chicago chapter. The New York group renamed itself Young Lords Party (YLP). The YLP subsequently organized several chapters in New York, California, New Jersey, Connecticut, Pennsylvania, and Wisconsin. Chapters were organized around three levels of command: "cadres" of rank-and-file members, "ministries" (e.g., of education, defense, etc.), and a "central committee." To serve as the organization's guiding document, the YLP published a 13-Point Program and Platform that outlined its political positions and demands. The YLP's demands included the self-determination of Puerto Ricans and all Latinas/os; an end to racism; equality for women; a cessation of U.S. militarism; freedom for political prisoners; and the creation of a socialist society.

The YLP also sought to address violence and crime in its communities by establishing a drug-rehabilitation program. Resistance from local drug dealers and organized crime stifled the group's ability to succeed. In response to the death of one of their members, **Julio Roldán**, while in police custody, the YLP took over the Methodist Church for a second time in 1970. Roldan was just one of a series of African Americans and Latinos who were found hung in jail cells in New York City, leading the YLP to again take over the church to demand justice in the case of Julio Roldán.

In the months that followed, the YLP led demonstrations for the independence of Puerto Rico and even attempted to establish itself on the island. The group was not embraced by any political party or rights organization in Puerto Rico, however, and internal debates ensued about whether the YLP should concentrate on the independence struggle or the problems **Puerto Ricans** faced in the diaspora. In July 1972, the YLP became the Puerto Rican Revolutionary Worker's Organization (PRRWO) under the leadership of Gloria Fontáñez. Its stated mission was to organize Latina/o workers toward building a revolutionary party in the United States. The PRRWO embraced Marxist-Leninist-Maoist thought, but deep internal ideological divisions persisted.

Contemporary Activism: Immigration and Criminal Justice

Latina/o activism now builds on a long legacy. Current actions include protest and lobbying efforts against ballot initiatives that target undocumented immigrants. In 1994 in California, for example, Proposition 187 mandated that school districts and post-secondary institutions stop educational services altogether for undocumented students. Students unable to verify their status were to be reported to the INS and to the California attorney general. The initiative also prohibited hospitals from providing nonemergency care to undocumented aliens, and mandated that hospitals report sick people whose status was in question. The initiative passed 2 to 1 with more than 5 million votes. In 1996, Proposition 209 prohibiting public institutions from considering race, sex, or ethnicity for admission and advancement was passed. Propositions 187 and 209 mobilized the Latina/o community, and Latina/o immigrants developed networks to deal with future legislation. In the ensuing years activists were successful in blocking English–only and other anti-immigrant initiatives.

Arizona now has become the focus of the immigration battle because its new law, SB 1070, requires government workers to report undocumented immigrants who seek public benefits, and allows police to question anyone "suspected" of being undocumented. Arizona activists have opposed these attempts to legalize and mandate **racial profiling** and discrimination, and also have taken issue with polarizing political rhetoric and unfounded claims about the nature and extent of crime committed by undocumented immigrants. Arizona Governor Brewer, for instance, repeatedly has claimed that crime along the **border** has risen sharply, whereas FBI reports show the opposite. Brewer also has made more-sensational claims, including that, "Our law enforcement agencies have found bodies in the desert either buried or just lying out there that have been beheaded" (*La Prensa San Diego* 2010). The public face of the Arizona law is not the governor, however; rather, Sherriff Arpaio has managed to assume that role. Arpaio's enforcement tactics include using tents as make-shift jails for undocumented immigrants, and giving speaking tours and interviews in which he routinely demonizes undocumented Mexican immigrants and defends the policy of local police serving as immigration agents. As a result, his office in Maricopa County and the venues of his public appearances have become sites of protests.

Police behavior always has been a central issue for Latina/o activists, many of whom suffered mistreatment by the police. The history of tensions between the police and Chicana/o communities has been well documented. In a study commissioned by the **National Council of La Raza**, *Lost Opportunities: The Reality of Latinos in the U.S. Criminal Justice System*, police practices in Latina/o neighborhoods were identified as a key factor behind the overrepresentation of Latinas/os in prison: "Latinos receive more severe treatment at all stages of the criminal justice system, beginning with police **stops** and ending with longer periods of incarceration, than similarly-situated White Americans" (Walker et al. 2004, 1). Police relations with Latina/o communities remain strained because police officers who abuse their authority by mistreating Latinas/os still are unlikely to suffer any real consequences. As the NCLR study points out: "Sadly, however, the justice system sometimes fails to live up to expectations. Individual police officers have engaged in brutality against suspected offenders, brutal or corrupt police officers often go unpunished" (Walker et al. 2004, 46).

The historic and systemic problem of lack of police accountability to Latina/o communities increasingly has become a central focus of community and movement organizations. Among them is the **National Congress for Puerto Rican Rights (NCPRR),** which has merged earlier models of activism with a political philosophy centered on community intervention, control, and oversight of police policies, plans, and conduct.

The NCPRR was co-founded in the early 1980s by **Richie Pérez (1944–2004)**, a former Young Lord. In New York City, the NCPRR participated in bringing together the families that formed Mothers Against Police Brutality (MAPB) in 1994. The founder of the MAPB, **Iris Báez**, unsuccessfully sought justice after her son Anthony was choked to death by police officer Francis Livoti. It turned out that Livoti had numerous civilian complaints against him—including for brutality—and that he previously had assaulted a police sergeant. Yet, NYPD official Louis Anemone praised Livoti after the killing, saying that the city needed more officers like him. Livoti's account that he did not use excessive force and that Báez put up a struggle was corroborated by other officers who arrived at the scene, but eventually was refuted by officer Daisy Boria. After her testimony, Boria required police protection, including bomb-sniffing dogs. As a result, she resigned from the NYPD.

The Báez case became noteworthy for yet another reason. Street organizations (**gangs**), particularly the Latin Kings, became involved with the MAPB and the NCPRR's **Justice Committee** because of the issue of police brutality and the Báez case in particular. As Pérez said, it resonated with Latino youth throughout New York City. The participation of gangs drew publicity and added controversy to a movement that otherwise would have been uncontroversial, at least in the *barrio*; a movement of mothers that sought police accountability and justice for the murder of their children by wayward police officers.

Over the years, the Justice Committee has remained active in organizing against police violence and racism. Inspired by its founder and leader, Richie Pérez, it remains dedicated to community organizing and education and to supporting victims of police violence and their families. Other locally based groups also have formed. One is El Grito de Sunset Park, which has been active in a Brooklyn community that has long complained of mistreatment and harassment at the hands of police officers. The group's most recent activities have involved organizing cop-watch efforts and pressuring local political representatives into taking steps to protect the community from police misconduct and use of excessive force.

Activism Focused on Gangs: Alex Sánchez and Homies Unidos

Police and government sources claim that Latina/o gangs are a problem that is getting worse; not only with increased size and involvement in violent crime, but also with supposedly rapidly developing international criminal conspiracies. The problem has been framed by these sources in such a manner as to help justify the position that the only viable option for dealing with gangs is increased suppression and criminalization of young people. As **Alex Sanchez**, founder of **Homies Unidos**, puts it, "They're criminalizing the youth, they're criminalizing the immigrants, they're criminalizing just about anything that they don't want in this country anymore" (quoted in Morín 2009, 139).

Homies Unidos was founded in 1996 in El Salvador by rival gang members in response to a rapidly escalating cycle of gang violence. The Los Angeles branch was co-founded by Sanchez in 1997. Homies has received wide praise and support for its intervention work, including its Epiphany Project, which provides classes for gang members to transform them into "peacemakers," and its Family Wellness Workshops, which deal with relationship and communication problems in the family context. Yet, Homies remains controversial. The fact that it works with gang members without requiring them to quit their organizations has made it possible for the Los Angeles Police Department and Federal Bureau of Investigation to depict it as "gang friendly" and to call its motives and commitments into question. Previous deportation efforts and recent felony charges against Sánchez have been widely condemned as politically motivated. He now is accused of being the person who "calls the shots" for MS-13, even though transcripts of telephone calls that serve as the basis for the indictment make it clear that Sánchez no longer is an active member. Activists and community organizers have interpreted the treatment of Homies by authorities as sending a clear message that they are stay to out of the way. Activists respond that this cannot be done without abandoning a large segment of youth as a lost cause.

See also: Part I essays: Policing and Latina/o Communities; Incarceration and Latinas/os in the United States; Gangs in the United States and Latina/o Communities; Crime and the U.S.-Mexican Border. Part II entries: Chicanas/os; Civil Rights; Civilian Oversight of Police; Community-Based Latina/o Advocacy Organizations; Legal Advocacy Groups; Puerto Ricans.

Further Reading

Abramson, Michael. 1971. *Palante: Young Lords Party*. New York, NY: McGraw-Hill.

Acuña, Rodolfo. 2004. *Occupied America: A history of Chicanos*. New York, NY: Pearson Longman.

Barrera, Mario. 1979. *Race and class in the Southwest: A theory of racial inequality*. Notre Dame, IN: University of Notre Dame Press.

Camarillo, Albert. 1996. *Chicanos in a changing society*. Cambridge, MA: Harvard University Press.

Chavez, Ernesto. 2002. *Mi raza primero: Nationalism, identity and insurgency in the Chicano Movement*. Berkeley, CA: University of California Press.

Democracy Now. 2009. "Influential Puerto Rican activist group the Young Lords marks 40th anniversary" [transcript]. Broadcast aired August 21, 2009. http://www.democracynow.org/2009/8/21/young_lords.

DeSipio, Louis, and Rodolfo de Garza. 1998. Immigration and immigration policy. In *Making Americans, remaking Americans: Immigration & immigrant policy*, edited by L. DeSipio and R. de Garza. Boulder, CO: Westview Press.

El Plan Espiritual de Aztlán. [n.d.]. http://www.insearchofaztlan.com/plan.html.

Escobar, Edward J. 1999. *Race, police and the making of a political identity*. Berkeley, CA: University of California Press.

Former PRRWO Cadres. [n.d.]. The degeneration of PRRWO: From revolutionary organization to neo-Trotskyite sect. http://www.mltranslations.org/US/degenprrwo.htm. Accessed November 14, 2015.

Gomez-Quinones, Juan. 1990. *Chicano politics: Reality and promise, 1940–1990*. Albuquerque, NM: University of New Mexico Press.

Gonzales, Rodolfo ("Corky"). 2005 (April 15). I am Joaquin. *CounterPunch*. http://www.counterpunch.org/gonzales04152005.html.

Gutierrez, Gregory (ed.). 2004. *The Columbia history of Latinos in the United States since 1960*. New York, NY: Columbia University Press.

Guzmán, Pablo. 1998. *La vida pura:* A Lord of the barrio. In *The Puerto Rican movement: Voices from the Diaspora*, edited by A. Torres and J. E. Velázquez, 155–72. Philadelphia, PA: Temple University Press.

Haney López, Ian F. 2003. *Racism on trial: The Chicano fight for justice*. Cambridge, MA: Belknap/Harvard University Press.

Herz, Ansel. 2009. *The Young Lords party: Examining its deficit of democracy and decline*. http://athomehesaturista.wordpress.com/2009/09/01/the-young-lords-party-examining-its-deficit-of-democracy-and-decline/. Accessed November 30, 2010.

In Search of Aztlán. [n.d.]. *The program of el plan de Aztlán, March 1969*. http://www.insearchofaztlan.com/plan.html. Accessed November 14, 2015.

Justice Committee. [n.d.]. http://www.justicecommittee.org/. Accessed November 14, 2015.

La Prensa San Diego. 2010. Sheriff Arpaio, SB 1070, and Gov. Brewer galvanizing the Hispanic community into action. http://laprensa-sandiego.org/editorial-and-commentary/editorial/sheriff-arpaio-sb-1070-and-gov-brewer-galvanizing-the-hispanic-community-into-action. Accessed November 14, 2015.

Latino Like Me. 2010. Brown Berets "Ten Point Program." Reprinted in *Brown Berets: Serve, observe, and protect*. 1968 (June 7). http://latinolikeme.wordpress.com/2010/09/22/latino-history-month-1. Accessed November 14, 2015.

Magana, Lisa, and Armando Xavier Mejia. 2004. Protest politics. In *Latino Americans and political participation: A reference handbook*, edited by S. A. Navarro and A. X. Mejia. Santa Barbara, CA: ABC-CLIO.

McCaffrey, Katherine. 2002. Military power and popular protest: The U.S. Navy in Vieques, Puerto Rico. New Brunswick, NJ: Rutgers University Press.

Melendez, Miguel. 2003. *We took the streets: Fighting for Latino rights with the Young Lords*. New York, NY: St. Martin's Press.

Montejano, David. 1986. *Anglos and Mexicans in the making of Texas*. Austin, TX: University of Texas Press.

Moore, Joan, and Harry Pachon. 1985. *Hispanics in the United States*. Englewood Cliffs, NJ: Prentice Hall.

Morales, Iris. 1998. ¡Palante, Siempre Palante! The Young Lords. In *The Puerto Rican movement: Voices from the diaspora*, edited by A. Torres and J. E. Velázquez, 210–27. Philadelphia, PA: Temple University Press.

Morín, José Luis. 2009. *Latino/a rights and justice in the United States*. Durham, NC: Carolina Academic Press.

Movimiento Estudiantil Chicano de Aztlán. [n.d.]. The Philosophy of MEChA. http://www.nationalmecha.org/philosophy.html#historical%20foundation. Accessed November 14, 2015.

Naples, Nancy. 1998. *Grassroots warriors: Activist mothering, community work, and the war on poverty*. New York, NY: Routledge Press.

National Young Lords. [n.d.]. Jose (Cha-Cha) Jimenez. http://nationalyounglords.com/Jose%20bio.html. Accessed November 30, 2010.

National Young Lords. [n.d.]. Jose (Cha-Cha) Jimenez. http://nationalyounglords.com/?page_id=15. Accessed November 14, 2015.

Navarro, Sharon, A., and Armando Xavier Mejia (eds.). 2004. *Latino Americans and political participation: A reference handbook*. Santa Barbara, CA: ABC-CLIO.

Pérez, Richie. 2000. A Young Lord remembers. http://libcom.org/library/young-lord-remembers. Accessed November 14, 2015.

Plan of Santa Barbara. 1969. http://www.nationalmecha.org/documents/EPSB.pdf. Accessed November 14, 2015.

Romero, Mary. 2005. Brown is beautiful. *Law and Society Review* 39: 211–35.

Taylor, Ronald, B. 1975. *Chavez and the farmworkers*. Boston, MA: Beacon Press.

Torres, Andrés, and José E. Velázquez. 1998. *The Puerto Rican movement: Voices from the diaspora*. Philadelphia, PA: Temple University Press.

Trujillo, Josmar. 2015 (June 9). Puerto Rican pride as Sunset Park fights off police brutality. *Huffington Post*. http://www.huffingtonpost.com/josmar-trujillo/puerto-rican-pride-as-sun_b_7540022.html.

Vazquez, Blanca (ed.). 2005. Interview with Richie Perez: Founder, National Congress for Puerto Rican Rights & the Justice Committee. http://www.andersongoldfilms.com/everymothersson/resources/Richieperez.pdf. Accessed November 14, 2015.

Walker, Nancy E., J. Michael Senger, Francisco A. Villarruel, and Angela M. Arboleda. 2004. *Lost Opportunities: The reality of Latinos in the U.S. criminal justice system*. Washington, DC: National Council of La Raza. http://www.nclr.org/content/publications/detail/27567/.

Whalen, Carmen Teresa. 1998. Bridging homeland and barrio politics: The Young Lords in

Philadelphia. In *The Puerto Rican movement: Voices from the diaspora*, edited by A. Torres and J. E. Velázquez, 107–23. Philadelphia, PA: Temple University Press.

Young Lords. [n.d.]. Young Lord's 13 point program and platform. http://palante.org/YLPProg.html. Accessed November 14, 2015.

Prevention. *See* Part I essays: Gangs in the United States and Latina/o Communities; Latinas and the U.S. Criminal Justice System; Crime and the U.S.-Mexican Border; Latinas/os and the U.S. Criminal Justice System; Incarceration and Latinas/os in the United States; Latina/o Youth and Criminal Justice. Part II entries: Colombians; Community-Based Latina/o Advocacy Organizations; Hate Crimes; Homicide; Lesbian, Gay, Bisexual, and Transgender (LGBT).

Prison Industrial Complex. *See* Part I essays: Incarceration and Latinas/os in the United States; Latina/o Youth and Criminal Justice. Part II entries: Chicanas/os; Immigrant Detention Centers.

Prisoner Reentry. *See* Part I essays: Latinas/os and the U.S. Criminal Justice System; The U.S. War on Drugs and Latina/o Communities; Incarceration and Latinas/os in the United States.

Public Opinion. *See* Part I essays: Latinas/os and the U.S. Criminal Justice System; Gangs in the United States and Latina/o Communities. Part II entry: Media Depictions.

Puerto Rican Legal Defense and Education Fund (PRLDEF)/LatinoJustice PRLDEF. *See* Part II entries: Civil Rights; Community-Based Latina/o Advocacy Organizations; *Hernandez v. New York*, 500 U.S. 352 (1991); Latina/o Fraternal Law Enforcement Organizations; Legal Advocacy Groups; Puerto Ricans.

Puerto Ricans

Hector W. Soto, Marco Fernando Navarro, and José Luis Morín

Puerto Ricans living in the United States are the second largest Latina/o population in the nation. Data for 2013 shows that there are approximately 5.1 million Puerto Ricans living throughout the 50 states (Pew Research Center Hispanic Trends 2015). In recent years, the Puerto Rican population in the United States has exceeded the total population of the island, which in 2013 declined to 3.6 million persons (Cohn, Patten & Lopez 2014). In comparison to other U.S. Latinas/os, Puerto Ricans tend to have poorer socioeconomic indicators. As one recent report reveals, "[t]hey have lower median household incomes and a lower homeownership rate, and are more likely to be poor" (Cohn, Patten, & Lopez 2014). Low socioeconomic status and a history of disadvantage and unequal treatment including ethnic-racial discrimination and **racial profiling** have made Puerto Ricans in the United States a group vulnerable to negative criminal justice outcomes.

Historical Background: Colonization, Racism, and Socioeconomic Dislocation

Ever since Puerto Rico was taken as part of the Spanish empire in 1493, it has been under the control of another nation. Through what U.S. policy makers called the "splendid little war," Puerto Rico's colonial status under Spain ended in 1898, and the United States became the new "owner" of Puerto Rico as its prize for winning the war. Disregarding the autonomy Puerto Rico had obtained from Spain in 1897, the United States established a colonial government on the island nation that banned Spanish from the schools and denied any semblance of local control until the late 1940s.

United States territorial conquests over Puerto Rico and other territories of the Caribbean, Pacific, and West and Southwestern parts of North America were part of a larger plan to become a global economic and political power. The ideological justification for building an empire came in the form of "**Manifest Destiny**," which promoted the notion that the United States was preordained to expand its territory and influence by virtue of being a country founded by white Anglos-Saxons, whose race, religion, and culture were far superior to those it deigned to conquer. Puerto Ricans were among the "savage and backward" peoples to whom the United States would be tendering the benefits of its civilization.

To this day, under U.S. law the legal relationship between Puerto Rico and the United States is grounded in the 1898 Treaty of Paris, which ended the war with Spain and granted the U.S. Congress full authority to decide the civil rights and political status of the inhabitants of the conquered territories; the Territorial Clause of the U.S. Constitution (article IV, section 3, paragraph 2), which accords to Congress "plenary" or absolute powers over U.S. territories; and the *Insular Cases*, a series of U.S. Supreme Court cases from the turn of the 20th century that provide the rationale for restricting the rights of the peoples of the newly acquired lands.

"**Race**" played a major role in deciding to limit the rights of Puerto Ricans and other persons from the former Spanish colonies. One of the *Insular Cases*, the 1901 case *Downes v. Bidwell*, included among the reasons for identifying Puerto Rico as an "unincorporated territory" "belonging to but not a part of" the United States, was that it, along with the other recently acquired territories, was inhabited by "alien races." So inferior were these "alien races" that they could not be trusted with being considered "part of" the United States nor be entitled to equal rights as whites under the U.S. Constitution or U.S. laws. Even after U.S. citizenship was imposed on Puerto Ricans in 1917, the *Congressional Record* makes clear that naming them as "citizens" was meant euphemistically, so as not to call them "subjects," but that Congress was not granting to "those people any right that the American people do not want them to have" (Cabranes 1979, 37, quoting Senator Foraker, 33 Cong. Rec. 2473–74 (1900)).

In another Insular Case, *Balzac v. People of Porto Rico* [sic] (1922), the U.S. Supreme Court established that, because Puerto Rico remained an "unincorporated territory," those living on the island are not entitled to any rights that Congress has not specifically decided to grant to them—consistent with the Treaty of Paris and the Territorial Clause of the Constitution—despite Puerto Ricans being U.S. citizens. Even with U.S. congressional legislative action in the 1950s to allow Puerto Rico to be considered a "commonwealth," the legislative record makes evident that "The bill [S.3336] under consideration would not change Puerto Rico's fundamental political, social and economic relationship to the United States" (House of Representatives, 82nd Congress, 2nd session, Report 1832, April 30, 1952, p. 3, *quoted in* Fernandez 1994, at 85).

The *Downes* and *Balzac* cases never have been overturned, and therefore these U.S. Supreme Court decisions still determine the legal status and rights of Puerto Ricans. Pursuant to this case law, Puerto Ricans remain defined as an "alien race" incapable of being conferred equal rights. Although Puerto Ricans born on their island nation are U.S. "citizens" at birth, they cannot vote for the

President of the United States who can send them to war; they have no voting representation in the U.S. Congress, which makes decisions affecting the island; they have no power over treaties or foreign affairs that might impact Puerto Rico; the United States controls all trade, maritime, immigration, and monetary policies; Puerto Ricans do not necessarily benefit equally from federal laws and protections; and Puerto Rico falls under the jurisdiction of the U.S. federal courts system—a system that operates in English, not Spanish.

Under current circumstances, academics and analysts—including all major political parties on the island—find that Puerto Rico today is "the oldest colony in the world" (Trías Monge 1997; Rivera Ramos 2001; Torruella 1988; Denis 2015). With "commonwealth" status, the United States has considered international law no longer applicable to the case of Puerto Rico. Since the 1970s, however, Puerto Rico's colonial situation has and continues to be the subject of international scrutiny at the United Nations before the special committee mandated to oversee the decolonization process around the world in accordance with General Assembly Resolution 1514(XV) of 1960—the Declaration on the Granting of Independence to Colonial Countries and Peoples—the authoritative international law document on decolonization. (For more on Puerto Rico and Puerto Ricans see **Latinas/os and the U.S. Criminal Justice System: An Overview of Socio-Historic and Contemporary Issues** in this volume.)

Colonialism and the economic dislocation that has accompanied it have taken a toll on Puerto Rico and its people. The industrialization scheme initiated in the 1940s that was supposed to boost the economy caused a massive out-migration from the island, as Puerto Ricans seeking to escape poverty and unemployment were attracted to jobs in New York and other major U.S. cities. By 2006, economists determined that living standards for Puerto Ricans were further "from the U.S. average . . . than they were in 1970, and [had] a per capita income . . . only about half that of the poorest [U.S.] state" (Collins, Bosworth, & Soto-Class 2006, 2).

Today, Puerto Rico is experiencing an economic crisis of monumental proportions and waves of Puerto Ricans are leaving for the United States. Puerto Rico's debt is estimated at more than $70 billion dollars; unemployment is at 15.4 percent—well over the U.S. rate; poverty is at 45 percent—almost twice the rate of Mississippi, the poorest state in the United States; and per capita income is $15,200—roughly a third of what it is in the United States (Denis 2015, 259–61). Because it does not control major aspects of its own economy, Puerto Rico's options for resolving the crisis are limited. The result has been an exodus from the island to the United States, with more Puerto Ricans living in the states (4.9 million) than on the island itself (3.5 million, as of 2012) (Cohn, Patten, & Lopez 2014).

Race and the Criminalization of Puerto Ricans in the United States

As "**race**" has been central in defining the legal status of Puerto Ricans on the island, race and racialized notions about Puerto Ricans have influenced how they are viewed and treated once within the 50 states of the Union, particularly in relation to the criminal justice system. Puerto Ricans who have come to the United States seeking to evade poverty and despair on the island frequently have endured low socioeconomic status and discrimination in housing, voting rights, employment, and health care. They tended to reside in poor and working-class neighborhoods in major east coast urban centers segregated from whites. In spite of being U.S. citizens, they were not embraced as such. Puerto Ricans in the United States have experienced high levels of poverty and socioeconomic disadvantage, **residential segregation**, and racial and ethnic discrimination—all which correlate highly with negative criminal justice outcomes.

Perceived to be foreigners and as racially "other," Puerto Ricans were readily portrayed in the press as being prone to criminality. In New York City, where the greatest number of Puerto Ricans in the post–World War migration settled, the 1959 murders by **gang** member **Salvador Agron (1943–1986)**—better known in the media as "**Capeman**" for the cloak he was alleged to have worn—received immense publicity. Although he is said to have transformed himself to become a youth counselor later in life, he is remembered most for his criminal exploits for which he was sentenced to death, a sentence that later was commuted. His case is so well-known that Paul Simon even wrote a play about him, *The Capeman*, which debuted on Broadway in 1998.

Salvador Agron's case was to become emblematic of youth crime and delinquency and inextricably linked to Puerto Ricans. His obituary in the *New York Times* notes how his gang activity resembles the narrative in the popular Broadway musical, *West Side Story*. Added to the long history of negative Latina/o depictions, the image of Puerto Ricans as knife-carrying thugs and gang members persists to this day. The popularity of *West Side Story* and notoriety of other plays, such as *The Capeman*, as well as movies, television shows, and the news reports have left an indelible impression on generations of persons throughout the United States about Puerto Ricans and Latinas/os. Newspaper and television news media have been known for playing major roles in portraying youth of color as members of predatory gangs or "wolf packs"—as in the 1989 wrongful conviction of four African Americans and one Puerto Rican youth for raping a white woman in Central Park.

Generally, relations between the police and Puerto Rican communities in the United States have been strained. From the late 1960s and into the 1970s, Puerto Rican youth under the banner of the **Young Lords** worked in communities in Philadelphia, New York, and Chicago based on a platform against police brutality and injustices in the criminal justice system. In New York City, the Young Lords rallied the community members to contest the official story that the death of **Julio Roldán** in prison was a suicide. Similar to other youth activist organizations of the time, such as the **Brown Berets** and the Black Panthers, the Young Lords sought to address many intractable social and political ills suffered by Puerto Rican communities around the nation—the lack of adequate health care, housing, and education among them—which propelled them to embrace an agenda for fundamental political change. Contesting that ways the criminal justice system viewed and treated Puerto Ricans and other people of color in the United States became an enduring part of the Young Lords' legacy well after the organization ceased to exist in the early 1970s. **Police brutality** and **racial profiling** have and continue to be among the top criminal justice concerns for groups active in Puerto Rican communities around the country.

In later years, the **National Congress for Puerto Rican Rights**—which has chapters around the United States—focused attention on many issues of concern to Puerto Ricans, among them problems related to the operations of the criminal justice system and the police. Led by former Young Lords member, **Richie Pérez (1944–2004)**, the **Justice**

Committee of the National Congress for Puerto Rican Rights in New York City was among the organizations that worked with Puerto Ricans/Latina/o communities and across racial and ethnic lines to address numerous cases of persons who were killed or abused by police officers. The National Congress actively organized around many cases of excessive force, racially motivated violence, and police misconduct, including that of **Anthony Báez (1965–1994)**. Báez, a Puerto Rican, in 1994 was killed by a police officer who used a chokehold on him—one banned under NYPD rules—after Báez's football accidentally fell on the officer's patrol car. An officer with at least 11 previous civilian complaints against him, Officer Frances Livoti nevertheless was acquitted of the murder of Anthony Báez in state court, with the apparent support of police officers willing to perjure themselves in court. Livoti was dismissed from the police force for violating department rules and in a subsequent court case was found guilty of violating federal civil rights laws.

Activism focused on police misconduct and abuse continues among Puerto Ricans in the United States today. Anthony Báez's mother, **Iris Báez**, has become an activist and advocate in her own right since 1994. She founded the Anthony Báez Foundation with funds that were awarded to her in a wrongful death action against the City of New York. The funds enabled her to continue to work supporting other victims of police violence. She has been especially active with other mothers whose sons were killed by police officers, which became the subject of a documentary film, *Every Mother's Son*, released in 2004. The film profiles three mothers who join forces in pursuit of justice following the deaths of their sons at the hands of NYPD officers.

The Justice Committee continues the legacy of its founder and leader, Richie Pérez. It sees its mission as building a movement against police violence and racism and it dedicates itself to leadership development, education, direct action, and support to victims and their families. El Grito de Sunset Park is another group organizing in a largely Puerto Rican Brooklyn community that has a growing number of other Latina/o groups, all of which have been experiencing what they consider police brutality and harassment. El Grito de Sunset Park accuses the police of inciting melees and of beating and harassing Latina/o street vendors and other community residents. It has organized copwatch activities and called on political representatives to take action to protect the communities from the police.

Puerto Ricans in the United States have been at the forefront of criminal justice matters in other ways. A leading civil rights organization since the 1970s, the **Puerto Rican Legal Defense and Education Fund** (now called **Latino Justice/PRLDEF**) not only has litigated major housing, education, and voting rights cases on behalf of Puerto Ricans and other Latino/a groups, it also spearheaded litigation on behalf of Latina/o police officers to enhance Latina/o representation in the New York Police Department. In one of the cases, *Hispanic Society of the New York City Police Department et al. v. New York City Police Department* (1986), the organization succeeded in challenging non-job-related examinations that had the effect of barring Latino/a officers from obtaining promotions.

Puerto Ricans working in law enforcement also have played important roles in creating and setting the agenda for organizations that represent and advocate for Latina/o police officers. They were instrumental in leading the **Hispanic Society of the New York City Police Department** and in initiating litigation challenging the NYPD exams that served as barriers to diversifying the police force. Their work was essential in opening the doors for many Latinas/os who wanted to pursue law enforcement careers in the NYPD.

Since the mid-1990s, the National Latino Officers Association (NLOA) has been a vocal and visible advocate for Latinas/os in law enforcement. Headed by a Puerto Rican, **Anthony Miranda**, a retired NYPD sergeant, NLOA has been active on many fronts, including on issues of racial and ethnic discrimination and injustice. It has taken legal action on behalf of Latina/o officers believed to have been treated unfairly by their department and has challenged the NYPD in instances in which a hostile work environment for Latinas/os has been alleged. The NOLA membership consists of uniformed and civilian personnel "employed by law enforcement agencies on the city, state, and federal level and . . . non-law enforcement personnel employed in the private and public sectors (National Latino Officers Association 2014).

Despite numerous socioeconomic factors that tend to hinder the progress of Puerto Ricans in the United States, there are Puerto Ricans who have achieved national prominence in the legal profession—among them U.S. Supreme Court Justice Sonia Sotomayor, Second Circuit Judge José A. Cabranes, and New York State Court of Appeals judges Jenny Rivera (current) and Carmen Beauchamp Ciparick (former). Their achievements, however, mask a dramatic underrepresentation of Puerto Ricans in the legal profession and the serious repercussions for the Puerto Rican community of not having lawyers, judges, prosecutors, law professors, and other legal professionals available to represent and advocate for them.

Specific data on the number of Puerto Ricans in the legal profession is not available, but the overall numbers of Latina/o lawyers, judges, and other law professionals indicate a severe lack of representation in the profession. Of an estimated 776,625 lawyers in the United States in 2000, only 28,630 (3.2 percent) were Latinas/os, (with 2 percent being male and 1.2 percent being female); of 58, 355 judges only 2,650 (4.54 percent) were Latina/o (U.S. Census Bureau 2000; Rivera & Roure 2012). Based on these extremely low rates of Latina/o representation in the profession, scholars have extrapolated that Puerto Rican participation must be even less—raising concerns about the impact of having so few advocates and legal professionals within an ever-growing population in the United States.

Within the criminal justice system (as discussed elsewhere in this volume) the call for **cultural competency** among academics and advocates has been virtually universal (*see, e.g.,* Arya et al. 2009; Californians for Safety and Justice 2014). It is believed that having more Puerto Rican/Latina/o legal professionals would create greater access to justice, as there ostensibly would be more culturally competent professionals able to serve the community at all levels of the justice system.

To increase the numbers of Puerto Ricans in the legal profession and in policy making positions in the criminal justice system, the Puerto Rican community in the United States must overcome very onerous hurdles. Although Puerto Ricans have greater levels of education than Latinas/os in general (about 16 percent of Puerto Ricans age 25 years and older have obtained at least a bachelor's degree as compared to 13 percent of all Latinas/os), their levels of academic achievement still are significantly lower than those of the U.S. population (29 percent of which has least a bachelor's degree). Most disconcerting is that Puerto Ricans in the United States have a greater rate of poverty (28 percent) than that of the overall U.S. population (16 percent) and even of all Latinas/os (26 percent) (Brown & Patten 2013). These harsh socioeconomic realities have prompted analysts to advocate a comprehensive approach to improving academic success that includes development of "pipeline" programs and other support services, and increased funding for scholarships and need-based financial assistance.

See also: Part I essays: Latinas/os and the U.S. Criminal Justice System; Policing and Latina/o Communities; The U.S. War on Drugs and Latina/o Communities; Incarceration and Latinas/os in the United States. Part II entries: Community-Based Latina/o Advocacy Organizations; Latina/o Fraternal Law Enforcement Organizations; Media Depictions; Political Activist Groups; Segregation; Underrepresentation of Latinas/os in the Legal Profession.

Further Reading

Acosta-Bélen, Edna, and Carlos E. Santiago. 2006. *Puerto Ricans in the United States: A contemporary portrait.* Boulder, CO: Lynne Rienner.

Arya, Neelum, Francisco Villarruel, Cassandra Villanueva, and Ian Augarten. 2009. America's invisible children: Latino youth and the failure of justice. Washington, DC: Campaign for Youth Justice and National Council of La Raza. http://www.campaignforyouthjustice.org/documents/CFYJPB_InvisibleChildren.pdf.

Berg, Charles Ramírez. 2002. *Latino images in film: Stereotypes, subversion, resistance.* Austin, TX: University of Texas Press.

Brantley, Ben. 1998 (January 30). The lure of gang violence to a Latin beat. *New York Times.* http://www.nytimes.com/1998/01/30/movies/theater-review-the-lure-of-gang-violence-to-a-latin-beat.html. Accessed November 14, 2015.

Brown, Anna, and Eileen Patten. 2013. *Hispanics of Puerto Rican origin in the United States, 2011.* Washington, DC: Pew Research Center Hispanic Trends. http://www.pewhispanic.org/2013/06/19/hispanics-of-puerto-rican-origin-in-the-united-states-2011/.

Burns, Sarah. 2011. *The Central Park Five: The untold story behind one of New York City's most infamous crimes.* New York: Vintage Books.

Cabranes, José, A. 1979. *Citizenship and the American empire.* New Haven: Yale University Press.

Californians for Safety and Justice. 2014. *Latino voices: The Impacts of crime and criminal justice on Latinos.* Oakland, CA: Californians for Safety and Justice. http://libcloud.s3.amazonaws.com/211/04/1/430/LatinoReport_7.8.14v1.pdf.

Cohn, D'Vera, Eileen Patten, and Mark Hugo Lopez. 2014. Puerto Rican population declines on island, grows on U.S. mainland. Washington, DC: Pew Research Center Hispanic Trends. http://www.pewhispanic.org/2014/08/11/puerto-rican-population-declines-on-island-grows-on-u-s-mainland/.

Collins, Susan M., Barry P. Bosworth, and Miguel A. Soto-Class (eds.). 2006. *The economy of Puerto Rico: Restoring growth.* San Juan, Puerto Rico: Center for the New Economy/Brookings Institution Press.

Denis, Nelson A. 2015. *War against all Puerto Ricans: Revolution and terror in America's colony.* New York: Nation Books.

Enck-Wanzer, Darrel (ed.). 2010. *The Young Lords: A reader.* New York: New York University Press.

Falcón, Angelo. 2002. Opening the courthouse doors: The need for more Hispanic judges. New York: The Puerto Rican Legal Defense and Education Fund.

Fernandez, Ronald. 1994. *Prisoners of colonialism: The struggle for justice in Puerto Rico.* Monroe, ME: Common Courage Press.

Gold, Tami, and Kelly Anderson. 2004. *Every mother's son* (documentary film). POV/PBS.

Gonzalez, Juan. 2011. *Harvest of empire: A history of Latinos in America.* Revised ed. New York: Penguin Books.

Hsiao, Andrew. 2001. Mothers of invention: The families of police-brutality victims and the movement they've built. In *Zero tolerance: Quality of life and the new police brutality in New York City*, edited by Andrea McArdle and Tanya Erzen, 179–95. New York: New York University Press.

Human Rights Watch. 1998. *Shielded from justice: Police brutality and accountability in the United States*. New York: Human Rights Watch.

James, George. 1986 (April 24). "Cape Man": Life of killer is over at 42. *New York Times*. http://www.nytimes.com/1986/04/24/nyregion/cape-man-life-of-killer-is-over-at-42.html.

Johnson, Marilynn. 2003. *Street justice: A history of police violence in New York City*. Boston: Beacon Press.

Justice Committee. 2013. About us. http://www.justicecommittee.org/. Accessed November 14, 2015.

Maldonado-Denis, Manuel. 1972. *Puerto Rico: A socio-historic interpretation.* New York: Vintage.

Martínez, Ramiro, Jr. 2002. *Latino homicide: Immigration, violence and community*. New York: Routledge.

McArdle, Andrea, and Tanya Erzen (eds.). 2001. *Zero tolerance: Quality of life and the new police brutality in New York City*. New York: New York University Press.

Morales, Iris. 1998. ¡Palante, Siempre Palante! The Young Lords. In *The Puerto Rican movement: Voices from the diaspora*, edited by A. Torres and J. E. Velázquez, 210–27. Philadelphia, PA: Temple University Press.

Morín, José Luis. 2009. *Latino/a rights and justice in the United States: Perspectives and approaches*, 2nd ed. Durham, NC: Carolina Academic Press.

National Latino Officers Association. 2014. About us. http://nloaus.org/. Accessed November 14, 2015.

Pérez y González, María. 2000. *Puerto Ricans in the United States*. Westport, CT: Greenwood.

Pew Research Center Hispanic Trends. 2015. Statistical portrait of Hispanics in the United States, 1980–2013. Washington, DC: The Pew Charitable Trusts. http://www.pewhispanic.org/2015/05/12/statistical-portrait-of-hispanics-in-the-united-states-1980-2013/.

Rivera, Jenny, and Jodie G. Roure. 2012. So you want to be a lawyer. Puerto Ricans and their journey into the legal profession: Overcoming challenges. *Centro Journal* 24(2): 160–99.

Rivera Ramos, Efrén. 2001. *The legal construction of identity: The judicial and social legacy of American colonialism in Puerto Rico*. Washington, DC: American Psychological Association.

Smith, Peter H. 2013. *Talons of the eagle: Latin America, the United States, and the world.* 4th ed. New York: Oxford University Press.

Stephanson, Anders. 1995. *Manifest Destiny: American expansion and the empire of right*. New York: Hill and Wang.

Torruella, Juan R. 1988. *The Supreme Court and Puerto Rico: The doctrine of separate and unequal*. Río Piedras, Puerto Rico: Universidad de Puerto Rico.

Trías Monge, José 1997. *Puerto Rico: The trials of the oldest colony in the world.* New Haven: Yale University Press.

Trujillo, Josmar. 2015 (June 9). Puerto Rican pride as Sunset Park fights off police brutality. *Huffington Post*. http://www.huffingtonpost.com/josmar-trujillo/puerto-rican-pride-as-sun_b_7540022.html.

U.S. Census Bureau. 2000. Demographic profile of selected economic characteristics: 2000. http://factfinder2.census.gov/faces/tableservices/jsf/pages/productview.xhtml?pid=DEC_00_SF4_DP3&prodType=table/. Accessed November 14, 2015.

Weiser, Benjamin. 1998 (October 9). "Former officer gets 7 1/2 years in man's death."

New York Times. http://www.nytimes.com/1998/10/09/nyregion/former-officer-gets-7-1-2-years-in-man-s-death.html. Accessed November 14, 2015.

Young Lords Party. 1971. *Palante: Voices and photographs of the Young Lords, 1969–1971*. Chicago, IL: Haymarket Books.

Zinn, Howard. 2003. *People's history of the United States: 1492–present*. New York: Perennial Classics.

Cases Cited

Balzac v. People of Porto Rico [sic], 258 U.S. 298 (1922).

Downes v. Bidwell, 182 U.S. 244 (1901).

Hispanic Society of the New York City Police Department et al. v. New York City Police Department, 42 Fair Employment Prac. Cas. (BNA) 905, 40 Employment Prac. Decisions (CCH) P36, 385 (S.D.N.Y. 1986), *aff'd*, 806 F.2d 1147 (2d Cir. 1986).

R

Race and Ethnicity. *See* Introduction; Part I essays: Latinas/os and the U.S. Criminal Justice System; Latina/o Immigrants, Crime, and Justice; Incarceration and Latinas/os in the United States; Latina/o Youth and Criminal Justice. Part II entries: Chicanas/os; Columbians; Cultural Criminology; Death Penalty; Dominicans; Hate Crimes; *Hernandez v. New York,* 500 U.S. 352 (1991); *Hernandez v. Texas,* 347 U.S. 475 (1954); Homicide; International Human Rights; Language Rights in the Courts; Latina/o Fraternal Law Enforcement Organizations; Legal Advocacy Groups; Lesbian, Gay, Bisexual, and Transgender (LGBT); Mexicans and Mexican Americans; Political Activist Groups; Segregation; Slavery; *Terry v. Ohio,* 398 U.S. 1 (1968); Vigilantism.

Racial and Ethnic Discrimination. *See* Part I essays: Latinas/os and the U.S. Criminal Justice System; Latina/o Immigrants, Crime, and Justice; Latinas and the U.S. Criminal Justice System; Incarceration and Latinas/os in the United States; Gangs in the United States and Latina/o Communities; Latina/o Youth and Criminal Justice. Part II entries: Chicanas/os; Civil Rights; Colombians; Cultural Criminology; Dominicans; Hate Crimes; *Hernandez v. New York*, 500 U.S. 352 (1991); *Hernandez v. Texas*, 374 U.S. 475 (1954); International Human Rights; Language Rights in the Courts; Latina/o Fraternal Law Enforcement Organizations; Legal Advocacy Groups; Mexicans and Mexican Americans; Political Activist Groups; Segregation; Slavery; *Terry v. Ohio*, 398 U.S. 1 (1968); Vigilantism.

Racial Profiling. *See* Part I essays: Latinas/os and the U.S. Criminal Justice System; Latina/o Immigrants, Crime, and Justice; Policing and Latina/o Communities; Incarceration and Latinas/os in the United States; Latina/o Youth and Criminal Justice. Part II entries: Civil Rights; Colombians; Cultural Criminology; Dominicans; International Human Rights; Media Depictions; Political Activist Groups; Puerto Ricans; Segregation; *Terry v. Ohio*, 398 U.S. 1 (1968); *United States v. Brignoni-Ponce,* 422 U.S. 873 (1975); *United States v. Martinez-Fuerte*, 428 U.S. 543 (1976).

Racialization. *See* Part I essays: Latinas/os and the U.S. Criminal Justice System; Policing and Latina/o Communities; Incarceration and Latinas/os in the United States. Part II entries: *Hernandez v. Texas*, 374 U.S. 475 (1954). Mexicans and Mexican Americans; Puerto Ricans; Segregation.

Ramirez, Luis. *See* Part II entry: Hate Crimes.

Rampart Scandal. *See* Part I essays: Policing and Latina/o Communities; Gangs in the United States and Latina/o Communities. Part II entries: Civilian Oversight of Police; Victims.

raúlrsalinas. *See* Part II entries: Chicanas/os; Salinas, Raúl R. (raúlrsalinas) (1934–2008).

Removal. *See* Part I essays: Latinas/os and the U.S. Criminal Justice System; Latina/o Immigrants, Crime, and Justice; Crime and the U.S.-Mexican Border. Part II entries: Deportation; Deportation Laws; Immigrant Detention Centers; Immigration and Customs Enforcement (ICE).

Residential Segregation. *See* Part I essays: Latinas/os and the U.S. Criminal Justice System; Policing and Latina/o Communities; Latina/o Youth and Criminal Justice. Part II entries: Chicanas/os; Civil Rights; International Human Rights; Puerto Ricans; Segregation.

Reyna, Juan. *See* Part I essays: Latinas/os and the U.S. Criminal Justice System; Policing and Latina/o Communities. Part II entry: Civilian Oversight of Police.

Rockefeller Drug Laws. *See also:* Part I essays: Latinas/os and the U.S. Criminal Justice System; Policing and Latina/o Communities; The U.S. War on Drugs and Latina/o Communities; Latinas and the U.S. Criminal Justice System; Incarceration and Latinas/os in the United States; Latina/o Youth and Criminal Justice. Part II entry: Colombians.

Roldán, Julio. *See* Part I essay: Policing and Latina/o Communities. Part II entries: Political Activist Groups; Puerto Ricans.

Rosario, Antonio. *See* Part I essay: Policing and Latina/o Communities.

S

Salazar, Rúben.
See Part II entry: Chicanas/os.

Salinas, Raúl R. (raúlrsalinas) (1934–2008)

Louis Mendoza

> "somewhere beyond Majestic Mount Rainier in dungeons built by evil men are brothers/sisters (prisoners) who are still not free As i am still not free . . . though i walk Seattle's streets."
>
> Crash Landing

The above lines illustrate Raúl R. Salinas' (raúlrsalinas) ongoing concern for the incarcerated—an issue that would be a consistent driving force in his post-prison politics and poetics. In many respects, the life of this ***pachuco*** turned pinto turned poet-activist exemplifies the contentious, vexed, and often over-determined relationship that Latinos have with the criminal justice system in the United States. Born in San Antonio, Texas in 1934, Salinas was raised in Austin where he attended Catholic elementary school and public high school until he was given a "choice" by a judge to go to jail, join the military, or leave town. Faced with the prospect of institutionalization he opted to enter the migrant stream, a decision that took him to the fields of northern California at the age of 17.

Salinas' life often was in conflict with mainstream institutional and cultural mores; thus, in many respects, he was both representative and exceptional. During his childhood, the city of Austin's segregationist policies were being codified to ensure that East Austin was comprised exclusively of ethnic minorities. It was within the *barrios* of this deliberately marginalized community, composed of several African American and Mexican neighborhoods, that Salinas first learned his "place" in society. As an adolescent he experienced continuous harassment by police and school officials for any aspect of his behavior or appearance that signaled difference from a narrowly defined cultural norm—be it his style of dress, hair, tattoos, or language usage, all of which had their specific manifestation in a defiant *pachuchismo* that he eagerly embraced. His alignment with this counterculture visibly marked him as a troublemaker even as he excelled in school. Labeled a "delinquent," local police developed a dossier on Salinas when he was at a young age, an action that made him easy prey for police. This resulted in Salinas serving short stints in local and state juvenile detention centers.

A *pachuco* hipster with an affinity for jazz and blues music, Salinas "came of age" in 1952—the same year that *The New York Times* heralded the emergence of the beat literary movement. Salinas identified with the rejection of cultural and social conventions promoted by these young artists.

California offered Salinas a respite from the oppressive conventions and expectations of society and family in the post-war boom period. As a streetwise young man, his lifestyle soon included the consumption and selling of **drugs**. In 1957, Salinas was convicted in Los Angeles of "violating the health and safety code for sale and possession of marihuana" and he was sent to Soledad State Penitentiary, also known as the "Gladiator School." Not counting his experience in juvenile detention centers, Soledad would be Salinas' first home behind bars. It was here that he began to write poetry for the first time. He was released on parole in 1959.

In November 1961, Salinas was arrested in Austin, Texas, was convicted on possession of marijuana charges, and was sent to Huntsville State Prison where he stayed until May of 1965. In Huntsville, he joined the production team of the monthly prison newspaper, *The Echo* and wrote Quartered Notes, a jazz column. These early writings were penned under his childhood name of Roy Salinas. It was not until he was in Leavenworth that Salinas reclaimed his birth name of Raúl. Later, inspired by e. e. cummings, he began using the lowercased name, "raúlrsalinas."

When sent to Leavenworth on a felony drug charge in 1967, Salinas' outlaw perspective was turned inside out by Ramón Chacón, a convict from South Texas who introduced him to the writings of Ernesto "Ché" Guevara and Frantz Fanon. He also was befriended by Standing Deer (alias: Robert Wilson) and Rafael Cancel Miranda, a Puerto Rican *independentista* in prison for his participation in a 1954 armed protest in congressional chambers. Through his interaction with these men, Salinas began to see how race and class functioned in prison and in the outside world to keep people from discovering constructive solutions to individual and group empowerment.

Just as there was a clear relationship between his pre-prison experience of social marginalization and his eventual incarceration, there was also a direct link between his prison experience and his development as an intellectual-activist. The transformation he underwent led him to engage fellow convicts, prison authorities, friends, and political activists in the outside world. It is within the context of a highly politicized and racist prison culture that Salinas came to terms with his Mexicano-**Chicano**-Indigenous identity; and it is through a Xicanindio identity that he acquired political insight, found individual and collective fulfillment, and initiated a life-long struggle to advance human liberation. Originally a prisoner because of "social crimes" (drug possession and distribution), Salinas' experience exemplifies the ways in which a convict is transformed by—and transforms—the prison system. His 1972 relocation from Leavenworth to the Marion control unit clearly marks prison authorities' recognition of his metamorphosis from a social prisoner to a political prisoner as he was marked for "behavior modification" due to his prolific activity on behalf of fellow convicts.

Salinas' transformation was a process that was both solitary and communal. The emotional, spiritual, and political substance of this transformation is mapped out in his writings and makes his life one worthy of study, one that provides insight on society and the human capacity to persevere, adapt, and rebuild oneself. Salinas' writing and activism can be seen as interventions in the ahistorical and dehumanizing popular discourse on prisoners and crime that often preempts any critical discussion of the faults, limitations, and corrupt nature of the justice system. As part of a prisoner rights movement, he and his cohorts forged a radical cultural praxis that linked issues of identity and power with notions of history and justice.

By 1970, Salinas had undergone a major ideological shift due to his contact with political prisoners, his extensive reading, as well as the educational and organizational experiences obtained through his membership in *Chicanos Organizados Rebeldes de Aztlán* (CORA), a political action group in Leavenworth. His editorial and literary contributions to the important prison publications, *Aztlán de Leavenworth*, *New Era*, *Entrelíneas*, and *Signet* document the evolution of his political consciousness. Having developed his skills and reputation under austere circumstances, Salinas' writing and activism eventually earned him international recognition as a spokesperson for causes ranging from prisoner rights and national liberation struggles to gang intervention and **youth** arts advocacy.

Salinas first received recognition as a writer in 1969 when what was to become his signature poem, "Un Trip Through the Mind Jail," was published to wide critical acclaim. He then published three collections of poetry, a collection of prison writings, and three spoken-word CDs. A consistent motif in Salinas' writing is that of the journey. His exceptional journey from individual alienation to rage to resistance was linked to social movements occurring within and outside of prison. Although prison served as a catalyst for his political consciousness, what was extraordinary about Salinas was his decision upon leaving prison to devote his life to the pursuit of social, political, and economic justice.

Salinas gained his final release from prison in 1972 with the help of faculty and graduate students at the University of Washington. Unable to return to Texas or California due to parole restrictions, Salinas chose to be exiled in Seattle. Immediately following his arrival, he joined a multiracial, Latino-led coalition of community groups that had seized control of an abandoned school building. Successful in their effort, they formed *El Centro de La Raza*. His reputation as a poet and activist blossomed as he entered full-force into the national Chicano literary scene.

Salinas joined the Native American fishing rights struggle in the Seattle-Tacoma region, working with the Nisqually/Puyallup peoples. It was through *El Centro de La Raza* that his international vision and his ideas regarding Indian-Chicano unity were cultivated. In 1975, he traveled to Cuba for the first time. Later that year, he met and worked with American Indian Movement (AIM) member Leonard Peltier. In 1976, he coordinated the Trail of Self-Determination, a seven-month cross-country caravan led by the Survival of American Indians Association that arrived in Washington, DC, on July 4th to present an indigenous perspective on the bicentennial. In 1977, Salinas co-founded the National Leonard Peltier Defense Committee. Four years later he would be selected as part of an International Indian Treaty Council delegation sent to represent Peltier at a human rights symposium in Geneva.

In 1981, after completing the terms of his parole with the Texas Department of Corrections, Salinas returned to Austin where he began teaching critical media studies at the University of Texas and joined the League of United Chicano Artists (LUChA). Almost immediately he established Resistencia Bookstore/Casa de Red Salmon Press; it remains open to this day. In 1985, Salinas moved to St. Louis for a year to head the national office of the Leonard Peltier Defense Committee. As part of his ongoing work with the International Indian Treaty Council, Salinas traveled to Nicaragua; Libya; Cuba; Panama; Chiapas, Mexico; and Vieques, Puerto Rico.

From 1989 to 1992, Salinas worked as a counselor with South Austin Youth Services. This work led him to become a specialist in gang intervention and conflict resolution, skills he utilized locally and nationally. A popular poet and speaker on social justice issues at universities and political and cultural venues, Salinas' dedication to literacy and empowerment earned him a reputation as a steadfast cultural and political force in Austin. Resistencia Bookstore became a haven for emerging writers and young activists, serving as home base for local chapters of AIM, the Leonard Peltier Defense Committee, the *Comité en Solidaridad con Chiapas y Mexico*, SOY (Save Our Youth) arts program, a read-in of *Live from Death Row* (part of the Free Mumia Campaign), as well as numerous other political committees addressing local, state, national, and international causes.

Salinas' contributions as a cultural worker were extensive. In addition to conducting youth writing workshops and maintaining a busy schedule on the reading circuit, he taught courses at St. Edwards University. He won many accolades for his work, including a Senate Resolution from the State of Texas for his community arts work with youth, a Best Supporting Actor in a Comedy in the City of Austin Award, the Guadalupe Cultural Arts Center Distinguished Writer Award, the Luis Reyes Rivera Lifetime Achievement Award, the 2004 National Association for Latino Art and Culture (NALAC) Lifetime Achievement Award, and a 2006 Macondo Foundation Gloria Anzaldúa Milagro Award. In 1994, the first installment of Salinas' personal archives was obtained by Stanford University; this was followed by additional materials acquired by Stanford following Salinas' death on February 13, 2008.

An activist and writer of the prison rebellion movement, Salinas' work helped heighten social consciousness about the unjust and disproportionate imprisonment of people of color in the United States. His work should be seen alongside the work of other prison writers and activists, such as Ricardo Sánchez, Luis Talamantez, Jimmy Santiago Baca, and Judy Lucero, as well as important African American anti-prison activists and artists such as Etheridge Knight, Malcolm X, Angela Davis, George Jackson, and Assata Shakur. Salinas is a representative figure inasmuch as his pre-prison life and his incarceration are all too typical of the prison population; his experiences of social disenfranchisement, under-education, participation in the lumpen economy, migrancy, and other forms of displacement are indicators of experience and social location that he and many other prisoners share.

Salinas' literary legacy is eclectic and masterful in its creative bilingual engagement with multiple literary and music traditions. The continuation of Red Salmon Arts and Resistencia Bookstore stand as testimony to his influence as a teacher and inspirational cultural worker for many generations of writers, thinkers, and advocates for social justice. Salinas never forgot his prison past and the ongoing injustices perpetuated by the criminal justice system. He took every opportunity available to visit prisoners to provide discussions, free readings, and workshops. This lifelong dedication to ameliorating the inhumanity of prisons is perhaps best articulated by Salinas on the final page of *My Weapon is My Pen* (2006), where he asserts a declaration of struggle: "In honor of those who did not survive the 'prison rebellion' years, and in solidarity with those prison fighters who continue to struggle, I commit the remainder of my life to exposing the inhumanity of the jail machine. '*A luta continua.*' "

See also: Part I essay: Incarceration and Latinas/os in the United States. Part II entry: Chicanas/os.

Further Reading

Gómez, Alan Eladio. 2006. Resisting living death at Marion Federal Penitentiary, 1972. *Radical History Review* 96: 58–86.

Mendoza, Louis. 2003. The re-education of a Xicanindio: Raúl Salinas and the poetics of Pinto transformation. *MELUS: Multi-Ethnic Literatures and the Idea of Social Justice* 28(1): 39–60.

Olguín, Ben V. 2010. *La pinta: Chicana/o prisoner literature, culture, and politics*. Austin: University of Texas Press.

raúlrsalinas. 1995. *East of the freeway: Reflections de mi pueblo*. Austin: Red Salmon Press.

raúlrsalinas. 1999. *Un trip through the mind jail y otras excursions*. San Francisco, CA: Editorial Pocho-Ché, 1980; Houston, TX: Arte Público Press.

raúlrsalinas. 2006. *Indio trails: A Xicano odyssey thru Indian Country*. San Antonio: Wings Press.

raúlrsalinas. 2006. *raúlrsalinas and the jail machine: My weapon is my pen. Selected prison writings (1963–1974)*, edited by L. Mendoza. Austin: University of Texas Press.

Sánchez, Alex (1971–). *See* Part I essay: Gangs in the United States and Latina/o Communities Part II entry: Political Activist Groups.

School-to-Prison Pipeline. *See* Part I eassy: Latina/o Youth and Criminal Justice. Part II entry: Segregation.

Segregation

Judith Perez Caro

Latinas/os have experienced a history of unequal treatment in the United States, including segregation or the discriminatory separation of persons by race, class, or ethnicity. The segregation of Latinas/os has been linked to issues of **race** and **racialization**. The racialization of Latinas/os in the United States stems from a belief that Latinas/os fall into or belong in a category of non-white "others" in relation to the dominant Anglo-American society and its social norms and standards. Differences in skin color, language, and other cultural characteristics and norms consequently are perceived as inferior. Through racialization, Latinas/os ultimately are seen as "foreigners" in relation to the dominant culture and norms of U.S. society.

Although it is the case that racial and ethnic groups tend to form ethnic enclaves for support and reasons other than discrimination, the segregation of Latinas/os in housing, schools, public accommodations, and other areas of life also has been symptomatic of the **racial and ethnic discrimination** they have faced based on the dominant's society's perception of Latinos/os as racially "other." The impact of segregation has affected many facets of the Latina/o experience in the United States, including interaction with the criminal justice system.

Throughout their history in the United States, Latinas/os have been subject to **de jure segregation** (segregation sanctioned by law), as well as **de facto segregation** (racial and ethnic segregation that occurs despite it being illegal), as is the case in the contemporary United States. The most common forms of segregation that Latinas/os have encountered have been in housing and education. Separation and exclusion, however, also have been evident in the Latina/o experience with the criminal justice system. Every form of segregation has fostered the marginalization and increased social distance of Latinas/os from the larger society, and has diminished opportunities for economic advancement and justice within U.S. society. Latinas/os living in segregated communities—enclaves where few educational and economic opportunities for advancement are available—are vulnerable to being perceived negatively, and as a result are treated more harshly by law enforcement and the criminal justice system than are whites.

Racial and Ethnic Segregation

Residential segregation refers to the separation of racial and ethnic minorities through residence and housing patterns. Residential segregation perpetuates urban poverty and inequality in the provision of many basic services, public amenities, privileges, and rights in the United States. In addition to African Americans, Latinas/os were among the groups in the United States subject to de jure and de facto residential segregation in the 20th century. Before segregation in the public domain was outlawed legally, neighborhoods and communities were forcefully segregated, ensuring that whites and non-whites remained within suitable social distance. After the abolition of slavery, a new era of de jure segregation—Jim Crow segregation—began. It replaced the institution of slavery thereby ensuring the continuation of white supremacy and privilege. Similar to the experience of African Americans, Mexican Americans were forced to live in designated geographical areas roughly during the same period that Jim Crow laws were in effect.

Mexican Americans living in the Southwest were most often subject to residential segregation. They also faced lawful segregation in public parks and recreation centers, restaurants, drugstores, public pools, and maternity wards. As with African Americans, Mexican Americans also were segregated in courthouses and restrooms, and used separate drinking fountains and cafeterias in government and municipal buildings. Signage announcing "No Mexicans allowed" or "No Colored People" was commonplace in these public spaces. In other cases, Mexican Americans were also denied burials in white-only cemeteries. In 1940s California, "Mexican Monday" was the day designated for Mexicans to use the public pool, as it was the day the pool was the dirtiest and the day before the pool was to be cleaned for whites to use. The Latina/o experience with their exclusion from many aspects of U.S. society drew national attention in the 1947 case *Mendez v. Westminster School District of Orange County*, which involved the segregation of Latina/o school children, and the 1954 case ***Hernandez v. Texas***, which dealt with the systematic rejection of Mexican Americans from juries. Segregation prevented Latinas/os and their families from basic opportunities and rights enjoyed by whites, even the basic constitutional right to a trial by a jury of your peers.

De facto segregation is both a historical and contemporary social problem. Sociologists have found that de facto segregation in housing can result from the decision by whites to choose to live in primarily white neighborhoods where few ethnic minorities live in close proximity. This phenomenon is often referred to as "white flight." Scholars note that racial attitudes and prejudice are permanent forces supporting racial segregation and divisions within the United States. These divisions do not just occur within the confines of where people live—they affect how people live. The segregation of underrepresented ethnic groups, such as Latinas/os, often is rooted in social, racial, structural, and income discriminatory practices. Residential segregation blocks equal access to vital community resources, such as well-performing school districts, employment and labor-market opportunities, adequate and affordable health services, green spaces, healthy environmental exposure, and well-funded community organizations and services. Communities of color, including Latinas/os, are at a societal disadvantage without equal access to quality services and resources. Thus, residential segregation affects not only the potential for upward mobility; it affects a person's total quality of life (Massey & Denton 1993).

Proximity and Social Distance

A study conducted by the Harvard Civil Rights Project found that segregation has increased for Latinas/os in all regions of the United States. Compared to African Americans, Latinas/os tend to live in closer proximity to whites, especially in suburban townships. Yet residence in the suburbs has proven to be a contentious experience for some Latina/o groups, where full racial integration has not been achieved, conflating both racial and socio-economic class dimensions.

A byproduct of social distance and residential segregation is that Latinos often reside in *barrios*—highly segregated spaces composed of various generations of Spanish-speaking Latinos from low-income backgrounds. Although some Latinos might choose to reside in these *barrios* or ethnic enclaves for community solidarity purposes, many are relegated to living in *barrios* that have poor housing stock and substandard community and educational resources. Geographically, *barrios* tend to be located on the periphery of central cities, and their remote locales could make it harder for residents to gain access to important resources and services. Specifically, isolation caused by insular residential social distance and segregation inhibit access to labor market and employment opportunities, which can lead to participation in underground criminal activities.

Limited educational and employment opportunities, residential segregation, and social distance contribute to joblessness and high incarceration rates among young men of color. In fact, studies show that many Latino and African American men reside in unhealthy neighborhoods—where the lack of resources and opportunities are highly concentrated. As a consequence, their environment places them "directly in harm's way" for negative health outcomes, harmful behavior is reinforced, and the chances of going to prison are magnified.

Institutional practices such as racial and ethnic steering help maintain segregation. Some real estate agents have been known to show racial minority home buyers residential units only in heavily concentrated minority neighborhoods or in white neighborhoods that are in economic decline, thereby ensuring that communities are kept segregated. Some agents also have encouraged segregation by steering whites away from homes near people of color for fear that the value of the property will diminish after purchase. Although this practice is illegal, racial and ethnic steering is a contemporary example of how a system of de facto segregation is maintained.

The problem of residential segregation has been longstanding and persistent. In 2009, media attention was drawn to the U.S. Department of Housing and Urban Development (HUD) investigation of practices in Westchester County, a suburb of New York City, which was failing to advance fair housing standards. HUD officials found that affordable housing was clustered in low-income areas where mostly people of color reside, and away from middle-class white neighborhoods. It is a system that has kept people of color at a distance from the county's wealth and resources. Yet, after entering into a consent degree in court with HUD in 2009 to build 750 affordable housing units and implement a plan to ensure fair housing, Westchester County has made no progress. Making reference to the county's long history of residential segregation, a 2015 *New York Times* editorial characterized the barriers to fair housing in the county as functioning as "invisible 'Whites Only' signs," calling upon Westchester County officials to end their recalcitrance.

School Segregation

Latinas/os have a longstanding history with de jure school segregation in the United States. The first successful federal lawsuit to challenge Latina/o student segregation was *Mendez v. Westminster School District of Orange County* (1947). The *Mendez* case, a precursor to the landmark 1954 *Brown v. Board of Education* Supreme Court decision, involved a challenge to the separation of Mexican and white students into different schools in Orange County, California. Through this lawsuit, Latina/o parents in the school district successfully ended California's practice of placing "Mexican" children in separate public schools.

The struggle to end segregation of Latina/o school children, however, did not end with the *Mendez* case. In the 1973 case of *Keyes v. School District No. 1*, the Supreme Court once again ruled in favor of plaintiffs who petitioned the court to end school segregation in Denver, Colorado. One decade later, in the case of the *United States et al. v. Yonkers Board of Education,* the City of Yonkers, New York, was found liable for intentionally and systematically isolating African Americans and Latinas/os from white residential areas and the predominantly white public school districts in the city.

Despite these legal victories, Latina/o children still experience high levels of segregation in schools throughout the country. Latino students experience school segregation from whites more frequently than any other racial and ethnic group, including African Americans. According to a 2006 report by the Harvard Civil Rights Project, "[t]he average black student attends a school that is 30 percent white and the average Latino student, 28 percent. . . . Growing segregation of black and Latino students from white students is a basic educational trend" (Orfield & Lee 2006, 8, 15).

Studies since 2006 show an ominous pattern and trajectory: School segregation is worsening, not improving. An examination of school segregation from 1968 to 2011 reveals that major shifts have occurred in school enrollment, with white student enrollment dropping 28 percent, African American student enrollment increasing 19 percent, and Latina/o student enrollment skyrocketing 495 percent (Orfield et al. 2014, 6). Along with these remarkable changes in enrollment have come marked increases in school segregation, with Latina/o school children in particular suffering extremely high levels of school segregation. New York State, a state with an overall Latina/o population of 18.4 percent in 2013, is considered to have the most segregated school system in the United States (U.S. Bureau of the Census 2015a; Kucsera with Gary Orfield 2014). No other state has more African American and Latina/o students attending schools where whites comprise less than 10 percent of student enrollment (Kucsera with Gary Orfield 2014, 3). With a 28.6 percent Latina/o population, New York City also is one of the most segregated city public school systems in the country (U.S. Bureau of the Census 2015b; Kucsera with Gary Orfield 2014, 3).

Segregation and the "School-to-Prison" Pipeline

Currently, Latinas/os are the most segregated minority groups in public schools nationwide. "In 2005–06, one-fifth of Latino students in large cities attended schools of almost absolute racial isolation (where 99–100% of the students were nonwhite)" (MALDEF and The Civil Rights Project at UCLA 2008, 3). Latina/o school segregation has increased in every region of the country and Latinas/os typically attend school districts with poor classroom conditions, shortened school years, tracking problems, greater numbers of students labeled "special needs," limited access to college preparatory high schools, and less challenging school curricula. The need for more integration to enhance educational opportunities to prevent Latina/o children from continuing to be part of the "**school-to-prison pipeline**" is significant.

The maintenance of segregated schools promotes what commonly is called the "school-to-prison pipeline," which refers to the systemic and institutional problems and processes that make it more possible for Latina/o and African American school children to end up in the criminal justice system than to complete school. Attending highly segregated schools has been associated with the school-to-prison pipeline. In addition to all of the inadequacies and problems found in segregated schools, children of color—more so than white children—are susceptible to school disciplinary action, often for minor infractions. This leads to increased numbers of suspensions, expulsions, and even arrests of children of color. Some studies show that African American and Latina/o students have been overrepresented among school children most vulnerable to tough disciplinary action and zero tolerance policies, as has been the case in the state of Texas (Texas Appleseed 2007).

Among the most controversial trends over the last few decades has been the placement of police officers and personnel in schools. Beginning in 1998, in New York City, where a majority of students in the public school system are students of color, the New York City Police Department (NYPD) deployed more than 5,000 School Safety Officers and other personnel—including almost 200 armed police officers—in public schools throughout the city. The NYPD's presence in these schools was equivalent to the fifth largest police force in the United States and greater than the police forces in Baltimore, Boston, Dallas, Detroit, Las Vegas, Phoenix, San Diego, San Francisco, and Washington, DC. Although school crime had been dropping before 1998, police presence in New York City public schools continued to grow, and with this growth came increasing numbers of complaints about police abuse in the schools, including instances of wrongful arrests and use of excessive force by police in cases involving minor disciplinary matters. In a much publicized case, a child was handcuffed and detained for hours by the police for doodling on a desk with erasable ink.

In the context of segregated schools, civil liberties groups and others have expressed concerns about the aggressive over-policing of schools resulting in incidents of police abuse and arrests of students for minor noncriminal violations of school rules. These groups argue that low-income African American and Latina/o youth have been subjected to harassment, excessive **stops and frisks**, and other forms of abuse by police personnel in their schools. As spaces and places render Latina/o youth vulnerable to aggressive law enforcement policies and practices, segregated communities and segregated school systems appear to be a significant factor contributing to the school-to-prison pipeline.

By 2014, evidence had mounted pointing to zero tolerance and tough school disciplinary actions as having disproportionately negative criminal justice outcomes for students of color. With data showing that "more than half of students involved in school-related arrests or referred to law enforcement were Hispanic or black," the Obama administration issued new guidelines to curb the discriminatory effects of zero tolerance school disciplinary policies that buttressed the school-to-prison pipeline (Hefling 2014). The nonbinding guidelines that were released called for, among other things, the retraining of school personnel on handling disciplinary matters to ensure that police officers are not deployed in routine disciplinary matters.

Residential Segregation and Criminal Justice

According to the U.S. Census Bureau, residential segregation increased significantly between 1980 and 2000. During that same period, metropolitan areas with the greatest increases in Latina/o population generally experienced larger increases in segregation than did metropolitan areas with smaller Latina/o populations. The census data revealed the five most-segregated metropolitan areas for Latinas/os were predominantly located in the Northeast—the area of Providence-Fall River-Warwick, Rhode Island; New York City; Newark, New Jersey; and Hartford, Connecticut. The cities of Los Angeles and Long Beach, California, round out the list. Metropolitan areas showing the greatest percentage declines (or lowest increases) in Latino residential segregation include San Antonio, Texas; Tampa-St. Petersburg-Clearwater and Miami, Florida; and St. Louis, Missouri. Geographically, there was a decline in the residential segregation of Latinas/os in Southern metropolitan areas, and an increase in residential segregation in Western metropolitan areas over the same period.

From a criminal justice perspective, it is noteworthy that it was in large metropolitan centers that have greater Latina/o populations—such as Los Angeles and New York—that the largest increases in segregation were recorded from 1980 to 2000. These generally are metropolitan areas that also have long histories of tensions between police and Latina/o communities. The racialized and segregated Latino *barrio* of Los Angeles, for example, is known to have been a contributing factor in the social and racial divide and the strain between law enforcement and the Latino community dating back many years—from the **Zoot Suit Riot** of the early 1940s to the police hostility toward the **Chicano** movement of the 1960s to more contemporary and controversial police practices that arguably target Latina/o **youth** and purport that they are suspected of being **gang** members.

Residential segregation perpetuates social distance by preventing opportunities for engagement between those who work in law enforcement and the criminal justice system and people of color from disadvantaged communities. Judges, attorneys, and other criminal justice personnel often do not reside in the same communities as those whom they are prosecuting. Therefore they are unfamiliar with and are prone to misunderstand or treat Latinas/os differently than those from their own racial, ethnic, and socioeconomic background.

The effects of residential segregation coupled with **felony disenfranchisement** laws—state laws that restrict a prisoner's right to vote based on a felony conviction—reduce the political power of Latina/o communities. A 2003 study of the impact of felony disenfranchisement on the voting rights of Latinas/os in 10 selected states (Arizona, California, Florida, Nebraska, Nevada, New York, North Carolina, Texas, Virginia, and Washington) concluded that

> significant numbers of Latinos are prohibited from voting by felony disenfranchisement laws. . . . Latinos have

> disproportionately higher rates of disenfranchisement compared to their presence in the voting age population. . . . Latinos are more likely to be disenfranchised than the general population due to felony disenfranchisement laws [and] . . . [w]hen the disenfranchisement rates are compared to only citizens of voting age (removing the non-citizens), the impact of the felony disenfranchisement laws on Latino citizens is greater (Demeo & Ochoa 2003, ii).

Given that Latina/o communities, particularly in metropolitan areas, are greatly segregated, the absence of a segment of the voting age population in electoral districts with large Latina/o populations diminishes the voting power—and consequently the political strength—of Latinas/os. Although some states have moved forward with reforming their laws to repeal lifetime disenfranchisement or to provide information about the restoration of voting rights upon release, decades of Latina/o overrepresentation in prison appears to have had a considerable impact on the political power of Latina/o communities nationwide.

Prisoners from communities of color, including Latina/o communities, have been sent to serve sentences in prisons located in largely white electoral districts. Districts then have counted the prisoners as part of that particular county's population for purposes of political apportionment. This practice is known as "prison-based gerrymandering." Arguably, it violates the "one person, one vote" principle that political representation be apportioned in accordance with the size of the population in an electoral district to assure equal access to political power.

The practice politically and economically empowered white upstate New York counties unfairly, and disempowered communities of color in New York City by allowing these upstate counties to count prisoners from New York City as part of the county population. Many of these prisoners are Latina/o and African American, and are included in the white county's population to qualify for greater entitlement funds and to increase legislative representation—at the expense of the downstate districts from which the prisoners come. Although some states, for example New York, have ended prison-based gerrymandering, it is a practice that has for many years given white communities unfair political and economic advantages. The practice continues in many states throughout the country despite the efforts to eradicate it. Without the high levels of segregation in the United States, prison-based gerrymandering would be difficult if not impossible.

Residential Segregation and Hate Crimes

Hate violence against people of color has been one way in which racial and ethnic exclusion and segregation have been maintained. In examining the history of **hate crimes**, scholars have identified patterns of anti-integrationist crime and the persistence of residential segregation. In other words, "move-in violence"—including cross burning, arson, vandalism, physical assault, and varying forms of intimidation—often has surfaced when attempts are made to integrate neighborhoods. People of color thereby are victimized twice: they are kept from moving to better neighborhoods with improved schools, services, and other amenities, and they are subjected to acts of criminal violence and intimidation. For Latinas/os, racially motivated violence of this type is not new, as the attacks on Latino day-laborers and the firebombing of a Latina/o immigrant family home in Farmingville, New York, in 2003 demonstrate.

Recent studies suggest that exposing children to better neighborhoods at an early age has a significant impact on improving economic fortunes and a family's upward social mobility. Distressingly, research also demonstrates not only that African Americans and Latinas/os, on average, reside in areas where poverty is considerably greater than in white neighborhoods, but even middle-class African American and Latina/o households (incomes of about $55,000 to $60,000) usually live in neighborhoods "similar to those of very poor white households (those with incomes of roughly $12,000) . . . [and] even high income black and Hispanic households do not achieve neighborhood income parity with similar-income white households" (Reardon, Fox, & Townsend 2015, 94). Given the gravity of the information available on the persistence of residential segregation, scholars suggest that factors that promote such disparities and inequalities—including the role of hate crimes—require more attention and action, and that legal remedies, such as **civil rights** actions, should be pursued.

Segregation and Policing

A consequence of residential segregation is the tendency for over-policing of low-income minority neighborhoods. As criminologist Marc Mauer (2009) points out, segregation leads to crime-control policies that result in increased numbers of arrests of young African American and Latino men. Moreover, that Latinas/os generally can be found living in particular neighborhoods makes it common for law enforcement to engage in more aggressive police tactics under the premise that certain forms of criminality are more rampant in Latina/o and African American communities. Although Latinas/os are no more likely to use **drugs** than are other racial and ethnic groups, police frequently categorize Latina/o communities as being "high-crime areas" to justify frequent stops and frisks of Latinas/os in their neighborhoods.

Over-policing affects the perceptions of communities of color by making them feel that they are being targeted systematically. Aggressive law enforcement practices typically deployed in low-income neighborhoods enhance the probability of tense community-police relations. Residents of border communities are subjected to aggressive strategies by **Immigration and Customs Enforcement** agents. Together with police tactics that target young Latino adult males, an unfavorable perception of the police is a likely result among Latinos.

The existence of distinct and highly segregated low-income Latina/o communities can contribute to the stereotype or generalized belief that those communities are deserving of "get tough" police tactics. As a result, trust between Latinos and police is damaged, and community cooperation consistent with effective **community policing** is undermined. The long history of distrust and negative interactions between Latina/o community members and law enforcement officials from New York to Los Angeles parallels the long history of segregation and marginalization of Latina/o communities.

In a study of police **racial profiling** in San Jose, California, Koehler (2007) found that this discriminatory practice is a form of state-sanctioned preservation of space, place, and race between whites and people of color. Stratification in the housing sector makes possible the targeting of particular low-income areas for aggressive law enforcement tactics, and it makes it possible to derive large segments of the prison population from these disadvantaged communities.

The segregation of Latinas/os in distinct neighborhoods and the illegal practice of racial profiling often intersect. The underlying premise of racial profiling is that certain persons are prone to criminal behavior based on their racial or ethnic background. Although discriminatory and illegal, the use of race or ethnicity as the determining factor for law enforcement officers reinforces the separation and separateness of Latinas/os and other people of color from whites. Distinctions by geographic area enable law enforcement officers to perceive certain communities, and hence persons from those communities, to be criminally inclined. The idea that a certain neighborhood is a "high -rime" area becomes a proxy for illegal singling out of persons of color for aggressive police tactics. Scholars have observed that space and place correspond to incidents in which Latina/o youth are singled out as criminals even before they have committed any crime. Analysts thus have associated segregation along with contemporary criminal justice policies as factors associated with the **mass imprisonment** of African Americans and Latinas/os.

Prison Population Segregation

The segregation of prisoners by **race and ethnicity** has been a subject of considerable controversy in recent years. California, which has the largest state prison system in the nation, has become a prime example of segregation within prisons. Thirty-nine percent of California's inmate population is Latina/o. California's prison system was under long-term investigation for using racial and ethnic categories as a determinant in housing upon an inmate's intake. Investigators found that Latino inmates from Northern and Southern California, for example, were kept apart because of a history of gang conflicts, and Latinas/os were segregated from other ethnic groups and racially profiled for fear of gang-related **violence**. In 2005, the Supreme Court in *Johnson v. California* ruled that racial segregation of prisoners in their cells and elsewhere in the prison involves a form of racial classification for which a court must apply strict scrutiny. As a result of the Court's 5-to-3 decision, the State of California has begun to integrate its prison system.

Legal Challenges to Exclusion in the Criminal Justice System

In addition to forms of segregation discussed above, Latinas/os have faced exclusion in other ways through the operation of the criminal justice system. In the case of ***Hernandez v. Texas*, 347 U.S. 475 (1954)**, Hernandez and his attorneys challenged the systematic exclusion of Mexicans from service as jury commissioners, grand jurors, and petit jurors in the Texas county in which he was indicted and tried for murder. The evidence showed that there were people of Mexican descent in the county qualified to serve on the jury, and their absence deprived Hernandez from equal protection of the laws pursuant to the Fourteenth Amendment of the U.S. Constitution. The Supreme Court ruled unanimously in favor of Hernandez, based on a finding that "persons of Mexican descent constitute a separate class" and therefore they merit representation on juries.

By contrast, ***Hernandez v. New York* (1991)** is a case that challenged a prosecutor's exclusion of prospective Latina/o jurors because they spoke Spanish, for a trial involving a Spanish-speaking criminal defendant. The Supreme Court allowed the exclusion under the rationale that the rejection of potential jurors was not based on racial or national origin discrimination, but on language. This case, discussed elsewhere in this volume, remains controversial, as it is often viewed as failing to consider the impact that the decision would have on Latina/o representation on juries.

Segregation and exclusion have been effective means by which Latinas/os have been denied full civil and human rights. Although racial and ethnic segregation is unconstitutional and illegal, segregation remains commonplace in U.S. society and is manifested in ways that are subtle and sometimes difficult to discern. The persistence of segregation continues to affect all aspects of the lives of Latinas/os today, and its impact on criminal justice outcomes for Latinas/os can be severe. As a result, scholars suggest that legal challenges will have to continue to be utilized so that justice and equality can be advanced. Specifically with respect to hate crimes intended to keep Latinas/os and other people of color from moving into white neighborhoods, federal civil rights laws—including litigation under Section 241 of U.S. Code Title 18, and Section 3631 of the Fair Housing Act—have been used to prosecute anti-integration violence as well as a variety of federal, state, and local hate crimes statutes and criminal laws.

It is also significant that on June 25, 2015, in addressing the problem of housing discrimination, the U.S. Supreme Court in the case of *Texas Department of Housing and Community Affairs v. The Inclusive Communities Project, Inc.* held that one need not necessarily show intentional discrimination to prove illegal housing discrimination. For the civil rights advocates and for many who are frequently affected by discrimination, including Latina/o communities in the United States, the decision represents an important victory in addressing less obvious and indirect forms of discrimination by allowing complainants to show that certain acts are having a disparate impact that is discriminatory.

See also: Part I essays: Latinas/os and the U.S. Criminal Justice System; Policing and Latina/o Communities; Incarceration and Latinas/os in the United States; Latina/o Youth and Criminal Justice. Part II entries: Chicanas/os; Community Policing; *Hernandez v. New York*, 500 U.S. 352 (1991); *Hernandez v. Texas*, 347 U.S. 475 (1954); Legal Advocacy Groups.

Further Reading

Alba, Richard D., and John R. Logan. 1993. Minority proximity to whites in suburbs: An individual-level analysis of segregation. *The American Journal of Sociology* 98: 1388–1427.

Alba, Richard D., John R. Logan, and Brian J. Stults. 2000. The changing neighborhood contexts of the immigrant metropolis. *Social Forces* 79: 58–621.

Bell, Jeannine. 2007. Hate thy neighbor: Violent racial exclusion and the persistence of segregation. *Ohio State Journal of Criminal Law* 5: 47–77.

California Endowment. 2010. *Healthy communities matter: The importance of place to the health of boys of color*. Los Angeles, CA: The California Endowment, http://www.calendow.org/Article.aspx?id=4494. Accessed November 21, 2010.

Chetty, Raj, Nathaniel Hendren, and Lawrence F. Katz. 2015. The effects of exposure to better neighborhoods on children: New evidence from the moving to opportunity experiment (Working Paper 21156). Cambridge, MA: National Bureau of Economic Research. http://www.nber.org/papers/w21156.pdf.

Clegg, Roger. 2009. Color-coding the suburbs: The social engineers come to Scarsdale. *National Review Online*. http://www.nationalreview.com/corner/185785/color-coding-suburbs-social-engineers-come-scarsdale-roger-clegg?target=author&tid=1046. Accessed November 15, 2015.

Cobas, José, Jorge Duany, and Joe E. Feagin (eds.). 2009. *How the United States racializes Latinos: White hegemony and its consequences*. Boulder, CO: Paradigm.

Corcoran, Mary, Colleen M. Heflin, and Belinda L. Reyes. 1999. The economic progress of Mexican and Puerto Rican women. In *Latinas and African American Women at Work*, edited by I. Browne, 105–38. New York: Russell Sage Foundation.

Cordero-Guzman, Hector, Robert Smith, and R. Grosfoguel (eds.). 2001. Migration, transnationalization, and race in a changing New York. Philadelphia: Temple University Press.

Demeo, Marisa J., and Steven A. Ochoa. 2003. *Diminished voting power in the Latino community: The impact of felony disenfranchisement laws in ten targeted states.* Los Angeles, CA: Mexican American Legal Defense and Education Fund.

Editorial Board. 2015 (June 12). Westchester's Tortured Road. *New York Times*. http://www.nytimes.com/2015/06/13/opinion/westchesters-tortured-road.html?emc=eta1&_r=3. Accessed November 15, 2015.

Egelko, Bob. 2004 (March 2). U.S. Supreme Court to take prison segregation case: Fear of violence prompts state policy for reception centers. *San Francisco Chronicle* at A-13.

Escobar, Edward J. 1999. *Race, police, and the making of a political identity: Mexican Americans and the Los Angeles Police Department 1900–1945.* Berkeley: University of California Press.

Ferg-Cadima, James. 2004. *Black, white and brown: Latino school desegregation efforts in the pre- and post-Brown v. Board of Education era.* Mexican American and Legal Defense Fund. http://api.ning.com/files/JMPLiJz8JrOP-aK*m6d2ww1SGIfWuYKnryinYKg6gIJMasOFGu44M7bpWQIdu5UjhE3WWAZPmtXxNTpH6eumkYqZ1gcxq5zx/FergCadima2004.pdf. Accessed November 22, 2010.

Gootman, Elissa. 2003 (August 18). Old tensions over immigrants surface after firebombing. *New York Times*.

Haney López, Ian F. 2003. *Racism on trial: The Chicano fight for justice.* Cambridge, MA: Belknap/Harvard University Press.

Hefling, Kimberly. 2014 (January 8). Government offers new recommendations to combat "school-to-prison" pipeline. *Huffington Post*. http://www.huffingtonpost.com/2014/01/08/school-to-prison-pipeline_n_4560737.html. Accessed November 15, 2015.

Hipp, John. 2000. Income inequality, race, and place: Does the distribution of race and class within neighborhoods affect crime rates? *Criminology* 45(3): 665–97.

Kochhar, Rakesh. 2005. *The occupational status and mobility of Hispanics*. Washington, DC: Pew Hispanic Center. http://pewhispanic.org/files/reports/59.pdf. Accessed November 22, 2010.

Koehler, Robert. 2007. Petit apartheid and the "TB" syndrome: Police racial profiling of Chicano youths in San Jose, California. *Ethnic Studies Review* 30(1 & 2): 1–37.

Kucsera, John, with Gary Orfield. 2014. New York State's extreme school segregation inequality, inaction and a damaged future. Los Angeles, CA: The Civil Rights Project/*Proyecto Derechos Civiles*, UCLA.

MALDEF and The Civil Rights Project at UCLA. 2008. *Preserving integration options for Latino children: A manual for educators, civil rights leaders, and the community.* http://maldef.org/resources/publications/IntegrationOptionsManual.pdf. Accessed November 15, 2015.

Martínez, Jr., Ramiro. 2007. Incorporating Latinos and immigrants into policing research. *Criminology & Public Policy* 6: 157–64.

Massey, Douglas S., and Nancy A. Denton. 1993. American apartheid: Segregation and the making of the underclass. Cambridge: Harvard University Press.

Mauer, Marc. 2009. Two tiered justice: Race, class, and crime policy. In *The integration debate: Competing futures for American cities,* edited by C. Hartman and G. D. Squires, 169–83. New York: Routledge.

Misra, Joya. 1999. Latinas and African American women in the labor market: Implications for policy. In *Latinas and African American women at work,* edited by

I. Browne, 408–31. New York: Russell Sage Foundation.

Morín, José Luis. 2009. *Latino/a rights and justice in the United States: Perspectives and approaches*. 2nd ed. Durham, NC: Carolina Academic Press.

Mukherjee, Elora. 2007. *Criminalizing the classroom: The over-policing of New York City schools*. New York: New York Civil Liberties Union and the American Civil Liberties Union.

NAACP Legal Defense and Education Fund. 2010. Captive constituents: Prison-based gerrymandering and the distortion of our democracy. New York: NAACP Legal Defense and Education Fund. http://www.thedefendersonline.com/2010/06/02/captive-constituents-prison-based-gerrymandering-and-the-distortion-of-our-democracy. Accessed November 19, 2010.

New York Civil Liberties Union. [n.d.]. New 2 weeks after class action lawsuit filed over police in NYC schools. Another Child Arrested for Desk Doodling. http://www.nyclu.org/news/2-weeks-after-class-action-lawsuit-filed-over-police-nyc-schools-another-child-arrested-desk-do.

New York Times. 2009 (August 11). Fair housing in the suburbs. Editorial. A20.

New York Times. 2010 (August 22). An end to prison gerrymandering. Editorial.. http://www.nytimes.com/2010/08/23/opinion/23mon3.html?_r=1. Accessed November 19, 2010.

Ofer, Udi, Angela Jones, Johanna Miller, Deinya Phenix, Tara Bahl, Christina Mokhtar, and Chase Madar. 2009. *Safety with dignity: Alternatives to the over-policing of schools*. New York: New York Civil Liberties Union, Annenberg Institute for School Reform at Brown University and Make the Road New York.

Orfield, Gary, and Chungmei Lee. 2006. *Racial transformation and the changing nature of segregation*. Cambridge, MA: The Civil Rights Project at Harvard University.

Orfield, Gary, and Erica Frankenberg, with Jongyeon Ee and John Kuscera. 2014. Brown at 60: Great progress, a long retreat and an uncertain future. Los Angeles, CA: UCLA, The Civil Rights Project/*Proyecto Derechos Civiles*, UCLA.

Págan, Eduardo Obregón 2003. *Murder at Sleepy Lagoon: Zoot suits, race, and riot in wartime L.A*. Chapel Hill, North Carolina: University of North Carolina Press.

Prison Policy Initiative. [n.d.]. Prison gerrymandering. http://www.prisonpolicy.org/research/prison_gerrymandering/. Accessed November 15, 2015.

Reardon, Sean F., Lindsay Fox, and Joseph Townsend. 2015. Neighborhood income composition by household race and income, 1990–2009. *Annals of the American Academy* 660: 78–97. doi: 10.1177/0002716215576104.

Rodriguez, Clara E. 2000. *Changing race: Latino/as, the census, and the history of ethnicity in the United States*. New York, NY: New York University Press.

Rogers, Robert. 2010 (August 16). Integrated state prison cells still distant. *The Bay Citizen*. http://www.baycitizen.org/crime/story/integrating-california-prison-cells. Accessed November 20, 2010.

South, Scott J., Kyle Crowder, and Erick Chavez. 2005. Migration and spatial assimilation among U.S. Latino/as: Classical versus segmented assimilation. *Demography* 42(3): 497–521.

Steinmetz, Erika, and John Iceland. 2003. *Racial and ethnic residential housing patterns in places: 2000*. U.S. Census Bureau, 1–17. Paper presented at the annual meetings of the Population Association of America, Minneapolis, MN.

Texas Appleseed. 2007. *Texas' school-to-prison pipeline: Dropout to incarceration: The impact of school discipline and zero tolerance*. Austin, TX: Texas Appleseed.

Tita, George, Tricia L. Petras, and Robert T. Greenbaum. 2006. Crime and residential choice: A neighborhood level analysis of the impact of crime on housing prices. *Journal of Quantitative Criminology* 22: 299–317.

United Nations. 1966. International covenant on civil and political rights. Done at New York, Dec. 16, 1966. Entered into force, Mar. 23, 1976. U.N.G.A. Res. 2200(XXI), 21 U.N. GAOR, Supp. (No. 16) 52, U.N. Doc. A/RES/6316 (1967), reprinted in 6 I.L.M. 368 (1967). Ratified, United States, 1994.

U.S. Bureau of the Census. 2008. *Residential segregation of Hispanics or Latinos: 1980–2000*. Washington, DC Housing and Household Economic Statistics Division. http://www.census.gov/hhes/www/housing/housing_patterns/pdf/ch6.pdf. http://www.census.gov/hhes/www/housing/housing_patterns/ch6.html. Revised: August 11, 2008.

U.S. Bureau of the Census. 2015a. State and County QuickFacts: New York. http://quickfacts.census.gov/qfd/states/36000.html. Accessed November 15, 2015.

U.S. Bureau of the Census. 2015b. State and County QuickFacts: New York (City), New York. http://quickfacts.census.gov/qfd/states/36/3651000.html. Accessed November 15, 2015.

U.S. Department of Education Office for Civil Rights. 2014. Civil Rights data collection, data snapshot: School discipline (Issue Brief No. 1, March 2014). Washington, DC: U.S. Department of Education.

U.S. Department of Housing and Urban Development. 2009. *Anti-discrimination Center of Metro New York vs. Westchester County. Stipulation and order of settlement and dismissal*. No. 06 Civ. 2860 (DLC). http://www.hud.gov/content/releases/settlement-westchester.pdf. Accessed November 15, 2015.

Vargas-Ramos, Carlos, and Andrew Maroko. 2006. *Settlement patterns and residential segregation of Puerto Ricans in the United States*. New York, NY: Centro de Estudios Puertorriqueños, Hunter College (City University of New York).

Yinger, John. 1995. *Closed doors, opportunities lost: The continuing costs of housing discrimination*. New York, NY: Russell Sage Foundation.

Cases Cited

Brown v. Board of Education, 347 U.S. 483 (1954).

Hernandez v. New York, 500 U.S. 352 (1991).

Hernandez v. Texas, 347 U.S. 475 (1954).

Johnson v. California, 543 U.S. 499 (2005).

Keyes v. School Dist. No. 1, 413 U.S. 189 (1973).

Mendez v. Westminster School District of Orange County, 64 F. Supp. 544, 549 (S.D. Cal. 1946), *aff'd*, 161 F.2d 774 (9th Cir. 1947).

Texas Department of Housing and Community Affairs v. The Inclusive Communities Project, Inc., No. 13-1371, 2015 U.S. LEXIS 4249 (2015).

United States et al. v. Yonkers Board of Education, 624 F. Supp.1276 (1985); 837 F.2d 1181 (2d Cir. 1987).

Selective Prosecutions. *See* Part I essays: Policing and Latinas/o Communities; Incarceration and Latinas/os in the United States.

Sentencing Project, The. *See* Part I essays: Latinas/os and the U.S. Criminal Justice System; Latinas and the U.S. Criminal Justice System; Incarceration and Latinas/os in the United States. Part II entries: Death Penalty; Felon Disenfranchisement; International Human Rights.

Sex Crimes. *See* Part I essays: Crime and the U.S.-Mexican Border; Latinas and the U.S. Criminal Justice System. Part II entries: Deportation Laws; Hate Crime; Human Trafficking; International Human Rights; Intimate Partner Violence/Domestic Violence; *Miranda v. Arizona*, 384 U.S. 436 (1966); Slavery; Transnational Crime; Victims.

Slavery

Maria Swimm

Slavery, generally defined as the control of a person bound in servitude by an individual, group, or institution through the use of persistent threat or use of **violence**, often is considered to have been eradicated generations ago. Slavery, however, is very much a modern-day phenomenon. Having touched every part of the globe over thousands of years, slavery is viewed by the international community as an intolerable crime and a gross violation of fundamental human rights. It is well-established under international law that all countries are obligated to protect persons from slavery, and as such, "[t]he practice of slavery has thus been universally accepted as a crime against humanity" (Weissbrodt & Anti-Slavery International 2002, 3). Nevertheless, contemporary forms of slavery take many forms today, and it is a form of exploitation that has persistently plagued the most vulnerable populations. Although the practice of slavery has been condemned around the world, it has succeeded in remaining a consistently lucrative industry. Latinas/os have tended to be extremely vulnerable to slavery as a result of pervasive poverty in their home countries in Latin America in which many are susceptible to forced labor, debt bondage, and sexual exploitation. Conservative estimates approximate that 27,000,000 slaves exist today worldwide (Bales 2007).

Globally, modern-day slavery has been able to thrive primarily through the ubiquitous **human trafficking** industry. Human trafficking, explained as the coerced transporting or harboring of a vulnerable person for the purpose of abusive activities, provides exploiters with the means to profit from the degradation and suffering of its **victims**. Trafficking results in the direct victimization of men, women, and children as they are forced into commercial sexual exploitation, domestic servitude, and factory and textile work, made to produce revenue for the keepers who maintain their control through the threat or use of violence. Slaves are employed in homes, on farms, in mines, fields, restaurants, hotels, brothels, or wherever traffickers can employ them, working long, arduous work days for little or no compensation.

Contrary to popular beliefs, slavery is not a phenomenon experienced only by persons of African descent. Instead, it is a crisis greatly suffered by Latina/o men, women, and children as well. In the United States, "mulattos" and "mestizos," along with blacks, automatically were subject to slavery under slave codes, as found in South Carolina. The broad racial distinction between whites and non-whites laid the foundation for a system of treatment post-slavery, in which those who are racially "other"—including African Americans and Latinas/os—would be treated unequally by the "dominant 'white' social structure" (Morín 2008, 15). Though Latinas/os can be trafficked between South and Central America and into Europe and Asia, a significant number are transported into the United States each year, primarily exploited as domestic servants and as cheap labor in the agriculture and textile industries.

Although the modern-day slave is not shackled or branded, he or she is imprisoned, divested of dignity, and forced to remain dependent on a keeper who views him or her as nothing more than an instrument for personal profit. Because of the coercive and cruel qualities of human trafficking, it is appropriately likened to a contemporary form of slavery. Although there is nothing legal binding between "owner" and "slave" as there was in the chattel slave trade, dehumanization remains a prevalent and central feature of human trafficking. Individuals are continually threatened, harmed, and forced to work against their will and are viewed as merchandise that is useful only until he or she can be replaced with a more profitable, more vulnerable victim. According to the United Nations' Office of the High Commissioner of Human Rights, "patterns of discrimination are internalized by both perpetrators and victims, who more or less consciously envisage themselves as 'masters' and 'servants'" (Office of the High Commissioner of Human Rights 2010, 14).

The slave trade is said to have been able to endure for centuries for various reasons, including economic globalization, consistent population growth that tends to be concentrated in third-world countries, as well as persistent universal tolerance on the part of innumerable governments that have chosen to ignore obvious human rights infringements and the far-reaching grasp slavery has on its victims and affected communities. The unremitting indifference exhibited by leaders of corrupt governments has allowed the conditions that promote slavery to flourish in marginalized societies across nations, with traffickers continuing to profit from the blood of the most vulnerable, all while fearing no due penalty.

As poverty and the absence of legitimate work opportunities are significant contributors to the existence of human trafficking, indigenous persons in Latin America are particularly vulnerable to the slave trade. Throughout South, Central, and North America, indigenous ethnic groups are viewed as low caste and coerced into providing unrecompensed labor, primarily in domestic services and in the commercial sex industry. Market opportunities are exacerbated by additional problems that plague indigenous communities, including a lack of educational opportunities and racial and class bias, making them prime targets for the most virulent forms of oppression.

Although political, economic, and social transformations have occurred worldwide over time, the fundamental tenets and methods used to preserve slavery have changed little. Exemplary of the way that slavery as an industry has retained its configuration through the centuries is to review the three basic forms of slavery: chattel and contract slaveries and debt bondage. Persons born or sold into permanent slavery are victims of chattel slavery. Individuals are referred to and treated as property and remain in captivity for a lifetime, although they might be sold from one owner to another. Contract slavery is that in which individuals are deceived into work that, on the surface, looks legitimate. Soon after agreeing to fulfill specified obligations, individuals find themselves coerced into exploitative labor and sexual exploitation. The on-its-face legitimacy of contract slavery is alarming because it has been documented that victims unknowingly sign themselves into slavery for years, decades, or however long the contractor decides to retain them.

The most common form of contemporary slavery, however, is that of debt bondage in which an individual pledges him or herself against a monetary loan. Some persons looking to migrate from one region to the next might exchange labor for passage, thereby agreeing to indentured servitude to pay off their debt. Upon arrival to the new region, however, the monetary amount to be paid off is increased many times over, forcing the individual to work under dire circumstances for an undetermined period with no hope for relief. Extortion methods such as this are exemplary of the way in which traffickers retain control of their victims through endless greed and tyranny. The level of deception often is so severe that the slave—an individual with no other means of support, financially, socially, or politically—is exploited in ways unimaginable to the average person.

Although ownership is not formally asserted over the individual, physical and psychological control prevail and the victim incurs a debt that is ever-growing and inherited by future generations. Debt bondage has maintained its position as the most widely employed form of slavery because of its tremendous profitability for holders, bringing in high returns in exchange for uncompensated, unrestricted servitude.

The domestic work industry is one in which many Latinas/os find themselves fixed in a life of slavery. Domestic work includes cooking, cleaning, gardening, and caring for children and the elderly, either in or for a household. Across the globe, such work remains dominated by women and girls. Domestic work opportunities lure migrant workers with little to no formal education as it does not require certification as do other types of work and it often provides workers with a place to live. Due to their immigration status and complete dependence on their employers, many domestic workers are paid well below minimum wage, are forced to reside in inferior living conditions, are expected to be "on call" up to 20 hours a day, and often are denied adequate rest, vacation, and maternity leave. The ease with which many perpetrators are able to exploit these workers is extraordinary and Latina/o victims are often forced to live months, years, or even decades as a slave or in slave-like circumstances.

Perhaps the most disconcerting reality of slavery is that people are treated as disposable commodities that are viewed by their keepers to be worthy of concern only when they are profitable. Much of the literature on contemporary slavery in recent years speaks to the alarming rate at which people are discarded once they are not able to maximize personal production. This disregard for the slave by the owner is said to be much different than the early slave trade in which owners cared for those in their possession because, economically, their longevity and worth were dependent upon good health. Impoverished, desperate communities that are preyed upon today provide cheap slaves who are viewed as replaceable goods. As a result, these contemporary slaves are considered not worth maintaining if they have exceeded their value or merely become a liability. It is not uncommon for victims to be abandoned in waters, on streets, and in fields after bouts of illness or injury, or to have aged out of value.

People from Latin America fleeing violence and other forms of abuse, including contemporary forms of slavery, is a matter deserving of continued attention. The arrival of unaccompanied minors on the U.S. border from countries such as El Salvador, Guatemala, and Honduras in recent years should provide us with adequate notice about the need to understand the conditions and circumstances that have led these children to travel many miles alone to reach the United States—circumstances that could include some form of modern-day slavery. In its 2014 study of the situation, the United Nations High Commissioner for Refugees (UNHCR) has called for the full implementation of international legal protections to ensure the rights of unaccompanied children from Central America and Mexico to safety, security, and well-being as they seek refugee status or some other form of protection in coming to the United States (UNHCR 2014). It is equally important to guard against human trafficking, sexual exploitation, and other abuses targeting vulnerable Latinas/os, as poverty and other social and economic conditions render many in Latinas/os susceptible to contemporary forms of slavery.

Although the circumstances that lead to slavery and the conditions that individuals must abide by and endure might differ, human suffering is common to all who live as slaves worldwide. The dehumanization of individuals to be used as for-profit commodities is a problem that appears not to be subsiding. Today, there is an ever-growing number of organizations that seek to terminate slavery worldwide and advocacy groups who attempt to give former slaves a chance to attain personal agency. Although the attention given the issue of human trafficking has increased over the last decade—thereby creating a platform for the empowerment of victims—greater awareness about slavery, its pervasiveness, and the urgency of addressing the problem is needed. It will not be until the demand for cheap labor and sexual exploitation diminishes and fair and equal conditions of employment are guaranteed to migrants and marginalized communities through the enforcement of domestic and international law that such a scourge will cease to exist.

See also: Part I essay: Latinas and the U.S. Criminal Justice System. Part II entries: Human Trafficking; International Human Rights; Transnational Crime; Victims.

Further Reading

Bales, Kevin. 2004. *Disposable people: New slavery in the global economy, revised edition*. Berkeley, CA: University of California Press.

Bales, Kevin. 2007. *Ending slavery: How we free today's slaves*. Berkeley, CA: University of California Press.

Bales, Kevin. 2009. *The slave next door: Human trafficking and slavery in America today*. Berkeley, CA: University of California Press.

Free the Slaves. 2009. http://www.freetheslaves.net/. Accessed August 8, 2009.

Morín, José Luis. 2008. Latinas/os and U.S. prisons: Trends and challenges. *Latino Studies* 6: 11–34.

Office of the High Commissioner of Human Rights. 2010. *Report of the Special Rapporteur on contemporary forms of slavery, including its causes and consequences, Gulnara Shahinian*. Geneva Switzerland: United Nations Human Rights: Office of the High Commissioner of Human Rights.

Save the Children, UK. 2007. *The small hands of slavery: Modern day child slavery: A report by Save the Children UK*. London, UK. http://resourcecentre.savethechildren.se/library/small-hands-slaverymodern-day-child-slavery. Accessed November 15, 2015.

Sutton, Alison. 1994. *Slavery in Brazil: A link in the chain of modernization*. London: Anti-Slavery International.

United Nations High Commissioner for Refugees. 2014. *Children on the run; Unaccompanied children leaving Central America and Mexico and the need for international protection*. Washington, DC: UNHCR. http://www.unhcrwashington.org/sites/default/files/UAC_UNHCR_Children%20on%20the%20Run_Full%20Report.pdf. Accessed November 15, 2015.

Weissbrodt, David, and Anti-Slavery International. 2002. *Abolishing slavery and its contemporary forms*. New York, NY: United Nations Office of the United Nations High Commissioner for Human Rights. http://www.ohchr.org/Documents/Publications/slaveryen.pdf. Accessed November 15, 2015.

Sleepy Lagoon. *See* Part I essays: Latinas/os and the U.S. Criminal Justice System; Gangs in the United States and Latina/o Communities. Part II entries: Chicanas/os; Cultural Criminology; Civilian Oversight of Police; Media Depictions.

Stops and Frisks. *See* Part I essays: Latinas/os and the U.S. Criminal Justice System; Policing and Latina/o Communities; Incarceration and Latinas/os in the United States; Latina/o Youth and Criminal Justice. Part II entries: Civil Rights; Civilian Oversight of Police; Colombians; Deportation Laws; *Immigration and Naturalization Service (INS) v. Lopez-Mendoza et al.*, 468 U.S. 1032 (1984); Political Activist Groups; Segregation; *Terry v. Ohio*, 398 U.S. 1 (1968).

Sucuzhañay, José Osvaldo. *See* Part II entries: Hate Crimes; International Human Rights; Lesbian, Gay, Bisexual, and Transgender (LGBT).

Sucuzhañay, Romel. *See* Part II entries: Hate Crimes; International Human Rights; Lesbian, Gay, Bisexual, and Transgender (LGBT).

T

"Talk, The." *See* Part I essay: Policing and Latina/o Communities.

Terrorism. *See* Part I essays: Latinas/os and the U.S. Criminal Justice System; Incarceration and Latinas/os in the United States; Gangs in the United States and Latina/o Communities; Latina/o Youth and Criminal Justice. Part II entries: Colombians; Deportation; Deportation Laws; Immigrant Detention Centers; Immigration and Customs Enforcement (ICE); LatCrit: Latina & Latino Critical Legal Theory, Inc.; Transnational Crime.

Terry v. Ohio, 398 U.S. 1 (1968)

Sandra Del Valle

The Supreme Court's ruling in *Terry v. Ohio* (1968), the Court's seminal decision on "stops and searches," substantially limited the Constitution's Fourth Amendment protections against unreasonable searches and seizures. This case is directly implicated in the current controversy about the racial and immigrant profiling by law enforcement personnel along or near the **U.S.-Mexico border**. With *Terry*, the Court took a forceful step in allowing police officers to stop and search people based on officers' "suspicion." In its subsequent **border patrol** decisions, the Court loosened the requirements of the Fourth Amendment even more, which some argue has allowed the use of racial, ethnic, and linguistic profiling as a basis to stop and search vehicles and individuals.

Prior to *Terry*, the Fourth Amendment had been read as requiring that **police** officers have probable cause to believe that a crime had been committed, was being committed, or was imminent before an individual could be seized by the police and searched. Although the probable cause standard is written right into the Amendment, the *Terry* Court enunciated a lesser, "reasonable suspicion" standard for pre-arrest interactions between the police and the public.

In *Terry*, a police officer, McFadden, watched two men, Terry and Chilton, as they met and spoke on the street, talked back and forth, were joined by another man, separated and came together again. Based upon his experience as a police officer, McFadden believed that the men were preparing to rob a store. He approached them, identified himself, and asked them their names. He suspected that either or both of the men could be carrying a weapon. When the men mumbled a response, McFadden grabbed Terry, spun him around, searched his coat pockets, and found a revolver. McFadden then grabbed and searched Chilton and found a gun. Terry and Chilton were arrested and charged with carrying concealed weapons. On motions to suppress the evidence (the revolvers), the trial court found that the revolvers were lawfully obtained. It found that, although McFadden clearly did not have probable cause for arresting Terry and Chilton until after he found the weapons, based upon his experience as a police officer he did have a "reasonable suspicion" that a crime was about to be committed sufficient to interrogate and then search the men.

The Supreme Court took up the case on appeal. It recognized that a seizure had indeed occurred. Although Terry and Chilton were not handcuffed and taken away, as soon as they felt that they were not free to leave they effectively were seized. Further, the "exploration" of the men's clothing for concealed weapons was nothing less than a search. As such, the Fourth Amendment was implicated. The Court, however, declared a new, lesser standard for these pre-arrest police interactions: To justify an investigatory seizure and search, police officers must be able to point to "specific and articulable facts which, taken together with rational inferences from those facts, reasonably warrant that intrusion." The Court emphasized that it was trying to develop an objective standard susceptible to judicial review and to not open the door to searches based on nothing more than "inarticulate hunches." The Court, however, also cautioned that the Fourth Amendment not be allowed to become "mere words." Justice Douglas in his dissent insisted that the new "reasonable suspicion" standard was indeed a blow to the Fourth Amendment's integrity. Douglas argued that the probable cause standard had made a meaningful distinction between an officer's "mere inkling" and the presence of facts that an officer can reasonably draw upon to question and search a suspect (*Terry v. Ohio* 398 U.S. 1, 21–22, 38 (1968)).

Douglas's fear that a "mere inkling" would become the new standard in the eyes of many scholars has come to pass. If officers are allowed to rely on "hunches" or "inklings," the concern then is that people of color are most likely to be subjected to discriminatory or unequal treatment by police. This likelihood is greater in the interactions between border patrol officers and motorists along the U.S.-Mexican border.

A sovereign nation's right to control its borders and to protect itself by stopping and examining persons entering the country is well established in accordance with *Carroll v. United States* (1925). Searches that occur at the point of entry into the country can be made without warrant or probable cause or even the degree of suspicion required for other investigatory **stops.** The judicial analysis of the Fourth Amendment interests at stake in border control favors the government's position (*United States v. Ramsey* (1977); *United States v. Montoya de Hernandez* (1985).

The Supreme Court in *United States v. Montoya de Hernandez,* however, made clear that the *Terry* standard could apply to prolonged searches that extend beyond what normally is required for a customs check, although *Terry* cannot necessarily limit the length or intrusiveness of the search and seizure. It is in those cases that have arisen some miles away from the actual border that the jurisprudence has become murky. The courts have been accepting of the government's position that it must restrict unauthorized immigration from Mexico and of actions of the border patrol officers who are tasked with protecting Mexico's 2,000 mile border with the United States (***United States v. Brignoni-Ponce*** (1975); ***United States v. Martinez-Fuerte*** (1976)). The Supreme Court's decisions favoring broad governmental authority at the border to some—including some members of the Court itself who dissented—to countenance the indiscriminate harassment of motorists simply because they appear to be of Mexican descent and are traveling near the border.

In a series of cases the Supreme Court has sought to apply the *Terry* standard to a new context: border enforcement in an age of increased unauthorized immigration. In attempting to do so, the Court has made distinctions between roving border patrols and fixed check points, between degrees of intrusions and pushes the question of whether a "hunch" sometimes is enough after all. In *Almeida-Sanchez v. United States* (1973) and *United States v. Brignoni-Ponce* (1975), the Court took up the issue of roving border patrols. In the case of *Almeida-Sanchez*, the border patrol stopped a Mexican citizen's car when he was 25 air miles from the border and on a road that did not intersect with the border. The officers had no warrant nor did they assert either probable cause or reasonable suspicion for the stop. Instead, they relied on a provision of the Immigration and Nationality Act and its implementing regulation which authorizes warrantless searches of vehicles within 100 air miles of the border (U.S.C. § 1357(a)(3); 8 C.F.R. sec. 287.1). In the Prohibition era, the Court previously had found that officers could search vehicles without a warrant but insisted that the probable cause standard still applied (see *Carroll v. United States* 1925). The Court in *Almeida-Sanchez* found that the search was a violation of the Fourth Amendment despite the government's argument that it needed the type of freedom that the statute provided to effectively control unlawful immigration. Because the United States did not offer any basis for its search however, the Court did not have to decide whether it was the probable cause or the reasonable suspicion standard that applied.

In *United States v. Brignoni-Ponce*, the Court did indeed take up this question. The Court held that border patrol officers could not base a decision to stop and question occupants of a vehicle about their immigration status solely on the physical appearance of the occupants. The officers had asserted that the only reason they had stopped a vehicle was because the occupants appeared to be of Mexican descent. Applying the *Terry* standard the Court found the rationale for the stop insufficient. It justified the lesser standard, however, because of the "modest" nature of the intrusion when balanced against the significant law enforcement needs. It insisted that questioning or investigation beyond that limited nature would require probable cause. The Court undercut any rigor that could be found in its decision, however, by indicating a broad range of circumstances that could coalesce into reasonable suspicion. The examples it gave included whether a vehicle was a station wagon, whether it was heavily loaded, or whether its occupants dressed the way officers believed Mexican nationals dressed.

In *United States v. Martinez-Fuerte* (1976), the Court was called upon to decide the applicable standards in the context of fixed checkpoints established without a judicial warrant and at least 25 miles from the border. The border patrol had created a two-tiered checkpoint system. At the first stop the officers decided which cars to send to a secondary inspection point; there the vehicle occupants were questioned about their citizenship and immigration status. The Court adopted a benign view of fixed checkpoints. It found that the citing decision was based on permissible factors, that the visual inspection of the vehicle at the first point did not amount to a search at all, and that the questioning that occurred at the second checkpoint did not rise to the level of intrusion that would trigger *Terry*. In a breathtaking break with precedent, the Court specifically found that even if the decision to defer vehicles to the second inspection point was based solely on the appearance of being of Mexican descent, the search and seizure could be lawful. The Court stated that because the intrusion was "sufficiently minimal . . . no particularized reason" was required to justify it. Instead, "Border Patrol officers must have wide discretion in selecting motorists to be diverted for the brief questioning involved" (*United States v. Martinez-Fuerte* 1976, 563).

The *Martinez-Fuerte* decision has sparked considerable controversy and consternation among Latinas/os. Indeed, Justice William Brennan's dissent foresaw not only the manner in which this decision would be interpreted and implemented but also the bitterness that it would engender.

> Every American citizen of Mexican ancestry and every Mexican alien lawfully in this country must know after today's decision that he travels the fixed checkpoint highways at the risk of being subjected not only to a stop, but also to detention and interrogation, both prolonged and to an extent far more than for non-Mexican appearing motorists.

Brennan further predicted, "That deep resentment will be stirred by a sense of unfair discrimination is not difficult to foresee" (*United States v. Martinez-Fuerte* 1976, 572–73).

The deterioration of the Fourth Amendment's protections especially at the border has led legal scholars to suggest that the Court had created a "Mexican exception" to the Fourth Amendment. That is, the Supreme Court's decision in *Martinez-Fuerte* ostensibly provides an opening for law enforcement and immigration agents to engage in racial profiling, or at least national-origin discrimination.

The implications of the *Terry* decision and its progeny are especially concerning in view of the increase in contact between Latinas/os and the U.S. criminal justice system. In a 2009 study, the Pew Hispanic Center found that approximately 56 percent of Latinos surveyed said that they or someone in their immediate family had interacted with the criminal justice system in the five years preceding the survey. Fifty-nine percent of those had interacted in a way that at least suggests an accusation of criminal behavior, including attending court on a criminal, non-traffic-related matter, being arrested, being on probation or parole, and serving time in prison. Lopez and Livingston found that the Latino exposure to the criminal justice system has risen faster than has their share of the U.S. adult population (Lopez & Livingston 2009).

Interactions between Latinas/os and the criminal justice system appear to be increasingly negative, for the number of Latinos who have little confidence that they or other people of color will be treated fairly is quite low. A recent study shows that 47 percent of Latinas/os surveyed did not believe that police would avoid using excessive force on suspects and only 45 percent thought that they would be treated fairly by police. Perhaps not surprisingly, immigrant Latinos reported less confidence in the fairness of the legal system than did native-born Latinos: 58 percent of immigrants had little confidence versus 50 percent of the native-born respondents (Lopez & Livingston 2009). These findings raise significant questions for policy makers, local law enforcement departments, and all who seek to enhance civic engagement and confidence that the U.S. justice system is fair and equitable to all.

See also: Part I essays: Latinas/os and the U.S. Criminal Justice System; Policing and Latina/o Communities; Crime and the U.S.-Mexican Border. Part II entries: Civil Rights; Mexicans and Mexican Americans.

Further Reading

Cole, David. 1999. *No equal justice: Race and class in the American criminal justice system*. New York, NY: New Press.

Lopez, Mark Hugo, and Gretchen Livingston. 2009. *Hispanics and the criminal justice system: Low confidence, high exposure*. Washington, DC: Pew Hispanic Center.

Mirandé, Alfredo. 2003. Is there a "Mexican Exception" to the Fourth Amendment? *Florida Law Review* 55: 365–89.

Morín, José Luis. 2009. *Latino/a rights and justice in the United States: Perspectives and approaches*. 2nd ed. Durham, NC: Carolina Academic Press.

Cases Cited

Almeida-Sanchez v. United States, 413 U.S. 266 (1973).

Carroll v. United States, 267 U.S. 132 (1925).

Terry v. Ohio, 398 U.S. 1 (1968).

United States v. Brignoni-Ponce, 422 U.S. 873 (1975).

United States v. Martinez-Fuerte, 428 U.S. 543 (1976).

United States v. Montoya de Hernandez, 473 U.S. 531 (1985).

United States v. Ramsey, 431 U.S. 606 (1977).

Texas Rangers

Isabel Martínez

The Texas Rangers—or "*los rinches,*" as they were referred to by many Mexican American residents of South Texas—is a Texas government law enforcement organization known for its history of cruelty and animus toward Mexicans. Founded in the early 1800s, the Texas Rangers created a culture of terror, first against Native Americans and then against Mexicans prior to, during, and after the U.S.-Mexican War. In the name of nation-state and border development for the United States government, Texas Rangers enforced a violent system of subordination of Mexican-Americans in Texas, often acting in concert with Anglo civilian vigilantes in capturing and killing Mexicans. By the early- to mid-20th century, the purpose of the Texas Rangers shifted towards internal affairs, namely to breaking union strikes and dispersing civil rights protests. In spite of their changing roles, however, most indelible in the United States imagination is the memory of their ruthless acts to extend Anglo interests through force and the intimidation of Mexican-American residents.

Since the creation of the Texas Rangers, its members have been mythologized to exemplify the model American male and citizen. In an era of national expansion, the United States government lauded the Texas Rangers as being composed of men who—because of their fearlessness in fighting Native Americans and Mexicans, and their allegiance to national security—were worthy of being citizens of the United States. During Western expansion, manhood and citizenship were constructed in relation to Anglo male membership in militias and their commitment to protect and pursue Anglo expansion at the expense of Mexicans and in the name of Manifest Destiny.

History of the Texas Rangers

Traced back to the early 1820s, the Texas Rangers began as an unofficial team of men organized to protect a colony of early Anglo settlers in present-day Texas from Native American attack. Prior to Mexico's independence from Spain in 1821, the Spanish government allowed Anglo settlers to establish colonies in what now is Texas as long as they pledged their allegiance to the Spanish crown. Settling in lands controlled by Native Americans, however, placed their safety and the future colony development under threat for attack. In the name of defense, one of the main architects of the Texas revolution—Stephen F. Austin—with approval from the Spanish governor, created private ranger companies, employing men to protect his colony from Native Americans, including the Karankawa and Tonkawa tribes.

Although independent ranging companies were established as early as 1823 to protect and assist westward Anglo settlement, it was not until 1835 that the Texas Rangers organization formally was established. On the eve of the U.S.-Mexican War, a council of revolutionary colonists approved the formation of a corps of rangers to protect the frontiers between the Colorado, Brazos, and Trinity rivers. Unlike the official revolutionary army and militia that were targeting Mexicans, this group of approximately 150 men was responsible for using its own horses and arms to target Indians (Samora, Bernal, & Peña 1979; Webb 1965).

Until 1845, however, their employment was inconsistent and as needed with duties ranging from patrolling to spying. During the U.S.-Mexican War, however, various accounts exist that discuss their fighting deep in Mexico and their overall role in the defeat of Mexican forces. Charged only with accompanying other resources and other military units, the Texas Rangers were known to engage in extreme violence against Mexicans after provoking them. Samora, Bernal, and Peña (1979), for example, recount how a Mexican was shot dead after a Ranger stole candies from him. In another account, 80 Mexicans were killed by Texas Rangers in Mexico City in response to the murder of one Texas Ranger.

In 1861, the organization became an official division of Texas law enforcement. As an official law enforcement agency of the newly formed state of Texas, the Texas Rangers' purpose was to be accountable to all citizens, both Anglo and Mexican. Their loyalties, however, were anything but to the entire community in Texas; instead, the group's focus was to advance the interests of a few wealthy robber baron settlers. This meant expanding the economic interests of Anglo settlers by displacing Mexican Texans after the U.S.-Mexican war.

The Texas Rangers relied on a variety of tactics to assist wealthy Texas landowners in their economic and political expansion. The organization relied mostly on intimidating and exploiting Mexicans so that they would voluntarily flee and relinquish their properties. Unable to evict Mexicans by legal means, Texas landowners, such as Richard King—owner of the King Ranch—and Mifflin Kennedy enlisted the support of Texas Rangers to increase their holdings. In the case of King, he provided both beef and money to the Rangers for their protection and assistance.

To both protect the Mexico-Texas border and advance the individual property interests of Anglo settlers, however, Texas Rangers engaged in extralegal activities that extended beyond reasonable means. Although officially responsible for rooting out potential Mexican revolutionaries or cattle rustlers, Texas Rangers often used these pretexts to harass and kill Mexicans. In numerous cases, Rangers confiscated cattle for Anglo settlers that had been stolen from Mexicans in the first place. In other cases, Rangers killed innocent Mexicans without provocation, accusing them of revolutionary activities. Although the Mexican Border Commission refuted claims that the acts of the Texas Rangers were lawful, the Rangers continued to act with impunity. Carrigan and Webb (2003, 2013) estimated that thousands of Mexicans were lynched at the hands of the Texas Rangers, acts for which the Rangers never were held accountable. If unarmed Mexican "villains" were found lynched or shot, blame would lie not with the Rangers, but rather with the Mexicans, who were alleged to have killed themselves.

Resistance to Texas Rangers

Texas Rangers, however, did not enact violence on Mexicans without meeting resistance. Key Mexican American figures who challenged the Texas Rangers include Gregorio Cortez and Juan Cortina. Gregorio Cortez was a Mexican ranch hand who, in 1901, was accused of being a horse thief. After law enforcement officials shot and wounded his brother and then shot at him, Cortez shot and killed one of the men. Hundreds of men, including the Texas Rangers, sought his capture across the U.S.-Mexico border and finally, after 10 days, a fellow Mexican told officials where Cortina could be found.

Juan Cortina was a Mexican landowner who, in 1859 in Brownsville, Texas, shot and killed a federal marshal after witnessing the marshal pistol-whipping a Mexican prisoner who had been his former servant. Soon after, Cortina organized 100 men and declared a raid on Brownsville, freeing prisoners and calling for greater protections for Mexicans living in this territory. Eventually, Texas Rangers backed by U.S. Army troops began a reign of terror against Mexicans in Brownsville, Texas, eventually defeating and detaining Cortina. After several appeals, Cortina was acquitted of murdering a landowner and pardoned for the murder of a sheriff. Upon his release, Mexicans and *Tejanos* along the border hailed him a hero for standing up for the rights of Mexican/*Tejano* border residents.

Texas Rangers As Strike Breakers

By the middle of the 20th century, Texas Rangers continued as instruments of the state and business interests, but their focus shifted to unions and civil rights activists. Mirroring the shifts in power during the 20th century, the targets of the Texas Rangers slowly became more associated with union membership, which, although less overt, still possessed racial undertones. In 1967, Texas Rangers were sent to dismantle the Starr County farm workers strike. After dismantling the predominantly Mexican American strike, Texas Rangers were accused of using excessive force in arresting picketing union members. Reaching the Supreme Court, the Texas Rangers were found guilty of these charges.

Contemporary Depictions of Texas Rangers

By relying on documents and accounts penned by Anglo settlers, most Texas historians have celebrated Texas Rangers as heroes, as "quiet, deliberate, gentle men," and honorable fighters for truth and justice (Mirandé 1987; Webb 1965). Juxtaposed against criminal Mexicans, Texas Rangers are praised for their bravery and selflessness in protecting fellow Anglo settlers from these vagrants. For their service, Anglo settlers associated Texas Rangers with justice and the American way, sanctioning their violent tactics against Native Americans and Mexicans as necessary for the ousting of criminal elements from Texas.

These heroic representations have continued to influence contemporary ideas about the Texas Rangers. In one of its most famous incarnations, the CBS television show, "Walker, Texas Ranger," Chuck Norris was cast as a modern-day Texas Ranger who fought crime using vigilante justice. Aired from 1993 to 2001 and now in syndication on cable networks Hallmark and USA, this long-running show was lauded for its family-friendly appeal. In the TV program, although Norris performed violent acts, his acts were deemed necessary to dramatize the themes of good versus evil and to depict him as a champion of moral justice. In 2010, Texas Governor Rick Perry appointed Norris an honorary Texas Ranger for this role and for the "renewed attention" that Norris brought to the Texas Rangers. Perry described his portrayal of a Texas Ranger as "iconic," and believed that Norris accurately characterized the Rangers as individuals who are "observant, meticulous and honorable" (Ball 2010).

Other scholars have refuted this image, and instead have provided evidence of the Rangers' cruelty, criminality, and law breaking. Based on interviews with Mexicans and Anglos, as well as examination of documents and other artifacts, several historians have concluded that the Texas Rangers engaged in excessively violent tactics and injustices. During their reign of terror, innumerable *corridos* (Mexican folklore songs) characterized an alternate view of the Texas Rangers. The earliest border *corrido* described the experiences of Juan Cortina and the conflict in Brownsville, but one of the most famous chronicled the conflict between the Texas Rangers and Gregorio Cortez. *El Corrido de Gregorio Cortez* still is performed by singers near the border to inform and educate border residents of this event. In 1982, Embassy Pictures Corporation and the National Endowment of the Arts brought the story of Gregorio Cortez to film, first on PBS and then in movie theaters. Chicano scholars, however, complained that the movie—although well-intended—failed to portray the extent of not only racism against Mexicans in South Texas at the turn of the century, but also the Mexican community's response to the Anglo injustices and its support for Cortez. Given the opportunity to glimpse into the lives of Mexicans under the reign of Texas Rangers, many Chicano scholars believe that Hollywood fell short.

Rarely held accountable for their actions by the state, the Texas Rangers operated as a law and justice organization. The Texas Rangers often used unauthorized violence to intimidate Mexicans, oftentimes even resorting to murder. Supported by the U.S. government, and later by wealthy Anglo landowners, Texas Rangers acted to establish and then maintain white hegemony in the state of Texas. Acting without fear of punishment, the Texas Rangers intimidated *Tejanos* to flee their land and, in the worst cases, murdered resistant and even submissive Mexicans and *Tejanos*. The Texas Ranger legacy in Texas has been a violent one, overshadowed by state-sanctioned vigilantism targeting Mexicans.

See also: Part I essays: Latina/o Immigrants, Crime, and Justice; Crime and the U.S.-Mexican Border. Part II entries: Hate Crimes; Media Depictions; Vigilantism.

Further Reading

Ball, Linda Stewart. 2010 (December 3). Chuck Norris named honorary Texas Ranger. *The El Paso Times*. http://www.elpasotimes.com/news/ci_16764442.

Carrigan, William D., and Clive Webb. 2003. The lynching of persons of Mexican Origin or descent in the United States, 1848–1928. *Journal of Social History* 37(2): 411–38.

Carrigan, William D., and Clive Webb. 2013. *Forgotten dead: Mob violence against Mexicans in the United States, 1848–1928*. Oxford, UK: Oxford University Press.

Delgado, Richard. (2009). The law of the noose: A history of Latino lynching. *Harvard Civil Rights and Civil Liberties Review* 44: 297–312.

Fregoso, Rosa Linda. 1993. *The bronze screen: Chicana and Chicano film culture*. Minneapolis, MN: University of Minnesota Press.

Mertz, Richard J. 1974. No one can arrest me: The story of Gregorio Cortez. *Journal of South Texas* 1: 1–17.

Mindiola, Tatcho, Jr. 1984. Film critique: The ballad of Gregorio Cortez. *La Red/The Net* 80: 11–17.

Mirandé, Alfredo. 1987. *Gringo justice*. Notre Dame, IN: University of Notre Dame Press.

Paredes, Americo. 1958. *With his pistol in his hand: A border ballad and its hero*. Austin, TX: University of Texas Press.

Rodríguez, Juan Carlos. El corrido de Gregorio Cortez. 2012. *Handbook of Texas Online*. http://www.tshaonline.org/handbook/online/articles/xee02. Accessed November 15, 2015.

Samora, Julian, Joe Bernal, and Albert Peña. 1979. *Gunpowder justice: A reassessment of the Texas Rangers*. Notre Dame, IN: University of Notre Dame Press.

Webb, Walter Prescott.1965. *The Texas Rangers*. Austin, TX: University of Texas Press.

Transnational Crime

Isabel Martínez

Transnational crime refers to types of illegal activities punishable under domestic or international penal law which extend beyond nation-state borders into other nation-states' legal jurisdictions. In recent years, activities have increased and diversified to include acts ranging from those committed by highly organized transnational criminal organizations (TCOs) to those committed by individuals. Across the Americas, human, drug, and arms **trafficking**, as well as money laundering, dominate the list of transnational crimes committed across borders.

In the United States, transnational crime often has been conflated with concerns about **immigration** and with **violence** often mistakenly attributed to immigrants. As a result, much of the immigration debate in the United States erroneously has included attributes that strictly belong to transnational crime organizations. Anti-immigrant figures have coupled the violence occurring in Mexico with immigration to fan fears about immigrant crime in the United States. Instead, the United States' border states and cities or the spaces across which these activities become transnational in the United States have remained among the safest areas in the Americas. Although unauthorized immigration rates increased at the end of the 20th century, rates of both violent and nonviolent crimes have diminished across the United States and in border states and cities such as Arizona and El Paso, Texas.

This entry broadly discusses transnational crime as it has emerged and has been addressed in the Americas, with a special focus on regional actors, conditions, and challenges found in Latin America. The rhetoric and role of the United States in the emergence of transnational crimes in the Americas will also be explored, with special attention given not only to the complicity of the United States policies, but also to the ways in which **immigration** and transnational crime have been conflated inaccurately and used as a tool for anti-immigrant campaigns. Lastly, human rights abuses occurring at the hands of TCOs and in response to crackdowns against TCOs is explored.

Characteristics and Contexts: Transnational Crime Organizations in the Americas

Characteristics of transnational criminal organizations include the ability to extend their reach into other countries via crime cells; alliances with other criminal organizations; and relationships with corrupt political leaders in countries other than their own. These crime organizations typically have similar structures and organization, mirroring traditional, legal, for-profit organizations. That is, they usually are organized with a hierarchical model of administration, strict divisions of labor, established organizational rules, as well as reliable, vast caches of capital that, in some cases, surpass the economic resources of many countries (Lee 1999). In Mexico, for example, drug cartels are well-known to possess *capos*, or cartel leaders, who oversee the entire organization, including employees ranging from regional directors, to *sicarios* (hitmen), to underage lookouts, drug runners, and errand boys and girls. These organizations earn an estimated $30 billion a year through the drug trade—about 3 to 4 percent of Mexico's $1.2 trillion annual GDP (Lee 2014).

The ability of cartels to operate in between traditional approaches to state security, as well as their financial capabilities, makes their disbandment especially difficult. For one, these crime organizations are able to elude traditional approaches to public security by operating across and in between domestic legal security organizations, effectively dodging each state's criminal justice systems (Shirk 2011). Their protection is financed within and across the states' criminal justice and security systems, and includes **police** officers, judges, and U.S. federal officials such as **Immigration and Customs Enforcement (ICE)** and **Border Patrol** agents. In fact, ICE and U.S. Border Patrol agents have been indicted in aiding and abetting transnational crime organizations in smuggling goods into the United States. According to the Department of Homeland Security, between 2003 and 2009, 129 U.S. Border Patrol agents and Customs and Border Protection officers were arrested on corruption charges that involved aiding drug and **human trafficking** (Graham 2011).

In other cases, transnational crime organizations work with the protection of states' criminal justice systems. Because of their extensive financial capabilities, TCOs oftentimes are protected by politicians, both domestically and abroad. Like legal organizations, TCOs often contribute to and influence particular electoral candidates and political campaigns to produce results and public policies that benefit and protect them. Their political influence can extend across national borders, as some transnational criminal organizations are able to negotiate protection with corrupt foreign leaders who enable TCO activity in their own countries. Across the Americas, countries with vast social inequalities, weak governmental, financial, and judicial institutions and finance laws, and permeable borders with drug-producing countries have been particularly vulnerable to the emergence and penetration of transnational crime organizations. Ecuador, for example, has become increasingly attractive to organizations such as those engaged in transnational criminal activity, including the FARC (the Revolutionary Armed Forces of Colombia). Several of former Ecuadoran President Correa's aides have been implicated in assisting and benefitting from the FARC's activities, such as money laundering and illegal arms sales. Central American countries such as Guatemala also have experienced increases in the presence of transnational crime organizations. After regional conflicts, the structural weaknesses of Central American states have enabled transnational criminal **gangs** to take root and thrive. In Mexico, the election of PAN candidate Vicente Fox Quesada and the end of one-party rule in Mexico in 2000 also coincided with the multiplication of more competitive and violent transnational criminal organizations.

Comparisons between the transnational crime emerging in Colombia in the 1980s and 1990s and that of today's Mexico often are drawn, sometimes in error. For example, the strategic and financial package provided to Mexico by the United States is modeled after the one provided to Colombia. In 2010, former Secretary of State Hillary Clinton concluded that particular characteristics of the Colombia conflict—including violence targeting journalists and politicians—were the same as those observed in Mexico, concluding that the "tactics of Mexican cartels looked increasingly like those of **Colombian** insurgents" (Ellingwood 2010). A closer look, however, shows that Clinton was mistaken to draw such a broad comparison when significant distinctions exist between the two countries' experiences. As a result of much criticism from Mexican officials, President Obama and Secretary Clinton backed off such unfounded comments.

The situation in Mexico also is not complicated by a regional conflict that involves insurgent activities of guerilla fighters, as in Colombia. In the case of Colombia, a fight for political control of the country has coincided with the emergence of a multi-billion-dollar transnational drug industry to create a dangerous mix of **drugs**, corruption, and insurgency, with each giving rise to violence. Mexican drug cartels only count on corruption and drugs, focusing on obtaining large profits from illicit activities. Unlike Colombian guerillas and cartels, Mexican transnational crime organizations have relied less on government disruption. Instead, they have depended more on the government to protect their businesses. Mexican TCOs exploit their relationships with corrupt government officials in exchange for protection of routes and illicit merchandise free from all legal accountability or liability. Thus, they rely on government corruption to enable the TCOs to act with impunity. In contrast, Colombian guerillas largely have been opposed to government, singling out political and legal figures for assassination rather than targeting rival organizations.

In terms of territorial control, FARC-controlled areas of Colombia were ceded to it by the government. Mexican cartels control areas of Mexico through violence and intimidation. The boundaries of guerilla groups were distinctly demarcated by the Colombian government and the guerilla groups, with the FARC possessing approximately 5 percent of current Colombia territory and guerillas. Mexican cartels do not control set territories in Mexico, although particular areas of the country are loosely considered to be under their control for financial purposes. The Mexican cartels also constantly are challenged by other cartels. The territorial boundaries have been contested predominantly through gun violence. This also is significant because—unlike in Colombia, where explosives were a significant element in the Colombian guerilla arsenal—bombs are not extensively used by Mexican cartels.

The Role of Regional Conflicts in the Emergence of Transnational Crime

In several Latin American countries, political, social, and economic instability during and after regional or internal military conflict have increased their vulnerability to the emergence of transnational criminal organizations. After the end of periods of armed conflict, tens of thousands of former guerillas and soldiers who were trained to commit acts of violence are left without jobs or land. Many arms and ammunition remain in the country long after military clashes have dissipated. Arms traffickers typically sell and smuggle unused arms to crime organizations and guerillas, and existing corrupt and incompetent law enforcement agencies have been incapable of or unwilling to quell criminal activities.

During the periods of armed conflict in Central America from the 1950s through the 1980s, for instance, the United States provided military assistance to a series of right-wing regimes—including dictatorships in such countries as Nicaragua, Guatemala, and El Salvador—to undermine left or center-left political groups in Latin America.

In Nicaragua, U.S. support for the counterrevolutionary forces, or *contras*, composed largely of the military personnel loyal to the Somoza dictatorship after the Somoza regime was toppled, implicated the United States in one of the largest political scandals in recent history—the Iran-Contra Affair. In the attempt to ensure the defeat of so-called "communists" in Central America during the 1980s, the U.S. government, via National Security Council representative Oliver North, funneled millions of dollars from illegal arms sales to Iran to support the Contras, all with the National Security Advisor and President Reagan's approval. The Contras were engaging in drug trafficking to the United States with the knowledge of the Reagan administration. Investigations concluded that the Central Intelligence Agency (CIA) knowingly concealed—among other things—drug trafficking routed directly into U.S. neighborhoods. In addition to these illicit activities, according to congressional documents, the Contras were found to have performed gross human rights violations against Nicaraguan citizens. The U.S. government's involvement in supporting corrupt governments and others engaged in arms and drug trafficking and human rights abuses has implicated the United States in the rise of transnational criminal activity, not only in Nicaragua but throughout Latin America.

Perceptions of Transnational Crimes in the United States

In the United States, transnational crime most often has been characterized and perceived as having originated in the developing world (Latin America) and unidirectionally spilling over into the United States. Only recently has it been more accurately distinguished as multi-directional, including the flow of criminal activities originating in the United States and moving into Latin American countries. Although the supply of drugs and human trafficking originate in Latin American countries, these activities have emerged to meet market demands in the United States, particularly illicit drug consumption and prostitution. Admitting U.S. complicity in 2009, former Secretary of State Hillary Clinton stated that the United States possesses an "insatiable demand" for drugs. In 2011, annual drug consumption in the United States was generated approximately $65 billion (Office of National Drug Control Policy 2011). Additionally, the livelihood of drug cartels is dependent on arms smuggling and money laundering occurring in the United States with upwards of 80 percent of arms used by drug cartels originating in the United States (Astorga & Shirk 2010).

Foremost in discussions of transnational crime in the United States is the threat of "spillover violence," or "drug-related violence that targets innocent civilians or law enforcement on U.S. soil" (Burnett 2011). Numerous studies, however, challenge the popular notion that uncontrollable spillover violence exists. Studies based on city and county FBI data conclude that for areas where criminal overflows have been suspected as most likely to occur—such as the U.S.-Mexico border and identified cartel hubs away from the border—there has been no statistically significant increase in violent crimes. In fact, prior to the expensive border security upsurge—including the construction of a wall and the dispatching of thousands of law enforcement officers to the region—rates of violent crime have been falling and continue to fall. In 2008, Texas border cities such as Laredo, Brownsville, and McAllen reported total **homicides** in single digits—11, 9, and 3, respectively. In El Paso, the Texas border city located directly across from one of the deadliest cities in the world, Ciudad Juarez, Chihuahua, only one case related to spillover violence has been identified in the previous three years. Border officials believe that because it is not in organizations' best interests to attract the attention of U.S. law enforcement on their own soil, cartels have prevented violent crime from seeping over the U.S.-Mexico border.

Despite a lack of substantial evidence linking Latin American drug cartels to violent crimes in the United States, U.S. political leaders called on former Secretary of State Hillary Clinton to designate Mexican drug cartels as "**terrorist**" groups because of perceived potential threats to United States security. There is little to no evidence, however, that Mexican transnational criminal organizations are interested in threatening the security of U.S. nationals or the national security (national defense, foreign relations, and economic interests) of the United States. Rather, these TCOs appear more interested in accumulating monetary wealth than in securing political or ideological power. Not surprisingly, within Mexico most people reject the idea that Mexico poses a national security threat to the United States.

Transnational Crime Organizations

At the end of the 20th century, the dominant transnational crime organizations in the Americas engaged in drug supply-demand relationships between Colombia and the United States. In the early 1980s, the Medellin Cartel evolved from a street gang into the largest Colombian cartel, eventually supplying half of the world's cocaine. Founded by Jorge Luis-Ochoa Vazquez, Pablo Emilio Escobar-Gaviria, Jose Gonzalo Rodriguez-Gacha, and Carlos Enrique Lehder-Rivas, this cartel was the primary target of U.S.-Colombian anti-narcotics initiatives.

Although most of their violence targeted other drug actors in the early 1990s, Colombian cartels directed their attention against the Colombian government to protest plans to extradite traffickers to the United States, and engaged in numerous violent attacks against Colombian politicians and governmental institutions. By the late 1980s, Medellin Cartel leader Pablo Escobar was imprisoned. He escaped from prison in 1992 only to be gunned down by Colombian police in 1993. His death marked the end of the Medellin Cartel and of large Colombian cartels in general. To fill the void left by the Medellin Cartel's dissipation, smaller drug organizations emerged to continue cocaine production and distribution.

The second largest Colombian cartel was the Cali Cartel. Founded in the late 1970s and early 1980s, the Cali Cartel was distinguished from the Medellin Cartel by its low profile and a focus on business management. By maintaining a low profile, the Cali Cartel avoided much of the legal attention afforded to the Medellin Cartel. Instead, during the most severe anti-narcotics initiatives, the Cali Cartel thrived while the Medellin Cartel suffered. Aside from drug production and distribution, the group also engaged in money laundering.

Drug trafficking groups such as the Medellin and Cali cartels existed at first parallel to and eventually in collaboration with guerrilla and paramilitary groups for a range of activities to ensure their protection, as well as to contract them to perform extortion and assassinations. Guerilla groups such as the Revolutionary Armed Forces of Colombia, for example, turned to narcotics production and trafficking in regions of Colombia to finance their political efforts with monies garnered from these endeavors. By 2000, the FARC earned up to $600 million a year in drug production.

The start of the 21st century reflects a shift in attention from Colombia to Mexican and

Central American transnational crime organizations. During this period, Mexican and Central American criminal organizations completed their evolution from *mulas*—drug-trafficking agents for Colombian crime organizations—to leaders of the illicit commodity trade in the Western Hemisphere. Currently, Mexican and Central American crime organizations produce a more diversified cache of drugs than do their Colombian counterparts, including most of the marijuana, methamphetamine, and heroin trafficked to the United States. In 2012, approximately 90 percent of the cocaine supplied to the United States was trafficked through Mexico, up from 77 percent from 2003 to 2014 (Lee 2014).

Currently, Central American and Mexican crime organizations are of most concern to United States federal law enforcement. Based in Central America, two transnational gangs, MS-13 ("Mara Salvatrucha") and the 18th Street Gang (M-18) are composed of displaced refugees from U.S.-sponsored Central American conflicts and have established cells in Central America, Mexico, and the United States. Legal tactics against these gangs have included prosecuting gang members under the Racketeer Influence and Corrupt Organizations (RICO) statute, as well as relying on criminal and immigration enforcement laws resulting in **deportation**s. Effectively strengthening the transnational ties between gang cells and members, deportations have led to a "revolving door" syndrome, or the return of transnational gang members to Central America and Mexico where they are able to spread U.S. gang culture and then return to the United States.

In Mexico, one of the drug cartels of greatest interest has been Los Zetas. Made of former elite Mexican military members, this cartel previously provided armed security forces for the Gulf Cartel located in northeastern Mexican states, including Tamaulipas and Nuevo Leon. After a break with the Gulf Cartel in early 2010, Los Zetas evolved into its own crime organization and has been fighting for control of the northeastern Mexican corridor for trafficking drugs, humans, and other illicit commodities. Los Zetas has been identified as being responsible for the recent unprecedented rash of kidnappings, murders, and mass burials of Central American and Mexican immigrants traveling to the United States and, overall, it has emerged as the most violent dangerous threat to Mexican security, causing significant shifts in strategies employed in former Mexican President Càlderon's war against drugs. In the United States, President Obama signed an Executive Order naming Los Zetas as a criminal group that could threaten the United States' interests and security, and calling for the barring of members' entry into the United States. Additionally, the order requires financial sanctions against members of the group as well as individuals who aid and abet them inside U.S. borders. This would include members of several U.S.-based gangs contracted by the Zetas, including Barrio Azteca, MS-13, and the Texas Syndicate. These groups have been retained by Los Zetas for particular low-threat operations such as smuggling and illicit storage.

Although the source or "supply-side" of illegal drugs commonly is the focus of attention, little is mentioned of demand-side forces which maintain and encourage transnational crime and that originate in the United States. The demands of U.S. citizens for drugs and for bodies (for both labor and sex) fuel transnational crimes. For one, the United States' vast addiction to illegal drugs drives the drug trade in the Americas. Even former Secretary of State Hillary Clinton has acknowledged U.S. involvement in contributing to drug trafficking from Latin America to the United States (Landler 2009). United States employers also stimulate transnational human smuggling through their desire for both cheap, exploitable, unauthorized labor and for sexual partners. The 2006 report, *Trafficking in Persons*, estimated that the numbers of people trafficked into the United States ranged from 600,000 to 800,000 a year (U.S. State Department 2006).

Efforts to Address Transnational Crime

Efforts to prevent and deter transnational crime have employed different tactics, based on the size and source of the criminal activity and organization. These tactics reflect different degrees of cross-border interventions, from enacting legislation that targets transnational crime organizations and leaders' activities to providing cross-border funds to establishing counter-criminal law enforcement offices in the home countries of transnational crime organizations.

Several United States–sponsored policies, ranging from highly interventionist to more collaborative, have had minimal impact on transnational drug production and distribution between the United States and Latin America, and many analysts have declared that the more than 30-year-long **war on drugs** has failed. The 1989 Panama Invasion ("Operation Just Cause"), for example, targeted former School of the Americas graduate, Panamanian head of state, and alleged "drug kingpin" Manuel Noriega. After his capture and extradition to the United States, it was found that Noriega was not quite the drug kingpin he was touted to be by Washington and in the U.S. media. Moreover, his capture did little to nothing to curb illicit drug distribution originating from Panama.

Other country-specific, comprehensive strategies aimed at diminishing transnational criminal activities in the Americas have included broader-based aid packages and legislation, such as the controversial Plan Colombia and the Merida Initiative. Under Colombian President Pastrana, Plan Colombia began in 1998 as an effort to end the 40-year regional conflict that had plagued Colombia, promote peace and economic development, and curb drug trafficking. Designed to be transnational in nature, funding primarily was split between Colombia and the United States. With the goal of obstructing drug trafficking to the United States, U.S. funds totaling more than $7 billion have targeted the eradication of coca and poppy crops, training, and support for the Colombian military and law enforcement agents, alternative crop development, and the development and protection of infrastructure that assists in providing Colombians with legal sources of income. Since 2000, however, the United States has continued to fund these efforts through the Andean Counterdrug Initiative (ACI) as well as the Foreign Military Financing Program and the Department of Defense counter-narcotics account.

Disagreement on the success of Plan Colombia exists. Colombian leaders insist that coca cultivation has been reduced to less than a third of its production at the inception of Plan Colombia, but critics believe that reduction has been temporary, pushing drug production beyond Colombian borders to surrounding Andean countries such as Ecuador and other countries in the Andean region. Additionally, Plan Colombia has been plagued with accusations of numerous human rights violations conducted by the government, including the murders of innocent civilians by the Colombian military in an effort to claim progress on the war on drugs. In recent analyses of the success of Plan Colombia, scholars have found evidence of the use of United States dollars for paramilitary efforts promoting electoral fraud and intimidation.

At the start of the 21st century, the U.S. and Mexican governments' response to transnational crimes has been the Merida Initiative. Although this $1.8 billion comprehensive partnership originally was designed to combat **drug trafficking** and organized crime between the United States and Central America, the Dominican Republic, and Haiti, Mexico has been the recipient of most of the funds. Much like Plan Colombia, between 2008 and 2010 these funds were focused on developing and equipping law enforcement, as well as counterinsurgency and counterterrorism efforts modeled after those practiced in Iraq and Afghanistan. More recently, the Obama administration has proposed a shift in the objectives of the Merida Initiative to include increased emphasis on institutional and community development.

As with Plan Colombia, the Merida Initiative's efficacy has been called into question. Promised funds had not been released in a timely manner, and the funds have been spent on training the armed services that have a long history of corruption and human rights violations. The renewal of funding has occurred with much criticism, as Mexico has experienced approximately 60,000 drug-related deaths over a six-year period and the rates of trafficking into the United States and drug-related violence have continued (Beittell 2013).

Approved by Mexican President Felipe Calderon, a United States military intelligence megaplex, the Office of Bilateral Intelligence (OBI) opened in Mexico City on August 31, 2010. The OBI is modeled after the Texas-based El Paso Intelligence Center (EPIC), which is credited with creating and implementing the strategies against broad-based drug trafficking and organized crime in Mexico. The OBI houses offices for the Pentagon, the Department of Justice (DOJ), the Central Intelligence Agency (CIA), the Federal Bureau of Investigation (FBI), the Department of Homeland Security, the Department of Treasury, and other law enforcement offices. The OBI manages all tactical efforts, counterinsurgency operations, and counterterrorism efforts against drug cartels in Mexico. It also oversees the resources provided by Washington via the Merida Initiative to combat the drug war in Mexico. Two remote offices in Juarez and Tijuana also are in operation.

The presence of United States military and law enforcement agents in Mexico continues to expand. In the summer of 2011, the United States increased its physical presence on Mexican soil by embedding greater numbers of CIA operatives and American civilian military employees in Mexico, all with the approval of the Calderon administration. These personnel are working with Mexican officials to plan strategic anti-cartel operations and to collect intelligence. Perhaps most controversial, however, has been the deployment of unmanned drones from the United States deep into Mexican territory. Although flown along the U.S.-Mexico border since the early 2000s, this initiative, coordinated by both the Department of Homeland Security and the Department of Defense but supervised by the Mexican air force and other agencies, has brought previously unseen U.S. surveillance tactics to Mexican territories.

The growing presence of U.S. agents operating on Mexican soil has sparked concern among **Mexicans** who recall previous U.S. violations of Mexican sovereignty including U.S. occupation of Mexican territory. Largely a response to U.S. occupations, Mexican laws prohibit the presence of foreign military and police. In this case, however, U.S. and Mexican officials both assert that they have been careful to comply with Mexican law. United States and Mexican officials have also attributed U.S. interventionist actions in Mexico as having been conducted at the behest of Mexico, not to conditions attached to receiving U.S. aid. Lastly, an ongoing concern among Mexicans involves U.S. assistance provided since 1999 to train the notoriously corrupt Mexican military and law enforcement forces. These U.S. funds inadvertently resulted in the training of founding Los Zetas members. Overall, competing agendas and interests on both sides of the U.S.-Mexican border pose grave challenges for binational cooperation. It is difficult for countries to effectively eradicate criminal activities on both sides of and across state borders if countries perceive the problem and the solutions differently.

In the effort to combat transnational crime across the Americas, broad-based law enforcement organizations have been developed. One such example is Ameripol, founded in 2007 to coordinate police actions across the Americas. Modeled after Europol, the institution's primary function is to draw upon regional police forces in operations that reduce crime spanning across nation-state borders. Intelligence sharing, standardizing police training, and coordinating investigations are among its top priorities.

Ameripol's creation was a response to several shortcomings in the "war" against transnational crime. Although transnational crime organizations exercised smooth coordination across borders, local and regional law enforcement agencies did not. In the past, other global organizations targeting transnational crime—such as Interpol and the United States Drug Enforcement Agency—had to rely on individual local police forces to gather information on TCOs' activities within nation-state borders and local areas. Ameripol serves as a clearinghouse for information criminal activities across the region and represents an attempt to respond to criticism that the military tactics resulting in human rights violations have been overused to combat transnational crime and that few parties have been held accountable for these violations.

Ameripol has not been without criticism, however. The selection of Mexican Secretary of Public Security Genaro Garcia Luna as the Secretary General of Ameripol (2010–2013) received scrutiny, as his closest supporters and agents have been linked with Mexican cartels, namely that of Sinaloa and Beltran Leyva. So serious are the concerns, that Garcia Luna and his former office have been the subjects of investigations by the Mexican attorney general.

Legislative counter-narcotics strategies include the 1999 Foreign Narcotics Kingpin Designation Act. Based on the previous legislation, the Blocking Assets and Prohibiting Transactions Act which gained prominence in addressing the flow of narcotics arriving from Colombia, the Foreign Narcotics Kingpin Designation Act has been used against Mexican drug cartels and their financial and commercial activities. Part of a multi-agency response to transnational crime that includes the State Department, the Justice Department, and other U.S. government agencies, this law allows the United States Treasury department to freeze any assets traced back to drug kingpins. In 2010, three Mexican drug cartels were added to the list of targeted drug-running organizations, including the Sinaloa Cartel, La Familia Michoacana, and Los Zetas.

Legislation that held the promise of significantly curbing transnational crime is the inter-American arms treaty banning the sale of assault weapons in the United States.

Expired in 2004, Mexican President Calderon hoped that the Obama administration would keep its campaign promise and ban assault weapons, but its renewal by the U.S. Congress is viewed as being unlikely. Instead, smaller piecemeal gains have been made. Acknowledging that gun smuggling from the United States to Mexico is a significant challenge to fighting the war on drugs, the Obama administration has supported legal standards requiring gun dealers in border states, such as Texas, Arizona, New Mexico, and California, to report the multiple purchases of certain arms to the Bureau of Alcohol, Tobacco, Firearms, and Explosives (ATF). This effort seeks to prevent the sale of high-powered weapons to drug cartels. Through this initiative, ATF officials hope to disrupt the easy flow of high-power firearms to transnational crime organizations, especially in Mexico.

The pursuit of major drug traffickers continued under the administration of Mexican President Enrique Peña Nieto. In 2014, a key figure in the drug trade, Joaquín "El Chapo" Guzmán Loera of the Sinaloa Cartel, was captured along with 750 pounds of cocaine and three other cartel members, including its infamous kingpin's first cousin. Despite his arrest and the apprehension of other major drug traffickers, however, Mexican authorities believe that such losses are "not necessarily devastating" for the illegal drug industry because drug cartels maintain vast resources at their disposal (Thompson & Archibold 2014). In the meantime, public frustration in Mexico with President Peña Nieto has grown in response to his failure to satisfactorily handle a case involving the disappearance and apparent mass execution of 43 students—a case that has implicated local police, a drug gang, and even a mayor and his wife in the southern Mexican state of Guerrero. The political motivations and governmental and police corruption in combination with a violent drug cartel all appears to have converged, resulting in human rights violations on a massive scale.

Current/Contemporary Issues Involving Transnational Crime

In the United States, the specter of transnational crime has been used to justify aggressive anti-immigration policies. Immigration-related legislation—such as Proposition 187 (California, 1994), the Illegal Immigration Relief Act Ordinance (Hazelton, Pennsylvania, 2006), and S.B. 1070 (Arizona, 2010)—has been passed in numerous states on the assertion that immigrants are causing crime rates to increase. Research shows that the opposite is true. Although nationwide, unauthorized immigration doubled to 12 million between 1994 and 2004, violent crime rates decreased by 35 percent during the same period (Nadler 2008; Rumbaut & Ewing 2007). More specifically, states that have experienced the greatest levels of unauthorized immigration at the start of the 21st century, including Arizona, are experiencing marked declines in crime rates. According to the United States Bureau of Justice Statistics, since 2006, border states have shown steep reductions in all types of crime, including violent crime (murder, assault, and rape) and property crimes. In Arizona, for example, violent crime rates dropped from 512 per 100,000 persons in 2005 to 447 per 100,000 persons in 2008, and property crime rates declined from 5,850 per 100,000 persons in 2005 to 4,291 per 100,000 persons in 2008 (Ewing 2010).

Other studies demonstrate that persons born in the United States are more prone to commit crimes than are immigrants. Across the United States, incarceration rates of native-born U.S. citizens are significantly higher than those of immigrants, with border states exhibiting significant differences in institutionalization and incarceration rates. In the United States, the incarceration rate of native males ages 18 to 39 years was five times greater than for the same-aged foreign male population, 3.5 percent and 0.7 percent, respectively (Rumbaut & Ewing 2007). In border states such as California this trend also is evident. The 2008 California Counts report from the Public Policy Institute of California found that of both male and female adults of the entire native and foreign-born adult populations in California, U.S.-born adults make up nearly three times the foreign-born incarceration rate (0.8 percent and 0.3 percent, respectively). Of native-born males between the ages of 18 and 40 years—the largest institutionalized population—the institutionalization (e.g., prisons, jails, halfway houses) rate was 10 times greater than that of foreign-born men (4.2 percent and 0.42 percent, respectively). Additionally, although comprising 35 percent of the California population, foreign-born men make up only 17 percent of the California adult prison population (Butcher & Piehl 2008). The analysis of institutionalization rates across the United States and in the border states with the broadest and perhaps most punitive institutional system demonstrates that the conflation of crime with immigrants is wholly false. Instead, immigrants including those most perceived to be associated with crime—Mexicans—are far less likely to commit crimes than are natives.

This data notwithstanding, the perception of immigrants as criminals has increased in the post-September 11 climate. Despite evidence that shows border crime dropping precipitously even before efforts to increase homeland security accelerated, politicians and the media have continued to pursue a grossly inaccurate portrait of out-of-control border violence in which immigrants are deemed the culprits. Erroneously conflating immigration and crime, anti-immigrant supporters have called for a range of punitive actions including legislation that forces state and local law enforcement officials to verify immigration status, a function of federal agencies consistent with the U.S. Constitution. Tactics linking immigration to crime have led to the expansion of the use of drones along the U.S.-Mexico border to monitor human and drug trafficking activities. The producers of these costly vehicles that range between $18 million and $20 million per drone have contributed handsomely to the campaigns of a number of U.S. senators and representatives, including border senators, such as Henry Cuellar (Democrat, Laredo, TX) (Barry 2011). Fanning fears about immigration and crime has been viewed by analysts as a ready-made path to personal and political gain for a number of legislators.

The Role of Neoliberal Trade Policies in Transnational Crime

Shifts in global economic policies have ushered in new opportunities for transnational criminal organizations to extend their illicit activities into the United States. One of the most consequential shifts in transnational economic policy between the United States and Latin America came with the passage of the North American Free Trade Agreement (NAFTA), which became effective on January 1, 1994. NAFTA not only facilitated the cross-border flow of legal goods and services across the U.S.-Mexico border, but also produced an open border for the flow of illegal goods and services across the border. To enable the transport of goods across the U.S.-Mexican border, border and customs protections were loosened. To combat human and drug trafficking, the U.S.-Mexico border has become increasingly militarized, and calls for the expansion of a border wall have become a rallying point for conservative politicians and anti-immigrant activists.

Trade agreements and NAFTA in particular, however, generated partnerships between countries that are asymmetrical economically, legally, and politically. These asymmetries have produced unintended consequences that have led to a growth of transnational criminal activity, such as increased human, narcotics, and arms trafficking. Structural adjustment programs set by NAFTA have had a disproportionate economic impact on sustenance farmers and small-farm owners in Mexico. The decline of import substitution and an inability to compete in the marketplace against cheaper, foreign crops, has left rural farmers unable to even engage in sustenance farming, instead turning to immigration to support their families. To meet the demand for immigration, human smugglers—working both independently and operating in networks—have emerged to meet this demand. Another effect of economic "dislocation" by transnational trade policies is the adoption of illicit activities for economic survival. Rural areas that have been disproportionately affected by economic asymmetries and neoliberal policies have responded by relying on the harvesting of illicit drugs for household economic survival. Illicit activities in some cases have provided economic safety valves for workers, especially youth, dislocated by changing economic circumstances.

Transnational criminal organizations also increasingly have engaged women and minors in their activities. In Mexico, between 2007 and 2010, women and minors were voluntarily or involuntarily working for cartels in various capacities, including as high-level assassins, drug traffickers, lookouts, and in some cases as bosses. Between 2007 and 2010, Mexican minors arrested on charges related to organized crime increased from 8 to 214 (Graham 2011). Hiring women and minors and paying up to three times the national average, transnational criminal organizations have provided employment and wages that the formal labor market has been unable to supply.

Critics of the latest U.S. trade initiative, the Trans-Pacific Partnership (TPP), claim that the TPP impact on Latin American countries will be similar to that of NAFTA and the other major trade agreement, the Dominican Republic-Central American Free Trade Agreement (DR-CAFTA). As with NAFTA and DR-CAFTA, poverty, unemployment, and environmental damage are predicted, causing harm to the Latin American countries likely to participate, which include Mexico, Peru, and Chile. Presidential "fast-track" authorization has been assured—permitting only an up or down vote in Congress on a trade agreement negotiated in secret—thus it is believed that the TTP is likely to move forward.

Human Rights Violations and Transnational Crime Counter-Efforts

In most instances, efforts to counter transnational crime organizations have been accompanied by rampant human rights abuses by United States–backed nation-state militaries. Several Latin American countries, including Colombia and Mexico, hold abysmal human rights records and their governments have been unable or unwilling to investigate and prosecute human rights violators, including their own agents. The heavy reliance on the military to combat transnational crime organizations is responsible, in part, for high rates of human rights violations. In the name of waging war against drugs and crime, many Latin American armed forces—financed and trained by the United States—have engaged in the repression of civil society and widespread human rights abuses, including forced disappearances, torture, and extrajudicial killings. Militaristic approaches and tactics too often have taken precedence over practices focused on promoting civilian policing and public safety.

Colombia, a country with one of the worst human rights records in the world, has been ineffective in addressing and prosecuting human rights violators. In many cases, the government's own military is implicated in committing human rights atrocities. The military, paramilitary forces, guerilla insurgents, and drug traffickers use violence to combat each other and to maintain power bases in Colombia. A 2015 Human Rights Watch report found mounting evidence that top military leaders in Colombia engaged in massive numbers of systematic extrajudicial killings of civilians from 2002 to 2008. The report states that these high-ranking officials have never been held accountable and many actually have been promoted.

Under the guise of restoring order, military and paramilitary forces have used excessive force on innocent civilians. Violence against innocent civilians has been committed in the effort to reign in guerrilla groups, such as the FARC, ELN (the National Liberation Army), and ELP (the People's Liberation Army)—groups that themselves have been accused of human rights violations. Both military and guerilla forces have collaborated with paramilitary groups which act as their enforcers, often using extralegal means to accomplish their goals. Since 1977, more than 3,000 cases of kidnappings have been reported in Colombia, with few cases solved. Additionally, between 1985 and 2000, approximately 200 judges and investigators, 1,200 police officers, and 300,000 civilians were killed due to conflicts in the area fought between military, paramilitary, guerrilla groups, and drug traffickers (Pardo 2000). Despite reports of such crimes, less than 3 percent of reported crimes had been prosecuted by the year 2000 (Seagrave 2001).

In spite of Colombia's written and spoken support for the exercise of human rights, little has been done by the national judicial system to prosecute human rights violations and bring perpetrators to justice. In absence of concerted efforts by the Colombian government to enforce human rights standards, the Inter-American Commission on Human Rights has proposed that international humanitarian law is most appropriate to apply to the thousands of crimes that have gone uninvestigated and unprosecuted.

From the moment that former Mexican President Felipe Calderon deployed the military to combat transnational crime organizations, allegations of human rights abuses escalated exponentially. Between 2006 and 2009, human rights abuse complaints increased from 182 to nearly 2,000. By 2011, the number of allegations levied against the military since Calderon took office totaled more than 5,000 (Human Rights Watch 2011a). Ranging from use of unlawful force and detention, to rape, sexual abuse, torture, and extrajudicial killings, the Mexican government repeatedly has failed to sufficiently investigate human rights cases. In the rare instance when attempts are made to bring military personnel to justice, cases that have been pursued often are tried in closed military courts, in which justice frequently has been denied to **victims** and their relatives and they were unable to file appeals. In the summer of 2011, after much lobbying of human rights groups such as Amnesty International, Human Rights Watch, and the Mexican National Human Rights Commission, the Mexican Supreme Court ruled that military personnel should be tried in a civilian court when accused of human rights violations. This unanimous ruling marked a welcome change for human rights advocates who have long been calling for reform to the handling of military cases.

Regardless of Mexico's lax efforts to investigate and prosecute human rights abuses, however, the United States has continued to express full support and fund Mexico's anti-organized crime initiatives. Originally, the release of 15 percent of Plan Mexico funds was tied to following human rights guidelines, but despite evidence of Mexico's lack of compliance, the United States has released more than $1.5 billion since 2007. The Obama administration, including former Secretary of State Clinton, lauded former President Calderon's initiatives despite evidence that the war on drugs has been a failure and regardless of the increases in violence and deaths occurring since 2006. Going as far as stating that she was a "fan" of the public security policies, Hillary Clinton and the Obama administration registered full support of the Merida Initiative.

See also: Part I essays: Latina/o Immigrants, Crime, and Justice; The U.S. War on Drugs and Latina/o Communities; Incarceration and Latinas/os in the United States; Gangs in the United States and Latina/o Communities; Crime and the U.S.-Mexican Border. Part II entries: Colombians; Deportation; Homicide; Human Trafficking; Immigration and Customs Enforcement (ICE); Mexicans and Mexican Americans; Slavery; Victims.

Further Reading

Agren, David. 2014 (November 7). Mexicans increasingly angry at President Peña Nieto amid disappearance of 43 students. *Fox News Latino.* http://latino.foxnews.com/latino/news/2014/11/07/mexicans-increasingly-angry-at-president-pena-nieto-job-amid-disappearance-43/.

Andreas, Peter. 2000. *Border games: Policing the U.S.-Mexico divide.* Ithaca, NY: Cornell University Press.

Associated Press. 2011 (July 26). U.S. imposes sanctions on 4 international criminal groups. *New York Times.* http://www.nytimes.com/2011/07/26/us/politics/26cartel.html. Accessed November 15, 2015.

Astorga, Luis, and David A. Shirk. 2010. *Drug trafficking organizations and counter-drug strategies in the U.S.-Mexican context.* Working Paper, Mexico and the United States: Confronting the Twenty-First Century Series. https://www.wilsoncenter.org/sites/default/files/Chapter%201-Drug%20Trafficking%20Organizations%20and%20Counter-Drug%20Strategies%20in%20the%20U.S.-Mexico%20Context.pdf. Accessed November 15, 2015.

Barry, Tom. 2011 (November 30). How the drone warfare industry took over our Congress. *Alternet.org.* http://ww.alternet.org/story/153278/how_the_drone_warfare_industry_took_over_our_congress. Accessed October 18, 2015.

Barry, Tom, Harry Browne, and Beth Sims. 1994. *Crossing the line: Immigrants, economic integration and drug enforcement on the U.S.-Mexico border.* Albuquerque, NM: Resource Center Press.

Beith, Malcolm. 2010 (April 15). Are Mexico's drug cartels terrorist groups? *Slate.com.* http://www.slate.com/articles/news_and_politics/foreigners/2010/04/are_mexicos_drug_cartels_terrorist_groups.html. Accessed November 15, 2015.

Beittell, June S. 2013 (April 15). *Mexico's drug trafficking organizations: Source and scope of the violence.* CRS Report for Congress. Washington, DC: Congressional Research Service.

Bennet, Brian. 2011 (July 9). U.S. can't justify its drug war spending, report says. *Los Angeles Times.* http://articles.latimes.com/2011/jun/09/world/la-fg-narco-contract-20110609. Accessed November 15, 2015.

Burnett, John. 2011 (July 6). "Spillover" violence from Mexico: Trickle or flood? *NPR.*

http://www.npr.org/2011/07/06/137445310/spillover-violence-from-mexico-a-trickle-or-flood. Accessed November 15, 2015.

Butcher, Kristin F., and Anne Morrison Piehl. 2005, November. Why are immigrants' incarceration rates so low? Evidence on selective immigration, deterrence, and deportation. Working Paper 2005–19. Chicago, IL: Federal Reserve Bank of Chicago.

Camarena, Rodrigo. 2011 (June 7). Felipe Calderon's cartel war dead-end. *The Guardian UK.*

Carter, Jimmy. 2011 (June 16). Call off the global drug war. *New York Times.* http://www.nytimes.com/2011/06/17/opinion/17carter.html. Accessed November 15, 2015.

Ceballos Melguiza, Ramiro, and Francine Cronshow. 2001 (January). The evolution of armed conflict in Medellin: An analysis of the major actors. *Latin American Review* 28(1): 110–31.

Chen, Michelle. 2011 (March 21). Wars on the U.S.-Mexico border divide and conquer. *Colorlines.com.* http://colorlines.com/archives/2011/03/wars_on_the_us-mexico_border_divide_and_conquer.html. Accessed November 15, 2015.

Chen, Michelle. 2011 (March 26). Clinton admits U.S. blame on drugs. *BBC News.* http://news.bbc.co.uk/2/hi/7963292.stm. Accessed November 15, 2015.

CNN México. 2010 (October 16). México encabezara por 3 años la communidad de policías de America. http://mexico.cnn.com/nacional/2010/10/10/mexico-encabezara-por-3-anos-la-comunidad-de-policias-de-america. Accessed November 15, 2015.

CNN México. 2011 (May 26). Colombia Amenazo con cancelar cooperación con Mexico por corrupción. http://mexico.cnn.com/nacional/2011/05/26/colombia-amenazo-con-cancelar-cooperación-con-mexico-por-corrupción. Accessed November 15, 2015.

Del Bosque, Melissa. 2009 (April 17). Lights! Camera! Mayhem! The national media invades El Paso—and gets the story wrong. *Texas Observer.* http://www.texasobserver.org/3014-lights-cameras-mayhem/. Accessed November 15, 2015.

Dorsey, James. 2010 (February 2). Ecuador emerges as hub for international crime. *Deutsche Welle.* http://www.dw.de/ecuador-emerges-as-hub-for-international-crime/a-5201759. Accessed November 15, 2015.

Dube, Oeindrila, and Suresh Naidu. 2010. Bases, bullets and ballots: The effect of U.S. military aid on political conflict in Colombia. Working Paper 197, Center for Global Development: Washington, DC.

Ellingwood, Ken. 2010 (March 21). Abuse allegations rise against Mexican army. *Los Angeles Times.*

Ewing, Walter A. 2010 (April 28). Arizona's punishing new immigration law doesn't fight crime. http://immigrationimpact.com/2010/04/28/arizona%E2%80%99s-punishing-new-immigration-law-doesn%E2%80%99t-fight-crime/. Accessed November 15, 2015.

Fetterhoff, Christina M. 2011 (October 19). Military justice reform in Mexico amid increased violence. *The Human Rights Brief.* http://hrbrief.org/2011/10/military-justice-reform-in-mexico-amid-increased-violence. Accessed November 15, 2015.

Florez, Carl P., and Bernadette Boyce. 1990. Colombian organized crime. *Police Studies: International Review Police Development* 81: 81–89.

Franco, Celinda. 2008. The MS-13 and 18th Street gangs: Emerging transnational gang threats? CRS Report RL34233. Washington, DC: Congressional Research Service, Library of Congress.

Gomez, Alan, Jack Gillum, and Kevin Johnson. 2011 (June 6). Female assassins a growing part of drug cartels. *The Brownsville Herald.* http://www.brownsvilleherald.com/news/valley/article_f399a6b8-c334-5558-98b2-ea5498122c59.html. Accessed November 15, 2015.

Gomez, Alan, Jack Gillum, and Kevin Johnson. 2011 (July 15). U.S. border cities prove havens from Mexico's drug violence. *USA Today*. http://www.usatoday.com/news/washington/2011-07-15-border-violence-main_n.htm. Accessed November 15, 2015.

Gonzalez, Maria de luz. 2010 (October 10). México asume Secretaría Ejecutiva de Ameripol. *El Universal*. http://www.eluniversal.com.mx/notas/715170.html. Accessed November 15, 2015.

Graham, Dave. 2011 (June 17). Mexican teenage girls train as drug cartel killers. *Reuters*. http://www.reuters.com/article/2011/06/17/us-mexico-drugs-teenagers-idUSTRE75G5F820110617. Accessed November 15, 2015.

Holden, Robert H., and Eric Zolov (eds.). 2011. *Latin America and the United States: A documentary history*. 2nd ed. New York: Oxford University Press.

Human Rights Watch. 2011a (May 26). The monster and Monterrey: The politics and cartels of Mexico's drug war. www.hrw.org/print/news/2011/05/26/monster-and-monterrey. Accessed November 15, 2015.

Human Rights Watch. 2011b (November 10). Mexico: Widespread rights abuses in "war on drugs." http://www.hrw.org/news/2011/11/09/mexico-widespread-rights-abuses-war-drugs. Accessed November 15, 2015.

Human Rights Watch. 2015. Colombia: Top brass linked to extrajudicial executions generals, colonels implicated in "false positive" killings. New York, NY: HRW. https://www.hrw.org/news/2015/06/24/colombia-top-brass-linked-extrajudicial-executions.

Immigration Policy Center. 2008 (February 25). Immigrants and crime: Are they connected? A decade of research finds that crime rates for immigrants are lower than for the native-born. http://www.immigrationpolicy.org/just-facts/immigrants-and-crime-are-they-connected-century-research-finds-crime-rates-immigrants-are. Accessed November 15, 2015.

Isacson, Adam. 2005–2006. Failing grades: Evaluating the results of Plan Colombia. *Yale Journal of International Affairs* 1: 138–55.

James, Frank. 2010 (September 9). Obama rejects Hillary Clinton Mexico-Colombia comparison. National Public Radio. http://www.npr.org/blogs/thetwo-way/2010/09/09/129760276/obama-rejects-hillary-clinton-mexico-colombia-comparison. Accessed November 15, 2015.

Jeffs, Jennifer. 2011. Get off the sidelines, Canada. Join Ameripol. *The Globe and Mail*. http://embamex.sre.gob.mx/canada/index.php?option=com_content&view=article&id=2372:get-off-the-sidelines-canada-join-ameripol-the-globe-and-mail&catid=265:martes-1-de-marzo-2011&Itemid=101. Accessed November 15, 2015.

Landler, Mark. 2009 (March 25). Clinton says U.S. feeds Mexico drug trade. *New York Times*. http://www.nytimes.com/2009/03/26/world/americas/26mexico.html. Accessed November 15, 2015.

Lee, Brianna. 2014 (March 5). Mexico's drug war. *Council on Foreign Relations*. http://www.cfr.org/mexico/mexicos-drug-war/p13689. Accessed November 15, 2015.

Lee, Matthew T. 2003. *Crime on the border: Immigration and homicide in urban communities*. New York, NY: LFB Scholarly Publishing LLC.

Lee, Matthew T., Ramiro Martínez, Jr., and Richard Rosenfeld. 2001. Does immigration increase homicide? Negative evidence from three border cities. *The Sociological Quarterly* 42(4): 559–80.

Lee, Rensselaer W. 1999. Transnational organized crime: An overview. In *Transnational crime in the Americas,* edited by T. Farer, 1–38. New York, NY: Routledge.

Logan, Sam. 2009 (March 16). The evolution of "Los Zetas," a Mexican crime organization. *ISN Security Watch*. http://www.freerepublic.com/focus/f-news/2217689/posts. Accessed November 15, 2015.

Logan, Sam. 2011 (July 13). Mexican drug cartels remain low key in South Texas. *The Brownsville Herald*. http://www.brownsvilleherald.com/articles/groups-128789-low-crossing.html. Accessed November 15, 2015.

Martínez, Jr., Ramiro. 2006. Coming to America: The impact of new immigration on crime. In *Immigration and crime: Race, ethnicity and violence*, edited by Ramiro Martínez, Jr. and Abel Valenzuela, 1–19. New York, NY: New York University Press.

Mexidata. 2007 (December 3). "Ameripol," a Latin America regional police force, is being formed. http://mexidata.info/id1633.html. Accessed November 15, 2015.

Millet, Richard, and Shannon Stiles. 2008. Peace without security: Central America in the 21st Century. *The Whitehead Journal of Diplomacy and International Relations* 9(1): 31–41. http://www.ciaonet.org/journals/shjdir/v9i1/index.html.

Morín, José Luis. 2009. *Latino/a rights and justice in the United States: Perspectives and approaches*. 2nd ed. Durham, NC: Carolina Academic Press.

Nadler, Richard. 2008. *Immigration and the wealth of States*. Overland Park, Kansas: Americas Majority Foundation.

Newman, Alex. 2010 (January 18). Obama backs Mexico's failed "war on drugs." *The New American*.

Office of National Drug Control Policy. 2011. *National Southwest border counternarcotics strategy*. Washington DC: Executive Office of the President of the United States.

Orrenius, Pia M., and Roberto Coronado. 2005. *The effect of illegal immigration and border enforcement on crime rates along the U.S-Mexico border*. San Diego, CA: Center for Comparative Immigration Studies.

Ortiz, Ildefonso. 2011 (November 17). Trickle or flood? Groups clash over true extent of violence spillover from Mexico. *Brownsville Herald*.

Otis, John. 2001. Is the FARC a drug cartel? *Houston Chronicle*, August 5. http://www.chron.com/news/article/Is-the-FARC-a-drug-cartel-2014390.php. Accessed November 15, 2015.

Padgett, Tim. 2011 (July). Day of the dead. The drug war is Mexico's tragedy; now its survivors are fighting back. *Time*.

Pardo, Rafael. 2000. Colombia's two front war. *Foreign Affairs*. http://www.foreignaffairs.com/articles/56238/rafael-pardo/colombias-two-front-war. Accessed November 15, 2015.

Pérez-Rocha, Manuel, Julia Paley, and Foreign Policy In Focus. 2014 (November 24). What "free trade" has done to Central America. *TheNation.com*. http://www.thenation.com/article/what-free-trade-has-done-central-america/. Accessed November 15, 2015.

Powell, Steward M. 2011 (May 23). U.S. lags in vow to help battle cartels: After 3 years, much equipment still hasn't been to Mexico. *Houston Chronicle*. http://www.chron.com/news/houston-texas/article/U-S-lags-in-promise-to-help-Mexico-battle-cartels-1683396.php. Accessed November 15, 2015.

Rosenberg, Tina. 2011 (July 10). The stimulant stimulus: Could something other than Ricky Perry's business-friendly policies be keeping the Texas economy buzzing? *New York Magazine*. http://nymag.com/news/intelligencer/rick-perry-2011-7/.

Rumbaut, Ruben G., and Walter A. Ewing. 2007. The myth of immigrant criminality and the paradox of assimilation: Incarceration rates among native and foreign-born men. Washington: DC: Immigration Policy Center.

Savage, Charles. 2011 (July 11). New reporting rules on multiple sales of guns near border. *New York Times*.

Seagrave, Alan. 2001. Conflict in Colombia: How can rebel forces, paramilitary groups, drug traffickers, and government forces be held liable for human rights violations in a country where impunity reigns supreme? *Nova Law Review* 25: 525–41.

Shirk, David. 2011. *The drug war in Mexico: Confronting a shared threat*. New York, NY: Council of Foreign Relations, Center for Preventive Action.

Smith, Peter H. 1999. Semi-organized international crime: Drug trafficking in Mexico. In *Transnational crime in the Americas,* edited by T. Farer, 193–216. New York, NY: Routledge.

Smith, Peter H. 2013. *Talons of the eagle: Latin America, the United States, and the world*. 4th ed. New York, NY: Oxford University Press.

Stevenson, Mark. 2010 (May 10). Leaked documents suggest Mexico drug corruption. *Huffington Post*. http://www.huffingtonpost.com/huff-wires/20100510/lt-mexico-drug-war/.

Stevenson, Mark. 2009 (January 25). Top Mexico cops charged with links to cartels. *MSNBC*. http://www.msnbc.msn.com/id/28832995/ns/world_news-americas/t/top-mexico-cops-charged-links-cartels/.

Thompson, Ginger. 2011 (August 6). U.S. widens its role in battle against Mexican drug cartels. *New York Times*.

Thompson, Ginger, and Randal C. Archibold. 2014 (February 25). El Chapo's arrest unlikely to break Mexican cartel. *New York Times*. http://www.nytimes.com/2014/02/26/world/americas/arrest-unlikely-to-break-cartel.html. Accessed November 15, 2015.

U.S. State Department. 2006. *Trafficking in persons report*. Washington, DC: Office to monitor and combat trafficking in persons. U.S. State Department.

Webb, Gary. 2006 (August 18). The truth in "dark alliance." *Los Angeles Times*. http://articles.latimes.com/print/2006/aug/18/opinion/oe-schou18. Accessed November 15, 2015.

Weisman, Jonathan. 2015 (June 24). Trade authority bill wins final approval in Senate, *New York Times*. http://www.nytimes.com/2015/06/25/business/trade-pact-senate-vote-obama.html?_r=0. Accessed November 15, 2015.

Zatz, Marjorie S., and Hilary Smith. 2012. Immigration, crime, and victimization: Rhetoric and reality. *Annual Review of Law and Social Science* 8: 141–59.

Zavala, Armando Escobar. 2010 (November 1). El flagelo de la corrupción. *La Jornada Guerrero*. http://www.lajornadaguerrero.com.mx/2010/11/01/index.php?section=opinion&article=002a1soc. Accessed November 15, 2015.

U

Underrepresentation of Latinas/os in the Legal Profession

Leonard Baynes

On August 6, 2009, by a vote of 68 to 31, the U. S. Senate confirmed Sonia Sotomayor as an Associate Justice of the U.S. Supreme Court. On August 8, 2009, she was sworn in and became the Supreme Court's 111th justice but its first Latina/o justice and its third female justice. Sotomayor, who is of **Puerto Rican** ancestry, was born in the Bronx, New York. In 1976, Sotomayor graduated summa cum laude from Princeton University. She was awarded her Juris Doctor degree from Yale Law School in 1979, where she also served as an editor at the *Yale Law Journal*. Her elevation to the Supreme Court makes her a role model and trailblazer for women, Latinas/os, and other people of color who aspire to join the legal profession. Sotomayor's ascent has a great deal of symbolic value. As the first Latina and the third woman to be appointed to the Supreme Court, however, her success could appear very singular. It is important to work to ensure that other Sotomayors are in the pipeline into the profession to reflect the demographic increases among U.S. Latinas/os. A gap exists between the number of Latinas/os in the United States and lawyers of those same backgrounds who can linguistically or culturally represent this demographic group, including in the area of criminal justice.

Recent census data have shown the Latino/a population in the United States is growing rapidly. Between 2000 and 2010, the Latina/o population in the U. S. increased by 15.2 million, "accounting for over half of the 27.3 million increase in the total population of the United States" (Ennis, Ríos-Vargas, & Albert 2011, 2). During this same 10-year period, the Latina/o population increased by 43 percent—more than "four times the growth in the total population at 10 percent" (Ennis, Ríos-Vargas, & Albert 2011, 2). In 2013, an estimated 17 percent of the U.S. population was Latinas/os, with the Census Bureau projecting that this demographic group would comprise 28 percent of the U.S. population by 2050 (U.S. Bureau of the Census 2014a). Latinas/os, along with African Americans, Asian Americans, and Native Americans, by then will make up more than half of the U.S. population.

The legal profession has not kept pace with these changing demographics. In 2000, only 9.7 percent of attorneys in the United States were members of racial/ethnic minority groups, with roughly 4 percent being of African descent and another 2.5 being of Asian ancestry (Chambliss 2000, 1). Of approximately 776,625 lawyers in the United States in 2000, only 28,630 or 3.2 percent were Latinas/os (2 percent being male and 1.2 percent being female) (Rivera & Roure 2012). The percentage of minority groups in the legal profession is less than their representation in other professions, that is, 21 percent of accountants, 24 percent of physicians, and 18 percent of university professors (Stern 2009).

The percentage of Hispanics or Latinas/os who serve as federal judges was 5.1 percent in 2014 (McMillion 2014) and 3.5 percent of state court judges in 2010 (American Bar Association Standing Committee on Judicial Independence [n.d.]). Four-fifths of Latina/o federal judges serve at the district court level, the rest serve on the circuit court (McMillion 2014). Approximately three-quarters of Latina/o federal judges serve in California and Texas (Federal Judicial Center [n.d.]; McMillion 2014). The rest of the Latina/o judges are concentrated in 18 states, generally those having large Latina/o populations, and 30 states have no Latina/o federal judges (Federal Judicial Center [n.d.]). A study of the 105th Congress found that Senate approval time for white nominees for federal judges averaged 186 days as compared to 246 days for minority-group nominees (Falcón 2002, 6, 10). Another study found that the federal confirmation process for white men took approximately five months as compared to eight months for women and other members of minority groups (Biskupic 2000, 1A).

There is also a dearth of Latina/o law professors. Latinas/os comprise only 3.1 percent of law professors in the United States (ABA Commission on Hispanic Legal Rights and Responsibilities 2013, 69). The Association of American Law Schools (AALS) Committee on the Retention and Recruitment of Minorities examined the disparity in hiring and tenure outcomes for faculty members from underrepresented backgrounds in comparison to those from majority backgrounds and found that both the absolute number and the proportion of minority law professors hired had decreased and that the racial gap in tenure rates increased. Of the cohort of law professors hired in 1996–1997, for example, "73 percent of white law professors but only 47 percent of minority law professors were awarded tenure by year eight" (AALS 2005, 3). The data also showed that Latina/o faculty members are particularly underrepresented and leave the profession at the highest rate without obtaining tenure. Of the 11 Latina/o law faculty hired in 1996–1997, none received tenure after eight years. The AALS attributed the disparity in tenure rates as often resulting from isolation, lack of mentoring, and the failure of law schools in conveying the unwritten rules for attaining tenure, and the imposition of caretaking roles for the minority community that does not exist for majority faculty members (AALS 2005, 4).

The number of Latinas/os in the education pipeline and available to enter the legal profession is inadequate in proportion to the increase in Latinas/os in the U.S. population. To enter the legal profession, an individual must have at least completed a bachelor's degree. The U.S. Census reports that only 13.1 percent of Latinas and 11.5 percent of Latinos, older than age 25 have a bachelor degree, as compared to 27.9 percent of men and 26.2 percent of women in the general population holding a bachelor's degree (U.S. Bureau of the Census 2006). Between 1990 and 2006, the total first year law school enrollment increased from 43,000 students to 46,000 students, a slightly less than 10 percent increase (Johnson 2009). A Society of American Law Schools study revealed that, although Mexican American and African American entry credentials also increased during this same period, first-year African American and Mexican American enrollment declined 8.6 percent, from a combined 3,937 in 1992 to 3,595 in 2005 (Columbia Law School [n.d.]).

A study conducted by Associate Dean John Nussbaumer showed that 62 percent of African American and 47 percent of Mexican American applicants are rejected by every law school to which they apply as compared to 34 percent of white law school applicants (Nussbaumer, n.d.). This disparity could be attributable to the difference in median Law School Admission Test (LSAT) scores for each of these different racial groups. The median score for all LSAT test takers is approximately 152, for African American test takers it is 144, and for Mexican American test takers it is approximately 150 (Johnson 2009). For other Latina/o demographic groups, the median LSAT score could be as low as 138 (Dalessandro, Suto, & Reese 2009, 13).

The underrepresentation of Latinas/os in the law schools produces underrepresentation in the number of Latinas/os eligible to be judges and lawyers. In turn, underrepresentation ultimately can undermine the integrity and credibility of the legal profession, because a significant underrepresentation of this demographic group could lead to doubts about the fairness of legal outcomes, including outcomes in the criminal justice system. Analysts posit that more Latina/o lawyers would foster more respect for the law in those communities (*see, e.g.,* Falcón 2002). Increasing diversity in the legal profession also would improve the chances that decision making would be more inclusive, engendering an environment in which more fully formed and considered decisions are made. Moreover, law school students attending law schools that lack racial and ethnic diversity are more likely to be unprepared to work in a world in which diversity is a part of everyday life.

Latina/o attorneys and other lawyers of color through local and national bar associations have been active over the years to press for greater diversity in the profession, among them the Hispanic National Bar Association. In 2013, the American Bar Association (ABA) Commission on Hispanic Legal Rights and Responsibilities released a report on the state of Latinas/os in relation to a broad spectrum of U.S. justice issues. On the question of the lack of Latinas/os in the legal profession, the report noted that Latina/o attorneys called on both the ABA (as the leading national association for lawyers) and law schools to meet the challenge facing the country. In the words of Adria D. Maddaleni of the Wisconsin Hispanic Lawyers Association, Midwest,

> [I]f the ABA accepts that law schools have the obligation to prepare students for the practice of law, it then follows that law schools must account for the changing demographics in our country when fulfilling this obligation. The growing need for Spanish-speaking lawyers cannot be ignored and must be addressed by our law schools (ABA Commission on Hispanic Legal Rights and Responsibilities 2013, 69).

Although there are few studies examining how well Latinas and Latinos fare once they are in the legal profession, two studies point to the persistence of barriers to access and retention in the profession. A 2009 nationwide study of Latina lawyers conducted by the Hispanic National Bar Association Commission on Latinas in the Legal Profession suggests that Latinas frequently encounter many obstacles in their careers. Strong prejudices and stereotypes lead many employers, clients, coworkers, and members of the general public to question Latinas' abilities and qualifications. Many Latinas, for instance, often reported being mistaken for "court reporters, interpreters or paralegals" (Cruz & Molina 2009, 384–85). A subsequent study of Latinas specifically in public-interest legal employment found that Latinas also too readily were devalued in the workplace in addition to being in an employment sector that already is undervalued—despite its importance to the operations of a fair system of justice and to Latinas/os (Cruz, Molina, & Rivera 2010). Both studies suggest that, in addition to increasing the number of Latina/o attorneys in the country, to retain larger numbers of Latina/o attorneys over time requires paying attention to Latinas/os who have been successful in entering the profession. These studies call for improvements in mentoring and support, and for increased recognition for Latinas in the profession.

Strengthening the Educational Pipeline

To address the issue of underrepresentation, pipeline programs have been developed to increase the representation among minorities in the legal profession. In 1968, the Council on Legal Education Opportunity (CLEO) was founded as a nonprofit project of the American Bar Association Fund for Justice and Education. It is intended to expand opportunities for minority and low-income students to attend law school. During a six-week summer program, CLEO provides students with workshops on legal methods and techniques that emphasize developing the students' abstract-thinking, analysis, and synthesizing skills. Additionally, courses in legal writing and briefing also are provided (Council on Legal Education Opportunity [n.d.]).

Some law schools have intensive study programs designed to increase access to the legal profession. St. John's School of Law, for example, has a comprehensive and award-winning pipeline program called "The Ronald H. Brown Prep Program for College Students," which this author created while a faculty member of St. John's School of Law. Now, as Dean, I have re-instituted a similar program at the University of Houston Law Center called "The UHLC Pre-Law Pipeline Program." Both programs are rigorous and specifically designed to provide students from underrepresented backgrounds with exposure to law school classes, internships, and intensive LSAT preparation (University of Houston Law Center [n.d.]). Some Latina/o legal organizations, as in the case of **LatinoJustice PRLDEF,** also have sought to expand the number of Latina/o attorneys by running programs to help prepare students for the LSAT and the law school application process (LatinoJustice PRLDEF [n.d.]).

Just as there are programs to assist in creating access to law school admission, there are several types of programs available for lawyers interested in joining the teaching profession. Harvard Law School, for instance, has the Reginald Lewis Fellowship. The Lewis Fellowship program supports the training of prospective law teachers who will enhance the diversity of the profession. The Lewis Fellow is required to prepare a major article for publication and has an opportunity to audit courses at the Law School (Harvard Law School [n.d.]). The University of Wisconsin Law School has a two-year LLM program called the William H. Hastie Fellowship Program, which is also designed to increase the diversity of the legal profession (University of Wisconsin Law School [n.d.]). St. John's University School of Law has a research professorship and fellowship in the Ronald H. Brown Center position that is designed to increase the diversity of the profession. These efforts each help increase the diversity of the legal profession.

Latina/o academics and community organizations firmly believe that increasing the number of Latina/o legal professionals could substantially enhance the chances that justice and fairness prevail, and that Latina/o communities would be best served by having more culturally competent professionals working at all levels of the justice system (Falcón 2002; Rivera & Roure 2012). Analysts, thus, must urge for a comprehensive approach to serve the growing U.S. Latina/o population by—among other things—developing academic pipeline programs and providing various forms of support, including increased funding for scholarships, and need-based financial assistance (Rivera & Roure 2012). As Janet Murguia, president and CEO of the **National Council of La Raza**, has expressed to the American Bar Association, the "ABA's ability to serve its members, improve the profession, eliminate bias, and advance the rule of law hinges on its ability to integrate Latinos in all aspects of its work" (ABA Commission on Hispanic Legal Rights and Responsibilities 2013, 69).

See also: Part I essay: Latinas and the U.S. Criminal Justice System. Part II entries: Civil Rights; Legal Advocacy Groups; Puerto Ricans.

Further Reading

American Bar Association Commission on Hispanic Legal Rights and Responsibilities. 2013. Latinos in the United States: Overcoming obstacles, engaging in civic life. Chicago, IL: ABA. http://www.americanbar.org/content/dam/aba/images/commission_on_hispanic_legal_rights_responsibilities/hispanicreportnew.pdf#page=75&zoom=70,-32,747. Accessed November 15, 2015.

American Bar Association Standing Committee on Judicial Independence. National database on judicial diversity in state courts. http://apps.americanbar.org/abanet/jd/display/national.cfm. Accessed November 15, 2015.

Association of American Law Schools. 2005. *The racial gap in the promotion to tenure of law professors: Report of the Committee on the Recruitment and Retention of Minority Law Teachers Committee commentary.* Washington, DC: Association of American Law Schools.

Biskupic, Joan. 2000 (August 25). Minorities face hurdles in judicial quest. *USA Today*.

Chambliss, Elizabeth. 2000. *Miles to go 2000: Progress of minorities in the legal profession.* Chicago, IL: American Bar Association Commission on Racial and Ethnic Diversity in the Profession, American Bar Association.

Columbia Law School. [n.d.]. Web site shows drop in minority enrollment at U.S. law schools: New Columbia Law School web site documents disturbing decline in minority enrollment at U.S. law schools. New York, NY: Columbia Law School. http://www.law.columbia.edu/media_inquiries/news_events/2007/December07/law_enroll. Accessed November 15, 2015.

Council on Legal Education Opportunity. n.d. What is CLEO. Washington, DC: Council on Legal Education Opportunity. http://www.cleoscholars.com/index.cfm?fuseaction=Page.viewPage&pageId=482. Accessed November 15, 2015.

Cruz, Jill L., and Melinda S. Molina. 2009. *Few and far between: The reality of Latina lawyers*. Washington, D.C.: Hispanic National Bar Association, Commission on Latinas in the Legal Profession. http://198.171.230.232/files/warehouse_attachment_1399872518.pdf.

Cruz, Jill L., Melinda S. Molina, and Jenny Rivera. 2010. *La voz de la abogada Latina: Challenges and rewards in serving the public interest.* Washington, D.C.: Hispanic National Bar Association, Commission on Latinas in the Legal Profession. http://198.171.230.232/files/warehouse_attachment_1399880167.pdf.

Dalessandro, Susan P., Deborah A. Suto, and Lynda M. Reese. 2009. *LSAT performance with regional, gender, and racial/ethnic breakdowns: 2001–2001 through 2007–2008 testing years*. Newtown, PA: Law School Admission Council.

Ennis, Sharon R., Merarys Ríos-Vargas, and Nora G. Albert. 2011. The Hispanic population: 2010. U.S. Bureau of the Census, U.S. Department of Commerce, Economics and Statistics Administration. http://www.census.gov/prod/cen2010/briefs/c2010br-04.pdf.

Falcón, Angelo. 2002. *Opening up the courthouse doors: The need for more Hispanic judges*. New York, NY: Puerto Rican Legal Defense and Education Fund.

Federal Judicial Center. [n.d.]. Diversity on the bench; Biographical directory of federal judges. http://www.fjc.gov/history/home.nsf/page/research_categories.html. Accessed November 15, 2015.

Harvard Law School. [n.d.]. The Reginald F. Lewis Fellowships for Law Teaching. http://www.law.harvard.edu/academics/fellowships/the-reginald-f.-lewis-fellowships-for-law-teaching.html. Accessed November 15, 2015.

Johnson, Conrad. 2009. A disturbing trend in law school diversity. New York: Columbia University School of Law. http://blogs.law.columbia.edu/salt/. Accessed November 15, 2015.

LatinoJustice PRLDEF. [n.d.]. Legal education. http://latinojustice.org/legal_education/. Accessed November 15, 2015.

Lopez, Mark Hugo, Ana Gonzalez-Barrera, and Danielle Cuddington. 2013. Diverse origins: The nation's 14 largest Hispanic-origin groups. Washington, DC: Pew Research Center/Hispanic Trends. http://www.pewhispanic.org/2013/06/19/diverse-origins-the-nations-14-largest-hispanic-origin-groups/.

McMillion, Barry M. 2014. U.S. circuit and district court judges: Profile of select characteristics. R43426. Congressional Research Service. http://fas.org/sgp/crs/misc/R43426.pdf.

Motel, Seth, and Eileen Patten. 2012. The 10 largest Hispanic origin groups: Characteristics, rankings, top counties. Washington, DC: Pew Hispanic Center. http://www.pewhispanic.org/2012/06/27/the-10-largest-hispanic-origin-groups-characteristics-rankings-top-counties/.

Nussbaumer, John. [n.d.]. Unpublished data. On file with author and available upon request.

Rivera, Jenny, and Jodie G. Roure. 2012. So you want to be a lawyer. Puerto Ricans and their journey into the legal profession: Overcoming challenges. *Centro Journal*, 24 (2): 160–99.

Sherman, Mark. 2013 (May 12). Supreme Court saw only one African-American lawyer in last 75 hours of arguments. *Huffington Post*. http://www.huffingtonpost.com/2013/05/12/supreme-court-minority-lawyers_n_3262475.html. Accessed November 15, 2015.

Stern, Gary. 2009 (August 18). Breaking the minority drought: Why it's time to minimize use of the LSAT in law school admissions. *Pacific Standard*. http://www.psmag.com/politics-and-law/breaking-the-minority-attorney-drought-3525.

St. John's University School of Law. [n.d.]. Ronald H. Brown Center for Civil Rights and Economic Development: Prep program for college students. New York, NY: St. John's University of Law. http://www.stjohns.edu/academics/graduate/law/academics/centers/ronbrown.

University of Houston Law Center. [n.d.]. UHLC Pre-Law Pipeline Program. Houston, TX: University of Houston Law Center. http://www.law.uh.edu/pipeline/. Accessed November 15, 2015.

University of Wisconsin Law School. [n.d.]. William H. Hastie Fellowship Program: *Increasing the diversity of the law teaching profession. Madison, WI: University of Wisconsin Law School*. http://www.law.wisc.edu/grad/fellow_hastie.html. Accessed November 15, 2015.

U.S. Bureau of the Census. 2006. Hispanics in the United States. Washington DC: U.S. Bureau of the Census. http://www.census.gov/population/hispanic/publications/hispanics_2006.html. Accessed November 15, 2015.

U.S. Bureau of the Census. 2014a. Changing nation: Percent Hispanic of the U.S. population: 1980–2050. http://www.census.gov/content/dam/Census/newsroom/facts-for-features/2014/cb14-ff22_graphic.pdf. Accessed November 15, 2015.

U.S. Bureau of the Census. 2014b. Facts for features: Hispanic Heritage Month 2014. Sept. 15 to Oct. 15. http://www.census.gov/content/dam/Census/newsroom/facts-for-features/2014/cb14ff-22_hispanic.pdf. Accessed November 15, 2015.

Uniform Crime Report. *See* Introduction; Part I essays: Policing and Latina/o Communities; Incarceration and Latinas/os in the United States.

***United States ex rel. Negron v. New York*, 434 F.2d 386 (2d Cir. 1970).** *See* Part II entries: International Human Rights; Language Rights in the Courts.

***United States v. Brignoni-Ponce*, 422 U.S. 873 (1975).** *See* Part I essays: Policing and Latina/o Communities; Crime and the U.S.-Mexican Border. Part II entries: *Immigration and Naturalization Service (INS) v. Lopez-Mendoza et al.*, 468 U.S. 1032 (1984); *Terry v. Ohio*, 398 U.S. 1 (1968).

***United States v. Martinez-Fuerte*, 428 U.S. 543 (1976).** *See* Part I essays: Policing and Latina/o Communities; Crime and the U.S.-Mexican Border. Part II entries: *Immigration and Naturalization Service (INS) v. Lopez-Mendoza et al.*, 468 U.S. 1032 (1984); *Terry v. Ohio*, 398 U.S. 1 (1968).

V

Vega, Hilton. *See* Part I essay: Policing and Latina/o Communities.

Victims

Maria Swimm

Studies show that there has long existed a propensity for various news and **media** groups in the United States to represent Latina/o and African American communities as breeding grounds for criminal perpetration directed against the white citizens in the United States. This propensity stems from a protracted history of racial and ethnic bias and discrimination against Latinas/os and African Americans, exacerbated in recent years by persistent fears over the growth of the Latina/o immigrant population in the country. The inclination to immediately associate Latinas/os with criminals instead of victims has resulted in a generally misinformed society that fails to recognize that whites are more likely to be victimized by whites, and that whites actually are more likely to victimize Latinas/os than the converse. Victimization data reveal that reported **hate crimes** against Latinas/os have continually increased over time nationwide, with federal crime statistics showing a 40 percent increase in such attacks from 2003 to 2007 (Potok 2008; Federal Bureau of Investigation 2007). Although significant attention continues to be focused on Latinas/os as criminal offenders rather than as victims, the susceptibility of Latinas/os to criminal victimization appears to be an area worthy of intense focus and concern.

As is evident in the general criminal justice literature, the most likely male victim is one who is young, unmarried, poor, and lives in an urban area. Although Latinas/os are at decreased risk for specific violent crimes such as homicide in comparison to African Americans, they are a racial class at considerable risk for property and personal crimes, particularly robbery, assault, and **intimate partner violence**. In addition to these forms of victimization, many immigrant Latinas/os have fallen prey to labor exploitation both in the formal and informal work domain, and others still are forced into forms of contemporary **slavery** that can involve appalling violations of human rights, as in the case of victims of **human trafficking**. Although criminal victimization in all its degrees is a phenomenon experienced by many Latinas/os, the underreporting of victimization within the Latina/o community is a common yet explicable reality.

According to official data obtained by the federal government, from 1993 to 2000, Latinas/os aged 12 years and older were the victims of approximately 700,000 violent crimes in the United States. More specifically, Latinas/os experienced 11 percent of all violent crimes against persons, no matter what racial classification, over this 7-year period. Latinas/os were the victims of robbery, assault, aggravated assault, rape, and sexual assault at a rate of almost 28 for every 1,000 Latina/o persons (Rennison 2002). Overall, simple assault was found to be the crime predominantly experienced by people of Latina/o ethnicity, followed by robbery and aggravated assault.

Although these statistics are compiled from self-reports via the National Crime Victimization survey, an annual national effort, and are indicative of a critical criminal justice concern, the exact number of victimization episodes experienced by this population cannot be secured. More specifically, those criminal incidences suffered by individuals not surveyed, including persons under the age of 12 and those persons still unwilling to discuss their criminal victimization histories, are not captured in the data. Thus the actual rate and frequency of crimes experienced by the Latina/o population are even greater than that officially compiled by government officials. Bureau of Justice Statistics data for 2013 show that Latinas/os have a greater prevalence of being victims (1.3 percent) than do whites (1.1 percent) (Truman & Langton 2014, 6). African Americans had the same prevalence rate as Latinas/os in 2013.

Although criminal victimization can be experienced in different forms under different circumstances, it is important to note that, according to official data, Latinas/os are more likely to be victimized by strangers or persons unknown to them—a condition very different from that generally experienced by non-Latinas/os. This point is significant in that among whites, African Americans, and Asians, offenders most often are intimate partners, relatives, friends, and acquaintances. The unique finding with regard to Latinas/os can be interpreted to indicate that they could be more likely to be targeted because of their race than are non-Latinas/os. Additionally, because many Latinas/os migrate from Mexico, Central America, and South America to the United States for work without their families or close friends, they therefore are less likely to live with people to whom they are closely connected, and are more likely to encounter unfamiliar individuals on a daily basis.

Another important finding in the victimology literature states that, in comparison to those of other races, Latinas/os are more likely to be victimized by more than one offender in individual criminal episodes as compared to non-Latinas/os. Data from the Bureau of Justice Statistics indicates that Latinas/os were the group most likely to be targeted by multiple individuals in incidences of assault and robbery, specifically. Motivation perhaps could stem from the perceived unlikelihood that Latinas/os will report their criminal victimization to police, therefore individuals normally who would not engage in criminal activity could find it beneficial or profitable to do so when the situation presents itself.

Although robbery and assault are personal crimes most frequently experienced by Latina/o victims, intimate partner violence—commonly referred to as **domestic violence**—is a crime for which Latina women are at increased risk. Although children and same-sex partners undoubtedly can experience household violence, scholarly research often focuses on women who are wives or significant others of males who are physically, psychologically, and emotionally abusive. The domestic episodes experienced by these women can range from isolated incidences of physical battery to daily occurrences of emotional torment over an extended period.

In addition to assault, robbery, and intimate partner violence, Latinas/os also are at increased risk of falling victim to labor exploitation which can be explained as the unjust treatment of workers for the purpose of financial gain. Abuses include inadequate compensation, wage discrimination, unsafe or unhealthy working conditions, subjection to sexual harassment, and an outright disregard for conventional labor rights. Because Latinas/os often migrate to the United States for the purpose of finding work to support family members in their country of origin, some are undocumented and either bypassed border inspection or have overstayed their visa or work permit. Therefore they can obtain only low-wage hourly jobs or work as day laborers. Although this situation is ripe for victimization, reasoning behind the low if non-existent level of reporting of labor exploitation to police is explicable. Many individuals fear repercussion on the part of employers, resulting in the inability to gain work. Some victims also think that if they were to report nothing can or would be done on the part of law enforcement or labor agencies, specifically because of the victim's immigrant status. It is assumed by the victim that his or her situation is insignificant, and merely is a part of life as a migrant worker in America. It should be stated that, although this issue certainly coincides with the larger issue of human trafficking—a crime in which individuals are coercively transported or harbored for the purpose of exploitative activities such as slave labor, domestic servitude, and sex work—it is very much a crime experienced by documented persons as well as those migrants not trafficked into the United States.

Though statistics indicate that Latinas/os are as likely to report their criminal victimization to police as are non-Latinas/os—specifically, whites and African Americans—there exist some unique factors that weigh heavily on Latinas/os and sway them to not report a crime when they are victimized. Language barriers often make the reporting process difficult and although many law enforcement agencies have made some attempts to recruit Spanish-speaking officers, native Spanish speakers often feel that they cannot communicate properly or they become frustrated when attempting to do so. In addition to language barriers, among the undocumented population fear of reprisal due to immigration status is an obvious deterrent to reporting victimization.

Many Latinas/os also come from countries where the police force is not trustworthy and they therefore place little faith in the effectiveness of American authorities. Individuals from Mexico and regions in South America, for example, are familiar only with the police as a corrupt organization that abuses power, and whose concern is not with helping citizens in need but rather is self-advancement and profit. Additionally—perhaps stemming from the reasons previously described—many Latinas/os feel as though their victimization episodes, no matter how serious, will not be taken seriously and that little if anything will be done to bring perpetrators to justice.

The experience of Latinas/os with bias and discrimination in the United States has served to erode confidence in the criminal justice system. In particular, a long history of heightened tensions between police departments and Latina/o communities has been an obstacle to cooperation and communication. From the **Zoot Suit Riots** of the early 1940s, to the **Rampart Scandal** in Los Angeles and Street Crimes Unit controversy in New York City in the 1990s, to the police **stop-and-frisk** tactics in more recent years—the numerous documented cases of corruption and unfair treatment in which police departments have been implicated serve as a fairly constant source of distrust.

Although significant progress in learning more about Latinas/os as victims of crime has been made in recent years, much more scholarly research is needed. Trends in criminal victimization across Latina/o ethnicities, fear of victimization among Latina/o victims of different crime types, individuals victimized in suburban versus urban areas, differences in levels of fear among documented versus undocumented persons, participation in the U.S. criminal justice process, and access to victim assistance services in the Latina/o community are only some of the areas that deserve further exploration. Additionally, the myth that Latinas/os and African Americans are responsible for a majority of person-on-person crimes against whites must be dispelled from the media and throughout the general public. Perhaps then the appropriate attention, concern, and public-policy support for Latinas/os victims might be realized.

See also: Part I essays: Latinas/os and the U.S. Criminal Justice System; Latina/o Immigrants, Crime, and Justice; Policing and Latina/o Communities; Latinas and the U.S. Criminal Justice System; Incarceration and Latinas/os in the United States; Latina/o Youth and Criminal Justice. Part II entries: Central Americans; Cultural Criminology; Death Penalty; Hate Crimes; Homicide; Human Trafficking; Intimate Partner Violence/Domestic Violence; Lesbian, Gay, Bisexual, and Transgender (LGBT); Media Depictions; Slavery.

Further Reading

Davis, Robert C., and Edna Erez. 1998. *Immigrant populations as victims: Toward a multicultural criminal justice system. Research in Brief.* Washington, DC: U.S. Department of Justice, National Institute of Justice.

Federal Bureau of Investigation. 2007. Hate crime statistics, 2007. Washington, DC: U.S. Department of Justice. http://www.fbi.gov/about-us/cjis/ucr/ucr.

Karmen, Andrew. 2009. *Crime victims: An introduction to victimology.* 7th ed. New York, NY: Wadsworth Publishing.

Morín, José Luis. 2009. *Latino/a rights and justice in the United States.* 2nd ed. Durham, NC: Carolina Academic Press.

Potok, Mark. 2008. Anti-Latino hate crimes rise for fourth year in a row. Montgomery, AL: Southern Poverty Law Center. http://www.splcenter.org/blog/2008/10/29/anti-latino-hate-crimes-rise-for-fourth-year/.

Rennison, Callie Marie. 2002. *Hispanic victims of violent crime, 1993–2000: Bureau of Justice Statistics Special Report.* NCJ 191208. Washington, DC: U.S. Department of Justice, Bureau of Justice Statistics.

Rodriguez Pizarro, Gabriela. 2008. Human trafficking in Latin America in the context of international migration. In *Trafficking in humans: Social, cultural, and political dimensions*, edited by S. Cameron and E. Newman, 206–23. New York, NY: United Nations University Press.

Truman, Jennifer L., and Lynn Langton. 2014. *Criminal victimization, 2013* (NCJ 247648). Washington, DC: Bureau of Justice Statistics.

Walker, Samuel, Cassia Spohn, and Miriam DeLone. 2012. *The color of justice: Race, ethnicity, and crime in America.* 5th ed. Belmont, CA: Wadsworth Publishing.

Vigilantism

Isabel Martínez

Vigilantism, or self-appointed unauthorized acts of coercion or force committed by a group or committee that seeks to mete out justice, typically occurs when the state is unable to protect particular interests or quell challenges to the state and the ruling class. Rather than work through established avenues to seek redress or challenge the state through orthodox means, vigilantes concentrate on perpetrating disruption and seeking to destroy what they consider threats to social order. A "vigilante" is someone who belongs to "an unauthorized group organized for the express purpose of maintaining order and apprehending criminals" (Mirandé 1987, 53). Vigilantes target individuals or groups of persons for extrajudicial or unauthorized enforcement of what they believe the law to be, even though their actions fall outside of legally acceptable means of resolving crime and thereby are inconsistent with the law.

Latinas/os in the United States have been the victims of vigilante violence over many years—from the 1800s when vigilantes labeled Mexicans "bandits" and used violence to expel Mexicans from their own lands, to more contemporary acts of violence by groups intent on stopping purported "illegal aliens." Vigilantes usually rely on intimidation, violence, and paranoia to challenge perceived threats to the status quo or social order. To gain public or state support and approval for the use of such tactics, vigilantes often invoke three themes to justify their actions: national security and counterterrorism, the rule of law, and xenophobia and **nativism**. In tandem, these three themes often also have the effect of "solidifying society and reinforcing civic virtue" (Delgado 2009, 301).

Vigilante violence and terror typically seek to intimidate and instill fear and take a heavy psychological and social toll on individuals and groups subjected to such acts. Beyond the psychological damage it causes, vigilantism can have long-lasting institutional effects—especially on Latina/o communities—including "economic exploitation, racism, and decremental deprivation" (Mirandé 1987, 54). The impact of vigilante violence was felt historically among Mexicans who lost their land, property, and even their lives at the hands of Anglos seeking to settle in the Southwest. Its impact, however, is felt today among many Latino communities, including those living near the U.S.-Mexican border area and other locations around the country that remain sites of disproportionate inequality and poverty and where law enforcement protections are weak. In response to perceived government lapses in enforcement of immigration laws on the border following the events of September 11, 2001, and to increased immigration from Latin America, vigilantism in recent years has grown in strength, stirring up xenophobic tensions and further marginalizing already disadvantaged Latina/o communities.

Historical Acts of Vigilantism

Although the United States experienced a resurgence of vigilantism in the post-9/11 era, vigilante activity against Latinos in the United States has an extended history. Both prior to and after the conquest of the present-day United States Southwest, loosely organized Anglo settlers systematically victimized and terrorized Mexicans along the border. After the end of the U.S.-Mexican War in 1848, Anglo settlers believed that land acquired through war was public domain. They invoked **Manifest Destiny**—the notion that Anglo Americans have a right to expand their land holdings because of their racial, religious, and cultural superiority—to justify their efforts to procure these "public" lands for their own use and benefit. Despite the many shortcomings associated with the 1848 Treaty of Guadalupe-Hidalgo which ended the U.S. war with Mexico, Mexican land owners, on occasion, were able to protect their property rights in the U.S. courts utilizing the treaty. When unsuccessful in the courts, Anglo settlers often turned to vigilantism to wrest lands and economic opportunities from Mexicans.

Economic competition served as a catalyst for employing intimidation and terror to force Mexicans to relinquish their lands. Many native Mexicans, who after 1848 involuntarily became United States citizens, were highly successful in both the agricultural and mining industries in these newly acquired regions, and Anglo settlers were eager to drive Mexicans out of these industries and off of their lands. Anglo settlers quickly enacted new laws and policies that disadvantaged Mexican owners and even challenged their claims to these lands. The protections under the Treaty of Guadalupe-Hidalgo soon carried little weight. Historians make clear that "[m]ost Anglos in the American Southwest cared very little for the welfare of Mexicans. . . . The [government] made no effort whatsoever to protect Mexicans from mob violence, to investigate actions by lynchers, or to hold mob leaders accountable. Instead, they willfully ignored or cruelly celebrated the mob violence that led Mexicans to be expelled from their own lands, to be stripped of their property, and to be killed without trial or legal process" (Carrigan & Webb 2013, 96).

Motivated by Manifest Destiny, Anglo settlers readily engaged in campaigns of lawlessness and discrimination, using both formal and informal institutions and actors to commit acts of violence against Mexicans with impunity. Most common were violations of property rights. In the early 1850s, for instance, Anglo Americans confiscated the lands owned by 2,000 native New Mexicans. One such confiscation resulted in the Salt War in 1877 involving the Anglo takeover of El Paso salt deposits that met with intense Mexicans resistance.

Redefining "citizenship" and designating Mexicans as "foreigners" played an essential part in the confiscation of lands and the expulsion of Mexicans from their lands. Newly recognized as foreigners, Mexicans were subject to unfair economic policies, such as the Foreign Miners Tax—a $20 tax imposed on noncitizen miners—which, if violated, resulted in a harsh penalty. Despite provisions of the Treaty of Guadalupe-Hidalgo that granted them full legal citizenship, Mexican Americans were subject to these fines as if they were foreigners in violation of the law, and faced severe consequences if they resisted. This tax was only enforced against Latin American miners, and if it went unpaid then miners faced eviction and violence, especially if they were defiant.

Most often, vigilantes first sought to incite Mexican Americans, then when encountering Mexican resistance to illegal and unfair laws and enforcement, Anglo Americans would "react" by taking oppressive measures. Scholars have documented incidences of vigilante "justice" and of vigilantes agitating Mexican Americans and then acting violently against them when Mexicans sought to defend themselves. **Lynching** became a common response of Anglo Americans, and between 1848 and 1928 more than 600 Mexicans were lynched by vigilantes (Walker 2007). Although most victims of lynching were men, women were lynched as well—most often after resisting the sexual advances of Anglo settlers.

First informally organized, vigilantism soon became politically institutionalized. Anglo settlers formed vigilante organizations, some of which operated under the auspices of the state government. One widely controversial legal organization, the **Texas Rangers**, was authorized by the Texas state government. It continues to exist today. Although organized during the Texas revolt in 1835 as an unofficial state militia, the Texas Rangers group was approved as a state-sanctioned organization in 1861, and was responsible for protecting the Texas frontier from both violent Indian uprisings and criminal Mexicans. Soon after the authorization, however, duties—justified under Manifest Destiny—focused on the economic exploitation of Mexican Texans. Increasingly, the subordination of Mexican Texans became the Rangers' main organizational priority, an objective that included assisting Anglo settlers in confiscating Mexican/Tejanos' properties.

Other organizations along the frontier also emerged, but they did not have legal authority. Non–state sanctioned organizations, such as the Santa Barbara Mounted Riflemen and the San Francisco Vigilante Committee of the mid-1800s, emerged to drive Mexicans from their properties and industries. The Santa Barbara Mounted Riflemen, a paramilitary group composed of former United States military members, was organized to pressure the local Mexican-led Santa Barbara city government to enforce more stringent laws against Mexicans and Mexican sympathizers. The San Francisco Vigilante Committee organized to expel foreign miners from the Sonora mines. Predominantly Latin American, miners were driven out of town so that Anglo settlers could take over their sites.

Local **media** assisted vigilante groups to enlist more supporters, as well as celebrated their violent activities. Newspapers such as the Santa Barbara *Gazette* openly called for the organization of vigilante groups as well as for acts against immigrant sympathizers —including the local mayor. Other papers covered Latina/o lynchings, reporting on these public performances as if a spectator sport, with perpetrators oftentimes mutilating bodies and displaying body parts like trophies.

Contemporary Vigilantism

Contemporary vigilantism against Latina/os in the United States has its roots in two 21st-century phenomena: the events of September 11, 2011, and the perceived heightened threat to national security; and the influx of undocumented immigrants from Mexico and Central America into the United States. Despite the U.S. government's costly militarization of the border, contemporary vigilante groups view these efforts as ineffective in keeping foreign intruders out of the country and have taken up border security themselves. More than 150 years after its demarcation, both state-sanctioned and unauthorized vigilantism continue to plague the United States-Mexican border.

Many analysts and immigration rights activists consider the Maricopa County Sheriff's Office (MCSO) in Arizona as the scene of a highly controversial form of state-sanctioned vigilantism. Led by celebrity sheriff Joe Arpaio, MCSO's efforts to enforce immigration laws at the local level originally were sanctioned by former Arizona governor and the director of the Department of Homeland Security, Janet Napolitano. Sheriff Arpaio—often referred to as "America's Toughest Sheriff"—launched a "reign of terror" against Latinos in small Arizona towns, searching for undocumented Latina/o immigrants to turn over to **Immigration and Customs Enforcement**. During raids, the Sheriff's Department racially profiled residents, and stopped and asked Latina/o residents for identification to prove their citizenship. Rather than arresting large numbers of undocumented immigrants, however, Arpaio conducted sweeps in areas in which he had no jurisdiction, disrupting town business, creating dangerous situations for his and the town's law enforcement, and intimidating Latina/o residents into staying inside their homes.

Sheriff Arpaio subsequently was stripped of his authority to conduct street patrols in search of undocumented immigrants and was placed under federal investigation for conducting unconstitutional raids. By 2013, a federal court had ruled that Sheriff Arpaio had engaged in unconstitutional sweeps of Latina/o communities and racial profiling. Civil rights organizations, in the case of *Ortega Melendres et al. v. Arpaio et al.* (2013), succeeded in showing that Sheriff Arpaio and MCSO had violated the rights of Latinas/os under the Fourth Amendment and the Fourteenth Amendment to the U.S. Constitution, and the court ordered the illegal practices to cease. Despite the court's ruling, Sheriff Arpaio has remained defiant.

The Minuteman Project

The most publicized unauthorized vigilante group, the **Minuteman Project**, was founded in October 2004 by Jim Gilchrist. Claiming that the government has been ineffective in stopping unauthorized immigration and controlling the U.S. border with Mexico, the Minuteman Project was formed with the intent—according to its mission statement—to bring "peaceful and respectful resolve" to undocumented immigrants' apparent disregard for the "rule of the law" (Walker 2007). Paradoxically, the group has not become known for using peaceful means, but instead for violent acts against Mexicans. It also has financial links to Aryan Nation, a known **hate group** with an anti-immigrant or nativist agenda. According to Gilchrist, however, these acts have been conducted by copycat splinter groups, some known as *cazamigrantes*, or immigrant hunters, with no direct affiliation to his organization.

The group's potency has been on the decline, with infighting and allegations of financial mismanagement against Gilchrist. Fiscal crises have led to the group breaking up into other border-monitoring groups. The "Minuteman Civil Defense Corps," for instance, began to function separately from the "Minuteman Project" in 2005, following an internal clash about finances. Being implicated in crimes against Mexicans and Latinas/os immigrants, however, has damaged the reputation of the various groups that go under the "Minuteman" name.

Although the Minuteman Project and similar organizations have from time to time garnered public support and credibility from certain elected government officials—Tom Tancredo, who once served as the Republican Congressman from Colorado and chaired the Congressional Immigration Reform Caucus, for example, was a keynote speaker at a Minuteman rally—these groups have been linked to hostile anti-immigrant hate rhetoric and violence. The Southern Poverty Law Center (SPLC), an organization nationally recognized for monitoring hate groups, has reported that vigilante militias have been virulent in apprehending, "pistol-whipping and very possibly shooting Latin American immigrants in Cochise County [Arizona] since the late '90s." The SPLC has documented the statements made by members of these border militia groups, including one retired Special Forces veteran who said unequivocally, "It should be legal to kill illegals. . . . Just shoot 'em on sight. That's my immigration policy recommendation. You break into my country, you die" (Holthouse 2005). In 2011, Shawna Forde, head of Minuteman American Defense, was arrested along with two others for the killing a 9-year old girl and her father and for wounding a woman after allegedly dressing as law enforcement officers and breaking into their home.

The Minuteman Project's effectiveness rested largely on its purported large membership and support. The organization claims to have more than 1,000 members, mere private citizens who are seeking to end undocumented immigration from south of the U.S.-Mexican border through the enforcement of immigration laws. These numbers have been challenged by human rights organizations, as the Minuteman Project never has been able to visibly turn out large groups of supporters to patrol the border.

Other vigilante groups, including Ranch Rescue and the Barnett Boys, have garnered support by summoning private citizens to protect their own individual properties. Frustrated by the immigrants' trespassing as they travel to their ultimate destinations, these vigilante groups have patrolled the border on horseback, armed with assault rifles and conducting citizen's arrests of the immigrants. Upon their capture, immigrants are released to the U.S. **Border Patrol**. Collectively, these groups claim detaining more than 5,000 undocumented border-crossers. Immigrant rights and human rights advocates contest the lawfulness of these groups' actions. They assert that state laws outline the conditions for citizen's arrests, and that when held up to these standards, most of the groups' actions are unconstitutional—even if done in the name of national security, the human rights of immigrants have been violated without redress.

Border-watch militia groups and their supporters continue to claim that the government has not aggressively sought to enforce immigration laws, particularly along the U.S. border with Mexico. Yet, under President Barak Obama, deportations have been at record highs. Six years into Obama's presidency, the number of persons deported surpassed the two million mark—an amount greater than under any other president in recent history.

Effects of Vigilante Groups

Some critics of the present-day approach toward vigilante groups find the media complicit in vigilantism in their reporting of these groups' activities, thus providing vigilantes with a public forum to misinform the public about unauthorized immigration from Mexico and to reinforce stereotypes about Latinas/os in the United States. In 2005 alone, the Minuteman Project was covered in more than 1,500 news articles (Walker 2007). Immigrant and human rights advocates challenging the work of the modern-day vigilante groups claim that these groups not only magnify the shortcomings of the government's border enforcement, but they also succeed in helping shape a criminal narrative around unauthorized immigration, and that, as in the past, present-day media wittingly or unwittingly persists in being an accessory to vigilantism.

Historically, there have been instances where vigilantism exercised against Latinas/os has received state imprimatur. Some argue that, today, practices by private citizens to intimidate and oppress Latinas/os also have received tacit if not overt support from some in government and in the media, under the premise that Latinas/os pose a threat to the nation's political and economic security. Whether viewed from an historical lens of the early incarnations of the Texas Rangers or from the actions of modern-day groups such as the Minuteman Project, vigilantism remains a concern of both native and foreign-born Latinas/os and their communities.

See also: Part I essay: Crime and the U.S.-Mexican Border. Part II entries: Hate Crimes; Legal Advocacy Groups; Lesbian, Gay, Bisexual, and Transgender (LGBT); Mexicans and Mexican Americans; Texas Rangers.

Further Reading

Carrigan, William D., and Clive Webb. 2013. *Forgotten dead: Mob violence against Mexicans in the United States, 1848–1928.* Oxford: Oxford University Press.

Christie, Bob. 2011 (January 23). Shawna Forde, Minuteman leader, arrested in double killing in Arizona. *Huffington Post.* http://www.huffingtonpost.com/2009/06/13

/shawna-forde-minutemen-le_n_215246 .html. Accessed November 15, 2015.

Delgado, Richard. 2009. The law of the noose: A history of Latino lynching. *Harvard Civil Rights-Civil Liberties Law Review* (44): 297–312.

Finnegan, William. 2009 (July). Sheriff Joe. *The New Yorker*.

Geis, Sonya. 2007 (March 13). Minuteman project in turmoil over financial allegations. *Washington Post*. http://www.washington post.com/wp-dyn/content/article/2007/03/12 /AR2007031201297.html. Accessed November 15, 2015.

Gonzales-Day, Ken. 2006. *Lynching in the West: 1850–1935*. Durham, NC: Duke University Press.

Grado, Gary. 2009 (October 6). Feds strip Arpaio of immigration authority. *East Valley Tribune*.

Holthouse, David. 2005. Minutemen, other anti-immigrant militia groups stake out Arizona border. *Intelligence Report*, 118. https://www.splcenter.org/fighting-hate /intelligence-report/2005/minutemen-other -anti-immigrant-militia-groups-stake-out -arizona-border. Accessed November 15, 2015.

Mirandé, Alfredo. 1987. *Gringo Justice*. Notre Dame, IN: University of Notre Dame Press.

Schwartz, David. 2014 (October 29). Judge orders Arizona Sheriff Joe Arpaio to undergo training to stop racial profiling. *Reuters*. http://www.huffingtonpost.com/2014/10/29 /joe-arpaio-racial-profiling-training_n _6065792.html. Accessed November 15, 2015.

Thompson, Ginger, and Sarah Cohen. 2014 (April 6). More deportations follow minor crimes, records show. *New York Times*. http://www.nytimes.com/2014/04/07/us /more-deportations-follow-minor-crimes -data-shows.html?_r=0.

Walker, Christopher. 2007. Border vigilantism and comprehensive immigration reform. *Harvard Latino Law Review* (10): 135–74.

Case Cited

Ortega Melendres et al. v. Arpaio et al. 989 F. Supp. 2d 822 (D.C. Ariz. 2013).

Violence. *See* Part I essays: Latina/o Immigrants, Crime, and Justice; Latinas and the U.S. Criminal Justice System; Gangs in the United States and Latina/o Communities; Latina/o Youth and Criminal Justice. Part II entries: Central Americans; Civil Rights; Colombians; Deportation; Deportation Laws; Hate Crimes; Homicide; Human Trafficking; International Human Rights; Lesbian, Gay, Bisexual, and Transgender (LGBT); Political Activist Groups; Segregation; Slavery; Victims.

Violence Prevention. *See* Part I essays: Latinas/os and the U.S. Criminal Justice System; Gangs in the United States and Latina/o Communities; Latina/o Youth and Criminal Justice.

W

War on Drugs. *See* Part I essays: Latinas/os and the U.S. Criminal Justice System; Latina/o Immigrants, Crime, and Justice; Policing and Latina/o Communities; The U.S. War on Drugs and Latina/o Communities; Latinas and the U.S. Criminal Justice System; Incarceration and Latinas/os in the United States; Gangs in the United States and Latina/o Communities; Latina/o Youth and Criminal Justice. Part II entries: Central Americans; Colombians; Transnational Crime.

Y

Young Lords. *See* Part I essays: Policing and Latina/o Community; Gangs in the United States and Latina/o Communities. Part II entries: Chicanas/os; Civilian Oversight of Police; Community-Based Latina/o Advocacy Organizations; Legal Advocacy Groups; Political Activist Groups; Puerto Ricans.

Youth. *See* Part I essays: Latinas/os and the U.S. Criminal Justice System; Latina/o Immigrants, Crime, and Justice; Incarceration and Latinas/os in the United States; Gangs in the United States and Latina/o Communities; Latina/o Youth and Criminal Justice. Part II entries: Central Americans; Chicanas/os; Cultural Criminology; Homicide; International Human Rights; Media Depictions; Political Activist Groups; Salinas, Raúl R.; Segregation.

Youth Crime. *See* Part I essays: Latinas/os and the U.S. Criminal Justice System; Gangs in the United States and Latina/o Communities; Latina/o Youth and Criminal Justice. Part II entry: Media Depictions.

Z

Zambrano-Montes, Antonio. *See* Part I essay: Policing and Latina/o Communities.

Zoot Suit Riots. *See* Part I essays: Latinas/os and the U.S. Criminal Justice System; Latina/o Immigrants, Crime, and Justice; Policing and Latina/o Communities; Gangs in the United States and Latina/o Communities; Latina/o Youth and Criminal Justice. Part II entries: Chicanas/os; Civilian Oversight of Police; Cultural Criminology; International Human Rights; Media Depictions; Mexicans and Mexican Americans; Segregation; Victims; Vigilantism.

The Editor, Contributors, and Advisory Board

Editor

José Luis Morín is a professor at John Jay College of Criminal Justice (CUNY) in the Department of Latin American and Latina/o Studies. His areas of academic specialization include domestic and international criminal justice, civil rights, international human rights, Latina/o studies, and Latin American studies. He is author of *Latino/a Rights and Justice in the United States: Perspectives and Approaches*. Professor Morín also has held various administrative positions in higher education, including founding vice president for Academic Affairs, and provost of Stella and Charles Guttman Community College; interim dean of Undergraduate Studies at John Jay College; and chair of John Jay College's Department of Latin American and Latina/o Studies. Prior to joining the faculty at John Jay, Professor Morín was a visiting professor at the Center for Hawaiian Studies at the University of Hawai'i at Mānoa, and he worked for many years as a civil rights and human rights litigator and advocate with organizations such as the Center for Constitutional Rights and the Puerto Rican Legal Defense and Education Fund (PRLDEF) (now known as LatinoJustice PRLDEF). Professor Morín is a graduate of Columbia University and New York University School of Law.

Contributors

Luis Barrios is a professor at John Jay College of Criminal Justice in the Department of Latin American and Latina/o Studies, and a member of the Ph.D. faculty in social/personality psychology, Graduate Center, City University of New York. Dr. Barrios recently served as a visiting professor of Research and Methodology and Criminal Justice in the School of Law and Political Science (Facultad de Ciencias Jurídicas y Politicas) of the Universidad Autónoma de Santo Domingo (UASD) and the Facultad Latinoamericana de Ciencias Sociales-Flacso, Ecuador.

Leonard Baynes, JD, is the dean of the University of Houston Law Center. He previously served as a professor of law and the inaugural director of the Ronald H. Brown Center for Civil Rights and Economic Development at St. John's University Law School. Baynes' areas of expertise include business organizations, communications law, regulated industries, and race and the law. He is the recipient of numerous awards, including "The Extraordinary Service Award" for his teaching, scholarship, and service given by the Second National People of Color Conference, and has received the New York State Bar Association Diversity Trailblazer Award.

Juan Cartagena is a constitutional and civil rights attorney and the president and general counsel of LatinoJustice PRLDEF, one of the nation's leading civil rights public interest law offices that represents Latinas and Latinos throughout the country and works to increase their entry into the legal profession. A graduate of Dartmouth College and Columbia University School of Law, Mr. Cartagena currently lectures on constitutional and civil rights law at Rutgers University in New Brunswick. Juan has written numerous articles on constitutional and civil rights issues and the political representation of poor and marginalized communities—especially Puerto Rican and Latino communities—and has recently begun litigating and publishing articles on the effects of policing and mass imprisonment on Latino communities.

Ric Curtis is the chair of the Department of Anthropology at John Jay College of Criminal Justice at the City University of New York. Much of his research on crime, drugs, gangs, sex markets, HIV, and other health- and crime-related issues is conducted in the New York City area.

Sandra Del Valle was senior associate counsel at the Puerto Rican Legal Defense and Education Fund for 12 years where she specialized in language rights and the rights of day laborers. She also was a criminal defense attorney at the Legal Aid Society of Nassau County. She is currently a high school English teacher in New York City.

Nitza Milagros Escalera is the assistant dean of Student Affairs at Fordham University's School of Law. She also teaches a course at Fordham in negotiation and mediation from a cross-cultural perspective. Additionally, Dean Escalera serves as an adjunct professor at John Jay College of Criminal Justice.

Hernando A. Estévez was born in Bogota, Colombia, where he first began his studies in philosophy. He received his master's in Liberal Studies from Indiana University in 1988 and earned a PhD in Latin American Philosophy from DePaul University. Some of the primary influences in Dr. Estévez' work include critical race theory, deconstruction, phenomenology, and critical theory. His work focuses on the articulation of identity and its histories, unfolding the conflict between political identity and cultural identity, from a Latin American perspective. Central to this work are the critical analysis of the relationships between culture and politics in Latin American thought and the articulation of the modalities that sustain 20th century continental philosophy.

Rosa Maria Gonzalez-Guarda, PhD, is an assistant professor at the University of Miami School of Nursing and Health Studies. Throughout her career, Dr. Gonzalez-Guarda has addressed health disparities affecting Hispanics and other vulnerable groups through community-based participatory research and community health projects addressing substance abuse, violence, risky sexual behaviors, and mental health.

Nancy Guarneros currently is a doctoral candidate at Claremont Graduate University in California and lecturer for the UCLA Labor Center. She completed her master's in social science and comparative education with a focus on race and ethnicity in 2010 from UCLA's Graduate School of Education. Her research interests include undocumented youth in higher education, spatial analysis, and geographic information systems as social justice tools to study immigrant communities.

Melissa Guzman received her PhD in sociology from The University of California, Santa Barbara, in December 2015. Her research focuses on Latina/o immigration, citizenship, and religion. Dr. Guzman currently is working as a research associate for a project exploring Latina/o Protestant Congregations in the United States.

David Manuel Hernández is an assistant professor of Latina/o Studies at Mount Holyoke College. His research focuses on immigration enforcement, in particular the U.S. detention regime. He is completing a book on this institution, tentatively entitled, *Undue Process: Immigrant Detention and Lesser Citizenship*. His article "Pursuant to Deportation: Latinos and Immigrant Detention" recently was reprinted for the second time in *Governing Immigration through Crime: A Reader* (Stanford University Press). Hernández is co-editor of *Critical Ethnic Studies: A Reader*, forthcoming with Duke University Press.

Manuel A. Huerta is a filmmaker, community-based public historian, and college educator from East Los Angeles. He is a member of Film Independent (FIND) and the National Art Education Association (NAEA). A graduate of UCLA and Columbia University, Mr. Huerta is working on a documentary film project about perspectives on Mexican identity in the Southwestern United States.

Joshua G. Kellison, PhD, is a staff psychologist in the Division of Psychology at Phoenix Children's Hospital where he currently is developing a LGBTQI (Lesbian, Gay, Bisexual, Transgender, Queer, and Intersexed) Youth and Families Clinic. His research interests include Latino/a health, LGBTQI families, and the development of culturally sensitive preventive interventions. He recently completed his postdoctoral residency in LGBT veterans' health at the VA Pacific Islands Health Care System in Honolulu, Hawaii.

Louis Kontos is an assistant professor of Sociology at John Jay College of Criminal Justice in New York City.

Yolanda C. Martín, PhD, is an assistant professor and program coordinator in Criminal Justice, Social Sciences, Human Services and Criminal Justice at the Borough of Manhattan Community College, City University of New York. She teaches in the areas of criminal justice, critical criminology, corrections, and drug use and abuse.

Isabel Martínez, PhD, is an assistant professor in the Department of Latin American and Latina/o Studies at John Jay College of Criminal Justice. She currently is completing a manuscript tentatively titled, *Making Transnational Workers from Youths: Independent Mexican Teenage Migrants and Pathways of Survival and Social Mobility*. She has received fellowships and grants from the Woodrow Wilson National Fellowship Foundation, the Consortium for Faculty Diversity, the Association of Black Sociologists, the Spencer Foundation, and the Society for the Study of Social Problems, and is the founding director of the Unaccompanied Latin American Minor Project (ULAMP).

Ramiro Martínez, Jr., PhD, is professor in the School of Criminology and Criminal Justice and in the Department of Sociology at Northeastern University. His research interests include race, ethnicity, and immigration; crime; and the criminal justice system.

Louis Mendoza is the Director of the School of Humanities, Arts, and Cultural Studies at Arizona State University. He is the author of *Historia: The Literary Making of Chicana and Chicano History* (2001), the editor of *raúlrsalinas and the Jail Machine: My Weapon is My Pen, Selected Prison Writings* (2006), and the author of *Conversations Across Our America: Talking about Immigration and the Latinoization in the U.S.* (2012), and *A Journey Around Our America: A Memoir on Cycling, Immigration, and the Latinoization of the U.S.*

Brian Montes, PhD, is an assistant professor in the Department of Latin American and Latina/o Studies at John Jay College, City University of New York.

Marco Fernando Navarro is a PhD student in communication and rhetoric at Rensselaer Polytechnic Institute. He has taught as an adjunct faculty member in the Department of Latin American and Latina/o Studies at John Jay College of Criminal Justice.

Judith Perez Caro, PhD, is a sociologist who focuses her research on the Caribbean Latino middle class. She currently serves as the director of Diversity at Stone Ridge School of the Sacred Heart, in Bethesda, Maryland.

Lisandro Pérez is professor and chair of the Department of Latin American and Latina/o Studies at John Jay College of Criminal Justice, City University of New York. Until the summer of 2010 Dr. Pérez served for 25 years on the faculty of Florida International University (FIU) in Miami where he founded and directed its Cuban Research Institute. He also served as the editor of the journal *Cuban Studies* from 1999 to 2004, and is co-author of the book *The Legacy of Exile: Cubans in the United States*.

François Restrepo-Serrano, Esq., was an adjunct instructor in the Latina/o American Studies Department at John Jay College of Criminal Justice, where he taught courses on the Latino/a experience in relation to social justice, human rights, and civil rights. He was also John Jay College's assistant director to the Ronald H. Brown Law School Prep Program at St. John's University School of Law. He currently is defending tenants' rights as an attorney in the Housing Unit for Manhattan Legal Services.

Robert Riggs is a PhD candidate in sociology at New York University (NYU). He holds a Graduate Research Fellowship from the National Science Foundation and a MacCracken Fellowship from NYU. His current research focuses on how formerly incarcerated people build their social networks after release, and investigates whether and how social connections mediate the negative impacts of incarceration and facilitate successful reintegration into society.

Victor M. Rios, PhD, is a professor in the Department of Sociology at the University of California, Santa Barbara. He is the author of *Punished: Policing the Lives of Black and Latino Boys* (New York University Press). Dr. Rios conducts research on youth-police relations and gang culture. He teaches courses on juvenile justice, Latino studies, and urban ethnography.

Jenny Rivera is an associate judge of the Court of Appeals in the State of New York. Judge Rivera has clerked for the Honorable Sonia Sotomayor at the Southern District of New York and for the Second Circuit Court of Appeals Pro Se Law Clerk's Office. She has also worked for the Legal Aid Society's Homeless Family Rights Project, and the Puerto Rican Legal Defense and Education Fund (renamed LatinoJustice/PRLDEF). Additionally, she has served as special deputy attorney general for Civil Rights in New York State, and as an administrative law judge for the New York State Division for Human Rights. At the City University of New York School of Law, she was a tenured faculty member, and founder and director of the Law School's Center on Latino and Latina Rights and Equality.

Evin R. Rodkey, PhD, is an adjunct assistant professor in Anthropology at the University of Illinois at Chicago. His research in the Dominican Republic concerns the economic and social survival strategies of deportees from the United States.

Hector W. Soto, JD, is an assistant professor at Hostos Community College in New York, where he teaches courses on policing, criminal justice, and law. He is a former New York City Police Department Advocate as well as former executive director of both New York City's Civilian Complaint Review Board and Philadelphia's Police Advisory Commission. He is a member of the Board of Directors of Citizen's Union as well as chair of the Public Safety Sub-Committee of its Municipal Affairs Committee.

Maria Swimm is a social science researcher with an interest in victimology, focusing specifically on the victimization of vulnerable populations. She has worked on numerous state-funded and federally funded victim-oriented research projects examining topics such as the victimization of unauthorized Latino day laborers in New York State, sexually exploited youth in New York City, and sexual abuse in the Catholic Church.

Manuel D. Vargas is senior counsel with the Immigrant Defense Project in New York. A nationally known expert on the immigration consequences of criminal convictions, he is the author of several legal resource materials for advocacy on behalf of immigrants accused of crimes, including *Representing Immigrant Defendants in New York* (4th ed. 2006).

Charles R. Venator-Santiago holds a joint appointment in the Department of Political Science and El Instituto: Institute for Caribbean, Latino/a and Latin American Studies at the University of Connecticut-Storrs. He teaches courses in public law, political theory, Latino/a politics, and Latinos/as and the law. He currently is studying the legal and political history of the federal status and citizenship legislation for the remaining U.S. unincorporated territories (Puerto Rico, U.S. Virgin Islands, American Samoa, Guam, and the Commonwealth of the Northern Mariana Islands). His most recent book is *Puerto Rico and the Origins of U.S. Global Empire: The Disembodied Shade* (Routledge 2015).

Advisory Board

Sandra Del Valle is a civil rights attorney and educator.

Kevin R. Johnson is dean, Mabie-Apallas Professor of Public Interest Law, and professor of Chicana/o studies at the University of California at Davis School of Law.

Louis Kontos is an assistant professor at John Jay College of Criminal Justice.

Francisco A. Villarruel is the associate chair for Education and Outreach, Department of Human Development and Family Studies, and University Outreach and Engagement Senior Fellow at Michigan State University.

Index

Main entries in **bold**

CPSIA information can be obtained
at www.ICGtesting.com
Printed in the USA
BVHW010423050221
599395BV00028B/97